Lecture Notes in Artificial Intelligence   5749

Edited by R. Goebel, J. Siekmann, and W. Wahlster

Subseries of Lecture Notes in

Silvio Ghilardi   Roberto Sebastiani (Eds.)

Frontiers of Combining Systems

7th International Symposium, FroCoS 2009
Trento, Italy, September 16-18, 2009
Proceedings

 Springer

Series Editors

Randy Goebel, University of Alberta, Edmonton, Canada
Jörg Siekmann, University of Saarland, Saarbrücken, Germany
Wolfgang Wahlster, DFKI and University of Saarland, Saarbrücken, Germany

Volume Editors

Silvio Ghilardi
Università degli Studi di Milano
Department of Computer Science
Via Comelico 39, 20135 Milano, Italy
E-mail: ghilardi@dsi.unimi.it

Roberto Sebastiani
Università di Trento, Facoltà di Scienze
Dipartimento di Ingegneria e Scienza dell'Informazione
Via Sommarive 14, 38050 Povo, Trento, Italy
E-mail: rseba@disi.unitn.it

Library of Congress Control Number: 2009933479

CR Subject Classification (1998): I.2, I.2.3, D.3.1, F.4, I.1, F.2

LNCS Sublibrary: SL 7 – Artificial Intelligence

ISSN   0302-9743
ISBN-10   3-642-04221-X Springer Berlin Heidelberg New York
ISBN-13   978-3-642-04221-8 Springer Berlin Heidelberg New York

springer.com

© Springer-Verlag Berlin Heidelberg 2009
Printed in Germany

Typesetting: Camera-ready by author, data conversion by Scientific Publishing Services, Chennai, India
Printed on acid-free paper   SPIN: 12747566   06/3180   5 4 3 2 1 0

Preface

This volume contains the proceedings of the 7th International Symposium of Frontiers of Combining Systems (FroCoS 2009) held during September 16-18, 2009 in Trento, Italy. Previous FroCoS meetings were organized in Munich (1996), Amsterdam (1998), Nancy (2000), Santa Margherita Ligure (2002), Vienna (2005), and Liverpool (2007). In 2004, 2006, and 2008 FroCoS joined IJCAR, the International Joint Conference on Automated Reasoning.

Like its predecessors, FroCoS 2009 offered a forum for the presentation and discussion of research activities on the combination, integration, analysis, modularization and interaction of formally defined systems, with an emphasis on logic-based ones. These issues are important in many areas of computer science such as logic, computation, program development and verification, artificial intelligence, automated reasoning, constraint solving, declarative programming, and symbolic computation.

There were 35 submissions to FroCoS 2009. Each submission was reviewed by at least three Program Committee members. After a careful evaluation, the committee decided to accept the 19 papers which are published in this volume. The volume also includes four invited contributions by Alessandro Armando (DIST Genova), Thomas Eiter (TU Wien), Boris Motik (OUCL Oxford), and Ashish Tiwari (SRI Stanford).

Many people and institutions contributed to the success of FroCoS 2009. We are indebted to the members of the Program Committee and to the additional referees for the thorough reviewing work, to the members of the FroCoS Steering Committee for their support, and to Andrej Voronkov for free use of the EasyChair conference management system. We would also like to mention and thank the institutions that supported FroCoS 2009 either as financial sponsors or by other means: Rettorato and Dipartimento di Scienze dell'Informazione of Università degli Studi di Milano, Università degli Studi di Trento, and Microsoft Research. A special final thanks is due to everyone at the Ufficio Convegni of Università degli Studi di Trento for their excellent work concerning Web management and local organization.

June 2009

Silvio Ghilardi
Roberto Sebastiani

Conference Organization

Program Chairs

Silvio Ghilardi
Roberto Sebastiani

Program Committee

Franz Baader	Technische Universität Dresden, Germany
Peter Baumgartner	NICTA, Canberra, Australia
Torben Brauner	Roskilde University, Denmark
Leonardo de Moura	Microsoft Research, Redmond, WA, USA
Bernhard Gramlich	Technische Universität Wien, Austria
Sava Krstic	Intel Corporation, Santa Clara, CA, USA
Viktor Kuncak	Ecole Polytechnique Fédérale de Lausanne, Switzerland
Albert Oliveras	Technical University of Catalonia, Spain
Silvio Ranise	University of Verona, Italy
Christophe Ringeissen	LORIA, Nancy, France
Ulrike Sattler	University of Manchester, UK
Renate Schmidt	University of Manchester, UK
Luciano Serafini	FBK-Irst, Trentino, Italy
Viorica Sofronie-Stokkermans	Max-Planck-Institut für Informatik, Saarbrücken, Germany
Cesare Tinelli	University of Iowa, IA, USA
Frank Wolter	University of Liverpool, UK
Michael Zakharyaschev	London Knowledge Laboratories, UK

Local Organization

Silvio Ghilardi
Roberto Sebastiani

External Reviewers

Jesse Alama	Nikolaj Bjorner
Carlos Ansotegui	Thomas Bolander
Carlos Areces	Maria Paola Bonacina
Gilles Audemard	Roberto Bruttomesso

Frank Ciesinski
Jean-Francois Couchot
David Deharbe
Clare Dixon
Uwe Egly
Levent Erkok
Germain Faure
Chris Fermüller
Pascal Fontaine
Alain Giorgetti
Isabelle Gnaedig
Bernardo Cuenca Grau
Jim Grundy
Marcus Grösser
Alan Hu
Ullrich Hustadt
Steffen Holldobler
Carsten Ihlemann
Swen Jacobs
Barbara Jobstmann
Boris Konev
Roman Kontchakov
Konstantin Korovin
Oliver Kutz
Pascal Lafourcade

Carsten Lutz
Ines Lynce
Marco Maratea
Maja Milicic
Eric Monfroy
Enrica Nicolini
Michael Norrish
Bijan Parsia
Grant Olney Passmore
Wieslaw Pawlowski
Emma Rollon
Vladislav Ryzhikov
Gernot Salzer
Felix Schernhammer
Thomas Schneider
Christoph Sticksel
Aaron Stump
Philippe Suter
Dmitry Tishkovsky
Dmitry Tsarkov
Xavier Urbain
Jurgen Villadsen
Arild Waaler
Dirk Walther

Table of Contents

Building SMT-Based Software Model Checkers: An Experience Report

Alessandro Armando

Artificial Intelligence Laboratory (AI-Lab)
DIST - University of Genova, Italy
armando@dist.unige.it

Abstract. In this paper I report on my experience on developing two SMT-based software model checking techniques and show—through comparison with rival state-of-the-art software model checkers—that SMT solvers are key to the effectiveness and scalability of software model checking.

1 Introduction

Software model checking is one of the most promising techniques for automatic program analysis. This is witnessed by the growing attention that this technique is receiving by leading software industries which have already introduced in their software production cycle:

> *Things like even software verification, this has been the Holy Grail of computer science for many decades but now in some very key areas, for example, driver verification we're building tools that can do actual proof about the software and how it works in order to guarantee the reliability.*

Bill Gates [Gat02]

As the name suggests, software model checking owns its origins to model checking [Cla00], a powerful technique capable to perform a complete and fully automatic exploration of the behaviors of a finite state system by using sophisticated data structures and algorithms (most notably OBDDs and SAT solvers).

Model checking has been (and still is) remarkably successful in the analysis of hardware and communication protocols. However the application of model checking to software is considerably more difficult as most programs deal with very large or even infinite data structures and are therefore inherently infinite-state. The development of software model checking tools asks for a technology that supports automated reasoning about data structures commonly occurring in programs (e.g. integers, lists, arrays, bit-vectors). This goes clearly beyond the scope of OBDDs and SAT solvers.

The development of decision procedures for theories of data structures is a long standing problem in Automated Reasoning. The Satisfiability Modulo Theory (SMT) problem is the problem of determining whether a formula is satisfied

S. Ghilardi and R. Sebastiani (Eds.): FroCoS 2009, LNAI 5749, pp. 1–17, 2009.

by at least one model of a given theory $\mathcal{T}$. Of course, theories whose SMT problem is decidable are of special interest. State-of-the-art SMT-solvers provide decision procedures for a number of decidable theories used in program verification, including propositional logic, linear arithmetics, the theory of uninterpreted function symbols, the theory of arrays, the theory of records and the combination thereof. (See [Seb07] for an extensive survey on SMT.)

In this paper I report on my experience in developing two SMT-based software model checking techniques. The first technique carries out a bounded analysis of the input program through a reduction to a SMT problem. The second technique is based on the CounterExample-Guided Abstraction Refinement (CEGAR) paradigm and heavily relies on SMT solving during the refinement phase. Both techniques have been implemented in prototype model checking tools. I also show—through experimental comparison with rival state-of-the-art software model checkers—that SMT solvers are key to the effectiveness and scalability of the tools.

Structure of the paper. Section 2 shows that bounded model checking of software can greatly benefit if SMT solvers are used instead of SAT Solvers. Section 3 introduces the CEGAR paradigm and shows the prominent role played by SMT-solvers in this context. A brief survey of the related work is given in Sect. 4. Some concluding remarks are drawn in Sect. 5.

2   Bounded Model Checking of Software

For simplicity in this paper we focus on fragments of the C programming language containing the usual control-flow constructs (e.g. if, while, and assert), (recursive) function definitions, and with assignments (over numeric variables and arrays) and function calls as atomic statements. Programs may also contain *conditional expressions*, i.e. expressions of the form $(c?e_1:e_2)$ whose value is the value of e_1 if the value of c is different from 0 and is the value of e_2 otherwise. We also assume that the failure of an assert statement leads the program to a special control location denoted by 0. If a is a program variable of type array, then $size(a)$ denotes its size.

The *bounded reachability problem for a program* P is the problem of determining whether there exists an execution path of P of at most a given length reaching a given control location of P. Here I focus on the *bounded 0-reachability problem for* P, i.e. the problem of determining whether there exists an execution path of P of bounded length reaching control location 0. In this section I show how to reduce this problem to a SMT problem. (For the sake of simplicity, in this section I assume that = is the only assignment operator occurring in P and that no pointer variables nor conditional expressions occur in P.)

Given an integer k, the procedure generates an SMT formula whose models (if any) correspond to execution traces (of length bounded by k) leading to an assertion violation. Finding assertion violations (of length up to k) therefore boils down to solving SMT problems.

Preliminarily to the generation of the formula, we apply a number of simplifying transformations to P, thereby obtaining a simplified program S, whose execution paths correspond to finite prefixes of the execution paths of P. These transformations are described in Section 2.1. We then build two sets of quantifier-free formulae C_S and P_S such that

$$C_S \models_T \bigwedge P_S \tag{1}$$

for some given background theory T if and only if no execution path of S violates any assert statement. The generation of C_S and P_S is the described in Sect. 2.2. The usage of SAT and SMT solvers to tackle (1) is discussed in Sect. 2.3 and in Sect. 2.3 respectively.

2.1 The Preprocessing Phase

The preprocessing activity starts by unwinding loops, i.e. by replacing them with a sequence of nested if statements. This is done by removing while loops through the application of the following transformation k times:

while(e) { P' } $\longrightarrow$ if(d) { P' while(c) { P' } }

and by replacing the remaining while loop with an *unwinding assertion* of the form assert(!c);. The failure of an unwinding assertion indicates that the bound k is not sufficient to adequately model the problem at hand, thereby indicating that it must be increased. Non-recursive function calls are then inlined. Recursive function calls are unwound similarly to loop statements. Let Q be the program obtained from P by applying the above transformations. It is easy to see that the execution paths of Q correspond to finite prefixes of the execution paths of P.

Next, program Q is put in *Static Single Assignment* (SSA) form. Let R be the resulting program. A program in SSA form [CFR+89] is a program in which every variable is assigned at most once. The transformation in SSA form is done by

1. replacing all the assignments of the form a[e_1]=e_2; with a=store(a,e_1,e_2);, where store is a function such that store(a,e_1,e_2) returns the array obtained from a by setting the element at position e_1 with the value of e_2;
2. replacing the occurrences of the variables that are target of assignments (say x) with new, indexed versions x_0, x_1, ...;
3. replacing all the occurrences of the variables that are not target of assignments with appropriate versions so to preserve the semantics of the original program; and
4. adding a new assignment of the form x_{j_3}=(c?x_{j_1}:x_{j_2}); (for suitable values of j_1, j_2, and j_3) after each conditional statement of the form if(c) Q_1 [else Q_2] where x occurs as target of an assignment in Q_1 [or in Q_2].

An example of transformation in SSA form is given in Fig. 1. As the first two statements of Q have the same target variable (namely i), the target of the corresponding assignments in R are two distinct versions of the same variable (namely i_1 and i_2). The assignment at line 3 of R uses in its right-hand side the version of the variable that is target of the assignment at line 2, namely i_1. The same considerations apply to the two occurrences of x that are target of the assignments at lines 6 and 8. Notice that the additional assignments at lines 9 and 11 of R are added to provide a unique definition for the future uses of x.

```
1  // Program Q
2  i=a[0];
3  i=i+1;
4  if(x>0) {
5    if(x<10)
6      x=x+1;
7    else
8      x=x-1;
9  }
10 assert(x>0 && x<10);
11 a[x]=i;
```

```
1  // Program R
2  i₁=a₀[0];
3  i₂=i₁+1;
4  if(x₀>0) {
5    if(x₀<10)
6      x₁=x₀+1;
7    else
8      x₂=x₀-1;
9    x₃=(x₀<10?x₁:x₂);
10 }
11 x₄=(x₀>0?x₃:x₀);
12 assert(x₄>0 && x₄<10);
13 a₁=store(a₀,x₄,i₂);
```

Fig. 1. Example program Q (left) and corresponding program in SSA form R (right)

Notice that by turning a program into SSA form we are trading assignments (e.g. x=x+1;) for equalities (e.g. $x_1 = x_0 + 1$). This is why, preliminarily to the generation of the encoding, it is convenient to apply this transformation.

The program R is now turned in *Conditional Normal form*, i.e. into a sequence of statements of the form if (c) r, where r is either an assignment or an assertion and does not contain conditional expressions. We refer to statements of the form if (c) r as *conditional statements*. Notice that this normalization step removes the **else** constructs and pushes the **if** statements downwards in the abstract syntax tree of the program until they are applied to atomic statements only.

The program in Conditional Normal form S corresponding to the program R on the right of Fig. 1 is shown on the left of Fig. 2. As the execution of statements at lines 2, 3, 12 and 13 of R does not depend on any condition, the guard of the corresponding conditional statements in S is **true**. The assignment at line 6 of R is executed only if the conditions of the two preceding **if** statements hold. Therefore the corresponding assignment at line 4 in S is guarded by the conjunction of these two conditions. Similar considerations apply for the guard of the assignment at line 5 in S. The assignment at line 9 (11) of R is turned into the pair of conditional statements at lines 6 and 7 (8 and 9, resp.) of S.

It must be noted that S is not necessarily in SSA form. However, all the variables that are assigned more than once (e.g. x_3 and x_4 in the program of Fig. 2) are guarded by mutually exclusive conditions.

Notice that, for suitable values of k, all the above transformations (i.e. the transformations leading from the input program P to Q, from Q to R, and from

```
 1  // Program S
 2  if(true)  i₁=a₀[0];
 3  if(true)  i₂=i₁+1;
 4  if(x₀>0  &&  x₀<10)  x₁=x₀+1;
 5  if(x₀>0  &&  !(x₀<10))  x₂=x₀-1;
 6  if(x₀>0  &&  x₀<10)  x₃=x₁;
 7  if(x₀>0  &&  !(x₀<10))  x₃=x₂;
 8  if(x₀>0)  x₄=x₃;
 9  if(!(x₀>0))  x₄=x₀;
10  if(true)  assert(x₄>0  &&  x₄<10);
11  if(true)  a₁=store(a₀,x₄,i₂);
```

$$\mathcal{C}_S = \{ \ (\text{TRUE} \Rightarrow i_1 = \text{select}(a_0, 0)),$$
$$(\text{TRUE} \Rightarrow i_2 = i_1 + 1),$$
$$((x_0 > 0 \wedge x_0 < 10) \Rightarrow x_1 = x_0 + 1),$$
$$((x_0 > 0 \wedge \neg(x_0 < 10)) \Rightarrow x_2 = x_0 - 1),$$
$$((x_0 > 0 \wedge x_0 < 10) \Rightarrow x_3 = x_1),$$
$$((x_0 > 0 \wedge \neg(x_0 < 10)) \Rightarrow x_3 = x_2),$$
$$(x_0 > 0 \Rightarrow x_4 = x_3),$$
$$(\neg(x_0 > 0) \Rightarrow x_4 = x_0),$$
$$(\text{TRUE} \Rightarrow a_1 = \text{store}(a_0, x_4, i_2))\}$$
$$\mathcal{P}_S = \{\text{TRUE} \Rightarrow (x_4 > 0 \wedge x_4 < 10)\}$$

Fig. 2. Program in Conditional Normal S (left) and corresponding encoding (right)

R to the program S) are such that each execution path in the input program corresponds to an execution path in the output program and vice versa, and both paths contain the same (modulo renaming of the variables) sequence of atomic statements, and all atomic statements are guarded by the same (modulo renaming of the variables) conditions. From this fact it readily follows that the bounded reachability problem for P can be reduced to the reachability problem for S.

2.2 The Encoding Phase

Let $S = s_1 \cdots s_m$ be the program in Conditional Normal form resulting from the application of the transformations described in Section 2.1 to the input program P for a given value of k. We now show how to build two sets of quantifier-free formulae $\mathcal{C}_S$ and $\mathcal{P}_S$ such that $\mathcal{C}_S \models_\mathcal{T} \bigwedge \mathcal{P}_S$ if and only if no execution path of S violates any **assert** statement.

For simplicity we assume that the variables of S are either of type **int** or are arrays of elements of type **int**. We define $\mathcal{T}$ to be the union of a theory of the integers and the theory of arrays. We also assume that the language of $\mathcal{T}$ contains *(i)* a variable v_j of sort INT for each variable v_j of S of type **int** and *(ii)* a variable a_j of sort array for each variable a_j of S ranging over arrays. Let e be a program expression. By e^* we indicate the term of the language of $\mathcal{T}$ obtained from e by replacing all program variables (say v_j) with the corresponding variables of $\mathcal{T}$ (say v_j) and the operators occurring in e with the corresponding function and predicate symbols in $\mathcal{T}$. For instance, if $e = (a_1[v_1+1] <= v_0+2)$, then $e^* = (\text{select}(a_1, v_1 + 1) \le v_0 + 2)$.

For each statement in S of the form if(c) v_j=e;, $\mathcal{C}_S$ contains the formula $(c^* \Rightarrow (v_j = e^*))$ and for each statement of the form if(c) **assert**(e); in S, $\mathcal{P}_S$ contains the formula $(c^* \Rightarrow e^*)$. An example of the encoding is given in Fig. 2.

If S is a program in conditional normal form with m statements, then $\mathcal{C}_S \models_\mathcal{T}$ $\mathcal{P}_S$ if and only if all complete execution paths of S end in control location $m + 1$. This result (proved in [AMP09]) guarantees that the encoding given by $\mathcal{C}_S$ and $\mathcal{P}_S$

is sound and complete, i.e. the bounded 0-reachability problem can be reduced to a SMT problem.

2.3 The Solving Phase

Solving the Formulae with a SAT Solver. In [KCY03] checking problems of the form (1) is reduced to a propositional satisfiability problem which is then fed to a SAT solver. This is done by modeling variables of basic data types (e.g. `int`) as fixed-size bit-vectors and by considering the equations in $\mathcal{C}_S$ and in $\mathcal{P}_S$ as bit-vector equations. Each array variable a is also replaced by $\text{size}(a)$ distinct variables $a^0, \dots, a^{\text{size}(a)-1}$ and each formula of the form $c \Rightarrow (a_{j+1} = \text{store}(a_j, e_1, e_2))$ occurring in $\mathcal{C}_S$ is replaced by the formula $\bigwedge_{i=0}^{\text{size}(a)-1} a_{j+1}^i = ((c \wedge e_1 = i) \, ? \, e_2 : a_j^i)$, where $v = (c \, ? \, e_1 : e_2)$ abbreviates the formula $(c \Rightarrow v = e_1) \wedge (\neg c \Rightarrow v = e_2)$. Finally each term of the form $\text{select}(a_j, e)$ is replaced by a new variable, say x, and $\bigwedge_{i=0}^{\text{size}(a)-1}((e = i) \Rightarrow x = a_j^i)$ is added to $\mathcal{C}_S$.

The resulting set of bit-vector equations is then turned into a propositional formula. Notice that the size of the propositional formula generated in this way depends *(i)* on the size of the bit-vector representation of the basic data types as well as *(ii)* on the size of the arrays used in the program. More generally, if the program contains a multi-dimensional array a with dimensions $d_1, \dots, d_m$, then the number of added formulae grows as $O(d_1 \cdot d_2 \cdot \dots \cdot d_m)$.

Solving the Formulae with a SMT Solver. The alternative approach, first proposed in [AMP06], is to use a SMT solver to directly check whether $\mathcal{C}_S \models_{\mathcal{T}} \bigwedge \mathcal{P}_S$. By proceeding in this way the size of the formula given as input to the SMT solver does not depend on the size of the bit-vector representation of the basic data types nor on the size of the arrays occurring in the program. Moreover the use of a SMT solver gives additional freedom in the modeling the basic data types. In fact, program variables of numeric type (e.g. `int`, `float`) can be modeled by variables ranging over bit-vectors or over the corresponding numerical domain (e.g. $\mathbb{Z}$, $\mathbb{R}$, resp.). If the modeling of numeric variables is done through fixed-size bit-vectors, then the result of the analysis is precise but it depends on the specific size considered for the bit-vectors. If, instead, the modeling of numeric variables is done through the corresponding numerical domain, then the result of the analysis is independent from the actual binary representation.

2.4 Experimental Results

SMT-CBMC is an SMT-based bounded model checker for sequential programs that implements the ideas described in Sect. 2. SMT-CBMC consists of four main modules. The first module parses the input program, the second carries out the preprocessing, the third builds the quantifier-free formula, and the fourth module solves the formula by invoking CVC Lite [BB04] as a SMT solver. The latter module also builds and prints the error trace whenever a counterexample is returned by CVC Lite. SMT-CBMC can represent numeric data types with corresponding numeric domains as well as with fixed-size bit-vectors. Moreover the user can specify the maximum number of unwindings to be considered.

We have thoroughly assessed the approach by running SMT-CBMC and CBMC against the following families of C programs:

- SelectSort.c(N), an implementation of the Selection Sort algorithm [Knu97],
- BellmanFord.c(N), an implementation of the Bellman Ford algorithm [Bel58] for computing single-source shortest paths in a weighted graph, and
- m_k_Gray_codes.c(N), an implementation of an algorithm for the generation of (m, k)-Gray code [Bla05], a generalization of the binary Gray code.

Each family of programs is parametric in a positive integer N such that both the size of the arrays occurring in the programs and the number of iterations done by the programs depend on N. Therefore the instances become harder as the value of N increases.

The results of the experiments are reported in Fig. 3. All the experiments presented here and in the rest of this paper have been carried out on a 2.4GHz Pentium IV running Linux with memory limit set to 800MB and time limit set to 30 minutes. The time (in seconds) spent by the tools to tackle each individual instance is given in the plots on the left. The size of the encodings (in bytes) generated by the tools are given by the plots on the right. CBMC has been invoked by manually setting the unwinding bound and by disabling simplification as these functionalities are not available in SMT-CBMC.

On the instances in the SelectSort.c(N) family, CBMC runs out of memory for $N > 17$, while SMT-CBMC can still analyze programs for $N = 75$. A comparison between the size of the formulae generated by SMT-CBMC and CBMC substantiates our remarks about the size of the encodings: the formula built by SMT-CBMC for $N = 17$ is almost two orders of magnitude smaller than the one built by CBMC. Similar considerations apply on the results obtained by running the tools against the instances of the BellmanFord.c(N) and m_k_Gray_Code.c(N) families.

It is worth pointing out that in our experiments we modeled the basic data types with bit-vectors thereby exploiting the decision procedure for the theory of bit-vectors available in CVC Lite during the solving phase. Experimental results indicate that similar performances are obtained by letting the numerical variables range over the integers and thereby using the decision procedure for linear arithmetic available in CVC Lite during the solving phase.

3   Counterexample-Guided Abstraction Refinement

Given a program P as input, a model checking procedure based on CEGAR amounts to the iteration of the following steps (see also Fig. 4):

Abstraction. An abstract program $\widehat{P}$ is generated from P. By construction every execution trace of P is also an execution trace of $\widehat{P}$. However, some trace of $\widehat{P}$ may not correspond to a trace of P.

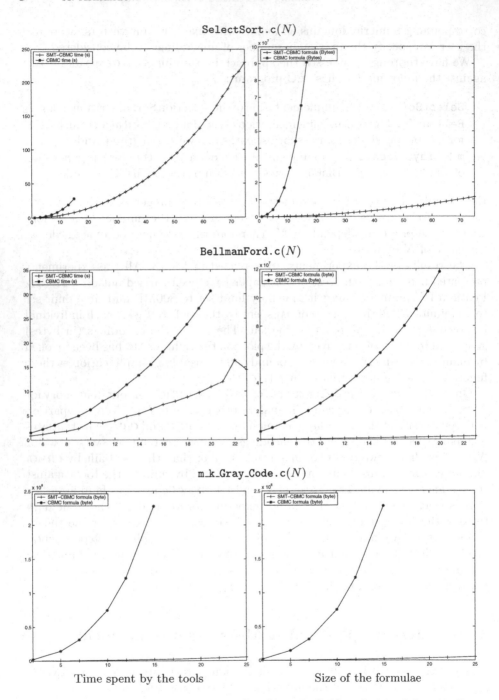

Fig. 3. SMT-CBMC vs. CBMC: time spent by the tools (left) and size of the encodings (right)

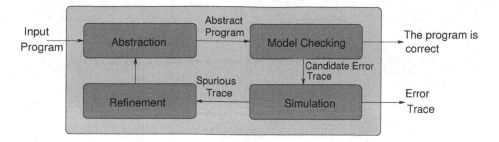

Fig. 4. The CEGAR Loop

Model Checking. The abstract program $\widehat{P}$ is model-checked. If $\widehat{P}$ is found to be safe (i.e. correct w.r.t. given properties), so is the original program P and this is reported to the user. If an error trace is found in $\widehat{P}$, then it is given as input to the next step.

Simulation. The error trace of $\widehat{P}$ found in the previous step is *simulated* on P in order to determine its feasibility, i.e. if it corresponds to an error trace of P. The feasibility check is usually carried out with the aid of an SMT solver. If the trace is feasible, then the error trace is reported to the user, otherwise the procedure continues with the next step.

Refinement. The information gathered from the SMT solver during the simulation step (typically a proof of the unfeasibility of the trace) is used to generate a new abstract program which *(i)* is more precise than the previous abstraction, and *(ii)* does not contain the spurious error trace found by the model checking phase.

The procedure outlined above can be instantiated in a variety of ways depending on the abstraction chosen. This choice has an important impact on the effectiveness of the whole procedure as it affects the complexity of the component steps (namely how difficult is *(i)* to model check abstract programs, *(ii)* to check abstract error traces, and *(iii)* to compute refined versions of the current abstract program whenever a spurious counterexample is found) as well as the number of iterations needed by the procedure to terminate.

3.1   Boolean Programs and CEGAR with Predicate Abstraction

The most widely applied instance of CEGAR (e.g. SLAM [BR01], BLAST [HJMS02], SATABS [CKSY05]) is based on predicate abstraction and uses boolean programs as target of the abstraction, i.e. programs whose variables range over the booleans and model the truth values of predicates corresponding to properties of the program state. The nice feature of boolean programs is that their reachability problem is decidable. A model checker for boolean programs based on the OBDDs technology is described in [BR00].

To illustrate, consider the programs in Fig. 5. These programs are obtained by applying a CEGAR procedure based on predicate abstraction to program

```
 1 | /* Program P */        | /* Program P̂₀ */      || /* Program P̂₁ */      | /* Program P̂₂ */      | 1
 2 | int numUnits;          |                        || bool nUO;              | bool nUO;              | 2
 3 | int level;             |                        ||                        |                        | 3
 4 |                        |                        ||                        |                        | 4
 5 | void getUnit() {       | void getUnit() {       || void getUnit() {       | void getUnit() {       | 5
 6 |  int canEnter=F;       |  ;                     ||  ;                     |  bool cE=F;            | 6
 7 |  if(numUnits==0) {     |  if(U) {               ||  if(nUO) {             |  if(nUO) {             | 7
 8 |   if(level>0) {        |   if(U) {              ||   if(U) {              |   if(U) {              | 8
 9 |    NewUnit();          |    ;                   ||    ;                   |    ;                   | 9
10 |    numUnits=1;         |    ;                   ||    nUO=F;              |    nUO=F;              | 10
11 |    canEnter=1;         |    ;                   ||    ;                   |    cE=T;               | 11
12 |   }                    |   }                    ||   }                    |   }                    | 12
13 |  } else canEnter=1;    |  } else ;              ||  } else ;              |  } else cE=T;          | 13
14 |  if(canEnter==1) {     |  if(U) {               ||  if(U) {               |  if(cE) {              | 14
15 |   if(numUnits==0)      |   if(U)                ||   if(nUO)              |   if(nUO)              | 15
16 |    ERROR: ;            |    ERROR: ;            ||    ERROR: ;            |    ERROR: ;            | 16
17 |   else                 |   else                 ||   else                 |   else                 | 17
18 |    gotUnit();          |    ;                   ||    ;                   |    ;                   | 18
19 |  }                     |  }                     ||  }                     |  }                     | 19
20 | }                      | }                      || }                      | }                      | 20
```

Fig. 5. Application of CEGAR with Predicate Abstraction

P. Program $\widehat{P}_0$ is the first abstraction of P and is obtained by replacing all the atomic statements by the skip statement (;) and all the expressions occurring in conditionals statements and in assertions with the U symbol (standing for *undefined*). A model checker for boolean programs determines that line 16 reachable in $\widehat{P}_0$ and returns 6,7,14,15,16 as execution trace. This trace is found to be spurious by simulating its execution on P. In fact, numUnits==0 cannot be false at line 7 and true at line 15. Program $\widehat{P}_0$ is thus refined into a program $\widehat{P}_1$ containing a new boolean variable nUO that is true when numUnits==0 and false otherwise. The model checker now determines that line 16 is still reachable in $\widehat{P}_1$ with error trace 6,7,8,14,15,16. Simulation on P reveals that also this trace is spurious. In fact, the assignment at line 6 sets canEnter to 0 and hence canEnter==1 at line 13 cannot possibly be true. Thus $\widehat{P}_1$ is refined to $\widehat{P}_2$ which contains a new boolean variable cE that is true when canEnter==1 and false otherwise. The model checker now concludes that line 16 is not reachable in $\widehat{P}_2$ and the CEGAR procedure can thus halt and return that line 16 in not reachable in P as well.

Predicate abstraction has proved effective on important application domains such as operating systems device drivers [BBC+06]. But it must be noted that device drivers are inherently control-intensive (i.e. the control flow largely prevails over the data flow). The effectiveness of predicate abstraction refinement on other kinds of software is still to be ascertained. As a matter of fact, CEGAR based on predicate abstraction performs poorly when applied to data intensive programs (e.g. programs performing non trivial manipulations of numeric variables and/or arrays): the abstractions that are built are too coarse, too many iterations of the abstraction refinement loop are usually required, and the refinement phase often fails to determine the boolean variables needed to build a more accurate model.

3.2   Linear Programs and CEGAR with Array Abstraction

Linear Programs (with arrays) are C programs where variables (and array elements) range over a numeric domain and expressions involve linear combinations of variables and array elements. By *Linear Arithmetic* we mean standard arithmetic (over $\mathbb{R}$ or $\mathbb{Z}$) with addition (i.e. $+$) and the usual relational operators (e.g. $=$, $<$, $\leq$, $>$, $\geq$) but without multiplication. By the *theory of arrays* we mean the theory concisely presented by the following axiom:

$$\forall a, i, j, e. \ \ \mathrm{select}(\mathrm{store}(a, i, e), j) = (j = i \ ? \ e : \mathrm{select}(a, j)) \tag{2}$$

where (_ ? _ : _) is a conditional term constructor with the obvious semantics.

An CEGAR procedure for model checking linear programs with arrays was is forward in [ABM07]. At the core of the procedure lies the model checker for linear programs described in [ACM04] and uses array indexes instead of predicates for the abstraction: the input program is abstracted w.r.t. sets of array indexes, the abstraction is a linear program (without arrays), and refinement looks for new array indexes. Thus, while predicate abstraction uses boolean programs as the target of the abstraction, in this approach linear programs are used for the same purpose. This is particularly attractive as linear programs can directly and concisely represent complex correlations among program variables and a small number of iterations of the abstraction refinement loop usually suffice to either prove or disprove that the input program enjoys the desired properties.

```
1 /* Program P */          /* Program P̂₀ */        /* Program P̂₁ */             1
2 void main() {            void main() {            void main() {               2
3   int i, a[30];            int i;                   int i, a¹;                 3
4   a[1] = 9;                ;                        a¹ = (1==1)?9:a¹;          4
5   i = 0;                   i = 0;                   i = 0;                     5
6   while(a[i]!=9) {         while(𝔘!=9) {            while(((i==1)?a¹:𝔘)!=9) {  6
7     a[i] = 2*i;            ;                          a¹ = (i==1)?2*i:a¹;      7
8     i = i+1; }             i = i+1; }                 i = i+1; }               8
9   assert(i<=1); }          assert(i<=1); }          assert(i<=1); }           9
```

Fig. 6. Application of CEGAR with Array Abstraction

To illustrate, consider the linear program with arrays P in Fig. 6. The procedure starts by abstracting P into $\widehat{P}_0$. This done by replacing every occurrence of array expressions with the symbol $\mathfrak{U}$ (denoting an arbitrary number) and every assignment to array elements with a skip statement (;). By applying a model checker for linear programs to $\widehat{P}_0$ we get the execution trace 4, 5, 6, 7, 8, 6, 7, 8, 6, 9, 0 witnessing the violation of the assertion at line 9. The feasibility check of the above trace w.r.t. P is done by generating a set of quantifier-free formulæ whose satisfying valuations correspond to all possible executions of the sequence of statements of P corresponding to the trace under consideration. This is done by first putting the trace in SSA form, then by replacing **while** statements with **assume** statements as shown in Tab. 1. Finally, quantifier-free formulæ encoding the behavior of the statements are generated.

Table 1. Checking the trace for feasibility

Step	Line	Original Statement	Renamed Statement	Formula
1	4	`a[1]=9;`	`a₁[1]=9;`	$a_1 = store(a_0, 1, 9)$
2	5	`i=0;`	`i₁=0;`	$i_1 = 0$
3	6	`while(a[i]!=9);`	`assume(a₁[i₁]!=9);`	$select(a_1, i_1) \neq 9$
4	7	`a[i]= 2*i;`	`a₂[i₁]=2*i₁;`	$a_2 = store(a_1, i_1, 2 * i_1)$
5	8	`i=i+1;`	`i₂=i₁+1;`	$i_2 = i_1 + 1$
6	6	`while(a[i]!=9);`	`assume(a₂[i₂]!=9);`	$select(a_2, i_2) \neq 9$
7	7	`a[i]=2*i;`	`a₃[i₂]=2*i₂;`	$a_3 = store(a_2, i_2, 2 * i_2)$
8	8	`i=i+1;`	`i₃=i₂+1;`	$i_3 = i_2 + 1$
9	6	`while(a[i]!=9);`	`assume(!(a₃[i₃]!=9));`	$\neg(select(a_3, i_3) \neq 9)$
10	8	`assert(i<=1);`	`assert(i₃<=1);`	$\neg(i_3 \leq 1)$

The resulting set of formulæ is then fed to an SMT solver. If it is found unsatisfiable (w.r.t. the union of the theory of arrays and the theory of bit-vectors), then the trace is not executable in P. If it is found satisfiable, then we can conclude that the trace is also executable in P. In our example the set of formulæ (see rightmost column in Table 1) is unsatisfiable and the proof of unsatisfiability found by the SMT solver is the following:

$$\cfrac{\cfrac{\cfrac{\cfrac{\cfrac{\cfrac{\cfrac{Q(i_2, a) \vdash select(a_2, i_2) \neq 9 \quad \vdash i_2 = i_1 + 1}{Q(i_1 + 1, a) \vdash select(a_2, i_1 + 1) \neq 9 \quad \vdash a_2 = store(a_1, i_1, 2 * i_1)}}{Q(i_1 + 1, a) \vdash select(store(a_1, i_1, 2 * i_1), i_1 + 1) \neq 9 \quad (2)}}{Q(i_1 + 1, a) \vdash (i_1 + 1 = i_1 \; ? \; 2 * i_1 : select(a_1, i_1 + 1)) \neq 9}}{Q(i_1 + 1, a) \vdash select(a_1, i_1 + 1) \neq 9 \qquad \vdash i_1 = 0}}{Q(1, a) \vdash select(a_1, 1) \neq 9 \qquad \vdash a_1 = store(a_0, 1, 9)}}{Q(1, a) \vdash select(store(a_0, 1, 9), 1) \neq 9 \qquad (2)}}{\cfrac{Q(1, a) \vdash (1 = 1 \; ? \; 9 : select(a_0, 1)) \neq 9}{Q(1, a) \vdash \bot}}$$

It is easy to see that the formulæ contributing to the proof are those associated with steps 1, 2, 4, 5, and 6. Moreover, the only term of the form $select(a, e)$ occurring in these formulæ is $select(a_2, i_2)$ (with $i_2 = 1$ given by the context). Thus, in order to rule out the above trace, we must refine $\widehat{P_0}$ by including the element of a at position 1. The resulting program, $\widehat{P_1}$, is obtained by replacing every expression of the form `a[e]` with the conditional expression `((e==1)?a¹:𝔘)` and every assignment of the form `a[e₁]=e₂;` with the assignment `a¹=((e₁==1)?e₂:a¹);` where a^1 is a new variable of numeric type corresponding to the array element of index 1. The model checker can now conclude that node 0 cannot be reached in $\widehat{P_1}$ and from this it follows that it is not reachable in P as well.

3.3   Experimental Results

The procedure presented in Sect. 3.2 has been implemented in the EUREKA tool [ABC+07]. We have tested EUREKA against a number of programs that involve reasoning on both arithmetic and arrays and thus allow to thoroughly assess

Table 2. Experimental results

Safe instances

Benchmark	EUREKA			BLAST		SATABS		
	N	total time	refined/total array elems	N	total time	N	ref. time	total time
STRING COPY	1000*	127.89	$1/2N$	Incorrect		10	105.98	144.69
STRING COMPARE	1000*	28.62	$2/2N$	Incorrect		9	210.619	296.20
GRAY CODE	60	62.75	16/28	Incorrect		Inconclusive		
PARTITION	40	108.23	$1/N$	Incorrect		Inconclusive		
BUBBLE SORT	9	77.67	N/N	Incorrect		2	24.39	30.42
INSERTION SORT	16	60.86	N/N	Incorrect		2	51.43	74.74
SELECTION SORT	9	64.20	N/N	Incorrect		2	75.53	115.86

Unsafe Instances

Benchmark	EUREKA			BLAST		SATABS		
	N	total time	refined/total array elems	N	total time	N	ref. time	total time
STRING COPY	1000*	73.70	$0/2N$	100*	167.98	21	724.40	819.77
STRING COMPARE	1000*	15.07	$0/2N$	100*	435.26	12	292.19	348.19
GRAY CODE	1000*	1.70	12/28	1000*	7.62	Inconclusive		
PARTITION	1000*	61.42	$0/N$	10*	214.31	21	127.91	186.63
BUBBLE SORT	50*	26.19	$0/N$	15*	395.38	7	327.33	460.76
INSERTION SORT	100*	190.74	$0/N$	20*	316.00	5	131.58	270.64
SELECTION SORT	500*	41.15	$0/N$	20*	506.81	7	101.97	291.20

the effectiveness and the scalability properties of the tool. On the same problems we have tested two well-known software model checkers based on predicate abstraction, namely BLAST and SATABS. All problems consist of a family of programs parametric in a positive integer N. The size of the arrays occurring in the programs and/or the number of iterations carried out by the loops increase as N increases. Thus the higher is the value of N, the bigger is the search space to be analyzed.

The results in Table 2 refers to safe and unsafe (i.e. with a bug injected) instances of the above benchmarks. Each entry shows the greatest instance the tools are able to analyze and the time in seconds. Also, we give the time taken by the refinement phase of SATABS, the number of array elements found by EUREKA during the refinement phase, and the sum of the sizes of the arrays involved in the programs. Numbers with * indicate that the tool can analyze greater instances than the one shown.

The analysis of linear programs with arrays is obtained by letting each tool deal with arrays in its own way: EUREKA abstracts and refines them w.r.t. array indexes, SATABS models them faithfully as adjacent sequences of variables, and BLAST applies some abstraction techniques. (Expressions of the for $a[i]$ and $a[i+r]$, as well as $*(a+i)$ and $*(a+i+r)$, with $r>0$ are indistinguishable for BLAST [HJMS02].)

As shown in Table 2, on most safe problems BLAST reports an incorrect answer, that is, it concludes that the program is unsafe when it is safe instead. On unsafe instances BLAST exhibits a better behavior than on safe ones, but still it exhibits scalability problems.

SATABS employs a SAT solver in the abstraction and refinement phases, thus allowing a precise encoding of pointer arithmetic, bit-level constructs, etc. Table 2 reveals (as expected) that SATABS does not output false positives nor negatives, and that scalability is often an issue. The results of the experiments demonstrate the great effort required by the refinement phase despite the efficiency of current SAT solvers.

The experimental results confirm the effectiveness of the array abstraction and reveal the difficulties of the approaches based on predicate abstraction when dealing with programs featuring a tight interplay between arithmetic and array manipulation.

4   Related Work

Bultan, Gerber, and Pugh are probably among the first to investigate model checking of infinite-state systems. In [BGP99] they propose a model checking technique for concurrent systems where transition systems are specified using Presburger formulæ over the integers. The systems are formalized in an *ad-hoc* event-action input language which no provision for arrays. Termination of the procedure process is ensured by means of widening techniques [CC77].

Besides BLAST and SATABS, which we analyzed in the previous sections, a number of other tools based on predicate abstraction have been developed. The early SLAM project[1] has now given raise to the Static Driver Verifier tool[2].

F-Soft [ISGG05] is a model checker for C programs developed at NEC Labs America. F-Soft treats pointers and arrays precisely, but this is done by fully expanding arrays and using an explicit representation of the internal memory. Since F-Soft is not publicly available no experimental comparison has been possible.

The approach proposed in [CR06] reduces the problem of finding execution paths of finite length that violate some given properties to a Constraint Satisfaction Problem (CSP). This is done by building a boolean constraint system whose solutions correspond to the execution paths of the control-flow graph of the program. A SAT solver is then used to enumerate the execution paths. For each execution path found by the SAT solver a constraint system encoding the reachability of an error statement is built and fed to a constraint solver for finite domains. The approach is thus clearly exponential in the number of execution paths of the control-flow graph of the program.

Flanagan [Fla04] provides an in-depth analysis of the connection between Constraint Logic Programs (CLPs), imperative, and object oriented programs. CLPs are embedded in the CEGAR paradigm in order to combine and unify theorem proving (performed with CLP over a numeric domain) and model checking

---

[1] See http://www.research.microsoft.com/~slam
[2] See http://www.microsoft.com/whdc/devtools/tools/sdv.mspx

of boolean programs (performed using CLP over the booleans). However, to the best of our knowledge, no implementation is publicly available.

ESC/Java [FLL$^+$02] analyzes user-annotated Java programs by generating verification conditions (representing the initial states from which no execution can lead to a violation of the given properties) which are then checked with the Simplify theorem prover [DNS03]. Since the generation of the verification conditions is an undecidable problem, several heuristics are used to drive this activity, but this may lead the tool to report unsound results.

5   Conclusions

SMT solvers are a key technology for the development of effective software model checkers. In this paper I have shown that by leveraging the strengths of SMT solvers it is possible to build software model checkers that outperform state-of-the-art tools based on OBDDs and SAT solvers.

Acknowledgments

I am indebted to Jacopo Mantovani, Lorenzo Platania, and Massimo Benerecetti for their collaboration on the development of the software model checking techniques presented in the paper. Most of the work I have reported here would not have been possible without their contribution. I am also grateful to Dario Carotenuto and Pasquale Spica for their help in the development of the EUREKA tool.

This work was partially supported by the PRIN Project no. 20079E5KM8 "Integrating automated reasoning in model checking: towards push-button formal verification of large-scale and infinite-state systems" funded by the Italian Ministry of University and Research.

References

[ABC$^+$07]   Armando, A., Benerecetti, M., Carotenuto, D., Mantovani, J., Spica, P.: The EUREKA tool for software model checking. In: Stirewalt, R.E.K., Egyed, A., Fischer, B. (eds.) ASE, pp. 541–542. ACM, New York (2007)

[ABM07]   Armando, A., Benerecetti, M., Mantovani, J.: Abstraction refinement of linear programs with arrays. In: Grumberg, O., Huth, M. (eds.) TACAS 2007. LNCS, vol. 4424, pp. 373–388. Springer, Heidelberg (2007)

[ACM04]   Armando, A., Castellini, C., Mantovani, J.: Software model checking using linear constraints. In: Davies, J., Schulte, W., Barnett, M. (eds.) ICFEM 2004. LNCS, vol. 3308, pp. 209–223. Springer, Heidelberg (2004)

[AMP06]   Armando, A., Mantovani, J., Platania, L.: Bounded Model Checking of Software using SMT Solvers instead of SAT Solvers. In: Valmari, A. (ed.) SPIN 2006. LNCS, vol. 3925, pp. 146–162. Springer, Heidelberg (2006)

[AMP09]   Armando, A., Mantovani, J., Platania, L.: Bounded Model Checking of Software using SMT Solvers instead of SAT Solvers. International Journal on Software Tools for Technology Transfer (STTT) 11(1), 69–83 (2009)

[BB04]   Barrett, C., Berezin, S.: CVC Lite: A new implementation of the cooper-
            ating validity checker. In: Alur, R., Peled, D.A. (eds.) CAV 2004. LNCS,
            vol. 3114, pp. 515–518. Springer, Heidelberg (2004)
[BBC⁺06]   Ball, T., Bounimova, E., Cook, B., Levin, V., Lichtenberg, J., McGarvey,
            C., Ondrusek, B., Rajamani, S.K., Ustuner, A.: Thorough static analy-
            sis of device drivers. In: EuroSys 2006: Proceedings of the 2006 EuroSys
            conference, pp. 73–85. ACM Press, New York (2006)
[Bel58]   Bellman, R.E.: On a Routing Problem. Quarterly of applied mathemat-
            ics 16, 87–90 (1958)
[BGP99]   Bultan, T., Gerber, R., Pugh, W.: Model-checking concurrent systems with
            unbounded integer variables: symbolic representations, approximations,
            and experimental results. ACM Transactions on Programming Languages
            and Systems 21(4), 747–789 (1999)
[Bla05]   Black, P.E.: Gray code, in dictionary of algorithms and data structures
            (2005), http://www.nist.gov/dads/HTML/graycode.html
[BR00]   Ball, T., Rajamani, S.K.: Bebop: A symbolic model checker for boolean
            programs. In: Havelund, K., Penix, J., Visser, W. (eds.) SPIN 2000. LNCS,
            vol. 1885, pp. 113–130. Springer, Heidelberg (2000)
[BR01]   Ball, T., Rajamani, S.K.: Automatically validating temporal safety prop-
            erties of interfaces. In: Dwyer, M.B. (ed.) SPIN 2001. LNCS, vol. 2057, pp.
            103–122. Springer, Heidelberg (2001)
[CC77]   Cousot, P., Cousot, R.: Abstract interpretation: A unified lattice model for
            static analysis of programs by construction or approximation of fixpoints.
            In: POPL, Los Angeles, USA, pp. 238–252. ACM, New York (1977)
[CFR⁺89]   Cytron, R., Ferrante, J., Rosen, B.K., Wegman, M.N., Zadeck, F.K.: An ef-
            ficient method of computing static single assignment form. In: Proceedings
            of POPL (ACM SIGPLAN-SIGACT Symposium on Principles of Program-
            ming Languages), pp. 25–35. ACM, New York (1989)
[CKSY05]   Clarke, E., Kroening, D., Sharygina, N., Yorav, K.: SATABS: SAT-based
            predicate abstraction for ANSI-C. In: Halbwachs, N., Zuck, L.D. (eds.)
            TACAS 2005. LNCS, vol. 3440, pp. 570–574. Springer, Heidelberg (2005)
[Cla00]   Clarke, E.: Model Checking. MIT Press, Boston (2000)
[CR06]   Collavizza, H., Rueher, M.: Exploration of the capabilities of constraint
            programming for software verification. In: Hermanns, H., Palsberg, J. (eds.)
            TACAS 2006. LNCS, vol. 3920, pp. 182–196. Springer, Heidelberg (2006)
[DNS03]   Detlefs, D.L., Nelson, G., Saxe, J.B.: Simplify: a Theorem Prover for Pro-
            gram Checking. Technical Report 148, HP Labs (2003)
[Fla04]   Flanagan, C.: Software model checking via iterative abstraction refinement
            of constraint logic queries. In: CP+CV 2004 (2004)
[FLL⁺02]   Flanagan, C., Leino, K.R.M., Lillibridge, M., Nelson, G., Saxe, J.B., Stata,
            R.: Extended static checking for java. In: PLDI 2002: Proceedings of the
            ACM SIGPLAN 2002 Conference on Programming language design and
            implementation, pp. 234–245. ACM Press, New York (2002)
[Gat02]   Gates, B.: Keynote address at WinHEC 2002 (2002),
            http://www.microsoft.com/presspass/exec/billg/speeches/
            2002/04-18winhec.aspx
[HJMS02]   Henzinger, T.A., Jhala, R., Majumdar, R., Sutre, G.: Lazy abstraction.
            In: POPL, Portland, USA, pp. 58–70. ACM, New York (2002)

[ISGG05] Ivanicic, F., Shlyakhter, I., Gupta, A., Ganai, M.K.: Model checking c
          programs using f-soft. In: ICCD 2005: Proceedings of the 2005 Interna-
          tional Conference on Computer Design, Washington, DC, USA, pp. 297–
          308. IEEE Computer Society, Los Alamitos (2005)
[KCY03]   Kroening, D., Clarke, E., Yorav, K.: Behavioral consistency of C and Ver-
          ilog programs using bounded model checking. In: Proc. of DAC 2003, Ana-
          heim, USA, pp. 368–371. ACM Press, New York (2003)
[Knu97]   Knuth, D.: The Art of Computer Programming, Volume 3: Sorting and
          Searching, vol. 3. Addison-Wesley, Reading (1997)
[Seb07]   Sebastiani, R.: Lazy satisability modulo theories. JSAT 3(3-4), 141–224
          (2007)

Combining Nonmonotonic Knowledge Bases with External Sources*

Thomas Eiter[1], Gerhard Brewka[2], Minh Dao-Tran[1], Michael Fink[1],
Giovambattista Ianni[3], and Thomas Krennwallner[1]

[1] Institut für Informationssysteme, Technische Universität Wien
Favoritenstraße 9-11, A-1040 Vienna, Austria
{eiter,dao,fink,tkren}@kr.tuwien.ac.at
[2] Universität Leipzig, Augustusplatz 10-11, 04109 Leipzig, Germany
brewka@informatik.uni-leipzig.de
[3] Dipartimento di Matematica, Universitá della Calabria, I-87036 Rende (CS), Italy
ianni@mat.unical.it

Abstract. The developments in information technology during the last decade have been rapidly changing the possibilities for data and knowledge access. To respect this, several declarative knowledge representation formalisms have been extended with the capability to access data and knowledge sources that are external to a knowledge base. This article reviews some of these formalisms that are centered around Answer Set Programming, viz. HEX-programs, modular logic programs, and multi-context systems, which were developed by the KBS group of the Vienna University of Technology in cooperation with external colleagues. These formalisms were designed with different principles and four different settings, and thus have different properties and features; however, as argued, they are not unrelated. Furthermore, they provide a basis for advanced knowledge-based information systems, which are targeted in ongoing research projects.

1 Introduction

The developments in information technology during the last decade have been rapidly changing the possibilities for data and knowledge access. The World Wide Web and the underlying Internet provide a backbone for the information systems of the 21st century, which will possess powerful reasoning capabilities that enable one to combine various pieces of information, possibly stored in heterogeneous formats and with different semantics, such that the wealth of information can be more profitably exploited. In that, information from plain sources and software packages with simple semantics (such as, e.g., from a route planner) will have to be mixed with semantically richer sources like expert knowledge bases, in a suitable manner, bridging the gap between different sources.

Driven by this need, extensions of declarative knowledge representation formalisms have been developed with the capability to access external data and knowledge sources.

---

* This work has been supported by the Austrian Science Fund (FWF) projects P20840 & P20841, the EC ICT Integrated Project Ontorule (FP7 231875), and the Vienna Science and Technology Fund (WWTF) project ICT08-020.

S. Ghilardi and R. Sebastiani (Eds.): FroCoS 2009, LNAI 5749, pp. 18–42, 2009.

Often, this is realized via an interface in the style of an API; examples of such rule based formalisms are Prolog engines, or extensions of Answer Set Programming (ASP), which is based on nonmonotonic logic programs. A particular application area where extensions of nonmonotonic formalisms received a lot of attention recently is the Semantic Web, cf. [35,41,1], and especially combinations of rules with external ontologies; see [14,10] for overviews and discussions.

However, such extensions are non-trivial, especially if the flow of information between a knowledge base and the external sources is bidirectional. That is, the external source influences the reasoning of the knowledge base, which in turn influences the behavior of the external source. To define suitable semantics for such scenarios, in the presence of heterogeneity and distribution, is a challenging problem.

At the Knowledge Based Systems (KBS) Group of the Vienna University of Technology, people have been working on this problem in several past and ongoing projects, with a focus on combining nonmonotonic knowledge bases with external sources, in cooperation with other researchers. The aim of this article is to give a short survey of some of the formalisms that have been developed, and to provide (for the first time) a more systematic view of these approaches, according to some characteristic features which, on the one hand derive from the underlying setting and on the other hand also determine the properties of the formalisms. Comparison to related work will be largely omitted here, and we refer to the original papers for this.

Historic Background. The work at KBS on access to external sources in the last years has precursors dating back more than a decade ago, in different areas: the action language for the IMPACT agent platform [39] in the area of agents, and logic programs with generalized quantifiers [13], in the area of nonmonotonic logic programming.

The IMPACT agent language [20,39] is a rule-based language for specifying the behavior of a single agent, in terms of actions she may take, depending on the agent state and input perceived from the environment and other agents via a message box. As the agent program sits on top of internal data structures, access to such data structures via *code calls* (available through APIs) in special *code call atoms* had been devised. As these code calls are in fact logically independent of the physical realization, they can be equally viewed as access to external data sources (as done in some system demos). A suite of semantics has been defined for agent programs, including nonmonotonic ones like minimal model and stable semantics.

Nonmonotonic logic programs with generalized quantifiers (GQLPs) were proposed in [13] to increase the expressiveness of logic programs under answer set semantics, by incorporating *Generalized Quantifiers (GQs)* akin to Lindström quantifiers in first-order logic (such as majority quantifiers; see [40]); similar extensions had been conceived for database query languages like SQL, to model aggregate functions, or to incorporate transitive closure. Special *GQ atoms* allowed to evaluate GQs (which, semantically boils down to decide whether a particular structure, determined by input predicates, belongs to a class of first-order structures). Viewing logic programs as GQs, [13] developed an approach to modular logic programming in which a program module can access other modules through an interface, which returns inferences of a module depending on input provided by the calling module.

Table 1. Classification of formalisms

reduct world view	GL-style	FLP
local model	GQLPs	HEX
globale state	MCS	MLPs

However, the formalisms in [20,13] have some limitations and shortcomings. Both suffer from groundedness issues in the semantics, in that atoms might be true in "models" without "founded" support in terms of rules that derive these atoms (a ubiquitous problem in knowledge representation and reasoning, most prominently discussed in Autoepistemic Logic; see [31]). Furthermore, in IMPACT, the focus was on efficient executability over (heterogenous) data structures, which was realized with rule unfolding and pre-compilation; only a very rudimentary (monotonic) fragment of the language was implemented. GQLPs were geared towards accessing sources with inherent logical properties of admissible classes of structures, and modular logic programs on top did not allow for recursion in module calls; furthermore, no implementation was available.[1]

Recent Work. Motivated by the growing desire for extensions of ASP to access external sources, which especially arose in the Semantic Web area, HEX-programs were proposed in [17] as a basic formalism for this purpose, abstracting from the more special description logic (dl-)programs [19] that combine ASP and OWL ontologies. To overcome the problems of modular logic programming via GQLPs, a refined approach has been recently presented in [7] which redefines the semantics of modular logic programs and, noticeably, allows for arbitrary (mutual) recursion between modules. Orthogonal to these formalisms are multi-context systems [2], which were motivated from a different angle, namely reasoning with contexts. Here, beliefs between several contexts, which can be seen as agents with different views of a scenario, have to be exchanged; naturally, this amounts to knowledge bases with external knowledge access, where nonmonotonicity is a desired feature.

As detailed in later sections, modular logic programs (MLPs) can be viewed as a special setting for HEX-programs where external sources are nonmonotonic logic programs themselves. In contrast, multi-context systems (MCSs) can be viewed as a generalization of HEX-programs, in which information exchange is moved to the meta-level above the knowledge bases that instantiate a generic logic. However, this view is superficial and neglects important aspects that make the formalisms rather different.

From a principled view, the most important are the following two orthogonal aspects:

environment view. The definition of the semantics takes either an individual or a societal view; in the former, even though there is a collection of programs (or knowledge bases) $KB_1, \ldots, KB_n$, the semantics is merely defined in terms of *local models* for each individual knowledge base KB_i; the semantics of the collection implicitly emerges from the local models. In contrast, in the societal view,

---

[1] The first systems supporting answer set semantics became available at that time; Gerald Pfeifer, one of the chief developers of the DLV system, deemed GQLPs in 1997 as very interesting and put a respective task on his growing todo list (it is still there).

the collection has a *global state*, which consists of a collection of local models, one for each KB_i, that is explicitly accessible. The latter allows, e.g., to define preference over global states, and to single out most preferred ones. Protagonists of the local-model semantics are GQLPs and HEX-programs, while MLPs and MCSs have global-state semantics. Loosely speaking, in game-theoretic terms the former semantics are akin to Nash equilibria, while the latter strive for *Pareto-optimality*.

program reduct. All formalisms involve, in the tradition of answer set semantics, a notion of reduct which alters the rules of a program. The classical definition of answer set semantics [24] uses the *Gelfond-Lifschitz (GL) reduct* [23], which given an interpretation roughly removes grounded rules whose negative body part is false in the interpretation, and strips off negative literals from the remaining rules. Later, the *Faber-Leone-Pfeifer (FLP) reduct* [21] was presented which simply removes all grounded rules with a false body. While the two reducts are equivalent for ordinary logic programs, they behave differently for language extensions; an attractive feature of the FLP reduct is that it retains minimality of models, which helps to ensure groundedness of the semantics. Of the formalisms considered here, GQLPs and MCSs use a GL-style reduct, while HEX-programs and MLPs use the FLP-reduct.

In summary, this leads to a systematic classification of approaches shown in Table 1. Each of the possible combinations, which comes with different features and properties, is in fact populated by a formalism from above. Other formalisms we developed also fit into this classification; e.g., dl-programs [19] are local-model/GL-style reduct.

The different combinations are not unrelated, and in some cases, one type of combination might coincide with another one or be reducible to it. For example, in special cases, the choice of the reduct does not play a role (this holds, e.g., for the premier fragment of dl-programs, cf. [17]). Furthermore, as we show in Section 5, under a natural condition MCSs can be encoded into HEX-programs. Finally, the classification also shows ways for possible variations of existing formalisms (e.g., MCS).

Roadmap. The rest of this article is structured as follows. In the next section, we recall the answer set semantics of nonmonotonic logic programs, where we provide both the original definition [24] and the equivalent one in terms of the FLP-reduct [21]. In the Sections 3–5, we then consider HEX-programs, modular logic programs, and multi-context systems and discuss their relationship. After that, we present in Section 6 ongoing work and projects, together with issues for research. The final Section 7 gives a short summary and conclusions.

2 Preliminaries

In this section, we recall the answer set semantics of logic programs (over classical literals) [24], which extends the stable model semantics [23] with *classical* (or, more appropriately, *strong*) *negation*. For more background, see [24,22,15].

Syntax. Ordinary logic programs are built over a first-order vocabulary Φ with nonempty finite sets $\mathcal{P}, \mathcal{C}, \mathcal{F}$ of predicate, constant, and function symbols (of arity $n \geq 1$), and a set $\mathcal{X}$ of variables. *Terms* are inductively built as usual from $\mathcal{C}$ and $\mathcal{X}$ using function symbols from $\mathcal{F}$. *Atoms* are expressions of the form $p(t_1, \ldots, t_n)$, where $p \in \mathcal{P}$ has arity $n \geq 0$ and $t_1, \ldots, t_n$ are terms. A *classical literal* (simply *literal*) l is an atom α or a negated atom $\neg\alpha$; its *complement* is $\neg\alpha$ (resp., α). A *negation-as-failure literal* (or simply *NAF-literal*) is a literal l or a default-negated literal *not* l.

A *(disjunctive) rule* r is of the form

$$\alpha_1 \vee \cdots \vee \alpha_k \leftarrow \beta_1, \ldots, \beta_m, \text{not } \beta_{m+1}, \ldots, \text{not } \beta_n \qquad (1)$$

where $k + n > 0$ and all α_i and β_j are literals. The disjunction $\alpha_1 \vee \cdots \vee \alpha_k$ is the *head* of r, and the conjunction $\beta_1, \ldots, \beta_m, \text{not } \beta_{m+1}, \ldots, \text{not } \beta_n$ is the *body* of r, where $\beta_1, \ldots, \beta_m$ (resp., not $\beta_{m+1}, \ldots, \text{not } \beta_n$) is the *positive* (resp., *negative*) *body* of r. We use the notation $H(r) = \{\alpha_1, \ldots, \alpha_k\}$ and $B(r) = B^+(r) \cup B^-(r)$, where $B^+(r) = \{\beta_1, \ldots, \beta_m\}$ and $B^-(r) = \{\beta_{m+1}, \ldots, \beta_n\}$.

If $B(r) = \emptyset$, then r is a *(disjunctive) fact*; we also omit "$\leftarrow$" in this case. If $H(r) = \emptyset$, then r is a *constraint*. If $k = 1$, then r is called *normal*, and if $m = n$, then r *is positive* (or *not-free*).

A *(disjunctive) program* is a finite set of rules. A program P is *normal* (resp., *positive*), if each rule $r \in P$ is normal (resp., *positive*).

While we have defined here programs with function symbols, traditional Answer Set Programming does not consider function symbols, as they lead to undecidability; however, more recently, decidable fragments have received attention, cf. [9]. Furthermore, Φ is often implicit from the rules of program P, i.e., $\Phi = \Phi_P$; if no constant appears in P, an arbitrary constant symbol is added to $\mathcal{C}$.

Semantics. The answer set semantics is defined in terms of consistent sets of classical literals. Positive programs are assigned the minimal consistent sets of classical ground literals that satisfy all rules; the semantics of arbitrary programs is defined by a reduction to positive programs.

As usual, a term, atom etc. is *ground*, if no variable occurs in it. Let HU_P be the *Herbrand universe* of a program P, which consists of all ground terms over Φ_P. The *Herbrand base* of P, denoted HB_P, is the set of all ground (classical) literals with predicate symbols from $\mathcal{P}$ and terms from HU_P.

An *interpretation* I relative to P is a consistent subset of HB_P. Satisfaction of ground literals, rules, and programs relative to I is as follows. I is a model of

- a ground literal α ($I \models \alpha$) iff $\alpha \in I$;
- a ground rule r ($I \models r$) iff $I \models H(r)$ whenever $I \models B(r)$, where (i) $I \models H(r)$ iff there is some $\alpha_i \in H(r)$ such that $I \models \alpha_i$, and (ii) $I \models B(r)$ iff $I \models \beta_j$ for all $\beta_j \in B^+(r)$ and $I \not\models \beta_j$ for all $\beta_j \in B^-(r)$.
- a set of ground rules R ($I \models R$) iff $I \models r$ for all $r \in R$.

Models of nonground rules r and programs P, are defined with respect to their groundings $grnd(r)$ and $grnd(P) = \bigcup_{r \in P} grnd(r)$, where $grnd(r)$ consists of all ground instances of r. A program P is (classically) *satisfiable*, if it has some model.

Then, for a positive program P, an *answer set* of P is any interpretation I such that $I \models P$ and $J \not\models P$ for every $J \subset I$, i.e., I is a minimal model of P under set inclusion.

Definition 1 (Gelfond-Lifschitz reduct). *The* Gelfond-Lifschitz reduct, *of a program P relative to an interpretation $I \subseteq HB_P$, denoted P^I, is the ground positive program that results from $grnd(P)$ by*

(i) *deleting every rule r such that $B^-(r) \cap I \neq \emptyset$, and*
(ii) *deleting the negative body from every remaining rule.*

An *answer set* of a (disjunctive) program P is any interpretation $I \subseteq HB_P$ such that I is an answer set of P^I. The set of all answer sets of a program P is denoted by $ans_{GL}(P)$.

Example 1. Consider the normal logic program P, consisting of the following rules, where g is an atom:

$$g \leftarrow \text{not } \neg g; \qquad \neg g \leftarrow \text{not } g. \tag{2}$$

Then, the answer sets of P are given by $M_1 = \{g\}$ and $M_2 = \{\neg g\}$. Informally, the rules allow to choose between g and $\neg g$; the single disjunctive fact $g \vee \neg g$ yields the same result.

Example 2. The following rules select from a set (stored in a predicate p) one element:

$$sel(X) \leftarrow p(X), \text{not } \neg sel(X).$$
$$\neg sel(X) \vee \neg sel(Y) \leftarrow p(X), p(Y), X \neq Y.$$

Informally, the first rule says that an element is picked by default, and the second that from two elements, at least one is not picked (here "$\neq$" is a built-in predicate that can easily be defined). Adding facts $F = \{p(c_i) \mid 1 \leq i \leq n\}$, the resulting program P has the answer sets $M_i = F \cup \{\neg sel(c_j) \mid 1 \leq j \neq i \leq n\} \cup \{sel(c_i)\}, i = 1, \ldots, n$.

We note that strong negation does not increase expressivity and can be easily compiled away, by viewing $\neg p$ as a fresh predicate symbol and adding the constraint $\leftarrow p(X_1, \ldots, X_n), \neg p(X_1, \ldots, X_n)$; thus, in ASP formalisms (e.g., in HEX-programs) strong negation is often omitted for simplicity.

Answer Sets using the FLP-reduct. Answer sets can be alternatively defined in many ways, cf. [29]. For our concerns, the following is of particular interest.

Definition 2 (Faber-Leone-Pfeifer reduct). *The* Faber-Leone-Pfeifer (FLP) reduct *of a program P relative to an interpretation $I \subseteq HB_P$, denoted fP^I, is the ground program consisting of rules $r \in grnd(P)$ such that $I \models B(r)$.*

An *FLP answer set* of a disjunctive program P is an interpretation $I \subseteq HB_P$ such that $I \models fP^I$ and no $J \subset I$ exists such that $J \models fP^I$. The set of all FLP answer sets of a program P is denoted by $ans_{FLP}(P)$. Thus, FLP answer sets differ from the usual ones only by the use of fP^I instead of P^I. Faber *et al.* [21] show that this is immaterial.

Proposition 1 ([21]). *For every (disjunctive) program P, $ans_{GL}(P) = ans_{FLP}(P)$.*

This property does not generalize to extensions of logic programs in which the building blocks α_i and β_j in a rule (1) may be other constructs than literals. This is the case e.g. for aggregate atoms [21], or for GQ atoms in [13] and external atoms in [17].

3   HEX-Programs

HEX-programs are a basic formalism featuring *a) external atoms* for accessing outer information in logic programs, and *b)* constructs for performing higher-order reasoning [17,18]. HEX-programs take inspiration and generalize their ancestors, such as the action language of the IMPACT agent platform [20,39], dl-programs [19,16] and the DLV-EX formalism [6,5]. Higher-order constructs enable a form of reasoning at the terminological level, overcoming some limitations of traditional logic programming under answer set semantics in this respect. This latter issue falls outside the scope of this paper; thus, among the two main extensions characterizing HEX-programs, we will focus next on external atoms.

3.1   Motivation and Outline

The conception of HEX-programs stems from some of its closest ancestors, that is dl-programs [19,16], and the DLV-EX extension to the DLV system [6,5].

Focusing on interoperability with description logic bases, dl-programs make use of *dl-atoms* to deal with this single species of external knowledge. Such atoms enable dl-programs to query an external source of knowledge, expressed in a description logic of choice, and allow a bidirectional flow of information about concept membership and role assertions to and from external sources. Notably, dl-programs assume a known and finite domain of individual constants. In general, invention of unknown values coming from external sources is both an important theoretical issue, and a desirable practical feature.

On the other hand, DLV-EX focused on the possibility to introduce general purpose external predicates, explicitly allowing to bring new constants from the outer realms into play. Nonetheless, this framework has a flow of information based on constants and values, without relations and higher order data as possible in HEX.

HEX-programs combine benefits of both frameworks within the notion of external atoms: there can be many sorts of external atoms, each of which is connected to a different kind of external knowledge and/or computation; also, it is possible to have relational information flow from and to the logic program at hand.

Informally, one can exploit external predicates through *external atoms* such as the RDF atom $\&rdf[urls, graphs](X, Y, Z)$. Here, *graphs* and *urls* constitute the input list, while X, Y and Z refer to the attributes of a ternary relation which can be considered as the output relation of the external atom. The extension of the output relation of an external atom depends on the input list, and on the definition of the external predicate $\&rdf$. Actually, the definitions of external predicates such as $\&rdf$, are associated with computable functions that take an input list $l_1, \ldots, l_n$ and an interpretation I, and return an output relation. The availability of I as input value makes relational extensions of predicates accessible to external atoms. Usually the names of predicates whose extensions are accessed are mentioned in the input list, together with other input values. Consider for instance the atom $\&reach[knows, john](X)$: the predicate $\&reach$ might be defined in a way such that $\&reach[knows, john](x)$ evaluates to true for any x which is reachable from *john* through the current extension of the binary predicate *knows*.

We now give a more formal overview of this simple, yet powerful framework.

$$subRelation(brotherOf, relativeOf). \qquad (4)$$

$$brotherOf(john, al). \quad relativeOf(john, joe). \quad brotherOf(al, mick). \qquad (5)$$

$$invites(john, X) \lor skip(X) \leftarrow X \neq john, \& reach[relativeOf, john](X). \qquad (6)$$

$$R(X, Y) \leftarrow subRelation(P, R), P(X, Y). \qquad (7)$$

$$someInvited \leftarrow invites(john, X). \qquad (8)$$

$$\leftarrow not\ someInvited. \qquad (9)$$

$$\leftarrow \& degs[invites](Min, Max), Max > 2. \qquad (10)$$

Fig. 1. Example HEX-program

3.2   Formal Concepts

Syntax of HEX-Programs. The vocabulary Φ comprises besides C and $\mathcal{X}$ also *external predicate names* $\mathcal{G}$, which are prefixed with "$\&$". We note that constant symbols serve both as individual and predicate symbols (no $\mathcal{P}$ is needed).

A *higher-order atom* (or *atom*) is a tuple $(Y_0, Y_1, \ldots, Y_n)$, where $Y_0, \ldots, Y_n$ are terms and $n \geq 0$. Intuitively, Y_0 is the predicate name, thus we use the familiar notation $Y_0(Y_1, \ldots, Y_n)$. The atom is *ordinary*, if Y_0 is a constant. For example, $(x, rdf\!:\!type, c)$, $node(X)$, and $D(a, b)$, are atoms; the first two are ordinary.

An *external atom* is of the form

$$\& g[Y_1, \ldots, Y_n](X_1, \ldots, X_m) , \qquad (3)$$

where $Y_1, \ldots, Y_n$ and $X_1, \ldots, X_m$ are two lists of terms (called *input* and *output* lists, respectively), and $\& g \in \mathcal{G}$ is an external predicate name. We assume that $\& g$ has fixed lengths $in(\& g) = n$ and $out(\& g) = m$ for input and output lists, respectively. An external atom provides a way for deciding the truth value of an output tuple depending on the extension of a set of input predicates: in this respect, an external predicate $\& g$ is equipped with a function $f_{\& g}$ evaluating to true for proper input values.

A HEX-*rule* r is of the form (1), where all α_i are (higher-order) atoms and each β_j is a (higher-order) atom or an external atom; strong negation is disregarded. $H(r)$, $B(r)$, $B^+(r)$, and $B^-(r)$ are as in Section 2; r is *ordinary*, if it contains only ordinary atoms.

Definition 3. *A* HEX-*program is a finite set P of* HEX-*rules. It is* ordinary, *if all rules are ordinary.*

Example 3 ([17]). Consider the HEX-program P in Figure 1. Informally, this program randomly selects a certain number of John's relatives for invitation. The first line states that *brotherOf* is a subrelation of *relativeOf*, and the next line gives concrete facts. The disjunctive rule (6) chooses relatives, employing the external predicate $\& reach$. This latter predicate takes in input a binary relation e and a node name n, returning the nodes reachable from n when traversing the graph described by e (see the following Example 5). Rule (7) axiomatizes subrelation inclusion exploiting higher-order atoms; that is, for those couples of binary predicates p, r for which it holds *subRelation*(p, r), it must be the case that $r(x, y)$ holds whenever $p(x, y)$ is true.

The constraints (9) and (10) ensure that the number of invitees is between 1 and 2, using (for illustration) an external predicate $\&\,degs$ from a graph library. Such a predicate has a valuation function $f_{\&\,degs}$ where $f_{\&degs}(I, e, min, max)$ is true iff min and max are, respectively, the minimum and maximum vertex degree of the graph induced by the edges contained in the extension of predicate e in interpretation I.

Semantics of HEX-Programs. In the sequel, let P be a HEX-program. As for ordinary programs, unless specified otherwise, $\mathcal{C}$ and $\mathcal{G}$ are implicitly given by P. The *Herbrand base* of P, denoted HB_P, is the set of all ground atoms and external atoms (we disregard here negative literals). The grounding of a rule r, $grnd(r)$, and of a program P, $grnd(P)$, are analog as above.

Example 4 ([17]). Given $\mathcal{C} = \{edge, arc, a, b\}$, ground instances of $E(X, b)$ are, e.g., $edge(a, b)$, $arc(a, b)$, $a(edge, b)$, and $arc(arc, b)$. The ground instances of the external atom $\&\,reach[edge, N](X)$ are all possible combinations where N and X are replaced by elements from $\mathcal{C}$; some examples are $\&\,reach[edge, edge](a)$, $\&\,reach[edge, arc](b)$, and $\&\,reach[edge, edge](edge)$.

An *interpretation relative to* P is any subset $I \subseteq HB_P$ containing only atoms. The notion of satisfaction (model) of rules and programs relative to I is defined as in Section 2, using for ground higher-order atoms and external atoms the following clauses:

- I satisfies a ground higher-order atom $a \in HB_P$ ($I \models a$) iff $a \in I$.
- I satisfies a ground external atom $a = \&\,g[y_1, \ldots, y_n](x_1, \ldots, x_m)$ ($I \models a$) iff $f_{\&g}(I, y_1, \ldots, y_n, x_1, \ldots, x_m) = 1$, where $f_{\&g}$ is a (fixed) $(n+m+1)$-ary Boolean function associated with $\&\,g \in \mathcal{G}$ that assigns each tuple $(I, y_1 \ldots, y_n, x_1, \ldots, x_m)$ either 0 or 1, where $n = in(\&\,g)$, $m = out(\&\,g)$, $I \subseteq HB_P$, and $x_i, y_j \in \mathcal{C}$.

Example 5 ([17]). Let us associate with the external atom $\&\,reach$ a function $f_{\&reach}$ such that $f_{\&reach}(I, E, A, B) = 1$ iff B is reachable in the graph E from A. Let $I = \{e(b, c), e(c, d)\}$. Then, $I \models \&\,reach[e, b](d)$ since $f_{\&reach}(I, e, b, d) = 1$.

Note that in contrast to the semantics of higher-order atoms, which in essence reduces to first-order logic as customary (cf. [37]), the semantics of external atoms is in spirit of second order logic since it involves predicate extensions.

A HEX-program P is *satisfiable*, if it has some model. Carrying the definition of FLP-reduct fP^I from Section 2 over naturally, we then have:

Definition 4. $I \subseteq HB_P$ *is an* answer set *of a* HEX-*program* P *iff* I *is a minimal model of* fP^I.

Considering example 3, as John's relatives are determined to be Al, Joe, and Mick, P has six answer sets, each of which contains one or two of the facts $invites(john, al)$, $invites(john, joe)$, and $invites(john, mick)$.

In principle, the truth value of an external atom depends on its input and output lists and on the entire model of the program. In practice, however, we can identify certain types of input terms that allow to restrict the input interpretation to specific relations. The Boolean function associated with the external atom $\&\,reach[edge, a](X)$ for instance will only consider the extension of the predicate $edge$ and the constant value a for computing its result, and simply ignore everything else of the given input interpretation.

An important property of answer sets, which is guaranteed by the use of the FLP-reduct, is groundedness.

Proposition 2 ([17]). *Every answer set of a* HEX-*program P is a minimal model of P.*

This would not be generally the case if instead of fP^I we would use the GL-reduct from Section 2; however, it is if all external atoms α in P are *monotonic*, i.e., whenever $I \subseteq J \subseteq HB_P$ and $I \models \alpha'$ for a ground instance α' of α, then $J \models \alpha'$. Then the following result, which generalizes Proposition 1, can be easily shown. Let $ans_{FLP}(P)$ and $ans_{GL}(P)$ denote the answer sets of P defined using the FLP-reduct and the GL-reduct, respectively.

Theorem 1. *Suppose P is a* HEX-*program such that all external atoms in P are monotonic. Then $ans_{GL}(P) = ans_{FLP}(P)$.*

3.3 Evaluation of HEX-Programs

Some concerns might be raised regarding practical evaluation of HEX-programs. Arguably, the features of HEX-programs (mainly, the possibility of combining higher-order constructs with external atoms, with no restriction on their usage) enforce some design constraint that would compromise the practical adoption of this formalism in its full generality. To this end, although keeping desirable advantages, feasible classes of HEX-programs for implementation were identified in [18], together with a general method for combining and evaluating sub-programs belonging to arbitrary classes, thus enlarging the variety of programs whose execution is practicable. As detailed in [38] HEX-programs can be evaluated by means of calls to a traditional answer set solver, interleaved with calls to external atom functions. The evaluation order is given by means of a generalization of the splitting sets method [30]. A recently explored way to further improve evaluation is program decomposition, by exploiting independence information of the external atoms, which is used to restrict the evaluation domain in each decomposed program [12].

3.4 Implementation and Applications

HEX-programs have been implemented within the dlvhex prototype,[2] which is based on a flexible and modular architecture. The evaluation of the external atoms is realized by plugins, which are loaded at run-time. Third-party developers can easily contribute by adding new external predicates to the (rich) pool of available external predicates.

HEX-programs have been deployed to a number of applications in different contexts, of which we mention some here. Hoehndorf et al. [28] showed how to combine multiple biomedical upper ontologies by extending the first-order semantics of terminological knowledge with default logic. The corresponding prototype implementation of such kind of system is given by mapping the default rules to a HEX-program. Fuzzy

---

[2] http://www.kr.tuwien.ac.at/research/systems/dlvhex/

extensions of answer-set programs in relation with HEX-programs are given in [33,27]. While [33] maps fuzzy answer set programs to HEX-programs, [27] defines a fuzzy semantics for HEX-programs and gives a translation to standard HEX-programs. In [34], the planning language $\mathcal{K}^c$ was introduced which features external function calls in spirit of HEX-programs. Also, HEX-programs have been applied to optimal credential selection in the context of trust negotiation processes [38].

4   Modular Nonmonotonic Logic Programming

We now turn to Modular Nonmonotonic Logic Programs (MLPs) [7], which have their roots in *Logic Programs with Generalized Quantifiers* (GQLPs) [13] and HEX-programs. GQLPs extend logic programs by *generalized quantifiers (GQs)*, i.e., formulas $Q\boldsymbol{x}[R(\boldsymbol{x})]$ with generalized quantifier $Q\boldsymbol{x}$ over a structure defined by the relation R (cf. [40] for background). For instance, for the transitive closure GQ Q_{tc}, the rule

$$t(X,Y) \leftarrow Q_{tc}[e](X,Y) \tag{11}$$

sets t to the transitive closure of the binary relation defined by e. Naturally, we may view GQs as interfaces to logic programs; thus Q_{tc}, may be defined as the logic program

$$tc(X,Y) \leftarrow e(X,Y). \tag{12}$$
$$tc(X,Y) \leftarrow tc(X,Z), tc(Z,Y). \tag{13}$$

with "input" predicate e and "output" predicate tc. Then, (11) may be seen as a module that calls a submodule defined by (12) and (13). Following this line, GQLPs can be used as a host to define a semantics for modular logic programs.

In [7], the modular logic programs allow for representing disjunctive logic programs in modules, which can use module atoms to access and update knowledge in other logic programs. Module atoms can be seen as an abstract way to interface with other programs, since the update mechanism of this kind of atoms gives rise to multiple instances of logic programs. HEX-programs share this similarity of updating external knowledge sources, but, unlike MLPs, these updates play only a role "locally," while updates in MLPs have the potential to trigger the creation of new "module instances," which act as new "global" entities. We will reconsider this issue later in this section. Next, we compare MLPs with HEX-programs and GQLPs.

MLP vs. GQLPs and HEX-Programs. The first stepping stone towards modular logic programs were GQLPs, which are programs that have besides standard literals also generalized quantifier literals in the body of rules. On top of that, the interface to the modules of a modular logic program can be conceived as GQs.

This approach has been enhanced in HEX-programs which use the FLP-reduct to deal with negation-as-failure, and have disjunctive heads. Essentially, HEX-programs are similar to GQLPs, and external atoms are in the same vein as GQLPs.

Both formalisms have limitations. In GQLPs, only *hierarchical* modular logic programs were defined, i.e., programs whose subprograms do not refer back to the calling program. If one defines in a HEX-program external atoms as interfaces to logic program modules, this restriction is not explicit; however, there is an implicit understanding that external sources are independent of the calling HEX-program, and thus that modules are acyclic. Hence, the first problem worth to overcome is the acyclic module topology, and to define a semantics that can deal with arbitrarily intertwined modules, where each of them can call each other (or themselves), possibly in a recursive way.

A second shortcoming of GQLPs is that their answer sets lack *groundedness*. E.g.,

$$P = \{ \, p(a) \leftarrow C_\forall[p] \, \}$$

has two answer sets, viz. $M_1 = \emptyset$ and $M_2 = \{p(a)\}$. While M_1 is a minimal model of P (and thus intuitively grounded), M_2 is not; hence, answer sets of GQLPs may be "unfounded." This anomaly is due to the use of a Gelfond-Lifschitz style reduct that treats external atoms like not-literals; in this way, self-supporting beliefs are possible, similar as in Autoepistemic Logic (AEL); indeed, P paraphrases the canonical AEL theory $T = \{Lp(a) \supset p(a)\}$ that has two stable expansions akin to M_1 and M_2 (cf. [31]). Similarly, cyclic logic program modules based on HEX-programs lack groundedness (the above example is easily recast to this setting using two cyclic modules).

The above shortcomings are remedied in MLPs: they impose no restriction on calls in a program and allow for modules that may recursively access other modules; unfounded answer sets are prevented by using the FLP-reduct, which ensures minimality of answer sets. Furthermore, taking into account that modules are parts of a global program, MLPs have a global-state semantics in which Pareto-optimal states are singled out.

4.1 Formal Concepts

Modular logic programs (MLPs) consist of modules as a means to structure logic programs. The modules allow for input provided by other modules, through call by value, and may call each other in (mutual) recursion. We illustrate this on an example.

Example 6. Suppose we have three modules named $P_1[\,]$, $P_2[q_2]$, and $P_3[q_3]$ with rules $R_1 = \{q(a). \; q(b). \; ok \leftarrow P_2[q].even.\}$,

$$R_2 = \left\{ \begin{array}{l} q_2'(X) \lor q_2'(Y) \leftarrow q_2(X), q_2(Y), \\ \qquad\qquad\qquad X \neq Y. \\ skip_2 \leftarrow q_2(X), not\ q_2'(X). \\ even \leftarrow not\ skip_2. \\ even \leftarrow skip_2, P_3[q_2'].odd. \end{array} \right\}, \quad R_3 = \left\{ \begin{array}{l} q_3'(X) \lor q_3'(Y) \leftarrow q_3(X), q_3(Y), \\ \qquad\qquad\qquad X \neq Y. \\ skip_3 \leftarrow q_3(X), not\ q_3'(X). \\ odd \leftarrow skip_3, P_2[q_3'].even. \end{array} \right\}$$

respectively. Informally, *ok* is computed true in P_1, if P_2 (having formal parameter q_2) computes *even* true on input of predicate q's value. P_2 does so in mutual recursion with P_3 (having formal parameter q_3), which computes *odd*; for this, they compute for the recursive call in q_i' the input q_i minus one randomly removed element (cf. Example 2).

Syntax of MLPs. The vocabulary Φ also has a set $\mathcal{M}$ of *module names* P with fixed associated lists $\boldsymbol{q} = q_1, \ldots, q_k$ $(k \geq 0)$ of predicate names $q_i \in \mathcal{P}$ (the formal input parameters), denoted $P[\boldsymbol{q}]$; function symbols are disregarded.

Ordinary atoms (simply atoms) have the form $p(t)$, where $p \in \mathcal{P}$ has arity $n \geq 0$ and $t = t_1, \ldots, t_n$ are terms. A *module atom* has the form

$$P[p_1, \ldots, p_k].o(t_1, \ldots, t_l) , \qquad (14)$$

where (i) $P \in \mathcal{M}$ with $P[q_1, \ldots, q_k]$, (ii) $p_1, \ldots, p_k$ is an input list of predicate names $p_i \in \mathcal{P}$ matching the arity of q_i, and (iii) $o(t_1, \ldots, t_l)$ is an ordinary atom (with $o \in \mathcal{P}$). Intuitively, a module atom provides a way for deciding the truth value of a (ground) atom $o()$ in a program P depending on a set of input predicates.

An *MLP-rule* r is of the form (1), where all α_i are atoms, each β_j is an atom or a module atom, and $k \geq 1$;[3] r is *ordinary*, if it contains only ordinary atoms.

A *module* $m = (P, R)$ consists of a module name $P \in \mathcal{M}$ and a finite set R of rules. *Main modules* have no input (i.e., have $P[\,]$), while *library modules* have arbitrary input. As usual, empty input $[\,]$ and argument lists $(\,)$ are omitted.

Definition 5. *A* modular logic program *(MLP) is of the form* $\mathbf{P} = (m_1, \ldots, m_n)$, $n \geq 1$, *where all* $m_i = (P_i, R_i)$ *are modules and at least one* m_i *is a main module.*

To have no unused modules, it is assumed that $\mathcal{M} = \{P_1, \ldots, P_n\}$. $\mathbf{P}$ is *ground*, iff each module M_i is *ground*, which means that all rules in R_i are ground.

The *call graph of an MLP* $\mathbf{P}$ is a labeled digraph $CG_{\mathbf{P}} = (V, E, l)$ with vertex set $V = VC(\mathbf{P})$ and an edge e from $P_i[S]$ to $P_k[T]$ in E iff $P_k[p].o(t)$ occurs in $R(m_i)$; furthermore, e is labeled with an input list p, denoted $l(e)$.

Example 7. The MLP in Example 6 consists of three modules $\mathbf{P} = (m_1, m_2, m_3)$, where $m_1 = (P_1, R_1)$ is the main module and $M_i = (P_i[q_i], R_i)$, $i = 2, 3$ are library modules. Furthermore, m_1 is ground while m_2 and m_3 are not.

Let $S_\emptyset^i = \emptyset$, $S_a^i = \{q_i(a)\}$, $S_b^i = \{q_i(b)\}$, and $S_{ab}^i = \{q_i(a), q_i(b)\}$. Then $VC(\mathbf{P}) = \{P_1[\emptyset], P_2[S_v^2], P_3[S_w^3]\}$, where $v, w \in \{\emptyset, a, b, ab\}$, and $CG_{\mathbf{P}}$ has edges $P_1[\emptyset] \xrightarrow{q} P_2[S_v^2]$, $P_2[S_v^2] \xrightarrow{q_2'} P_3[S_w^3]$, and $P_3[S_w^3] \xrightarrow{q_3'} P_2[S_v^2]$.

Semantics of MLPs. The semantics of MLPs is given in terms of grounding and Herbrand interpretations customary in logic programming. Naturally, also modules $(P[q], R)$ must be instantiated before they can be "used;" there is one instance per possible input for q (referred to as *value call*). To focus on "relevant" module instances, the call chain and an embracing context of value calls are considered, while others are (in essence) ignored.

The *Herbrand base* of an MLP $\mathbf{P}$ (implicitly defining $\Phi = \Phi_{\mathbf{P}}$) is the set $HB_{\mathbf{P}}$ of all ground ordinary and module atoms from vocabulary Φ. The grounding $grnd(r)$ of a rule and $grnd(R)$ of a rule set R are as usual; the grounding of a module $m = (P[q], R)$ is $grnd(m) = (P[q], grnd(R))$, and the grounding of an MLP $\mathbf{P} = (m_1, \ldots, m_n)$ is $gr(\mathbf{P}) = (grnd(m_1), \ldots, grnd(m_n))$.

To define module instances, we need the following notations. For any set S of ground atoms and lists $p = p_1, \ldots, p_k$ and $q = q_1, \ldots, q_k$ of predicate names, let $S|_p = \bigcup_{i=1}^k \{p_i(c) \in S\}$ and $S|_p^q = \bigcup_{i=1}^k \{q_i(c) \mid p_i(c) \in S\}$.

---

[3] Constraints $\leftarrow B(r)$ (banned for satisfiability) are easily emulated with $f \leftarrow$ not $f, B(r)$.

Then, for a module $m_i = (P_i[\boldsymbol{q_i}], R_i)$, a *value call with input* S is a pair (P_i, S) where $S \subseteq HB_\mathbf{P}|_{\boldsymbol{q_i}}$, also written as $P_i[S]$; its *instantiation with* S is the rule set $I_\mathbf{P}(P_i[S]) = R_i \cup S$. The possible instances of all modules m_i in $\mathbf{P}$ are naturally indexed by the set $VC(\mathbf{P})$ of all possible $P_i[S]$. Technically, they form an (indexed) tuple $I(\mathbf{P}) = (I_\mathbf{P}(P_i[S]) \mid P_i[S] \in VC(\mathbf{P}))$ called the *instantiation* of $\mathbf{P}$. The latter is a *rule base*, which are tuples $\mathbf{R} = (R_{P_i[S]} \mid P_i[S] \in VC(\mathbf{P}))$ of rule sets $R_{P_i[S]}$.

An *interpretation* $\mathbf{M}$ is now an (indexed) tuple $(M_i/S \mid P_i[S] \in VC(\mathbf{P}))$ of sets M_i/S of ordinary ground atoms. At a value call $P_i[S]$, it satisfies (is a model of)

– a ground atom $\alpha \in HB_\mathbf{P}$, denoted $\mathbf{M}, P_i[S] \models \alpha$, iff (i) $\alpha \in M_i/S$ when α is ordinary, and (ii) $o(\boldsymbol{c}) \in M_k/((M_i/S)|_{\boldsymbol{p}}^{\boldsymbol{q_k}})$, when $\alpha = P_k[\boldsymbol{p}].o(\boldsymbol{c})$ is a module atom;
– a ground rule r ($\mathbf{M}, P_i[S] \models r$), iff $\mathbf{M}, P_i[S] \models H(r)$ or $\mathbf{M}, P_i[S] \not\models B(r)$, where (i) $\mathbf{M}, P_i[S] \models H(r)$, iff $\mathbf{M}, P_i[S] \models \alpha$ for some $\alpha \in H(r)$, and (ii) $\mathbf{M}, P_i[S] \models B(r)$, iff $\mathbf{M}, P_i[S] \models \alpha$ for all $\alpha \in B^+(r)$ and $\mathbf{M}, P_i[S] \not\models \alpha$ for all $\alpha \in B^-(r)$;
– a set of ground rules R ($\mathbf{M}, P_i[S] \models R$) iff $\mathbf{M}, P_i[S] \models r$ for all $r \in R$.

Furthermore, $\mathbf{M}$ satisfies a rule base $\mathbf{R}$ ($\mathbf{M} \models \mathbf{R}$), if $grnd(R_{P_i[S]})$ at all $P_i[S]$ are satisfied by $\mathbf{M}$, and $\mathbf{M}$ satisfies $\mathbf{P}$ ($\mathbf{M} \models \mathbf{P}$), if $\mathbf{M} \models I(grnd(\mathbf{P}))$.

To focus on relevant module instances w.r.t. an interpretation $\mathbf{M}$, we use the *relevant call graph* $CG_\mathbf{P}(\mathbf{M})$ *of* $\mathbf{P}$, which is the subgraph of $CG_\mathbf{P}$ containing all edges $e :$ $P_i[S] \xrightarrow{l(e)} P_k[T]$ in $CG_\mathbf{P}$ such that $(M_i/S)|_{l(e)}^{q_k} = T$, with nodes induced by the edges plus all main module instantiations (called *relevant instances* w.r.t. $\mathbf{M}$).

Example 8. For the interpretation $\mathbf{M}$ such that $M_1/\emptyset = \{q(a), q(b), ok\}$, $M_2/S_{ab}^2 = \{q_2(a), q_2(b), q_2'(a), skip_2, even\}$, $M_2/\emptyset = \{even\}$, and $M_3/S_a^3 = \{q_3(a), skip_3, odd\}$, the nodes of $CG_\mathbf{P}(\mathbf{M})$ are $P_1[\emptyset]$, $P_2[S_{ab}^2]$, $P_2[\emptyset]$, and $P_3[S_a^3]$.

The nodes of $CG_\mathbf{P}(\mathbf{M})$ are the smallest set of module instances which is intuitively involved in building an answer set. As an over-approximation, a superset C of these nodes, called *context*, is used in [7]; we omit this here for simplicity.

To define answer sets, we first need minimal models, which are given as follows: let $\mathbf{M} \leq \mathbf{M}'$ iff $M_i/S \subseteq M_i'/S$ for all $P_i[S]$. Then a model $\mathbf{M}$ of $\mathbf{P}$ (resp., a rule base $\mathbf{R}$) is *minimal*, if $\mathbf{P}$ (resp., $\mathbf{R}$) has no model $\mathbf{M}' \neq \mathbf{M}$ such that $\mathbf{M}' \leq \mathbf{M}$.

Now the FLP-reduct is generalized to work on MLPs componentwise where module instantiations outside the relevant call graph are not touched. Formally, the *reduct* $f\mathbf{P}(P_i[S])^\mathbf{M}$ *of* $\mathbf{P}$ *at* $P_i[S]$ *w.r.t.* $\mathbf{M}$ is (i) the FLP-reduct $fI_{gr(\mathbf{P})}(P_i[S])^{M_i/S}$, i.e., $\{r \in I_{gr(\mathbf{P})}(P_i[S]) \mid \mathbf{M}, P_i[S] \models B(r)\}$, if $P_i[S]$ is in $CG_\mathbf{P}(\mathbf{M})$, and (ii) $I_{gr(\mathbf{P})}(P_i[S])$ otherwise. The *reduct of* $\mathbf{P}$ *w.r.t.* $\mathbf{M}$ is $f\mathbf{P}^\mathbf{M} = (f\mathbf{P}(P_i[S])^\mathbf{M} \mid P_i[S] \in VC(\mathbf{P}))$.

Definition 6. *An interpretation $\mathbf{M}$ of an MLP $\mathbf{P}$ is an* answer set *of $\mathbf{P}$, iff $\mathbf{M}$ is a minimal model of $f\mathbf{P}^\mathbf{M}$.*

Example 9. Recall interpretations of the form $\mathbf{M}$ from Example 8. It is easily verified that for every node $P_i[S]$ in $CG_\mathbf{P}(\mathbf{M})$, the respective interpretation M_i/S is minimal for $f\mathbf{P}(P_i[S])^\mathbf{M}$. Therefore, any such $\mathbf{M}$ is an answer set of $\mathbf{P}$ iff for every $P_i[S]$ outside $CG_\mathbf{P}(\mathbf{M})$, the interpretation M_i/S is a minimal model of $I_{gr(\mathbf{P})}(P_i[S])$.

4.2 Semantic Properties of MLPs

MLPs conservatively extend ordinary logic programs, and many of the nice semantic properties of the latter generalize to them. We recall below a couple of them from [7].

Proposition 3 ([7]). *Let R be an ordinary logic program. Then M is an answer set of R iff $\mathbf{M} = (M_1/\emptyset)$ with $M_1/\emptyset = M$ is an answer set of the MLP (m_1), where $m_1 = (P_1[\,], R)$ is a main module and P_1 is a module name.*

An important observation is that the answer sets of an MLP $\mathbf{P}$ are grounded; this is due to the use of the FLP-reduct (a GL-style reduct would behave differently).

Proposition 4. *Every answer set of $\mathbf{P}$ is a minimal model of $\mathbf{P}$.*

Moreover, in absence of negation-as-failure also the converse holds.

Proposition 5. *The answer sets of a positive MLP $\mathbf{P}$ coincide with its minimal models.*

For a suitable notion of intersection, we get that the models of a Horn MLP $\mathbf{P}$ are closed under intersection; hence, a Horn MLP has a canonical answer set.

Proposition 6. *Every Horn MLP $\mathbf{P}$ has a single answer set, which coincides with its least model.*

4.3 Computation

Exploiting Proposition 6, answer sets of Horn MLPs can be computed by means of a bottom up fixed-point computation. However, this is not effective, as many irrelevant module instantiations might be considered that do not contribute to the part of interest, given by the main modules. As has been shown in [7], in the general case, one has to deal with double exponential many instantiations, which is clearly infeasible in practice. This calls for refined methods that overcome the need to instantiate all possible modules.

Further work [8] addresses efficient evaluation of MLPs using a generalization of the splitting sets method [30] that takes relevance information into account. For a certain subclass of MLPs that obeys a notion of *call stratification* and *input stratification*, we have an algorithm that evaluates MLPs top-down, more importantly, expands only relevant instantiations during the evaluation, which speeds up the process.

5 Multi-context Systems

In this section, we turn to another nonmonotonic formalism that provides access to external sources in the realm of context-based reasoning. Informally, a multi-context system describes the information available in a number of contexts (e.g., to different agents or views) and specifies the information flow between those contexts. Furthering work in [32,25], the Trento School developed monotonic heterogeneous multi-context systems [26] with the aim to integrate different inference systems; informally, they viewed contexts as pairs $Context_i = (\{T_i\}, \Delta_{br})$ where each $T_i = (L_i, \Omega_i, \Delta_i)$ is a formal system, and Δ_{br} consists of *bridge rules* of the form

$$(c_1\ p_1), \ldots, (c_k\ p_k) \Rightarrow (c_j\ q_j)$$

using labeled formulas $(c\,p)$ where p is from the language L_c. Giunchiglia and Serafini gave a collection of such contexts a semantics in terms of local models plus compatibility conditions, which respects information flow across contexts via bridge rules. Noticeably, reasoning within/across contexts is monotonic.

Brewka et al. [4] extended the framework to Contextual Default Logic (CDL), improving on [36], where bridge rules with negation were considered. CDL integrates nonmonotonic inference systems of the same kind, viz. theories in Reiter's Default Logic. Here, defaults may refer to other contexts and play the role of bridge rules.

The Multi-Context Systems (MCS) of [2] generalized these approaches, by accommodating *heterogeneous* and both *monotonic* and *nonmonotonic* contexts, thus capable of integrating "typical" monotonic KR logics like description logics or temporal logics, and nonmonotonic logics like Reiter's Default Logic, Answer Set Programming, circumscription, defeasible logic, or theories in autoepistemic logic; in several of the latter, a knowledge base gives rise to multiple belief sets in general. In our taxonomy, MCSs have a "global-state" semantics, that is defined via bridge rules and follows the classical ASP definition, extended to this setting. Before we present MCSs in more detail, it is helpful to compare them to MLPs and HEX-programs.

MCSs vs. MLPs and HEX-Programs. Compared to MLPs, MCSs are more general since the contexts (viewed as modules) consist of general reasoning systems or logics, respectively, and not only of ASP programs. The MCS semantics is similar in spirit to the semantics of MLPs in [13], but global-state rather than local-state, and quite different from MLPs in [7], which are global-state and use FLP-reduct.

For HEX-programs, the comparison shows a more complex picture:

– MCSs are similar to HEX-programs where the external sources are knowledge bases.
– We may view MCSs as a more general, hybrid formalism than such HEX-programs, in which bridge rules for the information flow are distinguished (at the meta-level) from the formulas of the knowledge base; HEX-rules with external atoms can be seen as bridge rules, and HEX-rules without as rules of the knowledge base describing the local state.
– HEX-programs are local-state and use the FLP-reduct, while MCSs are global-state and use GL-style reducts. The local-state property prevents a naive encoding of MCSs into HEX (as local belief sets of other contexts can not be directly accessed); however, under some (weak) condition, such an encoding is possible; we discuss this in Section 5.2.
– In HEX-programs, we may abstractly access knowledge bases through powerful reasoning services of an API beyond checking formula membership in local belief sets.

5.1 Formal Concepts

In [2], a "logic" is, very abstractly, a tuple $L = (\mathbf{KB}_L, \mathbf{BS}_L, \mathbf{ACC}_L)$, where

– $\mathbf{KB}_L$ is a set of well-formed knowledge bases, each being a set (of formulas),
– $\mathbf{BS}_L$ is a set of possible belief sets, each being a set (of formulas), and
– $\mathbf{ACC}_L : \mathbf{KB}_L \to 2^{\mathbf{BS}_L}$ assigns each $kb \in \mathbf{KB}_L$ a set of acceptable belief sets;

L is *monotonic*, if $\mathbf{ACC}_L$ assigns each kb a single belief set (denoted S_{kb}), and $kb \subseteq kb'$ implies $S_{kb} \subseteq S_{kb'}$. We can think of knowledge bases as logic programs, classical theories etc; the possible belief sets are those which are syntactically admissible (e.g., deductively closed sets of sentences, set of literals, etc); and $\mathbf{ACC}_L$ respects that a knowledge base might have one, multiple, or even no acceptable belief set in the logic.

Access to other contexts is facilitated via bridge rules for heterogenous logics. Given logics $L = L_1, \ldots, L_n$, an L_i-bridge rule over L, $1 \leq i \leq n$, is of the form

$$s \leftarrow (r_1 : p_1), \ldots, (r_j : p_j), \mathbf{not}\ (r_{j+1} : p_{j+1}), \ldots, \mathbf{not}\ (r_m : p_m) \qquad (15)$$

where $r_k \in \{1 \ldots, n\}$ and p_k is an element of some belief set of L_{r_k}, $1 \leq k \leq m$, and $kb \cup \{s\} \in \mathbf{KB}_i$ for each $kb \in \mathbf{KB}_i$.

Multi-context systems are then defined as follows.

Definition 7. *A* multi-context system $M = (C_1, \ldots, C_n)$ *consists of contexts* $C_i = (L_i, kb_i, br_i)$, *where* $L_i = (\mathbf{KB}_i, \mathbf{BS}_i, \mathbf{ACC}_i)$ *is a logic,* $kb_i \in \mathbf{KB}_i$ *is a knowledge base, and* br_i *is a set of* L_i-*bridge rules over* $L = L_1, \ldots, L_n$, $1 \leq i \leq n$.

Example 10. As a simple example, we consider $M = (C_1, C_2)$, where the contexts are different views of a paper by its co-authors A_1 and A_2 who reason in different logics. In C_1, we have Classical Logic as L_1, the knowledge base $kb_1 = \{\ unhappy \supset revision\ \}$, and the bridge rules $br_1 = \{\ unhappy \leftarrow (2 : work)\ \}$. Intuitively, if A_1 is unhappy about the paper, then she wants a revision, and if A_2 finds that the paper needs more work, then A_1 feels unhappy. In C_2, we have Answer Set Programming as L_2, the knowledge base $kb_2 = \{\ accepted \leftarrow good, \mathbf{not}\ \neg accepted\ \}$ and bridge rules $br_2 = \{\ work \leftarrow (1 : revision); good \leftarrow \mathbf{not}\ (1 : unhappy)\}$. Intuitively, A_2 thinks that the paper, if good, is usually accepted; moreover, she infers that more work is needed if A_1 wants a revision, and that the paper is good if there is no evidence that A_1 is unhappy.

The semantics of an MCS is defined in terms of special belief states, which are sequences $S = (S_1, \ldots, S_n)$ such that each S_i is an element of $\mathbf{BS}_i$. Intuitively, S_i should be a belief set of the knowledge base kb_i; however, also the bridge rules must be respected; to this end, kb_i is augmented with the conclusions of its bridge rules that are applicable. More precisely, a bridge rule r of form (15) is *applicable in* S, if $p_i \in S_{r_i}$, for $1 \leq i \leq j$, and $p_k \notin S_{r_k}$, for $j + 1 \leq k \leq m$. Denote by $head(r)$ the head of r and by $app(R, S)$ the set of bridge rules $r \in R$ that are applicable in S. Then,

Definition 8. *A belief state* $S = (S_1, \ldots, S_n)$ *of a multi-context system* M *is an* equilibrium *iff* $S_i \in \mathbf{ACC}_i(kb_i \cup \{head(r) \mid r \in app(br_i, S)\})$, $1 \leq i \leq n$.

An equilibrium thus is a belief state which contains for each context an acceptable belief set, given the belief sets of the other contexts.

Example 11 (ctd). Reconsidering $M = (C_1, C_2)$ from Example 10, we find that M has two equilibria, viz.

- $E_1 = (Cn(\{unhappy, revision\}), \{work\})$ and
- $E_2 = (Cn(\{unhappy \supset revision\}), \{good, accepted\})$,

where $Cn(\cdot)$ is the set of all classical consequences. As for E_1, the bridge rule of C_1 is applicable in E_1, and $Cn(\{unhappy, revision\})$ is the (single) acceptable belief set of $kb_i \cup \{unhappy\}$; the first bridge rule of C_2 is applicable in E_1, but not the second; clearly, $\{work\}$ is the single answer set of $kb_2 \cup \{\ work\ \}$.

As for E_2, the bridge rule of C_1 is not applicable in E_1, and $Cn(\{unhappy \supset revision\} = Cn(kb_1)$; now the second bridge rule of C_2 is applicable but not the first, and $\{good, accepted\}$ is the single answer set of $kb_2 \cup \{good\}$.

The notion of equilibrium may remind of similar game-theoretic concepts, and in fact we may view each context C_i as a player in an n-person game where players choose belief sets. Assume that an outcome (i.e., belief state) $S = (S_1, \ldots, S_n)$, has for C_i reward 1 if $S_i \in \mathbf{ACC}_i(kb_i \cup \{head(r) \mid r \in app(br_i, S)\})$ and 0 otherwise. Then, it is easy to see that each equilibrium of M is a *Nash equilibrium* of this game (indeed, each player has optimal reward); on the other hand, there might be Nash equilibria that do not correspond to any equilibrium. This may happen e.g. if no acceptable belief sets are possible. For instance, the MCS $M = (C_1, C_2)$, where C_1 and C_2 are isolated answer set programs $\{a \leftarrow not\ a\}$, has no equilibrium, but $S = (\emptyset, \emptyset)$ is a Nash-equilibrium of the game. Clearly, if M has equilibria, then they coincide with the *Pareto-optimal* solutions of the game; under additional conditions (e.g., $\mathbf{ACC}_i(b_i \cup H_i) \neq \emptyset$ for each $H_i \subseteq \{h(r) \mid r \in br_i\}$) they coincide with the Nash equilibria.

Groundedness. Equilibria suffer, similar as the answer sets of modular logic programs in [13], from groundedness problems due to cyclic justifications. Informally, the reason is that bridge rules might be applied unfoundedly. E.g., in Example 10, *unhappy* has in $E_1 = (Cn(\{unhappy, revision\}), Cn(\{work\}))$ only a cyclic justification: it is accepted in C_1 via the bridge rule, as *work* is accepted in C_2; the latter is also via a bridge rule, as *revision* is accepted in C_1 (by modus ponens from *unhappy* $\supset$ *revision* and *unhappy*). Here, the application of the bridge rules is unfounded.

Inspired by the definition of answer set semantics, [2] proposed grounded equilibria to overcome this. They are defined in terms of a GL-style reduct which transforms $M = (C_1, \ldots, C_n)$, given a belief state $S = (S_1, \ldots, S_n)$, into another MCS $M^S = (C_1^S, \ldots, C_n^S)$ that behaves monotonically, such that a unique minimal equilibrium exists; if it coincides with S, we have groundedness.

Formally, $C_i^S = (L_i, red_i(kb_i, S), br_i^S)$, where $red_i(kb_i, S)$ maps kb_i and S to a monotonic core of L_i and br_i^S is the GL-reduct of br_i w.r.t. S, i.e., contains $s \leftarrow (r_1 : p_1), \ldots, (r_j : p_j)$ for each rule of form (15) in br_i such that $p_k \notin S_{r_k}, k = j+1, \ldots, m$.

In addition, the following *reducibility conditions* are assumed: (i) $red_i(kb_i, S_i)$ is antimonotonic in S_i, (ii) S_i is acceptable for kb_i iff $\mathbf{ACC}_i(red_i(kb_i, S_i)) = \{S_i\}$, and (iii) $red_i(kb_i, S) \cup H_i = red_i(kb_i \cup H, S)$, for each $H_i \subseteq \{head(r) \mid r \in br_i\}$. This condition is trivially satisfied by all monotonic logics, by Reiter's Default Logic, answer set programs, etc. Grounded equilibria are then defined as follows.

Definition 9. *A belief state $S = (S_1, \ldots, S_n)$ is a grounded equilibrium of M iff S is the unique minimal equilibrium of M^S, where minimality is componentwise w.r.t. $\subseteq$.*

Example 12 (ctd.). In our review example, naturally $red(kb_i, S)$ is identity and $red(kb_2, S)$ the GL-reduct. Then E_1 is not a grounded equilibrium: M^{E_1} has the single minimal equilibrium $(Cn(\{unhappy \supset revision\}), \emptyset)) \neq E_1$. On the other hand, E_2 is a grounded equilibrium of M.

Grounded equilibria are in fact equilibria of M, as well as minimal ones. Similar as for answer sets, the grounded equilibrium of M^S can be characterized as the least fixpoint of an operator [2].

5.2 Mapping MCSs into HEX-Programs

As mentioned above, the global state view of MCSs contrasts with the local-state and inference-based view of HEX-programs, but under some condition, an MCS can be encoded into a HEX-program.

Suppose that $M = (C_1, \ldots, C_n)$ is such that in all contexts C_i, every belief set $S \in \mathbf{ACC}(kb_i')$ has a *kernel* $\kappa(kb_i', S) = S \cap K_i$, for some (small finite) set K_i, that uniquely identifies S, where $kb_i \subseteq kb_i' \subseteq kb_i \cup \{head(r) \mid r \in br_i\}$. (As noted in [2], the usual logics have such kernels; e.g., for Answer Set Programming, $\kappa(kb_i', S) = S$ and K_i is the set of all ground literals.)

The equilibria of M can then be encoded by a HEX-program P_M as follows.

1. For each $p \in K_i$, set up rules

$$a_{p,i} \leftarrow \text{not } \bar{a}_{p,i}, \qquad \bar{a}_{p,i} \leftarrow \text{not } a_{p,i} \tag{16}$$

   where $a_{p,i}$ $\bar{a}_{p,i}$ are fresh atoms. They guess in an interpretation I a kernel $\kappa_i^I = \{p \mid a_{p,i} \in I\}$ for some belief set of $kb_i \cup H_i^I$, where $H_i^I = \{head(r) \mid r \in br_i, a_{s,i} \in I\}$.

2. For each formula $(r_l : p_l)$ in a bridge rule $r \in br_i$ of form (15), we set up an external atom $\& con\_r_l[\,](a_{p_l})$, whose associated $f_{con\_r_l}(I, a_{p_l})$ returns 1 iff p_l is in an acceptable belief set of $kb_{r_l} \cup H_{r_l}^I$ with kernel $\kappa_{r_l}^I$.

3. We then replace each $(r_l : p_l)$ in the body of r by $\& con\_r, l[\,](a_{p_l})$, and replace the head s by the atom $a_{s,i}$. So we have

$$\begin{aligned} a_{s,i} \leftarrow &\& con\_r_1[\,](a_{p_1}), \ldots, \& con\_r_j[\,](a_{p_j}), \\ &\text{not } \& con\_r_{j+1}[\,](a_{j+1}), \ldots, \text{not } \& con\_r_m[\,](a_{p_m}). \end{aligned} \tag{17}$$

4. Furthermore, we add

$$b_{s,i} \leftarrow \text{not } a_{s,i} \tag{18}$$

$$\leftarrow \text{not } \& con\_r_l[\,](a_\top), \tag{19}$$

   where b_s^i are fresh atoms. The rule (18) blocks minimization, while (19) eliminates an invalid guess for a kernel κ_i^I of some acceptable belief set of $kb_i \cup H_i^I$.

We then can establish the following result.

Theorem 2. *The answer sets I of P_M correspond 1-1 to the equilibria $S = (S_1, \ldots, S_n)$ of M, where each S_i is in $\mathbf{ACC}(kb_i \cup H_i^I)$ and has the kernel κ_i^I.*

Similarly, the grounded equilibria of a (reducible) M can be encoded elegantly into a HEX-program P_M^r, which results from P_M as follows:

- replace in the rules (17) $\& con\_r_l[\,](a_{p_l})$ with $\& con\_r_l{}^s[\,](a_{p_l})$, where $f_{con\_r_l s}(I, a_{p_l})$ returns 1 iff p_l is in the (single) acceptable belief set of $red(kb_{r_l} \cup H_{r_l}^I, S_{r_l})$, where S_{r_l} is the acceptable belief set of $kb_{r_l} \cup H_{r_l}^I$ with kernel $\kappa_{r_l}^I$,
- drop the rules (18), and
- for each $p \in K_i$, add the constraints

$$\leftarrow \text{not } \& con\_i[\,](a_p), a_{p,i}. \tag{20}$$

$$\leftarrow \& con\_i[\,](a_p), \text{not } a_{p,i}. \tag{21}$$

Informally, they check whether the single minimal equilibrium of M^S coincides with $S = (S_1, \ldots, S_n)$, by considering the guessed kernels κ_i^I of all S_i.

For the resulting program, one can show:

Theorem 3. *The answer sets I of P_M^r correspond to 1-1 to the grounded equilibria $S = (S_1, \ldots, S_n)$ of M where each S_i is in $\mathbf{ACC}(kb_i \cup H_i^I)$ and has the kernel κ_i^I.*

Refinements and alternative encodings, also for special cases, remain to be explored.

6   Ongoing Work

As demonstrated in the previous sections, combining knowledge bases with external sources based on answer set semantics is a major research focus of the KBS group at the Vienna University of Technology. Together with our external colleagues, we aim at furthering this work in several directions. Our research is driven by the general goal to develop the theoretical underpinnings for practicable and efficient implementations that serve the needs of relevant applications, as demonstrated by means of prototype implementations through experimentation and show-case applications.

Currently, we pursue the following two research projects on the topic:

– *Modular Hex programs*, funded by the Austrian Science Fund (FWF), with the goal to research and implement formalisms and reasoning techniques for providing a powerful reasoning framework in the context of modular logic programming.

– *Inconsistency Management for Knowledge-Integration Systems*, funded by the Vienna Science and Technology Fund (WWTF), with the goal to provide a general formalism and a suite of basic methods for inconsistency management in MCS, together with algorithms for their practical realization.

In the following, we summarize research issues to be addressed in these projects.

6.1   MLPs

A natural extension of MLPs is to allow program modules not only to call other modules, but also to assess external sources, i.e., 'modules' which are not necessarily specified as logic programs themselves. Intuitively, this is achieved by extending current MLP syntax and semantics to allow for HEX-programs in rule bases. While this is certainly of avail, also in a global view where modules are part of a 'global program' as an entity, optimization and relevance issues will gain importance for effective implementations. Thus, the crucial research question to address in this setting will be how to efficiently evaluate such MLPs. Some ideas to exploit generalizations of the splitting set method for restricted subclasses taking relevance information into account are briefly sketched at the end of Section 4, and initial results for the current MLP setting are reported in [8]. Further improvements, in particular when combining MLPs with HEX-programs, may be obtained by respecting further information that helps in pruning the evaluation to relevant parts. A particular case is when parts of the domain can be disregarded during the evaluation of program parts with external calls or module calls due to available independence information. Results for HEX-programs in this direction appear in [12], and experiments indicate promising improvements. An interesting related research issue is how to obtain such independence information. While it may often be easy to 'see' for the programmer, it is unclear how to proceed in a principled manner.

In a second step, we plan to carry over the MLP approach to a local-model view, with the aim to handle distributed settings appropriately, i.e., without the need of a global view for local evaluation. Semantically, this is achievable with a HEX-style state semantics for MLPs. Turning to such a distributed view will raise further challenging research issues. Concerning practical algorithms and efficient evaluation, additional characteristics of networks come into play, for instance, connection failures, scalability, or network latency. Moreover, the data traffic, i.e., the amount of data exchanged for external evaluation, must be kept low. To deal with these requirements, we envisage semantical relaxations and approximations in the vein of well-founded semantics or more general fixpoint semantics, algebraic techniques using operators, and/or multi-valued semantics.

Another aspect, which needs special attention in this setting, is the treatment of inconsistency. While in the global view, one might assume that the knowledge encoding is 'coordinated' (e.g., by a team of cooperating programmers), in a distributed setting we ought to assume that modules are created without a priori knowledge of their application, increasing the likelihood of arising conflicts. A research goal in this respect is to relax consistency requirements, in order to 'hide' conflicting information and ensure system operability. Resorting to partial models or paraconsistent reasoning techniques might be helpful. Furthermore, as mentioned earlier, incompleteness due to network errors may hinder distributed evaluation; appropriate methods are needed to cope with such situations. Techniques similar to open world reasoning might be developed for dealing with incomplete information in general, while three-valued (multi-valued) interpretations would allow to treat missing information due to network failures in an agnostic way. The MWeb framework [1] and [35] may give inspiration for this.

6.2 MCSs

MCSs constitute a promising approach to deal with important requirements for accessing and using data and knowledge in modern interconnected information systems, namely heterogeneity of formalisms and pointwise exchange of information rather than a central integration. However, for a practical realization, methods for adequate inconsistency handling are missing. Our research efforts address this issue at different levels. On the one hand, we are interested in applying MCS technology in order to facilitate genuine semantics of formalisms, e.g., context-based argumentation frameworks, together with ad hoc inconsistency management components. On the other hand, we aim at providing a platform for developing genuine inconsistency management of MCSs.

Argumentation. Argumentation Context Systems (ACSs) [3] specialize multi-context systems in one respect, and are more general in another. First of all, in contrast to the MCS of [2], they are homogeneous in the sense that all reasoning components in an ACS are of the same type, namely Dung style argumentation frameworks [11]. The latter are widely used as abstract models of argumentation. They are based on graphs whose nodes represent abstract arguments and edges describe attacks between arguments. Different semantics for argumentation frameworks have been defined; they specify *extensions*, i.e., subsets of the arguments which are considered jointly acceptable.

However, ACSs go beyond MCSs in two important aspects:

- The influence of an ACS module M_1 on another module M_2 can be much stronger than in an MCS. M_1 may not only provide information for M_2, it may directly affect M_2's KB and reasoning mode: M_1 may invalidate arguments or attack relationships in M_2's argumentation framework, and even determine the semantics to be used by M_2. In addition to peer-to-peer type forms of information exchange among modules, this allows one to capture hierarchical forms of argumentation as they are common in legal reasoning, where a judge may declare certain arguments as invalid, or where the type of trial requires a particular proof standard. Technically, this is achieved by an explicit representation of contexts in a genuine description language. Note that such a context is different from the usual one in MCSs: it acts as a modifier of a module's argumentation framework, and determines its semantics and reasoning mode (skeptical vs. credulous).
- A major focus in ACSs is on *inconsistency handling*. Modules are equipped with additional components called *mediators*. The main role of the mediator is to take care of inconsistencies in the information provided by connected modules. It collects the information coming in from connected modules and turns it into a consistent context for its module, using a pre-specified consistency handling method which may be based on preference information about other modules. The choice of the consistency handling method allows a broad range of scenarios to be modeled, from strictly hierarchical ones (a judge decides) to more "democratic" forms of decision making (based on voting).

We are currently investigating how to extend heterogeneous MCSs, which are not necessarily based on argumentation, in a similar fashion.

Inconsistency Management Architecture. When generalizing inconsistency management beyond specialized contexts, methods for inconsistency handling appropriate for homogenous settings cannot be utilized directly, and it is less clear how to deal with conflicts due to interaction of heterogenous knowledge bases. The objective is to abstract from techniques developed for particular formalisms with the eventual goal, to provide a general formalism and a suite of basic methods, which can be employed to declaratively specify suitable inconsistency management policies at different levels of sophistication on top of basic inconsistency management actions.

There are several research issues to achieve this goal, and different conceptual architectures can be conceived. Topologically, one may think of a hierarchical structure, where first of all each context is equipped with a local inconsistency manager, like the mediators in the above setting, acting locally and thus having access to all the information of its associated context and being capable of performing actions to ensure local consistency. This, however, will not guarantee consistency at a global level, i.e., the existence of an equilibrium for the MCS. For this purpose, a collection of contexts may agree to trust a dedicated entity to serve as their joint consistency manager, which has access to all bridge rules relevant for the contexts it is in charge of, as well as additional (but not all) information the contexts are willing to exhibit in order to resolve potential inconsistencies. Hierarchically extending this setting, with decreasing information exhibited from level to level, eventually a global inconsistency manager may take high-level decisions in order to ensure global consistency.

At each level, basic methods and algorithms for inconsistency handling need to be developed, such as for consistency checking, conflict explanation finding, conflict assessment, and methods for conflict resolution, taking into account the information that is available for the inconsistency manager. These basic methods shall be obtained building on ideas of existing techniques for specific formalisms. Corresponding algorithms shall be developed by reduction to computational logic, in particular HEX programming might be exploited, akin to the mapping of MCSs in HEX-programs presented in Section 5.2. Again, optimizations w.r.t. scalability and efficiency are deemed to be crucial, and shall be achieved by semantic relaxations and/or syntactic restrictions.

7 Conclusion

We have briefly reviewed some nonmonotonic formalisms that allow to access external information sources, focusing on HEX-programs, recent modular logic programs, and multi-context systems, which have been developed at the Knowledge-Based Systems Group of the Vienna University of Technology in joint work with other researchers. In a systematic view, we have classified them according two distinguishing properties, namely the kind of environment view (local-model versus global-state) and the reduct (GL-style or FLP) used for the definition of the semantics; accordingly, the formalisms have different properties.

We have also compared the formalisms at a more fine grained level, pointing out similar behaviors on fragments and possible mappings between them (in particular, from MCSs to HEX-programs). Ongoing work is concerned with further developing the formalisms, and with applications based on them in research projects, targeting inconsistency management in heterogenous knowledge bases and query answering in distributed global knowledge bases.

Despite the progress in the last years, much more research efforts are needed in order to satisfy the growing need for formalisms with external information access, besides formalisms which are based on Answer Set Programming. Suitable semantics for collections of knowledge bases, pooled together in different settings will be needed (e.g., in small closed systems of a few nodes, and in open peer to peer systems where (many) nodes may dynamically enter and leave a system), which take peculiarities and pragmatic constraints into account (like network topology, communication cost, loss of messages etc.).

Developing efficient algorithms for reasoning in a distributed environment is a further challenging issue, in particular in the presence of nonmonotonic negation. For this, sophisticated optimization techniques are needed to increase the performance of simple prototype implementations satisfactorily. In the end, reasonable scalability for expressive formalisms still needs to be achieved. Nevertheless, we are confident that a success similar to the one recently seen in paradigms like SAT solving, CSP and ASP is possible in this area as well.

References

1. Analyti, A., Antoniou, G., Damásio, C.V.: A principled framework for modular web rule bases and its semantics. In: Proc. 11th Int'l. Conf. Principles of Knowledge Representation and Reasoning (KR 2008), pp. 390–400. AAAI Press, Menlo Park (2008)
2. Brewka, G., Eiter, T.: Equilibria in Heterogeneous Nonmonotonic Multi-Context Systems. In: AAAI 2007, pp. 385–390. AAAI Press, Menlo Park (2007)
3. Brewka, G., Eiter, T.: Argumentation context systems: A framework for abstract group argumentation. In: LPNMR 2009. LNCS. Springer, Heidelberg (2009)
4. Brewka, G., Roelofsen, F., Serafini, L.: Contextual Default Reasoning. In: IJCAI 2007, pp. 268–273 (2007)
5. Calimeri, F., Cozza, S., Ianni, G.: External sources of knowledge and value invention in logic programming. Ann. Math. Artif. Intell. 50(3-4), 333–361 (2007)
6. Calimeri, F., Ianni, G.: External sources of computation for answer set solvers. In: Baral, C., Greco, G., Leone, N., Terracina, G. (eds.) LPNMR 2005. LNCS (LNAI), vol. 3662, pp. 105–118. Springer, Heidelberg (2005)
7. Dao-Tran, M., Eiter, T., Fink, M., Krennwallner, T.: Modular Nonmonotonic Logic Programming Revisited. In: Hill, P.M., Warren, D.S. (eds.) ICLP 2009. LNCS, vol. 5649, pp. 145–159. Springer, Heidelberg (2009)
8. Dao-Tran, M., Eiter, T., Fink, M., Krennwallner, T.: Relevance-driven evaluation of modular nonmonotonic logic programs. In: LPNMR 2009. LNCS. Springer, Heidelberg (to appear, 2009)
9. de la Banda, M.G., Pontelli, E. (eds.): Logic Programming (ICLP 2008). LNCS, vol. 5366. Springer, Heidelberg (2008)
10. Drabent, W., Eiter, T., Ianni, G., Krennwallner, T., Lukasiewicz, T., Małuszyński, J.: Hybrid reasoning with rules and ontologies. In: Bry, F., Małuszyński, J. (eds.) Semantic Techniques for the Web: The REWERSE perspective. LNCS, vol. 5500, p. 50. Springer, Heidelberg (2009)
11. Dung, P.M.: On the acceptability of arguments and its fundamental role in nonmonotonic reasoning, logic programming and n-person games. Artif. Intell. 77(2), 321–358 (1995)
12. Eiter, T., Fink, M., Krennwallner, T.: Decomposition of Declarative Knowledge Bases with External Functions. In: IJCAI 2009. AAAI Press, Menlo Park (2009)
13. Eiter, T., Gottlob, G., Veith, H.: Modular Logic Programming and Generalized Quantifiers. In: Fuhrbach, U., Dix, J., Nerode, A. (eds.) LPNMR 1997. LNCS, vol. 1265, pp. 290–309. Springer, Heidelberg (1997)
14. Eiter, T., Ianni, G., Krennwallner, T., Polleres, A.: Rules and Ontologies for the Semantic Web. In: Baroglio, C., Bonatti, P.A., Małuszyński, J., Marchiori, M., Polleres, A., Schaffert, S. (eds.) Reasoning Web 2008. LNCS, vol. 5224, pp. 1–53. Springer, Heidelberg (2008)
15. Eiter, T., Ianni, G., Krennwallner, T., Polleres, A.: Answer set programming: A primer. In: Tessaris, S., Franconi, E., Eiter, T., Gutierrez, C., Handschuh, S., Rousset, M.-C., Schmidt, R.A. (eds.) Reasoning Web 2009. LNCS, vol. 5689, pp. 40–110. Springer, Heidelberg (2009)
16. Eiter, T., Ianni, G., Lukasiewicz, T., Schindlauer, R., Tompits, H.: Combining answer set programming with description logics for the semantic web. Artif. Intell. 172(12-13), 1495–1539 (2008)
17. Eiter, T., Ianni, G., Schindlauer, R., Tompits, H.: A Uniform Integration of Higher-Order Reasoning and External Evaluations in Answer Set Programming. In: IJCAI 2005, pp. 90–96. Professional Book Center (2005)
18. Eiter, T., Ianni, G., Schindlauer, R., Tompits, H.: Effective Integration of Declarative Rules with external Evaluations for Semantic Web Reasoning. In: Sure, Y., Domingue, J. (eds.) ESWC 2006. LNCS, vol. 4011, pp. 273–287. Springer, Heidelberg (2006)

19. Eiter, T., Lukasiewicz, T., Schindlauer, R., Tompits, H.: Combining Answer Set Programming with Description Logics for the Semantic Web. In: KR 2004, pp. 141–151. Morgan Kaufmann, San Francisco (2004)
20. Eiter, T., Subrahmanian, V., Pick, G.: Heterogeneous Active Agents, I: Semantics. Artificial Intelligence 108(1-2), 179–255 (1999)
21. Faber, W., Leone, N., Pfeifer, G.: Recursive aggregates in disjunctive logic programs: Semantics and complexity. In: Alferes, J.J., Leite, J. (eds.) JELIA 2004. LNCS (LNAI), vol. 3229, pp. 200–212. Springer, Heidelberg (2004)
22. Gelfond, M.: Answer sets. In: van Harmelen, F., Lifschitz, V., Porter, B. (eds.) Handbook of Knowledge Representation, Foundations of Artificial Intelligence, ch. 7, pp. 285–316. Elsevier, Amsterdam (2007)
23. Gelfond, M., Lifschitz, V.: The Stable Model Semantics for Logic Programming. In: ICLP 1988, pp. 1070–1080. MIT Press, Cambridge (1988)
24. Gelfond, M., Lifschitz, V.: Classical negation in logic programs and deductive databases. New Generation Computing 9, 365–385 (1991)
25. Giunchiglia, F.: Contextual reasoning. Epistemologia XVI, 345–364 (1993)
26. Giunchiglia, F., Serafini, L.: Multilanguage hierarchical logics, or: How we can do without modal logics. Artificial Intelligence 65(1), 29–70 (1994)
27. Heymans, S., Toma, I.: Ranking services using fuzzy hex-programs. In: Calvanese, D., Lausen, G. (eds.) RR 2008. LNCS, vol. 5341, pp. 181–196. Springer, Heidelberg (2008)
28. Hoehndorf, R., Loebe, F., Kelso, J., Herre, H.: Representing default knowledge in biomedical ontologies: Application to the integration of anatomy and phenotype ontologies. BMC Bioinformatics 8(1), 377 (2007)
29. Lifschitz, V.: Twelve definitions of a stable model. In: Garcia de la Banda, M., Pontelli, E. (eds.) ICLP 2008. LNCS, vol. 5366, pp. 37–51. Springer, Heidelberg (2008)
30. Lifschitz, V., Turner, H.: Splitting a Logic Program. In: ICLP 1994, pp. 23–37. MIT Press, Cambridge (1994)
31. Marek, V., Truszczyński, M.: Nonmonotonic Logics – Context-Dependent Reasoning. Springer, Heidelberg (1993)
32. McCarthy, J.: Generality in artificial intelligence. Commun. ACM 30(12), 1029–1035 (1987)
33. Nieuwenborgh, D.V., Cock, M.D., Vermeir, D.: Computing Fuzzy Answer Sets Using dlvhex. In: Dahl, V., Niemelä, I. (eds.) ICLP 2007. LNCS, vol. 4670, pp. 449–450. Springer, Heidelberg (2007)
34. Nieuwenborgh, D.V., Eiter, T., Vermeir, D.: Conditional Planning with External Functions. In: Baral, C., Brewka, G., Schlipf, J. (eds.) LPNMR 2007. LNCS (LNAI), vol. 4483, pp. 214–227. Springer, Heidelberg (2007)
35. Polleres, A., Feier, C., Harth, A.: Rules with Contextually Scoped Negation. In: Sure, Y., Domingue, J. (eds.) ESWC 2006. LNCS, vol. 4011, pp. 332–347. Springer, Heidelberg (2006)
36. Roelofsen, F., Serafini, L.: Minimal and absent information in contexts. In: Proc. IJCAI 2005 (2005)
37. Ross, K.A.: Modular stratification and magic sets for datalog programs with negation. J. ACM 41(6), 1216–1266 (1994)
38. Schindlauer, R.: Answer-Set Programming for the Semantic Web. PhD thesis, Vienna University of Technology, Austria (December 2006)
39. Subrahmanian, V., Bonatti, P., Dix, J., Eiter, T., Kraus, S., Ozcan, F., Ross, R.: Heterogeneous Agent Systems: Theory and Implementation. MIT Press, Cambridge (2000)
40. Väänänen, J.: Generalized quantifiers, an introduction. In: Väänänen, J. (ed.) ESSLLI 1997. LNCS, vol. 1754, pp. 1–17. Springer, Heidelberg (2000)
41. Wang, K., Billington, D., Blee, J., Antoniou, G.: Combining description logic and defeasible logic for the Semantic Web. In: Antoniou, G., Boley, H. (eds.) RuleML 2004. LNCS, vol. 3323, pp. 170–181. Springer, Heidelberg (2004)

Combining Description Logics, Description Graphs, and Rules

Boris Motik

Computing Laboratory, University of Oxford, UK

Abstract. Recent practical experience with description logics (DLs) has revealed that their expressivity is often insufficient to accurately describe *structured objects*—objects whose parts are interconnected in arbitrary, rather than tree-like ways. To address this problem, we propose an extension of DL languages with *description graphs*—a modeling construct that can accurately describe objects whose parts are connected in arbitrary ways. Furthermore, to enable modeling the conditional aspects of structured objects, we also incorporate rules into our formalism. We present an in-depth study of the computational properties of such a formalism. In particular, we first identify the sources of undecidability of the general, unrestricted formalism, and then present a restriction that makes reasoning decidable. Finally, we present tight complexity bounds.

1 Introduction

The Web Ontology Language (OWL) is a well-known language for ontology modeling in the Semantic Web [25]. The World Wide Web Consortium (W3C) is currently working on a revision of OWL—called OWL 2 [8]—whose main goal is to address some of the limitations of OWL. The formal underpinnings of OWL and OWL 2 are provided by description logics (DLs)[3]–knowledge representation formalisms with well-understood formal properties.

DLs are often used to describe *structured objects*—objects whose parts are interconnected in complex ways. Such objects abound in molecular biology and the clinical sciences, and clinical ontologies such as GALEN, the Foundational Model of Anatomy (FMA), and the National Cancer Institute (NCI) Thesaurus describe numerous structured objects. For example, FMA models the human hand as consisting of the fingers, the palm, various bones, blood vessels, and so on, all of which are highly interconnected.

Modeling structured objects poses numerous problems to DLs and the OWL family of languages. The design of DLs has been driven by the desire to provide practically useful knowledge modeling primitives while ensuring decidability of the core reasoning problems. To achieve the latter goal, the modeling constructs available in DLs are usually carefully crafted so that the resulting language exhibits a variant of the *tree-model property* [30]: each satisfiable DL ontology always has at least one model whose elements are connected in a tree-like manner. This property can be used to derive a decision procedure; however, it also

S. Ghilardi and R. Sebastiani (Eds.): FroCoS 2009, LNAI 5749, pp. 43–67, 2009.

prevents one from accurately describing (usually non-tree-like) structured objects since, whenever a model exists, at least one model does not reflect the intended structure. This technical problem has severe consequences in practice [19]. In search of the "correct" way of describing structured objects, modelers often create overly complex descriptions; however, since the required expressive power is actually missing, such descriptions do not entail the consequences that would follow if the descriptions accurately captured the intended structure. We discuss the expressivity limitations of DLs in more detail in Section 3.

In order to address this lack of expressivity, in this paper we extend DLs with *description graphs*, which can be understood as schema-level descriptions of structured objects. To allow for the representation of conditional statements about structured objects, we also extend DLs with first-order rules [13]. In this way, we obtain a powerful and versatile knowledge representation formalism. It allows us, for example, to describe the structure of the hand using description graphs, statements such as "if a bone in the hand is fractured, then the hand is fractured as well" using rules, and nonstructural aspects of the domain such as "a medical doctor is a person with an MD degree" using DLs.

To study the computational properties of our formalism, we must select a particular logic for the DL component. The description logic $\mathcal{SHOIQ}^+$ seems like a reasonable choice since it provides the semantic underpinning of OWL 2. The combination of number restrictions, nominals, and inverse roles available in $\mathcal{SHOIQ}^+$, however, has shown to be notoriously difficult to handle [14]. In this paper we therefore focus on the simpler case of $\mathcal{SHOQ}^+$, and leave the more technically involved case of $\mathcal{SHOIQ}^+$ to [22].

Unsurprisingly, the resulting formalism is undecidable in its unrestricted form. It is widely recognized that reasoning algorithms are more likely to be effective in practice if the underlying logics are decidable. Therefore, we discuss the main causes of undecidability and investigate restrictions under which the formalism becomes decidable.

We have observed that structured objects can often be described by a possibly large, yet bounded number of parts. For example, a human body consists of organs all of which can be decomposed into smaller parts; however, further decomposition will eventually lead to parts that one does not want or know how to describe any further. In this vein, FMA describes the skeleton of the hand, but it does not describe the internal structure of the distal phalanges of the fingers. The number of parts needed to describe the hand is therefore determined by the granularity of the hierarchical decomposition of the hand. This decomposition naturally defines an acyclic hierarchy of description graphs. For example, the fingers can be described by description graphs that are subordinate to that of the hand; however, the description graph for the hand is not naturally subordinate to the description graphs for the fingers. We use this to define an *acyclicity* restriction on description graphs. Acyclicity bounds the number of parts that one needs to reason with, which, provided that there are no DL axioms, can be used to obtain a decision procedure for the basic reasoning problems.

If description graphs are used in combination with DL axioms, the acyclicity condition alone does not ensure decidability due to possible interactions between DL axioms, graphs, and rules [17]. To obtain decidability, we limit this interaction by imposing an additional condition on the usage of roles. In particular, we separate the roles (i.e., the binary predicates) that can be used in DL axioms from the roles that can be used in rules. We present a hypertableau-based [21] reasoning algorithm that decides the satisfiability problem for our formalism, together with tight complexity bounds.

Due to lack of space, we omit the proofs in this paper. All proofs, as well as additional decidability and complexity results for the case when DL axioms are expressed in $\mathcal{SHOIQ}^+$, can be found in [22].

2 Preliminaries

In this section, we present the basic definitions that our work builds upon.

2.1 The Description Logic $\mathcal{SHOQ}^+$

A $\mathcal{SHOQ}^+$ *signature* is a triple (N_C, N_R, N_I) consisting of mutually disjoint sets of *atomic concepts* N_C, *atomic roles* N_R, and *named individuals* N_I. In the rest of this paper, we assume that the signature is implicit in all relevant definitions. Also, we often call an atomic role simply a *role*.

An *RBox axiom* is an expression of the form $R_1 \sqsubseteq R_2$ (*role inclusion*) or $\mathsf{Tra}(R)$ (*transitivity*), where R, R_1, and R_2 are roles. For X a set of RBox axioms, let $\sqsubseteq_X^*$ be the reflexive-transitive closure of the $\sqsubseteq$-relation in X. A role R is *transitive* in X if a role R' exists such that $R' \sqsubseteq_X^* R$, $R \sqsubseteq_X^* R'$, and $\mathsf{Tra}(R') \in X$. A role S is *simple* in X if no transitive role R exists such that $R \sqsubseteq_X^* S$.

Given a set of RBox axioms X, the set of *concepts* w.r.t. X is the smallest set containing $\top$ (the *top concept*), $\bot$ (the *bottom concept*), A (*atomic concept*), $\{a\}$ (*nominal*), $\neg C$ (*negation*), $C \sqcap D$ (*conjunction*), $C \sqcup D$ (*disjunction*), $\exists R.C$ (*existential restriction*), $\forall R.C$ (*universal restriction*), $\exists S.\mathsf{Self}$ (*local reflexivity*), $\geq n\, S.C$ (*at-least restriction*), and $\leq n\, S.C$ (*at-most restriction*), where A is an atomic concept, a is an individual, C and D are concepts, R is a role, S is a simple role w.r.t. X, and n is a nonnegative integer. The set of *literal concepts* is defined as $N_L = N_C \cup \{\neg A \mid A \in N_C\}$. A *TBox* $\mathcal{T}$ is a finite set of RBox axioms and *general concept inclusion* (GCI) axioms $C \sqsubseteq D$, where C and D are concepts w.r.t. the subset of the RBox axioms of $\mathcal{T}$.

An *assertion* is an expression of the form $C(a)$ (*concept assertion*), $R(a, b)$ (*role assertion*), $a \approx b$ (*equality assertion*), and $a \not\approx b$ (*inequality assertion*), where C is a concept, R is a role, and a and b are named individuals. An *ABox* $\mathcal{A}$ is a finite set of assertions. Finally, a $\mathcal{SHOQ}^+$ *knowledge base* is a pair $(\mathcal{T}, \mathcal{A})$ where $\mathcal{T}$ is a TBox and $\mathcal{A}$ is an ABox. With $|\mathcal{K}|$ we denote the size of a knowledge base $\mathcal{K}$—that is, the number of symbols required to encode $\mathcal{K}$ on the input tape of a Turing machine (numbers can be coded in binary).

An *interpretation* for a signature (N_C, N_R, N_I) is a tuple $I = (\triangle^I, \cdot^I)$, where $\triangle^I$ is a nonempty set called the *interpretation domain* and $\cdot^I$ is a function

Table 1. Model-Theoretic Semantics of $\mathcal{SHOQ}^+$

Interpretation of Roles and Concepts		
$\top^I$	$=$	Δ^I
$\bot^I$	$=$	$\emptyset$
$\{s\}^I$	$=$	$\{s^I\}$
$(\neg C)^I$	$=$	$\Delta^I \setminus C^I$
$(C \sqcap D)^I$	$=$	$C^I \cap D^I$
$(C \sqcup D)^I$	$=$	$C^I \cup D^I$
$(\exists R.C)^I$	$=$	$\{x \mid \exists y : \langle x,y \rangle \in R^I \wedge y \in C^I\}$
$(\forall R.C)^I$	$=$	$\{x \mid \forall y : \langle x,y \rangle \in R^I \rightarrow y \in C^I\}$
$(\exists S.\mathsf{Self})^I$	$=$	$\{x \mid \langle x,x \rangle \in S^I\}$
$(\geq n\, S.C)^I$	$=$	$\{x \mid \sharp\{y \mid \langle x,y \rangle \in S^I \wedge y \in C^I\} \geq n\}$
$(\leq n\, S.C)^I$	$=$	$\{x \mid \sharp\{y \mid \langle x,y \rangle \in S^I \wedge y \in C^I\} \leq n\}$
Interpretation of Axioms and Assertions		
$I \models C \sqsubseteq D$	iff	$C^I \subseteq D^I$
$I \models R_1 \sqsubseteq R_2$	iff	$R_1^I \subseteq R_2^I$
$I \models \mathsf{Tra}(R)$	iff	$\forall x,y,z \in \Delta^I : \langle x,y \rangle \in R^I \wedge \langle y,z \rangle \in R^I \rightarrow \langle x,z \rangle \in R^I$
$I \models C(a)$	iff	$a^I \in C^I$
$I \models R(a,b)$	iff	$\langle a^I, b^I \rangle \in R^I$
$I \models a \approx b$	iff	$a^I = b^I$
$I \models a \not\approx b$	iff	$a^I \neq b^I$

Note: $\sharp N$ is the number of elements in N.

assigning an element $a^I \in \Delta^I$ to each named individual $a \in N_I$, a set $A^I \subseteq \Delta^I$ to each atomic concept $A \in N_C$, and a relation $R^I \subseteq \Delta^I \times \Delta^I$ to each atomic role $R \in N_R$. The extension of $\cdot^I$ to concepts and roles, and satisfaction of axioms and assertions in I is defined as shown in Table 1. An interpretation I is a *model* of $(\mathcal{T}, \mathcal{A})$, written $I \models (\mathcal{T}, \mathcal{A})$, if and only if all axioms of $\mathcal{T}$ and all assertions of $\mathcal{A}$ are satisfied in I.

The basic inference problem for $\mathcal{SHOQ}^+$ is checking whether $(\mathcal{T}, \mathcal{A})$ is *satisfiable*—that is, whether a model of $(\mathcal{T}, \mathcal{A})$ exists. Most reasoning problems used in practice can be reduced to knowledge satisfiability [3].

2.2 Extending DLs with Rules

Description logics can be extended with *rules*—clauses interpreted under standard first-order semantics—in a straightforward way [17,13,11]. Let N_V be a set of *variables* disjoint with the set of individuals N_I. An *atom* is an expression of the form $C(s)$, $R(s,t)$, or $s \approx t$, for s and t individuals or variables, C a concept, and R a role. A *rule* is an expression of the form

$$(1) \qquad U_1 \wedge \ldots \wedge U_m \rightarrow V_1 \vee \ldots \vee V_n$$

where U_i and V_j are atoms, $m \geq 0$, and $n \geq 0$. The conjunction $U_1 \wedge \ldots \wedge U_m$ is called the *body*, and the disjunction $V_1 \vee \ldots \vee V_n$ is called the *head*. Without

Table 2. Satisfaction of Rules in an Interpretation

$I, \mu \models C(s)$	iff	$s^{I,\mu} \in C^I$
$I, \mu \models R(s, t)$	iff	$\langle s^{I,\mu}, t^{I,\mu} \rangle \in R^I$
$I, \mu \models s \approx t$	iff	$s^{I,\mu} = t^{I,\mu}$
$I, \mu \models \bigwedge_{i=1}^{m} U_i \rightarrow \bigvee_{j=1}^{n} V_j$	iff	$I, \mu \models U_i$ for each $1 \leq i \leq m$ implies
		$I, \mu \models V_j$ for some $1 \leq j \leq n$
$I \models \bigwedge_{i=1}^{m} U_i \rightarrow \bigvee_{j=1}^{n} V_j$	iff	$I, \mu \models \bigwedge_{i=1}^{m} U_i \rightarrow \bigvee_{j=1}^{n} V_j$ for all mappings μ
$I \models \mathcal{R}$	iff	$I \models r$ for each rule $r \in \mathcal{R}$

loss of generality, we assume that no rule r contains $\approx$ in the body. The empty body and the empty head of a rule are written as $\top$ and $\bot$, respectively. A rule is *Horn* if the head of the rule contains at most one atom. Variables x and y are *directly connected* in a rule r if they occur together in some body atom of r; furthermore, *connected* is the transitive closure of directly connected. A rule r is *connected* if each pair of variables x and y occurring in r is connected in r.

Let $I = (\Delta^I, \cdot^I)$ be an interpretation and $\mu : N_V \rightarrow \Delta^I$ a mapping of variables to elements of the interpretation domain. Let $a^{I,\mu} = a^I$ for an individual a and $x^{I,\mu} = \mu(x)$ for a variable x. Satisfaction of an atom, rule, and a set of rules $\mathcal{R}$ in I and μ is defined in Table 2.

2.3   Hypertableau Calculus for $\mathcal{SHOQ}^+$

We now present an overview of the hypertableau calculus [21], which can be used to decide the satisfiability of a $\mathcal{SHOQ}^+$ knowledge base $(\mathcal{T}, \mathcal{A})$.

The algorithm first preprocesses $(\mathcal{T}, \mathcal{A})$ into a set of rules $\Xi_{\mathcal{T}}(\mathcal{T})$ and an ABox $\mathcal{A} \cup \Xi_{\mathcal{A}}(\mathcal{T})$. This transformation consists of three steps. First, transitivity axioms are eliminated from $\mathcal{T}$ by encoding them using general concept inclusions; similar encodings are well known in the context of various description and modal logics [29,28,18]. Second, axioms are normalized and complex concepts are replaced with atomic ones in a way similar to the structural transformation [26]. Third, the normalized axioms are translated into rules by using the correspondences between description and first-order logic [6]. We omit the details of the preprocessing for the sake of brevity; they can be found in [21, Section 4.1]. All steps are satisfiability preserving; thus, $\Xi_{\mathcal{T}}(\mathcal{T})$ and $\mathcal{A} \cup \Xi_{\mathcal{A}}(\mathcal{T})$ are equisatisfiable with $(\mathcal{T}, \mathcal{A})$. Preprocessing produces HT-rules—syntactically restricted rules on which the hypertableau calculus is guaranteed to terminate.

Definition 1. *We assume that the set of atomic concepts N_C contains a nominal guard concept O_a for each individual a, and that these concepts do not occur in any input knowledge base.*

An HT-rule is a rule r of the form (1) with $m \geq 0$ and $n \geq 0$, in which it must be possible to separate the variables into a center *variable x, a set of* branch *variables y_i, and a set of* nominal *variables z_j such that the following properties hold, for A an atomic concept, B a literal but not a nominal guard concept, O_a a nominal guard concept, R an atomic role, and S a role.*

- Each atom in the body of r is of the form $A(x)$, $R(x,x)$, $R(x,y_i)$, $A(y_i)$, or $A(z_j)$.
- Each atom in the head of r is of the form $B(x)$, $\geq h\,S.B(x)$, $B(y_i)$, $R(x,x)$, $R(x,y_i)$, $R(x,z_j)$, $x \approx z_j$, or $y_i \approx y_j$.
- Each y_i occurs in the body of r in an atom of the form $R(x,y_i)$.
- Each z_j occurs in the body of r in an atom of the form $O_a(z_j)$.

The following definition introduces the hypertableau calculus. It takes a set of HT-rules $\mathcal{R}$ and an input ABox $\mathcal{A}$, and it decides the satisfiability of $(\mathcal{R},\mathcal{A})$.

Definition 2.

Individuals. *Given a set of* named *individuals* N_I, *the set of* generalized *individuals* N_A *is the smallest set such that* $N_I \subseteq N_A$ *and, if* $x \in N_A$, *then* $x.i \in N_A$ *for each integer* i. *The individuals in* $N_A \setminus N_I$ *are* tree individuals.

An individual $x.i$ *is a* successor *of* x, *and* x *is a* predecessor *of* $x.i$. Descendant *and* ancestor *are the transitive closures of* successor *and* predecessor, *respectively.*

ABoxes. *The hypertableau algorithm operates on ABoxes that are obtained by extending the standard definition as follows.*

- *In addition to standard assertions, an ABox can contain* at-most *equalities and a special assertion* $\perp$ *that is false in all interpretations. Furthermore, assertions can refer to the individuals from* N_A *and not only from* N_I.
- *Each (in)equality* $s \approx t$ *($s \not\approx t$) also stands for the symmetric (in)equality* $t \approx s$ *($t \not\approx s$).*

An input *ABox* contains only named individuals and in which all concepts are literal.

Merge Target. *An individual* t *is a* merge target *for an individual* s *if* t *is a named individual, or* s *is a descendant of* t.

Pruning. *The ABox* $\text{prune}_\mathcal{A}(s)$ *is obtained from* $\mathcal{A}$ *by removing all assertions containing a descendent of* s.

Merging. *The ABox* $\text{merge}_\mathcal{A}(s \to t)$ *is obtained from* $\text{prune}_\mathcal{A}(s)$ *by replacing the individual* s *with the individual* t *in all assertions.*

Single Anywhere Blocking. *The* label of an individual s *is defined as*

$$\mathcal{L}_\mathcal{A}(s) = \{\, A \mid A(s) \in \mathcal{A} \text{ and } A \text{ is an atomic concept} \,\}.$$

Let $<$ *be a strict ordering (i.e., a transitive and irreflexive relation) on* N_A *containing the ancestor relation—that is, if* s' *is an ancestor of* s, *then* $s' < s$. *By induction on* $<$, *we assign to each individual* s *in* $\mathcal{A}$ *a* status *as follows:*

- *a tree individual* s *is* directly blocked *by a tree individual* t *if* t *is not blocked, $t < s$, and* $\mathcal{L}_\mathcal{A}(s) = \mathcal{L}_\mathcal{A}(t)$;
- *s is* indirectly blocked *if it has a predecessor that is blocked; and*
- *s is* blocked *if it is either directly or indirectly blocked.*

Table 3. Derivation Rules of the Hypertableau Calculus

Hyp-rule	If 1. $r \in \mathcal{R}$ with $r = U_1 \wedge \ldots \wedge U_m \rightarrow V_1 \vee \ldots \vee V_n$, and 2. a mapping σ from variables of r to the individuals of $\mathcal{A}$ exists s.t. 2.1 $\sigma(x)$ is not indirectly blocked for each variable $x \in N_V$, 2.2 $\sigma(U_i) \in \mathcal{A}$ for each $1 \le i \le m$, and 2.3 $\sigma(V_j) \notin \mathcal{A}$ for each $1 \le j \le n$ then $\mathcal{A}_1 := \mathcal{A} \cup \{\bot\}$ if $n = 0$; $\mathcal{A}_j := \mathcal{A} \cup \{\sigma(V_j)\}$ for $1 \le j \le n$ otherwise.
$\ge$-rule	If 1. $\ge n\, R.B(s) \in \mathcal{A}$, 2. s is not blocked in $\mathcal{A}$, and 3. $\mathcal{A}$ does not contain individuals $u_1, \ldots, u_n$ such that 3.1 $\{R(s, u_i), B(u_i) \mid 1 \le i \le n\} \cup \{u_i \not\approx u_j \mid 1 \le i < j \le n\} \subseteq \mathcal{A}$, and 3.2 u_i is not indirectly blocked in $\mathcal{A}$ for each $1 \le i \le n$ then $\mathcal{A}_1 := \mathcal{A} \cup \{R(s, t_i), B(t_i) \mid 1 \le i \le n\} \cup \{t_i \not\approx t_j \mid 1 \le i < j \le n\}$ where $t_1, \ldots, t_n$ are fresh distinct tree successors of s.
$\approx$-rule	If 1. $s \approx t \in \mathcal{A}$, 2. $s \ne t$, and 3. neither s not t is indirectly blocked then $\mathcal{A}_1 := \mathsf{merge}_{\mathcal{A}}(s \rightarrow t)$ if t is merge target for s, and $\mathcal{A}_1 := \mathsf{merge}_{\mathcal{A}}(t \rightarrow s)$ otherwise.
$\bot$-rule	If $s \not\approx s \in \mathcal{A}$ or $\{A(s), \neg A(s)\} \subseteq \mathcal{A}$ where s is not indirectly blocked then $\mathcal{A}_1 := \mathcal{A} \cup \{\bot\}$.

Derivation Rules. *Table 3 specifies* derivation rules *that, given an ABox $\mathcal{A}$ and a set of HT-rules $\mathcal{R}$, derive the ABoxes $\mathcal{A}_1, \ldots, \mathcal{A}_n$. In the Hyp-rule, σ is a mapping from the set of variables in the HT-rule to the individuals occurring in the assertions of $\mathcal{A}$, and $\sigma(U)$ is the result of replacing each variable x in the atom U with $\sigma(x)$.*

Clash. *An ABox $\mathcal{A}$ contains a* clash *iff $\bot \in \mathcal{A}$; otherwise, $\mathcal{A}$ is* clash-free.

Derivation. *For a set of HT-rules $\mathcal{R}$ and an ABox $\mathcal{A}$, a* derivation *is a pair (T, ρ) where T is a finitely branching tree and ρ is a function labeling the nodes of T with ABoxes such that the following properties hold for each $t \in T$:*

- *$\rho(t) = \mathcal{A}$ if t the root of T;*
- *t is a leaf of T if $\bot \in \rho(t)$ or no derivation rule is applicable to $\rho(t)$ and $\mathcal{R}$;*
- *t has children $t_1, \ldots, t_n$ such that $\rho(t_1), \ldots, \rho(t_n)$ are exactly the results of applying an arbitrarily chosen applicable rule to $\rho(t)$ and $\mathcal{R}$ in all other cases.*

A derivation is successful *if T contains a branch $t_1, t_2, \ldots$ such that each ABox $\rho(t_i)$ is clash-free.*

To check satisfiability of $(\mathcal{R}, \mathcal{A})$, one can construct a derivation for $(\mathcal{R}, \mathcal{A})$; then, $(\mathcal{R}, \mathcal{A})$ is satisfiable if and only if the derivation is successful.

3   Problems with Modeling Complex Structures

To understand the limitations of modeling structured objects in DLs (and hence in OWL as well), consider the problem of modeling the skeleton of the human hand, whose structure is shown in Figure 1a. The carpal bones form the base of the hand. The central part of the hand contains the metacarpal bones, one leading to each finger. The fingers consist of phalanges: the proximal phalanges are connected to the metacarpal bones, and all fingers apart from the thumb contain a middle phalanx between the proximal and the distal phalanx. This structure can be intuitively conceptualized as shown in Figures 1b–1e.[1]

This structure can be straightforwardly encoded in a DL ABox $\mathcal{A}$. ABox assertions, however, represent concrete data; thus, $\mathcal{A}$ would represent the structure of *one particular* hand. In this paper, we are concerned with modeling structured objects *at the schema level*—that is, we want to describe the general structure of *all* hands. We should be able to instantiate such a description many times. For example, if we say that each patient has a hand, then for each concrete patient we should instantiate a *different* hand, each with the structure as shown in Figures 1b–1e; depending on the properties of the patient and the axioms in the ontology, each such structure can then exhibit distinct features. This clearly cannot be achieved using ABox assertions.

We can give a logical, schema-level interpretation to Figures 1b–1e by treating vertices as concepts and arrows as *participation constraints* between the concepts. For example, vertices 1 and 6 would correspond to concepts *Hand* and *Index_finger*, whose instances would be all hands and all index fingers, respectively. Furthermore, the arrow from 1 to 6 would be interpreted as a statement that each hand has an index finger as its part. In DLs, such a participation constraint would commonly be represented by axioms (2)–(3).

(2) $$Hand \sqsubseteq \exists part.Index\_finger$$

(3) $$Hand \sqsubseteq \, \leq 1\, part.Index\_finger$$

Thus, the knowledge base $\mathcal{K}$ containing axioms (4)–(17) would provide a formalization of the structure shown in Figure 1e.[2]

(4) $$Index\_finger \sqsubseteq \exists part.Distal\_phalanx\_oif$$

(5) $$Index\_finger \sqsubseteq \exists part.Middle\_phalanx\_oif$$

(6) $$Index\_finger \sqsubseteq \exists part.Proximal\_phalanx\_oif$$

(7) $$Distal\_phalanx\_oif \sqsubseteq \exists attached\_to.Middle\_phalanx\_oif$$

(8) $$Middle\_phalanx\_oif \sqsubseteq \exists attached\_to.Distal\_phalanx\_oif$$

(9) $$Middle\_phalanx\_oif \sqsubseteq \exists attached\_to.Proximal\_phalanx\_oif$$

(10) $$Proximal\_phalanx\_oif \sqsubseteq \exists attached\_to.Middle\_phalanx\_oif$$

---

[1] The relationship *attached_to* is assumed to be bidirectional, so the edges labeled with it are not oriented.
[2] The suffix *_of_index_finger* has been abbreviated to *_oif*.

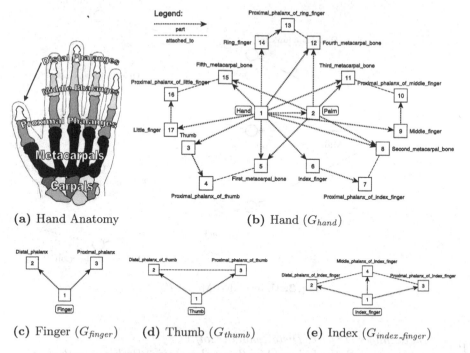

(a) Hand Anatomy   **(b)** Hand (G_{hand})

(c) Finger (G_{finger})   **(d)** Thumb (G_{thumb})   **(e)** Index (G_{index_finger})

Fig. 1. The Anatomy of the Hand and its Conceptual Models

$$(11) \qquad Index\_finger \sqsubseteq \; \leq 1 \, part.Distal\_phalanx\_oif$$

$$(12) \qquad Index\_finger \sqsubseteq \; \leq 1 \, part.Middle\_phalanx\_oif$$

$$(13) \qquad Index\_finger \sqsubseteq \; \leq 1 \, part.Proximal\_phalanx\_oif$$

$$(14) \qquad Distal\_phalanx\_oif \sqsubseteq \; \leq 1 \, attached\_to.Middle\_phalanx\_oif$$

$$(15) \qquad Middle\_phalanx\_oif \sqsubseteq \; \leq 1 \, attached\_to.Distal\_phalanx\_oif$$

$$(16) \qquad Middle\_phalanx\_oif \sqsubseteq \; \leq 1 \, attached\_to.Proximal\_phalanx\_oif$$

$$(17) \qquad Proximal\_phalanx\_oif \sqsubseteq \; \leq 1 \, attached\_to.Middle\_phalanx\_oif$$

Let I be an interpretation corresponding to Figure 1e in the obvious way. Clearly, I satisfies $\mathcal{K}$, which justifies the formalization of Figure 1e using $\mathcal{K}$.

Let us extend $\mathcal{K}$ with knowledge about bone fractures. For example, let $\mathcal{K}'$ be an extension of $\mathcal{K}$ with axiom (18) stating that, if the middle phalanx of the index finger is broken, then the index finger is broken as well:

$$(18) \qquad Index\_finger \sqcap \exists part.(Middle\_phalanx\_oif \sqcap Broken) \sqsubseteq Broken$$

Given the structure of the index finger shown in Figure 1e, we might expect $\mathcal{K}'$ to imply that if, the index finger has a distal phalanx that is attached to a broken middle phalanx, then the index finger is broken as well:

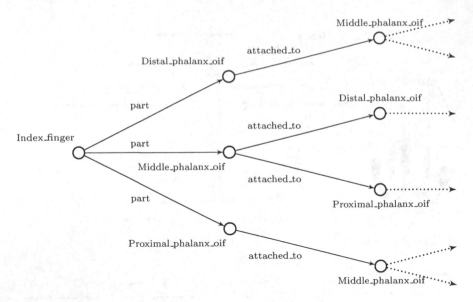

Fig. 2. Unintended Model I'

(19) $Index\_finger \sqcap \exists part.(Distal\_phalanx\_oif \sqcap$
$\exists attached\_to.(Middle\_phalanx\_oif \sqcap Broken)) \sqsubseteq Broken$

Unfortunately, $\mathcal{K}'$ is underconstrained, and some models of $\mathcal{K}'$ do not correspond to the structure of the index finger shown in Figure 1e. Axioms (5) and (7) both imply the existence of middle phalanges of the index finger, but $\mathcal{K}'$ does not capture the fact that, for any given index finger, these two middle phalanges must be the same object. Thus, the infinite interpretation I' shown in Figure 2 is also a model of $\mathcal{K}'$. In I', even if the middle phalanx of the index finger is broken, the middle phalanges at the second level of the model need not be broken; hence, axiom (18) does not necessarily derive that the index finger is broken and, consequently, axiom (19) is not a consequence of $\mathcal{K}'$.

That $\mathcal{K}'$ is underconstrained can also lead to problems with the performance of reasoning. In order to disprove an entailment, a DL reasoner will try to construct a "canonical" model of $\mathcal{K}'$—that is, a model that contains as little information derivable from $\mathcal{K}'$ as possible. Such models, however, are often highly repetitive and much larger than the intended ones, so constructing them can be costly. The interpretation I' is an example of such a "canonical" model, and it contains an infinite tree of phalanges instead of a finite structure shown in Figure 1e. In our experience, this is the main reason why DL reasoners cannot process complex ontologies such as FMA and certain versions of GALEN.

These problems could be addressed by ensuring that *all* models of $\mathcal{K}'$ resemble as much as possible the intended conceptualization shown in Figures 1b–1e. DL axioms, however, are syntactically restricted such that the resulting logic exhibits (a variant of) the *tree model property* [30]: whenever a DL knowledge base has a model, it has a model of a certain tree shape (such as I'). The tree model property is generally considered desirable because its absence often leads to the undecidability of reasoning; however, it also implies that we must leave the confines of DLs and OWL to faithfully represent structured objects.

Rule formalisms such as datalog [1] can routinely express conditions over non-tree structures; however, they typically do not provide for existential quantification. Such rules can thus be applied only to the individuals explicitly mentioned in a knowledge base and cannot express schema constraints such as "each patient has some (unknown) hand." Ontology languages such as OWL-Flight [10], Telos [24], and the logic programming variant of F-Logic [15] are based on datalog and therefore share its restrictions.

Combining rules with description logics overcomes the limitations of datalog and yields a very expressive knowledge representation formalism capable of axiomatizing nontree structures [13,17]. Similarly, the first-order version of F-Logic [15] provides a combination of existential quantification with rules. Such solutions, however, are quite complex and susceptible to modeling errors. Furthermore, the extension of DLs with rules is undecidable even for very simple DLs [17], and the same is the case for the first-order version of F-Logic.

A number of decidable combinations of DLs and rules have been proposed in practice, and decidability is typically achieved by syntactically restricting the applicability of the rules. For example, DL-safe rules [23] are restricted such that they apply only to the explicitly named objects. Role-safe [17] and weakly safe [27] rules also impose restrictions that prevent the application of the rules to arbitrary elements of the domain, and similar restrictions are also employed by various nonmonotonic rule extensions of DLs [12,27,20]. Consequently, such extensions are useful mainly for query answering, but not for schema modeling.

To address the problems outlined in this section, the DL $\mathcal{SROIQ}$ [16] provides *complex role inclusions*—axioms of the form $R_1 \circ \ldots \circ R_n \sqsubseteq S$, where $\circ$ stands for role composition. Such axioms are restricted in a way that ensures decidability of the basic reasoning problems. The use of complex role inclusions solves some of the identified problems; however, they still cannot axiomatize arbitrary structures such as the one in Figure 1b.

In the rest of this paper, we propose a formalism for modeling arbitrarily connected structured objects by extending DLs with *description graphs*. For example, Figure 1d can be seen as a description graph showing that each thumb has a proximal and a distal phalanx that are attached to each other. Different structured objects can be represented using separate description graphs, which can be appropriately connected. For example, the hand and the thumb can be represented using two different description graphs, which are connected to each other. Furthermore, structured objects often need to be modeled at different levels of abstraction. For example, we would like to describe the abstract structure common to all fingers as shown in Figure 1c, and then specialize it for, say, the index finger by introducing the middle phalanx as shown in Figure 1e. To this end, our formalism provides for graph specialization statements, which can represent the fact that one structure is more general than another. Finally, in order to represent conditional aspects of the domain, we also allow for arbitrary rules over the description graphs; for example, we can state that, if a bone in the hand is fractured, then the hand is fractured as well. We introduce the formalism in the following section, and show how it can be used to exclude unintended infinite models such as the one in Figure 2.

Our formalism is related to weakly guarded tuple generating dependencies [7] and the guarded fragment of first-order logic [2], which allow for axiomatizing nontree structures of bounded treewidth. Unlike these formalisms, however, graph-extended knowledge bases allow for functional roles and arbitrary rules; furthermore, we use different restrictions to achieve decidability of reasoning.

4   A Formalism for Modeling Complex Structures

In this section, we present our knowledge representation formalism. We start by defining the notion of a description graph.

Definition 3. *An ℓ-ary description graph $G = (V, E, \lambda, M)$ is a directed labeled graph where*

- $V = \{1, \ldots, \ell\}$ *is a set of ℓ vertices,*
- $E \subseteq V \times V$ *is a set of edges,*
- λ *is a function assigning a set of literal concepts $\lambda\langle i \rangle \subseteq N_L$ to each vertex $i \in V$ and a set of atomic roles $\lambda\langle i, j \rangle \subseteq N_R$ to each edge $\langle i, j \rangle \in E$, and*
- $M \subseteq N_C$ *is a set of main concepts for G.*

For A an atomic concept, V_A is the set of vertices that contain A in their label; that is, $V_A = \{k \in V \mid A \in \lambda\langle k \rangle\}$.

We define the vertices of G to be integers in order to be able to use them as indices. The main concepts of G identify the objects whose structure is defined by G. In Figure 1, main concepts are framed with rounded rectangles. Thus, the main concepts for the description graph shown in Figure 1b are *Hand* and *Palm*, implying that this graph defines the structure of all hands and palms.

As a notational convenience, we sometimes use $i \xrightarrow{R} j$ to denote that a description graph contains an R-labeled edge from a vertex i to a vertex j.

In order to represent conditions over the structure of a graph, our formalism allows for graph rules. The following definition refines the general notion of a rule introduced in Section 2.2.

Definition 4. *A graph atom is an atom of the form $G(t_1, \ldots, t_\ell)$, where G is an ℓ-ary description graph and $t_i \in N_I \cup N_V$ for $1 \leq i \leq \ell$. A graph rule is a rule in which all concepts and roles in atoms are atomic, and whose head and body can contain graph atoms.*

Next, we introduce graph specializations, which allow us to represent structured objects at different levels of abstraction. For example, we can capture the abstract structure common to all fingers by a description graph G_{finger} shown in

Figure 1c, and we can specialize this structure for the thumb by introducing a description graph G_{thumb} shown in Figure 1d. The following graph specialization axiom captures the relationship between these two description graphs:

$$(20) \qquad\qquad G_{finger} \lhd G_{thumb}$$

Definition 5. *A* graph specialization *is an axiom of the form* $G_1 \lhd G_2$, *where* $G_1 = (V_1, E_1, \lambda_1, M_1)$ *and* $G_2 = (V_2, E_2, \lambda_2, M_2)$ *are description graphs such that* $V_1 \subseteq V_2$.

Next, we introduce axioms that allow us to appropriately connect graph instances. For example, the description graph G_{hand} shown in Figure 1b contains the vertices 3 and 4 that represent the thumb and its proximal phalanx, which correspond to the vertices 1 and 3 of the description graph G_{thumb} shown in Figure 1d. We can specify this correspondence using the following *graph alignment*:

$$(21) \qquad\qquad G_{hand}[3, 4] \leftrightarrow G_{thumb}[1, 3]$$

This axiom ensures that, whenever two instances of G_{hand} and G_{thumb} share the thumb vertex, they also share a proximal phalanx vertex as well, and vice versa.

Definition 6. *A* graph alignment *has the form* $G_1[v_1, \ldots, v_n] \leftrightarrow G_2[w_1, \ldots w_n]$, *where* G_1 *and* G_2 *are description graphs with sets of vertices* V_1 *and* V_2, *respectively, and* $v_i \in V_1$ *and* $w_i \in V_2$ *for* $1 \leq i \leq n$.

Finally, we define GBoxes and graph-extended knowledge bases.

Definition 7. *A* graph box *(GBox) is a tuple* $\mathcal{G} = (\mathcal{G}_G, \mathcal{G}_S, \mathcal{G}_A)$ *where* $\mathcal{G}_G$, $\mathcal{G}_S$, *and* $\mathcal{G}_A$ *are finite sets of description graphs, graph specializations over* $\mathcal{G}_G$, *and graph alignments over* $\mathcal{G}_G$, *respectively. The definition of ABoxes from Section 2.1 is extended to allow for* graph assertions *of the form* $G(a_1, \ldots, a_\ell)$ *where* G *is an ℓ-ary graph and each* a_i, $1 \leq i \leq \ell$, *is an individual. A* graph-extended knowledge base *is a 4-tuple* $\mathcal{K} = (\mathcal{T}, \mathcal{P}, \mathcal{G}, \mathcal{A})$ *where* $\mathcal{T}$ *is a TBox,* $\mathcal{P}$ *is a finite set of connected graph rules,* $\mathcal{G}$ *is a GBox, and* $\mathcal{A}$ *is an ABox.*

Next, we define the semantics of the formalism.

Definition 8. *An interpretation* $I = (\triangle^I, \cdot^I)$ *is defined as usual, with the addition that it interprets each ℓ-ary description graph G as an ℓ-ary relation over* $\triangle^I$—*that is,* $G^I \subseteq (\triangle^I)^\ell$. *Each tuple in G^I is called a* graph instance *of G. A* graph assertion *is satisfied in I, written* $I \models G(a_1, \ldots, a_\ell)$, *if and only if* $\langle a_1^I, \ldots, a_\ell^I \rangle \in G^I$. *Satisfaction of a description graph, graph specialization, and graph alignment in I is defined in Table 4. A knowledge base* $\mathcal{K} = (\mathcal{T}, \mathcal{P}, \mathcal{G}, \mathcal{A})$ *is satisfied in I, written* $I \models \mathcal{K}$, *if all its components are satisfied in I.*

The key and disjointness properties in Table 4 ensure that no two distinct instances of G can share a vertex; for example, different instances of G_{hand} cannot share the vertex that represents the thumb. These properties are required to ensure that the representation of the structured objects is bounded. For example,

Table 4. Satisfaction of GBox Elements in an Interpretation

$I \models G$ for $G = (V, E, \lambda, M)$ iff

Key property:

$\forall x_1, \ldots, x_\ell, y_1, \ldots, y_\ell \in \Delta^I :$
$$\langle x_1, \ldots, x_\ell \rangle \in G^I \wedge \langle y_1, \ldots, y_\ell \rangle \in G^I \wedge \bigvee_{1 \leq i \leq \ell} x_i = y_i \rightarrow \bigwedge_{1 \leq j \leq \ell} x_j = y_j$$

Disjointness property:

$\forall x_1, \ldots, x_\ell, y_1, \ldots, y_\ell \in \Delta^I : \langle x_1, \ldots, x_\ell \rangle \in G^I \wedge \langle y_1, \ldots, y_\ell \rangle \in G^I \rightarrow \bigwedge_{1 \leq i < j \leq \ell} x_i \neq y_j$

Start property: for each atomic concept $A \in M$,

$\forall x \in \Delta^I : x \in A^I \rightarrow \exists x_1, \ldots, x_\ell \in \Delta^I : \langle x_1, \ldots, x_\ell \rangle \in G^I \wedge \bigvee_{k \in V_A} x = x_k$

Layout property:

$\forall x_1, \ldots, x_\ell \in \Delta^I :$
$$\langle x_1, \ldots, x_\ell \rangle \in G^I \rightarrow \bigwedge_{i \in V, \, B \in \lambda \langle i \rangle} x_i \in B^I \wedge \bigwedge_{\langle i,j \rangle \in E, \, R \in \lambda \langle i,j \rangle} \langle x_i, x_j \rangle \in R^I$$

$I \models G_1 \lhd G_2$ iff

$\forall x_1, \ldots, x_{\ell_2} \in \Delta^I : \langle x_1, \ldots, x_{\ell_1}, \ldots, x_{\ell_2} \rangle \in G_2^I \rightarrow \langle x_1, \ldots, x_{\ell_1} \rangle \in G_1^I$

$I \models G_1[v_1, \ldots, v_n] \leftrightarrow G_2[w_1, \ldots w_n]$ iff, for each $1 \leq i \leq n$,

$\forall x_1, \ldots, x_{\ell_1}, y_1, \ldots, y_{\ell_2} \in \Delta^I :$
$$\langle x_1, \ldots, x_{\ell_1} \rangle \in G_1^I \wedge \langle y_1, \ldots, y_{\ell_2} \rangle \in G_2^I \wedge x_{v_i} = y_{w_i} \rightarrow \bigwedge_{1 \leq j \leq n} x_{v_j} = y_{w_j}$$

Note: $\ell_{(i)}$ is the arity of the description graph $G_{(i)}$.

---

they prevent the existence of infinite "chains" of instances of G_{hand}, which is crucial for the decidability of our formalism.

The start property in Table 4 ensures that each instance of a main concept A of G occurs in an instance of G. For example, since **Hand** is a main concept for G_{hand}, each instance of **Hand** must occur as vertex 1 in an instance of G_{hand}. Similarly, vertex 3 of G_{hand} is labeled with **Thumb**, which is the main concept of G_{thumb}; hence, each vertex 3 in an instance of G_{hand} is also a vertex 1 in an instance of G_{thumb} (but not the other way around). The disjunction in the start property handles the case when a main concept labels multiple vertices. For example, if we were to describe the hand and the five fingers in a single graph without a distinction between the five fingers, then, given an instance of a **Finger**, we would have to guess which of the five fingers we are dealing with. Finally, the layout property ensures that each instance of G is labeled and connected as specified in the definition of G.

Graph specializations are interpreted as inclusions over the graph relations; for example, axiom (20) states that each instance of a thumb is also an instance of a finger. The two graphs share all the vertices of the more general graph, and the more specific graph can introduce additional vertices.

Finally, graph alignments state that, whenever two graphs share some vertex from the specified list, then they share all other vertices from the list as well. For example, alignment (21) states that, whenever instances of G_{hand} and G_{thumb} share vertices 3 and 1, respectively, then they must also share vertices 4 and 3, respectively.

The main reasoning problem for graph-extended knowledge bases is satisfiability checking, since concept subsumption and instance checking can be reduced to satisfiability as usual.

Description graphs allow us to faithfully represent the nontree connections between the parts of a structured object. For example, consider the graph-extended knowledge base $\mathcal{K}'' = (\mathcal{T}'', \emptyset, \mathcal{G}'', \emptyset)$ where $\mathcal{T}''$ contains axioms (11)–(18), and $\mathcal{G}''$ contains description graph $G_{index\text{-}finger}$ shown in Figure 1e. The GBox $\mathcal{G}''$ correctly axiomatizes the structure of the index finger and, unlike the DL knowledge base $\mathcal{K}'$ from Section 3, the graph-extended knowledge base $\mathcal{K}''$ entails axiom (19).

Note that Definition 8 does not ensure that objects in an instance of a description graph G are connected only by the edges as specified in G—that is, the maximum cardinality of the edges in an instance of G is not fixed. Because of that, axioms (11)–(17) are strictly necessary for the inference from the previous paragraph. Although Definition 8 could be straightforwardly extended with conditions that impose appropriate cardinality restrictions, we refrain from doing so for several reasons. First, cardinalities can always be axiomatized explicitly as shown in the previous example, so the presented formalism is more general. Second, the adopted approach allows us to study at a finer-grained level the impact of various constructs on the decidability of reasoning.

5   Undecidability of Reasoning

Checking the satisfiability of a graph-extended knowledge base $\mathcal{K}$ is clearly undecidable since the combination of simple DLs with unrestricted Horn rules is already undecidable [17]. The arbitrary combination of DLs and rules is, however, not the only source of undecidability. In this section, we show that the interactions between DL axioms and graphs (even without rules), as well as between graphs and Horn rules (even without DL axioms) lead to undecidability.

Proposition 1. *Checking the satisfiability of a graph-extended knowledge base $\mathcal{K} = (\mathcal{T}, \emptyset, \mathcal{G}, \mathcal{A})$ with $\mathcal{T}$ a TBox in $\mathcal{ALCF}$ and $\mathcal{G} = (\mathcal{G}_G, \emptyset, \emptyset)$ is undecidable.*

Proposition 2. *Checking the satisfiability of a graph-extended knowledge base $\mathcal{K} = (\emptyset, \mathcal{P}, \mathcal{G}, \mathcal{A})$ where all rules in $\mathcal{P}$ are Horn and $\mathcal{G} = (\mathcal{G}_G, \emptyset, \emptyset)$ is undecidable.*

The proofs of Propositions 1 and 2 are given in [22]. Proposition 1 is proved by a reduction from the unbounded domino tiling problem [5]; roughly speaking, one can axiomatize an infinite sequence of description graphs using $\mathcal{G}$, and arrange the graphs into a grid using functionality axioms in $\mathcal{T}$. Proposition 2 is proved by a reduction from the emptiness of the intersection of the context-free languages.

The proofs of Propositions 1 and 2 suggest that undecidability is partly due to the fact that graph-extended knowledge bases can axiomatize models containing unbounded sequences of instances of one or more description graphs. In practice, however, structured objects are usually modeled up to a certain level of granularity, which naturally determines a bound on the sequence of graphs one needs to represent. In such cases, we can describe the structure of an object by an acyclic hierarchy of parts; for example, carpal bones are parts of the hand, but the hand is not a part of the carpal bones. To reflect the acyclic nature of such a representation, it therefore seems reasonable to impose an acyclicity condition in our formalism. Intuitively, this condition ensures that the description graphs are arranged in a hierarchical manner and that their instantiation always provides a bounded representation.

Definition 9. *Let* $\mathcal{G} = (\mathcal{G}_G, \mathcal{G}_S, \mathcal{G}_A)$ *be a GBox and* $\lhd$ *the reflexive–transitive closure of* $\lhd$ *in* $\mathcal{G}_S$. *The GBox* $\mathcal{G}$ *is* acyclic *if a strict (i.e., an irreflexive and transitive, but not necessarily total) order* $\prec$ *on* $\mathcal{G}_G$ *exists such that, for each* $G = (V, E, \lambda, M)$ *and* $G' = (V', E', \lambda', M')$ *in* $\mathcal{G}_G$ *with* $G \not\preceq G'$, *and for each* $A \in M'$, *the following two conditions hold:*

- $G' \lhd G$ *implies* $\neg A \in \lambda\langle i \rangle$ *for each* $i \in V \setminus V'$; *and*
- $G' \not\lhd G$ *implies* $\neg A \in \lambda\langle i \rangle$ *for each* $i \in V$.

A graph-extended knowledge base is acyclic *if its GBox is acyclic.*

Intuitively, $G_1 \prec G_2$ means that an instance of G_1 is allowed to imply the existence of an instance of G_2. In our example, we would have $G_{hand} \prec G_{finger}$ and $G_{hand} \prec G_{thumb}$, which allows an instance of a hand to imply the existence of a finger and/or a thumb. We would also have $G_{finger} \prec G_{thumb}$, since finger is more general than thumb. The conditions in Definition 9 state that, if $G_1 \not\prec G_2$, then an instance of G_2 cannot imply the existence of an instance of G_1 because each node of G_2 must be labeled with a negation of each start concept of G_1. For example, since $G_{thumb} \not\prec G_{hand}$, no vertex in an instance of G_{thumb} should ever become labeled with a main concept of G_{hand}. Effectively, this prevents cyclic implications between instances of description graphs.

Requiring the GBox to be acyclic invalidates Proposition 2. In fact, checking the satisfiability of $\mathcal{K} = (\emptyset, \mathcal{P}, \mathcal{G}, \mathcal{A})$ with $\mathcal{G}$ acyclic is decidable: $\mathcal{G}$ can then imply the existence only of bounded structures (that can be obtained by unfolding $\mathcal{G}$ in a straightforward way), so it does not matter if the rules in $\mathcal{P}$ are not tree-like.

Even if $\mathcal{P}$ is empty, however, the acyclicity of $\mathcal{G}$ is not sufficient to ensure decidability if $\mathcal{T}$ is allowed to contain inverse roles. Since we do not consider inverse roles in this paper, we do not go into further detail in this section; please refer to [22] for more information.

6   Reasoning with Graph-Extended Knowledge Bases

Let $\mathcal{K} = (\mathcal{T}, \mathcal{P}, \mathcal{G}, \mathcal{A})$ be a graph-extended KB. In Section 5, we proposed acyclicity of $\mathcal{G}$ as a way to limit the size of the structures whose existence is implied by

$\mathcal{G}$. Furthermore, to prevent undecidability due to an interaction between rules and DL axioms, we place restrictions on the usage of roles in $\mathcal{T}$, $\mathcal{P}$, and $\mathcal{G}$, as shown in the following definition.

Definition 10. *A graph extended knowledge base $\mathcal{K} = (\mathcal{T}, \mathcal{P}, \mathcal{G}, \mathcal{A})$ is weakly admissible if $\mathcal{P}$ does not share any roles with $\mathcal{T}$.*

Let $\mathcal{R}$ be a set of rules, $\mathcal{G}$ a GBox, $\mathcal{A}$ an ABox. The triple $(\mathcal{R}, \mathcal{G}, \mathcal{A})$ is weakly admissible *if the set of rules $\mathcal{R}$ can be split into disjoint subsets $\mathcal{R}_{\mathcal{T}}$ and $\mathcal{R}_{\mathcal{P}}$ of $\mathcal{T}$- and $\mathcal{P}$-rules, respectively, such that*

- *each rule $r \in \mathcal{R}_{\mathcal{T}}$ is an HT-rule,*
- *each rule $r \in \mathcal{R}_{\mathcal{P}}$ is a connected graph rule, and*
- *$\mathcal{R}_{\mathcal{P}}$ does not share any roles with $\mathcal{R}_{\mathcal{G}}$.*

Furthermore, $(\mathcal{R}, \mathcal{G}, \mathcal{A})$ is acyclic *if $\mathcal{G}$ is acyclic.*

Let $\mathcal{K} = (\mathcal{T}, \mathcal{P}, \mathcal{G}, \mathcal{A})$ be a graph-extended KB, $\Xi_{\mathcal{T}}(\mathcal{T})$ and $\mathcal{A}' = \mathcal{A} \cup \Xi_{\mathcal{A}}(\mathcal{T})$ the result of preprocessing $\mathcal{T}$ using the preprocessing transformation from [21, Section 4.1], and $\mathcal{R} = \mathcal{P} \cup \Xi_{\mathcal{T}}(\mathcal{T})$. It is straightforward to see that, if $\mathcal{P}$ does not share any roles with $\mathcal{T} \cup \mathcal{R}$, then $(\mathcal{R}, \mathcal{G}, \mathcal{A}')$ is weakly admissible. Furthermore, if $\mathcal{G}$ is acyclic, then $(\mathcal{R}, \mathcal{G}, \mathcal{A}')$ is acyclic as well. Finally, since there is no interaction between $\mathcal{T}$ and $\mathcal{P}$, transitivity axioms in $\mathcal{T}$ can be encoded into GCIs in the same way as in [21, Section 4.1] without affecting satisfiability. The knowledge base $\mathcal{K}$ is thus equisatisfiable with $(\mathcal{R}, \mathcal{G}, \mathcal{A}')$. For the sake of brevity, we omit the details of the preprocessing phase and present an algorithm that decides the satisfiability of a weakly admissible triple $(\mathcal{R}, \mathcal{G}, \mathcal{A})$.

We next present an algorithm that can be used to check the satisfiability of a weakly separated knowledge base $\mathcal{K}$. The formal definitions of the algorithm are rather intricate, so we first outline the main ideas by means of an example. Consider the following graph-extended knowledge base $\mathcal{K}_1 = (\mathcal{T}_1, \mathcal{P}_1, \mathcal{G}_1, \mathcal{A}_1)$:

$$(22) \quad \begin{array}{l} \mathcal{T}_1 = \{\, C \sqsubseteq \exists R.A, \\ \qquad\quad B \sqsubseteq \{b\} \quad \} \\ \mathcal{P}_1 = \emptyset \\ \mathcal{A}_1 = \{\, C(a)\, \} \end{array} \qquad \begin{array}{l} \mathcal{G}_1 \text{ contains the following description graph:} \\[4pt] G: \quad \begin{array}{lll} V = \{1,2,3\} & \lambda\langle 1\rangle = \{A\} & 1 \xrightarrow{S} 2 \\ M = \{A\} & \lambda\langle 2\rangle = \{B\} & 2 \xrightarrow{T} 3 \\ & \lambda\langle 3\rangle = \{C\} & 1 \xrightarrow{U} 3 \end{array} \end{array}$$

The preprocessing of $\mathcal{T}_1$ produces the ABox $\Xi_{\mathcal{A}}(\mathcal{T}_1) = \{O_b(b)\}$ and the following set of rules $\Xi_{\mathcal{T}}(\mathcal{T}_1)$:

$$(23) \qquad\qquad\qquad\qquad C(x) \rightarrow (\exists R.A)(x)$$
$$(24) \qquad\qquad\qquad B(x) \wedge O_b(y_b) \rightarrow x \approx y_b$$

Let $\mathcal{R}_1 = \Xi_{\mathcal{T}}(\mathcal{T}_1)$ and $\mathcal{A}_1^1 = \Xi_{\mathcal{A}}(\mathcal{T}_1) \cup \mathcal{A}_1$. Clearly, $(\mathcal{R}_1, \mathcal{G}_1, \mathcal{A}_1^1)$ is weakly admissible: all rules in $\mathcal{R}_1$ are HT-rules and $\mathcal{P} = \emptyset$.

By successively applying the derivation rules shown in Tables 3 and 5 to $\mathcal{R}_1$, $\mathcal{G}_1$, and $\mathcal{A}_1^1$, our algorithm tries to construct an ABox that represents a model of

$$
\begin{array}{lll}
& & A(s_1) \\
& & G(s_1, t_{1,1}, t_{1,2}) \\
& & S(s_1, t_{1,1}) \\
O_b(b) & & T(t_{1,1}, t_{1,2}) \\
C(a) & R(a, s_1) & U(s_1, t_{1,2}) \\
\exists R.A(a) & & B(t_{1,1}) \\
& & C(t_{1,2}) \\
& & \exists R.A(t_{1,2})
\end{array}
\qquad
\begin{array}{ll}
& A(s_2) \\
& G(s_2, t_{2,1}, t_{2,2}) \\
& S(s_2, t_{2,1}) \\
R(t_{1,2}, s_2) & T(t_{2,1}, t_{2,2}) \\
& U(s_2, t_{2,2}) \\
& B(t_{2,1}) \\
& C(t_{2,2})
\end{array}
\qquad
\begin{array}{l}
a = \triangleright.\nu_a \\
s_1 = \triangleright.\nu_a.\tau \\
t_{1,1} = \triangleright.\nu_a.\tau.\gamma_1 \\
t_{1,2} = \triangleright.\nu_a.\tau.\gamma_2 \\
s_2 = \triangleright.\nu_a.\tau.\gamma_2.\tau \\
t_{2,1} = \triangleright.\nu_a.\tau.\gamma_2.\tau.\gamma_1 \\
t_{2,2} = \triangleright.\nu_a.\tau.\gamma_2.\tau.\gamma_2
\end{array}
$$

Fig. 3. Example Derivation of the Hypertableau Algorithm

$(\mathcal{R}_1, \mathcal{G}_1, \mathcal{A}_1^1)$. The evolution of $\mathcal{A}_1^1$ is shown in Figure 3, where assertions derived by a single application of a derivation rule are separated by dotted lines. Note that the derivation rules from Table 5 closely follow the semantic conditions on description graphs given in Definition 8.

The *Hyp*-rule derives new assertions based on the contents of $\mathcal{R}$: if the body of some rule $r \in \mathcal{R}$ can be matched to assertions in an ABox, an assertion from the head of r is derived nondeterministically. Thus, from $C(a)$ and (23), the *Hyp*-rule derives the assertion $\exists R.A(a)$.

To satisfy this assertion, the $\geq$-rule introduces a fresh *tree successor* s_1 of a and it derives the assertions $R(a, s_1)$ and $A(s_1)$. To keep track of the successor relation, our algorithm represents individuals as finite strings of the form $\triangleright.\alpha_1. \dots .\alpha_n$, where α_i are *symbols*, and $\triangleright$ is a special symbol that is used to make certain definitions simpler. Thus, the individual a actually corresponds to the string $\triangleright.\nu_a$ where ν_a is a *name symbol*; furthermore, s_1 corresponds to the individual $\triangleright.\nu_a.\tau$, where τ is a *tree symbol*. That s_1 is a successor of a is evident from the fact that $a = \triangleright.\nu_a$ is a prefix of $s_1 = \triangleright.\nu_a.\tau$.

The concept A is a main concept in G so, due to the assertion $A(s_1)$, individual s_1 must occur in an instance of G at vertex 1; to ensure this, the hypertableau calculus uses the $G_\exists$-rule. An application of the $G_\exists$-rule to $A(s_1)$ derives the assertion $G(s_1, t_{1,1}, t_{1,2})$. Individuals $t_{1,1}$ and $t_{1,2}$ fresh *graph successors* of s_1, which is reflected in their string representation: we have $t_{1,1} = s_1.\gamma_1 = \triangleright.\nu_a.\tau.\gamma_1$ and $t_{1,2} = s_1.\gamma_2 = \triangleright.\nu_a.\tau.\gamma_2$ where γ_1 and γ_2 are *graph symbols*. A tree or named individual and all of its graph successors are said to form a *cluster*; individuals s_1, $t_{1,1}$, and $t_{1,2}$ are an example of such a cluster.

To connect and label all the vertices in an instance of G, the hypertableau calculus uses the G_L-rule. Its application to the current set of assertions adds, among others, the assertion $C(t_{1,2})$. These inferences can then be repeated: the *Hyp*-rule derives $\exists R.A(t_{1,2})$, the $\geq$-rule derives $R(t_{1,2}, s_2)$ and $A(s_2)$ where $s_2 = t_{1,2}.\tau = \triangleright.\nu_a.\tau.\gamma_2.\tau$, the $G_\exists$-rule derives the graph assertion $G(s_2, t_{2,1}, t_{2,2})$, and the G_L-rule connects and labels all the vertices. Let $\mathcal{A}_1^2$ be the ABox containing all assertions derived thus far; all assertions are shown in Figure 3.

Clearly, unrestricted application of the $\geq$- and $G_\exists$-rule would lead to nontermination. Therefore, just like the standard (hyper)tableau algorithms, our algorithm applies *blocking*. Roughly speaking, tree individuals s_1 and s_2 occur in $\mathcal{A}_1^2$ in the same concepts, so the former individual blocks the latter—that is, the $\geq$- and $G_\exists$-rule are not applied to (the successors of) the blocked individual. Blocking is applicable because the ABox $\mathcal{A}_1^2$ is of structure that generalizes the notion of forest-shaped ABoxes from Section 2.3. In particular, $\mathcal{A}_1^2$ can thus be seen as consisting of three clusters, shown in Figure 3 as the leftmost, middle, and right-most columns, connected by assertions $R(a, s_1)$ and $R(t_{1,2}, s_2)$.

Forest-shaped ABoxes contain several kinds of individuals, which we summarize next.

- *Named individuals* are the ones that occur in the input ABox.
- *Tree individuals* are introduced by the $\geq$-rule in order to satisfy the existential quantifiers in the TBox of the knowledge base.
- *Graph individuals* are introduced by the $G_\exists$-rule in order to satisfy the start property for the graphs in the GBox of the knowledge base.

The central concept in forest-shaped ABoxes is the notion of a cluster, whose formal definition ensures that all named individuals and all graph individuals of the form $\triangleright.\gamma_i$ form a single cluster, and that each tree individual t and all graph individuals of the form $t.\gamma_i$ form a cluster. The key idea behind clusters is that (i) individuals in the same cluster can be arbitrarily connected, but (ii) individuals from different clusters are connected in a tree-like manner. Thus, each forest-shaped ABox can be seen as a tree of clusters; we often call this structure a *tree backbone*. We exploit the tree backbone to generalize the notions of blocking and pruning from the standard (hyper)tableau algorithms.

In Lemma 1, we formalize the notion of forest-shaped ABoxes and show that, if $(\mathcal{R}, \mathcal{G}, \mathcal{A})$ is weakly separated, then the application of the hypertableau derivation rules to a forest-shaped ABox always produces a forest-shaped ABox. Intuitively, the arbitrarily shaped $\mathcal{P}$-rules in $\mathcal{R}$ can be applied only to assertions involving individuals in the same cluster, where they can introduce arbitrary connections; however, due to weak separation, they cannot affect the tree backbone. The tree backbone is constructed solely using the $\mathcal{T}$-rules in $\mathcal{R}$.

Nominals, however, introduce a slight complication. Consider again the ABox $\mathcal{A}_1^2$. From $B(t_{1,1})$, $O_b(b)$, and (24), the *Hyp*-rule derives $t_{1,1} \approx b$. The $\approx$-rule then *prunes* $t_{1,1}$ (i.e., it removes all graph and tree descendants or $t_{1,1}$) and replaces it with b; pruning is necessary in order to avoid nontermination due to repeated individual creation and merging, as in the so-called "yo-yo" problem [4]. After $t_{1,1}$ is replaced with b, the ABox contains the graph assertion $G(s_1, b, t_{1,2})$ in which b is not from the same cluster as s_1 and $t_{1,2}$; thus, the ABox is not forest shaped. This is remedied through *graph cleanup*: the mentioned assertion is replaced with $G(v_1, b, v_2)$, where $v_1 = \triangleright.\gamma_1$ and $v_2 = \triangleright.\gamma_2$ are fresh graph individuals from the cluster of b. The cluster of s_1 and $t_{1,2}$ is thus merged into the cluster of b in order to make the resulting ABox forest shaped. Furthermore, if graph cleanup is subsequently applied to an assertion of the form

$G(w_1, b, w_2)$, individuals w_1 and w_2 are replaced with v_1 and v_2, respectively. Reusing individuals in graph cleanup is sound because of the key property in Table 4, and it allows us to establish a bound on the number of thus introduced individuals.

We next define our algorithm formally.

Definition 11. *The hypertableau algorithm for checking the satisfiability of a weakly admissible triple* $(\mathcal{R}, \mathcal{G}, \mathcal{A})$ *is obtained by modifying parts of Definition 2 as follows.*

Individuals. *Let* Σ_τ, Σ_γ, *and* Σ_ν *be countably infinite and mutually disjoint sets of* tree, graph, *and* name symbols, *respectively, none of which contains the special symbol* $\triangleright$.

An individual *is a finite string of the form* $\triangleright.\alpha_1.\ \ldots\ .\alpha_n$ *with* $n \geq 1$ *such that*

- $\alpha_1 \in \Sigma_\nu \cup \Sigma_\gamma$,
- $\alpha_i \in \Sigma_\gamma \cup \Sigma_\tau$ *for* $2 \leq i \leq n$, *and*
- $\alpha_i \in \Sigma_\nu \cup \Sigma_\gamma$ *implies* $\alpha_{i+1} \notin \Sigma_\gamma$ *for* $1 \leq i \leq n$.

An individual with $\alpha_n \in \Sigma_\tau$ *(resp.* $\alpha_n \in \Sigma_\gamma$*) is a* tree *(resp.* graph*) individual. Furthermore, an individual of the form* $\triangleright.\alpha$ *is a* root *individual, and if* $\alpha \in \Sigma_\nu$, *the individual is* named. *Let* N_A *be the set of all individuals.*

For each individual $x.\alpha \in N_A$ *(with* x *possibly being equal to* $\triangleright$*), we say that* $x.\alpha$ *is a* successor *of* x, x *is* predecessor *of* $x.\alpha$, *and* descendant *and* ancestor *are the transitive closures of successor and predecessor, respectively.*

Cluster. *For each individual* $s \in N_A$, *the function* $\lfloor s \rfloor$ *is defined as follows:* $\lfloor s \rfloor = s$ *if* s *is a tree individual; otherwise,* $\lfloor s \rfloor = t$ *for* $s = t.\alpha$. *Individuals* s *and* t *are from the same* cluster *if* $\lfloor s \rfloor = \lfloor t \rfloor$.

Graph Cleanup. *Let* $\mathcal{A}$ *be an ABox containing an assertion* $G(u_1, \ldots, u_\ell)$ *where some* u_i *and* u_j *are not from the same cluster, and* $\lfloor u_i \rfloor$ *is an ancestor of* u_j. *A* cleanup *of* u_j *is an ABox obtained from* $\mathcal{A}$ *by pruning* u_j *and then replacing in all the remaining assertions* u_j *with an individual* t *defined as follows:*

- *if* $\mathcal{A}$ *contains another graph assertion* $G(v_1, \ldots, v_\ell)$ *such that* $u_i = v_i$ *and* v_j *is from the same cluster as* u_i, *then* $t = v_j$;
- *otherwise,* t *is a fresh graph successor of* $\lfloor u_i \rfloor$.

A graph cleanup *of* $\mathcal{A}$ *is obtained from* $\mathcal{A}$ *by iteratively applying a cleanup to candidate individuals as long as possible and in any sequence that satisfies the following restriction: whenever cleanup is applicable to* u_i *and* u_j *such that* u_i *is an ancestor of* u_j, *cleanup is applied first to* u_i.[3]

---

[3] Note that, due to the freedom in choice of t and the order in which cleanup is applied to candidate individuals, graph cleanup of $\mathcal{A}$ is not uniquely defined; however, for the purposes of our algorithm, *any* cleanup of $\mathcal{A}$ will suffice.

Table 5. Derivation Rules Related to Description Graphs

$G_\approx$-rule	If 1. $\{G(s_1, \ldots, s_\ell), G(t_1, \ldots, t_\ell)\} \subseteq \mathcal{A}$, 2. $s_i = t_i$ for some $1 \leq i \leq \ell$, 3. $\{s_j \approx t_j \mid 1 \leq j \leq \ell\} \not\subseteq \mathcal{A}$, and 4. neither s_i nor t_i is indirectly blocked for each $1 \leq i \leq \ell$ then $\mathcal{A}_1 := \mathcal{A} \cup \{s_j \approx t_j \mid 1 \leq j \leq \ell\}$.
$G_\perp$-rule	If 1. $\{G(s_1, \ldots, s_\ell), G(t_1, \ldots, t_\ell)\} \subseteq \mathcal{A}$, 2. $s_i = t_j$ for some $i \neq j$, and 3. neither s_i nor t_i is indirectly blocked for each $1 \leq i \leq \ell$ then $\mathcal{A}_1 := \mathcal{A} \cup \{\perp\}$.
$G_\exists$-rule	If 1. $A(s) \in \mathcal{A}$ such that $A \in M$ for some $G = (V, E, \lambda, M) \in \mathcal{G}_G$, 2. s is not blocked in $\mathcal{A}$, and 3. for each $v_i \in V_A = \{v_1, \ldots, v_n\}$, no individuals $u_1, \ldots, u_\ell$ exist such that $G(u_1, \ldots, u_\ell) \in \mathcal{A}$ and $u_{v_i} = s$ then $\mathcal{A}_i := \mathcal{A} \cup \{G(t_1, \ldots, t_\ell)\}$ for each $1 \leq i \leq n$ where $t_{v_i} = s$ and all other t_k are fresh graph successors of $\lfloor s \rfloor$.
G_L-rule	If 1. $G(s_1, \ldots, s_\ell) \in \mathcal{A}$ with $G = (V, E, \lambda, M)$, 2. $\{A(s_i) \mid A \in \lambda\langle i\rangle\} \cup \{R(s_i, s_j) \mid R \in \lambda\langle i, j\rangle\} \not\subseteq \mathcal{A}$, and 3. s_i is not indirectly blocked for each $1 \leq i \leq \ell$ then $\mathcal{A}_1 := \mathcal{A} \cup \{A(s_i) \mid A \in \lambda\langle i\rangle\} \cup \{R(s_i, s_j) \mid R \in \lambda\langle i, j\rangle\}$.
$G_\lhd$-rule	If 1. $G_1 \lhd G_2 \in \mathcal{G}_S$, 2. $G_2(s_1, \ldots, s_{\ell_2}) \in \mathcal{A}$, 3. $G_1(s_1, \ldots, s_{\ell_1}) \not\in \mathcal{A}$, and 4. s_i is not indirectly blocked for each $1 \leq i \leq \ell$ then $\mathcal{A}_1 := \mathcal{A} \cup \{G_1(s_1, \ldots, s_{\ell_1})\}$.
$G_\leftrightarrow$-rule	If 1. $G_1[v_1, \ldots, v_n] \leftrightarrow G_2[w_1, \ldots w_n] \in \mathcal{G}_A$, 2. $\{G_1(s_1, \ldots, s_{\ell_1}), G_2(t_1, \ldots, t_{\ell_2})\} \subseteq \mathcal{A}$, 3. $s_{v_i} = t_{w_i}$ for some $1 \leq i \leq n$, 4. $\{s_{v_j} \approx t_{w_j} \mid 1 \leq j \leq n\} \not\subseteq \mathcal{A}$, and 5. neither s_i nor t_i is indirectly blocked for each $1 \leq i \leq \ell$ then $\mathcal{A}_1 := \mathcal{A} \cup \{s_{v_j} \approx t_{w_j} \mid 1 \leq j \leq n\}$.

Merge Target. *An individual t is a merge target for an individual s if t is a named individual, or t is a root individual and s is not a named individual, or t is not a root individual and s is a descendant of $\lfloor t \rfloor$.*

Merging. *The ABox $\mathsf{merge}_\mathcal{A}(s \to t)$ is obtained from $\mathsf{prune}_\mathcal{A}(s)$ by replacing s with t in all assertions, and then applying a graph cleanup.*

Derivation Rules. *The derivation rules from Table 3 are extended with the ones from Table 5.*

Rule Precedence. *The $G_\exists$-rule is applicable to an ABox only if the $\perp$-, $\approx$-, $G_\perp$-, $G_\approx$-, $G_\lhd$-, and G_L-rule are not applicable to the ABox.*

We next prove soundness, completeness, and termination of our algorithm for the case when $\mathcal{K}$ is weakly admissible and acyclic. To this end, Lemma 1 formalizes the intuitive notion of forest-shaped ABoxes and shows that an application of a derivation rule always preserves this property. The proof of the lemma proceeds by an induction on the application of the derivation rules.

Lemma 1. *Let $\mathcal{R}$ be a set of rules, $\mathcal{G}$ a GBox, and $\mathcal{A}$ an ABox such that $(\mathcal{R}, \mathcal{G}, \mathcal{A})$ is simple and weakly admissible. Then, each ABox $\mathcal{A}'$ labeling a node of a derivation for $(\mathcal{R}, \mathcal{G}, \mathcal{A})$ satisfies the following properties, for a and b named individuals, $u_{(i)}$ individuals, $\gamma_i, \gamma_j \in \Sigma_\gamma$, and $\tau_i, \tau_j \in \Sigma_\tau$.*

1. *Each $R(s,t) \in \mathcal{A}'$ where R is a $\mathcal{T}$-role has the form $R(u, u.\tau_i)$, $R(u, a)$, or $R(u_1, u_2)$, where u_1 and u_2 are individuals from the same cluster.*
2. *Each $s \approx t \in \mathcal{A}'$ is of the form $a \approx u$, $u_1 \approx u_2$, $u_1 \approx u_2.\tau_i$, or $u.\tau_i \approx u.\tau_j$, where u_1 and u_2 are individuals from the same cluster.*
3. *In each $G(u_1, \ldots u_\ell) \in \mathcal{A}'$ and $U(u_1, u_2) \in \mathcal{A}'$ with U a $\mathcal{P}$-role, u_i are all from the same cluster. Furthermore, for each graph individual u_0 in $\mathcal{A}'$, an individual u_n from the same cluster as u_0 exists such that u_0 has a path to u_n in $\mathcal{A}'$ —that is, individuals $u_1, \ldots, u_{n-1}$ exist such that u_{i-1} and u_i occur together in a graph assertion in $\mathcal{A}'$ for each $1 \leq i \leq n$.*
4. *In each $O_a(u) \in \mathcal{A}'$ with O_a a nominal guard concept, the individual u is named. Furthermore, in each $\geq n\, R.B(u) \in \mathcal{A}'$, the concept B is not a nominal guard concept.*
5. *For each tree individual t_n in $\mathcal{A}'$, individuals $s_0, \ldots, s_n$ and $t_0, \ldots, t_{n-1}$ exist such that (i) s_0 is a named individual, (ii) for each $1 \leq i \leq n$, individuals s_i and t_{i-1} are from the same cluster, and (iii) for each $0 \leq i \leq n$, individual t_i is a tree successor of s_i, and $R_i(s_i, t_i) \in \mathcal{A}'$ for some $\mathcal{T}$-role R_i.*

Lemma 1 is used to prove the following theorem, which summarizes the properties of our algorithm.

Theorem 1. *The following properties hold for each set of rules $\mathcal{R}$, GBox $\mathcal{G}$, and ABox $\mathcal{A}$ such that $(\mathcal{R}, \mathcal{G}, \mathcal{A})$ is weakly admissible, simple, and acyclic:*

1. *if $(\mathcal{R}, \mathcal{G}, \mathcal{A})$ is satisfiable, then each derivation for $(\mathcal{R}, \mathcal{G}, \mathcal{A})$ is successful;*
2. *$(\mathcal{R}, \mathcal{G}, \mathcal{A})$ is satisfiable if a successful derivation for $(\mathcal{R}, \mathcal{G}, \mathcal{A})$ exists; and*
3. *each derivation for $(\mathcal{R}, \mathcal{G}, \mathcal{A})$ is finite.*

Since preprocessing of the TBox does not affect satisfiability, Theorem 1 implies that checking satisfiability of a a weakly separated acyclic graph-extended knowledge base $\mathcal{K} = (\mathcal{T}, \mathcal{P}, \mathcal{G}, \mathcal{A})$ is decidable.

7   Complexity of Reasoning

In this section we investigate the complexity bounds of checking the satisfiability of a graph-extended knowledge base $\mathcal{K} = (\mathcal{T}, \mathcal{P}, \mathcal{G}, \mathcal{A})$. We start the analysis by considering first the lower bound. A graph-extended knowledge base $\mathcal{K}$ contains a set $\mathcal{P}$ or disjunctive datalog rules, and checking the satisfiability of $\mathcal{P}$ is NEXPTIME-complete [9] (under standard first-order semantics), so one might intuitively expect this result to provide a lower bound for the complexity of checking the satisfiability of $\mathcal{K}$. To understand why this is not the case, consider the following intuitive explanation of the result from [9]. The satisfiability of $\mathcal{P}$ alone can be decided by the following three-step process:

1. Compute the grounding $\mathcal{P}_g$ of $\mathcal{P}$—that is, replace in $\mathcal{P}$ all variables in the rules with all individuals in all possible ways.
2. Nondeterministically guess an interpretation I for $\mathcal{P}_g$.
3. Check whether I is a model of $\mathcal{P}_g$.

Without restricting $\mathcal{P}$ in any way, the first and the third step can be implemented in exponential time, but the second step requires nondeterministic exponential time, so the overall complexity is NEXPTIME. If, however, the arity of the predicates occurring in $\mathcal{P}$ is bounded, then the number of ground atoms in $\mathcal{P}_g$ is polynomial in $|\mathcal{P}|$, so all interpretations I can be enumerated by an exponential algorithm. Similarly, if the number of variables in $\mathcal{P}$ is bounded, then $\mathcal{P}_g$ is polynomial in $|\mathcal{P}|$; furthermore, in the second step we can clearly restrict our attention to interpretations that contain only the ground atoms from $\mathcal{P}_g$, so we can again enumerate all relevant interpretations in exponential time. Thus, for the problem to be NEXPTIME-hard, $\mathcal{P}$ must be allowed to contain predicates of arbitrary arity as well as rules with an arbitrary number of variables.

The set of rules $\mathcal{P}$ of a graph-extended knowledge base $\mathcal{K}$ can contain rules with an unbounded number of variables, and it can contain graph atoms with arbitrary arity. The disjointness and key properties from Definition 8, however, impose restrictions on the interpretation of graph atoms in addition to $\mathcal{P}$, so the hardness result from [9] does not apply. In fact, we show that checking the satisfiability of $\mathcal{K}$ is NEXPTIME-hard even if the rules are allowed to contain only unary and binary predicates and at least four variables. We thus identify a new source of complexity of reasoning with graph-extended knowledge bases: description graphs can succinctly encode exponential structures. The proof of the following lemma is by a reduction from the succinct version of the bounded domino tiling problem [5].

Lemma 2. *Let $\mathcal{K} = (\emptyset, \mathcal{P}, \mathcal{G}, \mathcal{A})$ be a graph-extended KB where $\mathcal{G} = (\mathcal{G}_G, \emptyset, \emptyset)$ is an acyclic GBox and each rule in $\mathcal{P}$ contains only atomic concepts and roles and at most four variables. Then, checking the satisfiability of $\mathcal{K}$ is NEXPTIME-hard.*

For the upper complexity bound, note that the hypertableau procedure from Section 6 is not worst-case optimal even without description graphs and rules, and with $\mathcal{T}$ in $\mathcal{ALC}$ [21, Section 5.3]. This is because an ABox $\mathcal{A}'$ labeling a derivation node for a set of HT-rules $\mathcal{R} = \Xi_{\mathcal{T}}(\mathcal{T})$ and an ABox $\Xi_{\mathcal{A}}(\mathcal{T}) \cup \mathcal{A}$ can at any given point in time contain at most exponentially many nonblocked and directly blocked tree individuals; however, $\mathcal{A}'$ can contain a doubly exponential number of indirectly blocked individuals. The complexity of the hypertableau procedure can be reduced to NEXPTIME if we ensure that the label of each individual s is fully determined in $\mathcal{A}'$ before applying the $\geq$-rule to an assertion containing s: the rule application strategy then ensures that s cannot subsequently become blocked, so $\mathcal{A}'$ never contains indirectly blocked individuals. A similar approach was used in [11] to obtain a tableau algorithm for $\mathcal{ALC}$ running in NExpTime. For $\mathcal{SHOQ}^+$, such an algorithm is not worst-case optimal, since this DL is ExpTime-complete [3]. Description graphs increase the complexity at least to NExpTime, so the "excess" complexity of the modified hypertableau algorithm is not relevant. This allows us to prove the following theorem.

Theorem 2. *Checking the satisfiability of a weakly separated acyclic graph-extended knowledge base $\mathcal{K}$ is* NExpTime-*complete, provided that the numbers in $\mathcal{K}$ are coded in unary.*

8 Conclusion

We have presented an expressive formalism that extends DLs with description graphs and rules, allowing for more precise modeling of arbitrarily connected structures. Our formalism is applicable not only to anatomy, but to all domains in which the number of arbitrarily interconnected objects has a natural bound.

The main practical challenge is to validate the applicability of our formalism in these and other applications. To this end, we will extend the ontology editor Protégé 4 to support description graphs and apply our formalism in the identified practical scenarios.

References

1. Abiteboul, S., Hull, R., Vianu, V.: Foundations of Databases. Addison Wesley, Reading (1995)
2. Andréka, H., van Benthem, J., Németi, I.: Modal Languages and Bounded Fragments of Predicate Logic. Journal of Philosophical Logic 27(3), 217–274 (1998)
3. Baader, F., Calvanese, D., McGuinness, D., Nardi, D., Patel-Schneider, P.F. (eds.): The Description Logic Handbook: Theory, Implementation and Applications, 2nd edn. Cambridge University Press, Cambridge (2007)
4. Baader, F., Sattler, U.: An Overview of Tableau Algorithms for Description Logics. Studia Logica 69, 5–40 (2001)
5. Börger, E., Grädel, E., Gurevich, Y.: The Classical Decision Problem. Springer, Heidelberg (1996)
6. Borgida, A.: On the Relative Expressiveness of Description Logics and Predicate Logics. Artificial Intelligence 82(1-2), 353–367 (1996)
7. Calì, A., Gottlob, G., Kifer, M.: Taming the Infinite Chase: Query Answering under Expressive Relational Constraints. In: Proc. KR 2008, Sydney, NSW, Australia, pp. 70–80 (2008)
8. Grau, B.C., Horrocks, I., Motik, B., Parsia, B., Patel-Schneider, P., Sattler, U.: OWL 2: The next step for OWL. Journal of Web Semantics 6(4), 309–322 (2008)
9. Dantsin, E., Eiter, T., Gottlob, G., Voronkov, A.: Complexity and expressive power of logic programming. ACM Computing Surveys 33(3), 374–425 (2001)
10. de Bruijn, J., Polleres, A., Lara, R., Fensel, D.: OWL DL vs. OWL Flight: Conceptual Modeling and Reasoning on the Semantic Web. In: Proc. WWW 2005, Chiba, Japan, pp. 623–632 (2005)

11. Donini, F.M., Lenzerini, M., Nardi, D., Schaerf, A.: AL-log: Integrating Datalog and Description Logics. Journal of Intelligent Information Systems 10(3), 227–252 (1998)
12. Eiter, T., Lukasiewicz, T., Schindlauer, R., Tompits, H.: Combining Answer Set Programming with Description Logics for the Semantic Web. In: Proc. KR 2004, Whistler, Canada, pp. 141–151 (2004)
13. Horrocks, I., Patel-Schneider, P.F.: A Proposal for an OWL Rules Language. In: Proc. WWW 2004, New York, NY, USA, pp. 723–731 (2004)
14. Horrocks, I., Sattler, U.: A Tableau Decision Procedure for $\mathcal{SHOIQ}$. Journal of Automated Reasoning 39(3), 249–276 (2007)
15. Kifer, M., Lausen, G., Wu, J.: Logical foundations of object-oriented and frame-based languages. Journal of the ACM 42(4), 741–843 (1995)
16. Kutz, O., Horrocks, I., Sattler, U.: The Even More Irresistible $\mathcal{SROIQ}$. In: Proc. KR 2006, Lake District, UK, pp. 68–78 (2006)
17. Levy, A.Y., Rousset, M.-C.: Combining Horn Rules and Description Logics in CARIN. Artificial Intelligence 104(1-2), 165–209 (1998)
18. Motik, B.: Reasoning in Description Logics using Resolution and Deductive Databases. PhD thesis, Univesität Karlsruhe, Germany (2006)
19. Motik, B., Cuenca Grau, B., Sattler, U.: Structured Objects in OWL: Representation and Reasoning. In: Proc. WWW 2008, Beijing, China (2008)
20. Motik, B., Rosati, R.: A Faithful Integration of Description Logics with Logic Programming. In: Proc. IJCAI 2007, Hyderabad, India, pp. 477–482 (2007)
21. Motik, B., Shearer, R., Horrocks, I.: Hypertableau Reasoning for Description Logics. Technical report, University of Oxford (2008); Submitted to an international journal
22. Motik, B., Grau, B.C., Horrocks, I., Sattler, U.: Representing Ontologies Using Description Logics, Description Graphs, and Rules (2009); Submitted to a journal
23. Motik, B., Sattler, U., Studer, R.: Query Answering for OWL-DL with Rules. Journal of Web Semantics 3(1), 41–60 (2005)
24. Mylopoulos, J., Borgida, A., Jarke, M., Koubarakis, M.: Telos: Representing Knowledge about Information Systems. ACM Transactions of Information Systems 8(4), 325–362 (1990)
25. Patel-Schneider, P.F., Hayes, P., Horrocks, I.: OWL Web Ontology Language: Semantics and Abstract Syntax, W3C Recommendation, February 10 (2004), http://www.w3.org/TR/owl-semantics/
26. Plaisted, D.A., Greenbaum, S.: A Structure-Preserving Clause Form Translation. Journal of Symbolic Logic and Computation 2(3), 293–304 (1986)
27. Rosati, R.: $\mathcal{DL}+log$: A Tight Integration of Description Logics and Disjunctive Datalog. In: Proc. KR 2006, Lake District, UK, pp. 68–78 (2006)
28. Schmidt, R.A., Hustadt, U.: A Principle for Incorporating Axioms into the First-Order Translation of Modal Formulae. In: Baader, F. (ed.) CADE 2003. LNCS (LNAI), vol. 2741, pp. 412–426. Springer, Heidelberg (2003)
29. Tobies, S.: Complexity Results and Practical Algorithms for Logics in Knowledge Representation. PhD thesis, RWTH Aachen, Germany (2001)
30. Vardi, M.Y.: Why Is Modal Logic So Robustly Decidable? In: Proc. of a DIMACS Workshop on Descriptive Complexity and Finite Models, pp. 149–184 (1996)

Combining Equational Reasoning[*]

Ashish Tiwari

SRI International
Menlo Park, CA
tiwari@csl.sri.com

Abstract. Given a theory $\mathbb{T}$, a set of equations E, and a single equation e, the uniform word problem (UWP) is to determine if $E \Rightarrow e$ in the theory $\mathbb{T}$. We recall the classic Nelson-Oppen combination result for solving the UWP over combinations of theories and then present a constructive version of this result for equational theories. We present three applications of this constructive variant. First, we use it on the pure theory of equality ($\mathbb{T}_{EQ}$) and arrive at an algorithm for computing congruence closure of a set of ground term equations. Second, we use it on the theory of associativity and commutativity ($\mathbb{T}_{AC}$) and obtain a procedure for computing congruence closure modulo AC. Finally, we use it on the combination theory $\mathbb{T}_{EQ} \cup \mathbb{T}_{AC} \cup \mathbb{T}_{PR}$, where $\mathbb{T}_{PR}$ is the theory of polynomial rings, to present a decision procedure for solving the UWP for this combination.

1 Introduction

One of the most fundamental problems in computer science is deciding the validity of a formula in a given theory. This problem is parameterized by the choice of the theory $\mathbb{T}$ and the class of formulas whose validity is to be checked. A few examples of theories of interest include the pure theory of equality, Boolean logic, and the theory of integer or rational arithmetic. A typical choice for the class of formulas is the class of universal formulas (with no quantifier alternation). The $\mathbb{T}$-validity of universal formulas reduces to the $\mathbb{T}$-validity of universally quantified *clausal* formulas by converting formulas into a conjunction of clauses. A special subclass of (universally quantified) clauses is the class of Horn clauses: $\bigwedge_i e_i \Rightarrow e$, where e_i's and e are all atomic formulas in the theory. The $\mathbb{T}$-validity problem for universally quantified Horn clauses is also known as the *uniform word problem* for the theory $\mathbb{T}$, especially when the theory $\mathbb{T}$ is an equational theory wherein all atomic facts are equations.

In this paper, we will study the uniform word problem (UWP) for several different theories and the *combinations* of theories. A classic modularity result on the decidability of this problem was given by Nelson and Oppen, and is known as the Nelson-Oppen combination result (Section 2). This result says that we can

---

[*] Research supported in part by NSF grants CNS-0720721 and CNS-0834810 and NASA grant NNX08AB95A.

S. Ghilardi and R. Sebastiani (Eds.): FroCoS 2009, LNAI 5749, pp. 68–83, 2009.

decide the UWP for a union of disjoint theories by using the decision procedures for the individual components. The method relies on the individual decision procedures *sharing* with each other all the *Boolean combinations of equations over the shared variables* that they deduce. Since the individual decision procedures are treated as black boxes, the *deduction* of these equations to be shared is done by querying the black boxes multiple times.

In this paper, we present a combination result under certain assumptions about the internals of the black-box decision procedures. Specifically, we assume that, in each component theory, the UWP can be solved using classic *completion* or *saturation* procedures – such as standard Knuth-Bendix completion or completion modulo theories. The individual completion procedures can now be "forced" to generate the equations on shared variables by making the shared variables small in the ordering used for completion. Thus, we obtain a constructive variant of the Nelson-Oppen result for solving the UWP for combinations of theories (Section 3).

We then illustrate this constructive combination result through three applications:

1. First, we use the combination result on the pure theory of equality ($\mathbb{T}_{EQ}$). By viewing a signature containing uninterpreted function symbols as a disjoint union of singleton signatures, we study the UWP for the pure theory of equality as a combination problem. This results in an algorithm for computing congruence closure of a set of ground term equations along the lines of *abstract congruence closure* (Section 4).
2. Second, we use the combination result on the theory of associativity and commutativity ($\mathbb{T}_{AC}$). Again, by viewing the signature as a disjoint union of singleton sets, we only need to develop completion procedure for theories over *one* non-constant function symbols. When this function symbol is uninterpreted, we use standard congruence closure from above. When this function symbol is an AC symbol, we present a completion procedure. Using the constructive combination results, these different completion procedures can be combined and we obtain a procedure for computing congruence closure modulo AC (Section 5).
3. Finally, we use the combination result on the combination theory $\mathbb{T}_{EQ} \cup \mathbb{T}_{AC} \cup \mathbb{T}_{PR}$, where $\mathbb{T}_{PR}$ is the theory of polynomial rings, to present a decision procedure for solving the UWP for this combination (Section 6).

The idea of using a completion-based procedure for solving the uniform word problem in a theory is quite natural. There is a lot of work in this area related to deriving decision procedures for theories and automatically analyzing the complexity of such decision procedures [1,24]. We start by fixing the notation and recalling the classic Nelson-Oppen combination result in Section 2. The constructive variant of the result appears in Section 3 and is followed by the three applications described above in the next three sections.

2   Notation

A signature, Σ, is a (finite) set of function symbols. An arity function, *arity* : $\Sigma \mapsto \mathbb{N}$, assigns an arity to each function symbol. Symbols with arity 0, called *constants*, are denoted by a, b, c, d, e, with possible subscripts. The elements of a set $\mathcal{V}$ of *variables* are denoted by x, y, z with possible subscripts. The set $\mathcal{T}(\Sigma, \mathcal{V})$ of *terms* over Σ and $\mathcal{V}$, is the smallest set containing $\mathcal{V}$ and such that $f(t_1, \dots, t_m)$ is in $\mathcal{T}(\Sigma, \mathcal{V})$ whenever $f \in \Sigma$, $arity(f) = m$, and $t_1, \dots, t_m \in \mathcal{T}(\Sigma, \mathcal{V})$. A term t is called *ground* if t contains no variables. The set of ground terms is equal to $\mathcal{T}(\Sigma, \emptyset)$.

A *position* is a sequence of positive integers. If p is a position and t is a term, then $t|_p$ denotes the subterm of t at position p and $t[s]_p$ denotes the term obtained by replacing in t the subterm at position p by the term s. For example, if t is $f(a, g(b, h(c)), d)$, then $t|_{2.2.1} = c$, and $t[d]_{2.2} = f(a, g(b, d), d)$.

A *substitution* σ is a mapping from variables to terms. It can be homomorphically extended to a function from terms to terms. For example, if σ is $\{x \mapsto f(b, y), y \mapsto a\}$, then $\sigma(g(x, y))$ is $g(f(b, y), a)$.

A *rewrite rule* is a pair of terms (l, r), denoted by $l \to r$, with left-hand side l and right-hand side r. A *term rewrite system* (TRS) R is a finite set of rewrite rules. The *rewrite relation*, $\to_R$, induced by R is defined as: $s \to_R t$, if $s|_p = \sigma(l)$ and $t = s[\sigma(r)]_p$, for some $l \to r \in R$, position p, and substitution σ.

If $\to$ is a binary relation on a set S, then $\leftrightarrow$ is its symmetric closure, $\to^+$ is its transitive closure, $\leftarrow$ is its inverse, and $\to^*$ is its reflexive-transitive closure.

A *(rewrite) derivation* (from s) is a sequence of rewrite steps (starting from s), that is, a sequence $s \to s_1 \to s_2 \to \dots$. A TRS R is *terminating* if no infinite derivation $s_1 \to_R s_2 \to_R \cdots$ exists. A TRS R is *confluent* if for every s, u, v such that $s \to_R^* u$ and $s \to_R^* v$ there exists a term t such that $u \to_R^* t$ and $v \to_R^* t$. A TRS R is *convergent* if R is both confluent and terminating.

If E is a TRS, then $\leftrightarrow_E^*$ is the *equational theory* induced by E. By Birkhoff's theorem, we know that reasoning with axioms of equality ($\mathbb{T}_{EQ}$) and E is the same as reasoning about $\leftrightarrow_E^*$; in other words, $E \models_{\mathbb{T}_{EQ}} s = t$ iff $s \leftrightarrow_E^* t$. The theory of term rewriting reasons about $\leftrightarrow_E^*$ by "completing" E to a convergent system R such that $\leftrightarrow_E^*$ and $\leftrightarrow_R^*$ are identical relations. Such convergent presentations are important because of the following result.

Theorem 1. *If E is convergent, then the equational theory $\leftrightarrow_E^*$ is decidable.*

Construction of convergent presentations for equational theories uses well-founded *term orderings*. There are several such orderings.

Nelson-Oppen Combination Result

A *theory* is simply the (deductive closure) of a set of axioms; alternatively, a theory can be viewed as a collection of *models*. A theory is *stably infinite* if every satisfiable quantifier-free formula is satisfiable in an infinite model. For example, theories with only finite models are not stably infinite. For instance, the theory induced by the axiom $\forall x, y, z.(x = y \lor y = z \lor z = x)$ is not stably infinite. For examples of stably-infinite theories, note that if E is an equational theory, then $E \cup \{\exists x, y : x \neq y\}$ is stably-infinite. This follows from the fact that if M is a model for such a theory, then $M \times M$ is a model as well. Since M has atleast two elements, $M \times M$ will have atleast four elements, and using the argument repeatedly, by compactness, there will be an infinite model [7].

A theory is *convex* if whenever a conjunction of literals implies a disjunction of atomic formulas, it also implies one of the disjuncts. For example, the theory of integers over a signature containing $<$ is not convex. The formula $1 < x \wedge x < 4$ implies $x = 2 \vee x = 3$, but it does not imply either $x = 2$ or $x = 3$ independently. An example of convex theory is the theory of rationals over the signature $\{+, <\}$. All equational theories are convex, but they need not be stably-infinite in general. Also observe that a convex theory $\mathbb{T}$ with no trivial models is stably-infinite.

Theorem 2. *[Nelson-Oppen Combination Result [27,29]] Let $\mathbb{T}_1$ and $\mathbb{T}_2$ be consistent, stably-infinite theories over disjoint (countable) signatures. Assume satisfiability of (quantifier-free) conjunction of literals can be decided in $O(T_1(n))$ and $O(T_2(n))$ time respectively. Then,*

1. *The combined theory $\mathbb{T}$ is consistent and stably infinite.*
2. *Satisfiability of (quantifier-free) conjunction of literals in $\mathbb{T}$ can be decided in $O(2^{n^2} * (T_1(n) + T_2(n)))$ time.*
3. *If $\mathbb{T}_1$ and $\mathbb{T}_2$ are convex, then so is $\mathbb{T}$ and satisfiability in $\mathbb{T}$ is in $O(n^3 * (T_1(n) + T_2(n)))$ time.*

The main idea underlying the above result is that the two theories need to share boolean combinations of equalities between shared variables. There are $O(n)$ shared variables. There are $O(n^2)$ equalities and $O(n^2)$ disequalities between these variables. There are $O(2^{n^2})$ disjunctive formulas (clauses) over these equalities and disequalities. In general, the two theories need to share all such deducible clauses. Thus, the combination introduces an exponential multiplicative factor; see [30] for an example. For convex theories, however, we only need to share deduced equalities. We need to call the base decision procedure $O(n^2)$ times to find out *which* equality is implied and then we need to communicate it to the other component. We need to continue doing this for $O(n)$ times – since we can share at most n equations. Hence, the combination of convex theories introduces a $O(n^3)$ multiplicative factor.

3 Constructive Combination of Equational Theories

Given a disjunction of literals (clause), the clausal validity problem seeks to determine if the (universal closure of the) clause is $\mathbb{T}$-valid. The Nelson-Oppen combination result shows decidability of the clausal validity problem in the union of two disjoint theories. For a convex theory, clausal validity problem reduces to checking validity of a Horn clause, or the uniform word problem: given a set E of atomic facts and a single atomic fact e, determine if $E \Rightarrow e$ in the theory.

We are interested in deciding the uniform word problem in a combination of disjoint theories. We assume that the individual theories are equational theories which admit a finite convergent representation. Without loss of generality, we can assume that the input E and e are both ground (since, if they have variables, the variables can be treated as new constants).

Equational theories have some nice properties. Equational theories are always consistent. If E is a presentation for an equational theory and if $E \cup \{\exists x, y. x \neq y\}$ is consistent, then the theory E is also stably-infinite. Equational theories are convex. Therefore, using Theorem 2, satisfiability procedures can be combined with only a polynomial multiplicative factor. Recall that we need to share deducible atomic facts to perform satisfiability testing in combination of theories. So, how do we **deduce** such facts? In the classical Nelson-Oppen procedure, we **guess** (through enumeration) the shared facts and use the individual black-box decision procedures to verify the guess. In the case of equational theories, we can often deduce the facts to be shared using a decision procedure for the theory based on standard Knuth-Bendix completion. The key idea is to use an ordering that ensures that the facts to be shared are "smallest" in the term ordering. Thus, Theorem 2 can be instantiated for equational theories that are decided by a completion procedure as follows.

Theorem 3. *Let R_1, R_2 be two convergent presentations (for two equational theories over disjoint signatures Σ_1 and Σ_2).*

Let $Com_i(E, \succ)$ be a completion procedure that takes ground equations E over $\Sigma_i \cup K$, where K is a set of shared constants, and returns the completion of E (modulo R_i).

Let $\succ$ be an ordering over $\Sigma_i \cup K$ such that $c \not\succ t$ for any constant $c \in K$ and term $t \notin K$.

Then, the equational theory induced by $(R_1 \cup R_2) \cup E$, where E is a set of ground equations over $\Sigma_1 \cup \Sigma_2$ is decidable.

The idea behind the proof of Theorem 3 is that we can construct a convergent presentation for $(R_1 \cup R_2) \cup E$ over an *extended* signature using Com_i. Briefly, the procedure, which is adapted from the Nelson-Oppen combination procedure, is as follows:

1. Purify E: E is purified into $E_1 \cup E_2$, where E_i is over $\Sigma_i \cup K$
2. Componentwise completion: Perform completion of each component to get $E_1^{(1)}$ and $E_2^{(1)}$ as follows:

$$E_1^{(1)} := Com_1(E_1, \succ)$$
$$E_2^{(1)} := Com_2(E_2, \succ)$$

3. Share equalities between constants and repeat the above step

$$E_1^{(j+1)} := Com_1(E_1^{(j)} \cup E_2^{(j)}|_K, \succ)$$
$$E_2^{(j+1)} := Com_2(E_2^{(j)} \cup E_1^{(j)}|_K, \succ)$$

where $E|_K := E \cap (K \times K)$ denotes the the set of equational facts over the shared constants K that are in the set E.

Since the number of equations between shared variables that can be shared is at most $O(n)$, the loop above terminates in atmost $O(n)$ steps. It is easy to then show that the final system $(R_1 \cup R_2) \cup (E_1^\infty \cup E_2^\infty)$ is convergent. This shows that the combined equational theory is decidable.

The key point in the above procedure is that the requirement on the ordering – namely, that whenever $c \succ t$ for a constant c in K, then t is a constant in K – guarantees that equalities among shared constants appear explicitly during the completion procedure. Thus, generation of the equalities to be shared is "free". Moreover, since completion is an inherently incremental process, successive calls to Com_i can easily reuse the results from the previous calls.

If $T_{Com_i}(n)$ is the time complexity of completion for component i, then the total time for completion in the combined theory is $O(n*(T_{Com_1}(n)+T_{Com_2}(n)))$. Note that the n^3 factor is reduced to a linear factor because we do not need to guess the equalities to be shared. The shared equalities are deduced and there are at most $O(n)$ of these equalities. For more details and a formal presentation of the proof of the above theorem, the reader is referred to [34].

We will next present several applications of Theorem 3.

4   The Theory of Equality

As a first application of Theorem 3, we will derive a congruence closure algorithm by viewing it as a combination problem.

Let Σ be a signature consisting of function symbols and constants. Let E be a set of ground equation over Σ. The background equational theory is the empty theory, that is, we are working in the pure theory of equality ($\mathbb{T}_{EQ}$). The problem is to decide the equational theory, $\leftrightarrow_E^*$, induced by E. Computing the congruence closure of E is the classical approach for solving this problem.

Let us view the signature Σ as being the disjoint union of singleton sets Σ_i; that is, $\Sigma = \bigcup_i \Sigma_i$, $\Sigma_i \cap \Sigma_j = \emptyset$ and $\Sigma_i = \{f\}$ for some $f \in \Sigma$. Each Σ_i will be handled by a different component. The background theory in each component is identical; it is the empty theory. Now, our goal is to decide $\leftrightarrow_E^*$ using Theorem 3 by viewing the congruence closure over Σ as a problem of combining congruence closures over Σ_i.

Following the notation from Theorem 3, the convergent presentation R_i for each component i is the empty set $\emptyset$. The requirement on the ordering $\succ$ can be easily achieved using any ordering in which the function symbols in Σ_i have higher precedence than the shared symbols K. By Theorem 3, we only need the procedure $Com_i(E_i, \succ)$, where E_i is a set of ground equations over $\Sigma_i \cup K$, to obtain decidability of $\leftrightarrow_E^*$. In other words, we need the congruence closure algorithm for dealing with *one* function symbol and a finite set of constants.

Theory of Equality: Singleton Signature

The inference rules for computing a convergent presentation of E_i are given in Table 1. The inference rules consist of rules for computing the *union-find*

Table 1. Inference rules for completion of ground equations over a signature $\{f\} \cup K$, where K is a set of constants. Elements of K are denoted by $c, c', d, \ldots$.

Orient $\dfrac{c = d, E}{c \to d, E}$ if $c \succ d$		Delete $\dfrac{c = c, E}{E}$
Simplify $\dfrac{c = d, c \to d', E}{d' = d, c \to d', E}$		
Superpose $\dfrac{fc_1 \ldots c_k \to c, \ fc_1 \ldots c_k \to d, \ E}{c = d, \ fc_1 \ldots c_k \to c, \ E}$		
Collapse $\dfrac{f \ldots c \ldots \to d, \ c \to c', \ E}{f \ldots c' \ldots \to d, \ c \to c', \ E}$	Collapse $\dfrac{c \to d, c \to c', E}{c' = d, c \to c', E}$	
Compose $\dfrac{f \ldots \to c, \ c \to d, \ E}{f \ldots \to d, \ c \to d, \ E}$	Compose $\dfrac{c' \to c, c \to d, E}{c' \to d, c \to d, E}$	

data structure for a set of ground equations over K. The only novel deduction rule needed is the congruence rule which infers $c = d$ from the equations $f(c_1, \ldots, c_k) = c$ and $f(c_1, \ldots, c_k) = d$.

By combining then the above completion inference rules for each of the separate function symbols in Σ, we get a completion procedure for computing a congruence closure for E. Using the general observation made above, we can get a time complexity bound of $O(n * n \log(n))$ using this approach. This is because there is a linear $(O(n))$ combination factor combined with each component spending $O(n \log(n))$ time in maintaining its local copy of the union-find data structure. Of course, *the union-find data structure can be shared* across all theories and this will improve the time complexity.

We also note that the congruence closure procedure above is an instance of the abstract congruence closure presentation [6]. Note that by choosing appropriate strategies for applying the inference rules, the abstract congruence closure procedure can achieve $O(n \log(n))$ time complexity for computing a congruence closure. An example illustrating the use of the inference rules for computing a congruence closure of $E = \{a = f(a, b), \ f(f(a, b), b) = b\}$ is shown in Table 2.

5   The Theory of Associativity and Commutativity

As the second application of Theorem 3, we will derive an algorithm for deciding the equational theory induced by a set of ground equations over a signature that may contain some associative and commutative symbols.

Let Σ be a signature consisting of function symbols and constants, where some binary symbols in Σ are designated as satisfying the axioms for associativity and commutativity (AC). Let E be a set of ground equation over Σ. The background equational theory is the AC theory ($\mathbb{T}_{AC}$). The problem is to decide the equational theory, $\leftrightarrow^*_{E \cup AC}$, induced by E and the axioms for associativity and commutativity.

As before, by viewing the signature Σ as a disjoint union $\bigcup_i \Sigma_i$ of singleton sets Σ_i, we can again reduce the problem above to the problem of performing

Table 2. Illustrating the congruence closure inference rules. The input equations $\{a = fab, f(fab)b = b\}$ have three symbols: a, b, f. The first three columns handle these three symbols respectively. The last column carries the union-find data structure on the shared constants $\{c_1, c_2, c_3, c_4\}$ and is seen by all the three components. The rules that change are underlined.

$$a = fab,\, f(fab)b = b$$

$a \to c_1$	$b \to c_2$	$fc_1c_2 \to c_3,\, fc_3c_2 \to c_4$	$c_1 = c_3,\, c_4 = c_2$
$a \to c_1$	$b \to c_2$	$fc_1c_2 \to c_3,\, fc_3c_2 \to c_4$	$\underline{c_3 \to c_1},\, \underline{c_4 \to c_2}$
$a \to c_1$	$b \to c_2$	$fc_1c_2 \to c_3,\, \underline{fc_1c_2 \to c_4}$	$c_3 \to c_1,\, c_4 \to c_2$
$a \to c_1$	$b \to c_2$	$fc_1c_2 \to c_3$	$\underline{c_4 = c_3},\, c_3 \to c_1,\, c_4 \to c_2$
$a \to c_1$	$b \to c_2$	$fc_1c_2 \to c_3$	$\underline{c_2 = c_1},\, c_3 \to c_1,\, c_4 \to c_2$
$a \to c_1$	$b \to c_2$	$fc_1c_2 \to c_3$	$\underline{c_2 \to c_1},\, c_3 \to c_1,\, c_4 \to c_2$
$a \to c_1$	$b \to c_2$	$\underline{fc_1c_1 \to c_3}$	$c_2 \to c_1,\, c_3 \to c_1,\, c_4 \to c_2$
$a \to c_1$	$\underline{b \to c_1}$	$fc_1c_1 \to c_3$	$c_2 \to c_1,\, c_3 \to c_1,\, \underline{c_4 \to c_1}$

completion over a set of ground equations E_i over a signature $\Sigma_i \cup K$, where Σ_i contains either an uninterpreted symbol or an AC symbol. Thus, the component background theory is the the theory of commutative semigroups *if* Σ_i contains an AC symbol, and it is the empty theory *otherwise*. Since we already know how to perform completion in the latter case, we only need to see how to perform completion, $Com_i(E_i, \succ)$, where E_i is a set of ground equations over $\Sigma_i \cup K$, $\Sigma_i = \{f\}$, and f is an AC symbol.

Uniform Word Problem for Commutative Semigroups

A standard approach for dealing with an AC symbol f is based on treating f as a variable arity symbol satisfying the following equivalent axioms:

$$f(\ldots, f(\ldots), \ldots) = f(\ldots, \ldots, \ldots) \qquad (F)$$
$$f(\ldots, u, v, \ldots) = f(\ldots, v, u, \ldots) \qquad (P)$$

Now, we perform completion modulo the second equation, namely the permutation axiom (P), and treat the first equation, namely the flattening axiom (F), as a directed rule [4].

Let E_i be a set of ground equations over $\{f\} \cup K$, where f is AC. The inference rules for computing a convergent presentation of E_i are given in Table 1. All terms are implicitly flattened. Hence, we only have three different forms of equations: $f(c_1, \ldots, c_k) = f(d_1, \ldots, d_l)$; $f(c_1, \ldots, c_k) = c$; and $c = d$, where c, d are constants in K.

By looking at terms as power-products – the term $f(x, x, y)$ can be viewed as $x^2 y$ – we can define the ordering $\succ$ as the (total degree) lexicographic ordering on power-products. The inference rules for completing a set of ground equations modulo AC are given in Table 3; see [4] for more details.

It can be shown that the result of the completion procedure above is a system convergent modulo AC. The nontrivial part is showing termination of the

Table 3. Inference rules for completion of ground equations over a signature $\{f\} \cup K$, where K is a set of constants and f is an AC symbol. The symbols s, t are used to denote either constants in K or flat terms of the form $f(c_1, \ldots, c_k)$, where c_i's are constants in K. The symbols X, Y denote sequences of constants in K. Terms are assumed to be implicitly flattened. We do not show the rules for dealing with equations in K (given in Table 1).

	Orient $\dfrac{E, s = t}{E, s \to t}$	if $s \succ t$
Superpose	$\dfrac{E, f(X) \to s, f(Y) \to t}{E', f(s, Z) = f(t, Z')}$	for least Z, Z' s.t. $f(X, Z) = f(Y, Z')$ modulo AC, collapse inapplicable
	Collapse $\dfrac{E, f(X, Z) \to t, f(X) \to s}{E, f(s, Z) = t, f(X) \to s}$	
	Delete $\dfrac{E, s = s}{E}$	

Table 4. Illustrating the completion of a set of ground equations over the signature $\{f, 1\} \cup \{x, y\}$, where $x, y, 1$ are constants and f is an ACU symbol with unit 1. Flattened terms, such as $f(x, x, y)$ are written as power-products $x^2 y$ for brevity.

Input	$x^2 y = 1, \ xy^2 = y$
Orient	$x^2 y \to 1, \ xy^2 \to y$
Superpose	$x^2 y \to 1, \ xy^2 \to y, \ y = xy$
Orient	$x^2 y \to 1, \ xy^2 \to y, \ xy \to y$
Collapse	$xy = 1, \ y^2 = y, \ xy \to y$
Orient	$xy \to 1, \ y^2 \to y, \ xy \to y$
Collapse	$y = 1, \ y^2 \to y, \ xy \to y$
Orient	$y \to 1, \ y^2 \to y, \ xy \to y$
Collapse	$y \to 1, \ 1 = y, \ x = y$
Orient	$y \to 1, \ x \to y$

completion procedure above. Termination is guaranteed by the *collapse* rule and is based on using the Dickson's lemma: *If $s_1, s_2, \ldots$ is an infinite sequence of power products, then there exists i, j s.t. $i < j$ and s_i divides s_j.* To guarantee termination, we also need to assume that the "same inference" is not applied repeatedly. For complexity analysis, see [25].

The inference rules for an AC symbol can be easily extended to deal with ACU symbols – that is, AC symbols that also have a unit element 1. An example illustrating the inference rules of Table 3, extended to handle the unit element 1, is given in Table 4.

Let $\mathbb{T}_{EQ}$ be the theories of equality and let $\mathbb{T}_{AC}$ ($\mathbb{T}_{ACU}$) be the theory of associativity and commutativity (with unit). Let T_{EQ}, T_{AC} and T_{ACU} be the functions for the time complexity of completion of a set of ground equations in the respective theories. Then, Theorem 3, combined with the completion algorithm for AC and ACU outlined above, shows that the UWP for $\mathbb{T}_{EQ} \cup \mathbb{T}_{AC} \cup \mathbb{T}_{ACU}$ is solvable in time $O(n * (T_{AC}(n) + n \log(n) + T_{ACU}(n)))$.

6   The Theory of Polynomial Rings

We can now go beyond the theory of commutative monoids (ACU) and consider the theory of polynomial rings, which has two ACU symbols; namely, $+$, which forms a commutative group with unit element 0 and inverse operator $-$, and, $*$, which forms a commutative monoid with unit element 1. The signature Σ of the theory of polynomial rings is $\{\mathbb{Q}, +, -, *, x_1, \ldots, x_n\}$, where $\mathbb{Q}$ is a base domain (such as the rational numbers) containing the constants 0 and 1, $+, *$ are binary operators, $-$ is a unary operator, and $x_1, \ldots, x_n$ are constants. The underlying theory $\mathbb{T}_{PR}$ is the theory of polynomial rings; that is, we have the axioms for rings along with axioms for polynomial expressions.

An example of a system of ground equations in this theory is $E = \{x_1 x_2 = x_1, x_1^2 = x_1 + 1\}$. The goal is to decide the equational theory induced by $E \cup \mathbb{T}_{PR}$. We want to decide it using a completion-based procedure, which will then enable us to use Theorem 3 to combine it with other theories. This completion procedure is well known. It is the Gröbner basis algorithm for transforming E to a convergent canonical basis [10,11,3].

First, we should remark that there is a convergent presentation, modulo AC, for the underlying $\mathbb{T}_{PR}$. This convergent rewrite system essentially rewrites any expression to its canonical polynomial form. For example, the expression $x_1 * (x_2 + -1)$ rewrites to $x_1 x_2 + -x_1$ using this convergent presentation for the underlying theory $\mathbb{T}_{PR}$. Let us denote this convergent presentation by P/AC; see [5] for details.

We will assume that all terms are normalized by the underlying convergent system and hence all expressions are implicitly written as polynomials. We are given a set E of ground equations containing equations of the form $p = 0$, where p a polynomial in $\mathbb{Q}[x_1, \ldots, x_n]$. For example, $E := \{x_1 x_2 - x_1 = 0, x_1^2 - x_1 - 1 = 0\}$. The inference rules for completing the set E modulo the underlying theory, namely the rules for Gröbner basis computation, are showin in Table 5. As before, we need an ordering $\succ$ in which selected constants can be made smaller than other terms. Again, we can use the total-degree lexicographic ordering on power-products, but extended to polynomials using a multiset extension. Table 5 shows only the important inference rules required to obtain a convergent presentation for E. It is missing some simplification rules that are essential for efficiency, but not for correctness.

The correctness of the inference rules for computing Gröbner Basis, shown in Table 5, follows arguments that are similar to the correctness of the completion rules for commutative semigroups, shown in Table 3. In particular, the termination argument is the same as before and relies on the use of Dickson's lemma. The soundness and completeness theorem for the inference rules in Table 5 can be stated as follows:

Proposition 1. *If R is a result of applying the inference rules in Table 5 starting with E, then $\mathbb{T}_{PR} \models E \Rightarrow s = t$ iff $s \rightarrow^*_{R,P/AC} \circ \leftarrow^*_{R,P/AC} t$ for all s, t.*

In other words, equal terms (modulo $\mathbb{T}_{PR} \cup E$) have identical canonical forms with respect to $R \cup P/AC$. For example, in the theory of polynomial rings, the

Table 5. Computing Gröbner Basis. Application of the rules will result in expressions that are not polynomials, but we assume that these expressions are implicitly normalized by the underlying convergent presentation; that is, they are converted into polynomials. Furthermore, all equations $p = q$ are rewritten as equations of the form $p = 0$.

Orient	$\dfrac{E, cX + p = 0}{E, cX \rightarrow -p}$	if $X \succ p_0$
Superpose	$\dfrac{E, cX \rightarrow p, dY \rightarrow q}{E', d * p * Z = c * q * Z'}$	for least Z, Z' s.t. $X * Z = Y * Z'$, collapse not applicable
Collapse	$\dfrac{E, cXZ \rightarrow p, dX \rightarrow q}{E, d * p = c * Z * q, dX \rightarrow q}$	
Delete	$\dfrac{E, s = s}{E}$	

Table 6. Illustrating the inference rules for computing Gröbner basis

Input	$xy - x = 0,\ x^2 - x - 1 = 0$
Orient	$xy \rightarrow x,\ x^2 \rightarrow x + 1$
Superpose	$xy \rightarrow x,\ x^2 \rightarrow x + 1,\ x * x = y * (x + 1)$
Orient	$xy \rightarrow x,\ x^2 \rightarrow x + 1,\ x^2 \rightarrow xy + y$
Collapse	$xy \rightarrow x,\ x^2 \rightarrow x + 1,\ x + 1 = xy + y$
Orient	$xy \rightarrow x,\ x^2 \rightarrow x + 1,\ xy \rightarrow x - y + 1$
Collapse	$xy \rightarrow x,\ x^2 \rightarrow x + 1,\ x = x - y + 1$
Orient	$xy \rightarrow x,\ x^2 \rightarrow x + 1,\ y \rightarrow 1$
Collapse	$x = x,\ x^2 \rightarrow x + 1,\ y \rightarrow 1$
Delete	$x^2 \rightarrow x + 1,\ y \rightarrow 1$

equation $y = 1$ is implied by $E := \{xy = x, x^2 = x + 1\}$. The completion of E computed in Table 6 is $R := \{x^2 \rightarrow x + 1,\ y \rightarrow 1\}$. It is easy to see that the terms y and 1 have the same normal form, namely 1, with respect to this system.

The UWP for the Combined Theory $\mathbb{T} := \mathbb{T}_{EQ} \cup \mathbb{T}_{AC} \cup \mathbb{T}_{ACU} \cup \mathbb{T}_{PR}$

Now that we have a completion procedure for saturating a set of ground equations in the theory of equality (Section 4), the theory of commutative semigroups (Section 5), the theory of commutative monoids (Section 5), and the theory of polynomial rings (Section 6), we can use our main combination theorem, namely Theorem 3, to obtain a completion procedure for deciding the equational theory induced by a set of ground equations E over the **combination** of these theories.

Let Σ be the combined signature; that is, $\Sigma := \Sigma_{EQ} \cup \Sigma_{AC} \cup \Sigma_{ACU} \cup \Sigma_{PR}$, and let $\mathbb{T}$ denote the combination of the respective theories; namely, $\mathbb{T} := \mathbb{T}_{EQ} \cup \mathbb{T}_{AC} \cup \mathbb{T}_{ACU} \cup \mathbb{T}_{PR}$.

Given a set of ground equations E over the combined signature Σ, we can use Theorem 3 to get the following completion procedure to deduce equalities from $E \cup \mathbb{T}$:

- Purify E into $E_{EQ} \cup E_{AC} \cup E_{ACU} \cup E_{PR}$ by introducing a new set of shared constants K
- Use congruence closure (Section 4) on E_{EQ}
- Use AC(U) congruence closure on E_{AC} (E_{ACU})
- Use Gröbner basis algorithm on E_{PR}
- Share the deduced equations over K and repeat the process until no new equations over K are deduced by any of the components

Theorem 3 guarantees that the result is a convergent presentation of E (modulo $\mathbb{T}$), which can be used to decide the equational theory induced by $E \cup \mathbb{T}$. As before, the time complexity for solving the UWP in the combined theory has only a linear factor over the base theories.

Algebraically Closed Fields

We can enrich the theory of polynomial rings by adding a few extra axioms and considering the theory of algebraically closed fields ($\mathbb{T}_{ACF}$). Gröbner basis algorithm can be used to solve the uniform word problem for algebraically closed fields. In other words, given a set $E := \{p_1 = 0, \ldots, p_n = 0\}$ of polynomial equations and a polynomial p, we can decide if $E \Rightarrow p = 0$ in the theory of algebraically closed fields. This can be done by checking if the Gröbner basis of $\{p_1 = 0, \ldots, p_n = 0, py - 1\}$, where y is a new variable, contains a contradiction, such as $1 = 0$, over the base domain. The correctness of this procedure for solving the UWP for $\mathbb{T}_{ACF}$ follows from the Hilbert's Nullstellensatz [8].

Example 1. Using the same example from above, we saw that the equation $x_2 = 1$ is implied by $E := \{x_1 x_2 = x_1, x_1^2 = x_1 + 1\}$ in $\mathbb{T}_{PR}$. This implication is also valid in $\mathbb{T}_{ACF}$. To test this implication, we compute the Gröbner basis for $E \cup \{x_2 y - y = 1\}$. We can reuse the completion $R := \{x_1^2 \rightarrow x_1 + 1, \ x_2 \rightarrow 1\}$. of E computed in Table 6. The rule $x_2 \rightarrow 1$ immediately collapses the new equation $x_2 y - y - 1$ to -1, and we get $-1 = 0$ in the Gröbner basis – indicating that $y = 1$ is implied by E in $\mathbb{T}_{ACF}$.

It is tempting to speculate that the Gröbner basis R for E can be used directly to decide if $\mathbb{T}_{ACF} \models E \Rightarrow p = 0$ by checking if the R-normal form of p is 0 (as we did in the case of $\mathbb{T}_{PR}$). However, this is incorrect.

Example 2. Consider $E := \{x_1^5 = 0, x_2 = 0\}$. Note that the implication $E \Rightarrow x_1 = x_2$ is valid in $\mathbb{T}_{ACF}$, but it is not valid in $\mathbb{T}_{PR}$. This is because $x_1^5 = 0$ implies $x_1 = 0$ in $\mathbb{T}_{ACF}$, but not in $\mathbb{T}_{PR}$. The Gröbner basis for E can be computed as $\{x_1^5 \rightarrow 0, x_2 \rightarrow 0\}$. The normal form of x_1 is x_1, and the normal form of x_2 is 0. Thus x_1 and x_2 have different normal forms. However, if we compute a Gröbner basis for $E \cup \{x_1 y - x_2 y - 1 = 0\}$, we notice that we deduce $x \rightarrow 0$, which then gives us $-1 = 0$.

The theory of algebraically closed field is not equational and it is not convex. For example, we have $x_1 x_2 = 0$ implies $x_1 = 0 \lor x_2 = 0$, but it does not imply any of the disjuncts individually.

The theory of algebraically closed fields is an example of a theory for which a completion-based procedure can be used to decide the uniform word problem, but it can not be used to *deduce* equalities (between shared variables). In other words, while we can combine $\mathbb{T}_{ACF}$ with other theories using the classic Nelson-Oppen procedure (Theorem 2), we can not do so using Theorem 3.

7   Discussion and Other Combinations

Combination of Theory Validity Checkers with SAT Solvers. Several applications require reasoning in a combination of theories. One of the main application areas is formal verification. In bounded model checking and in checking of verification conditions during safety verification, one needs to check validity of arbitrary universally quantified formulas. In theory, a decision procedure for the clausal validity problem (equivalently, satisfiability of existentially quantified conjunctions of literals) also solves the more general problem of checking validity of an *arbitrary* universally quantified formula. However, this involves an exponential blowup in the form of converting an arbitrary formula into its CNF form. This can often be avoided by directly deciding validity of the given universal formula. This is achieved by cleverly *combining* a SAT-solver (based on the DPLL procedure) with decision procedures for the clausal validity problem. A solver that extends a DPLL-based SAT procedure with (single or multiple) theory solvers is called a *Satisfiability Modulo Theory* (SMT) solver [31,26,2,32,28]. There are several design choices and optimizations to be made when combining SAT solvers and theory solvers. Nevertheless, the essential ingredients for achieving an efficient combination are now well-understood [36,14,16,9,17]. Combining $\mathbb{T}$-validity checkers with SAT solvers requires that the $\mathbb{T}$-validity checkers satisfy some additional properties, such as incrementality. Completion-based procedures have some of these additional properties as well.

The Theory of Reals. We showed above how nonlinear equational constraints can be solved over algebraically closed fields. In practice, however, the theory of interest is the field of real numbers. All the inference rules in Table 5 for computing the Gröbner basis are also sound for reasoning about equations in the theory of reals. However, they are not sufficient to detect all possible inconsistencies. For example, the set $\{x^2 + 1 = 0\}$ is inconsistent over the reals. However, it is consistent in theory of ACF and the theory of polynomial rings. Moreover, the inference rules in Table 5 only reason about (possibly nonlinear) equations. The field of real numbers is an ordered field, and one also needs engines for reasoning about inequalities. The full first-order theory of the reals is decidable, but most of the known algorithms are lacking for the purposes of integration with other theories and integration with SAT solvers [33,12,22,21,8]. In [35], we presented a refutationally complete procedure, based on Gröbner basis computation and saturation, for solving the clausal validity problem in the theory of the reals. This procedure can also be viewed as a generalization of the Simplex algorithm [15], which solves the same problem for *linear* formulas.

Combining Abstract Interpreters. Combining $\mathbb{T}$-validity checkers is an important problem that arises in deductive verification or deductive falsification of systems. In contrast to the deductive verification approach, there are fixpoint approaches – based on performing abstract interpretation [13] – for performing safety verification of imperative programs. Such analysis procedures are called abstract interpreters. Since programs are naturally specified using symbols from a combination of theories, one needs to be build abstract interpreters that can reason about a combination of theories [18]. One way to achieve this is by combining abstract interpreters [19]. A $\mathbb{T}$-validity checker is only one of the components required to build an abstract interpreter. We need the following components:

- Join computation engine: A join is an over-approximation of the disjunction operator. For efficiency purposes, abstract interpreters work only on a subclass Φ of formulas. Given two formulas ϕ_1, ϕ_2 from this subclass, a *join* of ϕ_1 and ϕ_2 is a formula $\phi \in \Phi$ such that $\models_\mathbb{T} \phi_1 \Rightarrow \phi$ and $\models_\mathbb{T} \phi_2 \Rightarrow \phi$. Among all such $\phi \in \Phi$, the problem is to find the maximally strong ϕ. Note that if Φ contains all possible formulas, then the join of ϕ_1 and ϕ_2 is simply the disjunction $\phi_1 \vee \phi_2$. For some examples of join algorithms, see [20,23].
- Meet computation engine: A meet is an over-approximation of the conjunction operator. Given two formulas ϕ_1, ϕ_2 from some given class Φ, a *meet* of ϕ_1 and ϕ_2 is a formula $\phi \in \Phi$ such that $\models_\mathbb{T} \phi_1 \wedge \phi_2 \Rightarrow \phi$. Among all such $\phi \in \Phi$, the problem is to find the maximally strong ϕ. Note that if Φ is closed under conjunctions, then the meet of ϕ_1 and ϕ_2 is simply their conjunction $\phi_1 \wedge \phi_2$.
- Post computation engine: A post is an over-approximation of the existential quantification operator. Given a formula ϕ_1 from some given class Φ, and a variable x, a *post* of ϕ_1 is a formula $\phi \in \Phi$ such that $\models_\mathbb{T} (\exists x : \phi_1) \Rightarrow \phi$. Among all such $\phi \in \Phi$, the problem is to find the maximally strong ϕ.
- $\mathbb{T}$-validity checker: Given formulas ϕ_1, ϕ_2 in Φ, the problem is to decide if $\models_\mathbb{T} \phi_1 \Rightarrow \phi_2$.

Combining abstract interpreters entails combining the corresponding component engines. The Nelson-Oppen combination result allows us to combine $\mathbb{T}$-validity checkers. One needs to develop similar combination procedures for combining the other operators [19].

8   Conclusion

We presented a constructive variant of the classic Nelson-Oppen combination result for solving the clausal validity problem in a combination of theories. This constructive variant was instantiated in three different ways to finally give us a decision procedure for the uniform word problem in the combination of the theories of uninterpreted symbols, associative-commutative symbols, and polynomial rings.

References

1. Armando, A., Ranise, S., Rusinowitch, M.: Uniform derivation of decision procedures by superposition. In: Fribourg, L. (ed.) CSL 2001 and EACSL 2001. LNCS, vol. 2142, pp. 513–527. Springer, Heidelberg (2001)
2. Audemard, G., Bertoli, P., Cimatti, A., Kornilowicz, A., Sebastiani, R.: A SAT based approach for solving formulas over boolean and linear mathematical propositions. In: Voronkov, A. (ed.) CADE 2002. LNCS (LNAI), vol. 2392, pp. 195–210. Springer, Heidelberg (2002)
3. Bachmair, L., Ganzinger, H.: Buchberger's algorithm: A constraint-based completion procedure. In: Jouannaud, J.-P. (ed.) CCL 1994. LNCS, vol. 845, pp. 285–301. Springer, Heidelberg (1994)
4. Bachmair, L., Ramakrishnan, I.V., Tiwari, A., Vigneron, L.: Congruence closure modulo Associativity-Commutativity. In: Kirchner, H. (ed.) FroCos 2000. LNCS (LNAI), vol. 1794, pp. 245–259. Springer, Heidelberg (2000)
5. Bachmair, L., Tiwari, A.: D-bases for polynomial ideals over commutative noetherian rings. In: Comon, H. (ed.) RTA 1997. LNCS, vol. 1232, pp. 113–127. Springer, Heidelberg (1997)
6. Bachmair, L., Tiwari, A.: Abstract congruence closure and specializations. In: McAllester, D. (ed.) CADE 2000. LNCS (LNAI), vol. 1831, pp. 64–78. Springer, Heidelberg (2000)
7. Barrett, C., Dill, D., Stump, A.: A generalization of Shostak's method for combining decision procedures. In: Armando, A. (ed.) FroCos 2002. LNCS (LNAI), vol. 2309, p. 132. Springer, Heidelberg (2002)
8. Basu, S., Pollack, R., Roy, M.-F.: Algorithms in real algebraic geometry. Algorithms and Computation in Mathematics, vol. 10. Springer, Heidelberg (2003)
9. Bozzano, M., Bruttomesso, R., Cimatti, A., Junttila, T.A., Ranise, S., van Rossum, P., Sebastiani, R.: Efficient theory combination via boolean search. Information and Computation 204(10), 1493–1525 (2006)
10. Buchberger, B.: An algorithm for finding a basis for the residue class ring of a zero-dimensional ideal. PhD thesis, University of Innsbruck, Austria (1965)
11. Buchberger, B.: A critical-pair completion algorithm for finitely generated ideals in rings. In: Börger, E., Rödding, D., Hasenjaeger, G. (eds.) Rekursive Kombinatorik 1983. LNCS, vol. 171, pp. 137–161. Springer, Heidelberg (1984)
12. Collins, G.E.: Quantifier elimination for the elementary theory of real closed fields by cylindrical algebraic decomposition. In: Brakhage, H. (ed.) GI-Fachtagung 1975. LNCS, vol. 33, pp. 134–183. Springer, Heidelberg (1975)
13. Cousot, P., Cousot, R.: Abstract interpretation: A unified lattice model for static analysis of programs by construction or approximation of fixpoints. In: 4th ACM Symp. on Principles of Programming Languages, POPL 1977, pp. 238–252 (1977)
14. de Moura, L., Rueß, H., Sorea, M.: Lazy theorem proving for bounded model checking over infinite domains. In: Voronkov, A. (ed.) CADE 2002. LNCS (LNAI), vol. 2392, pp. 438–455. Springer, Heidelberg (2002)
15. Dutertre, B., de Moura, L.: A fast linear-arithmetic solver for DPLL(T). In: Ball, T., Jones, R.B. (eds.) CAV 2006. LNCS, vol. 4144, pp. 81–94. Springer, Heidelberg (2006)
16. Flanagan, C., Joshi, R., Ou, X., Saxe, J.: Theorem proving using lazy proof explication. In: Hunt Jr., W.A., Somenzi, F. (eds.) CAV 2003. LNCS, vol. 2725, pp. 355–367. Springer, Heidelberg (2003)

17. Ganzinger, H., Hagen, G., Nieuwenhuis, R., Oliveras, A., Tinelli, C.: DPLL(T): Fast decision procedures. In: Alur, R., Peled, D.A. (eds.) CAV 2004. LNCS, vol. 3114, pp. 175–188. Springer, Heidelberg (2004)
18. Gulwani, S., Tiwari, A.: Assertion checking over combined abstraction of linear arithmetic and uninterpreted functions. In: Sestoft, P. (ed.) ESOP 2006. LNCS, vol. 3924, pp. 279–293. Springer, Heidelberg (2006)
19. Gulwani, S., Tiwari, A.: Combining abstract interpreters. In: PLDI (June 2006)
20. Gulwani, S., Tiwari, A., Necula, G.C.: Join algorithms for the theory of uninterpreted symbols. In: Lodaya, K., Mahajan, M. (eds.) FSTTCS 2004. LNCS, vol. 3328, pp. 311–323. Springer, Heidelberg (2004)
21. Harrison, J.: Theorem proving with the real numbers. Springer, Heidelberg (1998)
22. Hong, H.: Quantifier elimination in elementary algebra and geometry by partial cylindrical algebraic decomposition version 13 (1995),
    http://www.gwdg.de/~cais/systeme/saclib,www.eecis.udel.edu/~saclib/
23. Karr, M.: Affine relationships among variables of a program. Acta Informatica 6, 133–151 (1976)
24. Lynch, C., Morawska, B.: Automatic decidability. In: IEEE Symposium on Logic in Computer Science, LICS 2002, pp. 7–16. IEEE Society, Los Alamitos (2002)
25. Mayr, E.W., Meyer, A.R.: The complexity of the word problems for commutative semigroups and polynomial ideals. Advances in Mathematics 46, 305–329 (1982)
26. Microsoft Research. Z3: An efficient SMT solver,
    http://research.microsoft.com/projects/z3/
27. Nelson, G., Oppen, D.: Simplification by cooperating decision procedures. ACM Transactions on Programming Languages and Systems 1(2), 245–257 (1979)
28. Nieuwenhuis, R., Oliveras, A.: Decision procedures for SAT, SAT modulo theories and beyond. The Barcelogictools. In: Sutcliffe, G., Voronkov, A. (eds.) LPAR 2005. LNCS (LNAI), vol. 3835, pp. 23–46. Springer, Heidelberg (2005)
29. Oppen, D.: Complexity, convexity and combinations of theories. Theoretical Computer Science 12, 291–302 (1980)
30. Pratt, V.R.: Two easy theories whose combination is hard. Technical report, MIT (1977)
31. SRI International. Yices: An SMT solver, http://yices.csl.sri.com/
32. Stump, A., Barrett, C.W., Dill, D.L.: CVC: A cooperating validity checker. In: Brinksma, E., Larsen, K.G. (eds.) CAV 2002. LNCS, vol. 2404, pp. 500–504. Springer, Heidelberg (2002)
33. Tarski, A.: A Decision Method for Elementary Algebra and Geometry, 2nd edn. University of California Press, Berkeley (1948)
34. Tiwari, A.: Decision procedures in automated deduction. PhD thesis, State University of New York at Stony Brook (2000)
35. Tiwari, A.: An algebraic approach for the unsatisfiability of nonlinear constraints. In: Ong, L. (ed.) CSL 2005. LNCS, vol. 3634, pp. 248–262. Springer, Heidelberg (2005)
36. Wolfman, S., Weld, D.: The LPSAT system and its application to resource planning. In: Proc. 16th Intl. Joint Conf. on Artificial Intelligence (1999)

Superposition Modulo Linear Arithmetic SUP(LA)

Ernst Althaus, Evgeny Kruglov, and Christoph Weidenbach

Max Planc Institute for Informatics, Campus E1 4
D-66123 Saarbrücken
{althaus,ekruglov,weidenbach}@mpi-inf.mpg.de

Abstract. The hierarchical superposition based theorem proving calculus of Bachmair, Ganzinger, and Waldmann enables the hierarchic combination of a theory with full first-order logic. If a clause set of the combination enjoys a sufficient completeness criterion, the calculus is even complete. We instantiate the calculus for the theory of linear arithmetic. In particular, we develop new effective versions for the standard superposition redundancy criteria taking the linear arithmetic theory into account. The resulting calculus is implemented in SPASS(LA) and extends the state of the art in proving properties of first-order formulas over linear arithmetic.

1 Introduction

The superposition calculus can be turned into a decision procedure for a number of decidable first-order fragments, e.g., [HSG04, ABRS09], and is therefore a good basis for actually proving decidability of fragments and obtaining terminating implementations. There are now four calculi available combining full first-order logic with linear arithmetic (LA). The hierarchic theorem proving approach SUP(T) for any theory T [BGW94], superposition and chaining for totally ordered divisible abelian groups [Wal01], superposition with linear arithmetic integrated [KV07], and DPPL(T) extended with saturation [dMB08]. In this paper we instantiate the hierarchic theorem proving approach [BGW94] to linear arithmetic SUP(LA), because it offers an abstract completeness result for the combination via a sufficient completeness criterion that goes beyond ground problems (needed for DPLL(T) completeness) and it enables the handling of the LA theory part in a modular way that can be eventually implemented via efficient off the shelf solvers (in contrast to [Wal01, KV07]).

Our contribution is the definition of effective redundancy criteria for SUP(LA) out of the abstract non-effective hierarchic redundancy criteria, and its implementation in SPASS(LA) together with some experiments. In particular, due to completeness, we show by examples that the approach can even decide *satisfiability* of first-order theories with universal quantification modulo LA extending the state of the art. Our presentation assumes an LA theory over the rationals.

The paper is organized as follows. After an introduction to the most important notions, Section 2, we present the SUP(LA) calculus with specific definitions for

S. Ghilardi and R. Sebastiani (Eds.): FroCoS 2009, LNAI 5749, pp. 84–99, 2009.

tautology deletion and subsumption that are then turned into effective procedures via a mapping to LP-solving technology, Section 4. Key aspects of the overall implementation of SPASS(LA) are provided in Section 5. SPASS(LA) is applied to reachability problems of transition systems in Section 6. Here we also discuss the sufficient completeness requirement with respect to container data structure axiomatizations using the example of lists. The paper ends with a discussion of the achieved results and the presentation of further directions of research (Section 7).

2 Definitions and Notations

For the presentation of the superposition calculus, we refer to the notation and notions of [Wei01], where for the specific notions serving the hierarchical combination we refer to [BGW94]. We won't introduce the full apparatus of the hierarchical theorem proving technology, but just the notions that enable us to state the inference rules, the sufficient completeness criterion, the completeness result and the redundancy notion.

A *hierarchic specification* is the extension of a base specification over a set of function symbols Ω with free function symbols Ω', $\Omega \subseteq \Omega'$. We assume a many-sorted setting with an explicit *base sort*, sorting Ω. The semantics of the base specification is given by a *base theory*, either through a set of axioms or a collection of models. The semantics of a hierarchic specification is then the extension of the base theory by the standard first-order semantics for the function symbols in $\Omega' \setminus \Omega$. Intuitively, if a hierarchic specification is sufficiently complete, Definition 10, then the restriction of a model of a hierarchic specification to the function symbols Ω of the base specification yields the base theory, in our particular case the standard LA model.

The terms build over Ω and base sort variables are called *base terms*. The base sort may contain further terms build over function symbols from Ω' and in particular $\Omega' \setminus \Omega$ ranging into the base sort. For variables of the base sort we write u, v, w possibly indexed or primed and for non-base sort variables we write x, y, z, possibly indexed and primed. We say that a term is *pure*, if it does not contain both a base operator and a non-base operator.

As usual in the superposition context, all considered atoms are equations where predicates are encoded by a mapping of a function to a distinguished element *true*. Non-equational atoms are thus turned into equations $P(t_1, \ldots, t_n) \approx$ *true* which are abbreviated $P(t_1, \ldots, t_n)$.

A substitution is called *simple*, if it maps every variable of a base sort to a base term. If σ is a simple substitution, $t\sigma$ is called a *simple instance* of t (analogously for equations and clauses). The set of simple ground instances of a clause C is denoted by $sgi(C)$, analogously $sgi(N)$ is the set of all simple ground instances of a clause set N.

For linear arithmetic over the rationals $\mathbb{Q}$ considered here we use the signature $\{+, -, \leq, <, \approx, >, \geq\} \subset \Omega$ plus additional symbols to represent the fractions which we denote in this paper simply by decimal numbers.

Clauses are of the form $\Lambda \parallel \Gamma \to \Delta$, where Λ is a sequence of base specification literals, only containing signature symbols from Ω plus variables, called the *clause constraint*. The sequences Γ, Δ of first-order atoms only contain signature symbols from the free first-order theory, i.e., equations over terms with variables over $\Omega' \setminus \Omega$. All parts share universally quantified variables. $\square$ denotes the empty clause. Semantically a clause is interpreted as the universal closure of the implication

$$\bigwedge \Lambda \wedge \bigwedge \Gamma \to \bigvee \Delta.$$

As usual Λ, Γ and Δ may be empty and are then interpreted as *true, true, false*, respectively. Different clauses are assumed to be variable disjoint. Upper Greek letters denote sequences of atoms $(\Lambda, \Gamma, \Delta)$ or theory literals, lower Greek letter substitutions (σ, τ), lower Latin characters non-variable terms (l, s, r, t) and variable terms (x, y, z, u, v, w) and upper Latin characters atoms (A, B, E). The function *vars* maps objects to their respective set of free variables, $dom(\sigma) = \{x \mid x\sigma \neq x\}$ and $cdom(\sigma) = \{t \mid x\sigma = t, x \in dom(\sigma)\}$ for any substitution σ.

The reduction ordering $\prec$ underlying the superposition calculus is as usual lifted to equational atoms, literals, and clauses [Wei01]. We distinguish inference from reduction rules, where the clause(s) below the bar, the conclusions, of an inference rule are added to the current clause set, while the clause(s) below the bar of a reduction rule replace the clause(s) above the bar, the premises. For example,

$$\mathcal{I} \frac{\Gamma_1 \to \Delta_1 \quad \Gamma_2 \to \Delta_2}{\Gamma_3 \to \Delta_3} \qquad \mathcal{R} \frac{\Gamma_1' \to \Delta_1' \quad \Gamma_2' \to \Delta_2'}{\Gamma_3' \to \Delta_3'}$$

an application of the above inference adds the clause $\Gamma_3 \to \Delta_3$ to the current clause set, while the above reduction replaces the clauses $\Gamma_1' \to \Delta_1'$, $\Gamma_2' \to \Delta_2'$ with the clause $\Gamma_3' \to \Delta_3'$. Note that reductions can actually be used to delete clauses, if there are no conclusions.

3   Superposition Modulo Linear Arithmetic

We will first define the calculus for the general case of a hierarchic specification [BGW94]. Later on, we will then instantiate the general rules for the case of LA.

Any given disjunction of literals can be transformed into a clause of the form $\Lambda \parallel \Gamma \to \Delta$, where Λ only contains base terms and all base terms in Γ, Δ are variables by the following transformation [BGW94]. Whenever a subterm t, whose top symbol is a base theory symbol from Ω, occurs immediately below a non-base operator symbol, it is replaced by a new base sort variable u ("abstracted out") and the equation $u \approx t$ is added to Λ. Analogously, if a subterm t, whose top symbol is not a base theory symbol from Ω, occurs immediately below a base operator symbol, it is replaced by a general variable x and the equation $x \approx t$ is added to Γ. This transformation is repeated until all terms in the clause are pure; then all base literals are moved to Λ and all non-base literals to Γ, Δ, respectively. Recall that Γ, Δ are sequences of atoms whereas Λ holds theory literals. Moreover, we need to "purify" clauses only once – just before saturating the clauses, since if the premises of an inference are abstracted clauses, then the conclusion is also abstracted. For example, the disjunction

$$S(u + 40, x) \lor v > 60 \lor \neg T(f(u - 3.5), y)$$

is abstracted to the clause

$$v' \approx u + 40, u' \approx u - 3.5, v \leq 60 \parallel T(f(u'), y) \to S(v', x).$$

During a derivation new base sort atoms $u \approx v$ may be created by inferences or reductions in the free part that are then moved to the constraint part.

Definition 1 (Superposition Left). *The hierarchic superposition left rule is*

$$\mathcal{I} \frac{\Lambda_1 \parallel \Gamma_1 \to \Delta_1, l \approx r \quad \Lambda_2 \parallel s[l'] \approx t, \Gamma_2 \to \Delta_2}{(\Lambda_1, \Lambda_2 \parallel s[r] \approx t, \Gamma_1, \Gamma_2 \to \Delta_1, \Delta_2)\sigma}$$

where σ is simple and a most general unifier of l and l', $l\sigma \not\prec r\sigma$, $s\sigma \not\prec t\sigma$, l' is not a variable, $(l \approx r)\sigma$ is strictly maximal in $(\Gamma_1 \to \Delta_1, l \approx r)\sigma$, and $(s[l'] \approx t)\sigma$ is maximal in $(s[l'] \approx t, \Gamma_2 \to \Delta_2)\sigma$.

For simplicity, we don't consider selection nor sort constraints. Note that we also do not consider the terms in the theory part of the clauses for our maximality criteria. As clauses are abstracted, this is justified by considering a suitable path ordering, like LPO, where the function symbols from Ω are smaller in the precedence than all symbols in $\Omega' \setminus \Omega$. The hierarchic superposition calculus suggested by Bachmair et al [BGW94] introduces a further refined maximality criterion with respect to simple grounding substitutions. The criterion is not decidable, in general. Therefore, we currently don't use it and define the inference rules such that they include the more restricted original versions but provide a decidable maximality criterion. The rules and redundancy criteria are implemented exactly in the way described below in SPASS(LA).[1]

Definition 2 (Superposition Right). *The hierarchic superposition right rule is*

$$\mathcal{I} \frac{\Lambda_1 \parallel \Gamma_1 \to \Delta_1, l \approx r \quad \Lambda_2 \parallel \Gamma_2 \to \Delta_2, s[l'] \approx t}{(\Lambda_1, \Lambda_2 \parallel \Gamma_1, \Gamma_2 \to \Delta_1, \Delta_2, s[r] \approx t)\sigma}$$

where σ is simple and a most general unifier of l and l', $l\sigma \not\prec r\sigma$, $s\sigma \not\prec t\sigma$, l' is not a variable, $(l \approx r)\sigma$ is strictly maximal in $(\Gamma_1 \to \Delta_1, l \approx r)\sigma$, and $(s[l'] \approx t)\sigma$ is strictly maximal in $(s[l'] \approx t, \Gamma_2 \to \Delta_2)\sigma$.

Definition 3 (Equality Factoring). *The hierarchic equality factoring rule is*

$$\mathcal{I} \frac{\Lambda \parallel \Gamma \to \Delta, l \approx r, l' \approx r'}{(\Lambda \parallel \Gamma, r \approx r' \to \Delta, l' \approx r')\sigma}$$

---

[1] The current implementation does not support equality but predicative reasoning (resolution). Equality reasoning will follow soon.

where σ is simple and a most general unifier of l and l', $l\sigma \not\approx r\sigma$, $l'\sigma \not\approx r'\sigma$, and $(l \approx r)\sigma$ is maximal in $(\Gamma \to \Delta, l \approx r, l' \approx r')\sigma$.

Definition 4 (Ordered Factoring). *The hierarchic ordered factoring rule is*

$$\mathcal{I}\frac{\Lambda \parallel \Gamma \to \Delta, E_1, E_2}{(\Lambda \parallel \Gamma \to \Delta, E_1)\sigma}$$

where σ is simple and a most general unifier of E_1 and E_2 and $E_1\sigma$ is maximal in $(\Gamma \to \Delta, E_1, E_2)\sigma$.

Definition 5 (Equality Resolution). *The hierarchic equality resolution rule is*

$$\mathcal{I}\frac{\Lambda \parallel \Gamma, s \approx t \to \Delta}{(\Lambda \parallel \Gamma \to \Delta)\sigma}$$

where σ is simple and a most general unifier of s and t and $(s \approx t)\sigma$ is maximal in $(\Gamma, s \approx t \to \Delta)\sigma$.

Definition 6 (Constraint Refutation). *The constraint refutation rule is*

$$\mathcal{I}\frac{\Lambda_1 \parallel \to \quad \dots \quad \Lambda_n \parallel \to}{\square}$$

where $\Lambda_1 \parallel \to \wedge \dots \wedge \Lambda_n \parallel \to$ is inconsistent in the base theory.

The completeness theorem will require compactness of the base theory to justify the constraint refutation rule. For the LA theory considered here, where we, e.g., do not consider shared parameters between clauses, the case $n = 1$ is sufficient.

We will now define new tautology deletion and subsumption deletion rules that will eventually be turned into effective algorithms for LA in Section 4.

Definition 7 (Tautology Deletion). *The hierarchic tautology deletion rule is*

$$\mathcal{R}\frac{\Lambda \parallel \Gamma \to \Delta}{}$$

if $\Gamma \to \Delta$ is a tautology or the existential closure of $\bigwedge \Lambda$ is unsatisfiable in the base theory.

Definition 8 (Subsumption Deletion). *The hierarchic subsumption deletion rule is*

$$\mathcal{R}\frac{\Lambda_1 \parallel \Gamma_1 \to \Delta_1 \qquad \Lambda_2 \parallel \Gamma_2 \to \Delta_2}{\Lambda_1 \parallel \Gamma_1 \to \Delta_1}$$

for a simple matcher σ with $\Gamma_1\sigma \subseteq \Gamma_2$, $\Delta_1\sigma \subseteq \Delta_2$, $vars(\Lambda_1\sigma) \subseteq vars(\Lambda_2)$, and the universal closure of $\bigwedge \Lambda_2 \Rightarrow \bigwedge \Lambda_1\sigma$ holds in the base theory.

In general, a matcher δ with $\Gamma_1\delta \subseteq \Gamma_2$ and $\Delta_1\delta \subseteq \Delta_2$ does not guarantee $vars(\Lambda_1\delta) \subseteq vars(\Lambda_2)$. The substitution $\sigma = \delta\tau$ can be obtained by first computing the standard subsumption matcher δ between and then establishing a simple theory matcher τ where $dom(\tau) = vars(\Lambda_1\delta) \setminus vars(\Lambda_2)$ and $vars(cdom(\tau)) \subseteq vars(\Lambda_2)$.

Note that $u \in vars(\Lambda_1\delta) \setminus vars(\Lambda_2)$ implies $u \notin (vars(\Gamma_1) \cup vars(\Delta_1))$. If the base theory enables quantifier elimination, then u could in fact be eliminated in $\Lambda_1 \parallel \Gamma_1 \to \Delta_1$ and eventually the need to find an additional theory matcher τ becomes obsolete. However, for LA there is a worst case exponential price to pay for eliminating all variables u as defined above. This is not tractable for subsumption deletion that typically needs to be checked several hundred thousand times for an "average" derivation. Therefore, in Section 4 we propose a polynomial transformation to linear programming for finding the matcher τ that eventually solves the clause constraint implication problem in polynomial time in the size of the two theory parts Λ_1, Λ_2. The basic idea is to map the above variables u to linear terms over variables from Λ_2.

Actually, efficient algorithms for establishing the theory matcher τ is a crucial part in getting the hierarchical superposition calculus to practically work for some base theory. In general, a decision procedure for an unsatisfiability check of clause constraints plus an implication test, potentially modulo a theory substitution are needed for the base theory.

Definition 9 (Hierarchic Redundancy [BGW94]). *A clause $C \in N$ is called redundant if for all $C' \in sgi(C)$ there are clauses $C'_1, \dots, C'_n \in sgi(N)$ such that $C'_1 \wedge \dots \wedge C'_n \models C'$ and $C'_i \prec C'$ for all i.*

Our definition of tautology deletion is an obvious instance of the hierarchic redundancy notion. This holds for subsumption deletion as well, because we only consider simple matchers, the notion on the free part is identical to the standard notion and the condition on the clause constraints is a reformulation of the above entailment requirement.

Definition 10 (Sufficient Completeness [BGW94]). *A set N of clauses is called sufficiently complete with respect to simple instances, if for every model $\mathcal{A}'$ of $sgi(N)$ and every ground non-base term t of the base sort there exists a ground base term t such that $t' \approx t$ is true in $\mathcal{A}'$.*

Note that if the base sort solely contains base terms, then any clause set N over the base and free sort is sufficiently complete.

Theorem 1 (Completeness [BGW94]). *If the base specification is compact, then the hierarchic superposition calculus is refutationally complete for all sets of clauses that are sufficiently complete with respect to simple instances.*

Here is an example of a clause set where the hierarchical calculus is not complete. Consider LA over the rationals and the two clauses

$$u < 0 \parallel f(v) \approx u \to$$
$$u' \geq 0 \parallel f(v') \approx u' \to$$

Then clearly these two clauses are unsatisfiable, however no superposition inference is possible. Note that equality resolution is not applicable as $\{u \mapsto f(v)\}$ is not a simple substitution. Even worse, the theory is no longer compact. Any finite set of ground instances of the two clauses is satisfiable. The two clauses are not sufficiently complete, because the clause set does not imply simple instances of the non-base term $f(v)$ of the base sort to be equal to a base term. Note that in this case a model $\mathcal{A}'$ of the clauses is a non-standard model of linear arithmetic. The equality to a base term can be forced by the additional clause

$$\| \to f(w) \approx w$$

and now the three clauses are sufficiently complete. For the three clauses there is a refutation where already the superposition left inference between the first and third clause yields

$$u < 0, w \approx u \,\|\to$$

and a constraint refutation application of the resulting clause yields the contradiction.   □

4   Linear Arithmetic Constraint Solving

As discussed in Section 3, we have to provide procedures for satisfiability and for an implication test for linear arithmetic, potentially modulo a theory matcher getting rid of extra constraint variables.

In the following, we use the standard notation from linear programming theory and assume that the reader is familiar with this topic. We write vectors in bold print. Vectors denoted with $\boldsymbol{a}, \boldsymbol{b}, \boldsymbol{c}$ or $\boldsymbol{d}$ refer to vectors of rational numbers, vectors $\boldsymbol{x}, \boldsymbol{y}, \boldsymbol{z}$ or $\boldsymbol{p}$ denote vectors of variables and using alternations $^-$, $^\sim$ and $^\wedge$ of those vectors like $\bar{\boldsymbol{x}}$ or $\tilde{\boldsymbol{x}}$ we denote assignments of values to the variables. $\boldsymbol{a}^T$ denotes the transposed vector of $\boldsymbol{a}$. A linear (in)equality is of the form $\boldsymbol{a}^T \boldsymbol{x} \circ c$ with $\boldsymbol{a} \in \mathbb{Q}^n, c \in \mathbb{Q}$, and $\circ \in \{\leq, <, \approx, >, \geq\}$. We can rewrite $\boldsymbol{a}^T \boldsymbol{x} = c$ as $\boldsymbol{a}^T \boldsymbol{x} \leq c \wedge \boldsymbol{a}^T \boldsymbol{x} \geq c$ and $\boldsymbol{a}^T \boldsymbol{x} \geq c$ as $-\boldsymbol{a}^T \boldsymbol{x} \leq -c$.

Matrices are denoted with capital letters like A, B, S, T, P and X, where A and B denote matrices of rational values and P, S, T, and X matrices of variables. A system of linear (in)equalities is the conjunction of a set of linear (in)equalities, its feasible region is typically written as $\{\boldsymbol{x} \in \mathbb{Q}^n \mid \boldsymbol{a}^{i^T} \boldsymbol{x} \circ_i c_i \text{ for all } 1 \leq i \leq m\}$ for $\boldsymbol{a}^i \in \mathbb{Q}^n$, $c_i \in \mathbb{Q}$ and $\circ_i \in \{\leq, <, \approx, >, \geq\}$. Let A be the matrix with rows $\boldsymbol{a}^{i^T}$, $\boldsymbol{c}$ be the vector with entries c_i and $\boldsymbol{o}$ be the vector with entries $\circ_i$. We can rewrite the feasible region of the system of linear (in)equalities above as $\{\boldsymbol{x} \in \mathbb{Q}^n \mid A\boldsymbol{x} \circ \boldsymbol{c}\}$. In the following, we often resign to give the dimensions of the defining matrices and vectors.

The description of the feasible region of any system of linear (in)equalities can be transformed into the standard form $\{\boldsymbol{x} \in \mathbb{Q}^n \mid A'\boldsymbol{x} \leq \boldsymbol{c}', A''\boldsymbol{x} < \boldsymbol{c}''\}$. For a matrix $A \in \mathbb{Q}^{m \times n}$, let A_i be the ith row of A.

It is well known that the feasibility of a linear program can be tested in weakly polynomial time using the Ellipsoid method. For further details we refer to [Sch89].

Assume the set of variables of the base theory part of a clause Λ is $\{x_1, \ldots, x_n\}$ and let $\boldsymbol{x}$ be the vector with entries $x_1, \ldots, x_n$. We can identify the base theory part of the clause as $\Lambda = \bigwedge_{i=1}^{m} {\boldsymbol{a}^i}^T \boldsymbol{x} \circ_i c_i$ for $\boldsymbol{a}^i \in \mathbb{Q}^n$, $c_i \in \mathbb{Q}$ and $\circ_i \in \{\leq, <, \approx, >, \geq\}$ with the subset of $\mathbb{Q}^n$ of satisfying assignments, i.e. the set $\{\boldsymbol{x} \in \mathbb{Q}^n \mid {\boldsymbol{a}^i}^T \boldsymbol{x} \circ_i c_i$ for all $1 \leq i \leq m\}$. The base theory part of the clause is satisfiable, if the corresponding subset of $\mathbb{Q}^n$ is non-empty. Hence the satisfiability of the theory part of a clause corresponds to testing the feasibility of a linear program.

Assume the base theory part of two clauses Λ_1, Λ_2 have the same set of variables. Λ_2 implies Λ_1 if the corresponding subset of $\mathbb{Q}^n$ of Λ_2 is contained in the subset corresponding to Λ_1 (all satisfying assignments for Λ_2 satisfy Λ_1). In Section 4.1, we show this containment problem can be reduced to testing the feasibility of a linear program.

For the subsumption test, we have, in addition, to compute a matcher τ such that Λ_2 implies $\Lambda_1 \delta \tau$ for given Λ_1, Λ_2, and δ. In Section 4.2, we show how to reduce this problem to testing the feasibility of a linear program when restricted to matchers that are affine transformations (see Figure 1).

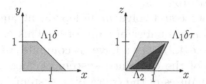

Fig. 1. In the left figure, we show the set $\Lambda_1 \delta = \{(x, y) \in \mathbb{Q}^2 \mid x \geq 0, y \geq 0, y \leq 1, 2x + 2y \leq 3\}$, choosing $\tau : \mathbb{Q} \mapsto \mathbb{Q}^2$ with $\tau(y) = -x + z/2 + 1$ gives the set $\Lambda_1 \delta \tau = \{(x, z) \in \mathbb{Q}^2 \mid x \geq 0, -x + z/2 \geq -1, -x + z/2 \leq 0, z \leq 1\}$ shown in light gray the right figure. $\Lambda_1 \delta \tau$ is implied by the set $\Lambda_2 = \{(x, z) \in \mathbb{Q}^2 \mid z \geq 0, z - x \leq 0, -x + z/2 \geq -1\}$ shown in dark gray as this set is contained in $\Lambda_1 \delta \tau$.

4.1 Implication Test

In this section we discuss our approach to solve the implication test, i.e. given $\Lambda_1 = \{\boldsymbol{x} \in \mathbb{Q}^n \mid A'\boldsymbol{x} \leq \boldsymbol{c}', A''\boldsymbol{x} < \boldsymbol{c}''\}$ and $\Lambda_1 = \{\boldsymbol{x} \in \mathbb{Q}^n \mid B'\boldsymbol{x} \leq \boldsymbol{d}', B''\boldsymbol{x} < \boldsymbol{d}''\}$, to tell if $\Lambda_2 \subseteq \Lambda_1$.

We first shortly discuss the case if all inequalities are non-strict, which is based on the well known Farkas' Lemma. Then we extend Farkas' Lemma to the case of mixed strict and non-strict inequalities, which can be used to solve the general case.

Recall the following variant of Farkas' Lemma (see e.g. [Sch89])

Lemma 1 (Farkas' Lemma (affine variant)). *Let $\Lambda = \{\boldsymbol{x} \in \mathbb{Q}^n \mid B\boldsymbol{x} \leq \boldsymbol{d}\}$ be non-empty. All points $\boldsymbol{x} \in \Lambda$ satisfy the inequality $\boldsymbol{a}^T \boldsymbol{x} \leq c$, iff there is $\boldsymbol{p} \geq 0$ such that $\boldsymbol{p}^T B = \boldsymbol{a}^T$ and $\boldsymbol{p}^T \boldsymbol{d} \leq c$.*

Informally speaking, if $\bar{\boldsymbol{p}}$ is a solution, we multiply every inequality $B_i \boldsymbol{x} \leq \boldsymbol{d}_i$ with $\bar{p}_i$ and sum up the obtained inequalities. This gives us for each feasible

$\bar{x}$ that $a^T \bar{x} = \sum_i \bar{p}_i^T B_i \bar{x} \leq \sum_i \bar{p}_i d_i \leq c$. We call the value $\bar{p}_i$ the multiplier of the inequality $B_i x \leq d_i$. Hence, if such a $\bar{p}$ exists, the inequality $a^T x \leq c$ clearly holds for every $x \in \Lambda$.

For the other direction, let $a^T x \leq c$ be an inequality that holds for all $x \in \Lambda$. Consider the linear program $\max\{a^T x \mid x \in \Lambda\}$ and its dual $\min\{p^T d \mid p^T B = a^T, p \geq 0\}$. As the first is feasible and bounded from above by c, we know from the Strong Duality Theorem that there is a solution p of the dual with value at most c.

From Lemma 1 we conclude:

Corollary 1. *A set $\{x \in \mathbb{Q}^n \mid Ax \leq c\}$ contains a non-empty set $\{x \in \mathbb{Q}^n \mid Bx \leq d\}$, iff each inequality $A_i x \leq c_i$ can be obtained by a non-negative linear combination of the inequalities of $Bx \leq d$, i.e. if there are $p^i \geq 0$ with $p^{i^T} B = A_i$ and $p^{i^T} d \leq c_i$.*

Rewriting the rows p^{i^T} as matrix P yields the existence of a matrix P with $PB = A$, $P \geq 0$ and $Pd \leq c$. Such a matrix P can be determined by testing the feasibility of a linear program.

Notice that so far, we could solve m independent small systems of linear constraints, where m is the number of rows of A. This is no longer possible in our subsumption test (see 4.2), as we have to compute a single substitution for which all (in)equalities of the contained system of linear (in)equalities can be derived from the (in)equalities of the containing system.

This result can be extended to strict inequalities as follows:

Lemma 2 (Farkas' Lemma for strict inequalities). *Let $\Lambda = \{x \in \mathbb{Q}^n \mid B'x \leq d', B''x < d''\}$. We assume that $\Lambda \neq \emptyset$ and that $B''x < d''$ includes the trivial inequality $0 < 1$.*

- *All points $x \in \Lambda$ satisfy the inequality $a^T x \leq c$, iff there are $p', p'' \geq 0$ such that $p'^T B' + p''^T B'' = a^T$ and $p'^T d' + p''^T d'' \leq c$.*
- *All points $x \in \Lambda$ satisfy the inequality $a^T x < c$, iff there are $p', p'' \geq 0$ such that $p'^T B' + p''^T B'' = a^T$, $p'^T d' + p''^T d'' \leq c$ and $p'' \neq 0$.*

For the proof please consider our technical report.

Corollary 2. *A set $\{x \in \mathbb{Q}^n \mid A'x \leq c', A''x < c''\}$ contains a non-empty set $\{x \in \mathbb{Q}^n \mid B'x \leq d', B''x < d''\}$, iff each inequality of the first system can be obtained by a non-negative linear combination of the inequalities of $B'x \leq d'$, $B'' < d''$, or $0 < 1$, where at least one multiplier of a strict inequality has to be different from zero if the inequality of the first system is strict.*

Assuming that the system $B''x < d''$ contains the inequality $0 < 1$, we have to test whether the following system of linear (in)equalities is feasible

$$\{(P_1, P_2, P_3, P_4) \in \mathbb{Q}^n \mid P_1, P_2, P_3, P_4 \geq 0,$$
$$P_1 B' + P_2 B'' = A',$$
$$P_3 B' + P_4 B'' = A'',$$
$$P_4 \mathbb{1} > 0,$$
$$P_1 d' + P_2 d'' \leq c',$$
$$P_3 d' + P_4 d'' \leq c''\},$$

where n is the total number of variables in the matrices P_1, P_2, P_3, and P_4 and $\mathbb{1}$ is the all ones vector with appropriate dimension.

Notice again, that we can solve m smaller systems of linear equations, where m is the total number of linear rows in A' and A''.

4.2   Subsumption Test

We discuss our approach for the subsumption test when all inequalities are nonstrict. The extension to strict inequalities is straight-forward with the discussion above.

Assume $\Lambda_1 = \{(x, y) \in \mathbb{Q}^{n_x + n_y} \mid A'x + A''y \leq c\}$ and $\Lambda_2 = \{(x, z) \in \mathbb{Q}^{n_x + n_z} \mid B'x + B''z \leq d\}$, where n_x, n_y, n_z equal the number of entries in the respective vectors. Furthermore let m_A be the number of rows in A' and A'' and m_B be the number of rows in B' and B''. Consider arbitrary affine transformations $y_i := s^i x + t^i z + \beta^i$ with $s^i \in \mathbb{Q}^{n_x}$, $t^i \in \mathbb{Q}^{n_z}$, $\beta^i \in \mathbb{Q}$ for $1 \leq i \leq n_y$. Let S be the matrix with rows $s_1^T, \dots s_{n_y}^T$, T be the matrix with rows $t_1^T, \dots t_{n_y}^T$ and β be the vector with entries β^i. Let $\tau(S, T, \beta)$ be the substitution corresponding to these affine transformations. Hence $y\tau(S, T, \beta) = Sx + Tz + \beta$ and $\Lambda_1 \delta\tau(S, T, \beta) = \{(x, z) \in \mathbb{Q}^{n_x + n_z} \mid A'x + A''Sx + A''Tz + A''\beta \leq c\}$.

We have to check whether there are S, T and β such that $\Lambda_1 \delta\tau(S, T, \beta)$ contains Λ_2.

With the approach described above these are S, T, β such that there are $p^1, \dots, p^{m_A} \in \mathbb{Q}^{m_B}$ with $p^1, \dots, p^{m_A} \geq 0$, $p^{i^T} B' = (A' + A''S)_i$, $p^{i^T} B'' = (A''T)_i$, and $p^{i^T} d + (A''\beta)_i \leq c_i$ for $1 \leq i \leq m_A$. Let P be the matrix with rows $p^1, \dots, p^{m_A}$. We have to test the feasibility of the following linear program

$$\{(P, S, T, \beta) \in \mathbb{Q}^n \mid PB' = A' + A''S, PB'' = A''T, P \geq 0 \text{ and } Pd + A''\beta \leq c\},$$

where $n = m_A \times m_B + n_x \times n_y + n_z \times n_y + n_y$

If the system contains strict inequalities, we have to find a solution of a system of linear (in)equalities that contains strict inequalities.

4.3   Summary

We summarize the discussion above by giving the complexity of the three tests. Let Λ_i consist of n_i variables and m_i linear (in)equalities for $i = 1, 2$.

The satisfiability of Λ_1 can be verified by testing the feasibility of a linear program with n_1 variables and m_1 linear (in)equalities.

The test whether Λ_1 implies Λ_2 can be verified by testing the feasibility of m_1 linear programs, each with m_2 variables and $n_1 + 1 = n_2 + 1$ linear (in)equalities, where we do not count the non-negativity conditions.

The test whether there is an affine matcher τ such that $\Lambda_1\tau$ contains Λ_2 can be verified by testing the feasibility of one linear program with $m_1 m_2 + (n_2+1)n'$ variables and $(n_2 + 1)m_1$ linear constraints, where n' is the number of variables that appear in Λ_1 but not in Λ_2.

All linear systems can contain strict and non-strict inequalities.

5   Implementation

The free part of the inference rules of the hierarchic superposition calculus described in Section 3 is identical to the standard calculus, except that only simple substitutions are considered. For the theory part of clauses an implementation needs to provide instantiation and union of two clause constraints.

The operations resulting from subsumption or tautology deletion are much more involved because here the clause constraints need to be mapped to linear programming problems. The existence of solutions to the linear programs eventually decides on the applicability of the reduction rules. As reductions are more often checked than inferences computed, it is essential for an efficient implementation to support the operations needed for reductions. Therefore, we decided to actually store the clause constraint not in a symbolic tree like representation, as it is done for first-order terms, but directly in the input format data structure of LP solvers, where for the published SPASS(LA) binary http://spass-prover.org/prototypes we rely on QSopt http://www2.isye.gatech.edu/~wcook/qsopt/.

QSopt uses the simplex-method to solve systems of linear constraints which is not polynomial time but very efficient in practice. Alternatively, we could use an interior-point method to become polynomial while staying efficient in practice.

Furthermore, QSopt relies on floating-point arithmetic and therefore is not guaranteed to find the correct answer. Using an exact solver like QSOpt_Ex http://www.dii.uchile.cl/~daespino/ESolver_doc/main.html would lead to a large increase in running-time. Currently we are integrating a floating-point-filter for linear programming [AD09], i.e. a method that certifies the feasibility of linear programs which are numerically not too difficult. This method will allow us to prove or disprove the feasibility of most of the linear programs without using exact arithmetic and hence gives a safe implementation without a large increase in running time. We verified that the linear programs that appear in the solution process of the examples in Section 6 are solved correctly.

A key aspect in implementing SPASS(LA) is the representation of the LA constraints. We decided to use a representation that is close to standard LP solver interfaces such that performing the satisfiability test can be done by calling the LP solver directly with our LA constraint representation. The LP format is a "column-oriented" sparse format, meaning that the problems are represented column by column (variable) rather than row by row (constraint) and only non-zero coefficients are stored. So given an LP by a system $A\boldsymbol{x} \circ \boldsymbol{c}$, the variable *numcols* holds the number of columns (or different variables) in the constraint matrix A, *numrows* holds the number of rows in the constraint matrix, *rhs* is an array containing the right-hand sides, *sense* is an array containing the sense vector for the different rows and finally, the three arrays *matval*, *matind*, and *matcnt* hold the values of the matrix A. The non-zero coefficients of the constraint matrix A are grouped by column in the array *matval*. Each column $A_{*,j}$ is stored in a separate array *matval[j]*, and *matcnt[j]* stores the number of entries in *matval[j]*. For each i and j, *matind[j][i]* indicates the row number of the corresponding coefficient A_{ij}, stored in *matval[j][i]*. For example, the clause constraint

$$\Lambda = -u_1 + 2u_2 + 3u_3 + 4.4u_4 \leq 0, \ 5u_2 + 6u_3 \leq 1, \ 7u_3 + 8u_4 < -2.5$$

is represented by the data structure shown in Figure 2.

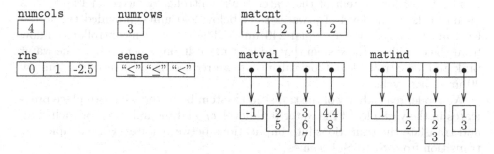

Fig. 2. Constraint Data Structures

The above representation implies that clause constraint satisfiability can directly be mapped from the clause constraint representation to a call of the LP solver. Furthermore, the SPASS variable normalization in clauses , done for sharing on the free theory part, fits perfectly to the above described LP format. All variables occurring in clauses are subsequently named starting with the "smallest" variable. In addition, the other operations on the free part eventually ranging into the constraints like the application of substitutions and the variable disjoint union of constraints can be efficiently mapped to the above suggested representation.

6   Example Applications

6.1   Transition Systems

In the following we present two examples showing that our notion on tautology and subsumption deletion is strong enough to decide formal safety properties of transition systems and our implementation SPASS(LA) is able to perform saturations in a reasonable amount of time. Furthermore, the proofs for the two presented properties of the examples are both satisfiability proofs and hence rely on the completeness of the calculus which is an important feature distinguishing our combination approach from others. Both examples are contained in the experimental SPASS(LA) version provided at http://spass-prover.org/prototypes/.

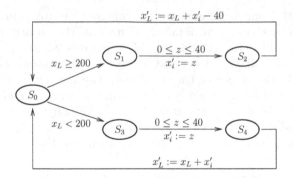

Fig. 3. Water Tank Controller

The transition system of the water tank controller depicted in Figure 3 is meant to keep the level of a water tank below 240 units, provided the initial level at state S_0 is less or equal 240 units. There is a non-controllable inflow from the outside of the system that adds at most 40 units per cycle to the water tank and a controllable outflow valve that can reduce the content of the tank by 40 units per cycle.

We model reachability of the transition system by introducing two place predicates in the variables of the water tank level x_L and the inflow x_i for each state and translate the transitions into implications between states. For example, the transition from S_1 to S_2 becomes

$$\forall u, v, w \, ((S_1(u,v) \wedge w \le 40 \wedge w \ge 0) \Rightarrow S_2(u,w))$$

and after normal form translation and abstraction the clause

$$w \le 40, w \ge 0 \parallel S_1(u,v) \rightarrow S_2(u,w)$$

and the transition from S_2 to S_0 eventually results in the clause

$$u' \approx u + v - 40 \parallel S_2(u,v) \rightarrow S_0(u',v)$$

The conjecture is translated into the formula

$$[\forall u, v \, ((u \le 240 \wedge S_0(u,v))] \Rightarrow [\exists u', v'(S_0(u',v') \wedge u' > 240))]$$

meaning that starting with an initial state S_0 with a level below 240 units we can reach a state S_0 with a level strictly above 240 units. SPASS(LA) finitely saturates this conjecture together with the theory of the transition system without finding the empty clause in less than one second on any reasonable PC hardware. Due to completeness this shows that the level of the water tank is always below 240 units. Obviously, the hierarchic superposition calculus is complete for this example, because there are no free function symbols at all. SPASS(LA) may also positively prove reachability conjectures. There is one such conjecture commented out in the example file of the distribution. For a number of classes of transition systems, it can actually be shown that the translation used here always results in a fragment where the hierarchic superposition calculus is complete[Non00, Dim09].

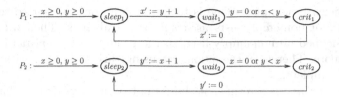

Fig. 4. Bakery Protocol

Note that the above clause set is out of reach for current SMT based approaches as their underlying calculus is typically not complete with respect to non-ground clauses and their instantiation based techniques are not able to show satisfiability. For example, Z3 "gives up" on the above (and the below) clause set. Both Z3 and any other Nelson-Oppen style solver are not complete for the two clause sets. The enhanced prover Z3(SP) [dMB08] is also not complete on both clause sets.

The bakery protocol is a protocol assuring mutual exclusion between two or more processes. We analyze the protocol for two processes by building the product transition system for the two processes shown in the Figure 4 and then modeling the transitions and states analogous to the water tank example.

The conjecture becomes

$$[\forall u, v \, ((u \geq 0 \wedge v \geq 0 \wedge \mathit{Sl1Sl2}(u, v))] \Rightarrow [\exists u', v' \; \mathit{Cr1Cr2}(u', v'))]$$

stating that if u and v are both greater than 0 and the processes in their respective sleep states, then the critical section of both processes can be reached simultaneously. Again, SPASS(LA) saturates this conjecture together with the theory of the two processes without finding the empty clause in less than one second. This shows that the protocol is safe, i.e., the critical sections cannot be reached simultaneously by both processes.

6.2 Container Data Structures

Sufficient completeness is a strong prerequisite for the completion of SUP(LA) that can be difficult to obtain, in general. However, in addition to the before shown results for transition systems, in the following we show how to obtain sufficient completeness for axiomatizations of container data structures using the example of lists. A well-known axiom clause set for lists is the following [ABRS09]

$$\begin{aligned}
\rightarrow \quad & car(cons(u, x)) \approx u \\
\rightarrow \quad & cdr(cons(u, x)) \approx x \\
\rightarrow \; & cons(car(x), cdr(x)) \approx x
\end{aligned}$$

where we assume u to be of LA base sort and x to be of sort list with according sort definitions for the functions. Then the above axiom set over the above signature including *nil* for the empty list is "almost" sufficiently complete. The function *car* ranges into the LA sort and the first axiom can reduce any ground *car* term to a base term except *car(nil)*. There are several ways to make the axioms sufficiently complete. One is to move to an ordered-sorted setting and define a sort of non-empty lists as a subsort of all lists. Then *nil* is of sort list, *car* is defined on non-empty lists, so the ground term *car*(*nil*) is not well-sorted anymore. Therefore, the axiom set using this extended sort structure is sufficiently complete.

The term *car*(*nil*) is a term that should not occur anyway as it has no well-defined meaning with respect to lists. Therefore, another possibility is simply to map the term *car*(*nil*) to some LA constant, e.g. 0. We add $\rightarrow car(nil) \approx 0$ to the above axioms making it sufficiently complete. Then in order to preserve the intended list semantics, we replace the third clause by $\rightarrow cons(car(x), cdr(x)) \approx x, x \approx nil$. The resulting set is sufficiently complete and preserves the list semantics. In general, additional atoms $t \approx nil$ have to be added to any clause containing a *car*(*t*) subterm.

Now having a complete axiom set it is subject to the same superposition based techniques for decidability results as they have been suggested, e.g., by Armando Et Al [ABRS09] for the standard superposition calculus. Sufficient completeness can also be obtained using the above described encodings for other container data structures, e.g., arrays, making SUP(LA) a complete calculus for the hierarchic combination of LA over the rationals and arrays.

7   Conclusion

We have presented an instance of the hierarchic superposition calculus [BGW94] with LA with effective notions for subsumption and tautology deletion. Compared to other approaches combining LA with first-order logic, the hierarchic superposition calculus is complete, if the actual clause sets enjoys the sufficient completeness criterion. We showed that for the theories of transition systems over LA and container data structures the sufficient completeness criterion can be fulfilled. The calculus is implemented in a first prototype version called SPASS(LA) for the resolution fragment of the hierarchic superposition calculus. By two examples we show that it can already be effectively used to decide satisfiability of clause sets that are out of scope for other approaches, in particular SMT based procedures. On the other hand the hierarchic approach cannot be extended to deal simultaneously with several different theories outside the free part in a straight forward way as it is the case for SMT based procedures using the Nelson-Oppen method, even if queries are ground. Here further research is needed.

For a bunch of examples we tested also SPASS(LA) with an SMT solver in place of the LP solver. In contrast to the results presented in [FNORC08], the LP solver turns out to be faster for our satisfiability and implication tests. Although we did not do enough experiments to arrive at a final conclusion, the usage of solvers in SPASS(LA) differs from the SMT scenario, because we do not incrementally/decrementally change the investigated LA theory as done by SMT solvers but ask for solving different "small" LA problems containing typically not more that 10–30 (dis)equations.

Finally, our definition of the calculus and the subsumption deletion and tautology deletion rules is not only applicable to a combination with LA, but potentially to any other theory providing an effective constraint satisfiability and implication test.

Acknowledgements. We thank our reviewers for their detailed and valuable comments. The authors are supported by the German Transregional Collaborative Research Center SFB/TR 14 AVACS.

References

[ABRS09]   Armando, A., Bonacina, M.P., Ranise, S., Schulz, S.: New results on rewrite-based satisfiability procedures. ACM Trans. Comput. Log. 10(1), 129–179 (2009)

[AD09]   Althaus, E., Dumitriu, D.: Fast and accurate bounds on linear programs. In: Vahrenhold, J. (ed.) SEA 2009. LNCS, vol. 5526, pp. 40–50. Springer, Heidelberg (2009)

[BGW94]   Bachmair, L., Ganzinger, H., Waldmann, U.: Refutational theorem proving for hierarchic first-order theories. Applicable Algebra in Engineering, Communication and Computing, AAECC 5(3/4), 193–212 (1994)

[Dim09]   Dimova, D.: On the translation of timed automata into first-order logic. In: Fietzke, A., Weidenbach, C. (supervisors) (2009)

[dMB08]   de Moura, L.M., Bjørner, N.: Engineering dpll(t) + saturation. In: Armando, A., Baumgartner, P., Dowek, G. (eds.) IJCAR 2008. LNCS (LNAI), vol. 5195, pp. 475–490. Springer, Heidelberg (2008)

[FNORC08] Faure, G., Nieuwenhuis, R., Oliveras, A., Rodríguez-Carbonell, E.: Sat modulo the theory of linear arithmetic: Exact, inexact and commercial solvers. In: Kleine Büning, H., Zhao, X. (eds.) SAT 2008. LNCS, vol. 4996, pp. 77–90. Springer, Heidelberg (2008)

[HSG04]   Hustadt, U., Schmidt, R.A., Georgieva, L.: A survey of decidable first-order fragments and description logics. Journal of Relational Methods in Computer Science 1, 251–276 (2004)

[KV07]   Korovin, K., Voronkov, A.: Integrating linear arithmetic into superposition calculus. In: Duparc, J., Henzinger, T.A. (eds.) CSL 2007. LNCS, vol. 4646, pp. 223–237. Springer, Heidelberg (2007)

[Non00]   Nonnengart, A.: Hybrid systems verification by location elimination. In: Lynch, N.A., Krogh, B.H. (eds.) HSCC 2000. LNCS, vol. 1790, pp. 352–365. Springer, Heidelberg (2000)

[Sch89]   Schrijver, A.: Theory of linear and integer programming. John Wiley & Sons, Inc., Chichester (1989)

[Wal01]   Waldmann, U.: Superposition and chaining for totally ordered divisible abelian groups. In: Goré, R.P., Leitsch, A., Nipkow, T. (eds.) IJCAR 2001. LNCS (LNAI), vol. 2083, pp. 226–241. Springer, Heidelberg (2001)

[Wei01]   Weidenbach, C.: Combining superposition, sorts and splitting. In: Robinson, A., Voronkov, A. (eds.) Handbook of Automated Reasoning, ch. 27, vol. 2, pp. 1965–2012. Elsevier, Amsterdam (2001)

Unification Modulo Homomorphic Encryption

Siva Anantharaman[1], Hai Lin[2], Christopher Lynch[2],
Paliath Narendran[3], and Michaël Rusinowitch[4]

[1] Université d'Orléans (Fr.)
siva@univ-orleans.fr
[2] Clarkson University, Potsdam, NY, USA
{linh,clynch}@clarkson.edu
[3] University at Albany-SUNY, USA
dran@cs.albany.edu
[4] Loria-INRIA Lorraine, Nancy (Fr.)
rusi@loria.fr

Abstract. Encryption 'distributing over pairs' is a technique employed in several cryptographic protocols. We show that unification is decidable for an equational theory HE specifying such an encryption. The method consists in transforming any given problem in such a way, that the resulting problem can be solved by combining a graph-based reasoning on its equations involving the homomorphisms, with a syntactic reasoning on its pairings. We show HE-unification to be NP-hard and in NEXPTIME.

1 Introduction

Several methods based on rewriting have been proposed with success, for the formal analysis of cryptographic protocols. The following Dolev-Yao (DY) system underlies many of them:

$$(\text{DY}) \quad \begin{array}{ll} p_1(x.y) \rightarrow x & dec(enc(x,y),y) \rightarrow x \\ p_2(x.y) \rightarrow y & enc(dec(x,y),y) \rightarrow x \end{array}$$

The '.' here is the 'pairing' operation on messages, p_1, p_2 are the respective projections from pairs, and 'dec' (resp. 'enc') stands for decryption (resp. encryption); the second argument of these latter functions are referred to as keys.

The so-called *public collapsing* theories, used in some works (e.g., [7]), are presented by rewrite systems where the rhs of every rule is a ground term or a variable. Some other results assume that the rhs of any rule is a proper subterm of the lhs. A general procedure for protocol security analysis has been given in [3] for such systems, extensively using equational unification and narrowing. Rewrite systems with such a 'subterm' property have been called *dwindling* in [1], where a decision procedure was given for passive deduction (i.e., detecting secrecy attacks by an intruder *not* interacting actively with the protocol sessions). The technique used is one that combines unification and narrowing with the notion of *cap closure* modeling the evolution of the intruder knowledge. The algorithm presented was also shown to be complete for passive deduction, for a class of rewrite systems strictly including the dwindling systems, and in particular the following

S. Ghilardi and R. Sebastiani (Eds.): FroCoS 2009, LNAI 5749, pp. 100–116, 2009.
© Springer-Verlag Berlin Heidelberg 2009

convergent, non-dwindling system, that we shall refer to as HE; it extends DY with the requirement that '*encryption distributes over pairs*':

(HE)
$$p_1(x.y) \to x$$
$$p_2(x.y) \to y$$
$$enc(dec(x,y),y) \to x$$
$$dec(enc(x,y),y) \to x$$

$$enc(x.y, z) \to enc(x, z).enc(y, z)$$
$$dec(x.y, z) \to dec(x, z).dec(y, z)$$

We shall refer to the equational theory defined by this system HE as *Homomorphic Encryption*, or just as HE. On protocols implementing encryption with the so-called ECB (Electronic Code Book) block chaining – performed sequentially on a block decomposition of the plain text, and under the assumption that message fields are assigned a round number of blocks – encryption can be modeled as an homomorphism on pairs; examples of such protocols can be found in e.g., [5]. As mentioned above, passive deduction is known to be decidable for protocols employing HE; but the problem of *active deduction* for such protocols, i.e., when the intruder is allowed to interact with the protocol steps (for instance, to forge the identity of some honest agent), has not been studied yet. Now, the decidability of unification modulo any given intruder theory E is known to be a necessary condition for deciding active deduction modulo E, cf. e.g., [5]; that motivated our interest in HE-unification. Note that the homomorphism $enc(-, y)$ defined on terms for any given y, admits an inverse homomorphism $dec(-, y)$ modulo HE; as a consequence, HE-unification cannot be reduced directly to unification modulo one-sided distributivity [12].

This paper is structured as follows: The needed preliminaries are given in Section 2. Unification modulo HE is shown to be decidable in Section 3. The main idea consists in reducing any given HE-unification problem into one of solving a set of 'simple' equations of the form $Z = enc(X, V)$ or $Z = dec(X, V)$, where none of the 1st arguments under enc get split into pairs by the other equations. Solving such a set of 'simple' equations is essentially the unification problem modulo the two rules for encryption and decryption:

$$dec(enc(x,y),y) \to x$$
$$enc(dec(x,y),y) \to x$$

which form a confluent, dwindling system, so has a decidable unification problem, cf. [10]. The method we propose in this work actually combines a graph-based algorithm reasoning modulo the group structure on homomorphisms – that is specific to 'simple' HE-unification problems – with one that reasons modulo a theory for pairings. We show that *even solving 'simple' HE-unification problems* (i.e., without pairings) *is NP-complete*. A couple of examples illustrating the method are given in Section 4.

2   Notation and Preliminaries

As usual, Σ will stand for a ranked signature, and $\mathcal{X}$ a countably infinite set of variables. $\mathcal{T} = \mathcal{T}(\Sigma, \mathcal{X})$ is the algebra of terms over this signature; terms in $\mathcal{T}$ will be denoted as $s, t, \ldots$, and variables as $u, v, x, y, z, \ldots$, all with possible suffixes.

The set of all positions on any term t is denoted as $Pos(t)$; if $q \in Pos(t)$, then $t|_q$ denotes the subterm of t at position q; and the term obtained from t by replacing the subterm $t|_q$ by any given term t' will be denoted as $t[q \leftarrow t']$; a similar notation is employed also for the substitution of variables of t by terms. We assume a simplification ordering $\succ$ on $\mathcal{T}$ that is total on ground terms (terms not containing variables). A rewrite rule is a pair of terms (l, r) such that $l \succ r$, and is represented as usual, as $l \to r$; a rewrite system is a finite set of rewrite rules. The notions of reduction and of normalization of a term by a rewrite system are assumed known, as well as those of termination and of confluence of the reduction relation defined by such a system on terms. A rewrite system R is *convergent* iff the reduction relation it defines on the set of terms is terminating and confluent.

By an HE-Unification problem we mean, as usual, any given finite set $\mathcal{P}$ of equations between terms over Σ; and a solution to the problem $\mathcal{P}$ is a substitution σ such that $\sigma s = \sigma t$ mod HE, for every equation $s = t$ in $\mathcal{P}$. For proving that HE-Unification is decidable, we shall be applying several reductions to the given problem. To start with, we shall assume (via usual reasonings mod HE) that the given problem $\mathcal{P}$ is in a *standard form*, in the following sense: each of its equations to solve, modulo HE, is assumed to have one of the following forms:

$$Z = T, \quad Z = X.Y, \quad Z = enc(X, Y), \quad Z = const,$$

where the $T, X, Y, Z, \ldots$ stand for variables, and $const$ is any ground constant. (If an equation in $\mathcal{P}$ is given in the form $U = dec(V, W)$, it is rewritten mod HE as $V = enc(U, W)$.) The equations in $\mathcal{P}$ of the *first* and *fourth* forms are said to be '*equalities*', equations of the second form are called '*pairings*' and those of the third form are said to be of the enc type. The second arguments of enc, in the equations of $\mathcal{P}$, are referred to as the *keys* or *key variables* of $\mathcal{P}$. If Y is a key variable which is also the lhs of an equation of the fourth form, i.e., the rhs is a constant, then Y as well as the constant of that equation will both be said to be a key constant of $\mathcal{P}$. Given a problem $\mathcal{P}$ in standard form, we denote by $\mathcal{X}_\mathcal{P}$ the set of its variables, and by $\mathcal{K}_\mathcal{P}$ the set of key variables (and key constants) of $\mathcal{P}$.

The *conjugate* of any enc equation $Z = enc(X, Y)$ in $\mathcal{P}$, is defined as the equation $X = dec(Z, Y)$; it will be said to be of the '*dec*' type. For every key variable/constant Y occurring in $\mathcal{P}$, let h_Y (resp. $\overline{h}_Y$) denote the homomorphism $enc(-, Y)$ (resp. $dec(-, Y)$) defined on terms. An enc equation $Z = enc(X, Y)$ can thus be written as $Z = h_Y(X)$, and its conjugate as $X = \overline{h}_Y(Z)$. We denote by $\mathcal{H} = \mathcal{H}_\mathcal{P}$ the finite set of all such homomorphisms associated with the key variables/constants of the problem $\mathcal{P}$. All our unification problems in the sequel will be assumed to be in standard form (unless mentioned otherwise explicitly).

The Dependency Graph of $\mathcal{P}$: We construct a graph of dependency $G = G_\mathcal{P}$ between the variables of the given problem $\mathcal{P}$: Its nodes will be the variables (or constants) of $\mathcal{P}$. From a node Z on G, there is an oriented arc to a node X on G iff the following holds:

a) $\mathcal{P}$ has an equation of the form $Z = h_Y(X)$ (resp. $X = h_Y(Z)$), for some $Y \in \mathcal{K}_\mathcal{P}$; the arc is then labeled with the symbol h_Y (resp. with $\overline{h}_Y$);

b) $\mathcal{P}$ has an equation of the form $Z = X.V$ (resp. $Z = V.X$): the arc is then labelled with p_1 (resp. with p_2).

Semantics: If G contains an edge of the form $Z \to^h X$, with $h \in \mathcal{H}$, then Z can be evaluated by applying the homomorphism h to the evaluation of X.

Note that there are *no 'equality' arcs* on the graph $G_\mathcal{P}$.

3   Unification Modulo HE

Theorem 1. *Unification modulo the theory HE is decidable.*

To facilitate understanding, we present briefly the outlines of the proof. An inference procedure will be applied to the unification problem $\mathcal{P}$, given in standard form. The transformation of $\mathcal{P}$ under the rules of this procedure (named *trimming* rules) will be based on the following guiding principles:

- Perfect Encryption: If $Z = enc(X, Y) \in \mathcal{P}$ and also $Z = enc(X, Y') \in \mathcal{P}$ (resp. $Z = enc(X', Y) \in \mathcal{P}$), then $Y = Y'$ (resp. $X = X'$) must be in $\mathcal{P}$.
- Pairing is free in HE: If $Z = X.Y$ and $Z = X'.Y'$ are both in $\mathcal{P}$, then the equalities $X = X', Y = Y'$ must be in $\mathcal{P}$.
- Split on Pairs: $Z = enc(X, Y) \in \mathcal{P}$ and if one of Z, X is the lhs of a pairing equation in $\mathcal{P}$, then the other must be so too.
- Irredundancy of the Dependency Graph: If Z', Z'' are two distinct nodes of $G_\mathcal{P}$, then $\mathcal{P}$ must not contain the equality $Z' = Z''$.

(The first principle says that, from any given message two different keys cannot generate the same encrypted message; the third says that no encrypted message may split into a pair, if the original message itself is not a pair.) Our objective is to transform the given problem into a 'trimmed' problem composed of two sub-problems which can be treated 'almost' separately: one containing only the pairings and equalities, and the other containing only the *enc* equations whose lhs variables (resp. first arguments under *enc*) are *not* splittable; the latter sub-problem will be solved by 'combinatorial' means as we shall be seeing farther down; and their solutions extend naturally as solutions for the entire problem, via combination with its equalities and pairings.

Among the four guiding principles above, the third necessitates introducing fresh 'splitting' variables, in general. For defining a measure on how deep we may need to go, for introducing such fresh variables starting from any given variable, we need the following relations on the set of variables $\mathcal{X} = \mathcal{X}_\mathcal{P}$ appearing in $\mathcal{P}$:

Definition 1. $U \sim V$ *is the finest equivalence relation on* $\mathcal{X}$ *such that:*

- *if* $U = V \in \mathcal{P}$ *then* $U \sim V$;
- *if* $U = enc(V, T) \in \mathcal{P}$ *or* $V = enc(U, T) \in \mathcal{P}$, *for some* T, *then* $U \sim V$;
- *if* $\mathcal{P}$ *contains two pairings of the form* $W = U.X$ *and* $W' = V.X'$ *(or of the form* $W = X.U$ *and* $W' = X'.V$*), where* $W \sim W'$, *then* $U \sim V$.

• *We write* $U \succ V$ *iff there is a loop-free chain from* U *to* V *formed of* $\sim$- *or* p_1/p_2-*steps, at least one of them being a* p_1- *or* p_2- *step.*

• *For any problem* $\mathcal{P}$ *and for any given* $Z \in \mathcal{X} = \mathcal{X}_\mathcal{P}$, *the* sp-*depth of* Z *(short for splitting depth of* Z, *and denoted as* $spd(Z)$*) is defined as the* maximum number of p_1- or p_2- steps *from Z to all possible $X \in \mathcal{X}$,* along the loop-free chains formed of $\sim$- or p_1/p_2-steps from Z to X.

A ground substitution on the set $\mathcal{X} = \mathcal{X}_\mathcal{P}$ is said to be *discriminating* iff distinct key variables of $\mathcal{P}$ are assigned distinct irreducible ground terms. A discriminating solution for $\mathcal{P}$ is such a substitution that also solves $\mathcal{P}$. A fifth guiding principle is that, in order that $\mathcal{P}$ admits such a solution, there can be no directed loop with a 'non-trivial label', and formed only of $h/\overline{h}$-arcs, from any node to itself on the graph $G_\mathcal{P}$. In formal terms: Let X, Y be any two nodes on G, and α any given word over the set $\mathcal{H}$ of homomorphisms. We shall write $X \rightarrowtail^\alpha Y$ iff there is a directed path from X to Y on G, the arcs of which are labeled respectively by the homomorphisms forming the word α. The following condition gives our fifth guiding principle:

(**SNF**): For any directed loop on $G = G_\mathcal{P}$ from any node Z on G to itself, such that the labels of its arcs form a word $\alpha \in \mathcal{H}^*$, the word α must simplify to the empty word under the following set of rules:

$$(\Delta) \qquad h_T \overline{h}_T \rightarrow \epsilon, \quad \overline{h}_T h_T \rightarrow \epsilon, \qquad T \in \mathcal{K}_\mathcal{P}.$$

This condition **SNF** is necessary for $\mathcal{P}$ to admit a discriminating solution: indeed, if σ is such a solution for $\mathcal{P}$, and $Z \rightarrowtail^\alpha Z$ is a non-trivial loop on G formed only of $h/\overline{h}$-arcs, it means the ground term $\sigma(\alpha)(\sigma Z)$ must normalize to $\sigma(Z)$, and that can be done only by the two rewrite rules to the bottom-left of the rewrite system HE.

Note that any non-discriminating solution to $\mathcal{P}$, i.e., one that does not assign distinct values to distinct key variables, can be seen as a discriminating solution to a *variant* of $\mathcal{P}$, obtained by 'equating some keys' by adding some further equalities to $\mathcal{P}$ (by applying inference rule 6 below). We are in a position now to formulate the rules of our inference system.

The Inference Rules: We denote by **Eq** (resp. **Pair, Enc**) the set of equalities (resp. pairings, the *enc*-equations) in $\mathcal{P}$, respectively.
Rule 1. (*Perfect Encryption*)

$$a) \quad \frac{\textbf{Eq; Pair; Enc} \sqcup \{Z = enc(X,Y),\, Z = enc(V,Y)\}}{\textbf{Eq} \cup \{V = X\};\ \textbf{Pair; Enc} \sqcup \{Z = enc(X,Y)\}}$$

$$b) \quad \frac{\textbf{Eq; Pair; Enc} \sqcup \{Z = enc(X,Y),\, Z = enc(X,T)\}}{\textbf{Eq} \cup \{T = Y\};\ \textbf{Pair; Enc} \sqcup \{Z = enc(X,Y)\}}$$

Rule 1'. (*Variable Elimination*)

$$\frac{\{U = V\} \sqcup \textbf{Eq; Pair; Enc}}{\{U = V\} \cup [V/U](\textbf{Eq});\ [V/U](\textbf{Pair});\ [V/U](\textbf{Enc})}$$

Rule 2. (*Pairing is free in HE*)

$$\frac{\textbf{Eq; Pair} \sqcup \{Z = U_1.U_2,\, Z = V_1.V_2\};\ \textbf{Enc}}{\textbf{Eq} \cup \{V_1 = U_1,\, V_2 = U_2\};\ \textbf{Pair} \sqcup \{Z = U_1.U_2\};\ \textbf{Enc}}$$

Rule 3. (*Split on Pairs*)

a)
$$\frac{\mathbf{Eq};\ \mathbf{Pair} \cup \{Z = Z_1.Z_2\};\ \mathbf{Enc} \sqcup \{Z = enc(X,Y)\}}{\mathbf{Eq};\ ;\ \mathbf{Pair} \sqcup \{X = X_1.X_2\};\ \mathbf{Enc} \sqcup \{Z_1 = enc(X_1,Y),\ Z_2 = enc(X_2,Y)\}}$$

b)
$$\frac{\mathbf{Eq};\ \mathbf{Pair} \cup \{X = X_1.X_2\};\ \mathbf{Enc} \sqcup \{Z = enc(X,Y)\}}{\mathbf{Eq};\ \mathbf{Pair} \sqcup \{Z = Z_1.Z_2\};\ \mathbf{Enc} \sqcup \{Z_1 = enc(X_1,Y),\ Z_2 = enc(X_2,Y)\}}$$

Rule 4. (*Occur check*)

$$\frac{\mathbf{Eq};\ \mathbf{Pair};\ \mathbf{Enc};\ \ Z \sim Z' \ and \ Z > Z'}{FAIL}$$

Rule 4'. (*Clash with Pair*)

$$\frac{\mathbf{Eq} \sqcup \{Z = a\};\ \mathbf{Pair} \sqcup \{Z = U_1.U_2\};\ \mathbf{Enc}}{FAIL}$$

Rule 4''. (*Clash with Constant*)

$$\frac{\mathbf{Eq} \sqcup \{Z = a, Z \sim b\};\ \mathbf{Pair};\ \mathbf{Enc}}{FAIL}$$

Rule 5. (**SNF** *Fails*)

$$\frac{\mathbf{Eq};\ \mathbf{Pair};\ \mathbf{Enc};\ \ Z \in G,\ \alpha \in \mathcal{H}^*,\ Z \longmapsto^\alpha Z,\ \alpha \not\to_\Delta^* \epsilon}{FAIL}$$

Rule 6. (*Equate Some Keys*)

$$\frac{\mathbf{Eq};\ \mathbf{Pair};\ \mathbf{Enc};\ \ U,\ V \text{ are keys of } \mathcal{P}}{\mathbf{Eq} \cup \{U = V\};\ \mathbf{Pair};\ \mathbf{Enc}}$$

The X_1, X_2 in rule 3a (resp. Z_1, Z_2 in rule 3b) are fresh variables – as indicated by the notation, the $\sqcup$ signifying *disjoint union*. Rules 1, 1' and 2 are referred to as "*Simplification Rules*", and rules 3a and 3b as "*Splitting Rules*". Rules 4, 4', 4'' and 5 are called "*Failure Rules*". All these rules together, i.e. the rules $1, 1', 2, 3, 4, 4', 4'', 5$, constitute our "*Trimming Rules*".

A problem $\mathcal{P}$ in standard form is said to be *trimmed* iff none of the trimming rules is applicable. The 'Occur-Check' rule 4 is meant to eliminate easy cases of unsolvability, such as when $\mathcal{P}$ contains two equations of the form $Z = enc(X,T), Z = X.Y$; similarly, rule 4' (resp. rule 4'') eliminates unsolvable cases such as $Z = a, Z = X.Y$ (resp. $Z = a, X = b, Z = enc(X,Y)$). The graph of the current problem is kept irredundant by rule 1'. The rules 3 – creating fresh splitting variables – are to be applied only if none of the other rules 1 through 5 are applicable; more precisely: rules $1a, 1b, 1'$ and 2 are to be applied with highest priority, followed by the Failure rules, then by rules 3. Rules 1, 2, 3 are *don't-care* nondeterministic. Rule 6 is *don't-know* nondeterministic; it is to be applied outside the scope of the trimming rules (in particular rule 1b), and its role is to produce variants of $\mathcal{P}$. It is easy to check that the set of solutions of $\mathcal{P}$ is equal to the union of the solution sets of the trimmed problems derived by applying *all* the above inference rules to $\mathcal{P}$.

We will show shortly that such an inference procedure terminates on any problem given in standard form. Hence only finitely many trimmed problems can be derived from any problem $\mathcal{P}$ given standard form. For proving termination, we shall be needing the following notions.

(1): Let $\mathcal{P}$ be any such given problem. We introduce a binary, infix operator '∘' representing pairs (but denoted differently, to avoid confusion); and define $\mathcal{T}_p(\mathcal{P}) = \mathcal{T}_p$ as the set of all terms formed over $\mathcal{X}$, the symbol '∘', and the set of all homomorphisms h_T – where T runs over all the keys of $\mathcal{P}$.

- Any pairing $X = X_1.X_2$ in $\mathcal{P}$, is seen as a rewrite rule: $X \to X_1 \circ X_2$;
- Any equation $Z = enc(X, T)$ in $\mathcal{P}$ gives rise to two rewrite rules:
  $Z \to^{h_T} X$, and $X \to^{\overline{h}_T} Z$.

Rules of the former type will be called pairing rules; those of the latter type will be respectively called h-rules or $\overline{h}$-rules, with key T, and with target X for the first among them, and Z for the second. We define $\mathcal{R}_\mathcal{P}$ to be the rewrite system formed of all such rules. By a *critical configuration* in $\mathcal{R}_\mathcal{P}$, we mean any given pair of distinct rewrite rules of $\mathcal{R}_\mathcal{P}$ such that:

- both rules have the same variable $X \in \mathcal{X}_\mathcal{P}$ to their left;
- if one of them is a h-rule (resp. $\overline{h}$-rule), then the other rule must be a
  pairing rule or a h-rule (resp. pairing rule or a $\overline{h}$-rule);
- if both are h-rules (or $\overline{h}$-rules), they have the same key or the same target.

The common lhs variable of a critical configuration is referred to as its *peak*.

(2): For any such given problem $\mathcal{P}$, and any given critical configuration wrt $\mathcal{R}_\mathcal{P}$ with $X \in \mathcal{X}$ as its peak, let n_X stand for the number of distinct nodes on $G_\mathcal{P}$ to which there is a loop-free, non-empty chain from X *formed only of* h- *or* $\overline{h}$- *arcs*. The *weight* of the critical configuration is then defined as the (lexicographically) ordered pair of integers $(spd(X), n_X)$.

Lemma 1. *Trimming terminates on problems given in standard form.*

Proof. Given $\mathcal{P}$ in standard form, we only need to consider the inferences other than $4, 4', 4'', 5$, which – to be applied whenever applicable – would yield 'FAIL'. We define the *measure* $m(\mathcal{P})$ of $\mathcal{P}$ as the lexicographic combination of 2 components: $m_1 = m_1(\mathcal{P})$, $m_2 = m_2(\mathcal{P})$, where:

- m_1 is the number of distinct key variables appearing in $\mathcal{P}$;
- m_2 is the *multiset of weights* of all the critical configurations over $\mathcal{R}_\mathcal{P}$.

Consider now any inference on $\mathcal{P}$, by a rule other than $4, 4', 4''$ and 5. It is not hard to check that none of the inference rules will increase the sp-depth of a variable. We then have the following:

- Inference rule $1b$ will lower m_1.
- Inference rules $1a, 2, 3a, 3b$ – followed by applying $1'$ *en bloc* – will
  all leave m_1 unchanged, but will lower m_2.

This is so, because if some nodes "become equal" under the inferences, and if the number of keys is *not* lower for the new problem derived, then:

- either some of the critical configurations have been eliminated, while the others remain unchanged;
- or some 'current' critical configurations have been replaced by new ones.

In the latter case, for any new critical configuration with Y as a peak, that replaces an old one with X as a peak, we should have either $spd(Y) < spd(X)$ (rules $3a, 3b$); or else $spd(Y) = spd(X)$ and $n_Y < n_X$ (rules $1a, 2$); the latter inequality is ensured, in particular because (by **SNF**) G contains no non-trivial directed loops containing only $h/\bar{h}$-arcs.   □

A trimmed problem $\mathcal{P}$ is divided into two sub-problems: one containing only the pairings and equalities of $\mathcal{P}$, and the other containing only its *enc* equations; this latter sub-problem will be referred to as the *kernel* of $\mathcal{P}$. *A problem $\mathcal{P}$ is said to be* simple *iff it is its own kernel.*

Example 1. (i) The following problem is not in standard form:
$T = Z$, $Z = enc(X, Y)$, $X = dec(T, Y)$, $X = U.V$, $Y = Y_1.Y_2$, $Y_2 = a$;
we first put it in standard form:
$T = Z$, $Z = enc(X, Y)$, $T = enc(X, Y)$, $X = U.V$, $Y = Y_1.Y_2$, $Y_2 = a$.
Under variable elimination (rule $1'$), we first get:
$\qquad T = Z$, $Z = enc(X, Y)$, $X = U.V$, $Y = Y_1.a$, $Y_2 = a$;
which has one critical configuration, namely: $Z \xleftarrow{h_Y} X \rightarrow U \circ V$. Only a splitting inference is applicable (on Z); and the trimmed equivalent that we get is:
$\qquad T = Z$, $Z = Z_1.Z_2$, $X = U.V$, $Y = Y_1.a$, $Y_2 = a$,
$\qquad\qquad Z_1 = enc(U, Y)$, $Z_2 = enc(V, Y)$.
(ii) The following problem:
$\qquad Z = enc(X, Y)$, $Y = enc(Z, T)$, $T = enc(Z, W)$, $Y = Y_1.Y_2$.
is in standard form, but not trimmed: we have one critical configuration, namely: $Z \xleftarrow{h_T} Y \rightarrow Y_1 \circ Y_2$, with peak at Y. Now $spd(Y) = 1$, but $n_Y = 3$ (we can go from Y to T, X, Z using only *enc/dec* arcs); so m_2 here is $\{(1,3)\}$, and the measure $m(\mathcal{P})$ of the problem is $(3, \{(1,3)\})$. The evolution of the dependency graph of the problem under splitting is illustrated below (where, for readability, we have not put in the $\bar{h}$-arcs).

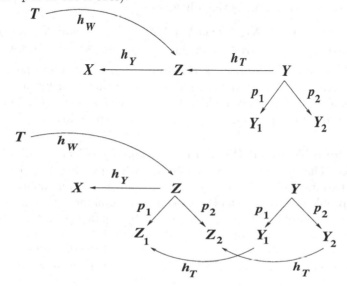

Trimming needs here several splitting steps. We first write $Z = Z_1.Z_2$, and replace the second enc equation by the 2 equations: $Y_1 = enc(Z_1, T), Y_2 = enc(Z_2, T)$; we get a problem with two critical configurations, both with peak at Z, $spd(Z) = 1$ and $n_Z = 2$; so the measure is lowered to $(3, \{(1, 2), (1, 2)\})$:

Next, we write $X = X_1.X_2$ and replace the first enc equation by $Z_1 = enc(X_1, Y), Z_2 = enc(X_2, Y)$, and get a problem with measure $(3, \{(1, 1)\})$:

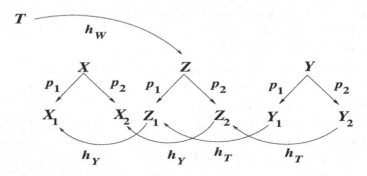

Finally, we write $T = T_1.T_2$ and replace the last enc equation by: $T_1 = enc(Z_1, W)$, $T_2 = enc(Z_2, W)$. We thus get the following trimmed equivalent, with measure $(3, \{(0, 0)\})$:

$$Z_1 = enc(X_1, Y), \quad Z_2 = enc(X_2, Y),$$
$$Y_1 = enc(Z_1, T), \quad Y_2 = enc(Z_2, T),$$
$$T_1 = enc(Z_1, W), \quad T_2 = enc(Z_2, W),$$
$$Y = Y_1.Y_2, \quad Z = Z_1.Z_2, \quad X = X_1.X_2, \quad T = T_1.T_2. \qquad \square$$

Remark 1. (i) The number of equations in a trimmed equivalent of a problem $\mathcal{P}$ given in standard form – derived at the end of the inference procedure, when it does not FAIL – can be exponential wrt the number of initial equations in $\mathcal{P}$; a typical illustrative example is the following:

$$X_1 = enc(X_2, U1) \qquad X_{11} = enc(X_{12}, U2) \qquad X_{111} = enc(X_{112}, U3)$$
$$X_1 = X_{11}.X_{12} \qquad\quad X_{11} = X_{111}.X_{112} \qquad\quad X_{111} = X_{1111}.X_{1112}$$

(ii) A key variable of a problem $\mathcal{P}$ (in standard form), can also be a 'message variable', as the Y, T of Example 1.(ii) above. Note that *as a key* it will remain unaffected under trimming even when it gets split as a 'message'. The number of keys of a problem thus remains unaffected under trimming. $\qquad \square$

The graph of a Trimmed Problem: *A trimmed problem will also be said to be admissible.* The dependency graph $G_\mathcal{P}$ of such a problem $\mathcal{P}$ is irredundant: if X, V are two distinct nodes on $G_\mathcal{P}$, then $X = V$ is *not* an equality in $\mathcal{P}$. An admissible problem $\mathcal{P}$ will actually be seen as a combination of its kernel $\mathcal{P}'$, and its 'other' subproblem $\mathcal{P}''$ consisting only of the pairings and equalities; and its graph $G = G_\mathcal{P}$ as a 'join' of the dependency graph $G' = G_{\mathcal{P}'}$ of its kernel $\mathcal{P}'$ – each arc of which is labeled with an h or an $\overline{h}$ – and the dependency graph G'' of the subproblem $\mathcal{P}''$, each arc of which is labeled with either p_1 or p_2.

Lemma 2. *(i) From any given node Z on G' there is at most one loop-free path on G' to any other given node X on G'.*

(ii) For any given word α over $\{p_1, p_2\}$, and any given node Z on G'', there is at most one directed path outgoing from Z that is labeled by the word α.

Proof. Assertion (i) follows from **SNF**, and assertion (ii) from Inference rule 2, and the fact that the dependency graph is irredundant (rule 1b).   □

Definition 2. *Between the variables of an admissible problem $\mathcal{P}$, we define a relation called* key-dependency *and denoted as* $\succ_k$:

- *$Z \succ_k X$ iff $Z \neq X$, and there is a directed path from Z to X on the graph $G_{\mathcal{P}}$ that contains an arc labeled with $h_{X'}$ or $\overline{h}_{X'}$, where $X' = X$ or $X' > X$.*

An admissible problem $\mathcal{P}$ and its graph $G_{\mathcal{P}}$ are said to satisfy the condition NKDC – short for 'No-Key-Dependency-Cycle', iff the following holds:

- *(NKDC): The graph $G = G_{\mathcal{P}}$ does not contain any node X such that $X \succ_k^+ X$, where $\succ_k^+$ is the transitive closure of the relation $\succ_k$.*

These relations play a key role in our method for solving a trimmed problem.

3.1   Discriminating Solutions for Admissible Problems

Let $\mathcal{P}$ be any given admissible problem. The case where the kernel of $\mathcal{P}$ is empty – i.e., when $\mathcal{P}$ contains only equalities and pairings – is trivial, as is easily checked; we shall therefore assume henceforth that $\mathcal{P}$ has a non-empty kernel $\mathcal{P}'$. Our objective in this section is to prove the following proposition:

Proposition 1. *An admissible problem admits a discriminating solution if and only if it satisfies NKDC.*

NKDC is Necessary: In this paragraph, θ stands for a discriminating substitution on the set $\mathcal{X}$. For any $X \in \mathcal{K}_{\mathcal{P}}$, $\tilde{h}_X$ stands for either h_X or its conjugate $\overline{h}_X$; and $C, C', \ldots$, referred to as contexts, stand for words over the $\tilde{h}_X$. For any term t, $|t|$ stands as usual for its size. If θ solves $\mathcal{P}$, then it must also solve $\mathcal{P}'$. Now, we know that solving $\mathcal{P}'$ amounts to solving the unification problem modulo the convergent system R formed of the following two rules:

$$(R): \quad enc(dec(x, y), y) \to x, \qquad dec(enc(x, y), y) \to x.$$

Lemma 3. *Assume that $Y = \tilde{h}_X(C[p \leftarrow t])$ for some context C, term t, and position $p \in \{1\}^*$. Then for any R-normalized ground substitution θ we have that $\theta(Y)$ is either a subterm of $\theta(t)$ or $\theta(X)$ is the outermost key of $\theta(Y)$.*

Proof. Case i) Where the encryption keys on top of $\theta(t)$ get cancelled by the decryption keys of the context C up to $\theta(X)$: in this case, $\theta(Y)$ must be a subterm of the term $\theta(t)$.

Case ii) Where the encryption by $\theta(X)$ is not cancelled by a decryption key just below, in the term $\theta(Y)$: By assumption θ assigns different terms to different variables; so, in this case $\theta(X)$ will remain the outermost key of $\theta(Y)$.   □

Lemma 4. *Assume that* $Y = \tilde{h}_{X'}(C[p \leftarrow X])$ *for some context* C, *and position* $p \in \{1\}^*$, *where* $X = X'$ *or* X *is a factor of* X' *for pairing. Then* $\theta(X')$ *is the outermost key of* $\theta(Y)$, *and* $|\theta(Y)| > |\theta(X)|$.

Proof. We apply the previous lemma with $t = X$; we will be in Case ii) of that proof, so we deduce that $\theta(X')$ is the outermost key of $\theta(Y)$. Since both $\theta(X)$, $\theta(Y)$ are in R-normal form, we also get the assertion on their sizes. □

Lemma 5. *If* $Y = C'[p' \leftarrow \tilde{h}_{X'}(C[p \leftarrow X])]$ *for some contexts* C, C', *and positions* $p, p' \in \{1\}^*$, *where* $X = X'$ *or* X *is a factor of* X' *for pairing, then* $\theta(t)$ *is a subterm of* $\theta(Y)$, *where* $t = \tilde{h}_{X'}(C[p \leftarrow X])$.

Proof. $\theta(X')$ is the outermost key of $\theta(t)$ by Lemma 4. And no reduction above $\theta(t)$ is possible, since θ is assumed discriminating. □

Corollary 1. *Let* $\mathcal{P}$ *be any trimmed admissible problem, and suppose the graph* $G_{\mathcal{P}}$ *of* $\mathcal{P}$ *does* not *satisfy the criterion NKDC; then there is no discriminating solution for the kernel* $\mathcal{P}'$ *of* $\mathcal{P}$, *so no discriminating solution for* $\mathcal{P}$.

Proof. If $G_{\mathcal{P}}$ does *not* satisfy NKDC, that means there is a key-dependency cycle; so, there are two nodes Y, Z on $G_{\mathcal{P}'}$ such that some arc on the the (unique) path on $G_{\mathcal{P}'}$ from Y to Z uses Y as key, and also that some arc on the (unique) path from Z to Y (which has to be the reverse of the path from Y to Z, cf. Lemma 2) uses Z as key. From the above lemma, we then deduce that for any discriminating substitution θ, $\theta(Y)$ and $\theta(Z)$ are subterms of each other, i.e., must be the same term – contradiction. □

Example 2. Consider the following (simple) problems:

(i) $\mathcal{P}_1$: $Y = enc(Z, X)$, $X = enc(Z, Y)$
(ii) $\mathcal{P}_2$: $Z = enc(X, X)$, $Z = dec(T, T)$
(iii) $\mathcal{P}_3$: $U = enc(X, Z)$, $Z = enc(U, Y)$, $Y = enc(U, X)$

(i) $\mathcal{P}_1$ does not admit any discriminating solution: Indeed we have $Y \succ_k X \succ_k Y$, so, if there is a solution, it must assign the same value to X, Y; thus, if the keys are to be unequal, then $\mathcal{P}_1$ would be unsolvable; or else, we could have guessed the key equality $X = Y$ (inference rule 6), and reduced the problem to one single equation $X = enc(Z, X)$, which is solvable as $Z = dec(X, X)$.

(ii) Problem $\mathcal{P}_2$ is unsolvable: First, we have $X \succ_k T \succ_k X$, so $\mathcal{P}_2$ does not admit any discriminating solution; if the keys are to be unequal, one deduces then that there is no solution. On the other hand, if we had guessed $X = T$, the problem to solve would reduce to: $Z = enc(X, X)$, $Z = dec(X, X)$, for which there can be no solution at all modulo the 2-rule system R.

(iii) No discriminating solution is possible for $\mathcal{P}_3$, since $X \succ_k Z \succ_k Y \succ_k X$. And guessing an equality on the keys, such as e.g., $Y = Z$, would transform the problem into one of the two problems just studied. □

NKDC is Sufficient: Let $\mathcal{P}$ be an admissible problem (with a non-empty kernel), satisfying NKDC. We propose then a method for constructing a discriminating solution, assuming that the graph G_P is connected (the general case follows). The idea is easily understood on an example. First a definition.

Definition 3. *Let Γ be any connected component on the graph G_P of P.*

i) A base-node *on Γ, for P and its kernel P', is any node $V_0 \in \Gamma$ that is minimal for the key-dependency relation $\succ_k$.*

ii) An end-node *for P on Γ is any node X such that:*
- there is an incoming path at X each arc of which is labeled with p_1 or p_2;
- there is no outgoing arc from the node X.

On any given component Γ, there may be several base-nodes and end-nodes; note also that *there may not be any end-node*.

Example 3. Consider the following trimmed problem:

$$(P): \quad Z = X.W, \; X = enc(U, V), \; U = enc(V, T), \; V = enc(Y, U)$$

whose kernel P' is formed of the three *enc*-equations. Its graph is connected, and there is a single maximal (loop-free) path between the nodes X and Y:

$$Z \xrightarrow[p_1]{\; p_2 \; W \;} X \underset{h_V}{\overset{\overline{h}_V}{\rightleftarrows}} U \underset{h_T}{\overset{\overline{h}_T}{\rightleftarrows}} V \underset{h_U}{\overset{\overline{h}_U}{\rightleftarrows}} Y$$

This graph satisfies NKDC: indeed, we only have two key-dependencies $X \succ_k V$ and $Y \succ_k U$; there are no key-dependency cycles, and both U and V are *minimal* for the relation $\succ_k$. So, either U or V can be chosen as a 'base-node'; W is the only 'end-node'. Thus, if we take U to be the base-node, the following substitution is a discriminating solution for P:

$$V = \overline{h}_T(U), \; Y = \overline{h}_U(V) = \overline{h}_U \overline{h}_T(U), \; X = h_V(U), \; Z = X.W$$

with U, T and W arbitrary. The value assigned by this solution to any given node/variable is obtained by 'propagating' the values assigned to the chosen base-node and end-node, along the unique paths from the given node to these latter nodes; propagation is done by using the homomorphisms (resp. pairings) labeling the arcs of these paths.   □

Lemma 6. *If P is admissible and satisfies NKDC, then P admits a discriminating solution.*

Proof. We show that the kernel of P admits a discriminating solution. (Such a substitution, under a condition of minimality, can be extended as a solution to the entire problem, as illustrated in the Example above, via propagation on every connected component of G_P. For a formal algorithm, see Section 3.2 below.) So we assume P itself to be simple, and G_P to be connected.

On every given connected component Γ of the graph $G = G_P$ of P, choose some base-node V; then, for any given node X on Γ, we solve for X by propagating to X any value v that is assignable to the chosen base-node V: i.e., we set $X = \alpha_{XV}(v)$, where α_{XV} is the word over $\mathcal{H}$ labeling the (unique) loop-free path from X to the base-node V. Such an assignment is sound; i.e., the term assigned to X is well-defined: indeed, none of the arcs along this path can be labeled with a h_X or $\overline{h}_X$: otherwise we would have $V \succ_k X$, and V wouldn't be $\succ_k$-minimal on Γ.

Note that if T is any key of $\mathcal{P}$ which is *not* also a node on $G_\mathcal{P}$, then T is 'unaffected' by such a substitution, i.e., it keeps its symbolic (or constant) value. Note also that if X, Y are any two distinct variables not 'made equal by any equalities' of $\mathcal{P}$, then they must correspond to distinct nodes of $G_{\mathcal{P}'}$, then (by admissibility), the words labeling the paths from X, Y to the base-node V must be distinct, consequently $\alpha_{XV}(v) \neq \alpha_{YV}(v)$ by Perfect Encryption. We deduce that the substitution constructed is indeed a discriminating solution. $\square$

To conclude this subsection, we observe that if σ is a non-discriminating solution for $\mathcal{P}$, then there is a variant $\mathcal{P}_1$ of $\mathcal{P}$, obtained by applying Inference Rule 6 to equate some further keys (possibly followed by further trimming rules) as appropriate, such that σ defines a discriminating solution for $\mathcal{P}_1$.

3.2   Solving a Problem in Standard Form

We can formulate now a non-deterministic decision procedure for solving any HE-unification problem, given in standard form. For that, we need the notion of a minimal discriminating solution for the kernel of a trimmed problem (condition needed for propagation as solution to the entire problem):

Definition 4. *Let $\mathcal{P}$ be a HE-unification problem in trimmed form, $\mathcal{P}'$ its kernel, and σ, τ two discriminating solutions for $\mathcal{P}'$. We define $\sigma \gg \tau$ iff:*

- *$Dom(\sigma) \supsetneq Dom(\tau)$, and*
- *$\exists$ variables Z, X of $\mathcal{P}$ such that $Z \succ X$ and $Z \in Dom(\sigma) \smallsetminus Dom(\tau)$.*

σ is said to be a minimal discriminating solution *for the kernel $\mathcal{P}'$ iff it is minimal for the strict relation $\gg$.*

A minimal discriminating solution for the kernel $\mathcal{P}'$, of a trimmed problem $\mathcal{P}$, thus does not instantiate any key variable that is not also a node on $G_{\mathcal{P}'}$.

Example 4. The following problem is in trimmed form :

$$V = V_1.V_2, \quad V_1 = enc(W_1, V), \quad V_2 = enc(W_2, V).$$

Its admissible kernel is formed of the two *enc*-equations above; its graph has two connected components, respectively with V_1 and V_2 as base-nodes (there are no end-nodes). Among the following two *discriminating solutions for this kernel*, constructed as described in the previous lemma:

$$\alpha: \quad W_1 = dec(V_1, V), \quad W_2 = dec(V_2, V), \quad V_1 = a, \quad V_2 = b,$$
$$\tau: \quad W_1 = dec(V_1, V), \quad W_2 = dec(V_2, V), \quad V_1 = a, \quad V_2 = b, \quad V = c$$

only α is minimal: we have $\tau \gg \alpha$. $\square$

The Algorithm $\mathcal{A}$: *Given:* $\mathcal{P}$ = an HE-unification problem $\mathcal{P}$, in standard form. G = the dependency graph for $\mathcal{P}$.

1a. Non-deterministically generate a non-Failing trimmed equivalent of $\mathcal{P}$.
1b. Replace $\mathcal{P}$ by the trimmed equivalent thus obtained; set
$\quad \mathcal{P}' = $ the kernel of $\mathcal{P}$; $G' = $ the sub-graph of $G_{\mathcal{P}}$ for $\mathcal{P}'$.
2a. Check for the criterion NKDC on every connected component of G';
2b. If NKDC is unsatisfied on some component, exit with 'Fail';
3a. On each connected component Γ of G', choose a *base-node* V_Γ for $\mathcal{P}'$
$\quad$ (i.e., a minimal node for the key-dependency relation $\succ_k$).
3b. Build a *minimal* discriminating substitution for the variables on each com-
$\quad$ ponent, derived via propagation from V_Γ to each of them (as described in the
$\quad$ previous lemma). Let σ' be the substitution, solution for $\mathcal{P}'$, thus obtained.
4a. On each connected component of G, choose all the end-nodes (if any).
4b. To the variables of the equalities and pairings of G that are not in G', assign
$\quad$ the values deduced (via propagation) from σ', and the values assigned to the
$\quad$ end-nodes (if any); return $\sigma = $ substitution thus obtained, as solution to $\mathcal{P}$.

Note that the Step 4b of the algorithm assigns a *unique, well-defined term modulo HE* to the variables of G which are not in G'; indeed $\mathcal{P}$ being trimmed, we have the following:

- No two distinct pairing equations of $\mathcal{P}$ can have the same variable to the left; and the variable to the left of any pairing equation is *not* a node on $G_{\mathcal{P}'}$.

- Variables to the left or to the right of the equalities of $\mathcal{P}$ have a unique representative node on the graph.

Proposition 2. *The algorithm $\mathcal{A}$ is sound and complete.*

Proof. Given $\mathcal{P}$ in standard form, and $\mathcal{P}_1$ a problem derived from $\mathcal{P}$ by applying $\mathcal{A}$, let σ_1 be a solution for $\mathcal{P}_1$; one can then deduce from σ_1 a solution σ for $\mathcal{P}$; so $\mathcal{A}$ is sound. The algorithm $\mathcal{A}$ is complete as well: this follows from the fact that NKDC is a necessary condition for any simple problem to admit a discriminating solution; and on the other hand, if there is a non-discriminating solution σ for $\mathcal{P}$, then, following $\mathcal{A}$, we can derive a trimmed variant of $\mathcal{P}$ (after an inference based on Rule 6), for which σ gives a discriminating solution. $\qquad\square$

Proposition 3. *Unification modulo HE, based on algorithm $\mathcal{A}$, is NP-hard and is in NEXPTIME wrt the number of initial equations for any problem $\mathcal{P}$ (given in standard form).*

Proof. We first observe that an upper bound $N(\mathcal{P})$ for the number of equations generated by trimming $\mathcal{P}$ can be given as follows: Let Variant$(\mathcal{P})$ be the set of all 'variants' of $\mathcal{P}$ obtained by adding some further equalities between the keys; let m be the sup of the number of equations in all these variants, and let d stand for the sup of the sp-depths of the variables in these variants. Then $N(\mathcal{P}) \leq m\, 2^d$.

Once $\mathcal{P}$ is trimmed, the algorithm $\mathcal{A}$ runs on its kernel $\mathcal{P}'$ in time NP wrt the number of equations in $\mathcal{P}'$: indeed, checking for the criterion NKDC on any component of $G_{\mathcal{P}'}$ can be done in time NP wrt the number of nodes on $G_{\mathcal{P}'}$; and solving for $\mathcal{P}$ in terms of the solutions for $\mathcal{P}'$ is also in NP. We therefore get a NEXPTIME upper bound for the algorithm $\mathcal{A}$.

The NP lower bound follows from our next Proposition, where we actually prove a more precise statement.   □

Proposition 4. *Solving simple HE-unification problems is NP-complete.*

Proof. We just saw that solving simple problems is in NP. So, we need only to prove the NP lower bound; that is done by reduction from the following so-called *Monotone 1-in-3 SAT* problem:

- Given a propositional formula without negation, in CNF over 3 variables, check for its satisfiability under the assumption that *exactly* one literal in each clause evaluates to true.

This problem is known to be NP-complete ([11]). Now consider the simple problem (without pairings) derived from the following unification problem over the 2-rule system R, involving 3 variables x_1, x_2, x_3:

$$dec(enc(dec(enc(dec(enc(a, b), x_1), b), x_2), b), x_3) =^? dec(enc(a, b), c).$$

Obviously, solving this problem amounts to saying that exactly one of the three variables x_1, x_2, x_3 is assigned the term c.   □

4   Illustrative Examples

The substitution that the algorithm $\mathcal{A}$ returns as a solution for a problem $\mathcal{P}$, is built "in a lazy style" in its steps $3a$ through $4b$: the variables of $\mathcal{P}$ get instantiated only if and when needed, as is shown in Example 5 below:

Example 5. Consider the following problem:

$$(\mathcal{P}'): \quad Z = enc(X, Y), \quad Y = enc(Z, T), \quad T = enc(Z, W).$$

The problem is simple, and its dependency graph is connected:

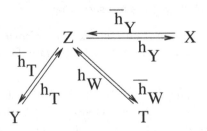

The graph does satisfy NKDC: the key-dependency relations are $X \succ_k Y \succ_k T$; so, T is the only base-node here. We solve for Z and Y, along the path from Y to T: namely $Y \to^{h_T} Z \to^{\overline{h}_W} T$; choosing arbitrarily T, W we get $Z = \overline{h}_W(T), Y = h_T\overline{h}_W(T)$ as solutions for Z, Y; and for the variable X, connected to this path at Z, we deduce $X = \overline{h}_Y(Z) = \overline{h}_Y\overline{h}_W(T)$. (Note: the base-node T has not been assigned any specific term here.)

Suppose now, the problem $(\mathcal{P}')$ is the kernel of a non-simple problem, e.g.:

$$(\mathcal{P}): \quad Z = enc(X,Y), \quad Y = enc(Z,T), \quad T = enc(Z,W), \quad X = a.$$

Then, for the above solution for its kernel to be valid, we need to check if $a = \overline{h}_Y \overline{h}_W(T)$ holds; this can be done by instantiating T, now, as $h_W h_Y(a)$. $\square$

Example 6. The following simple problem is unsolvable :

$$X = enc(Y,T), \quad Y = enc(Z,X), \quad Z = enc(W,V), \quad W = enc(V,S)$$

Indeed, its graph (is connected and) fails to satisfy NKDC:

$$X \underset{h_T}{\overset{\overline{h_T}}{\rightleftarrows}} Y \underset{h_X}{\overset{\overline{h_X}}{\rightleftarrows}} Z \underset{h_V}{\overset{\overline{h_V}}{\rightleftarrows}} W \underset{h_S}{\overset{\overline{h_S}}{\rightleftarrows}} V$$

Indeed we have $X \succ_k V \succ_k X$. So, no discriminating solution can exist; on the other hand, it is easy to check that, no matter which keys are 'made equal' (via inference rule 6), NKDC will continue to fail for the variant obtained. $\square$

5 Conclusion

We have presented a unification procedure for the theory HE modeling homomorphic encryption. The combination techniques employed seem to be general enough to be customizable for some other algebraic properties; we hope this would be a first step towards deriving a unification-based algorithm for protocol security, when the crypto-operators satisfy additional algebraic properties besides DY, cf. e.g., [4,9]. It is not difficult to show that unification modulo HE can be used to model protocols employing encryption based on ECB block chaining (with some minor adaptations if asymmetric keys are used). It would be of interest to propose a unification procedure for a rewrite system for homomorphic encryption that also captures encryption based on Cipher Block Chaining ([6]).

References

1. Anantharaman, S., Narendran, P., Rusinowitch, M.: Intruders with Caps. In: Baader, F. (ed.) RTA 2007. LNCS, vol. 4533, pp. 20–35. Springer, Heidelberg (2007)
2. Anantharaman, S., Lin, H., Lynch, C., Narendran, P., Rusinowitch, M.: Equational and Cap Unification for Intrusion Analysis. LIFO-Research Report, http://www.univ-orleans.fr/lifo/prodsci/rapports/RR/RR2008/RR-2008-03.pdf
3. Baudet, M.: Deciding security of protocols against off-line guessing attacks. In: Proc. of ACM Conf. on Computer and Communications Security, pp. 16–25 (2005)
4. Comon-Lundh, H., Shmatikov, V.: Intruder Deductions, Constraint Solving and Insecurity Decision in Presence of Exclusive-Or. In: Proc. of the Logic In Computer Science Conference, LICS 2003, pp. 271–280 (2003)
5. Cortier, V., Delaune, S., Lafourcade, P.: A Survey of Algebraic Properties Used in Cryptographic Protocols. Journal of Computer Security 14(1), 1–43 (2006)

6. Cortier, V., Rusinowitch, M., Zalinescu, E.: A resolution strategy for verifying cryptographic protocols with CBC encryption and blind signatures. In: Proc. of the 7th ACM SIGPLAN Symposium PPDP 2005, pp. 12–22 (2005)
7. Delaune, S., Jacquemard, F.: A decision procedure for the verification of security protocols with explicit destructors. In: Proc. of the 11th ACM Conference on Computer and Communications Security (CCS'04), Washington, D.C., USA, pp. 278–287. ACM Press, New York (2004)
8. Fujioka, A., Okamoto, T., Kazuo, O.: A Practical Secret Voting Scheme for Large Scale Elections. In: Zheng, Y., Seberry, J. (eds.) AUSCRYPT 1992. LNCS, vol. 718, pp. 244–251. Springer, Heidelberg (1993)
9. Lafourcade, P., Lugiez, D., Treinen, R.: Intruder deduction for the equational theory of Abelian groups with distributive encryption. Inf. Comput. 205(4), 581–623 (2007)
10. Narendran, P., Pfenning, F., Statman, R.: On the unification problem for Cartesian Closed Categories. In: Proc. of the Logic in Computer Science Conference LICS 1993, pp. 57–63 (1993)
11. Schaefer, T.J.: The complexity of satisfiability problems. In: Proc. of the 10th Annual ACM Symposium on Theory of Computing, pp. 216–226 (1978)
12. Tiden, E., Arnborg, S.: Unification Problems with One-sided Distributivity. Journal of Symbolic Computation 3(1-2), 183–202 (1987)

Argument Filterings and Usable Rules for Simply Typed Dependency Pairs*

Takahito Aoto[1] and Toshiyuki Yamada[2]

[1] Research Institute of Electrical Communication, Tohoku University, Japan
`aoto@nue.riec.tohoku.ac.jp`
[2] Graduate School of Engineering, Mie University, Japan
`toshi@cs.info.mie-u.ac.jp`

Abstract. Simply typed term rewriting (Yamada, 2001) is a framework of higher-order term rewriting without bound variables based on Lisp-like syntax. The dependency pair method for the framework has been obtained by extending the first-order dependency pair method and subterm criterion in (Aoto & Yamada, 2005). In this paper, we incorporate termination criteria using reduction pairs and related refinements into the simply typed dependency pair framework using recursive path orderings for S-expression rewriting systems (Toyama, 2008). In particular, we incorporate the usable rules criterion with respect to argument filterings, which is a key ingredient to prove the termination in a modular way. The proposed technique has been implemented in a termination prover and an experimental result is reported.

1 Introduction

Simply typed term rewriting [22] is a framework of higher-order term rewriting without bound variables based on *Lisp-like* syntax (e.g. (map F (cons 0 nil))) equipped with simple types (e.g. map : $(N \rightarrow N) \times L \rightarrow L$). Its untyped version has been called *S-expression rewriting* in [19]. To integrate these names, we refer to our framework as *simply typed S-expression rewriting* in this paper. Termination proof techniques for the (simply typed) S-expression rewriting system ((ST)SRS, for short) have been investigated in [1,3,19,20,22].

The dependency pair method [5] is a powerful termination proof technique for first-order term rewriting systems which virtually all modern termination provers are based on. The authors incorporated the dependency pair framework to the STSRSs in [3], which gave a characterization of minimal non-terminating simply typed S-expressions and extended the notions of dependency pairs and (estimated) dependency graphs into the simply typed framework. They also extended the subterm criterion [10] of first-order dependency pairs and introduced the head instantiation technique to make the simply typed dependency pair method effective even in the presence of function variables.

---

* An extended abstract [4] of a preliminary version of this paper has been appeared in the proceedings of HOR 2007.

S. Ghilardi and R. Sebastiani (Eds.): FroCoS 2009, LNAI 5749, pp. 117–132, 2009.

In this paper, we incorporate termination criteria using reduction pairs and related refinements into the simply typed dependency pair framework. For this, we use the recursive path ordering for S-expression rewriting systems [19,20]. We extend the notions of argument filterings [5] and usable rules [10,9] to the case of the simply typed framework. In particular, we incorporate the usable rules criterion with respect to argument filterings, which is a key ingredient to prove termination in a modular way. The proposed technique has been implemented in a termination prover and an experimental result is reported.

Related works and the contribution of the paper. Dependency pair methods for another similar framework of binder-free simply typed term rewriting based on *ML-like* syntax (the *applicative style simply typed framework*) have been studied by Kusakari, Sakai and others [13,14,15,16,17]. Although there are subtle differences between our approach and theirs, the main contributions of the paper and relations with results in [13,14,15,16,17] are summarized as follows.

- *Argument filtering in the simply typed setting based on the stability condition:* Argument filtering has been incorporated to the simply typed setting in the applicative style by Kusakari [13]. However, his method has some limitations that selective filtering for higher-order variables and rewrite rules of higher-order types are not considered. Extensions for such cases are not straightforward as the naive extension makes the technique unsound. This paper solves these issues by introducing a stability condition.
- *Simply typed usable rules with respect to argument filterings:* Usable rules without argument filterings [10] have been incorporated to simply typed setting in our preliminary version [4]. This paper also incorporates usable rules with respect to argument filterings [9]. Meanwhile, for the applicative style simply typed framework, usable rules without argument filterings appeared in [17] and very recently the ones with respect to argument filterings appeared in [16]. Unlike usable rules in [16,17], our usable rules need not to be closed with an (unusual) extra propagation rule.
- *Implementation in a termination prover and experiments:* In contrast to the termination proving in first-order term rewriting, few implementation of a termination prover are known for the higher-order setting. An implementation of extensions presented in the preceding clauses in a termination prover is reported for the first time in this paper.

2   Preliminaries

In this section, we briefly recall the terminology and the notations of simply typed S-expression rewriting (simply typed term rewriting in [22]).

A *simple type* is either the *base type* o or a *function type* $\tau_1 \times \cdots \times \tau_n \to \tau_0$. The set of all simple types is denoted by ST. For the sake of simplicity, we consider only a single base type, although all the results in this paper can be extended to the case of multiple base types. The sets of *constants* and *variables* of type τ

are denoted by Σ^τ and V^τ, while the sets of all constants and all variables are denoted by Σ and V. The set $S(\Sigma, V)^\tau$ of *simply typed S-expressions* of type τ is defined as follows: (i) $\Sigma^\tau \cup V^\tau \subseteq S(\Sigma, V)^\tau$, (ii) if $t_0 \in S(\Sigma, V)^{\tau_1 \times \cdots \times \tau_n \to \tau}$ and $t_i \in S(\Sigma, V)^{\tau_i}$ for all $i \in \{1, \ldots, n\}$ then $(t_0\ t_1 \cdots t_n) \in S(\Sigma, V)^\tau$. The set of all simply typed S-expressions is denoted by $S(\Sigma, V)^{\text{ST}}$. The type of a simply typed S-expression t is denoted by $\text{type}(t)$. By dropping type information, we obtain the set $S(\Sigma, V)$ of *untyped* S-expressions. We call a simply typed/untyped S-expression just an S-expression when we do not care whether it is simply typed or not. The set of variables in an S-expression t is denoted by $V(t)$. The *head symbol* of an S-expression is defined as follows: $\text{head}(a) = a$ for $a \in \Sigma \cup V$; $\text{head}((t_0\ t_1 \cdots t_n)) = \text{head}(t_0)$.

A simply typed *context* of type τ is a simply typed S-expression that contains one special symbol $\square^\tau$, called the *hole*, of type τ. The simply typed S-expression obtained by replacing the hole in a simply typed context C of type τ with a simply typed S-expression t of the same type τ is denoted by $C[t]$. A context of the form $\square^\tau$ is said to be *empty*. We omit the type of a hole when it is not important. The notion of context for untyped S-expressions is defined similarly. An S-expression s is a *subexpression* of an S-expression t (denoted by $s \trianglelefteq t$) if $C[s] = t$ for some context C, and is a *proper* subexpression (denoted by $s \vartriangleleft t$) when $s \neq t$ holds in addition. A simply typed *substitution* is a mapping $\sigma : V \to S(\Sigma, V)^{\text{ST}}$ such that $\text{type}(x) = \text{type}(\sigma(x))$ for all $x \in V$. An *instance* of a simply typed S-expression t is written as $t\sigma$. The notion of substitution for untyped S-expressions is defined similarly.

Every *simply typed rewrite rule* $l \to r$ must satisfy the following conditions: (1) $\text{type}(l) = \text{type}(r)$, (2) $\text{head}(l) \in \Sigma$, and (3) $V(r) \subseteq V(l)$. Let $\mathcal{R} = \langle \Sigma, R \rangle$ be a *simply typed S-expression rewriting system* (STSRS, for short). The set Σ_{d} of *defined symbols* of $\mathcal{R}$ is defined by $\Sigma_{\text{d}} = \{\text{head}(l) \mid l \to r \in R\}$. For *untyped rewrite rule* $l \to r$, we omit the conditions (1) and (2) and impose $(2')$ $l \notin V$ [19,20]. An *S-expression rewriting system* (SRS, for short) is a pair $\mathcal{R} = \langle \Sigma, R \rangle$ where Σ is a set of untyped constants and R is a set of untyped rewrite rules. The *rewrite relation* induced by (ST)SRS $\mathcal{R}$ is denoted by $\to_\mathcal{R}$; its reflexive closure, transitive closure, and reflexive transitive closure are denoted by $\to_\mathcal{R}^=$, $\to_\mathcal{R}^+$, and $\to_\mathcal{R}^*$, respectively.

The *root rewrite step* $\xrightarrow{\text{r}}_\mathcal{R}$ is defined as $s \xrightarrow{\text{r}}_\mathcal{R} t$ if $s = l\sigma$ and $t = r\sigma$ for some rewrite rule $l \to r$ and some substitution σ. The *head rewrite step* $\xrightarrow{\text{h}}_\mathcal{R}$ is defined recursively as follows: $s \xrightarrow{\text{h}}_\mathcal{R} t$ if (1) $s \xrightarrow{\text{r}}_\mathcal{R} t$ or (2) $s = (s_0\ u_1 \cdots u_n)$, $t = (t_0\ u_1 \cdots u_n)$, and $s_0 \xrightarrow{\text{h}}_\mathcal{R} t_0$. The non-head rewrite step is defined by $\xrightarrow{\text{nh}}_\mathcal{R} = \to_\mathcal{R} \setminus \xrightarrow{\text{h}}_\mathcal{R}$. An *argument context* is a context whose head symbol is the hole, more precisely, κ is an argument context of type τ if (1) $\kappa = \square^\tau$, or (2) $\kappa = (\kappa'\ t_1 \cdots t_n)$ for some argument context κ' of a function type and some S-expressions $t_1, \ldots, t_n$ of appropriate types. Then $s \xrightarrow{\text{h}}_\mathcal{R} t$ holds if and only if there exist a rewrite rule $l \to r$, a substitution σ, and an argument context κ such that $s = \kappa[l\sigma]$ and $t = \kappa[r\sigma]$.

Example 1 (simply typed S-expression rewriting). Let $\mathcal{R} = \langle \Sigma, R \rangle$ be an STSRS where $\Sigma = \{\ 0^\circ,\ \mathsf{s}^{\circ \to \circ},\ +^{\circ \to \circ \to \circ},\ []^\circ,\ :^{\circ \times \circ \to \circ},\ \mathsf{fold}^{(\circ \to \circ \to \circ) \times \circ \to \circ \to \circ},\ \mathsf{sum}^{\circ \to \circ}\ \}$, and $R =$

$$\left\{\begin{array}{lllr} ((+\ 0)\ y) & \to\ y & ((+\ (\mathsf{s}\ x))\ y) & \to\ (\mathsf{s}\ ((+\ x)\ y)) \\ ((\mathsf{fold}\ F\ x)\ []) & \to\ x & ((\mathsf{fold}\ F\ x)\ (:\ y\ ys)) & \to\ ((F\ y)\ ((\mathsf{fold}\ F\ x)\ ys)) \\ \mathsf{sum} \to (\mathsf{fold}\ +\ 0) \end{array}\right\}.$$

An example of rewrite sequence is $(\mathsf{sum}\ (:\ (\mathsf{s}\ 0)\ [])) \to_{\mathcal{R}} ((\mathsf{fold}\ +\ 0)\ (:\ (\mathsf{s}\ 0)\ []))$ $\to_{\mathcal{R}} ((+\ (\mathsf{s}\ 0))\ ((\mathsf{fold}\ +\ 0)\ [])) \to_{\mathcal{R}} ((+\ (\mathsf{s}\ 0))\ 0) \to_{\mathcal{R}} (\mathsf{s}\ ((+\ 0)\ 0)) \to_{\mathcal{R}} (\mathsf{s}\ 0)$.

The definition of simply typed dependency pairs is given as follows.

Definition 1 (dependency pairs [3]). A *simply typed dependency pair* (*untyped dependency pair*) is a pair of simply typed (resp. untyped) S-expressions. The set $DP(\mathcal{R})$ of all *dependency pairs* of an STSRS $\mathcal{R} = \langle \Sigma, R \rangle$ is the set of simply typed dependency pairs defined as follows:

$$DP(\mathcal{R}) = \{\langle l, r' \rangle \mid l \to r \in R,\ r' \trianglelefteq r,\ r' \ntrianglelefteq l,\ head(r') \in \Sigma_\mathsf{d} \cup V\}$$
$$\cup\ \{\langle l', r' \rangle \in Exp(l \to r) \mid l \to r \in R,\ head(r) \in \Sigma_\mathsf{d} \cup V\}$$

where the *argument expansion* $Exp(l \to r)$ is defined as follows: if $l \to r$ is of base type then $Exp(l \to r) = \emptyset$, otherwise $Exp(l \to r) = \{l' \to r'\} \cup Exp(l' \to r')$ where $l' = (l\ x_1\ \cdots\ x_n)$, $r' = (r\ x_1\ \cdots\ x_n)$, and $x_1, \ldots, x_n$ are distinct fresh variables of appropriate types. A (simply typed or untyped) dependency pair $\langle l, r \rangle$ is also written as $l \rightarrowtail r$.

Example 2 (dependency pairs). Let $\mathcal{R}$ be an STSRS in Example 1. Then $DP(\mathcal{R}) =$

$$\left\{\begin{array}{llll} ((+\ (\mathsf{s}\ x))\ y) & \rightarrowtail\ ((+\ x)\ y) & \mathsf{sum} & \rightarrowtail\ (\mathsf{fold}\ +\ 0) \\ ((+\ (\mathsf{s}\ x))\ y) & \rightarrowtail\ (+\ x) & \mathsf{sum} & \rightarrowtail\ \mathsf{fold} \\ ((\mathsf{fold}\ F\ x)\ (:\ y\ ys)) & \rightarrowtail\ ((F\ y)\ ((\mathsf{fold}\ F\ x)\ ys)) \\ ((\mathsf{fold}\ F\ x)\ (:\ y\ ys)) & \rightarrowtail\ (F\ y) & \mathsf{sum} & \rightarrowtail\ + \\ ((\mathsf{fold}\ F\ x)\ (:\ y\ ys)) & \rightarrowtail\ ((\mathsf{fold}\ F\ x)\ ys) & (\mathsf{sum}\ xs) & \rightarrowtail\ ((\mathsf{fold}\ +\ 0)\ xs) \end{array}\right\}.$$

In the simply typed framework, a root rewrite step using a dependency pair is not in general type-preserving and is distinguished from the rewrite relation.

Definition 2 (dependency relation [3]). Let $D \subseteq DP(\mathcal{R})$. The *dependency relation* $\rightarrowtail_D$ is defined as follows: $s \rightarrowtail_D t$ if there exist a dependency pair $l \rightarrowtail r \in D$ and a simply typed substitution σ such that $s = l\sigma$, $t = r\sigma$, and $head(t) \in \Sigma_\mathsf{d}$.

We say an S-expression s is *terminating* if there is no infinite rewrite sequence starting from s, otherwise *non-terminating*. We denote the set of non-terminating S-expressions by $NT(\mathcal{R})$. The set of minimal (w.r.t. the subexpression relation $\trianglelefteq$) non-terminating S-expressions is denoted by $NT_{\min}(\mathcal{R})$. Let $\mathcal{R}$ be an STSRS and D a set of simply typed dependency pairs of $\mathcal{R}$. A *dependency chain* of D is an infinite sequence $t_0, t_1, \ldots$ on $\mathrm{NT}_{\min}(\mathcal{R}) \cap \mathrm{S}(\Sigma, V)^{\mathrm{ST}}$ such that $t_i \xrightarrow{\mathrm{nh}}{}^*_{\mathcal{R}} \cdot \rightarrowtail_D t_{i+1}$ for all $i \geq 0$. For a set of dependency pairs D, we define $\mathbf{DC}(D)$ to be the set of all subsets of D that admit any dependency chain. We may omit the parameters $\mathcal{R}$ and D when they are not important.

Theorem 1 (termination by dependency chains [3]). An STSRS $\mathcal{R}$ is terminating if and only if $\mathbf{DC}(\mathrm{DP}(\mathcal{R})) = \emptyset$.

A relation $\gtrsim$ on a set of S-expressions is a *rewrite quasi-order* if it is a quasi-order that is closed under substitutions (i.e., $s \gtrsim t$ implies $s\sigma \gtrsim t\sigma$ for any s, t, σ) and closed under contexts (i.e., $s \gtrsim t$ implies $C[s] \gtrsim C[t]$ for any s, t, C). A pair $\langle \gtrsim, \succ \rangle$ of relations on S-expressions is a *reduction pair* if (1) $\gtrsim$ is a rewrite quasi-order, (2) $\succ$ is closed under substitutions, and (3) there is no infinite sequence $t_0 \gtrsim \cdot \succ t_1 \gtrsim \cdot \succ t_2 \cdots$.

Definition 3 (preservation of dependency chain). Let $\mathcal{R} = \langle \Sigma, R \rangle$ be an STSRS, D a set of simply typed dependency pairs of $\mathcal{R}$, $\varphi : \mathrm{S}(\Sigma, V)^{\mathrm{ST}} \to \mathrm{S}(\Sigma', V)$, R', D' sets of untyped rewrite rules on $\mathrm{S}(\Sigma', V)$, and $\psi : D \to D'$. A quadruple $\langle \varphi, R', D', \psi \rangle$ *preserves dependency chains* of D if (1) $s \xrightarrow{\mathrm{nh}}{}^*_{\mathcal{R}} \cdot \rightarrowtail_D t$ implies $\varphi(s) \to^*_{R'} \cdot \xrightarrow{\mathrm{r}}_{D'} \varphi(t)$, for all $s, t \in \mathrm{NT}_{\min}(\mathcal{R})$, and (2) for all $s, t \in \mathrm{S}(\Sigma, V)^{\mathrm{ST}}$ and $d \in D$, $s \rightarrowtail_{\{d\}} t$ implies $\varphi(s) \xrightarrow{\mathrm{r}}_{\{\psi(d)\}} \varphi(t)$.

Lemma 1 (preservation of dependency chain). Let $\mathcal{R} = \langle \Sigma, R \rangle$ be an STSRS and D a set of simply typed dependency pairs of $\mathcal{R}$, $\langle \gtrsim, \succ \rangle$ a reduction pair, $\langle \varphi, R', D', \psi \rangle$ a quadruple that preserves dependency chains of D such that $R' \subseteq \gtrsim$ and $D' \subseteq \gtrsim$. If $D \setminus D_\succ$ admits no dependency chains where $D_\succ = \{d \in D \mid \psi(d) \subseteq \succ\}$, then D also admits no dependency chains.

Most of modern termination provers for first-order term rewriting employ the DP framework [9]. Below we formulate a DP framework in the simply typed setting. We first formulate the notion of DP problems in a way similar to the first-order case.

Definition 4 (DP problems). A *DP problem* is a pair $\langle D, \mathcal{R} \rangle$ where $\mathcal{R}$ is an STSRS and D is a set of simply typed dependency pairs. A DP problem $\langle D, \mathcal{R} \rangle$ is *finite* if $\mathbf{DC}(D) = \emptyset$; it is *infinite* otherwise.

Using these notions, Theorem 1 is reformulated as follows.

Theorem 2 (termination by a DP problem). An STSRS $\mathcal{R}$ is terminating iff the DP problem $\langle \mathrm{DP}(\mathcal{R}), \mathcal{R} \rangle$ is finite.

The notion of DP processors for first-order DP problems [9] can be incorporated in a straightforward way.

Definition 5 (DP processors). A *DP processor* Φ on a set P of DP problems is a function from P to the set of finite sets of DP problems. A DP processor Φ on P is *sound* if, for any $p \in P$, the finiteness of all elements of $\Phi(p)$ implies that of the DP problem p.

In contrast to the first-order case, the head symbol of the rhs of a dependency pair may be a variable. Based on the *head instantiation* technique [3], however, it suffices to handle dependency pairs whose head symbols of rhs's are defined constants. Such dependency pairs are said to be *head-instantiated.* To be more precise, the head instantiation yields a sound DP processor Φ on the set of simply typed DP problems such that any $\langle D', \mathcal{R}' \rangle \in \Phi(\langle D, \mathcal{R} \rangle)$, $\mathcal{R}' = \mathcal{R}$ and D' is a set of head instantiated simply typed dependency pairs. Similarly, all techniques in [3] are reformulated in the term of DP processors, as in the first-order case [9].

Definition 6 (DP tree [9]). A *DP tree* over the DP processors Φ_i ($i \in I$) is a finite tree such that (1) each leaf node is labeled with a finite DP problem, and (2) each internal node is labeled with a DP problem p such that (a) there is a DP processors Φ_i on a domain that includes p and (b) its children nodes are precisely those labeled with each element from $\Phi_i(p)$.

The following is a corollary of this definition and Theorem 2, which is used as the basis of a design of termination provers.

Theorem 3 (termination by a DP tree). An STSRS $\mathcal{R}$ is terminating if there exists a DP tree over sound DP processors such that root node is labeled with the DP problem $\langle DP(\mathcal{R}), \mathcal{R} \rangle$.

The next theorem is an immediate consequence of Lemma 1, which is a basis of all main results presented in this paper.

Theorem 4 (termination by reduction pairs). Let $\mathcal{R} = \langle \Sigma, R \rangle$ be an STSRS, P a set of simply typed DP problems. Suppose Φ is a DP processor on P given by $\Phi(\langle D, \mathcal{R} \rangle) = \{\langle D \backslash D_{\succ}, \mathcal{R} \rangle\}$ if there exists a reduction pair $\langle \succsim, \succ \rangle$ such that some quadruple $\langle \varphi, R', D', \psi \rangle$ preserves dependency chains of D, $R' \subseteq \succsim$, $D' \subseteq \succsim$ where $D_{\succ} = \{d \in D \mid \psi(d) \subseteq \succ\}$, and $\Phi(\langle D, \mathcal{R} \rangle) = \{\langle D, \mathcal{R} \rangle\}$ otherwise. Then Φ is sound.

3   Argument Filterings

In the first-order case, an argument filtering associates each function symbol with argument positions to be selected. In the simply typed case, not only the head symbol but the depth of its occurrence in an S-expression needs to be considered additionally. For example, we may want to give different filterings for the same head symbol f in $(f \; x \; y)$ and $((f \; x \; y) \; z)$, occurring at different depths.

We first formulate the domain of argument filtering functions.

Definition 7 (depth and filtering domain). The *depth* of a simple type τ is defined as follows: $\text{depth}(o) = 0$; $\text{depth}(\tau_1 \times \cdots \times \tau_n \to \tau_0) = \text{depth}(\tau_0) + 1$. For a set X of simply typed constants and simply typed variables, the *filtering domain* is defined by $\text{FDom}(X) = \{\langle a, n \rangle \mid a \in X, 0 \leq n < \text{depth}(\text{type}(a))\}$.

By definition, $\text{depth}(\tau) > 0$ for any function type τ.

Example 3 (filtering domain). In Example 1, we have $\mathrm{FDom}(\Sigma \cup \{F^{\mathrm{o} \to \mathrm{o} \to \mathrm{o}}\}) = \{\langle \mathsf{s}, 0 \rangle, \langle :, 0 \rangle, \langle \mathsf{sum}, 0 \rangle, \langle +, 0 \rangle, \langle +, 1 \rangle, \langle F, 0 \rangle, \langle F, 1 \rangle, \langle \mathsf{fold}, 0 \rangle, \langle \mathsf{fold}, 1 \rangle\}$.

Definition 8 (recursive extraction of range type). For each $n \leq \mathrm{depth}(\tau)$, $\tau \downharpoonleft n$ is defined as follows: $\tau \downharpoonleft 0 = \tau$; $(\tau_1 \times \cdots \times \tau_m \to \tau_0) \downharpoonleft (n+1) = \tau_0 \downharpoonleft n$.

Example 4 (recursive extraction of range type). We have $((\mathrm{o} \to \mathrm{o}) \times (\mathrm{o} \to \mathrm{o}) \to \mathrm{o} \to \mathrm{o}) \downharpoonleft 2 = (\mathrm{o} \to \mathrm{o}) \downharpoonleft 1 = \mathrm{o}$.

Lemma 2 (property of depth). For each $\tau \in \mathrm{ST}$ and $n \leq \mathrm{depth}(\tau)$, (1) $\tau \downharpoonleft n$ is the base type iff $\mathrm{depth}(\tau) = n$, (2) $\tau \downharpoonleft n$ is a function type iff $\mathrm{depth}(\tau) > n$.

Proof. By induction on n. $\qquad\qquad\qquad\qquad\qquad\qquad\qquad\qquad\qquad\qquad$ □

Thus, for each $\langle a, n \rangle \in \mathrm{FDom}(X)$, $\mathrm{type}(a) \downharpoonleft n$ is a function type. So, we define $\mathrm{ArgPos}(a, n) = \{0, 1, \cdots, m\}$ when $\mathrm{type}(a) \downharpoonleft n = \tau_1 \times \cdots \times \tau_m \to \tau_0$.

Now we are ready to give the definition of argument filtering function.

Definition 9 (argument filtering). Let X be a set of simply typed constants and simply typed variables. A function $\pi : \mathrm{FDom}(X) \to \mathrm{List}(\mathbb{N}) \cup \mathbb{N}$ is an *argument filtering* for X if, for each $\langle a, n \rangle \in \mathrm{FDom}(X)$, either $\pi(a, n) = [i_1, \ldots, i_k]$ for some $i_1, \cdots, i_k \in \mathrm{ArgPos}(a, n)$ with $i_1 < \cdots < i_k$ or $\pi(a, n) \in \mathrm{ArgPos}(a, n)$. Note that if $k = 0$ then $[i_1, \ldots, i_k]$ is the empty list.

In order to select argument positions of a simply typed S-expression t specified by an argument filtering π, a natural number (together with a symbol) needs to be designated. A notion of head depth is introduced for this purpose.

Definition 10 (head depth). The *head depth* of a simply typed S-expression is defined as follows: $\mathrm{hdep}(a) = 0$ if a is a constant or a variable; $\mathrm{hdep}((t_0 \, t_1 \cdots t_n)) = \mathrm{hdep}(t_0) + 1$.

Lemma 3 (property of head depth). Let s be a simply typed S-expression and $\tau = \mathrm{type}(\mathrm{head}(s))$. Then (1) $\tau \downharpoonleft \mathrm{hdep}(s) = \mathrm{type}(s)$; (2) s has the base type iff $\mathrm{depth}(\tau) = \mathrm{hdep}(s)$; (3) s has a function type iff $\mathrm{depth}(\tau) > \mathrm{hdep}(s)$.

Proof. (1) By induction on s. (2)–(3) Use (1) and Lemma 2. $\qquad\qquad\qquad$ □

Thus, if $\mathrm{head}(s) \in X$ and s has a function type τ, then $\mathrm{hdep}(s) < \mathrm{depth}(\tau)$, and thus $\langle \mathrm{head}(s), \mathrm{hdep}(s) \rangle \in \mathrm{FDom}(X)$. The *head pair* of a simply typed S-expression t is defined by $\mathrm{hpair}(t) = \langle \mathrm{head}(t), \mathrm{hdep}(t) \rangle$. Note that a non-head rewrite step preserves both the head symbol and the head depth. Hence $s \stackrel{\mathrm{nh}}{\to} t$ implies $\mathrm{hpair}(s) = \mathrm{hpair}(t)$.

An argument filtering recursively selects the designated subexpressions.

Definition 11 (application of argument filtering). Let π be an argument filtering. For each simply typed S-expression t, the untyped S-expression $\pi(t)$ is defined as follows: (1) $\pi(a) = a$ if a is a constant or a variable; (2) $\pi((t_0 \, t_1 \cdots t_n)) = (\pi(t_{i_1}) \, \cdots \, \pi(t_{i_k}))$ if $\pi(\mathrm{hpair}(t_0)) = [i_1, \ldots, i_k]$; (3) $\pi((t_0 \, t_1 \cdots t_n)) = \pi(t_i)$ if $\pi(\mathrm{hpair}(t_0)) = i$.

Example 5 (application of argument filtering). We apply various argument filtering functions to a fixed simply typed S-expression $t = ((\text{fold } F \ x) \ y)$. If $\pi(\text{fold}, 1)$ is $[\ ]$, $[1]$ or 1, then $\pi(t)$ is $()$, (y), or y, respectively. Consider the case $\pi(\text{fold}, 1) = 0$. If $\pi(\text{fold}, 0)$ is $[0, 1, 2]$ or 1, $\pi(t)$ is $(\text{fold } F \ x)$ or F, respectively. Let $\pi(\text{fold}, 1) = [0, 1]$. If $\pi(\text{fold}, 0)$ is $[\ ]$, $[0, 1]$, or 0, then $\pi(t)$ is $(()\ y)$, $((\text{fold } F)\ y)$, or $(\text{fold } y)$, respectively.

Argument filtering can be soundly used for termination proofs provided that the filtering preserves dependency chains. However, by the presence of function variables and rewrite rules of function type, it does not always preserve dependency chains as demonstrated in the examples below.

Example 6 (unsound filtering). Let $\mathcal{R}_1 = \langle \Sigma_1, R_1 \rangle$ be an STSRS where $\Sigma_1 = \{ 0^\circ, \ f^{\circ \to \circ}, \ s^{\circ \to \circ} \}$ and $R_1 = \{ (\text{f } (F \ x)) \to (\text{f } (\text{s } x)) \}$. Its dependency pair $\langle \text{f } (F \ x), \text{f } (\text{s } x) \rangle$ admits a dependency chain $\text{f } (\text{s } x), \text{f } (\text{s } x), \cdots$. This chain is not preserved by an argument filtering π such that $\pi(\text{s}, 0) = 1$ and $\pi(\text{f}, 0) = \pi(F, 0) = [0, 1]$, because the filtered dependency pair $\langle \text{f } (F \ x), \text{f } x \rangle$ does not admit the filtered chain $\text{f } x, \text{f } x, \cdots$.

Let $\mathcal{R}_2 = \langle \Sigma_2, R_2 \rangle$ be an STSRS where $\Sigma_2 = \{ \text{f}^{\circ \to \circ}, \text{g}^{\circ \to \circ}, \text{h}^{\circ \to \circ} \}$ and $R_2 = \{ (\text{f } (\text{h } x)) \to (\text{f } (\text{g } x)), \text{g} \to \text{h} \}$. The dependency pair $\langle \text{f } (\text{h } x), \text{f } (\text{g } x) \rangle$ in combination with the rewrite rule $\text{g} \to \text{h}$ admits a dependency chain $\text{f } (\text{h } x), \text{f } (\text{h } x), \cdots$. This chain is not preserved by an argument filtering π such that $\pi(\text{f}, 0) = 1$, $\pi(\text{g}, 0) = [\ ]$, and $\pi(\text{h}, 0) = [1]$, because the filtered dependency pair $(x) \longmapsto ()$ does not admit the filtered chain (x), (x), $\cdots$. Note that the rule $\text{g} \to \text{h}$ can not be applied after filtering.

The first example suggests that filtering functions should consistently select the same argument positions from both an expression with a function variable and its instance. The second example suggests that filtering functions should consistently select the same argument positions in a subexpression when its head is rewritten by a rule of function type. The former suggestion is closely related to the extraction of the substitution part from filtered S-expressions. Notions of stabilization type and stable filtering functions are needed to show this.

Definition 12 (stabilization type). Let π be an argument filtering. For any simply typed S-expression t, the set $\text{Stab}(t) \subseteq \text{ST}$ of *stabilization types* of t is defined as follows:

$$\text{Stab}(t) = \begin{cases} \emptyset & \text{if } t \text{ is a constant or a variable} \\ \{\text{type}(t_0) \mid \text{head}(t_0) \in V\} \cup \bigcup_{j=1}^{k} \text{Stab}(t_{i_j}) \\ \quad \text{if } t = (t_0 \ t_1 \cdots t_n) \text{ and } \pi(\text{hpair}(t_0)) = [i_1, \ldots, i_k] \\ \{\text{type}(t_0) \mid \text{head}(t_0) \in V\} \cup \text{Stab}(t_i) \\ \quad \text{if } t = (t_0 \ t_1 \cdots t_n) \text{ and } \pi(\text{hpair}(t_0)) = i \end{cases}$$

Similarly to the first-order case, marking symbols of dependency pairs is useful to distinguish defined head symbols from other symbols. We define $\Sigma^\sharp = \Sigma \cup \{a^\sharp \mid a \in \Sigma_d\}$ where $a^\sharp$ is a new constant having the same type as a. For a simply typed S-expression t such that $\text{head}(t) \in \Sigma_d$, define $t^\sharp$ recursively as follows: $t^\sharp = a^\sharp$ if $t = a \in \Sigma_d$; $t^\sharp = (t_0^\sharp\, t_1 \cdots t_n)$ if $t = (t_0\, t_1 \cdots t_n)$. We also define $S^\sharp(\Sigma, V)^{\text{ST}} = S(\Sigma, V)^{\text{ST}} \cup \{t^\sharp \mid t \in S(\Sigma, V)^{\text{ST}}, \text{head}(t) \in \Sigma_d\}$.

Definition 13 (stability). Let π be an argument filtering for $\Sigma^\sharp \cup V$ and T a set of simple types. We say π is *stable* on T if for any $\langle a, n \rangle, \langle b, m \rangle \in \text{FDom}(\Sigma \cup V)$ and any $\tau \in T$, $\text{type}(a) \downarrow n = \text{type}(b) \downarrow m = \tau$ implies $\pi(a, n) = \pi(b, m)$. Note that restrictions are imposed on argument positions only for unmarked symbols.

For a simply typed substitution σ and an argument filtering π, the substitution σ_π is defined by $\sigma_\pi(x) = \pi(\sigma(x))$.

Lemma 4 (extraction of substitution). Let $t \in S^\sharp(\Sigma, V)^{\text{ST}}$ and $\sigma : V \to S(\Sigma, V)^{\text{ST}}$ be a simply typed substitution. Let π be an argument filtering for $\Sigma^\sharp \cup V$. If π is stable on $\text{Stab}(t)$ then $\pi(t\sigma) = \pi(t)\sigma_\pi$.

Proof. By induction on t. Use Lemma 3.   □

Definition 14 (stability w.r.t. rules). Let π be an argument filtering.

1. π is *stable* w.r.t. a set R of simply typed rewrite rules if for any rewrite rule $l \to r \in R$, π is stable on $\text{Stab}(l) \cup \text{Stab}(r)$ and if the rule is of function type τ then π is stable on $\{\tau, \ldots, \tau \downarrow (\text{depth}(\tau) - 1)\}$.
2. π is *stable* w.r.t. a set D of simply typed head-instantiated dependency pairs if π is stable on $\text{Stab}(l^\sharp) \cup \text{Stab}(r^\sharp)$ for every dependency pair $l \rightarrowtail r \in D$.

Example 7 (stability w.r.t. rules). Let $\mathcal{R} = \langle \Sigma, R \rangle$ be the STSRS in Example 1. An argument filtering π such that $\pi(\mathsf{s}, 0) = \pi(\mathsf{sum}, 0) = \pi(+, 1) = \pi(\mathsf{fold}, 1) = [1]$, $\pi(F, n) = [1]$ for all $F \in V^\tau$ and $n \in \mathbb{N}$ such that $\tau \downarrow n = \mathsf{o} \to \mathsf{o}$ is stable w.r.t. R. Note that for this argument filtering π, we have $\text{Stab}(((F\ y)\ ((\mathsf{fold}\ F\ x)\ ys))) = \{\mathsf{o} \to \mathsf{o}\}$ and thus the type $\mathsf{o} \to \mathsf{o} \to \mathsf{o} \notin \bigcup_{l \to r \in R}(\text{Stab}(l) \cup \text{Stab}(r))$. Furthermore, since there is no rules of type $\mathsf{o} \to \mathsf{o} \to \mathsf{o}$ in R, the stability w.r.t. R holds even if we have $\pi(+, 0) \neq \pi(F^{\mathsf{o} \to \mathsf{o} \to \mathsf{o}}, 0)$.

Let π be an argument filtering, R a set of rewrite rules, and D a set of head-instantiated dependency pairs. We write $D^\sharp = \{l^\sharp \rightarrowtail r^\sharp \mid l \rightarrowtail r \in D\}$, $\pi(R) = \{\pi(l) \to \pi(r) \mid l \to r \in R\}$, and $\pi(D^\sharp) = \{\pi(l^\sharp) \to \pi(r^\sharp) \mid l \rightarrowtail r \in D\}$. An argument filtering as a transformation of a set of dependency pairs satisfies condition (2) of dependency chain preservation in Section 2.

Lemma 5 (simulation of rewrite step). Let $\mathcal{R} = \langle \Sigma, R \rangle$ be an STSRS and D a set of head-instantiated dependency pairs. Suppose that an argument filtering π is stable w.r.t. R and D. If $s, t \in S(\Sigma, V)^{\text{ST}}$ then (1) $s \to_R t$ implies $\pi(s) \to_{\pi(R)}^= \pi(t)$, (2) $s \overset{\text{nh}}{\to}_R t$ implies $\pi(s^\sharp) \to_{\pi(R)}^= \pi(t^\sharp)$, and (3) $s \rightarrowtail_D t$ implies $\pi(s^\sharp) \overset{\text{r}}{\to}_{\pi(D^\sharp)} \pi(t^\sharp)$.

Proof. (1) By induction on s. Use Lemma 4. (2) By induction on s. (3) By Lemma 4.   □

Theorem 5 (argument filtering refinement). Let $\mathcal{R} = \langle \Sigma, R \rangle$ be an STSRS and P the set of simply typed DP problems. Suppose Φ is a DP processor on P given by $\Phi(\langle D, \mathcal{R} \rangle) = \{\langle D \backslash D_\succ, \mathcal{R} \rangle\}$ if all dependency pairs in D are head-instantiated and there exists a reduction pair $\langle \gtrsim, \succ \rangle$ on $S(\Sigma^\sharp, V)$ and an argument filtering π stable w.r.t. R and D, $\pi(R) \subseteq \gtrsim$, $\pi(D^\sharp) \subseteq \gtrsim$ where $D_\succ = \{l \longmapsto r \in D \mid \pi(l^\sharp) \succ \pi(r^\sharp)\}$, and $\Phi(\langle D, \mathcal{R} \rangle) = \{\langle D, \mathcal{R} \rangle\}$ otherwise. Then Φ is a sound DP processor on P.

Proof. By Lemma 5, $s \xrightarrow{\text{nh}}_* \cdot \longmapsto_D t$ implies $\pi(s^\sharp) \rightarrow^*_{\pi(R)} \cdot \xrightarrow{\text{r}}_{\pi(D^\sharp)} \pi(t^\sharp)$ for all $s, t \in S(\Sigma, V)^{\text{ST}}$. Hence the conclusion follows from Theorem 4.   □

Example 8 (termination proof (1)). Let $\mathcal{R}' = \langle \Sigma', R' \rangle$ be an STSRS where $\Sigma' = \{\ 0^\circ,\ s^{\circ \to \circ},\ []^\circ,\ :^{\circ \times \circ \to \circ},\ \mathsf{map}^{(\circ \to \circ) \times \circ \to \circ},\ \circ^{(\circ \to \circ) \times (\circ \to \circ) \to \circ \to \circ},\ \mathsf{twice}^{(\circ \to \circ) \to \circ \to \circ}\ \}$, and $R' =$

$$\left\{ \begin{array}{ll} (\mathsf{map}\ G\ []) & \to [] \\ (\mathsf{map}\ G\ (:\ x\ xs)) \to (:\ (G\ x)\ (\mathsf{map}\ G\ xs)) \end{array} \qquad \begin{array}{l} ((\circ\ G\ H)\ x) \to (G\ (H\ x)) \\ (\mathsf{twice}\ G) \quad \to (\circ\ G\ G) \end{array} \right\}.$$

Then two DP problems $\langle D_1, \mathcal{R}' \rangle, \langle D_2, \mathcal{R}' \rangle$ are obtained from the head-instantiation and dependency graph processors from the DP problem $\langle \mathsf{DP}(\mathcal{R}), \mathcal{R} \rangle$ where

$$D_1 = \left\{ (\mathsf{map}^\sharp\ G\ (:\ x\ xs)) \quad \longmapsto \quad (\mathsf{map}^\sharp\ G\ xs) \right\}, \text{ and } D_2 =$$

$$\left\{ \begin{array}{ll} ((\circ^\sharp\ (\circ\ U\ V)\ H)\ x) \longmapsto ((\circ^\sharp\ U\ V)\ (H\ x)) & ((\circ^\sharp\ G\ (\circ\ U\ V))\ x) \longmapsto ((\circ^\sharp\ U\ V)\ x) \\ ((\circ^\sharp\ (\mathsf{twice}\ U)\ H)\ x) \longmapsto ((\mathsf{twice}^\sharp\ U)\ (H\ x)) & ((\circ^\sharp\ G\ (\mathsf{twice}\ U))\ x) \longmapsto ((\mathsf{twice}^\sharp\ U)\ x) \\ ((\mathsf{twice}^\sharp\ G)\ x) \longmapsto ((\circ^\sharp\ G\ G)\ x) \end{array} \right\}.$$

The finiteness of $\langle D_1, \mathcal{R}' \rangle$ is shown using the subterm criterion processor [3]. We here show the finiteness of $\langle D_2, \mathcal{R}' \rangle$ based on the processor Φ given in Theorem 5. Take an argument filtering π such that $\pi(H^{\circ \to \circ}, 0) = \pi(\circ, 1) = \pi(\mathsf{twice}, 1) = 1$, $\pi(\mathsf{twice}, 0) = \pi(\mathsf{twice}^\sharp, 0) = \pi(\circ^\sharp, 1) = [0, 1]$, and $\pi(\mathsf{map}, 0) = \pi(:, 0) = \pi(\circ, 0) = \pi(\circ^\sharp, 0) = [0, 1, 2]$. Then π is stable w.r.t. R' and D_2, and we have $\pi(R') =$

$$\left\{ \begin{array}{ll} (\mathsf{map}\ G\ []) & \to [] \\ (\mathsf{map}\ G\ (:\ x\ xs)) & \to (:\ x\ (\mathsf{map}\ G\ xs)) \end{array} \qquad \begin{array}{ll} x & \to x \\ (\mathsf{twice}\ G) & \to (\circ\ G\ G) \end{array} \right\}, \pi(D_2^\sharp) =$$

$$\left\{ \begin{array}{ll} ((\circ^\sharp\ (\circ\ U\ V)\ H)\ x) \longmapsto ((\circ^\sharp\ U\ V)\ x) & ((\circ^\sharp\ G\ (\circ\ U\ V))\ x) \longmapsto ((\circ^\sharp\ U\ V)\ x) \\ ((\circ^\sharp\ (\mathsf{twice}\ U)\ H)\ x) \longmapsto ((\mathsf{twice}^\sharp\ U)\ x) & ((\circ^\sharp\ G\ (\mathsf{twice}\ U))\ x) \longmapsto ((\mathsf{twice}^\sharp\ U)\ x) \\ ((\mathsf{twice}^\sharp\ G)\ x) \longmapsto ((\circ^\sharp\ G\ G)\ x) \end{array} \right\}.$$

Take the reduction pair $\langle \gtrsim, \succ \rangle$ based on the lexicographic path ordering for S-expressions [19] with the precedence $\mathsf{twice} > \mathsf{twice}^\sharp > \circ^\sharp$, $\mathsf{twice} > \circ > \circ^\sharp$, and $\mathsf{map} > :$. Then $\pi(R) \subseteq \gtrsim$ and $\pi(D^\sharp) \subseteq \succ$ are satisfied. Therefore $\Phi(\langle D_2, \mathcal{R}' \rangle) = \{\langle \emptyset, \mathcal{R}' \rangle\}$. Hence the DP problem $\langle D_2, \mathcal{R}' \rangle$ is finite and thus $\mathcal{R}'$ is terminating.

4   Usable Rules

The termination of the STSRS $\mathcal{R} = \langle \Sigma, R \rangle$ in Example 1 can be proved using the dependency graph and the subterm criterion processors. However, the termination of combined STSRS $\mathcal{R} \cup \mathcal{R}' = \langle \Sigma \cup \Sigma', R \cup R' \rangle$ of $\mathcal{R}$ (in Example 1) and $\mathcal{R}' = \langle \Sigma', R' \rangle$ (in Example 8) can not be shown by the processors obtained so far. The problem is that no precedence produces the lexicographic path order satisfying $\pi(D_2^\sharp) \subseteq \succsim$, $\pi(R \cup R') \subseteq \succsim$—the additional constraint $\pi(R) \subseteq \succsim$ from $\mathcal{R}$ makes the reasoning in Example 8 failed. Usable rules criterion guarantees that only rewrite rules *usable* from a set of dependency pairs need to be oriented so that the termination proof can be applied in a modular way. The usable rules criterion for the first-order dependency pairs was first introduced for the innermost termination [5] and later it is extended to the general case [9,10].

By the presence of function variables, the usual first-order usable rules criterion [9,10] is not directly applicable in the simply typed setting. More precisely, the usable rules criterion does not hold for the following naive extension of first-order usable rules.

Definition 15 (naive usable rules). A relation $\blacktriangleright_R$ on Σ_{d} is the smallest quasi-order such that $f \blacktriangleright_R g$ for every simply typed rewrite rule $l \to r \in R$ with head(l) = f and $g \in \Sigma_{\mathrm{d}}(r)$. For a set D of head-instantiated dependency pairs, $\mathcal{U}_R(D^\sharp) = \{\, l \to r \in R \mid f \blacktriangleright_R \text{head}(l) \text{ for some } f \in \Sigma_{\mathrm{d}}(\mathrm{RHS}(D^\sharp)) \,\}$ where $\mathrm{RHS}(D^\sharp) = \{r' \mid l' \rightarrowtail r' \in D^\sharp\}$.

Example 9 (counterexample). Let $\mathcal{R} = \langle \Sigma, R \rangle$ be an STSRS where $\Sigma = \{\, 0^\circ,$ $\mathsf{f}^{(\circ \to \circ) \times \circ \to \circ}, \mathsf{g}^{\circ \to \circ} \,\}$ and $R = \{\, (\mathsf{f}\ F\ 0) \to (\mathsf{f}\ F\ (F\ 0)), (\mathsf{g}\ 0) \to 0 \,\}$. Then we have $\mathrm{DP}(\mathcal{R}) = \{\, (1)\ (\mathsf{f}\ F\ 0) \rightarrowtail (\mathsf{f}\ F\ (F\ 0)), (2)\ (\mathsf{f}\ F\ 0) \rightarrowtail (F\ 0) \,\}$. For $D = \{(1)\}$, there is a dependency chain $(\mathsf{f}\ \mathsf{g}\ 0) \rightarrowtail_D (\mathsf{f}\ \mathsf{g}\ (\mathsf{g}\ 0)) \to_{\mathcal{R}} (\mathsf{f}\ \mathsf{g}\ 0) \rightarrowtail_D \cdots$. However $\mathcal{U}_R(D^\sharp) = \emptyset$ and thus there is no infinite dependency chain on D and $\mathcal{U}_R(D^\sharp) \cup \{(\mathsf{cons}\ x\ y) \to x, (\mathsf{cons}\ x\ y) \to y\}$.

This example suggests that the way function variables may be instantiated should be taken into consideration. In what follows, we present a usable rules refinement for simply typed dependency pairs. As in the first-order case, the notion of interpretation [21] is crucial to obtain this.

Definition 16 (interpretation). Let $\mathcal{R} = \langle \Sigma, R \rangle$ be an STSRS, $\Gamma \subseteq \Sigma \times \mathbb{N}$, π an argument filtering, nil, cons fresh constants, and $t \in S^\sharp(\Sigma, V)^{\mathrm{ST}}$ a terminating expression with the property that $\{s \mid t \to_{\mathcal{R}}^* s\}$ is finite. Then the *interpretation* $\mathrm{I}_{\Gamma,\pi}(t)$ is an S-expression defined by

$$\mathrm{I}_{\Gamma,\pi}(t) = \begin{cases} \Pi(t) & \text{if hpair}(t) \notin \Gamma \\ (\mathsf{cons}\ \Pi(t)\ \mathrm{order}(\{\mathrm{I}_{\Gamma,\pi}(u) \mid t \to_{\mathcal{R}} u\})) & \text{if hpair}(t) \in \Gamma \end{cases}$$

where

$$\Pi(a) = a$$
$$\Pi((t_0\ t_1 \cdots t_n)) = \mathrm{I}_{\Gamma,\pi}(t_i) \qquad\qquad \text{if } \pi(\text{hpair}(t_0)) = i$$
$$\Pi((t_0\ t_1 \cdots t_n)) = (\mathrm{I}_{\Gamma,\pi}(t_{i_1}) \cdots \mathrm{I}_{\Gamma,\pi}(t_{i_k})) \quad \text{if } \pi(\text{hpair}(t_0)) = [i_1, \ldots, i_k]$$

$$\mathrm{order}(T) = \begin{cases} \mathsf{nil} & \text{if } T = \emptyset \\ (\mathsf{cons}\ t\ \mathrm{order}(T \setminus \{t\})) & \text{if } t \text{ is the minimum element of } T. \end{cases}$$

Here we assume an arbitrary but fixed total order on $S(\Sigma^\sharp, V)$. Our assumption on t implies that the S-expression order($\{I_{\Gamma,\pi}(u) \mid t \to_{\mathcal{R}} u\}$) is well-defined (via an inductive argument [10]). Clearly, when $I_{\Gamma,\pi}(t)$ is defined, $I_{\Gamma,\pi}(s)$ is defined for any subexpression s of t. We omit the subscript Γ, π when it is obvious from its context.

For a substitution σ such that $I(\sigma(x))$ is well-defined for all $x \in \text{Dom}(\sigma)$, we denote by σ_I a substitution defined by $\sigma_I(x) = I(\sigma(x))$.

Definition 17 (usable pairs w.r.t. an argument filtering). Let π be an argument filtering and $t \in S^\sharp(\Sigma, V)^{\text{ST}}$ a simply typed S-expression. Then the set $\text{UP}_\pi(t)$ of *usable pairs* in t w.r.t. π is defined as follows:

$$
\text{UP}_\pi(t) = \begin{cases}
\{\text{hpair}(t) \mid t \in \Sigma_d\} \text{ if } t \in \Sigma^\sharp \cup V \\
\{\text{hpair}(t) \mid \text{head}(t) \in \Sigma_d \cup V\} \cup \text{UP}_\pi(t_i) \\
\qquad \text{if } t = (t_0 \cdots t_n) \text{ and } \pi(\text{hpair}(t_0)) = i \\
\{\text{hpair}(t) \mid \text{head}(t) \in \Sigma_d \cup V\} \cup \bigcup_{j=1}^{k} \text{UP}_\pi(t_{i_j}) \\
\qquad \text{if } t = (t_0 \cdots t_n) \text{ and } \pi(\text{hpair}(t_0)) = [i_1, \ldots, i_k]
\end{cases}
$$

We also put $\text{UP}_\pi(T) = \{\text{UP}_\pi(t) \mid t \in T\}$ for any set $T \subseteq S^\sharp(\Sigma, V)^{\text{ST}}$.

Example 10 (usable pairs). Suppose $\pi(\text{fold}, 0) = \pi(\text{fold}, 1) = [0, 1]$. Then we have $\text{UP}_\pi(((\text{fold} + x) \; ys)) = \{\langle \text{fold}, 1 \rangle, \langle \text{fold}, 0 \rangle, \langle +, 0 \rangle\}$.

Let $\mathcal{C}_{\mathcal{E}} = \langle \Sigma^\sharp \cup \{\text{nil}, \text{cons}\}, \{(\text{cons } x \; y) \to x, (\text{cons } x \; y) \to y\} \rangle$ be an SRS.

Lemma 6 (extraction of substitution in interpretation). Let $\mathcal{R} = \langle \Sigma, R \rangle$ be an STSRS, $\Gamma \subseteq \Sigma_d \times \mathbb{N}$, and $t \in S^\sharp(\Sigma, V)^{\text{ST}}$. Suppose that σ is a simply typed substitution, π is an argument filtering which is stable on $\text{Stab}(t)$, and $I_{\Gamma,\pi}(t\sigma)$ is well-defined. Then (1) $I(t\sigma) \to_{\mathcal{C}_{\mathcal{E}}}^* \pi(t)\sigma_I$; (2) if $\text{UP}_\pi(t) \cap \Gamma = \emptyset$ and $\text{type}(F) \neq \text{type}(f) \downarrow k$ for any $\langle F, n \rangle \in \text{UP}_\pi(t)$, $\langle f, n + k \rangle \in \Gamma$ such that $F \in V$, then $I(t\sigma) = \pi(t)\sigma_I$.

Proof. By induction on t.   □

Definition 18 (simply typed usable rules). Let $\mathcal{R} = \langle \Sigma, R \rangle$ be an STSRS and π an argument filtering.

1. A relation $\blacktriangleright_{R,\pi}^{\text{ST}}$ on $(\Sigma_d \cup V) \times \mathbb{N}$ is the smallest quasi-order that satisfies:
   (1) $\text{hpair}(l) \blacktriangleright_{R,\pi}^{\text{ST}} \langle a, n \rangle$ for any $l \to r \in R \cup \text{Exp}(R)$ and $\langle a, n \rangle \in \text{UP}_\pi(r)$ where $\text{Exp}(R) = \bigcup_{l \to r \in R} \text{Exp}(l \to r)$,
   (2) $\langle F, n \rangle \blacktriangleright_{R,\pi}^{\text{ST}} \langle f, n + k \rangle$ for any $F \in V$, $f \in \Sigma_d$ and $n \in \mathbb{N}$ such that $\text{type}(F) = \text{type}(f) \downarrow k$, and
   (3) $\langle f, n + 1 \rangle \blacktriangleright_{R,\pi}^{\text{ST}} \langle f, n \rangle$ for any $f \in \Sigma_d$ and $n \in \mathbb{N}$.
2. Let D be a set of head-instantiated dependency pairs. We define the set of usable rules by $\mathcal{U}_{R,\pi}^{\text{ST}}(D^\sharp) = \{l \to r \in R \mid \langle a, n \rangle \blacktriangleright_{R,\pi}^{\text{ST}} \text{hpair}(l) \text{ for some } \langle a, n \rangle \in \text{UP}_\pi(\text{RHS}(D^\sharp))\}$.

Below we put $\mathcal{U}_{R,\pi}^{*\text{ST}}(D^\sharp) = \{l \to r \in R \cup \text{Exp}(R) \mid \langle a, n \rangle \blacktriangleright_{R,\pi}^{\text{ST}} \text{hpair}(l) \text{ for some } \langle a, n \rangle \in \text{UP}_\pi(\text{RHS}(D^\sharp))\}$. Note that $\mathcal{U}_{R,\pi}^{\text{ST}}(D^\sharp) = \mathcal{U}_{R,\pi}^{*\text{ST}}(D^\sharp) \cap R$.

Lemma 7 (property of usable rules). Let $\mathcal{R} = \langle \Sigma, R \rangle$ be an STSRS and D a set of head-instantiated dependency pairs, π an argument filtering. Let $U = \mathcal{U}^{\mathrm{ST}}_{R,\pi}(D^\sharp)$, $U^* = \mathcal{U}^{*\mathrm{ST}}_{R,\pi}(D^\sharp)$, $\Gamma = \{\langle f, m \rangle \mid \mathrm{hpair}(l) = \langle f, m' \rangle, m' \leq m, l \rightarrow r \in (R \cup \mathrm{Exp}(R)) \setminus U^*\}$, and $t \in \mathrm{RHS}(U^*) \cup \mathrm{RHS}(D^\sharp)$. (1) $\mathrm{UP}_\pi(t) \cap \Gamma = \emptyset$, (2) $\mathrm{type}(F) \neq \mathrm{type}(f) \downharpoonright k$ for any $\langle F, n \rangle \in \mathrm{UP}_\pi(t)$, $\langle f, n+k \rangle \in \Gamma$ such that $F \in V$.

Proof. Straightforward. $\qquad\square$

In the following lemma, only Lemma 7 for the case $t \in \mathrm{RHS}(U) \cup \mathrm{RHS}(D^\sharp)$ is needed.

Lemma 8 (preservation of rewrite step). Let $\mathcal{R} = \langle \Sigma, R \rangle$ be an STSRS, D a set of head-instantiated dependency pairs, and π an argument filtering. Let $U = \mathcal{U}^{\mathrm{ST}}_{R,\pi}(D^\sharp)$ such that π is stable w.r.t. U and D, $U^* = \mathcal{U}^{*\mathrm{ST}}_{R,\pi}(D^\sharp)$, $\Gamma = \{\langle f, m \rangle \mid \mathrm{hpair}(l) = \langle f, m' \rangle, m' \leq m, l \rightarrow r \in (R \cup \mathrm{Exp}(R)) \setminus U^*\}$, and $s, t \in \mathrm{S}^\sharp(\Sigma, V)$ such that $\mathrm{I}(s)$ and $\mathrm{I}(t)$ are well-defined. Then (1) $s \rightarrow_\mathcal{R} t$ implies $\mathrm{I}(s) \rightarrow^*_{\mathcal{C}_\mathcal{E} \cup \pi(U)} \mathrm{I}(t)$; (2) $s \rightarrowtail_{D^\sharp} t$ implies $\mathrm{I}(s) \rightarrow^*_{\mathcal{C}_\mathcal{E}} \cdot \xrightarrow{\mathrm{r}}_{\pi(D^\sharp)} \mathrm{I}(t)$.

Proof. (1) By induction on s. Use Lemmata 6 and 7. (2) By Lemmata 6 and 7. $\qquad\square$

We now arrive at the main result of this section.

Theorem 6 (simply typed usable rules refinement). Let $\mathcal{R} = \langle \Sigma, R \rangle$ be a finitely branching STSRS, and P a set of simply typed DP problems. Suppose Φ is a DP processor on P given by $\Phi(\langle D, \mathcal{R} \rangle) = \{\langle D \setminus D_\succ, \mathcal{R} \rangle\}$ if all dependency pairs in D are head-instantiated and there exists a reduction pair $\langle \succsim, \succ \rangle$ on $\mathrm{S}(\Sigma^\sharp, V)$ and an argument filtering π stable w.r.t. U and D, $\mathcal{C}_\mathcal{E} \cup \pi(U) \subseteq \succsim$, $\pi(D^\sharp) \subseteq \succsim$ where $U = \mathcal{U}^{\mathrm{ST}}_{R,\pi}(D^\sharp)$, $D_\succ = \{u \mapsto v \in D \mid \pi(u^\sharp) \succ \pi(v^\sharp)\}$, and $\Phi(\langle D, \mathcal{R} \rangle) = \{\langle D, \mathcal{R} \rangle\}$ otherwise. Then Φ is a sound DP processor on P.

Proof. Suppose $s, t \in \mathrm{NT}_{\min}(R)$ and $s \xrightarrow{\mathrm{nh}*} \cdot \rightarrowtail_D t$. Since $s, t \in \mathrm{NT}_{\min}(R)$ and R is finitely branching, $\mathrm{I}(s^\sharp), \mathrm{I}(t^\sharp)$ are well-defined. Hence $\mathrm{I}(s^\sharp) \rightarrow^*_{\mathcal{C}_\mathcal{E} \cup \pi(U)} \cdot \xrightarrow{\mathrm{r}}_{\pi(D^\sharp)} \mathrm{I}(t^\sharp)$ by Lemma 8. Hence the conclusion follows from Theorem 4. $\qquad\square$

Example 11 (termination proof (2)). Consider the combination $\mathcal{R} \cup \mathcal{R}' = \langle \Sigma \cup \Sigma', R \cup R' \rangle$ of the STSRS $\mathcal{R} = \langle \Sigma, R \rangle$ in Example 1 and $\mathcal{R}' = \langle \Sigma', R' \rangle$ in Example 8. Using the head-instantiation, dependency graph, subterm criterion processors, the finiteness of the DP problems other than $\langle D_2, \mathcal{R} \cup \mathcal{R}' \rangle$ is shown. We show the finiteness of the DP problem $\langle D_2, \mathcal{R} \cup \mathcal{R}' \rangle$ using the DP processor Φ given in Theorem 6. Take an argument filtering π such that $\pi(\circ^\sharp, 0) = [0, 1, 2]$, $\pi(\circ^\sharp, 1) = [0]$, $\pi(\circ, 0) = [0, 1, 2]$, $\pi(\circ, 1) = [\,]$, $\pi(\mathsf{twice}^\sharp, 0) = [0, 1]$, and $\pi(\mathsf{twice}^\sharp, 1) = [0]$. Then $U = \mathcal{U}^{\mathrm{ST}}_{R \cup R', \pi}(D_2^\sharp) = \emptyset$, π is stable w.r.t. $\emptyset$ and D_2, and

$$\pi(D_2^\sharp) = \left\{ \begin{array}{ll} ((\circ^\sharp \ (\circ \ U \ V) \ G)) \rightarrowtail ((\circ^\sharp \ U \ V)) & ((\circ^\sharp \ G \ (\circ \ U \ V))) \rightarrowtail ((\circ^\sharp \ U \ V)) \\ ((\circ^\sharp \ (\mathsf{twice} \ U) \ G)) \rightarrowtail ((\mathsf{twice}^\sharp \ U)) & ((\circ^\sharp \ G \ (\mathsf{twice} \ U))) \rightarrowtail ((\mathsf{twice}^\sharp \ U)) \\ ((\mathsf{twice}^\sharp \ G)) \qquad\qquad \rightarrowtail ((\circ^\sharp \ G \ G)) \end{array} \right\}.$$

Take the reduction pair $\langle \gtrsim, \succ \rangle$ as in Example 8. Then we have $C_{\mathcal{E}} \cup \pi(U) \subseteq \succ$ and $D_2^\sharp \subseteq \succ$. Thus $\Phi(\langle D_2, \mathcal{R} \cup \mathcal{R}' \rangle) = \{\langle \emptyset, \mathcal{R} \cup \mathcal{R}' \rangle\}$. Hence the DP problem $\langle D_2, \mathcal{R} \cup \mathcal{R}' \rangle$ is finite and thus we conclude that $\mathcal{R} \cup \mathcal{R}'$ is terminating.

5   Experiments

The techniques in this paper have been implemented based on the dependency pair method for simply typed S-expression rewriting [3], in which dependency pairs, dependency graph, and the subterm criterion have been incorporated from the first-order dependency pairs and the head instantiation technique is introduced. The program consists of about 8,000 lines of code written in SML/NJ. Constraints for ordering satisfiability problems are encoded as SAT-problems and an external SAT-solver is called from the program to solve them. Most of the SAT-encoding methods of these constraints are based on [6,18]. We employed the lexicographic path relation (comparing from left to right) for S-expressions based on quasi-precedence [19,20] for the reduction order. The dependency graph processor and the head instantiation are included in default.

For the experiment, the 125 examples used in the experiment in [3] are employed. They consists of typical higher-order functions such as fold, map, rec, filter of various types. All tests have been performed on a PC equipped with 4 Intel Xeon processors of 2.66GHz and a memory of 7GB.

The table below summarizes our experimental result. The columns below the title 'direct' show the results of experiments via our prover. The numbers of examples where termination has been proved are on the column 'success'. The numbers of examples which timeout (in 60 seconds) are on the column 'timeout'. The total time (in seconds) needed to perform the checks for all the examples are on the column 'total'. We compare our result with those obtained by the corresponding first-order dependency pair techniques applied to a (naive) first-order encoding [3] of our examples. They are listed on the columns below the title 'first-order encoding'. We also tested termination proving of our first-order encoded examples using competitive termination provers AProVE 07 [7] and TTT2 [10] for first-order TRSs.

	direct			first-order encoding		
	success	timeout	total	success	timeout	total
reduction pairs	28	0	3.439	43	0	3.830
+ argument filtering	73	0	17.397	53	0	16.606
+ usable rules	121	0	19.145	65	0	17.808
subterm criterion	98	0	3.824	59	0	3.435
+ reduction pairs	103	0	4.183	62	0	4.390
+ argument filtering	115	0	9.420	68	0	13.480
+ usable rules	121	0	12.162	68	0	13.761
AProVE				89	34	2,336.109
TTT2				94	6	1,245.639

The table shows the effectiveness of reduction pairs, argument filtering and usable rules directly formulated in the simply typed S-expression framework.

6   Related Works

Another similar framework of binder-free higher-order term rewriting is (simply-typed) *applicative* term rewriting [2,8,11,12], which is called term rewriting with higher-order variables or simply-typed term rewriting in [13,14,15,16,17]. Applicative terms can be seen as S-expressions on the signature whose function symbols are unary. Applications of first-order dependency pairs for such frameworks are studied in [2,8,11].

Dependency pairs and argument filterings for such frameworks are introduced in [13]. Besides the difference of the framework (applicative terms vs. S-expressions), the framework in [13] allows rewrite rules only of basic types. The characterization of dependency chains and dependency pairs in the presence of rewrite rules of function types are introduced by the authors in [3]. ([15] allows rewrite rules of function types but without the special treatment for dependency pairs from argument expansions as in [3].) Another notion of dependency pairs based on strong computability (SC-dependency pairs) is studied in [15,16,17].

The argument filtering in [13,14,15,17] is formulated as a function from Σ to List($\mathbb{N}$)—therefore, there are two limitations compared to the one in this paper: (1) variables are excluded from the domain of argument filterings (e.g., they always have $\pi(((F\ s_1)\ s_2)) = ((F\ \pi(s_1))\ \pi(s_2))$ when $F \in V$), and (2) eliminating head symbols is not allowed (that is, $\pi(((f\ s_1)\ s_2)) = f$ or $\pi(((f\ s_1)\ s_2)) = (f\ \pi(s_i))$ is allowed but $\pi(((f\ s_1)\ s_2)) = (\pi(s_1)\ \pi(s_2))$, $\pi(((f\ s_1)\ s_2)) = \pi(s_i)$, etc. are not). Besides these limitations, some extra conditions on the precedence, the form of the lhs of the rewrite rules and argument filterings are needed (Corollary 7.8 in [13], Theorem 6.12 in [14])—these conditions are simplified in [16] by introducing argument filterings which, instead of eliminating subexpressions, replaces them with new constants.

Compared to the usable rules in this paper, usable rules in [16,17] (for SC-dependency pairs) need to be closed with an (unusual) extra propagation rule $u \to (\rightarrowtail) v \blacktriangleright l \to r$ if $\langle F, n \rangle \in \mathrm{UP}_\pi(u)$, $F \in V(v)$, and type(l) $\downarrow k$ = type(F) so that they depend on lhs of the dependency pairs and rewrite rules. In contrast, our usable rules criterion conservatively extends the first-order case. Moreover, we obtain no larger set of usable rules than the one in [16,17] for the same set of dependency pairs. Hence our criterion is more effective to prove termination.

Acknowledgments

The authors thank Jeroen Ketema, Yoshihito Toyama, Yuki Chiba, and anonymous referees for their helpful comments. This work was partially supported by a grant from JSPS (No. 20500002).

References

1. Aoto, T., Yamada, T.: Termination of simply typed term rewriting systems by translation and labelling. In: Nieuwenhuis, R. (ed.) RTA 2003. LNCS, vol. 2706, pp. 380–394. Springer, Heidelberg (2003)
2. Aoto, T., Yamada, T.: Termination of simply-typed applicative term rewriting systems. In: Proc. of HOR 2004, pp. 61–65 (2004)

3. Aoto, T., Yamada, T.: Dependency pairs for simply typed term rewriting. In: Giesl, J. (ed.) RTA 2005. LNCS, vol. 3467, pp. 120–134. Springer, Heidelberg (2005)
4. Aoto, T., Yamada, T.: Argument filterings and usable rules for simply typed dependency pairs (extended abstract). In: Proc. of HOR 2007, pp. 21–27 (2007)
5. Arts, T., Giesl, J.: Termination of term rewriting using dependency pairs. Theoretical Computer Science 236(1-2), 133–178 (2000)
6. Codish, M., Lagoon, V., Stuckey, P.J.: Solving partial order constraints for LPO termination. In: Pfenning, F. (ed.) RTA 2006. LNCS, vol. 4098, pp. 4–18. Springer, Heidelberg (2006)
7. Giesl, J., Schneider-Kamp, P., Thiemann, R.: AProVE 1.2: Automatic termination proofs in the dependency pair framework. In: Furbach, U., Shankar, N. (eds.) IJCAR 2006. LNCS (LNAI), vol. 4130, pp. 281–286. Springer, Heidelberg (2006)
8. Giesl, J., Thiemann, R., Schneider-Kamp, P.: Proving and disproving termination of higher-order functions. In: Gramlich, B. (ed.) FroCos 2005. LNCS (LNAI), vol. 3717, pp. 216–231. Springer, Heidelberg (2005)
9. Giesl, J., Thiemann, R., Schneider-Kamp, P.: Mechanizing and improving dependency pairs. Journal of Automated Reasoning 37(3), 155–203 (2006)
10. Hirokawa, N., Middeldorp, A.: Tyrolean termination tool: Techniques and features. Information and Computation 205(4), 474–511 (2007)
11. Hirokawa, N., Middeldorp, A., Zankl, H.: Uncurrying for termination. In: Cervesato, I., Veith, H., Voronkov, A. (eds.) LPAR 2008. LNCS (LNAI), vol. 5330, pp. 667–681. Springer, Heidelberg (2008)
12. Kennaway, R., Klop, J.W., Sleep, R., de Vries, F.-J.: Comparing curried and uncurried rewriting. Journal of Symbolic Computation 21, 57–78 (1996)
13. Kusakari, K.: On proving termination of term rewriting systems with higher-order variables. IPSJ Transactions on Programming 42(SIG. 7 PRO. 11), 35–45 (2001)
14. Kusakari, K.: Higher-order path orders based on computability. IEICE Trans. on Inf. & Sys., E87–D(2), 352–359 (2004)
15. Kusakari, K., Sakai, M.: Enhancing dependency pair method using strong computability in simply-typed term rewriting. Applicable Algebra in Engineering, Communication and Computing 18(5), 407–431 (2007)
16. Kusakari, K., Sakai, M.: Static dependency pair method for simply-typed term rewriting and related techniques. IEICE Trans. on Inf. & Sys., E92–D(2), 235–247 (2009)
17. Sakurai, T., Kusakari, K., Sakai, M., Sakabe, T., Nishida, N.: Usable rules and labeling product-typed terms for dependency pair method in simply-typed term rewriting systems (in Japanese). IEICE Trans. on Inf. & Sys., J90–D(4), 978–989 (2007)
18. Schneider-Kamp, P., Thiemann, R., Annov, E., Codish, M., Giesl, J.: Proving termination using recursive path orders and SAT solving. In: Konev, B., Wolter, F. (eds.) FroCos 2007. LNCS (LNAI), vol. 4720, pp. 267–282. Springer, Heidelberg (2007)
19. Toyama, Y.: Termination of S-expression rewriting systems: Lexicographic path ordering for higher-order terms. In: van Oostrom, V. (ed.) RTA 2004. LNCS, vol. 3091, pp. 40–54. Springer, Heidelberg (2004)
20. Toyama, Y.: Termination proof of S-expression rewriting systems with recursive path relations. In: Voronkov, A. (ed.) RTA 2008. LNCS, vol. 5117, pp. 381–391. Springer, Heidelberg (2008)
21. Urbain, X.: Modular & incremental automated termination proofs. Journal of Automated Reasoning 32, 315–355 (2004)
22. Yamada, T.: Confluence and termination of simply typed term rewriting systems. In: Middeldorp, A. (ed.) RTA 2001. LNCS, vol. 2051, pp. 338–352. Springer, Heidelberg (2001)

DL-Lite with Temporalised Concepts, Rigid Axioms and Roles

Alessandro Artale[1], Roman Kontchakov[2], Vladislav Ryzhikov[1],
and Michael Zakharyaschev[2]

[1] KRDB Research Centre
Free University of Bozen-Bolzano
I-39100 Bolzano, Italy
`lastname@inf.unibz.it`
[2] School of Comp. Science and Inf. Sys.
Birkbeck College
London WC1E 7HX, UK
`{roman,michael}@dcs.bbk.ac.uk`

Abstract. We investigate the temporal extension of the description logic $DL\text{-}Lite_{bool}^{(\mathcal{RN})}$ with the *until* operator on concepts, rigid (time-independent) and local (time-dependent) roles, and rigid TBox axioms. Using an embedding into the one-variable fragment of first-order temporal logic and the quasimodel technique, we prove that (i) the satisfiability problem for the resulting logic is PSPACE-complete, and that (ii) by weakening *until* to *sometime in the future* we obtain an NP-complete logic, which matches the complexities of the propositional linear-time temporal logics with the corresponding temporal operators.

1 Introduction

Numerous temporal extensions of various description logics (DLs) have been constructed and investigated since 1993, when K. Schild published his seminal paper [19]. (We refer the reader to the monograph [15] and survey papers [3,9,17], where the history of the development of both interval- and point-based temporalised DLs is discussed in full detail.) There are various ways of introducing a temporal dimension in a DL. Temporal operators can be used as constructs for concepts, roles, TBox and ABox axioms—such concepts, roles or axioms are called *temporalised*. Alternatively, one may declare that a certain concept, role or axiom is *rigid* in the sense that its interpretation does not change in time. A number of complexity results have been obtained for different combinations of temporal operators and DLs. For instance, the following is known for combinations of $\mathcal{ALC}$ with the linear-time temporal logic $\mathcal{LTL}$: the satisfiability problem for the temporal $\mathcal{ALC}$ is

- *undecidable* if temporalised concepts together with rigid axioms and roles are allowed in the language is enough); see [15] and references therein;
- 2ExpTime-complete if the language allows rigid concepts and roles with temporalised axioms [10];

S. Ghilardi and R. Sebastiani (Eds.): FroCoS 2009, LNAI 5749, pp. 133–148, 2009.
© Springer-Verlag Berlin Heidelberg 2009

- ExpSpace-complete if the language allows temporalised concepts and axioms (but no rigid or temporalised roles) [15];
- ExpTime-complete if the language allows only temporalised concepts and rigid axioms (but no rigid or temporalised roles) [19,4].

In other words, as long as one wants to express the temporal behaviour of only axioms and concepts (but not roles), the resulting combination is likely to be decidable. As soon as the combination allows reasoning about the temporal behaviour of binary relations, it becomes undecidable, unless we limit the means to describe the temporal behaviour of concepts. Furthermore, we notice that a better computational behaviour is exhibited in cases where rigid axioms are used instead of more general temporalised ones.

In this paper, we are interested in the scenario where axioms are rigid, concepts are temporalised and roles may be rigid or local (i.e., may change arbitrarily). To regain decidability in this case, one has to restrict either the temporal [8] or the DL component [7]. A decidable (in fact, 2ExpTime-complete) logic $S5_{\mathcal{ALCQI}}$ [8] is obtained by combining the modal logic $S5$ with $\mathcal{ALCQI}$. This approach weakens the temporal dimension to the much simpler $S5$, but can nevertheless represent rigid concepts and roles and allows one to state that concept and role memberships change in time (but without discriminating between changes in the past and future).

Temporal extensions of 'weak' DLs from the recently introduced $DL\text{-}Lite$ and $\mathcal{EL}$ families with rigid roles and temporalised axioms and concepts were investigated in [7]. It was shown that even in this case the resulting temporal DLs turn out to be very complex: ExpSpace-complete for tractable $DL\text{-}Lite_{horn}^{\mathcal{N}}$ and undecidable for tractable $\mathcal{EL}$. An inspection of the lower bound proofs reveals, however, that they do not go through without the use of temporal and Boolean operators on TBox axioms. To find out the complexity of temporal $DL\text{-}Lite$ logics without these constructs is the main aim of this paper.

Our most expressive $DL\text{-}Lite$ logic $DL\text{-}Lite_{bool}^{(\mathcal{RN})}$ [2] features non-qualified number restrictions and role inclusion axioms (with limited interaction), full Booleans on concepts as well as some other constructs. In $DL\text{-}Lite_{bool}^{(\mathcal{RN})}$, the satisfiability problem is NP-complete for combined complexity, while instance checking is in AC^0 for data complexity. We also consider the fragment $DL\text{-}Lite_{core}^{(\mathcal{RN})}$ of $DL\text{-}Lite_{bool}^{(\mathcal{RN})}$ with primitive concept inclusion axioms, for which satisfiability is NLogSpace-complete for combined complexity and answering positive existential queries is in AC^0 for data complexity. (Because of this low data complexity of query answering, $DL\text{-}Lite$ logics form the basis of OWL 2 QL, one of the three profiles of OWL 2; see http://www.w3.org/TR/owl2-profiles/.)

We consider two temporal extensions, $T_{\lozenge}DL\text{-}Lite_{bool}^{(\mathcal{RN})}$ and $T_{\mathcal{U}}DL\text{-}Lite_{bool}^{(\mathcal{RN})}$, of $DL\text{-}Lite_{bool}^{(\mathcal{RN})}$. Both logics weaken $TDL\text{-}Lite_{bool}$ of [7] by allowing only rigid axioms; the temporalised concepts of $T_{\mathcal{U}}DL\text{-}Lite_{bool}^{(\mathcal{RN})}$ can be built using temporal operators *until* $\mathcal{U}$, *next-time* $\bigcirc$ and their derivatives, while in $T_{\lozenge}DL\text{-}Lite_{bool}^{(\mathcal{RN})}$ they are limited to *sometime in the future* $\lozenge$ and *always in the future* $\square$. We show that the satisfiability problem is NP-complete for $T_{\lozenge}DL\text{-}Lite_{bool}^{(\mathcal{RN})}$ and PSPACE-complete for $T_{\mathcal{U}}DL\text{-}Lite_{bool}^{(\mathcal{RN})}$, which matches the complexity of the component logics. (Note, however, that they are not simple fusions of their components.) The lower bounds hold also for the *core* fragments of $T_\Diamond DL\text{-}Lite_{bool}^{(\mathcal{RN})}$ and $T_\mathcal{U} DL\text{-}Lite_{bool}^{(\mathcal{RN})}$.

2   Temporal *DL-Lite* Logics

We begin by defining temporal extensions $T_\mathcal{U} DL\text{-}Lite_{bool}^{(\mathcal{RN})}$ and $T_\Diamond DL\text{-}Lite_{bool}^{(\mathcal{RN})}$ of the description logic $DL\text{-}Lite_{bool}^{(\mathcal{RN})}$ [1,2], which, in turn, extends the original $DL\text{-}Lite_{\sqcap,\mathcal{F}}$ language [11,12,13] with full Booleans over concepts as well as cardinality restrictions on roles and role inclusion axioms with limited interaction.

The language of $T_\mathcal{U} DL\text{-}Lite_{bool}^{(\mathcal{RN})}$ contains *object names* $a_0, a_1, \ldots$, *concept names* $A_0, A_1, \ldots$, *local role names* $P_0, P_1, \ldots$ and *rigid role names* $G_0, G_1, \ldots$; *role names* S, *roles* R, *basic concepts* B and *concepts* C are defined as follows:

$$S \quad ::= \quad P_i \quad | \quad G_i, \qquad\qquad\qquad R \quad ::= \quad S \quad | \quad S^-,$$

$$B \quad ::= \quad \bot \quad | \quad A_i \quad | \quad \geq q\,R,$$

$$C \quad ::= \quad B \quad | \quad \neg C \quad | \quad C_1 \sqcap C_2 \quad | \quad \geq q\,R.C \quad | \quad C_1 \mathcal{U} C_2,$$

where $q \geq 1$ is a natural number. The language $T_\Diamond DL\text{-}Lite_{bool}^{(\mathcal{RN})}$ is a proper sub-language of $T_\mathcal{U} DL\text{-}Lite_{bool}^{(\mathcal{RN})}$ in which the until operator $\mathcal{U}$ can occur only in concepts of the form $\top\,\mathcal{U}\,C$, where $\top = \neg\bot$. As usual in temporal logic, we denote $\top\,\mathcal{U}\,C$ by $\Diamond C$, and also write $\Box C$ for $\neg\Diamond\neg C$ and $\bigcirc C$ for $\bot\,\mathcal{U}\,C$ (so, $\bigcirc$ is a $T_\mathcal{U} DL\text{-}Lite_{bool}^{(\mathcal{RN})}$ concept construct). Other standard abbreviations we use are as follows: $C_1 \sqcup C_2 = \neg(\neg C_1 \sqcap \neg C_2)$, $\exists R = (\geq 1\,R)$ and $\leq q\,R = \neg(\geq q+1\,R)$.

A $T_\mathcal{U} DL\text{-}Lite_{bool}^{(\mathcal{RN})}$ *TBox* $\mathcal{T}$ is a finite set of *concept inclusions, role inclusions,* and *role disjointness, irreflexivity and reflexivity constraints* of the form:

$$C_1 \sqsubseteq C_2, \qquad R_1 \sqsubseteq R_2, \qquad \mathsf{Dis}(R_1, R_2), \qquad \mathsf{Irr}(S) \qquad \text{and} \qquad \mathsf{Ref}(S).$$

We write $inv(R)$ for S^- if $R = S$, and for S if $R = S^-$. Denote by $\sqsubseteq_\mathcal{T}^*$ the reflexive and transitive closure of $\{(R, R'), (inv(R), inv(R')) \mid R \sqsubseteq R' \in \mathcal{T}\}$. Say that R' is a *proper sub-role of* R in $\mathcal{T}$ if $R' \sqsubseteq_\mathcal{T}^* R$ and $R \not\sqsubseteq_\mathcal{T}^* R'$. The following syntactic conditions, limiting the interaction between number restrictions and role inclusions, are imposed on $T_\mathcal{U} DL\text{-}Lite_{bool}^{(\mathcal{RN})}$ TBoxes $\mathcal{T}$ (cf. [18,2]):

(inter) if R has a proper sub-role in $\mathcal{T}$ then $\mathcal{T}$ contains no *negative occurrences*[1] of number restrictions $\geq q\,R$ or $\geq q\,inv(R)$ with $q \geq 2$;

(exists) $\mathcal{T}$ may contain only positive occurrences of $\geq q\,R.C$, and if $\geq q\,R.C$ occurs in $\mathcal{T}$ then $\mathcal{T}$ does not contain negative occurrences of $\geq q'\,R$ or $\geq q'\,inv(R)$, for $q' \geq 2$.

It follows that no TBox can contain both a functionality constraint $\geq 2\,R \sqsubseteq \bot$ and an occurrence of $\geq q\,R.C$, for some $q \geq 1$ and some role R. (These conditions are required for NP-completeness of satisfiability in $DL\text{-}Lite_{bool}^{(\mathcal{RN})}$.)

---

[1] An occurrence of a concept on the right-hand (left-hand) side of a concept inclusion is called *negative* if it is in the scope of an odd (even) number of negations $\neg$; otherwise the occurrence is called *positive*.

An *ABox* $\mathcal{A}$ consists of assertions of the form:

$$\bigcirc^n B(a), \quad \Box B(a), \quad \bigcirc^n S(a,b), \quad \Box S(a,b), \quad \bigcirc^n \neg S(a,b) \quad \text{and} \quad \Box \neg S(a,b),$$

where B is a basic concept, S a (local or rigid) role name, a,b object names and $\bigcirc^n$ denotes the sequence of n *next-time operators* $\bigcirc$, for $n \geq 0$ (inverse roles could also be allowed in the ABoxes, but they are just syntactic sugar). The TBox and ABox together form the *knowledge base* (KB) $\mathcal{K} = (\mathcal{T}, \mathcal{A})$.

A $T_U DL\text{-}Lite_{bool}^{(\mathcal{RN})}$ *interpretation* $\mathcal{I}$ is a function on natural numbers $\mathbb{N}$:

$$\mathcal{I}(n) = (\Delta^{\mathcal{I}}, a_0^{\mathcal{I}}, \ldots, A_0^{\mathcal{I}(n)}, \ldots, P_0^{\mathcal{I}(n)}, \ldots, G_0^{\mathcal{I}(n)}, \ldots),$$

where $\Delta^{\mathcal{I}}$ is a non-empty set, the *domain of* $\mathcal{I}$, $a_i^{\mathcal{I}} \in \Delta^{\mathcal{I}}$, $A_i^{\mathcal{I}(n)} \subseteq \Delta^{\mathcal{I}}$ and $P_i^{\mathcal{I}(n)}, G_i^{\mathcal{I}(n)} \subseteq \Delta^{\mathcal{I}} \times \Delta^{\mathcal{I}}$, for all i and all $n \in \mathbb{N}$. Furthermore, $a_i^{\mathcal{I}} \neq a_j^{\mathcal{I}}$ for $i \neq j$ (which means that we adopt the *unique name Assumption*) and $G_i^{\mathcal{I}(n)} = G_i^{\mathcal{I}(m)}$, for all $n, m \in \mathbb{N}$. The role and concept constructs are interpreted in $\mathcal{I}$ as follows: for each moment of time $n \in \mathbb{N}$,

$$(S^-)^{\mathcal{I}(n)} = \{(y,x) \in \Delta^{\mathcal{I}} \times \Delta^{\mathcal{I}} \mid (x,y) \in S^{\mathcal{I}(n)}\}, \qquad \perp^{\mathcal{I}(n)} = \emptyset,$$

$$(\geq q\,R.C)^{\mathcal{I}(n)} = \{x \in \Delta^{\mathcal{I}} \mid \sharp\{y \in C^{\mathcal{I}} \mid (x,y) \in R^{\mathcal{I}(n)}\} \geq q\}, \quad (\neg C)^{\mathcal{I}(n)} = \Delta^{\mathcal{I}} \setminus C^{\mathcal{I}(n)},$$

$$(C \sqcap D)^{\mathcal{I}(n)} = C^{\mathcal{I}(n)} \cap D^{\mathcal{I}(n)}, \qquad\qquad (\geq q\,R)^{\mathcal{I}(n)} = (\geq q\,R.\neg\perp)^{\mathcal{I}(n)},$$

$$(C \,\mathcal{U}\, D)^{\mathcal{I}(n)} = \bigcup_{k>n}\left(D^{\mathcal{I}(k)} \cap \bigcap_{n<m<k} C^{\mathcal{I}(m)}\right),$$

where $\sharp X$ is the cardinality of X. The satisfaction relation $\models$ is defined as follows:

$$\mathcal{I} \models C_1 \sqsubseteq C_2 \quad \text{iff} \quad C_1^{\mathcal{I}(n)} \subseteq C_2^{\mathcal{I}(n)} \text{ for all } n \geq 0,$$

$$\mathcal{I} \models R_1 \sqsubseteq R_2 \quad \text{iff} \quad R_1^{\mathcal{I}(n)} \subseteq R_2^{\mathcal{I}(n)} \text{ for all } n \geq 0,$$

$$\mathcal{I} \models \mathsf{Dis}(R_1, R_2) \quad \text{iff} \quad \forall n \geq 0\,(R_1^{\mathcal{I}(n)} \cap R_2^{\mathcal{I}(n)} = \emptyset) \quad (R_1 \text{ and } R_2 \text{ are } \textit{disjoint}),$$

$$\mathcal{I} \models \mathsf{Irr}(S) \quad \text{iff} \quad \forall x \in \Delta^{\mathcal{I}} \,\forall n \geq 0 \,(x,x) \notin S^{\mathcal{I}(n)} \quad (S \text{ is } \textit{irreflexive}),$$

$$\mathcal{I} \models \mathsf{Ref}(S) \quad \text{iff} \quad \forall x \in \Delta^{\mathcal{I}} \,\forall n \geq 0 \,(x,x) \in S^{\mathcal{I}(n)} \quad (S \text{ is } \textit{reflexive}),$$

$$\mathcal{I} \models \bigcirc^n B(a) \text{ iff } a^{\mathcal{I}} \in B^{\mathcal{I}(n)}, \qquad \mathcal{I} \models \Box B(a) \text{ iff } \forall n > 0\, a^{\mathcal{I}} \in B^{\mathcal{I}(n)},$$

$$\mathcal{I} \models \bigcirc^n S(a,b) \text{ iff } (a^{\mathcal{I}}, b^{\mathcal{I}}) \in S^{\mathcal{I}(n)}, \quad \mathcal{I} \models \Box S(a,b) \text{ iff } \forall n > 0\, (a^{\mathcal{I}}, b^{\mathcal{I}}) \in S^{\mathcal{I}(n)},$$

$$\mathcal{I} \models \bigcirc^n \neg S(a,b) \text{ iff } (a^{\mathcal{I}}, b^{\mathcal{I}}) \notin S^{\mathcal{I}(n)}, \quad \mathcal{I} \models \Box \neg S(a,b) \text{ iff } \forall n > 0\, (a^{\mathcal{I}}, b^{\mathcal{I}}) \notin S^{\mathcal{I}(n)}.$$

We say that $\mathcal{I}$ is a *model* of a KB $\mathcal{K}$ if $\mathcal{I} \models \alpha$ for all α in $\mathcal{K}$; in this case we also write $\mathcal{I} \models \mathcal{K}$. A concept A (role R) is *satisfiable w.r.t.* $\mathcal{K}$ if there are a model $\mathcal{I}$ of $\mathcal{K}$ and $n \geq 0$ such that $A^{\mathcal{I}(n)} \neq \emptyset$ ($R^{\mathcal{I}(n)} \neq \emptyset$). Note that role symmetry $\mathsf{Sym}(S)$ and asymmetry $\mathsf{Asym}(S)$ constraints are syntactic sugar in this language: they can be equivalently replaced with $S^- \sqsubseteq S$ and $\mathsf{Dis}(S, S^-)$, respectively.

It should be noted that $T_U DL\text{-}Lite_{bool}^{(\mathcal{RN})}$ is not a simple fusion of $DL\text{-}Lite_{bool}^{(\mathcal{RN})}$ and $\mathcal{LTL}$. Indeed, consider $\mathcal{K} = (\{\Diamond \exists R^- \sqsubseteq \perp, \exists R \sqsubseteq \Diamond \exists R\}, \{\exists R(a)\})$. Clearly, $\mathcal{K}$ is not satisfiable in $T_U DL\text{-}Lite_{bool}^{(\mathcal{RN})}$. However, it is satisfiable both in $DL\text{-}Lite_{bool}^{(\mathcal{RN})}$ (if we substitute the temporal concepts by fresh $DL\text{-}Lite_{bool}^{(\mathcal{RN})}$ concepts) and in $\mathcal{LTL}$ (by substituting $\exists R$ concepts with fresh atomic propositions).

3 $T_{\mathcal{U}}DL\text{-}Lite_{bool}^{(\mathcal{RN})}$ and First-Order Temporal Logic

For a $T_{\mathcal{U}}DL\text{-}Lite_{bool}^{(\mathcal{RN})}$ KB $\mathcal{K} = (\mathcal{T}, \mathcal{A})$, let $ob(\mathcal{A})$ be the set of all object names occurring in $\mathcal{A}$. Let $role^{\pm}(\mathcal{K})$ be the set of rigid and local role names, together with their inverses, occurring in $\mathcal{K}$ and $grole^{\pm}(\mathcal{K})$ its subset of rigid roles. For $R \in role^{\pm}(\mathcal{K})$, let $Q_{\mathcal{K}}^{R}$ be the set of natural numbers containing 1 and all the numerical parameters q for which $\geq q\, R$ or $\geq q\, R.C$ occurs in $\mathcal{K}$.

With every object name $a \in ob(\mathcal{A})$ we associate the individual constant a of $\mathcal{QTL}^1$, the one-variable fragment of first-order temporal logic over $(\mathbb{N}, <)$, and with every concept name A the unary predicate $A(x)$ from the signature of $\mathcal{QTL}^1$. For each $R \in role^{\pm}(\mathcal{K})$, we also introduce $|Q_{\mathcal{K}}^{R}|$ fresh unary predicates $E_q R(x)$, for $q \in Q_{\mathcal{K}}^{R}$. Intuitively, for each $n \geq 0$, $E_1 R(x)$ and $E_1 R^{-}(x)$ represent the domain and range of R at moment n (i.e., $E_1 R(x)$ and $E_1 R^{-}(x)$ are interpreted by the sets of points with **at least one** R-successor and **at least one** R-predecessor at moment n, respectively), while $E_q R(x)$ and $E_q R^{-}(x)$ represent the sets of points with **at least q** distinct R-successors and **at least q** distinct R-predecessors at moment n.

Let us consider first the sub-language of $T_{\mathcal{U}}DL\text{-}Lite_{bool}^{(\mathcal{RN})}$ without qualified number restrictions and role constraints; we denote it by $T_{\mathcal{U}}DL\text{-}Lite_{bool}^{(\mathcal{RN})^{-}}$. Without loss of generality, we will assume that $Q_{\mathcal{K}}^{R} \subseteq Q_{\mathcal{K}}^{R'}$ whenever $R \sqsubseteq_{\mathcal{T}}^{*} R'$ (for if this is not the case we can always add the missing numbers to $Q_{\mathcal{K}}^{R'}$ by introducing fictitious concept inclusions of the form $\bot \sqsubseteq \geq q\, R'$). By induction on the construction of a $T_{\mathcal{U}}DL\text{-}Lite_{bool}^{(\mathcal{RN})^{-}}$ concept C we define the $\mathcal{QTL}^1$-formula C^*:

$$\bot^* = \bot, \qquad\qquad\qquad (A)^* = A(x),$$
$$(\geq q\, R)^* = E_q R(x), \qquad\qquad (\neg C)^* = \neg C^*(x),$$
$$(C_1 \sqcap C_2)^* = C_1^*(x) \wedge C_2^*(x), \qquad (C_1\, \mathcal{U}\, C_2)^* = C_1^*(x)\, \mathcal{U}\, C_2^*(x),$$

and then extend this translation to $T_{\mathcal{U}}DL\text{-}Lite_{bool}^{(\mathcal{RN})^{-}}$ TBoxes $\mathcal{T}$ by taking:

$$\mathcal{T}^* = \bigwedge_{C_1 \sqsubseteq C_2 \in \mathcal{T}} \Box^{+}\forall x \left(C_1^*(x) \to C_2^*(x)\right)$$
$$\wedge \bigwedge_{\substack{R \sqsubseteq R' \in \mathcal{T} \text{ or} \\ inv(R) \sqsubseteq inv(R') \in \mathcal{T}}} \bigwedge_{q \in Q_{\mathcal{K}}^{R}} \Box^{+}\forall x \left(E_q R(x) \to E_q R'(x)\right),$$

where $\Box^{+}\varphi = \varphi \wedge \Box\varphi$. For $R \in role^{\pm}(\mathcal{K})$, we need two $\mathcal{QTL}^1$-sentences:

$$\varepsilon_R = \exists x\, E_1 R(x) \;\to\; \exists x\, inv(E_1 R)(x), \tag{1}$$

$$\delta_R = \bigwedge_{\substack{q,q' \in Q_{\mathcal{K}}^{R}, \;\; q' > q \\ q' > q'' > q \text{ for no } q'' \in Q_{\mathcal{K}}^{R}}} \forall x \left(E_{q'} R(x) \to E_q R(x)\right), \tag{2}$$

where $inv(E_1 R)$ is the predicate $E_1 S^{-}(x)$ if $R = S$ and $E_1 S(x)$ if $R = S^{-}$, for a role name S. Sentence (1) says that if the domain of R is non-empty then its range is non-empty either; the meaning of (2) should be obvious.

Now we define 'temporal slices' of the ABox $\mathcal{A}$.[2] Denote by $N_\mathcal{A}$ the maximum n with $\bigcirc^n B(a) \in \mathcal{A}$, $\bigcirc^n S(a,b) \in \mathcal{A}$ or $\bigcirc^n \neg S(a,b) \in \mathcal{A}$ (or 0 if there are no such assertions in $\mathcal{A}$). For a *rigid* role $R \in role^\pm(\mathcal{K})$, we take:

$$\mathcal{A}_R^\square = \{R(a,b) \mid \bigcirc^n R'(a,b) \in \mathcal{A} \text{ or } \square R'(a,b) \in \mathcal{A}, \text{ and } R' \sqsubseteq_{\mathcal{T}}^* R\}$$

and $\mathcal{A}_R^n = \mathcal{A}_R^\square$, for all n, $0 \leq n \leq N_\mathcal{A}$. For a *local* role $R \in role^\pm(\mathcal{K})$, we take:

$$\mathcal{A}_R^\square = \{R(a,b) \mid \square R'(a,b) \in \mathcal{A}, \text{ for } R' \sqsubseteq_{\mathcal{T}}^* R\}$$
$$\cup \{R(a,b) \mid R'(a,b) \in \mathcal{A}_{R'}^\square, \text{ for } R' \sqsubseteq_{\mathcal{T}}^* R\},$$
$$\mathcal{A}_R^n = \{R(a,b) \mid \bigcirc^n R'(a,b) \in \mathcal{A}, \text{ for } R' \sqsubseteq_{\mathcal{T}}^* R\}$$
$$\cup \{R(a,b) \mid R'(a,b) \in \mathcal{A}_{R'}^\square, \text{ for } R' \sqsubseteq_{\mathcal{T}}^* R$$
$$\text{and either } R' \in grole^\pm(\mathcal{K}) \text{ or } n > 0\}.$$

We also set $\mathcal{A}^\square = \bigcup_{R \in role^\pm(\mathcal{K})} \mathcal{A}_R^\square$ and $\mathcal{A}^n = \bigcup_{R \in role^\pm(\mathcal{K})} \mathcal{A}_R^n$, for $0 \leq n \leq N_\mathcal{A}$. The $\mathcal{QTL}^1$ translation of the ABox $\mathcal{A}$ is defined as follows:

$$\mathcal{A}^* = \bigwedge_{\bigcirc^n B(a) \in \mathcal{A}} \bigcirc^n B^*(a) \wedge \bigwedge_{R(a,b) \in \mathcal{A}^n} \bigcirc^n E_{q_{R,a},\mathcal{A}^n} R(a) \wedge \bigwedge_{R(a,b) \in \mathcal{A}^\square} \square E_{q_{R,a},\mathcal{A}^\square} R(a)$$
$$\wedge \bigwedge_{\bigcirc^n \neg S(a,b) \in \mathcal{A}} (\bigcirc^n \neg S(a,b))^\perp \wedge \bigwedge_{\square \neg S(a,b) \in \mathcal{A}} (\square \neg S(a,b))^\perp,$$

where, for a role R, an ABox $\mathcal{A}'$ and $a \in ob(\mathcal{A}')$,

$$q_{R,a,\mathcal{A}'} = \max(\{0\} \cup \{q \in Q_\mathcal{K}^R \mid R(a,a_i) \in \mathcal{A}', 1 \leq i \leq q \ \& \ a_{i_1} \neq a_{i_2} \text{ if } i_1 \neq i_2\}),$$

and $(\bigcirc^n \neg S(a,b))^\perp = \perp$ if $S(a,b) \in \mathcal{A}^n$ and $\top$ otherwise, and $(\square \neg S(a,b))^\perp = \perp$ if $S(a,b) \in \mathcal{A}^\square$ or $S(a,b) \in \mathcal{A}^n$, for $0 < n \leq N_\mathcal{A}$, and $\top$ otherwise. Finally, let

$$\mathcal{K}^\ddagger = \mathcal{T}^* \wedge \bigwedge_{R \in role^\pm(\mathcal{K})} \square^+(\varepsilon_R \wedge \delta_R) \wedge \bigwedge_{T \in grole^\pm(\mathcal{K})} \bigwedge_{q \in Q_\mathcal{K}^T} \square^+ \forall x (E_q T(x) \leftrightarrow \square E_q T(x)) \wedge \mathcal{A}^*.$$

Observe that the length of $\mathcal{K}^\ddagger$ is linear in length of $\mathcal{K}$. It can be shown in a way similar to [7, Theorem 2 and Corollary 3]) that we have:

Lemma 1. *A* $T_\mathcal{U} DL\text{-}Lite_{bool}^{(\mathcal{RN})^-}$ *KB* $\mathcal{K} = (\mathcal{T}, \mathcal{A})$ *is satisfiable iff the* $\mathcal{QTL}^1$-*sentence* $\mathcal{K}^\ddagger$ *is satisfiable.*

Proof. ($\Leftarrow$) Let $\mathfrak{M}$ be a first-order temporal model with a *countable* domain D and let $(\mathfrak{M}, 0) \models \mathcal{K}^\ddagger$ (if $\mathcal{K}^\ddagger$ is satisfiable then such an $\mathfrak{M}$ clearly exists). We denote the interpretations of unary predicates P in $\mathfrak{M}$ at moment n by $P^{\mathfrak{M},n}$ and the interpretations of constants a in $\mathfrak{M}$ by $a^{\mathfrak{M}}$ (without loss of generality

---

[2] We slightly abuse notation and, for $R \in role^\pm(\mathcal{K})$, write $\bigcirc^n R(a_i, a_j) \in \mathcal{A}$ to indicate that $\bigcirc^n S(a_i, a_j) \in \mathcal{A}$ if $R = S$, or $\bigcirc^n S(a_j, a_i) \in \mathcal{A}$ if $R = S^-$, where S is a (local or rigid) role name; similarly for $\square R(a_i, a_j) \in \mathcal{A}$.

we assume that the $a^{\mathfrak{M}}$ are all distinct). We are going to construct a model $\mathcal{I}$ of $\mathcal{K}$ based on the domain $\Delta = \bigcup_{m=0}^{\infty} W_m$, where

$$W_0 = \{a^{\mathfrak{M}} \mid a \in ob(\mathcal{A})\} \subseteq D \qquad \text{and} \qquad W_{m+1} = W_m \cup (D \times \mathbb{N} \times \{m\}).$$

The interpretations of object names in $\mathcal{I}$ are given by their interpretations in $\mathfrak{M}$: $a^{\mathcal{I}(n)} = a^{\mathfrak{M}} \in W_0$. The interpretations $A^{\mathcal{I}(n)}$ of concept names A in $\mathcal{I}$ are set to be $A^{\mathcal{I}(n)} = \{w \in \Delta \mid (\mathfrak{M}, n) \models A^*[cp(w)]\}$, where $cp \colon \Delta \to D$ is defined by taking:

$$cp(w) = \begin{cases} w, & \text{if } w \in W_0, \\ d, & \text{if } w = (d, k, m) \in D \times \mathbb{N} \times \mathbb{N}. \end{cases}$$

We call w a *copy* of $cp(w)$.

It remains to define $S^{\mathcal{I}(n)}$ for each role S in $\mathcal{K}$ and $n \in \mathbb{N}$. Let us first consider a minimal role S for which $R \sqsubseteq_{\mathcal{T}}^* S$ implies $S \sqsubseteq_{\mathcal{T}}^* R$, for every $R \in role^{\pm}(\mathcal{K})$. Let $[S] = \{R \in role^{\pm}(\mathcal{K}) \mid R \sqsubseteq_{\mathcal{T}}^* S \text{ and } S \sqsubseteq_{\mathcal{T}}^* R\}$. Consider first the case when $[S] \cap grole^{\pm}(\mathcal{K}) = \emptyset$ (i.e., S is not equivalent to a rigid role). Fix some $n \in \mathbb{N}$. We set $S^{\mathcal{I}(n)} = \bigcup_{m=0}^{\infty} S^{n,m}$, where $S^{n,m} \subseteq W_m \times W_m$ are defined inductively (on $m \geq 0$) as follows. For the basis of induction, set

$$S^{n,0} = \{(a^{\mathfrak{M}}, b^{\mathfrak{M}}) \in W_0 \times W_0 \mid S(a,b) \in \mathcal{A}^n, n \leq N_{\mathcal{A}}, \text{ or } S(a,b) \in \mathcal{A}^{\square}, n > 0\}.$$

Suppose the $S^{n,m}$ have been defined. Given $R = S$ or S^-, the *required R-rank* $r^n(R, d)$ *of* $d \in D$ *at moment* n is $\max(\{0\} \cup \{q \in Q_{\mathcal{K}}^R \mid (\mathfrak{M}, n) \models E_q R[d]\})$. By (2), if $r^n(R, d) = q$ then, for every $q' \in Q_{\mathcal{K}}^R$, we have $(\mathfrak{M}, n) \models E_{q'} R[d]$ whenever $q' \leq q$ and $(\mathfrak{M}, n) \models \neg E_{q'} R[d]$ whenever $q < q'$. The *actual R-rank* $r_m^n(R, w)$ *of* $w \in \Delta$ *at moment* n *and step* m is $\sharp\{w' \in W_m \mid (w, w') \in R^{n,m}\}$, where $R^{n,m} = S^{n,m}$ if $R = S$ and $R^{n,m} = \{(w, w') \mid (w', w) \in S^{n,m}\}$ if $R = S^-$. It will follow from our construction that $r_m^n(S, w) \leq r^n(S, cp(w))$, for all $w \in W_m$ (we leave the easy inductive proof to the reader). Consider now the two sets of *defects* $\Lambda_S^{n,m}$ and $\Lambda_{S^-}^{n,m}$ in $S^{n,m}$, where

$$\Lambda_R^{n,m} \;=\; \{w \in W_m \mid r_m^n(R, w) < r^n(R, cp(w))\}.$$

The purpose of $\Lambda_R^{n,m}$ is to identify those 'defective' points $w \in W_m$ from which precisely $r^n(R, cp(w))$ distinct R-arrows should start (according to $\mathfrak{M}$), but some arrows are missing (only $r_m^n(R, w)$ many arrows exist). To 'cure' these defects, we need a pool $F_m \subseteq W_{m+1} \setminus W_m$ of witnesses that can be used at step m of the unravelling construction: more precisely, it contains, for each role R, a countably infinite supply of points w (*witnesses for* R) such that $cp(w) = d$ and $(\mathfrak{M}, n) \models inv(E_1 R)[d]$, provided that $(\mathfrak{M}, n) \models \exists x \big(E_1 R(x) \vee inv(E_1 R)(x)\big)$ (by (1), either both $E_1 R(x)$ and $inv(E_1 R)(x)$ are empty or both are non-empty). It should be emphasised that this set will be the same for all roles R and all moments of time n. We extend $S^{n,m}$ to $S^{n,m+1}$ according to the following rules:

$(\Lambda_S^{n,m})$ If $w \in \Lambda_S^{n,m}$, then let $q = r^n(S,d) - r_m^n(S,w)$ and $d = cp(w)$. We have $(\mathfrak{M},n) \models E_{q'}S[d]$ for some $q' \in Q_{\mathcal{K}}^S$. By (2), $(\mathfrak{M},n) \models E_1S[d]$. In this case we take q *fresh witnesses* $w_1,\ldots,w_q \in F_m$ for S, remove them from F_m and then add the pairs (w,w_i), $1 \le i \le q$, to $S^{n,m+1}$; we also add the pairs (w_i,w), $1 \le i \le q$, to $S^{n,m+1}$ if $S^- \in [S]$.

$(\Lambda_{S^-}^{n,m})$ The mirror image of $(\Lambda_S^{n,m})$.

In a way similar to [2, Section 5.3] one can show that, for all $n \ge 0$ and $R = S, S^-$

$$(\mathfrak{M},n) \models E_qR[cp(w)] \quad \text{iff} \quad w \in (\ge q\,R)^{\mathcal{I}(n)}. \tag{3}$$

Once we have defined $S^{\mathcal{I}(n)}$ for S, we set $(S')^{\mathcal{I}(n)} = S^{\mathcal{I}(n)}$ for all $S' \in [S]$ and $n \ge 0$ (observe that $\mathcal{A}_S^\square = \mathcal{A}_{S'}^\square$ and $\mathcal{A}_S^n = \mathcal{A}_{S'}^n$, for all n, if $S' \in [S]$). If $[S] \cap \boldsymbol{grole}^\pm(\mathcal{K}) \ne \emptyset$, then we perform the above unravelling procedure at moment 0 and set $S^{\mathcal{I}(n)} = S^{\mathcal{I}(0)}$ for all $n > 0$, and $(S')^{\mathcal{I}(n)} = S^{\mathcal{I}(n)}$, for all $S' \in [S]$ and $n \ge 0$ (observe that $\mathcal{A}_S^\square = \mathcal{A}_{S'}^\square = \mathcal{A}_S^n = \mathcal{A}_{S'}^n$, for all n, if $S' \in [S]$).

Suppose now that S has a proper sub-role and we have already defined the $R^{\mathcal{I}(n)}$ for all such proper sub-roles R. For S with $[S] \cap \boldsymbol{grole}^\pm(\mathcal{K}) = \emptyset$, the unravelling procedure is analogous to the one described above: the basis of induction is defined as above; then, at every step, we first expand $S^{n,m}$ with the pairs that belong to its proper sub-roles, i.e., $\bigcup_{R \sqsubseteq_{\mathcal{T}}^* S, S \not\sqsubseteq_{\mathcal{T}}^* R} R^{n,m}$, and only after that start curing the defects (remember that a point in F_m can never be used twice as a witness). As the actual rank may be greater than the required rank, we have the following: for all $n \ge 0$ and $R = S, S^-$,

$$\text{if } (\mathfrak{M},n) \models E_qR[cp(w)] \quad \text{then} \quad w \in (\ge q\,R)^{\mathcal{I}(n)}. \tag{4}$$

If $[S] \cap \boldsymbol{grole}^\pm(\mathcal{K}) \ne \emptyset$ then we perform the unravelling procedure only for the moment 0 and, at each step, first expand $S^{0,m}$ with the pairs that belong to its proper sub-roles at any moment of time (i.e., $\bigcup_{R \sqsubseteq_{\mathcal{T}}^* S, S \not\sqsubseteq_{\mathcal{T}}^* R} \bigcup_{n=0}^{\infty} R^{n,m}$) and only after that cure the defects (yet again a point in F_m can never be used twice as a witness). Finally, we set $S^{\mathcal{I}(n)} = S^{\mathcal{I}(0)}$, for all $n > 0$, and $(S')^{\mathcal{I}(n)} = S^{\mathcal{I}(n)}$, for all $S' \in [S]$ and $n \ge 0$.

It remains to show that the constructed interpretation $\mathcal{I}$ is indeed a model of $\mathcal{K}$. It follows from the construction that $\mathcal{I} \models R_1 \sqsubseteq R_2$, for each $R_1 \sqsubseteq R_2 \in \mathcal{T}$. It also follows that (3) holds for every role without proper sub-roles and, for a role that has proper sub-roles, (4) is enough in view of (**inter**): by induction on the structure of concepts, one can show that, for each concept inclusion $C_1 \sqsubseteq C_2 \in \mathcal{T}$, we have $\mathcal{I} \models C_1 \sqsubseteq C_2$ whenever $(\mathfrak{M},n) \models \forall x\,(C_1^*(x) \to C_2^*(x))$, for all $n \ge 0$. Thus, $\mathcal{I} \models \mathcal{T}$. We also have $\mathcal{I} \models \mathcal{A}$ and thus $\mathcal{I} \models \mathcal{K}$.

For ($\Rightarrow$) we refer the reader to [7, Theorem 2 and Corollary 3]. $\qquad\qquad\square$

Denote by $T_{\mathcal{U}}^0 DL\text{-}Lite_{bool}^{\mathcal{N}}$ the fragment of $T_{\mathcal{U}} DL\text{-}Lite_{bool}^{(\mathcal{RN})^-}$ such that (i) it has no rigid roles, (ii) its TBoxes contain only concept inclusions and (iii) its ABoxes contain only assertions of the form $\bigcirc^n B(a)$ and $\square B(a)$.

Lemma 2. *Given a* $T_{\mathcal{U}} DL\text{-}Lite_{bool}^{(\mathcal{RN})}$ *KB* $\mathcal{K}$, *one can construct (in polynomial time) an equisatisfiable* $T_{\mathcal{U}}^0 DL\text{-}Lite_{bool}^{\mathcal{N}}$ *KB* $\mathcal{K}'$.

Proof. As a first step, one can construct a $T_{\mathcal{U}}DL\text{-}Lite_{bool}^{(\mathcal{RN})^-}$ KB such that it is equisatisfiable with $\mathcal{K}$. The proof is based on the forest model property (cf. [2, Remark 5.15]) and is similar to that of [2, Lemma 5.17]. It shows how to get rid of qualified number restrictions, role disjointness, reflexivity and irreflexivity constraints. So, without loss of generality we may assume that $\mathcal{K}$ is a $T_{\mathcal{U}}DL\text{-}Lite_{bool}^{(\mathcal{RN})^-}$ KB.

Next, we set $\mathcal{K}' = (\{\top \sqsubseteq \bot\}, \emptyset)$ if $\bigcirc^n \neg S(a, b) \in \mathcal{A}$ and $S(a, b) \in \mathcal{A}^n$, or $\Box \neg S(a, b) \in \mathcal{A}$ and $S(a, b) \in \mathcal{A}^\Box$ or $S(a, b) \in \mathcal{A}^n$, $0 < n \leq N_{\mathcal{A}}$. Otherwise, let $\mathcal{A}_0$ be the part of $\mathcal{A}$ with assertions of the form $\bigcirc^n B(a)$ and $\Box B(a)$ only and let T_0 be the part of T that contains no role inclusion axioms. Consider $\mathcal{K}' = (T_0 \cup T'', \mathcal{A}_0 \cup \mathcal{A}'')$, where

$$T'' = \{\Box(\geq qT) \sqsubseteq (\geq qT), (\geq qT) \sqsubseteq \Box(\geq qT) \mid q \in Q_{\mathcal{K}}^T, T \in grole^{\pm}(\mathcal{K})\}$$

$$\cup \{(\geq qR) \sqsubseteq (\geq qR') \mid q \in Q_{\mathcal{K}}^R, R \sqsubseteq R' \in T \text{ or } inv(R) \sqsubseteq inv(R') \in T\},$$

$$\mathcal{A}'' = \{\bigcirc^n(\geq q_{R,a,\mathcal{A}^n} R)(a) \mid R(a, b) \in \mathcal{A}^n\} \cup \{\Box(\geq q_{R,a,\mathcal{A}^\Box} R)(a) \mid R(a, b) \in \mathcal{A}^\Box\}.$$

Clearly, $\mathcal{K}^{\ddagger} = (\mathcal{K}')^{\ddagger}$. The claim follows immediately from Lemma 1.   □

4   Satisfiability of $T_{\mathcal{U}}DL\text{-}Lite_{bool}^{(\mathcal{RN})}$ KBs Is PSpace-complete

It follows from Lemma 2 that satisfiability of $T_{\mathcal{U}}DL\text{-}Lite_{bool}^{(\mathcal{RN})}$ KBs is reducible to satisfiability of $T_{\mathcal{U}}^0 DL\text{-}Lite_{bool}^{\mathcal{N}}$ KBs. Our plan is as follows. First, we define a notion of *quasimodel* for a $T_{\mathcal{U}}^0 DL\text{-}Lite_{bool}^{\mathcal{N}}$ KB and prove that such a KB is satisfiable iff there exists a quasimodel for it. Then we show that if there is a quasimodel for a KB then there exists an *ultimately periodic quasimodel* such that both the length of the prefix and the length of the period are exponential in the length of the KB. The existence of such a quasimodel can be checked in non-deterministic polynomial space, which together with Lemma 2 provides us with a PSPACE upper complexity bound for satisfiability in $T_{\mathcal{U}}DL\text{-}Lite_{bool}^{(\mathcal{RN})}$; the matching lower bound follows from the complexity of $\mathcal{LTL}$.

Let $\mathcal{K} = (T, \mathcal{A})$ be a $T_{\mathcal{U}}^0 DL\text{-}Lite_{bool}^{\mathcal{N}}$ KB. We assume $ob(\mathcal{A}) \neq \emptyset$. Denote by $ev(\mathcal{K})$ the set of all concepts of the form $C \mathcal{U} D$ occurring in $\mathcal{K}$. We introduce, for every $C \mathcal{U} D \in ev(\mathcal{K})$, a fresh concept name $F_{C\mathcal{U}D}$, the *surrogate* of $C \mathcal{U} D$, and then, for a concept C, denote by $\overline{C}$ the result of replacing each $C' \mathcal{U} D'$ in C, which is not in the scope of another $\mathcal{U}$, with the surrogate $F_{C'\mathcal{U}D'}$. For a $T_{\mathcal{U}}^0 DL\text{-}Lite_{bool}^{\mathcal{N}}$ TBox T, denote by $\overline{T}$ the $DL\text{-}Lite_{bool}^{\mathcal{N}}$ TBox obtained by replacing every concept C in T with $\overline{C}$.

Let $cl(\mathcal{K})$ be the closure under negation of all concepts occurring in T together with the $\exists R$, for $R \in role^{\pm}(\mathcal{K})$, and the B, for $\bigcirc^n B(a) \in \mathcal{A}$ or $\Box B(a) \in \mathcal{A}$. A *type* for $\mathcal{K}$ is a subset $\mathbf{t}$ of $cl(\mathcal{K})$ such that

- $C \sqcap D \in \mathbf{t}$ iff $C, D \in \mathbf{t}$, for every $C \sqcap D \in cl(\mathcal{K})$;
- $\neg C \in \mathbf{t}$ iff $C \notin \mathbf{t}$, for every $C \in cl(\mathcal{K})$.

A type $\mathbf{t}$ for $\mathcal{K}$ is *realisable* if the concept $\sqcap_{C \in \mathbf{t}} \overline{C}$ is satisfiable w.r.t. $\overline{T}$.

A function r mapping $\mathbb{N}$ to types for $\mathcal{K}$ is called a *coherent* and *saturated run* for $\mathcal{K}$ if the following conditions are satisfied:

(real) $r(i)$ is realisable, for every $i \geq 0$,

(coh) for all $0 \leq j < i$ and $C \sqcup D \in ev(\mathcal{K})$, if $D \in r(i)$ and $C \in r(k)$, for all k, $j < k < i$, then $C \sqcup D \in r(j)$;

(sat) for all $i \geq 0$ and $C \sqcup D \in ev(\mathcal{K})$, if $C \sqcup D \in r(i)$ then there is $j > i$ such that $D \in r(j)$ and $C \in r(k)$ for all k, $i < k < j$.

Given a model $\mathcal{I}$ of $\mathcal{K}$ and $d \in \Delta^{\mathcal{I}}$, let $run_{\mathcal{I}}(d) \colon i \mapsto \{C \in cl(\mathcal{K}) \mid d \in C^{\mathcal{I}(i)}\}$. Clearly, each $run_{\mathcal{I}}(d)$ is a coherent and saturated run for $\mathcal{K}$. For a run r and a finite sequence $s = (s(0), \dots, s(n))$ of types for $\mathcal{K}$, we denote by s^k the k repetitions of s and let

$$r^{<i} = (r(0), \dots, r(i-1)), \qquad s^{\omega} = (s(0), \dots, s(n), s(0), \dots, s(n), \dots),$$
$$r^{\geq i} = (r(i), r(i+1), \dots), \qquad s \cdot r = (s(0), \dots, s(n), r(0), r(1), \dots).$$

A *witness* for $\mathcal{K}$ is a pair of the form (r, Ξ), where r is a coherent and saturated run for $\mathcal{K}$, $\Xi \subseteq \mathbb{N}$ and $|\Xi| \leq 1$. A *quasimodel* for $\mathcal{K}$ is a quadruple $\mathfrak{Q} = \langle W, K, K_0, L \rangle$, where W is a set of witnesses for $\mathcal{K}$ and K, K_0, L are natural numbers with $0 \leq K < K_0 < L$ such that:

(run) $W = \{(r_a, \emptyset) \mid a \in ob(\mathcal{A})\} \cup \{(r_R, \{i_R\}) \mid R \in \Omega\}$, for some $\Omega \subseteq role^{\pm}(\mathcal{K})$;

(rep) $r_R(K) = r_R(K_0)$, for each $(r_R, \{i_R\}) \in W$;

(obj) if $\bigcirc^n B(a) \in \mathcal{A}$ then $B \in r_a(n)$; if $\square B(a) \in \mathcal{A}$ then $B \in r_a(i)$ for all $i > 0$;

(role) for all $i \geq 0$ and $R \in role^{\pm}(\mathcal{K})$, if $\exists R^- \in r(i)$, for some $(r, \Xi) \in W$, then $(r_R, \{i_R\}) \in W$, $\exists R \in r_R(i_R)$ and either $i \leq i_R < K$ or $K \leq i_R < L$.

Theorem 1. *A $T^0_{\mathcal{U}}DL\text{-}Lite^{\mathcal{N}}_{bool}$ KB $\mathcal{K}$ is satisfiable iff there is a quasimodel $\mathfrak{Q} = \langle W, K, K_0, L \rangle$ for $\mathcal{K}$ with $L \leq N_{\mathcal{A}} + 2^{|cl(\mathcal{K})| \cdot |role^{\pm}(\mathcal{K})|} \cdot (|role^{\pm}(\mathcal{K})| + 1) + 2^{|cl(\mathcal{K})|} + 2$.*

Proof. Suppose $\mathcal{I} \models \mathcal{K}$. For $m \geq 0$, let

$$\mathbf{F}^m = \{R \in role^{\pm}(\mathcal{K}) \mid \text{ there is } i \geq m \text{ with } R^{\mathcal{I}(i)} \neq \emptyset\}.$$

Lemma 3. *For all $n, v \geq 0$, there exists m such that $n \leq m \leq n + v \cdot |\mathbf{F}^0|$ and, for every role $R \in \mathbf{F}^0$, either $R \in \mathbf{F}^{m+v+1}$ or $R \notin \mathbf{F}^{m+1}$.*

Proof. If a role R is non-empty infinitely often then $R \in \mathbf{F}^{m+v+1}$, for any m. So we have to consider only those roles that are non-empty finitely many times. Let $\mathbf{FG} = \{R \in role^{\pm}(\mathcal{K}) \mid \text{ there is } i \geq 0 \text{ with } R \notin \mathbf{F}^i\}$. For $R \in \mathbf{FG} \cap \mathbf{F}^0$, let $i_R = \min\{i \mid R \notin \mathbf{F}^{i+1}\}$ (i.e., i_R is the last moment when R is non-empty). If $\max\{i_R \mid R \in \mathbf{FG}\} \leq n + v \cdot |\mathbf{F}^0|$, we take $m = \max(\{n\} \cup \{i_R \mid R \in \mathbf{FG}\})$. Clearly, $\mathbf{FG} \cap \mathbf{F}^{m+1} = \emptyset$ (so all roles in $\mathbf{FG}$ are empty after m). Otherwise, $\mathbf{FG} \cap \mathbf{F}^0 \neq \emptyset$ and without loss of generality we may assume that $\mathbf{FG} \cap \mathbf{F}^0 = \{R_1, \dots, R_s\}$ and $i_{R_1} \leq i_{R_2} \leq \dots \leq i_{R_s}$. If $i_{R_1} > n + v$, we take $m = n$; then $\mathbf{FG} \cap \mathbf{F}^0 \subseteq \mathbf{F}^{m+v+1}$ (all roles in $\mathbf{FG} \cap \mathbf{F}^0$ are non-empty after $m + v$). Otherwise, $i_{R_1} \leq n + v$ and $i_{R_s} > n + v \cdot |\mathbf{F}^0|$, whence $i_{R_s} - i_{R_1} > (v-1) \cdot |\mathbf{F}^0|$. Let j_0 be the smallest j, $1 \leq j < s$, such that $i_{R_j} \geq n$ and $i_{R_{j+1}} - i_{R_j} > v$ (it exists as $s \leq |\mathbf{F}^0|$), and let $m = i_{R_{j_0}}$. We then clearly have $R_1, \dots, R_{j_0} \notin \mathbf{F}^{m+1}$ and $R_{j_0+1}, \dots, R_s \in \mathbf{F}^{m+v+1}$. $\qquad \square$

Let $V = 2^{|cl(\mathcal{K})| \cdot |role^{\pm}(\mathcal{K})|}$. By Lemma 3, there is M, $N_{\mathcal{A}} \leq M \leq N_{\mathcal{A}} + V \cdot |\mathbf{F}^0|$, such that, for every role $R \in \mathbf{F}^0$, either $R \in \mathbf{F}^{M+V+1}$ or $R \notin \mathbf{F}^{M+1}$. We set

$$i_R = \begin{cases} \min\{i \geq M+V+1 \mid R^{\mathcal{I}(i)} \neq \emptyset\}, & R \in \mathbf{F}^{M+V+1}, \\ \max\{i \mid R^{\mathcal{I}(i)} \neq \emptyset\}, & R \in \mathbf{F}^0 \setminus \mathbf{F}^{M+1}. \end{cases}$$

Clearly, for each $R \in \mathbf{F}^0$, either $i_R \leq M$ or $i_R \geq M + V + 1$. We fix some $d_R \in (\exists R)^{\mathcal{I}(i_R)}$ and set $r_R = run_{\mathcal{I}}(d_R)$, for each $R \in \mathbf{F}^0$. For $a \in ob(\mathcal{A})$, set $r_a = run_{\mathcal{I}}(a^{\mathcal{I}})$. Let

$$W = \big\{(r_a, \emptyset) \mid a \in ob(\mathcal{A})\big\} \cup \big\{(r_R, \{i_R\}) \mid R \in \mathbf{F}^0\big\}.$$

Clearly, **(run)** and **(obj)** hold for W. Also, $\exists R^- \in r(i)$ iff $\exists R \in r_R(i_R)$ and $(r_R, \{i_R\}) \in W$, for all $(r, \Xi) \in W$ and $i \geq 0$.

Observe that there are K, K_0 such that $M < K < K_0 \leq M + V + 1$ and $r_R(K) = r_R(K_0)$, for all $(r_R, \{i_R\}) \in W$. Let $L = K_0 + T + 1$. Next, for each $(r_R, \{i_R\}) \in W$ with $i_R \geq L$, we construct a new witness $(r'_R, \{i'_R\})$ such that $\exists R \in r'_R(i'_R)$ and $i'_R < L$: we remove every part $(r_R(n), \ldots, r_R(n'))$ of the run r_R such that $r_R(n) = r_R(n'+1)$, for $K_0 < n < n' < i_R$. Let $(r'_R, \{i'_R\})$ be the result of this operation. It should be clear that r'_R is a coherent and saturated run for $\mathcal{K}$ and, as there are only T different types for $\mathcal{K}$, we have $i'_R < L$. Denote by W' the resulting set of witnesses. It is as an exercise for the reader to check that $\mathfrak{Q} = \langle W', K, K_0, L \rangle$ is a quasimodel for $\mathcal{K}$.

($\Leftarrow$) Let $\mathfrak{Q} = \langle W, K, K_0, L \rangle$ be a quasimodel for $\mathcal{K}$. We construct a model for $\mathcal{K}^{\ddagger}$ which, by Theorem 1, will show that $\mathcal{K}$ is satisfiable. Let

$$\mathfrak{R} \quad = \quad \big\{r_a \mid (r_a, \emptyset) \in W\big\} \ \cup$$
$$\Big\{ \big(r_R^{<K} \cdot (r_R(K), \ldots, r_R(K_0 - 1))^i \cdot r_R^{\geq K_0}\big)^{\geq j} \mid (r_R, \{i_R\}) \in W, \ i > 0, \ j \geq 0 \Big\}.$$

Clearly, each $r \in \mathfrak{R}$ is a coherent and saturated run for $\mathcal{K}$. Moreover, if we have $(r_R, \{i_R\}) \in W$ and $i_R < K$ then, for all i, $0 \leq i \leq i_R$, there is $r' \in \mathfrak{R}$ with $\exists R \in r'(i)$. And if $(r_R, \{i_R\}) \in W$ and $i_R \geq K$ then, for all $i \geq 0$, there is $r' \in \mathfrak{R}$ with $\exists R \in r'(i)$. As follows from **(role)**, for each $R \in \Omega$, we have $R^- \in \Omega$ and either $i_R \geq K$ and $i_{R^-} \geq K$ or $i_R = i_{R^-} < K$. So, for all $i \geq 0$ and $r \in \mathfrak{R}$,

if $\exists R^- \in r(i)$ then there is $r' \in \mathfrak{R}$ such that $\exists R \in r'(i)$.

We construct a first-order temporal model $\mathfrak{M}$ based on the domain $D = \mathfrak{R}$ by taking $a^{\mathfrak{M}} = r_a$, for each $a \in ob(\mathcal{A})$, and $(B^*)^{\mathfrak{M},i} = \{r \in \mathfrak{R} \mid B \in r(i)\}$, for each $B \in cl(\mathcal{K})$ and $i \geq 0$. It should be clear that $(\mathfrak{M}, 0) \models \mathcal{K}^{\ddagger}$. $\qquad\square$

Theorem 2. *If there is a quasimodel $\mathfrak{Q} = \langle W, K, K_0, L \rangle$ for $\mathcal{K}$ then there is an ultimately periodic quasimodel $\mathfrak{Q}' = \langle W', K, K_0, L' \rangle$ for $\mathcal{K}$, that is, there are $L' \leq L + 2^N$ and $P \leq N \cdot 2^N$, where $N = |W| \cdot |cl(\mathcal{K})|$, such that $r'(i+P) = r'(i)$, for all $i \geq L'$ and $(r', \Xi') \in W'$.*

Proof. The proof is a straightforward modification of the standard $\mathcal{LTL}$ construction (see, e.g., [14]) with the set of propositions being $cl(\mathcal{K}) \times W$. $\square$

It follows from Lemma 2 and Theorems 1 and 2 that we have the following:

Theorem 3. *Satisfiability of* $T_{\mathcal{U}}DL\text{-}Lite_{bool}^{(\mathcal{RN})}$ *KBs is* PSPACE-*complete.*

5   Satisfiability of $T_\Diamond DL\text{-}Lite_{bool}^{(\mathcal{RN})}$ KBs Is NP-complete

We notice that Lemma 2 holds for $T_\Diamond DL\text{-}Lite_{bool}^{(\mathcal{RN})}$ and its respective fragment $T_\Diamond^0 DL\text{-}Lite_{bool}^{\mathcal{N}}$. Thus, to prove that satisfiability of $T_\Diamond DL\text{-}Lite_{bool}^{(\mathcal{RN})}$ KBs is in NP, it is enough to consider $T_\Diamond^0 DL\text{-}Lite_{bool}^{\mathcal{N}}$ KBs. We proceed as in Section 4. First we prove that a $T_\Diamond^0 DL\text{-}Lite_{bool}^{\mathcal{N}}$ KB is satisfiable iff there exists a quasimodel for it. Then we show that if there is a quasimodel for $\mathcal{K}$ then there exists an ultimately periodic quasimodel for $\mathcal{K}$ such that both the length of the prefix and the length of the period are *polynomial* in the length of $\mathcal{K}$. As the existence of such a quasimodel can be checked in non-deterministic polynomial time, we obtain the NP upper bound. The matching lower bound will be shown for a sublogic $T_\Diamond DL\text{-}Lite_{core}$ of $T_\Diamond DL\text{-}Lite_{bool}^{(\mathcal{RN})}$ with rather primitive concept inclusions.

Let $\mathcal{K} = (\mathcal{T}, \mathcal{A})$ be a $T_\Diamond^0 DL\text{-}Lite_{bool}^{\mathcal{N}}$ KB. We say that a type $\mathbf{t}$ for $\mathcal{K}$ is *stutter-invariant* if $\neg \Diamond C \in \mathbf{t}$ implies $\neg C \in \mathbf{t}$, for each $\Diamond C \in ev(\mathcal{K})$. A *quasimodel* for $\mathcal{K}$ is a triple $\mathfrak{Q} = \langle W, K, L \rangle$, where W is a set of witnesses for $\mathcal{K}$ and K, L are natural numbers with $0 \leq K \leq L$ such that they satisfy **(run)**, **(obj)**, **(role)** and the following condition

(stuttr) $r(K)$ and the $r(i)$, for $i \geq L$, are stutter-invariant for each $(r, \varXi) \in W$.

Theorem 4. *A* $T_\Diamond^0 DL\text{-}Lite_{bool}^{\mathcal{N}}$ *KB* $\mathcal{K}$ *is satisfiable iff there is a quasimodel* $\mathfrak{Q} = \langle W, K, L \rangle$ *for* $\mathcal{K}$ *such that* $L \leq N_{\mathcal{A}} + |ev(\mathcal{K})| \cdot (|role^{\pm}(\mathcal{K})| + 2) + 3.$

Proof. ($\Rightarrow$) Suppose $\mathcal{I} \models \mathcal{K}$. Let $V = |ev(\mathcal{K})|$. By Lemma 3, there exists M with $N_{\mathcal{A}} \leq M \leq N_{\mathcal{A}} + V \cdot |\mathbf{F}^0|$ such that, for every role $R \in \mathbf{F}^0$, either $R \in \mathbf{F}^K$ or $R \notin \mathbf{F}^{M+1}$, where $K = M + V + 1$. We then set

$$i_R = \begin{cases} \min\{i \geq K \mid R^{\mathcal{I}(i)} \neq \emptyset\}, & R \in \mathbf{F}^K, \\ \max\{i \mid R^{\mathcal{I}(i)} \neq \emptyset\}, & R \in \mathbf{F}^0 \setminus \mathbf{F}^{M+1}. \end{cases}$$

Clearly, for $R \in \mathbf{F}^0$, either $i_R \leq M$ or $i_R \geq K$. For each $R \in \mathbf{F}^0$, we fix some $d_R \in (\exists R)^{\mathcal{I}(i_R)}$ and set $r_R = run_{\mathcal{I}}(d_R)$. For $a \in ob(\mathcal{A})$, set $r_a = run_{\mathcal{I}}(a^{\mathcal{I}})$. Let

$$W = \{(r_a, \emptyset) \mid a \in ob(\mathcal{A})\} \cup \{(r_R, \{i_R\}) \mid R \in \mathbf{F}^0\}.$$

Clearly, **(run)** and **(obj)** hold. Also, we have $\exists R^- \in r(i)$ iff $\exists R \in r_R(i_R)$ and $(r_R, \{i_R\}) \in W$, for all $(r, \varXi) \in W$ and $i \geq 0$.

We now transform W by expanding and pruning runs in such a way that the $r(i)$ are never thrown out for $(r, \varXi) \in W$ and $i \in \varXi$.

Lemma 4. *For each coherent and saturated run* r,

$$\big|\{i \mid r(i) \text{ is not stutter-invariant}\}\big| \leq |ev(\mathcal{K})|.$$

Proof. Suppose that there are $0 \leq i_1 < \cdots < i_n$ such that $n > |ev(\mathcal{K})|$ and $r(i_1), \ldots, r(i_n)$ are not stutter-invariant, i.e., there are $\Diamond C_j \in ev(\mathcal{K})$ with $\neg \Diamond C_j, C_j \in r(i_j)$. Then there is $\Diamond C \in ev(\mathcal{K})$ such that $\neg \Diamond C, C \in r(i_j), r(i_{j'})$ for some $0 \leq i_j < i_{j'}$. As $C \in r(i_{j'})$, we have, by **(coh)**, $\Diamond C \in r(i_j)$, contrary to $\neg \Diamond C \in r(i_j)$. □

Step 1. By Lemma 4, for each $(r, \Xi) \in W$, there is j_r, $M < j_r \leq K$, such that $r(j_r)$ is stutter-invariant. Set

$$r' = r^{<j_r} \cdot r(j_r)^{K-j_r} \cdot r^{\geq j_r},$$
$$\Xi' = \{i \mid i \in \Xi,\ i \leq j_r\} \cup \{i + K - j_r \mid i \in \Xi,\ i > j_r\}.$$

Clearly, r' is a coherent and saturated run. Denote by W' the set of all (r', Ξ') constructed as above. Then, for each $(r', \Xi') \in W'$, $r'(K)$ is stutter-invariant. It is easy to see that, for each $R \in \mathbf{F}^0$, $(r'_R, \{i'_R\}) \in W'$ and either $i'_R \leq M$ or $i'_R \geq K$.

Step 2. For $(r', \Xi') \in W'$, let $\Xi^0 = \{i > K \mid r'(i) \text{ is not stutter-invariant}\}$. By Lemma 4, $|\Xi^0| \leq |ev(\mathcal{K})|$. If $\Xi^0 \cup \Xi' \neq \emptyset$, we prune the run r' by removing all stutter-invariant $r'(i)$ with $K < i < \max(\Xi^0 \cup \Xi')$. The resulting function r'' is a coherent and saturated run for $\mathcal{K}$. Set

$$\Xi'' = \{i \mid i \in \Xi',\ i \leq K\} \cup \{K + \sharp\{j \in \Xi^0 \cup \Xi' \mid j \leq i\} \mid i \in \Xi',\ i > K\}.$$

Let W'' be the set of all witnesses (r'', Ξ'') constructed as above and $L = K + V + 2$. Clearly, for each $(r'', \Xi'') \in W''$, all the types $r''(i)$ are stutter-invariant, for $i \geq L$. Thus, **(stuttr)** holds. It is easy to see that, for each $R \in \mathbf{F}^0$, we have $(r''_R, \{i''_R\}) \in W''$ and $K \leq i''_R < L$ if $R \in \mathbf{F}^K$, and $i''_R \leq M$ if $R \notin \mathbf{F}^{M+1}$. So **(role)** holds as well. It is readily seen now that $\mathfrak{Q} = \langle W'', K, L \rangle$ is as required.

($\Leftarrow$) Let $\mathfrak{Q} = \langle W, K, L \rangle$ be a quasimodel for $\mathcal{K}$. We construct a model for $\mathcal{K}^{\ddagger}$ which, by Theorem 1, will show that $\mathcal{K}$ is satisfiable. Let

$$\mathfrak{R} = \{r_a \mid (r_a, \emptyset) \in W\} \cup \{r_R^{\geq i} \mid (r_R, \{i_R\}) \in W,\ 0 \leq i \leq i_R\} \cup$$
$$\{r_R^{<K} \cdot (r_R(K))^{i - i_R} \cdot r_R^{\geq K} \mid (r_R, \{i_R\}) \in W,\ i > i_R \geq K\}.$$

Clearly, each $r \in \mathfrak{R}$ is a coherent and saturated run for $\mathcal{K}$. Moreover, if we have $(r_R, \{i_R\}) \in W$ and $i_R < K$ then, for all i, $0 \leq i \leq i_R$, there is $r' \in \mathfrak{R}$ with $\exists R \in r'(i)$. And if $(r_R, \{i_R\}) \in W$ and $i_R \geq K$ then, for all $i \geq 0$, there is $r' \in \mathfrak{R}$ with $\exists R \in r'(i)$. As follows from **(role)**, for each $R \in \Omega$, we have $R^- \in \Omega$ and either $i_R \geq K$ and $i_{R^-} \geq K$ or $i_R = i_{R^-} < K$. So, for all $i \geq 0$ and $r \in \mathfrak{R}$,

$$\text{if } \exists R^- \in r(i) \text{ then there is } r' \in \mathfrak{R} \text{ such that } \exists R \in r'(i).$$

We construct a first-order temporal model $\mathfrak{M}$ based on the domain $D = \mathfrak{R}$ by taking $a^{\mathfrak{M}} = r_a$, for each $a \in ob(\mathcal{A})$, and $(B^*)^{\mathfrak{M}, i} = \{r \in \mathfrak{R} \mid B \in r(i)\}$, for each $B \in cl(\mathcal{K})$ and $i \geq 0$. It should be clear that $(\mathfrak{M}, 0) \models \mathcal{K}^{\ddagger}$. □

Theorem 5. *If there is a quasimodel $\mathfrak{Q} = \langle W, K, L \rangle$ for $\mathcal{K}$ then there is an ultimately periodic quasimodel $\mathfrak{Q}' = \langle W', K, L \rangle$, that is, there is $P \leq |ev(\mathcal{K})|$ such that $r'(i + P) = r'(i)$, for all $i > L$ and $(r', \Xi') \in W'$.*

Proof. We begin the proof with the following observation:

Lemma 5. *Let r be a coherent and saturated run for $\mathcal{K}$ and let $l \geq 0$ be such that every $r(i)$, $i \geq l$, is stutter-invariant. Then there are $i_1, \ldots, i_{|ev(\mathcal{K})|} \geq l$ such that $r' = r^{\leq l} \cdot \left(r(i_1) \cdot \ldots \cdot r(i_{|ev(\mathcal{K})|}) \right)^{\omega}$ is a coherent and saturated run for $\mathcal{K}$.*

Proof. First we show that

$$r(l) \cap ev(\mathcal{K}) = r(j) \cap ev(\mathcal{K}), \quad \text{for all } j > l. \tag{5}$$

Suppose that there is $j > l$ and $\Diamond C \in r(l)$ such that $\Diamond C \notin r(j)$. As $r(j)$ is stutter-invariant, $C \notin r(j)$ and, by **(coh)**, $\Diamond C \notin r(j-1)$. By repeating this argument sufficiently many times, we obtain $\Diamond C \notin r(l)$, contrary to our assumption. The converse direction—i.e., for each $j > l$, if $\Diamond C \in r(j)$ then $\Diamond C \in r(l)$—follows from **(coh)**.

For each $\Diamond C \in ev(\mathcal{K})$, we can select an i, $i \geq l$, such that $C \in r(i)$ whenever $\Diamond C \in r(l)$. Let $i_1, \ldots, i_{|ev(\mathcal{K})|}$ be all such i. It remains to show that r' is coherent and saturated. For coherency of r', let $C \in r'(i)$, for $i \geq 0$. By **(coh)** for r, we have $\Diamond C \in r'(j)$, for each $0 \leq j < i$ such that $j \leq l$. It remains to consider j with $l < j < i$. It follows that $r'(i) = r(i_k)$, for some $1 \leq k \leq |ev(\mathcal{K})|$, from which, by **(coh)** for r, $\Diamond C \in r(l) = r'(l)$ and, by (5), $\Diamond C \in r'(j)$. For saturation of r', let $\Diamond C \in r'(i)$, for $i \geq 0$. If $\Diamond C \in r(l)$ then $C \in r(i_k)$ for $1 \leq k \leq |ev(\mathcal{K})|$ and, by the construction of r', there is $j > i$ such that $r'(j) = r(i_k)$. Thus $C \in r'(j)$. If $\Diamond C \notin r(l)$ then, by (5), $i < l$, from which $\Diamond C \in r(i)$. By **(sat)** for r, there is $j > i$ with $C \in r(j)$ and, by (5), $j \leq l$. Thus $C \in r(j) = r'(j)$. $\square$

Let $P = |ev(\mathcal{K})|$. For each (r, Ξ), we take $r' = r^{\leq L} \cdot (r(i_1) \cdot \ldots r(i_P))^{\omega}$ provided by Lemma 5. Denote the set of all (r', Ξ) by W'. It follows that $\mathfrak{Q}' = \langle W', K, L \rangle$ is an ultimately periodic quasimodel for $\mathcal{K}$ (with period P). $\square$

It is now easy to devise an NP algorithm which can check whether there exists a quasimodel for a $T_{\Diamond}DL\text{-}Lite_{bool}^{\mathcal{N}}$ KB. By Lemma 2 and Theorems 4 and 5, this means that satisfiability of $T_{\Diamond}DL\text{-}Lite_{bool}^{(\mathcal{RN})}$ KBs is in NP. We prove the matching lower bound for the fragment $T_{\Diamond}DL\text{-}Lite_{core}$ of $T_{\Diamond}DL\text{-}Lite_{bool}^{(\mathcal{RN})}$ that allows only concept inclusions of the form $A_1 \sqsubseteq A_2$, $A_1 \sqsubseteq \neg A_2$, $\Diamond A_1 \sqsubseteq A_2$ or $A_1 \sqsubseteq \Diamond A_2$, where A_1 and A_2 are concept names.

Lemma 6. *The satisfiability problem for $T_{\Diamond}DL\text{-}Lite_{core}$ KBs is NP-hard.*

Proof. We prove this by reduction of the graph 3-colourability (3-COL) problem, which is formulated as follows: given a graph $G = (V, E)$, decide whether there is an assignment of colours $\{1, 2, 3\}$ to vertices V such that no two vertices $a_i, a_j \in V$ sharing the same edge, $(a_i, a_j) \in E$, have the same colour. Let X_0, X_1, X_2, V, U and A_i, for $A_i \in V$, be concept names and a an object name. Consider the following KB $\mathcal{K}_G$:

$$V(a), \qquad V \sqsubseteq \Diamond A_i, \qquad A_i \sqsubseteq X_3, \qquad \text{for all } A_i \in V,$$
$$A_i \sqsubseteq \neg A_j, \quad \text{for all } (A_i, A_j) \in E,$$
$$V \sqsubseteq \neg U, \qquad \Diamond X_0 \sqsubseteq U, \qquad \Diamond X_1 \sqsubseteq X_0, \qquad \Diamond X_2 \sqsubseteq X_1, \qquad \Diamond X_3 \sqsubseteq X_2.$$

It is easy to see that $\mathcal{K}_G$ is satisfiable iff G is 3-colourable. $\qquad\qquad$ □

Thus we obtain the following theorem:

Theorem 6. *The satisfiability problem for* $T_\Diamond DL\text{-}Lite_{bool}^{(\mathcal{RN})}$ *KBs is*NP-*complete.*

It is also of interest to note that the fragment $T_\mathcal{U} DL\text{-}Lite_{core}$ of $T_\mathcal{U}^0 DL\text{-}Lite_{bool}^\mathcal{N}$ with concept inclusions of the form $A_1 \sqsubseteq A_2$, $A_1 \sqsubseteq \neg A_2$ or $A_1 \sqsubseteq A_2 \mathcal{U} A_3$ (the A_i concept names) turns out to be as complex as the whole logic $T_\mathcal{U} DL\text{-}Lite_{bool}^{(\mathcal{RN})}$:

Theorem 7. *The satisfiability problem for* $T_\mathcal{U} DL\text{-}Lite_{core}$ *KBs is* PSPACE-*hard.*

The proof can be found in the full version of the paper available online at `http://www.dcs.bbk.ac.uk/~roman/`.

6   Conclusions

The obtained complexity results look encouraging in view of possible applications for reasoning about temporal conceptual data models [4]. On the one hand, the logic $DL\text{-}Lite_{bool}^\mathcal{N}$ was shown to be adequate for representing different aspects of conceptual models: ISA, disjointness and covering for classes, domain and range of relationships, n-ary relationships, attributes and participation constraints [6]. On the other hand, the approach of [8] shows that rigid axioms and roles with temporalised concepts are enough to capture temporal data models.

The logic $T_\Diamond DL\text{-}Lite_{bool}$ presented in this paper can capture some form of *evolution constraints* [5,20,16] thanks to the $\Diamond$ operator. Furthermore, it also captures *snapshot* classes—i.e., classes whose instances do not change over time. However, by restricting the temporal component only to $\Diamond$ and $\Box$, we lose the ability to capture *temporary* entities and relationships whose instances have a limited lifespan. To overcome this limitation, we plan to extend the logics presented here with either past temporal operators or with a special kind of axioms that hold over finite prefix.

References

1. Artale, A., Calvanese, D., Kontchakov, R., Zakharyaschev, M.: DL-Lite in the light of first-order logic. In: Proc. of the 22nd AAAI Conf. on Artificial Intelligence, pp. 361–366. AAAI Press, Menlo Park (2007)
2. Artale, A., Calvanese, D., Kontchakov, R., Zakharyaschev, M.: The DL-Lite family and relations. Technical Report BBKCS-09-03, School of Computer Science and Information Systems, Birbeck College, London (2009),
   `http://www.dcs.bbk.ac.uk/research/techreps/2009/bbkcs-09-03.pdf`

3. Artale, A., Franconi, E.: Temporal description logics. In: Fisher, M., Gabbay, D., Vila, L. (eds.) Handbook of Time and Temporal Reasoning in Artificial Intelligence, pp. 375–388. Elsevier, Amsterdam (2005)
4. Artale, A., Franconi, E., Wolter, F., Zakharyaschev, M.: A temporal description logic for reasoning about conceptual schemas and queries. In: Flesca, S., Greco, S., Leone, N., Ianni, G. (eds.) JELIA 2002. LNCS (LNAI), vol. 2424, pp. 98–110. Springer, Heidelberg (2002)
5. Artale, A., Parent, C., Spaccapietra, S.: Evolving objects in temporal information systems. Annals of Mathematics and AI 50(1-2), 5–38 (2007)
6. Artale, A., Calvanese, D., Kontchakov, R., Ryzhikov, V., Zakharyaschev, M.: Reasoning over extended ER models. In: Parent, C., Schewe, K.-D., Storey, V.C., Thalheim, B. (eds.) ER 2007. LNCS, vol. 4801, pp. 277–292. Springer, Heidelberg (2007)
7. Artale, A., Kontchakov, R., Lutz, C., Wolter, F., Zakharyaschev, M.: Temporalising tractable description logics. In: Proc. of the 14th Int. Symposium on Temporal Representation and Reasoning (TIME). IEEE Computer Society, Los Alamitos (2007)
8. Artale, A., Lutz, C., Toman, D.: A description logic of change. In: Proc. of Int. Joint Conf. on Artificial Intelligence (IJCAI), pp. 218–223 (2007)
9. Baader, F., Küsters, R., Wolter, F.: Extensions to description logics. In: Description Logic Handbook, pp. 219–261. Cambridge University Press, Cambridge (2003)
10. Baader, F., Ghilardi, S., Lutz, C.: LTL over description logic axioms. In: Proc. of the 11th Int. Conf. on Principles of Knowledge Representation and Reasoning (KR), pp. 684–694. AAAI Press, Menlo Park (2008)
11. Calvanese, D., De Giacomo, G., Lembo, D., Lenzerini, M., Rosati, R.: DL-Lite: Tractable description logics for ontologies. In: Proc. of the 10th Nat. Conf. on Artificial Intelligence and the 17th Innovative Applications of Artificial Intelligence Conf., pp. 602–607. AAAI Press/The MIT Press (2005)
12. Calvanese, D., De Giacomo, G., Lembo, D., Lenzerini, M., Rosati, R.: Data complexity of query answering in description logics. In: Proc. of the 10th Int. Conf. on Principles of Knowledge Representation and Reasoning (KR), pp. 260–270. AAAI Press, Menlo Park (2006)
13. Calvanese, D., De Giacomo, G., Lembo, D., Lenzerini, M., Rosati, R.: Tractable reasoning and efficient query answering in description logics: The DL-Lite family. J. of Automated Reasoning 39(3), 385–429 (2007)
14. Gabbay, D., Hodkinson, I., Reynolds, M.: Temporal Logic: Mathematical Foundations and Computational Aspects, vol. 1. Oxford University Press, Oxford (1994)
15. Gabbay, D., Kurucz, A., Wolter, F., Zakharyaschev, M.: Many-Dimensional Modal Logics: Theory and Applications. Elsevier, Amsterdam (2003)
16. Hall, G., Gupta, R.: Modeling transition. In: Proc. of the 7th Int. Conf. on Data Engineering (ICDE), pp. 540–549. IEEE Computer Society, Los Alamitos (1991)
17. Lutz, C., Wolter, F., Zakharyaschev, M.: Temporal description logics: A survey. In: Proc. of the 14th Int. Symposium on Temporal Representation and Reasoning (TIME), pp. 3–14. IEEE Computer Society, Los Alamitos (2008)
18. Poggi, A., Lembo, D., Calvanese, D., De Giacomo, G., Lenzerini, M., Rosati, R.: Linking data to ontologies. J. on Data Semantics X, 133–173 (2008)
19. Schild, K.: Combining terminological logics with tense logic. In: Damas, L.M.M., Filgueiras, M. (eds.) EPIA 1993. LNCS, vol. 727, pp. 105–120. Springer, Heidelberg (1993)
20. Spaccapietra, S., Parent, C., Zimanyi, E.: Conceptual Modeling for Traditional and Spatio-Temporal Applications—The MADS Approach. Springer, Heidelberg (2006)

Runtime Verification Using a Temporal Description Logic

Franz Baader[1], Andreas Bauer[2], and Marcel Lippmann[1]

[1] TU Dresden
{baader,lippmann}@tcs.inf.tu-dresden.de
[2] The Australian National University
baueran@rsise.anu.edu.au

Abstract. Formulae of linear temporal logic (LTL) can be used to specify (wanted or unwanted) properties of a dynamical system. In model checking, the system's behavior is described by a transition system, and one needs to check whether all possible traces of this transition system satisfy the formula. In runtime verification, one observes the actual system behavior, which at any time point yields a finite prefix of a trace. The task is then to check whether all continuations of this prefix to a trace satisfy (violate) the formula.

In this paper, we extend the known approaches to LTL runtime verification in two directions. First, instead of *propositional* LTL we use $\mathcal{ALC}$-LTL, which can use axioms of the description logic $\mathcal{ALC}$ instead of propositional variables to describe properties of single states of the system. Second, instead of assuming that the observed system behavior provides us with complete information about the states of the system, we consider the case where states may be described in an incomplete way by $\mathcal{ALC}$-ABoxes.

1 Introduction

Formulae of linear temporal logic (LTL) [11] can be used to specify (wanted or unwanted) properties of a dynamical system. For example, assume that the system we want to model is a TV set, and consider the properties on, turn_off, and turn_on, which respectively express that the set is on, receives a turn-off signal from the remote control, and receives a turn-on signal from the remote control. The LTL formula $\phi_{tv} := \Box\,(\text{turn\_on} \rightarrow \mathsf{X}(\text{on} \wedge (\mathsf{X}\text{on})\,\mathsf{U}\,\text{turn\_off}))$ says that, whenever the set receives the turn-on signal, it is on at the next time point, and it stays on (i.e., is on also at the next time point) until it receives the turn-off signal (since we use a "strong until" this signal has to come eventually).

In model checking [7,4], one assumes that the system's behavior can be described by a transition system. The verification task is then to check whether all possible traces of this transition system satisfy the formula. In contrast, in runtime verification [8], one does not model all possible behaviors of the system by a transition system. Instead, one observes the actual behavior of the system, which at any time point yields a finite prefix u of a trace. The task is then to

S. Ghilardi and R. Sebastiani (Eds.): FroCoS 2009, LNAI 5749, pp. 149–164, 2009.
© Springer-Verlag Berlin Heidelberg 2009

check whether all continuations of this prefix to a trace satisfy (violate) the given LTL formula ϕ. Thus, there are three possible answers[1] to a runtime verification problem (u, ϕ):

- $\top$, if all continuations of u to an infinite trace satisfy ϕ;
- $\bot$, if all continuations of u to an infinite trace do not satisfy ϕ;
- ?, if none of the above holds, i.e., there is a continuation that satisfies ϕ, and one that does not satisfy ϕ.

For example, consider the two prefixes $u := \{\neg\text{on}, \neg\text{turn\_off}, \text{turn\_on}\}$ and $u' := \{\neg\text{on}, \neg\text{turn\_off}, \text{turn\_on}\} \{\neg\text{on}, \neg\text{turn\_off}, \neg\text{turn\_on}\}$ and the formula ϕ_{tv} from our example. For the prefix u, the answer is ?, whereas for u' it is $\bot$. For our specific formula ϕ_{tv}, there is no prefix for which the answer would be $\top$.

It should be noted, however, that runtime verification is not really about solving a single such problem (u, ϕ). In practice, one observes the behavior of the system over time, which means that the prefix is continuously extended by adding new letters. The runtime verification device should not simply answer the problems $(\varepsilon, \phi), (\sigma_0, \phi), (\sigma_0\sigma_1, \phi), (\sigma_0\sigma_1\sigma_2, \phi), \ldots$ independently of each other. What one is looking for is a monitoring device (called *monitor* in the following) that successively accepts as input the next letter, and then computes the answer to the next runtime verification problem in constant time (where the size of ϕ is assumed to be constant). This can, for example, be achieved as follows [5]. For a given LTL formula ϕ, one constructs a deterministic Moore automaton $\mathcal{M}_\phi$ (i.e., a deterministic finite-state automaton with state output) such that the state reached by processing input u gives as output the answer to the runtime verification problem (u, ϕ). If u is then extended to $u\sigma$ by observing the next letter σ of the actual system behavior, it is sufficient to perform one transition of $\mathcal{M}_\phi$ in order to get the answer for $(u\sigma, \phi)$. Since $\mathcal{M}_\phi$ depends on ϕ (which is assumed to be constant), but not on u, this kind of monitoring device can answer the runtime verification question for (u, ϕ) in time linear in the length of u. More importantly, the delay between answering the question for u and for $u\sigma$ is constant, i.e., it does not depend on the length of the already processed prefix u. Basically, such a monitor can be constructed from generalized Büchi automata for the formula ϕ and its negation $\neg\phi$.[2]

Using *propositional* LTL for runtime verification presupposes that (the relevant information about) the states of the system can be represented using propositional variables, more precisely conjunctions of propositional literals. If the states actually have a complex internal structure, this assumption is not realistic. In order to allow for a more appropriate description of such complex states, one can use the extension of propositional LTL to $\mathcal{ALC}$-LTL introduced in [3].[3]

---

[1] There are also variants of runtime verification that work with only two or even four possible answers [6].

[2] A generalized Büchi automaton for an LTL formula ψ accepts the LTL structures satisfying this formula, viewed as words over an appropriate alphabet [16,4].

[3] A comparison of $\mathcal{ALC}$-LTL with other temporal DLs [1,2,10] is beyond the scope of this introduction. It can be found in [3].

From the syntactic point of view, the difference between propositional LTL and $\mathcal{ALC}$-LTL is that, in the latter, $\mathcal{ALC}$-axioms (i.e., concept and role assertions as well as general concept inclusion axioms formulated in the description logic $\mathcal{ALC}$ [14]) are used in place of propositional letters. From the semantic point of view, $\mathcal{ALC}$-LTL structures are infinite sequences of $\mathcal{ALC}$-interpretations, i.e., first-order relational structures, rather than propositional valuations. In [3], the complexity of the satisfiability problem for $\mathcal{ALC}$-LTL formulae is investigated in detail. In particular, it is shown that this complexity depends on whether rigid concepts and roles (i.e., concepts/roles whose interpretation does not change over time) are available or not. The algorithms for deciding satisfiability of $\mathcal{ALC}$-LTL formulae developed in [3] are not based on generalized Büchi automata. Before we can adapt the monitor construction used for propositional LTL to the case of $\mathcal{ALC}$-LTL, we must first show how Büchi automata for $\mathcal{ALC}$-LTL formulae can be constructed. We will see that this construction becomes more complex in the presence of rigid concepts and roles.

In runtime verification for propositional LTL, one usually assumes that the observed prefix provides one with complete information about the relevant system properties. In the setting of runtime verification for $\mathcal{ALC}$-LTL, this completeness assumption would mean that, for every time point covered by it, the prefix must provide full information about the status of every $\mathcal{ALC}$-axiom occurring in the formula, i.e., it must say whether it is true at that time point or not. If one has only limited access to the system's behavior, this assumption may be too strict. In this paper we show that runtime verification is also possible under the weaker assumption that one has (possibly) incomplete knowledge about the system's behavior at a time point. Technically, this means that we assume that the prefix describing the system's behavior is a finite sequence of ABoxes. Given such an ABox and an axiom occurring in the formula, there are now three possible cases: the axiom may follow from the ABox, its negation may follow from the ABox, or neither of them follows from the ABox. The third case means that we do not know whether in this state of the system the axiom or its negation holds. Thus, in addition to the unknown continuation of the prefix in the future, the use of ABoxes as (possibly) incomplete descriptions of states adds another source of uncertainty, which may cause the monitor to answer with ?.

As a possible application of this kind of monitoring, consider an emergency ward, where the vital parameters of a patient are measured in short intervals (sometimes not longer than 10 minutes), and where additional information about the patient is available from the patient record and added by doctors and nurses. Using concepts defined in a medical ontology like SNOMED CT,[4] a high-level view of the medical status of the patient at a given time point can be given by an ABox. Critical situations, which require the intervention of a doctor, can then be described by an $\mathcal{ALC}$-LTL formula (see [3] for a simple example). As long as the monitor for this formula yields the output ?, we continue with monitoring. If it yields $\top$, we raise an alarm, and if it yields $\bot$ we can shut off this monitor.

---

[4] See http://www.ihtsdo.org/our-standards/

In the next section, we introduce the temporal description logic $\mathcal{ALC}$-LTL, and in Section 3 we show how to construct generalized Büchi automata for $\mathcal{ALC}$-LTL formulae. These generalized Büchi automata are then used in Section 4 to construct monitors for $\mathcal{ALC}$-LTL formulae.

2   The Temporal DL $\mathcal{ALC}$-LTL

The temporal DL $\mathcal{ALC}$-LTL introduced in [3] combines the basic DL $\mathcal{ALC}$ with linear temporal logic (LTL). First, we recall the relevant definitions for $\mathcal{ALC}$.

Definition 1. *Let N_C, N_R, and N_I respectively be disjoint sets of concept names, role names, and individual names. The set of $\mathcal{ALC}$-concept descriptions is the smallest set such that*

- *all concept names are $\mathcal{ALC}$-concept descriptions;*
- *if C, D are $\mathcal{ALC}$-concept descriptions and $r \in N_R$, then $\neg C$, $C \sqcup D$, $C \sqcap D$, $\exists r.C$, and $\forall r.C$ are $\mathcal{ALC}$-concept descriptions.*

A general concept inclusion axiom (GCI) *is of the form $C \sqsubseteq D$, where C, D are $\mathcal{ALC}$-concept descriptions, and an* assertion *is of the form $a : C$ or $(a,b) : r$ where C is an $\mathcal{ALC}$-concept description, r is a role name, and a, b are individual names. We call both GCIs and assertions $\mathcal{ALC}$-axioms. A Boolean combination of $\mathcal{ALC}$-axioms is called a* Boolean $\mathcal{ALC}$-knowledge base, *i.e.,*

- *every $\mathcal{ALC}$-axiom is a Boolean $\mathcal{ALC}$-knowledge base;*
- *if $\mathcal{B}_1$ and $\mathcal{B}_2$ are Boolean $\mathcal{ALC}$-knowledge bases, then so are $\mathcal{B}_1 \wedge \mathcal{B}_2$, $\mathcal{B}_1 \vee \mathcal{B}_2$, and $\neg \mathcal{B}_1$.*

An $\mathcal{ALC}$-TBox is a conjunction of GCIs, and an $\mathcal{ALC}$-ABox is a conjunction of assertions.

According to this definition, TBoxes and ABoxes are special kinds of Boolean knowledge bases. However, note that they are often written as sets of axioms rather than as conjunctions of these axioms. The semantics of $\mathcal{ALC}$ is defined through the notion of an interpretation.

Definition 2. *An $\mathcal{ALC}$-interpretation is a pair $\mathcal{I} = (\Delta^{\mathcal{I}}, \cdot^{\mathcal{I}})$ where the domain $\Delta^{\mathcal{I}}$ is a non-empty set, and $\cdot^{\mathcal{I}}$ is a function that assigns to every concept name A a set $A^{\mathcal{I}} \subseteq \Delta^{\mathcal{I}}$, to every role name r a binary relation $r^{\mathcal{I}} \subseteq \Delta^{\mathcal{I}} \times \Delta^{\mathcal{I}}$, and to every individual name a an element $a^{\mathcal{I}} \in \Delta^{\mathcal{I}}$. This function is extended to $\mathcal{ALC}$-concept descriptions as follows:*

- $(C \sqcap D)^{\mathcal{I}} = C^{\mathcal{I}} \cap D^{\mathcal{I}}, (C \sqcup D)^{\mathcal{I}} = C^{\mathcal{I}} \cup D^{\mathcal{I}}, (\neg C)^{\mathcal{I}} = \Delta^{\mathcal{I}} \setminus C^{\mathcal{I}}$;
- $(\exists r.C)^{\mathcal{I}} = \{x \in \Delta^{\mathcal{I}} \mid \text{there is a } y \in \Delta^{\mathcal{I}} \text{ with } (x,y) \in r^{\mathcal{I}} \text{ and } y \in C^{\mathcal{I}}\}$;
- $(\forall r.C)^{\mathcal{I}} = \{x \in \Delta^{\mathcal{I}} \mid \text{for all } y \in \Delta^{\mathcal{I}}, (x,y) \in r^{\mathcal{I}} \text{ implies } y \in C^{\mathcal{I}}\}$.

We say that the interpretation $\mathcal{I}$ satisfies the unique name assumption (UNA) *iff different individual names are interpreted by different elements of the domain. The interpretation $\mathcal{I}$ is a* model *of the $\mathcal{ALC}$-axioms $C \sqsubseteq D$, $a : C$, and $(a,b) : r$ iff it respectively satisfies $C^{\mathcal{I}} \subseteq D^{\mathcal{I}}$, $a^{\mathcal{I}} \in C^{\mathcal{I}}$, and $(a^{\mathcal{I}}, b^{\mathcal{I}}) \in r^{\mathcal{I}}$. The notion of a model is extended to Boolean $\mathcal{ALC}$-knowledge bases as follows:*

- $\mathcal{I}$ *is a model of* $\mathcal{B}_1 \wedge \mathcal{B}_2$ *iff it is a model of* $\mathcal{B}_1$ *and* $\mathcal{B}_2$;
- $\mathcal{I}$ *is a model of* $\mathcal{B}_1 \vee \mathcal{B}_2$ *iff it is a model of* $\mathcal{B}_1$ *or* $\mathcal{B}_2$;
- $\mathcal{I}$ *is a model of* $\neg\mathcal{B}_1$ *iff it is not a model of* $\mathcal{B}_1$.

We say that the Boolean $\mathcal{ALC}$-*knowledge base* $\mathcal{B}$ *is* consistent *iff it has a model. We say that* $\mathcal{B}$ *implies the* $\mathcal{ALC}$-*axiom* α *iff every model of* $\mathcal{B}$ *is a model of* α.

Instead of first introducing the propositional temporal logic LTL, we directly define its extension $\mathcal{ALC}$-LTL. The difference to propositional LTL is that $\mathcal{ALC}$-axioms replace propositional letters.

Definition 3. $\mathcal{ALC}$-*LTL formulae are defined by induction:*

- *if* α *is an* $\mathcal{ALC}$-*axiom, then* α *is an* $\mathcal{ALC}$-*LTL formula;*
- *if* ϕ, ψ *are* $\mathcal{ALC}$-*LTL formulae, then so are* $\phi \wedge \psi$, $\neg\phi$, $\phi\mathsf{U}\psi$, *and* $\mathsf{X}\phi$.

As usual, we use $\phi\vee\psi$ as an abbreviation for $\neg(\neg\phi\wedge\neg\psi)$, true as an abbreviation for $(a : A) \vee \neg(a : A)$, $\Diamond\phi$ as an abbreviation for true$\mathsf{U}\phi$ (*diamond*, which should be read as "some time in the future"), and $\Box\phi$ as an abbreviation for $\neg\Diamond\neg\phi$ (*box*, which should be read as "always in the future"). The semantics of $\mathcal{ALC}$-LTL is based on $\mathcal{ALC}$-LTL structures, which are sequences of $\mathcal{ALC}$-interpretations over the same non-empty domain Δ (constant domain assumption). We assume that every individual name stands for a unique element of Δ (rigid individual names), and we make the unique name assumption.

Definition 4. *An* $\mathcal{ALC}$-*LTL structure is a sequence* $\mathfrak{I} = (\mathcal{I}_i)_{i=0,1,\ldots}$ *of* $\mathcal{ALC}$-*interpretations* $\mathcal{I}_i = (\Delta, \cdot^{\mathcal{I}_i})$ *obeying the UNA (called* worlds*) such that* $a^{\mathcal{I}_i} = a^{\mathcal{I}_j}$ *for all individual names* a *and all* $i, j \in \{0, 1, 2, \ldots\}$. *Given an* $\mathcal{ALC}$-*LTL formula* ϕ, *an* $\mathcal{ALC}$-*LTL structure* $\mathfrak{I} = (\mathcal{I}_i)_{i=0,1,\ldots}$, *and a time point* $i \in \{0, 1, 2, \ldots\}$, *validity of* ϕ *in* $\mathfrak{I}$ *at time* i *(written* $\mathfrak{I}, i \models \phi$*) is defined inductively:*

$$
\begin{aligned}
&\mathfrak{I}, i \models C \sqsubseteq D && \textit{iff } C^{\mathcal{I}_i} \subseteq D^{\mathcal{I}_i} \\
&\mathfrak{I}, i \models a : C && \textit{iff } a^{\mathcal{I}_i} \in C^{\mathcal{I}_i} \\
&\mathfrak{I}, i \models (a, b) : r && \textit{iff } (a^{\mathcal{I}_i}, b^{\mathcal{I}_i}) \in r^{\mathcal{I}_i} \\
&\mathfrak{I}, i \models \phi \wedge \psi && \textit{iff } \mathfrak{I}, i \models \phi \textit{ and } \mathfrak{I}, i \models \psi \\
&\mathfrak{I}, i \models \neg\phi && \textit{iff not } \mathfrak{I}, i \models \phi \\
&\mathfrak{I}, i \models \mathsf{X}\phi && \textit{iff } \mathfrak{I}, i + 1 \models \phi \\
&\mathfrak{I}, i \models \phi\mathsf{U}\psi && \textit{iff there is } k \geq i \textit{ such that } \mathfrak{I}, k \models \psi \\
&&& \quad \textit{and } \mathfrak{I}, j \models \phi \textit{ for all } j, i \leq j < k
\end{aligned}
$$

As mentioned before, for some concepts and roles it is not desirable that their interpretation changes over time. For example, in a medical application, we may want to assume that the gender and the father of a patient do not change over time, whereas the health status of a patient may of course change. Thus, we will assume that a subset of the set of concept and role names can be designated as being rigid. We will call the elements of this subset *rigid concept names* and *rigid role names*. All other concept and role names are called *flexible*.

Definition 5. *We say that the $\mathcal{ALC}$-LTL structure $\mathfrak{I} = (\mathcal{I}_i)_{i=0,1,\ldots}$ respects rigid names iff $A^{\mathcal{I}_i} = A^{\mathcal{I}_j}$ and $r^{\mathcal{I}_i} = r^{\mathcal{I}_j}$ holds for all $i, j \in \{0, 1, 2, \ldots\}$, all rigid concept names A, and all rigid role names r. The $\mathcal{ALC}$-LTL structure $\mathfrak{I}$ is a model of the $\mathcal{ALC}$-LTL formula ϕ (w.r.t. rigid names) iff $\mathfrak{I}, 0 \models \phi$ (and $\mathfrak{I}$ respects rigid names). The $\mathcal{ALC}$-LTL formula ϕ is* satisfiable *(w.r.t. rigid names) iff there is an $\mathcal{ALC}$-LTL structure $\mathfrak{I}$ (respecting rigid names) such that $\mathfrak{I}, 0 \models \phi$. For clarity, if rigidity of names is not required, then we sometimes talk about satisfiable without rigid names.*

In [3], it is shown that satisfiability w.r.t. rigid names in $\mathcal{ALC}$-LTL is 2-EXP-TIME-complete, whereas satisfiability without rigid names is "only" EXPTIME-complete. The decision procedures developed in [3] to show the complexity upper bounds are not based on generalized Büchi automata. In the next section, we show, however, that the ideas underlying these decision procedures can also be used to obtain automata-based decision procedures.

3   Generalized Büchi Automata for $\mathcal{ALC}$-LTL Formulae

For propositional LTL, the satisfiability problem can be decided by first constructing a generalized Büchi automaton for the given formula, and then testing this automaton for emptiness. Generalized Büchi automata can be used to define ω-languages, i.e., sets of infinite words. For an alphabet Σ, we denote the set of all infinite words over Σ by Σ^ω.

Definition 6. *A* generalized Büchi automaton *$\mathcal{G} = (Q, \Sigma, \Delta, Q_0, \mathcal{F})$ consists of a finite set of states Q, a finite input alphabet Σ, a transition relation $\Delta \subseteq Q \times \Sigma \times Q$, a set $Q_0 \subseteq Q$ of initial states, and a set of sets of final states $\mathcal{F} \subseteq 2^Q$.*
*   Given an infinite word $w = \sigma_0 \sigma_1 \sigma_2 \ldots \in \Sigma^\omega$, a* run *of $\mathcal{G}$ on w is an infinite word $q_0 q_1 q_2 \ldots \in Q^\omega$ such that $q_0 \in Q_0$ and $(q_i, \sigma_i, q_{i+1}) \in \Delta$ for all $i \geq 0$. This run is* accepting *if, for every $F \in \mathcal{F}$, there are infinitely many $i \geq 0$ such that $q_i \in F$. The language accepted by $\mathcal{G}$ is defined as*

$$L_\omega(\mathcal{G}) := \{w \in \Sigma^\omega \mid \text{there is an accepting run of } \mathcal{G} \text{ on } w\}.$$

The emptiness problem *for generalized Büchi automata is the problem of deciding, given a generalized Büchi automaton $\mathcal{G}$, whether $L_\omega(\mathcal{G}) = \emptyset$ or not.*

We use *generalized* Büchi automata rather than normal ones (where $|\mathcal{F}| = 1$) since this allows for a simpler construction of the automaton for a given $\mathcal{ALC}$-LTL formula. It is well-known that a generalized Büchi automaton can be transformed into an equivalent normal one in polynomial time [9,4]. Together with the fact that the emptiness problem for normal Büchi automata can be solved in polynomial time [15], this yields a polynomial time bound for the complexity of the emptiness problem for generalized Büchi automata.

3.1   The Case without Rigid Names

In principle, given an $\mathcal{ALC}$-LTL formula ϕ, we want to construct a generalized Büchi automaton $\mathcal{G}_\phi$ that accepts exactly the models of ϕ. However, since there are infinitely many $\mathcal{ALC}$-interpretations, we would end up with an infinite alphabet for this automaton. For this reason, we abstract from the specific interpretations, and only consider their $\mathcal{ALC}$-types. We call an $\mathcal{ALC}$-axiom α a ϕ-*axiom* if it occurs in ϕ. A ϕ-*literal* is a ϕ-axiom or the negation of a ϕ-axiom. For example, the formula

$$\phi_{ex} := \mathsf{X}(a : A) \wedge ((A \sqsubseteq B) \, \mathsf{U} \, (a : \neg B)) \tag{1}$$

has $a : A, A \sqsubseteq B, a : \neg B, \neg(a : A), \neg(A \sqsubseteq B), \neg(a : \neg B)$ as its literals. In the following, we assume that an arbitrary (but fixed) $\mathcal{ALC}$-LTL formula ϕ is given.

Definition 7. *The set of ϕ-literals T is an $\mathcal{ALC}$-type for ϕ iff the following two properties are satisfied:*

1. *For every ϕ-axiom α we have $\alpha \in T$ iff $\neg\alpha \notin T$.*
2. *The Boolean $\mathcal{ALC}$-knowledge base $\mathcal{B}_T := \bigwedge_{\alpha \in T} \alpha$ is consistent.*

We denote the set of all $\mathcal{ALC}$-types for ϕ with Σ^ϕ.

For example, $\{a : A, A \sqsubseteq B, \neg(a : \neg B)\}$ is an $\mathcal{ALC}$-type for ϕ_{ex} whereas $\{a : A, A \sqsubseteq B, a : \neg B\}$ is not (since it violates the second condition).

Given an $\mathcal{ALC}$-interpretation $\mathcal{I}$, we define its ϕ-type $\tau_\phi(\mathcal{I})$ as the set of all ϕ-literals that $\mathcal{I}$ is a model of. It is easy to see that $\tau_\phi(\mathcal{I})$ is an $\mathcal{ALC}$-type for ϕ. Conversely, given an $\mathcal{ALC}$-type T for ϕ, the model $\mathcal{I}$ of $\mathcal{B}_T$ is such that $\tau_\phi(\mathcal{I}) = T$. The evaluation of ϕ in an $\mathcal{ALC}$-LTL structure only depends on the ϕ-types of the $\mathcal{ALC}$-interpretations in this structure. To be more precise, given an $\mathcal{ALC}$-LTL structure $\mathfrak{I} = (\mathcal{I}_i)_{i=0,1,\ldots}$, its ϕ-type is the following infinite word over Σ^ϕ: $\tau_\phi(\mathfrak{I}) := \tau_\phi(\mathcal{I}_0)\tau_\phi(\mathcal{I}_1)\tau_\phi(\mathcal{I}_2)\ldots$.

If $\mathfrak{I}, \mathfrak{J}$ are two $\mathcal{ALC}$-LTL structures whose ϕ-types coincide, then we have $\mathfrak{I}, i \models \phi$ iff $\mathfrak{J}, i \models \phi$ for all $i \geq 0$. In particular, $\mathfrak{I}$ is a model of ϕ iff $\mathfrak{J}$ is a model of ϕ. Instead of accepting the models of ϕ, the generalized Büchi automaton $\mathcal{G}_\phi$ will accept their ϕ-types.

The states of $\mathcal{G}_\phi$ are types that also take the structure (and not just the axioms) of the $\mathcal{ALC}$-LTL formula ϕ into account. A *sub-literal* of ϕ is a sub-formula or its negation. For example, the formula ϕ_{ex} in (1) has the sub-literals $\phi_{ex}, \mathsf{X}(a : A), a : A, (A \sqsubseteq B) \, \mathsf{U} \, (a : \neg B), A \sqsubseteq B, a : \neg B, \neg\phi_{ex}, \neg\mathsf{X}(a : A), \neg(a : A), \neg((A \sqsubseteq B) \, \mathsf{U} \, (a : \neg B)), \neg(A \sqsubseteq B), \neg(a : \neg B)$.

Definition 8. *The set T of sub-literals of ϕ is an $\mathcal{ALC}$-LTL-type for ϕ iff the following properties are satisfied:*

1. *For every sub-formula ψ of ϕ we have $\psi \in T$ iff $\neg\psi \notin T$.*
2. *For every sub-formula $\psi_1 \wedge \psi_2$ of ϕ we have $\psi_1 \wedge \psi_2 \in T$ iff $\{\psi_1, \psi_2\} \subseteq T$.*
3. *For every sub-formula $\psi_1 \, \mathsf{U} \, \psi_2$ of ϕ we have*

- $\psi_2 \in T \Rightarrow \psi_1 U \psi_2 \in T$,
- $\psi_1 U \psi_2 \in T$ and $\psi_2 \notin T \Rightarrow \psi_1 \in T$.

4. *The restriction of T to its ϕ-literals is an $\mathcal{ALC}$-type for ϕ.*

We denote the set of all $\mathcal{ALC}$-LTL-types for ϕ by Q^ϕ.

For example, $\{\phi_{ex}, X(a : A), a : A, (A \sqsubseteq B) U (a : \neg B), A \sqsubseteq B, \neg(a : \neg B)\}$ is an $\mathcal{ALC}$-LTL-type for ϕ_{ex}.

The conditions for until in the definition of an $\mathcal{ALC}$-LTL-type T allow an until-formula $\psi_1 U \psi_2 \in T$ to be satisfied either now ($\psi_2 \in T$) or later ($\psi_1 \in T$). The automaton $\mathcal{G}_\phi$ uses the generalized Büchi-acceptance condition to prevent that satisfaction of until formulae is deferred indefinitely. This automaton has the set of all $\mathcal{ALC}$-types for ϕ as its alphabet and the set of all $\mathcal{ALC}$-LTL-types for ϕ as its set of states.

Definition 9. *Given an $\mathcal{ALC}$-LTL formula ϕ, the corresponding generalized Büchi automaton $\mathcal{G}_\phi = (Q^\phi, \Sigma^\phi, \Delta^\phi, Q_0^\phi, \mathcal{F}^\phi)$ is defined as follows:*

- *$\Delta^\phi \subseteq Q^\phi \times \Sigma^\phi \times Q^\phi$ is defined as follows: $(q, \sigma, q') \in \Delta^\phi$ iff*
  - *σ is the restriction of q to its ϕ-literals;*
  - *$X\psi \in q$ implies $\psi \in q'$;*
  - *$\psi_1 U \psi_2 \in q$ implies that (i) $\psi_2 \in q$ or (ii) $\psi_1 \in q$ and $\psi_1 U \psi_2 \in q'$;*
- *$Q_0^\phi := \{q \in Q^\phi \mid \phi \in q\}$;*
- *$\mathcal{F}^\phi := \{F_{\psi_1 U \psi_2} \mid \psi_1 U \psi_2$ is a sub-formula of $\phi\}$ where*

$$F_{\psi_1 U \psi_2} := \{q \in Q^\phi \mid \psi_1 U \psi_2 \notin q \text{ or } \psi_2 \in q\}.$$

The following proposition states in which sense this construction of $\mathcal{G}_\phi$ is correct. Its proof is similar to the one for correctness of the automaton construction for propositional LTL [16,15].

Proposition 1. *For every infinite word $w \in (\Sigma^\phi)^\omega$, we have $w \in L_\omega(\mathcal{G}_\phi)$ iff there exists an $\mathcal{ALC}$-LTL structure $\Im$ such that $\tau_\phi(\Im) = w$ and $\Im, 0 \models \phi$.*

As an immediate consequence of this proposition, we obtain that the $\mathcal{ALC}$-LTL formula ϕ is satisfiable iff $L_\omega(\mathcal{G}_\phi) \neq \emptyset$. Thus, we have reduced the satisfiability problem in $\mathcal{ALC}$-LTL (without rigid names) to the emptiness problem for generalized Büchi automata. It remains to analyze the complexity of the decision procedure for satisfiability obtained by this reduction.

The size of the automaton $\mathcal{G}_\phi$ is obviously exponential in ϕ. In addition, this automaton can be computed in exponential time. Indeed, to compute the set Σ^ϕ, we consider all the exponentially many subsets of the set of ϕ-literals. Each such set T has a size that is polynomial in the size of ϕ. The only non-trivial test needed to check whether T is an $\mathcal{ALC}$-type for ϕ is the consistency test for $\mathcal{B}_T$. Since the consistency problem for Boolean $\mathcal{ALC}$-knowledge bases is ExpTime-complete [3], this test can be performed in exponential time. A similar argument can be used to show that Q^ϕ can be computed in exponential time. Obviously, given the exponentially large sets Σ^ϕ and Q^ϕ, the remaining components of $\mathcal{G}_\phi$ can also be computed in exponential time.

Since the emptiness problem for generalized Büchi automata can be solved in polynomial time, this yields an alternative proof for the fact (originally shown in [3]) that satisfiability of $\mathcal{ALC}$-LTL formulae (without rigid names) can be decided in exponential time.

3.2   The Case with Rigid Names

If rigid concept and role names must be taken into account, Proposition 1 is not sufficient to reduce satisfiability of ϕ w.r.t. rigid names to the emptiness problem for $\mathcal{G}_\phi$. The proposition says that, for any infinite word $T_0 T_1 T_2 \ldots \in L_\omega(\mathcal{G}_\phi)$, there is a model $\mathfrak{I} = (\mathcal{I}_i)_{i=0,1,\ldots}$ of ϕ with $\tau_\phi(\mathcal{I}_i) = T_i$ for $i \geq 0$. However, without additional precautions, there is no guarantee that the $\mathcal{ALC}$-interpretations $\mathcal{I}_i$ interpret the rigid concept and role names in the same way. In order to enforce this, the automaton has to keep track of which $\mathcal{ALC}$-types it has already read, and check the set of these types for consistency w.r.t. rigid names.

Definition 10. *The set $T = \{T_1, \ldots, T_k\}$ of $\mathcal{ALC}$-types for ϕ is r-consistent iff there are $\mathcal{ALC}$-interpretations $\mathcal{I}_1, \ldots, \mathcal{I}_k$ that share the same domain, coincide on the rigid concept and role names, and satisfy $\tau_\phi(\mathcal{I}_i) = T_i$ for $i = 1, \ldots, k$.*

The r-consistency of a set of $\mathcal{ALC}$-types can be decided using the renaming technique for flexible symbols introduced in [3]. Given a set $T = \{T_1, \ldots, T_k\}$ of $\mathcal{ALC}$-types for ϕ, we introduce renamed variants $A^{(i)}$ and $r^{(i)}$ ($i = 1, \ldots, k$) for every *flexible* concept name A and every *flexible* role name r. For a ϕ-literal α, its renamed variant $\alpha^{(i)}$ is obtained by replacing the flexible concept and role names occurring in α by the corresponding renamed variants. The following proposition is an easy consequence of the proof of Lemma 10 in [3].

Proposition 2. *Let $T = \{T_1, \ldots, T_k\}$ be a set of $\mathcal{ALC}$-types for ϕ. Then T is r-consistent iff the Boolean $\mathcal{ALC}$-knowledge base $\mathcal{B}_T$ is consistent, where*

$$\mathcal{B}_T := \bigwedge_{i=1,\ldots,k} \bigwedge_{\alpha \in T_i} \alpha^{(i)}.$$

The set of all r-consistent sets of $\mathcal{ALC}$-types for ϕ will be denoted by $\mathcal{C}_r^\phi$.

The automaton $\widehat{\mathcal{G}}_\phi$ that also takes care of rigid names has tuples (q_1, q_2) as states, where q_1 is a state of $\mathcal{G}_\phi$ and q_2 is an r-consistent set of $\mathcal{ALC}$-types for ϕ. In the first component, $\widehat{\mathcal{G}}_\phi$ works like $\mathcal{G}_\phi$, and in the second it simply collects all the $\mathcal{ALC}$-types it has read. The fact that the set in the second component must be r-consistent ensures that the semantics of rigid names is taken into account.

Definition 11. *For an $\mathcal{ALC}$-LTL formula ϕ with rigid names, the corresponding generalized Büchi automaton $\widehat{\mathcal{G}}_\phi = (\widehat{Q}^\phi, \Sigma^\phi, \widehat{\Delta}^\phi, \widehat{Q}_0^\phi, \widehat{\mathcal{F}}^\phi)$ is defined as follows:*

- *$\widehat{Q}^\phi := Q^\phi \times \mathcal{C}_r^\phi$;*
- *$\widehat{\Delta}^\phi \subseteq \widehat{Q}^\phi \times \Sigma^\phi \times \widehat{Q}^\phi$ is defined as follows: $((q_1, q_2), \sigma, (q_1', q_2')) \in \widehat{\Delta}^\phi$ iff $(q_1, \sigma, q_1') \in \Delta^\phi$ and $q_2' = q_2 \cup \{\sigma\}$;*

$- \; \widehat{Q}_0^\phi := \{(q_1, \emptyset) \mid q_1 \in Q_0^\phi\};$
$- \; \widehat{\mathcal{F}}^\phi := \{F \times \mathcal{C}_r^\phi \mid F \in \mathcal{F}^\phi\}.$

The following proposition states in which sense the construction of $\widehat{\mathcal{G}}_\phi$ is correct. It is an easy consequence of Proposition 1 and the definition of r-consistency.

Proposition 3. *For every infinite word* $w \in (\Sigma^\phi)^\omega$ *we have* $w \in L_\omega(\widehat{\mathcal{G}}_\phi)$ *iff there exists an* $\mathcal{ALC}$-*LTL structure* $\mathfrak{I}$ *respecting rigid names such that* $\tau_\phi(\mathfrak{I}) = w$ *and* $\mathfrak{I}, 0 \models \phi$.

As an immediate consequence of this proposition, we obtain that the $\mathcal{ALC}$-LTL formula ϕ is satisfiable w.r.t. rigid names iff $L_\omega(\widehat{\mathcal{G}}_\phi) \neq \emptyset$. Thus, we have reduced the satisfiability problem w.r.t. rigid names in $\mathcal{ALC}$-LTL to the emptiness problem for generalized Büchi automata. However, the complexity of this reduction is higher than for the case of satisfiability without rigid names.

The size of the automaton $\widehat{\mathcal{G}}_\phi$ is double-exponential in the size of ϕ. In fact, the set $\mathcal{C}_r^\phi$ of all r-consistent sets of $\mathcal{ALC}$-types for ϕ may contain double-exponentially many elements since there are exponentially many $\mathcal{ALC}$-types for ϕ. Each element of $\mathcal{C}_r^\phi$ may be of exponential size.

Next, we show that the automaton $\widehat{\mathcal{G}}_\phi$ can be computed in double-exponential time. In addition to computing $\mathcal{G}_\phi$, i.e., the automaton working in the first component of $\widehat{\mathcal{G}}_\phi$, one must also compute the set $\mathcal{C}_r^\phi$. For this, one considers all sets of $\mathcal{ALC}$-types for ϕ. There are double-exponentially many such sets, each of size at most exponential in the size of ϕ. By Proposition 2, testing such a set $\mathcal{T}$ for r-consistency amounts to testing the Boolean $\mathcal{ALC}$-knowledge base $\mathcal{B}_\mathcal{T}$ for consistency. Since the size of $\mathcal{B}_\mathcal{T}$ is exponential in the size of ϕ and the consistency problem for Boolean $\mathcal{ALC}$-knowledge bases is ExpTime-complete, this test can be performed in double-exponential time. Overall, the computation of $\mathcal{C}_r^\phi$ requires double-exponentially many tests each requiring double-exponential time. This shows that $\mathcal{C}_r^\phi$, and thus also $\widehat{\mathcal{G}}_\phi$, can be computed in double-exponential time.

Since the emptiness problem for generalized Büchi automata can be solved in polynomial time, this yields an alternative proof for the fact (originally shown in [3]) that satisfiability w.r.t. rigid names in $\mathcal{ALC}$-LTL can be decided in double-exponential time.

4   The Monitor Construction

The construction of the monitor is basically identical for the two cases (without rigid names, with rigid names) considered in the previous section since it only depends on the properties of the automata $\mathcal{G}_\phi$ and $\widehat{\mathcal{G}}_\phi$ respectively stated in Proposition 1 and Proposition 3, and not on the actual definitions of these automata. For this reason, we treat only the more complex case with rigid names in detail. However, we distinguish between two cases according to whether the monitor has complete or incomplete knowledge about the current state of the system.

4.1   The Case of Complete Knowledge

In this case, it is assumed that, at every time point, the monitor has complete information about the status of every $\mathcal{ALC}$-axiom occurring in the formula ϕ. To be more precise, assume that $\mathcal{I}_i$ is the $\mathcal{ALC}$-interpretation at time point i. Then the monitor receives its $\mathcal{ALC}$-type $\tau_\phi(\mathcal{I}_i)$ as input at this time point.

Before showing how a monitor for an $\mathcal{ALC}$-LTL formula ϕ can actually be constructed, let us first define how we expect it to behave. As mentioned in the introduction, such a monitor is a deterministic Moore automaton.

Definition 12. *A deterministic Moore automaton $\mathcal{M} = (S, \Sigma, \delta, s_0, \Gamma, \lambda)$ consists of a finite set of states S, a finite input alphabet Σ, a transition function $\delta : S \times \Sigma \to S$, an initial state $s_0 \in S$, a finite output alphabet Γ, and an output function $\lambda : S \to \Gamma$.*

The transition function and the output function can be extended to functions $\widehat{\delta} : S \times \Sigma^* \to S$ and $\widehat{\lambda} : \Sigma^* \to \Gamma$ as follows:

- *$\widehat{\delta}(s, \varepsilon) := s$ where ε denotes the empty word;*
- *$\widehat{\delta}(s, u\sigma) := \delta(\widehat{\delta}(s, u), \sigma)$ where $u \in \Sigma^*$ and $\sigma \in \Sigma$;*

and $\widehat{\lambda}(u) := \lambda(\widehat{\delta}(s_0, u))$ for every $u \in \Sigma^*$.

Given a finite sequence $\widetilde{\mathfrak{J}} = \mathcal{I}_0, \mathcal{I}_1, \ldots, \mathcal{I}_t$ of $\mathcal{ALC}$-interpretations, we say that it *respects rigid names* if these interpretations share the same domain and coincide on the rigid concept and role names. The ϕ-*type of* $\widetilde{\mathfrak{J}}$ is defined as $\tau_\phi(\widetilde{\mathfrak{J}}) := \tau_\phi(\mathcal{I}_0) \ldots \tau_\phi(\mathcal{I}_t)$. We say that the $\mathcal{ALC}$-LTL structure $\mathfrak{J} = (\mathcal{J}_i)_{i=0,1,\ldots}$ *extends* $\widetilde{\mathfrak{J}}$ iff $\mathcal{I}_i = \mathcal{J}_i$ for $i = 0, \ldots, t$. In principle, a monitor for ϕ needs to realize the following monitoring function m_ϕ:

$$
m_\phi(\widetilde{\mathfrak{J}}) := \begin{cases} \top & \text{if } \mathfrak{J}, 0 \models \phi \text{ for all } \mathcal{ALC}\text{-LTL structures } \mathfrak{J} \\ & \text{that respect rigid names and extend } \widetilde{\mathfrak{J}}, \\ \bot & \text{if } \mathfrak{J}, 0 \models \neg\phi \text{ for all } \mathcal{ALC}\text{-LTL structures } \mathfrak{J} \\ & \text{that respect rigid names and extend } \widetilde{\mathfrak{J}}, \\ ? & \text{otherwise.} \end{cases}
$$

Definition 13. *Let ϕ be an $\mathcal{ALC}$-LTL formula. The deterministic Moore automaton $\mathcal{M} = (S, \Sigma^\phi, \delta, s_0, \{\top, \bot, ?\}, \lambda)$ is a monitor w.r.t. rigid names for ϕ iff for all finite sequences $\widetilde{\mathfrak{J}}$ of $\mathcal{ALC}$-interpretations respecting rigid names we have $\widehat{\lambda}(\tau_\phi(\widetilde{\mathfrak{J}})) = m_\phi(\widetilde{\mathfrak{J}})$.*

Intuitively, this definition assumes that the system observed by the monitor respects rigid names, i.e., its states are $\mathcal{ALC}$-interpretations over the same domain and these interpretations coincide on the rigid concept and role names. At every time point, the monitor sees the $\mathcal{ALC}$-type of the current interpretation. Thus, if the states that the system successively entered up to time point t were $\mathcal{I}_0, \mathcal{I}_1, \ldots, \mathcal{I}_t$, then the monitor has received the word $\tau_\phi(\mathcal{I}_0) \ldots \tau_\phi(\mathcal{I}_t)$ over Σ^ϕ as input. The monitor now needs to tell (by its output) whether all possible extensions of the observed behavior satisfy ϕ (output $\top$, which says that the property ϕ will definitely be satisfied by this run of the system) or $\neg\phi$ (output $\bot$, which says that the property ϕ will definitely be violated by this run of the system); if neither is the case, then both satisfaction and violation are still possible, depending on the future behavior of the system. Since we assume that the system respects rigid names, only finite sequences $\mathcal{I}_0, \mathcal{I}_1, \ldots, \mathcal{I}_t$ that respect rigid names can actually be observed, and thus Definition 13 does not formulate any requirements for sequences not satisfying this restriction. Likewise, only $\mathcal{ALC}$-LTL structures respecting rigid names need to be considered as possible extensions in the definition of m_ϕ.

We will show now that a monitor w.r.t. rigid names for ϕ can in principle be obtained by first making the automata $\widehat{\mathcal{G}}_\phi$ and $\widehat{\mathcal{G}}_{\neg\phi}$ (viewed as automata working on *finite* words) deterministic and then building the product automaton of the deterministic automata obtained this way. The output for each state of this product automaton is determined through emptiness tests for generalized Büchi automata derived from $\widehat{\mathcal{G}}_\phi$ and $\widehat{\mathcal{G}}_{\neg\phi}$ by varying the initial states. If q is a state of $\widehat{\mathcal{G}}_\phi$ ($\widehat{\mathcal{G}}_{\neg\phi}$), then $\widehat{\mathcal{G}}_\phi^q$ ($\widehat{\mathcal{G}}_{\neg\phi}^q$) denotes the generalized Büchi automaton obtained from $\widehat{\mathcal{G}}_\phi$ ($\widehat{\mathcal{G}}_{\neg\phi}$) by replacing its set of initial states with the singleton set $\{q\}$. Note that $\widehat{\mathcal{G}}_\phi$ and $\widehat{\mathcal{G}}_{\neg\phi}$ are actually automata over the same alphabet (i.e., $\Sigma^\phi = \Sigma^{\neg\phi}$) since ϕ and $\neg\phi$ obviously contain the same $\mathcal{ALC}$-axioms.

Definition 14. *Let ϕ be an $\mathcal{ALC}$-LTL formula with rigid names, and let $\widehat{\mathcal{G}}_\phi = (\widehat{Q}^\phi, \Sigma^\phi, \widehat{\Delta}^\phi, \widehat{Q}_0^\phi, \widehat{\mathcal{F}}^\phi)$ be the generalized Büchi automaton corresponding to ϕ and $\widehat{\mathcal{G}}_{\neg\phi} = (\widehat{Q}^{\neg\phi}, \Sigma^{\neg\phi}, \widehat{\Delta}^{\neg\phi}, \widehat{Q}_0^{\neg\phi}, \widehat{\mathcal{F}}^{\neg\phi})$ be the generalized Büchi automaton corresponding to $\neg\phi$.*

The deterministic Moore automaton $\mathcal{M}_\phi = (S, \Sigma^\phi, \delta, s_0, \{\top, \bot, ?\}, \lambda)$ is defined as follows:

- $S := 2^{\widehat{Q}^\phi} \times 2^{\widehat{Q}^{\neg\phi}}$
- $s_0 := (\widehat{Q}_0^\phi, \widehat{Q}_0^{\neg\phi})$
- *For all $(P_1, P_2) \in S$ and $\sigma \in \Sigma^\phi$, we have $\delta((P_1, P_2), \sigma) := (P_1', P_2')$, where:*
  - $P_1' = \displaystyle\bigcup_{q_1 \in P_1} \{q_1' \in \widehat{Q}^\phi \mid (q_1, \sigma, q_1') \in \widehat{\Delta}^\phi\}$
  - $P_2' = \displaystyle\bigcup_{q_2 \in P_2} \{q_2' \in \widehat{Q}^{\neg\phi} \mid (q_2, \sigma, q_2') \in \widehat{\Delta}^{\neg\phi}\}$
- $\lambda : Q \to \{\top, \bot, ?\}$ *is defined as*

$$
\lambda((P_1, P_2)) := \begin{cases} \top & \text{if } (i)\ L_\omega(\widehat{\mathcal{G}}_{\neg\phi}^{q_2}) = \emptyset \text{ for all } q_2 \in P_2 \text{ and} \\ & \quad (ii)\ L_\omega(\widehat{\mathcal{G}}_\phi^{q_1}) \neq \emptyset \text{ for some } q_1 \in P_1 \\ \bot & \text{if } (i)\ L_\omega(\widehat{\mathcal{G}}_\phi^{q_1})) = \emptyset \text{ for all } q_1 \in P_1 \text{ and} \\ & \quad (ii)\ L_\omega(\widehat{\mathcal{G}}_{\neg\phi}^{q_2}) \neq \emptyset \text{ for some } q_2 \in P_2 \\ ? & \text{otherwise} \end{cases}
$$

Note that the conditions (ii) are necessary to have a unique output for every state of $\mathcal{M}_\phi$, and not just for the ones reachable from s_0. In fact, for the reachable ones, condition (i) implies condition (ii) (see the third and fourth item in Lemma 1 below). Let $\mathcal{M}_\phi = (S, \Sigma^\phi, \delta, s_0, \{\top, \bot, ?\}, \lambda)$ be the deterministic Moore automaton defined above. Given a state $s \in S$, we define $\widehat{\delta}_1(s)$ to be the first and $\widehat{\delta}_2(s)$ to be the second component of $\widehat{\delta}(s)$. The following lemma easily follows from Proposition 3.

Lemma 1. *Let $\widetilde{\mathfrak{I}}$ be a finite sequence of $\mathcal{ALC}$-interpretations respecting rigid names. Then the following equivalences hold:*

- *$m_\phi(\widetilde{\mathfrak{I}}) \neq \bot$ iff there exists $q_1 \in \delta_1(s_0, \tau_\phi(\widetilde{\mathfrak{I}}))$ such that $L_\omega(\widehat{\mathcal{G}}_\phi^{q_1}) \neq \emptyset$;*
- *$m_\phi(\widetilde{\mathfrak{I}}) \neq \top$ iff there exists $q_2 \in \delta_2(s_0, \tau_\phi(\widetilde{\mathfrak{I}}))$ such that $L_\omega(\widehat{\mathcal{G}}_{\neg\phi}^{q_2}) \neq \emptyset$;*
- *$L_\omega(\widehat{\mathcal{G}}_\phi^{q_1}) = \emptyset$ for all $q_1 \in \delta_1(s_0, \tau_\phi(\widetilde{\mathfrak{I}}))$ implies that there exists $q_2 \in \delta_2(s_0, \tau_\phi(\widetilde{\mathfrak{I}}))$ with $L_\omega(\widehat{\mathcal{G}}_{\neg\phi}^{q_2}) \neq \emptyset$;*
- *$L_\omega(\widehat{\mathcal{G}}_{\neg\phi}^{q_2}) = \emptyset$ for all $q_2 \in \delta_2(s_0, \tau_\phi(\widetilde{\mathfrak{I}}))$ implies that there exists $q_1 \in \delta_1(s_0, \tau_\phi(\widetilde{\mathfrak{I}}))$ such that $L_\omega(\widehat{\mathcal{G}}_\phi^{q_1}) \neq \emptyset$.*

The next theorem shows that this construction really yields a monitor according to Definition 13. Its proof is an easy consequence of Lemma 1.

Theorem 1. *The deterministic Moore automaton $\mathcal{M}_\phi$ introduced in Definition 14 is a monitor w.r.t. rigid names for ϕ.*

Since the size of the generalized Büchi automata $\widehat{\mathcal{G}}_\phi$ and $\widehat{\mathcal{G}}_{\neg\phi}$ is double-exponential in the size of ϕ, the size of the monitor $\mathcal{M}_\phi$ is triple-exponential in the size of ϕ, and it is easy to see that $\mathcal{M}_\phi$ can actually be computed in triple-exponential time.

4.2   The Case of Incomplete Knowledge

Instead of presupposing that, at every time point, the monitor has complete information about the status of every $\mathcal{ALC}$-axiom occurring in the formula ϕ, we now assume that the monitor receives incomplete information about the states of the system at different time points in the form of $\mathcal{ALC}$-ABoxes.[5] Given such an ABox $\mathcal{A}$ and an $\mathcal{ALC}$-axiom α occurring in ϕ, there are now three possible cases: (i) $\mathcal{A}$ implies α; (ii) $\mathcal{A}$ implies $\neg\alpha$; (iii) $\mathcal{A}$ implies neither α nor $\neg\alpha$. Under the assumption that all we know about the current state $\mathcal{I}$ of the system is that it is a model of $\mathcal{A}$, then in the third case we do not know whether α or $\neg\alpha$ holds in $\mathcal{I}$. This adds an additional source of uncertainty, which may cause the monitor to answer with ?.

In the following, we thus assume that the input alphabet $\widehat{\Sigma}$ for our monitor consists of all consistent $\mathcal{ALC}$-ABoxes. Formally speaking, a monitor over this alphabet can no longer be a deterministic Moore automaton since we have required the alphabet of such an automaton to be finite. It should be clear, however, that Definition 12 can trivially be extended to cover also the case of an infinite input alphabet. From a practical point of view, this means, of course, that one cannot precompute such an infinite monitor. Instead, one precomputes only the states of

---

[5] Instead of ABoxes we could also use arbitrary Boolean $\mathcal{ALC}$-knowledge bases here.

the monitor. Given such a state and an input ABox, one then needs to compute the transition (i.e., the successor state in the monitor) on-the-fly.

Before constructing the actual monitor, we formally define how we expect it to behave. Given a (finite) word $\widehat{w}$ over $\widehat{\Sigma}$, i.e., a finite sequence of $\mathcal{ALC}$-ABoxes $\widehat{w} = \mathcal{A}_0, \dots, \mathcal{A}_t$, the finite sequence $\widetilde{\mathfrak{I}} = \mathcal{I}_0, \mathcal{I}_1, \dots, \mathcal{I}_t$ of $\mathcal{ALC}$-interpretations is called a *model* of $\widehat{w}$ (written $\widetilde{\mathfrak{I}} \models \widehat{w}$) iff $\mathcal{I}_i$ is a model of $\mathcal{A}_i$ for $i = 1, \dots, t$. If $\widetilde{\mathfrak{I}}$ additionally respects rigid names, then we say that it is a *model w.r.t. rigid names*. The monitor w.r.t. partial knowledge for ϕ needs to realize the following monitoring function $\widehat{m}_\phi : \widehat{\Sigma}^* \to \{\top, \bot, ?\}$:

$$\widehat{m}_\phi(\widehat{w}) := \begin{cases} \top & \text{if } m_\phi(\widetilde{\mathfrak{I}}) = \top \text{ for all models w.r.t. rigid names of } \widehat{w}, \\ \bot & \text{if } m_\phi(\widetilde{\mathfrak{I}}) = \bot \text{ for all models w.r.t. rigid names of } \widehat{w}, \\ ? & \text{otherwise.} \end{cases}$$

Definition 15. *Let ϕ be an $\mathcal{ALC}$-LTL formula. The deterministic Moore automaton $\mathcal{M} = (S, \widehat{\Sigma}, \delta, s_0, \{\top, \bot, ?\}, \lambda)$ is a* monitor w.r.t. rigid names and incomplete knowledge *for ϕ iff for all finite sequences $\widehat{w}$ of $\mathcal{ALC}$-ABoxes, we have $\widehat{\lambda}(\widehat{w}) = \widehat{m}_\phi(\widehat{w})$.*

The monitor w.r.t. rigid names and incomplete knowledge for ϕ constructed in the following is almost identical to the monitor w.r.t. rigid names $\mathcal{M}_\phi$ constructed in the previous subsection. The only difference can be found in the definition of the transition functions. In $\mathcal{M}_\phi$, transitions are of the form $\delta(s, \sigma) = s'$ where σ is an $\mathcal{ALC}$-type for ϕ. In the monitor w.r.t. incomplete knowledge, the input symbol is a consistent $\mathcal{ALC}$-ABox $\mathcal{A}$ instead of an $\mathcal{ALC}$-type. Intuitively, $\mathcal{A}$ stands for all its models since all we know about the current state of the system is that it is a model of $\mathcal{A}$. The monitor must consider all the transitions (in the generalized Büchi automata $\widehat{\mathcal{G}}_\phi$ and $\widehat{\mathcal{G}}_{\neg\phi}$ for ϕ and $\neg\phi$) that can be induced by such models. To be more precise, the transitions in $\widehat{\mathcal{G}}_\phi$ and $\widehat{\mathcal{G}}_{\neg\phi}$ are made with the ϕ-types of these models as input symbols. In the following definition, we use the fact that σ is the ϕ-type of a model of $\mathcal{A}$ iff $\mathcal{A} \wedge \bigwedge_{\alpha \in \sigma} \alpha$ is consistent.

Definition 16. *Let ϕ be an $\mathcal{ALC}$-LTL formula with rigid names, and let $\widehat{\mathcal{G}}_\phi = (\widehat{Q}^\phi, \Sigma^\phi, \widehat{\Delta}^\phi, \widehat{Q}_0^\phi, \widehat{\mathcal{F}}^\phi)$ be the generalized Büchi automaton corresponding to ϕ and $\widehat{\mathcal{G}}_{\neg\phi} = (\widehat{Q}^{\neg\phi}, \Sigma^{\neg\phi}, \widehat{\Delta}^{\neg\phi}, \widehat{Q}_0^{\neg\phi}, \widehat{\mathcal{F}}^{\neg\phi})$ be the generalized Büchi automaton corresponding to $\neg\phi$.*

The deterministic Moore automaton $\mathcal{M}_\phi^{inc} = (S, \widehat{\Sigma}, \delta^{inc}, s_0, \{\top, \bot, ?\}, \lambda)$ is defined as follows:

- *S, s_0, and λ are defined as in Definition 14*
- *For all $(P_1, P_2) \in S$ and $\mathcal{A} \in \widehat{\Sigma}$, we have $\delta^{inc}((P_1, P_2), \sigma) := (P_1', P_2')$, where:*

$$P_1' = \bigcup_{\sigma \in \Sigma^\phi} \bigcup_{q_1 \in P_1} \{q_1' \in \widehat{Q}^\phi \mid (q_1, \sigma, q_1') \in \widehat{\Delta}^\phi \text{ and } \mathcal{A} \wedge \bigwedge_{\alpha \in \sigma} \alpha \text{ is consistent}\}$$

$$P_2' = \bigcup_{\sigma \in \Sigma^\phi} \bigcup_{q_2 \in P_2} \{q_2' \in \widehat{Q}^{\neg\phi} \mid (q_2, \sigma, q_2') \in \widehat{\Delta}^{\neg\phi} \text{ and } \mathcal{A} \wedge \bigwedge_{\alpha \in \sigma} \alpha \text{ is consistent}\}$$

Lemma 1 from the previous subsection can also be used to show correctness of the monitor construction in the case of incomplete knowledge.

Theorem 2. *The deterministic Moore automaton $\mathcal{M}_\phi^{inc}$ introduced in Definition 16 is a monitor w.r.t. rigid names and incomplete knowledge for ϕ.*

Since the input alphabet $\widehat{\Sigma}$ of $\mathcal{M}_\phi^{inc}$ is infinite, it only makes sense to measure the size of $\mathcal{M}_\phi^{inc}$ in terms of the size of its set of states. This set is identical to the set of states S of $\mathcal{M}_\phi$, and we have already seen that S is of triple-exponential size. Regarding the on-the-fly computation of the transitions in $\mathcal{M}_\phi^{inc}$, for a given input ABox $\mathcal{A}$, one needs to consider the exponentially many $\mathcal{ALC}$-types for ϕ, and, for each such type σ, check the Boolean $\mathcal{ALC}$-knowledge base $\mathcal{A} \wedge \bigwedge_{\alpha \in \sigma} \alpha$ for consistency. This test is exponential in the size of this knowledge base, and thus exponential in the size of ϕ and in the size of $\mathcal{A}$.

5 Conclusion

We have shown that the three-valued approach to runtime verification in propositional LTL [5] can be extended to $\mathcal{ALC}$-LTL and the case where states of the observed system may be described in an incomplete way by $\mathcal{ALC}$-ABoxes. The complexity of the monitor construction is quite high. We have seen that the size of our monitors is triple-exponential in the size of the formula ϕ.[6] However, the size of the formula is usually quite small, whereas the system is monitored over a long period of time. If we assume the size of the formula to be constant (an assumption often made in model checking and runtime verification), then our monitor works in time linear in the length of the observed prefix. Moreover, each input symbol (i.e., $\mathcal{ALC}$-type or consistent ABox) can be processed in constant time.

It should also be noted that the triple-exponential complexity of the monitor construction is a worst-case complexity. Minimization of the intermediate generalized Büchi automata and the monitor may lead to much smaller automata than the ones defined above. We have observed this behavior on several small example formulae. A more thorough empirical evaluation will be part of our future research.

From a worst-case complexity point of view, the large size of the monitor can probably not be avoided. In fact, the complexity lower bounds for the satisfiability problem in $\mathcal{ALC}$-LTL (ExpTime-hard without rigid names and 2-ExpTime-hard with rigid names) imply that our construction of the generalized Büchi automata $\mathcal{G}_\phi$ and $\widehat{\mathcal{G}}_\phi$ is optimal. Regarding complexity lower bounds for the size of the monitor, it is known [13,12] that, in the case of propositional LTL, the monitor must in general be of size at least exponential in the size of the formula. However, the constructions in the literature [5] actually yield monitors of double-exponential size, i.e., one exponential higher than the size of the generalized Büchi automata for propositional LTL.

---

[6] For the case without rigid names it is "only" double-exponential since the generalized Büchi automata are then smaller.

References

1. Artale, A., Franconi, E.: A survey of temporal extensions of description logics. Ann. of Mathematics and Artificial Intelligence 30, 171–210 (2000)
2. Artale, A., Franconi, E.: Temporal description logics. In: Gabbay, D., Fisher, M., Vila, L. (eds.) Handbook of Time and Temporal Reasoning in Artificial Intelligence. The MIT Press, Cambridge (2001)
3. Baader, F., Ghilardi, S., Lutz, C.: LTL over description logic axioms. In: Brewka, G., Lang, J. (eds.) Proc. of the 11th Int. Conf. on Principles of Knowledge Representation and Reasoning (KR 2008), pp. 684–694. Morgan Kaufmann, Los Altos (2008)
4. Baier, C., Katoen, J.-P.: Principles of Model Checking. The MIT Press, Cambridge (2008)
5. Bauer, A., Leucker, M., Schallhart, C.: Monitoring of real-time properties. In: Arun-Kumar, S., Garg, N. (eds.) FSTTCS 2006. LNCS, vol. 4337, pp. 260–272. Springer, Heidelberg (2006)
6. Bauer, A., Leucker, M., Schallhart, C.: Comparing LTL semantics for runtime verification. Journal of Logic and Computation (2009)
7. Clarke, E.M., Grumberg, O., Peled, D.A.: Model Checking. The MIT Press, Cambridge (1999)
8. Colin, S., Mariani, L.: Run-time verification. In: Broy, M., Jonsson, B., Katoen, J.-P., Leucker, M., Pretschner, A. (eds.) Model-Based Testing of Reactive Systems. LNCS, vol. 3472, pp. 525–555. Springer, Heidelberg (2005)
9. Gerth, R., Peled, D., Vardi, M.Y., Wolper, P.: Simple on-the-fly automatic verification of linear temporal logic. In: Proceedings of the Fifteenth IFIP WG6.1 International Symposium on Protocol Specification, Testing and Verification XV, London, UK, pp. 3–18. Chapman & Hall, Ltd., Boca Raton (1996)
10. Lutz, C., Wolter, F., Zakharyaschev, M.: Temporal description logics: A survey. In: Demri, S., Jensen, C.S. (eds.) Proc. of the 15th Int. Symp. on Temporal Representation and Reasoning (TIME 2008), pp. 3–14. IEEE Computer Society Press, Los Alamitos (2008)
11. Pnueli, A.: The temporal logic of programs. In: Proc. of the 18th Annual Symp. on the Foundations of Computer Science (FOCS 1977), pp. 46–57 (1977)
12. Roşu, G.: On safety properties and their monitoring. Technical Report UIUCDCS-R-2007-2850, Department of Computer Science, University of Illinois at Urbana-Champaign (2007)
13. Roşu, G., Havelund, K.: Rewriting-based techniques for runtime verification. Automated Software Engineering 12(2), 151–197 (2005)
14. Schmidt-Schauß, M., Smolka, G.: Attributive concept descriptions with complements. Artificial Intelligence 48(1), 1–26 (1991)
15. Vardi, M.Y., Wolper, P.: Reasoning about infinite computations. Information and Computation 115(1), 1–37 (1994)
16. Wolper, P., Vardi, M.Y., Prasad Sistla, A.: Reasoning about infinite computation paths. In: Proc. of the 24th Annual Symp. on the Foundations of Computer Science (FOCS 1983), pp. 185–194. IEEE Computer Society Press, Los Alamitos (1983)

Axiomatization and Completeness of Lexicographic Products of Modal Logics

Philippe Balbiani

CNRS — Université de Toulouse
Institut de recherche en informatique de Toulouse
118 ROUTE DE NARBONNE, 31062 TOULOUSE CEDEX 9, France
Philippe.Balbiani@irit.fr

Abstract. This paper sets out a new way of combining Kripke-complete modal logics: lexicographic product. It discusses some basic properties of the lexicographic product construction and proves axiomatization/completeness results.

Keywords: Modal logic, lexicographic product, axiomatization/completeness.

1 Introduction

From state transition systems for computer programs to semantic networks for knowledge representation, multifarious applications of modal logic to computer science and artificial intelligence require propositional languages combining different kinds of modal connectives for talking about time, action, knowledge, etc. Within the context of multi-agent distributed systems, we should consider, for example, the combination of temporal logic with epistemic logic considered by Fagin *et al.* [7] and the combination of dynamic logic with epistemic logic considered by van Ditmarsch *et al.* [5].

A lot of these combinations are products of modal logics. Given Kripke complete modal logics $L_1, \ldots, L_n$ in languages respectively based on $\Box_1, \ldots, \Box_n$, the product of $L_1, \ldots, L_n$ is defined as the modal logic $L_1 \times \ldots \times L_n = Log\{\mathcal{F}_1 \times \ldots \times \mathcal{F}_n \colon \mathcal{F}_1 \models L_1, \ldots, \mathcal{F}_n \models L_n\}$ in a language based on $\Box_1, \ldots, \Box_n$ where the product $\mathcal{F}_1 \times \ldots \times \mathcal{F}_n$ of frames $\mathcal{F}_1 = (W_1, R_1), \ldots, \mathcal{F}_n = (W_n, R_n)$ is the frame $\mathcal{F} = (W, S_1, \ldots, S_n)$ defined by putting $W = W_1 \times \ldots \times W_n$ and $(u_1, \ldots, u_n) \, S_i \, (v_1, \ldots, v_n)$ iff $u_1 = v_1, \ldots, u_{i-1} = v_{i-1}, u_i \, R_i \, v_i, u_{i+1} = v_{i+1}, \ldots, u_n = v_n$. See [9,10] for a detailed study of the axiomatization and the decidability of such a product of modal logics.

Given Kripke complete modal logics $L_1, \ldots, L_n$ in languages respectively based on $\Box_1, \ldots, \Box_n$, it also makes sense to consider the "lexicographic" product of $L_1, \ldots, L_n$ defined as the modal logic $L_1 \rhd \ldots \rhd L_n = Log\{\mathcal{F}_1 \rhd \ldots \rhd \mathcal{F}_n \colon \mathcal{F}_1 \models L_1, \ldots, \mathcal{F}_n \models L_n\}$ in a language based on $\Box_1, \ldots, \Box_n$ where the product $\mathcal{F}_1 \rhd \ldots \rhd \mathcal{F}_n$ of frames $\mathcal{F}_1 = (W_1, R_1), \ldots, \mathcal{F}_n = (W_n, R_n)$ is the frame $\mathcal{F} = (W, S_1, \ldots, S_n)$ defined by putting $W = W_1 \times \ldots \times W_n$ and $(u_1, \ldots, u_n) \, S_i$

S. Ghilardi and R. Sebastiani (Eds.): FroCoS 2009, LNAI 5749, pp. 165–180, 2009.

$(v_1, \ldots, v_n)$ iff $u_i \ R_i \ v_i$, $u_{i+1} = v_{i+1}$, $\ldots$, $u_n = v_n$. Although such a product of frames has been considered recently [1], the detailed study of the modal logics it gives rise to has never been undertaken.

We can best illustrate the importance of the notion of lexicographic product in computer science and artificial intelligence by considering the three following examples. First, within the context of time representation and temporal reasoning, several papers consider the need of ordering different events within a single instant. See [6] for a survey. To satisfy this need, one can think about using lexicographic products of temporal orderings. That is to say, given temporal orderings $\mathcal{F}_1 = (W_1, R_1)$ and $\mathcal{F}_2 = (W_2, R_2)$, one may use their lexicographic product $\mathcal{F} = (W, S_1, S_2)$ where the grained temporal domain concerned by S_1 is less coarse than the grained temporal domain concerned by S_2. Second, within the context of preference modelling and decision analysis, several papers consider the need of gathering together preferences associated to different criteria. See [16] for a survey. To satisfy this need, one can think about using lexicographic products of preference orderings. That is to say, given preference orderings $\mathcal{F}_1 = (W_1, R_1)$ and $\mathcal{F}_2 = (W_2, R_2)$, one may use their lexicographic product $\mathcal{F} = (W, S_1, S_2)$ where the criterion concerned by S_1 is less important than the criterion concerned by S_2. Third, within the context of human-computer interaction, computer programmers have to produce softwares for multifarious users while making them work as if they were produced for each individual user and several papers consider that the user-software interactions are such that the software must stand idle during the activity period of the user whereas the user may nondeterministically bustle about during the activity period of the software. See [17] for a survey. In this respect, given Kripke structures $\mathcal{F}_1 = (W_1, R_1)$ and $\mathcal{F}_2 = (W_2, R_2)$ capturing the behaviours of a human and a computer, their lexicographic product $\mathcal{F} = (W, S_1, S_2)$ captures the behaviour of the system made up of the human and the computer.

The section-by-section breakdown of the paper is as follows. In section 2, we introduce the syntax and the semantics of our modal logics. Section 3 defines the notion of lexicographic product of frames whereas section 4 defines the notion of lexicographic product of Kripke complete modal logics. In section 5, we consider the interactions between modal connectives which will result in certain lexicographic products. Taking into account what we have observed in section 5, section 6 addresses the axiomatization/completeness issue related to lexicographic products. In section 7, we suggest several open problems. We assume the reader is at home with tools and techniques in modal logic (homomorphism, bounded morphism, bisimulation, etc). For more on these see [4]. *Every modal logic considered in this paper is normal.* In all our figures, black circles represent irreflexive possible worlds whereas white circles represent reflexive possible worlds. See [2] for a long version of this paper that contains the proofs of all its propositions.

2   Syntax and Semantics of Our Modal Logics

In this section, we introduce the syntax and the semantics of our modal logics.

2.1   Syntax

Suppose that we have a denumerably infinite set BV of Boolean variables (with typical members denoted p, q, ...). A modal language is a structure of the form $\mathcal{L} = (BV, MS)$ where MS is a countable set of modality symbols (with typical members denoted α, β, ...). The set of formulas of $\mathcal{L}$ (with typical members denoted ϕ, ψ, ...) is defined as follows:

- $\phi ::= p \mid \perp \mid \neg\phi \mid (\phi \vee \phi) \mid \Box_\alpha\phi$.

It is usual to omit parentheses if this does not lead to any ambiguity. We adopt the standard definitions for the remaining Boolean connectives. As usual, we define $\Diamond_\alpha\phi ::= \neg\Box_\alpha\neg\phi$ for each $\alpha \in MS$. The length of formula ϕ, denoted by $length(\phi)$, is defined to be the number of symbols in ϕ. The closure of ϕ, denoted by $Cl(\phi)$, is defined to be the least set S of formulas such that $\phi \in S$ and S is closed under subformulas. It is a simple matter to check that $Card(Cl(\phi)) \leq length(\phi)$. We shall say that ϕ is variable-free iff it contains no Boolean variables. Let MS_1 and MS_2 be disjoint countable sets of modality symbols. We define the union

$$\mathcal{L}_1 \otimes \mathcal{L}_2$$

of the language $\mathcal{L}_1 = (BV, MS_1)$ and the language $\mathcal{L}_2 = (BV, MS_2)$ as the language $(BV, MS_1 \cup MS_2)$.

2.2   Semantics

Let $\mathcal{L} = (BV, MS)$ be a language. A frame for $\mathcal{L}$ is a structure of the form $\mathcal{F} = (W, \{R_\alpha : \alpha \in MS\})$ where W is a nonempty set of possible worlds and R_α is a binary relation on W for each $\alpha \in MS$. We shall say that $\mathcal{F}$ is rooted iff there exists $u_0 \in W$ such that $\mathcal{F}$ is generated by u_0. Such a u_0 is called a root of $\mathcal{F}$. The notion of generated subframe is standard. We adopt the standard definitions for the notions of homomorphism, bounded morphism, bisimulation, etc. A model for $\mathcal{L}$ is a structure of the form $\mathcal{M} = (\mathcal{F}, m)$ where $\mathcal{F} = (W, \{R_\alpha : \alpha \in MS\})$ is a frame for $\mathcal{L}$ and m is a valuation on $\mathcal{F}$ for $\mathcal{L}$, i.e. a function m: $BV \mapsto 2^W$. Satisfaction is a 3-place relation $\models$ between a model $\mathcal{M} = (W, \{R_\alpha : \alpha \in MS\}, m)$, a possible world $u \in W$ and a formula ϕ. It is inductively defined as usual. In particular, for all $\alpha \in MS$,

- $\mathcal{M} \models_u \Box_\alpha\phi$ iff $\mathcal{M} \models_v \phi$ for each possible world $v \in W$ such that $u\, R_\alpha\, v$.

Let ϕ be a formula. We shall say that ϕ is true in model $\mathcal{M} = (W, \{R_\alpha : \alpha \in MS\}, m)$, in symbols $\mathcal{M} \models \phi$, iff $\mathcal{M} \models_u \phi$ for each possible world $u \in W$. ϕ is said to be valid in frame $\mathcal{F}$, in symbols $\mathcal{F} \models \phi$, iff $(\mathcal{F}, m) \models \phi$ for each valuation m on $\mathcal{F}$. We shall say that ϕ is valid in class $\mathcal{C}$ of frames, in symbols $\mathcal{C} \models \phi$, iff $\mathcal{F} \models \phi$ for each frame $\mathcal{F}$ in $\mathcal{C}$. Let $Log(\mathcal{C}) = \{\phi : \mathcal{C} \models \phi\}$.

2.3 Modal Logics

Let $\mathcal{L} = (BV, MS)$ be a language. A modal logic for $\mathcal{L}$ is a subset L of the set of formulas of $\mathcal{L}$ such that L contains all Boolean tautologies, L is closed under modus ponens, L is closed under uniform substitution, L contains the set of formulas of $\mathcal{L}$ of the form $\Box_\alpha(\phi \to \psi) \to (\Box_\alpha\phi \to \Box_\alpha\psi)$ for each $\alpha \in MS$ and L is closed under generalization, i.e. if $\phi \in L$ then $\Box_\alpha\phi \in L$ for each $\alpha \in MS$. Let $\mathsf{Fr}L = \{\mathcal{F}: \mathcal{F}$ is a frame validating all formulas in $L\}$ and $\mathsf{Fr}^rL = \{\mathcal{F}: \mathcal{F}$ is a rooted frame validating all formulas in $L\}$. We shall say that L is consistent iff $\bot \notin L$. Given a set Σ of formulas of $\mathcal{L}$, let $L \oplus \Sigma$ be the least modal logic for $\mathcal{L}$ containing L and Σ. The notion of a conservative extension is standard. We adopt the standard definitions for the notions of Kripke complete modal logic and canonical modal logic. Let MS_1 and MS_2 be disjoint countable sets of modality symbols. We define the fusion

$$L_1 \otimes L_2$$

of a modal logic L_1 for (BV, MS_1) and a modal logic L_2 for (BV, MS_2) as the least modal logic for $(BV, MS_1 \cup MS_2)$ containing L_1 and L_2. See [10,18] for a detailed study of fusions of modal logics. The modal logics that will be used in this paper are the modal logic K and the modal logics

- $K4.3 = K \oplus \{\Box p \to \Box\Box p, \Diamond p \wedge \Diamond q \to \Diamond(p \wedge q) \vee \Diamond(p \wedge \Diamond q) \vee \Diamond(\Diamond p \wedge q)\}$,
- $S5 = K \oplus \{\Box p \to p, \Box p \to \Box\Box p, \Diamond p \to \Box\Diamond p\}$,
- $S4.3 = K \oplus \{\Box p \to p, \Box p \to \Box\Box p, \Diamond p \wedge \Diamond q \to \Diamond(p \wedge \Diamond q) \vee \Diamond(\Diamond p \wedge q)\}$,
- $T = K \oplus \{\Box p \to p\}$,
- $DAlt = K \oplus \{\Box p \to \Diamond p, \Diamond p \to \Box p\}$,
- $D = K \oplus \{\Box p \to \Diamond p\}$,
- $S4 = K \oplus \{\Box p \to p, \Box p \to \Box\Box p\}$,
- $B = K \oplus \{\Box p \to p, p \to \Box\Diamond p\}$,
- $Triv = K \oplus \{\Box p \to p, p \to \Box p\}$,
- $KB4 = K \oplus \{p \to \Box\Diamond p, \Box p \to \Box\Box p\}$,
- $K4 = K \oplus \{\Box p \to \Box\Box p\}$,
- $KB = K \oplus \{p \to \Box\Diamond p\}$.

3 Lexicographic Products of Frames

We define the l-product of a frame $\mathcal{F}_1 = (W_1, \{R_1^j\}^{j=1\ldots k_1})$ and a frame $\mathcal{F}_2 = (W_2, \{R_2^j\}^{j=1\ldots k_2})$ as the frame of the form

$$\mathcal{F}_1 \rhd \mathcal{F}_2 = (W_1 \times W_2, \{S_1^j\}^{j=1\ldots k_1}, \{S_2^j\}^{j=1\ldots k_2})$$

in which for all $u_1, v_1 \in W_1$, for all $u_2, v_2 \in W_2$,

- $(u_1, u_2)\, S_1^j\, (v_1, v_2)$ iff $u_1\, R_1^j\, v_1$ and $u_2 = v_2$ for each $j \in \{1, \ldots, k_1\}$,
- $(u_1, u_2)\, S_2^j\, (v_1, v_2)$ iff $u_2\, R_2^j\, v_2$ for each $j \in \{1, \ldots, k_2\}$.

Such a frame will be called a l-product frame. Remark that if R_2^j is the universal relation on W_2 then S_2^j is the universal relation on $W_1 \times W_2$ for each $j \in \{1, \ldots, k_2\}$. In the case where $k_1 = 1$ and $k_2 = 1$ for example, the reader may easily verify, in figure 1, that the frame $\mathcal{F} = (W, S_1, S_2)$ is the l-product of the frames $\mathcal{F}_1 = (W_1, R_1)$ and $\mathcal{F}_2 = (W_2, R_2)$.

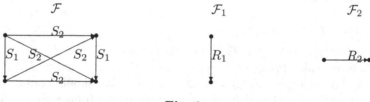

Fig. 1.

There exists frames $\mathcal{F}_1$, $\mathcal{F}_2$ such that $\mathcal{F}_1 \triangleright \mathcal{F}_2$ is not isomorphic to $\mathcal{F}_2 \triangleright \mathcal{F}_1$. We should consider, in the case where $k_1 = 1$ and $k_2 = 1$ for instance, the frames $\mathcal{F}_1 = (W_1, R_1)$ and $\mathcal{F}_2 = (W_2, R_2)$ defined in figure 2.

Fig. 2.

Nevertheless,

Proposition 1. *Let $\mathcal{F}_1$, $\mathcal{F}_2$ and $\mathcal{F}_3$ be frames. $(\mathcal{F}_1 \triangleright \mathcal{F}_2) \triangleright \mathcal{F}_3$ is isomorphic to $\mathcal{F}_1 \triangleright (\mathcal{F}_2 \triangleright \mathcal{F}_3)$.*

Hence, the notion of l-product frame can be extended to finitely many frames in a straightforward manner. The l-product of frames $\mathcal{F}_1 = (W_1, \{R_1^j\}^{j=1\ldots k_1})$, ..., $\mathcal{F}_n = (W_n, \{R_n^j\}^{j=1\ldots k_n})$ is the frame of the form

$$\triangleright(\mathcal{F}_1, \ldots, \mathcal{F}_n) = (W_1 \times \ldots \times W_n, \{S_i^j\}_{i=1\ldots n}^{j=1\ldots k_i})$$

where

$- (u_1, \ldots, u_n) \, S_i^j \, (v_1, \ldots, v_n)$ iff $u_i \, R_i^j \, v_i$, $u_{i+1} = v_{i+1}$, ..., $u_n = v_n$

for each $u_1, v_1 \in W_1$, ..., for each $u_n, v_n \in W_n$, for each $i \in \{1, \ldots, n\}$, for each $j \in \{1, \ldots, k_i\}$. Remark that if R_n^j is the universal relation on W_n then S_n^j is the universal relation on $W_1 \times \ldots \times W_n$ for each $j \in \{1, \ldots, k_n\}$. The reader may easily verify that

Proposition 2. *Let $\mathcal{F}_1$, ..., $\mathcal{F}_n$ be frames. $\triangleright(\mathcal{F}_1, \ldots, \mathcal{F}_n)$ is isomorphic to the following frames:*

$$- (\ldots(\mathcal{F}_1 \triangleright \mathcal{F}_2)\ldots \triangleright \mathcal{F}_n),$$
$$- \ldots,$$
$$- (\mathcal{F}_1 \triangleright \ldots (\mathcal{F}_{n-1} \triangleright \mathcal{F}_n)\ldots).$$

In other respects,

Proposition 3. *Let $\mathcal{F}_1, \ldots, \mathcal{F}_n$ be frames. Let $\mathcal{I}_1, \ldots, \mathcal{I}_n$ be frames. If $\mathcal{I}_1, \ldots, \mathcal{I}_n$ are such that $\mathcal{F}_i$ is isomorphic to $\mathcal{I}_i$ for each $i \in \{1,\ldots,n\}$ then $\triangleright(\mathcal{F}_1,\ldots,\mathcal{F}_n)$ is isomorphic to $\triangleright(\mathcal{I}_1,\ldots,\mathcal{I}_n)$.*

But there exists frames $\mathcal{F}_1, \ldots, \mathcal{F}_n$, there exists frames $\mathcal{I}_1, \ldots, \mathcal{I}_n$ such that $\mathcal{I}_i$ is a strong homomorphic image of $\mathcal{F}_i$ for each $i \in \{1,\ldots,n\}$ and $\triangleright(\mathcal{I}_1,\ldots,\mathcal{I}_n)$ is not a strong homomorphic image of $\triangleright(\mathcal{F}_1,\ldots,\mathcal{F}_n)$. We should consider, in the case where $n = 2$, $k_1 = 1$ and $k_2 = 1$ for example, the frames $\mathcal{F}_1 = (W_1, R_1)$, $\mathcal{F}_2 = (W_2, R_2)$, $\mathcal{I}_1 = (Z_1, U_1)$ and $\mathcal{I}_2 = (Z_2, U_2)$ defined in figure 3.

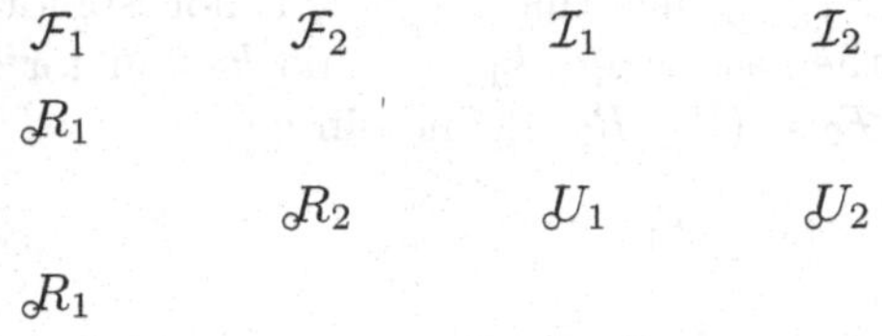

Fig. 3.

Nevertheless,

Proposition 4. *Let $\mathcal{F}_1, \ldots, \mathcal{F}_n$ be frames. Let $\mathcal{I}_1, \ldots, \mathcal{I}_n$ be frames. If $\mathcal{I}_1, \ldots, \mathcal{I}_n$ are such that $\mathcal{I}_i$ is a bounded morphic image of $\mathcal{F}_i$ for each $i \in \{1,\ldots,n\}$ then $\triangleright(\mathcal{I}_1,\ldots,\mathcal{I}_n)$ is a bounded morphic image of $\triangleright(\mathcal{F}_1,\ldots,\mathcal{F}_n)$.*

The truth of the matter is that

Proposition 5. *Let $\mathcal{F}_1, \ldots, \mathcal{F}_n$ be frames. Let $\mathcal{I}_1, \ldots, \mathcal{I}_n$ be frames. If $\mathcal{I}_1, \ldots, \mathcal{I}_n$ are such that $\mathcal{F}_i$ is strongly bisimilar to $\mathcal{I}_i$ for each $i \in \{1,\ldots,n\}$ then $\triangleright(\mathcal{F}_1,\ldots,\mathcal{F}_n)$ is strongly bisimilar to $\triangleright(\mathcal{I}_1,\ldots,\mathcal{I}_n)$.*

4   Lexicographic Products of Kripke Complete Logics

Given a class $\mathcal{C}_1$ of frames and a class $\mathcal{C}_2$ of frames, we define their l-product as the class of frames of the form

$$\mathcal{C}_1 \triangleright \mathcal{C}_2 = \{\mathcal{F}_1 \triangleright \mathcal{F}_2 \colon \mathcal{F}_1 \in \mathcal{C}_1 \text{ and } \mathcal{F}_2 \in \mathcal{C}_2\}.$$

Let L_1 and L_2 be two Kripke complete modal logics formulated in languages $\mathcal{L}_1$ and $\mathcal{L}_2$. We define the l-product of L_1 and L_2 as the modal logic

$$L_1 \triangleright L_2 = Log(\mathsf{Fr}L_1 \triangleright \mathsf{Fr}L_2)$$

in the language $\mathcal{L}_1 \otimes \mathcal{L}_2$. For instance, $K4.3 \triangleright K$ is the set of all formulas ϕ in the language $(BV, \{1,2\})$ such that $\mathcal{F}_1 \triangleright \mathcal{F}_2 \models \phi$ for each frame $\mathcal{F}_1 = (W_1, R_1)$ validating $K4.3$, for each frame $\mathcal{F}_2 = (W_2, R_2)$ whereas $K \triangleright K4.3$ is the set of all formulas ϕ in the language $(BV, \{1, 2\})$ such that $\mathcal{F}_1 \rhd \mathcal{F}_2 \models \phi$ for each frame $\mathcal{F}_1 = (W_1, R_1)$, for each frame $\mathcal{F}_2 = (W_2, R_2)$ validating $K4.3$. There exists Kripke complete modal logics L_1 and L_2 formulated in languages $\mathcal{L}_1$ and $\mathcal{L}_2$ such that $L_1 \rhd L_2 \not\supseteq Log(\mathsf{Fr}^r L_1 \rhd \mathsf{Fr}^r L_2)$. Take the case of the logics $L_1 = K4.3$ and $L_2 = K$ in languages $\mathcal{L}_1 = (BV, \{1\})$ and $\mathcal{L}_2 = (BV, \{2\})$, seeing that

- $\Box_1 \bot \to \Box_2(\Box_1 \bot \vee \Diamond_1 \Box_1 \bot) \notin K4.3 \rhd K$,
- $\Box_1 \bot \to \Box_2(\Box_1 \bot \vee \Diamond_1 \Box_1 \bot) \in Log(\mathsf{Fr}^r K4.3 \rhd \mathsf{Fr}^r K)$.

Leaving the proof that $\Box_1 \bot \to \Box_2(\Box_1 \bot \vee \Diamond_1 \Box_1 \bot) \in Log(\mathsf{Fr}^r K4.3 \rhd \mathsf{Fr}^r K)$ to the reader, let us demonstrate that $\Box_1 \bot \to \Box_2(\Box_1 \bot \vee \Diamond_1 \Box_1 \bot) \notin K4.3 \rhd K$. Let $\mathcal{F}_1 = (W_1, R_1)$ and $\mathcal{F}_2 = (W_2, R_2)$ be the frames defined in figure 4.

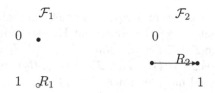

Fig. 4.

Obviously, $\mathcal{F}_1$ validates $K4.3$. Let m be a valuation on $\mathcal{F}_1 \rhd \mathcal{F}_2$. Obviously, $(\mathcal{F}_1 \rhd \mathcal{F}_2, m) \not\models_{(0,0)} \Box_1 \bot \to \Box_2(\Box_1 \bot \vee \Diamond_1 \Box_1 \bot)$. Consequently, $(\mathcal{F}_1 \rhd \mathcal{F}_2, m) \not\models \Box_1 \bot \to \Box_2(\Box_1 \bot \vee \Diamond_1 \Box_1 \bot)$. Therefore, $\mathcal{F}_1 \rhd \mathcal{F}_2 \not\models \Box_1 \bot \to \Box_2(\Box_1 \bot \vee \Diamond_1 \Box_1 \bot)$. Since $\mathcal{F}_1$ validates $K4.3$, then $\Box_1 \bot \to \Box_2(\Box_1 \bot \vee \Diamond_1 \Box_1 \bot) \notin K4.3 \rhd K$. Nevertheless,

Proposition 6. *Let L_1 and L_2 be two Kripke complete modal logics formulated in languages $\mathcal{L}_1$ and $\mathcal{L}_2$. $L_1 \rhd L_2 \subseteq Log(\mathsf{Fr} L_1 \rhd \mathsf{Fr}^r L_2)$.*

Proposition 7. *Let L_1 and L_2 be two Kripke complete modal logics formulated in languages $\mathcal{L}_1$ and $\mathcal{L}_2$. $L_1 \rhd L_2 \subseteq Log(\mathsf{Fr}^r L_1 \rhd \mathsf{Fr}^r L_2)$.*

In other respects,

Proposition 8. *Let L_1 and L_2 be two Kripke complete modal logics formulated in languages $\mathcal{L}_1$ and $\mathcal{L}_2$. $L_1 \rhd L_2 \supseteq Log(\mathsf{Fr} L_1 \rhd \mathsf{Fr}^r L_2)$.*

There exists consistent Kripke complete modal logics L_1 and L_2 formulated in languages $\mathcal{L}_1$ and $\mathcal{L}_2$ such that $L_1 \rhd L_2$ is not a conservative extension of L_2. Take the case of the logics $L_1 = K$ and $L_2 = K4.3$ in languages $\mathcal{L}_1 = (BV, \{1\})$ and $\mathcal{L}_2 = (BV, \{2\})$, seeing that

- $\Diamond_2 p \wedge \Diamond_2 q \to \Diamond_2(p \wedge q) \vee \Diamond_2(p \wedge \Diamond_2 q) \vee \Diamond_2(\Diamond_2 p \wedge q) \notin K \rhd K4.3$,
- $\Diamond_2 p \wedge \Diamond_2 q \to \Diamond_2(p \wedge q) \vee \Diamond_2(p \wedge \Diamond_2 q) \vee \Diamond_2(\Diamond_2 p \wedge q) \in K4.3$.

Leaving the proof that $\Diamond_2 p \wedge \Diamond_2 q \to \Diamond_2(p \wedge q) \vee \Diamond_2(p \wedge \Diamond_2 q) \vee \Diamond_2(\Diamond_2 p \wedge q) \in K4.3$ to the reader, let us demonstrate that $\Diamond_2 p \wedge \Diamond_2 q \to \Diamond_2(p \wedge q) \vee \Diamond_2(p \wedge \Diamond_2 q) \vee \Diamond_2(\Diamond_2 p \wedge q) \notin K \rhd K4.3$. Let $\mathcal{F}_1 = (W_1, R_1)$ and $\mathcal{F}_2 = (W_2, R_2)$ be the frames defined in figure 4. Obviously, $\mathcal{F}_2$ validates $K4.3$. Let m be a valuation on $\mathcal{F}_1 \rhd \mathcal{F}_2$ such that $m(p) = \{(0, 1)\}$ and $m(q) = \{(1, 1)\}$. Obviously, $(\mathcal{F}_1 \rhd \mathcal{F}_2, m) \not\models_{(0,0)}$

$\Diamond_2 p \wedge \Diamond_2 q \rightarrow \Diamond_2(p \wedge q) \vee \Diamond_2(p \wedge \Diamond_2 q) \vee \Diamond_2(\Diamond_2 p \wedge q)$. Consequently, $(\mathcal{F}_1 \rhd \mathcal{F}_2, m)$ $\not\models \Diamond_2 p \wedge \Diamond_2 q \rightarrow \Diamond_2(p \wedge q) \vee \Diamond_2(p \wedge \Diamond_2 q) \vee \Diamond_2(\Diamond_2 p \wedge q)$. Therefore, $\mathcal{F}_1 \rhd \mathcal{F}_2 \not\models$ $\Diamond_2 p \wedge \Diamond_2 q \rightarrow \Diamond_2(p \wedge q) \vee \Diamond_2(p \wedge \Diamond_2 q) \vee \Diamond_2(\Diamond_2 p \wedge q)$. Since $\mathcal{F}_2$ validates $K4.3$, then $\Diamond_2 p \wedge \Diamond_2 q \rightarrow \Diamond_2(p \wedge q) \vee \Diamond_2(p \wedge \Diamond_2 q) \vee \Diamond_2(\Diamond_2 p \wedge q) \notin K \rhd K4.3$. Nevertheless,

Proposition 9. *Let L_1 and L_2 be two consistent Kripke complete modal logics formulated in languages $\mathcal{L}_1$ and $\mathcal{L}_2$. $L_1 \rhd L_2$ is a conservative extension of L_1.*

In other respects,

Proposition 10. *Let L_1 and L_2 be two consistent Kripke complete modal logics formulated in languages $\mathcal{L}_1$ and $\mathcal{L}_2$. Let ϕ be a variable-free formula in the language $\mathcal{L}_2$. $\phi \in L_1 \rhd L_2$ iff $\phi \in L_2$.*

We shall say that the consistent Kripke complete modal logic L_1 formulated in language $\mathcal{L}_1$ distributes over the consistent Kripke complete modal logic L_2 formulated in language $\mathcal{L}_2$ iff for all frames $\mathcal{F} = (W, S_1, S_2)$, if $\mathcal{F} \models L_1 \rhd L_2$ then there exists frames $\mathcal{F}_1 = (W_1, R_1)$, $\mathcal{F}_2 = (W_2, R_2)$ such that $\mathcal{F}_1 \models L_1$, $\mathcal{F}_2 \models L_2$ and $\mathcal{F}$ is a bounded morphic image of $\mathcal{F}_1 \rhd \mathcal{F}_2$.

Proposition 11. *Let L_1, L_2 and L_3 be three consistent Kripke complete modal logics formulated in languages $\mathcal{L}_1$, $\mathcal{L}_2$ and $\mathcal{L}_3$. If L_1 distributes over L_2 then $(L_1 \rhd L_2) \rhd L_3 \supseteq L_1 \rhd (L_2 \rhd L_3)$.*

Proposition 12. *Let L_1, L_2 and L_3 be three consistent Kripke complete modal logics formulated in languages $\mathcal{L}_1$, $\mathcal{L}_2$ and $\mathcal{L}_3$. If L_2 distributes over L_3 then $(L_1 \rhd L_2) \rhd L_3 \subseteq L_1 \rhd (L_2 \rhd L_3)$.*

Concerning the question whether $(K \rhd K) \rhd K = K \rhd (K \rhd K)$, it remains open, seeing that, as we will show it in section 5.5, K does not distribute over itself. Nevertheless,

Proposition 13. $(S5 \rhd S5) \rhd S5 = S5 \rhd (S5 \rhd S5)$.

Now, we extend the notion of l-product of classes of frames to finitely many classes of frames as follows. The l-product of classes $\mathcal{C}_1, \ldots, \mathcal{C}_n$ of frames is the class of frames of the form

$$\rhd(\mathcal{C}_1, \ldots, \mathcal{C}_n) = \{\rhd(\mathcal{F}_1, \ldots, \mathcal{F}_n) \colon \mathcal{F}_1 \in \mathcal{C}_1, \ldots, \mathcal{F}_n \in \mathcal{C}_n\}.$$

Hence, we can take as the definition of the l-product of finitely many Kripke complete modal logics $L_1, \ldots, L_n$ formulated in languages $\mathcal{L}_1, \ldots, \mathcal{L}_n$ the equality

$$\rhd(L_1, \ldots, L_n) = Log(\rhd(\mathsf{Fr}L_1, \ldots, \mathsf{Fr}L_n))$$

in the language $\mathcal{L}_1 \otimes \ldots \otimes \mathcal{L}_n$. It should be clear from the definition that we have

Proposition 14. *Let $L_1, \ldots, L_n$ be consistent Kripke complete modal logics formulated in languages $\mathcal{L}_1, \ldots, \mathcal{L}_n$. Let $i \in \{1, \ldots, n\}$ be such that $i < n$. $\rhd(L_1, \ldots, L_n)$ is a conservative extension of $\rhd(L_1, \ldots, L_i)$.*

In other respects,

Proposition 15. *Let L_1, ..., L_n be consistent Kripke complete modal logics formulated in languages $\mathcal{L}_1$, ..., $\mathcal{L}_n$. Let $i \in \{1, ..., n\}$ be such that $i < n$. Let ϕ be a variable-free formula in the language $\mathcal{L}_{i+1} \otimes ... \otimes \mathcal{L}_n$. $\phi \in \triangleright(L_1, ..., L_n)$ iff $\phi \in \triangleright(L_{i+1}, ..., L_n)$.*

To end this section, we present results analog to the results presented in Theorem 16 and Theorem 17 in [12].

Proposition 16. *Let L_1, ..., L_n be Kripke complete modal logics formulated in languages $\mathcal{L}_1$, ..., $\mathcal{L}_n$ such that $\mathsf{Fr}L_1$, ..., $\mathsf{Fr}L_n$ are definable by a set of first-order sentences. $\triangleright(L_1, ..., L_n)$ is determined by the class of its countable frames.*

Proposition 17. *Let L_1, ..., L_n be Kripke complete modal logics formulated in languages $\mathcal{L}_1$, ..., $\mathcal{L}_n$ such that $\mathsf{Fr}L_1$, ..., $\mathsf{Fr}L_n$ are definable by a recursive set of first-order sentences. $\triangleright(L_1, ..., L_n)$ is recursively enumerable.*

5   Examples

The aim of this section is to consider the interactions between $\square_1$ and $\square_2$ which will result in certain l-products of two Kripke complete modal logics L_1 and L_2 formulated in languages $\mathcal{L}_1 = (BV, \{1\})$ and $\mathcal{L}_2 = (BV, \{2\})$.

5.1 $S5 \triangleright S5$

Let us consider the l-product $S5 \triangleright S5$. The modal logic $S5$ is determined by the class of all frames $\mathcal{F} = (W, R)$ satisfying the following first-order sentences:

- $\forall u(u \; R \; u)$,
- $\forall u \forall v(\exists w(u \; R \; w \wedge w \; R \; v) \rightarrow u \; R \; v)$,
- $\forall u \forall v(\exists w(w \; R \; u \wedge w \; R \; v) \rightarrow u \; R \; v)$.

As a result, the l-product $\mathcal{F} = (W, S_1, S_2)$ of a frame $\mathcal{F}_1 = (W_1, R_1)$ and a frame $\mathcal{F}_2 = (W_2, R_2)$ such that $\mathcal{F}_1 \models S5$ and $\mathcal{F}_2 \models S5$ satisfies the following first-order sentences:

- $\forall u(u \; S_1 \; u)$,
- $\forall u \forall v(\exists w(u \; S_1 \; w \wedge w \; S_1 \; v) \rightarrow u \; S_1 \; v)$,
- $\forall u \forall v(\exists w(w \; S_1 \; u \wedge w \; S_1 \; v) \rightarrow u \; S_1 \; v)$,
- $\forall u(u \; S_2 \; u)$,
- $\forall u \forall v(\exists w(u \; S_2 \; w \wedge w \; S_2 \; v) \rightarrow u \; S_2 \; v)$,
- $\forall u \forall v(\exists w(w \; S_2 \; u \wedge w \; S_2 \; v) \rightarrow u \; S_2 \; v)$,
- $\forall u \forall v(u \; S_1 \; v \rightarrow u \; S_2 \; v)$.

Moreover,

Proposition 18. *Let $\mathcal{F} = (W, S_1, S_2)$ be a countable rooted frame satisfying the above first-order sentences. There exists frames $\mathcal{F}_1 = (W_1, R_1)$, $\mathcal{F}_2 = (W_2, R_2)$ such that $\mathcal{F}_1 \models S5$, $\mathcal{F}_2 \models S5$ and $\mathcal{F}$ is a bounded morphic image of $\mathcal{F}_1 \triangleright \mathcal{F}_2$.*

Thus,

Proposition 19. $S5 \triangleright S5 = (S5 \otimes S5) \oplus \{\Box_2 p \to \Box_1 p\}$.

Let us remark that

Proposition 20. $S5 \triangleright S5$ *is a conservative extension of* $S5$ *in the language* $\mathcal{L}_2$.

According to [14,15], all extensions of $S5$ are finitely axiomatizable. Let us prove the

Proposition 21. *Let* L_1 *and* L_2 *be two consistent Kripke complete modal logics formulated in languages* $\mathcal{L}_1 = (BV, \{1\})$ *and* $\mathcal{L}_2 = (BV, \{2\})$ *such that* $S5 \subseteq L_1$ *and* $S5 \subseteq L_2$. $L_1 \triangleright L_2$ *is finitely axiomatizable.*

5.2 $S4.3 \triangleright S4.3$

Let us consider the l-product $S4.3 \triangleright S4.3$. The modal logic $S4.3$ is determined by the class of all frames $\mathcal{F} = (W, R)$ satisfying the following first-order sentences:

- $\forall u (u \ R \ u)$,
- $\forall u \forall v (\exists w (u \ R \ w \wedge w \ R \ v) \to u \ R \ v)$,
- $\forall u \forall v (\exists w (w \ R \ u \wedge w \ R \ v) \to u \ R \ v \vee v \ R \ u)$.

As a result, the l-product $\mathcal{F} = (W, S_1, S_2)$ of a frame $\mathcal{F}_1 = (W_1, R_1)$ and a frame $\mathcal{F}_2 = (W_2, R_2)$ such that $\mathcal{F}_1 \models S4.3$ and $\mathcal{F}_2 \models S4.3$ satisfies the following first-order sentences:

- $\forall u (u \ S_1 \ u)$,
- $\forall u \forall v (\exists w (u \ S_1 \ w \wedge w \ S_1 \ v) \to u \ S_1 \ v)$,
- $\forall u \forall v (\exists w (w \ S_1 \ u \wedge w \ S_1 \ v) \to u \ S_1 \ v \vee v \ S_1 \ u)$,
- $\forall u (u \ S_2 \ u)$,
- $\forall u \forall v (\exists w (u \ S_2 \ w \wedge w \ S_2 \ v) \to u \ S_2 \ v)$,
- $\forall u \forall v (\exists w (w \ S_2 \ u \wedge w \ S_2 \ v) \to u \ S_2 \ v \vee v \ S_2 \ u)$,
- $\forall u \forall v (u \ S_1 \ v \to u \ S_2 \ v)$,
- $\forall u \forall v (u \ S_1 \ v \to v \ S_2 \ u)$.

Moreover,

Proposition 22. *Let* $\mathcal{F} = (W, S_1, S_2)$ *be a countable rooted frame satisfying the above first-order sentences. There exists frames* $\mathcal{F}_1 = (W_1, R_1)$, $\mathcal{F}_2 = (W_2, R_2)$ *such that* $\mathcal{F}_1 \models S4.3$, $\mathcal{F}_2 \models S4.3$ *and* $\mathcal{F}$ *is a bounded morphic image of* $\mathcal{F}_1 \triangleright \mathcal{F}_2$.

Thus,

Proposition 23. $S4.3 \triangleright S4.3 = (S4.3 \otimes S4.3) \oplus \{\Box_2 p \to \Box_1 p, p \to \Box_1 \Diamond_2 p\}$.

Let us remark that

Proposition 24. $S4.3 \triangleright S4.3$ *is a conservative extension of* $S4.3$ *in the language* $\mathcal{L}_2$.

According to [8,11], all extensions of $S4.3$ are finitely axiomatizable. Nevertheless, we do not know whether for all consistent Kripke complete modal logics L_1 and L_2 formulated in languages $\mathcal{L}_1 = (BV, \{1\})$ and $\mathcal{L}_2 = (BV, \{2\})$, if $S4.3 \subseteq L_1$ and $S4.3 \subseteq L_2$ then $L_1 \triangleright L_2$ is finitely axiomatizable.

5.3 $T \triangleright T$

Let us consider the l-product $T \triangleright T$. The modal logic T is determined by the class of all frames $\mathcal{F} = (W, R)$ satisfying the following first-order sentence:

- $\forall u(u \, R \, u)$.

As a result, the l-product $\mathcal{F} = (W, S_1, S_2)$ of a frame $\mathcal{F}_1 = (W_1, R_1)$ and a frame $\mathcal{F}_2 = (W_2, R_2)$ such that $\mathcal{F}_1 \models T$ and $\mathcal{F}_2 \models T$ satisfies the following first-order sentences:

- $\forall u(u \, S_1 \, u)$,
- $\forall u(u \, S_2 \, u)$,
- $\forall u \forall v(\exists w(u \, S_1 \, w \wedge w \, S_2 \, v) \rightarrow u \, S_2 \, v)$,
- $\forall u \forall v(\exists w(w \, S_1 \, u \wedge w \, S_2 \, v) \rightarrow u \, S_2 \, v)$,
- $\forall u \forall v(\exists w(u \, S_2 \, w \wedge w \, S_1 \, v) \rightarrow u \, S_2 \, v)$.

Moreover,

Proposition 25. *Let $\mathcal{F} = (W, S_1, S_2)$ be a countable rooted frame satisfying the above first-order sentences. There exists frames $\mathcal{F}_1 = (W_1, R_1)$, $\mathcal{F}_2 = (W_2, R_2)$ such that $\mathcal{F}_1 \models T$, $\mathcal{F}_2 \models T$ and $\mathcal{F}$ is a bounded morphic image of $\mathcal{F}_1 \triangleright \mathcal{F}_2$.*

Thus,

Proposition 26. $T \triangleright T = (T \otimes T) \oplus \{\Box_2 p \rightarrow \Box_1 \Box_2 p, \Diamond_2 p \rightarrow \Box_1 \Diamond_2 p, \Box_2 p \rightarrow \Box_2 \Box_1 p\}$.

Let us remark that

Proposition 27. $T \triangleright T$ *is a conservative extension of T in the language $\mathcal{L}_2$.*

5.4 $DAlt \triangleright DAlt$

Let us consider the l-product $DAlt \triangleright DAlt$. The modal logic $DAlt$ is determined by the class of all frames $\mathcal{F} = (W, R)$ satisfying the following first-order sentence:

- $\forall u \exists v(u \, R \, v)$,
- $\forall u \forall v(\exists w(w \, R \, u \wedge w \, R \, v) \rightarrow u = v)$.

As a result, the l-product $\mathcal{F} = (W, S_1, S_2)$ of a frame $\mathcal{F}_1 = (W_1, R_1)$ and a frame $\mathcal{F}_2 = (W_2, R_2)$ such that $\mathcal{F}_1 \models DAlt$ and $\mathcal{F}_2 \models DAlt$ satisfies the following first-order sentences:

- $\forall u \exists v(u \, S_1 \, v)$,
- $\forall u \forall v(\exists w(w \, S_1 \, u \wedge w \, S_1 \, v) \rightarrow u = v)$,
- $\forall u \exists v(u \, S_2 \, v)$,
- $\forall u \forall v(\exists w(u \, S_1 \, w \wedge w \, S_2 \, v) \rightarrow u \, S_2 \, v)$,
- $\forall u \forall v(\exists w(w \, S_1 \, u \wedge w \, S_2 \, v) \rightarrow u \, S_2 \, v)$,
- $\forall u \forall v(\exists w(u \, S_2 \, w \wedge w \, S_1 \, v) \rightarrow u \, S_2 \, v)$.

We do not know whether for all countable rooted frames $\mathcal{F} = (W, S_1, S_2)$ satisfying the above first-order sentences, there exists frames $\mathcal{F}_1 = (W_1, R_1)$, $\mathcal{F}_2 = (W_2, R_2)$ such that $\mathcal{F}_1 \models DAlt$, $\mathcal{F}_2 \models DAlt$ and $\mathcal{F}$ is a bounded morphic image of $\mathcal{F}_1 \triangleright \mathcal{F}_2$. Nevertheless,

Proposition 28. $DAlt \triangleright DAlt = (DAlt \otimes D) \oplus \{\Box_2 p \to \Box_1 \Box_2 p, \Diamond_2 p \to \Box_1 \Diamond_2 p, \Box_2 p \to \Box_2 \Box_1 p\}$.

Let us remark that $DAlt \triangleright DAlt$ is not a conservative extension of $DAlt$ in the language $\mathcal{L}_2$. We should consider, for example, the formula $\Diamond_2 p \to \Box_2 p$ which is in $DAlt$ but not in $DAlt \triangleright DAlt$. Leaving the proof that $\Diamond_2 p \to \Box_2 p$ is in $DAlt$ to the reader, let us demonstrate that $\Diamond_2 p \to \Box_2 p$ is not in $DAlt \triangleright DAlt$. Let $\mathcal{F}_1 = (W_1, R_1)$ and $\mathcal{F}_2 = (W_2, R_2)$ be the frames defined in figure 5.

$$\mathcal{F}_1 \qquad\qquad\qquad \mathcal{F}_2$$

$$0 \quad R_1$$

$$\qquad\qquad\qquad\qquad 0 \quad R_2$$

$$1 \quad R_1$$

Fig. 5.

Obviously, $\mathcal{F}_1$ validates $DAlt$ and $\mathcal{F}_2$ validates $DAlt$. Let m be a valuation on $\mathcal{F}_1 \triangleright \mathcal{F}_2$ such that $m(p) = \{(0,0)\}$. Obviously, $(\mathcal{F}_1 \triangleright \mathcal{F}_2, m) \not\models_{(0,0)} \Diamond_2 p \to \Box_2 p$. Consequently, $(\mathcal{F}_1 \triangleright \mathcal{F}_2, m) \not\models \Diamond_2 p \to \Box_2 p$. Therefore, $\mathcal{F}_1 \triangleright \mathcal{F}_2 \not\models \Diamond_2 p \to \Box_2 p$. Since $\mathcal{F}_1$ validates $DAlt$ and $\mathcal{F}_2$ validates $DAlt$, then $\Diamond_2 p \to \Box_2 p \notin DAlt \triangleright DAlt$. Nevertheless, we have

Proposition 29. $DAlt \triangleright DAlt$ *is a conservative extension of D in the language* $\mathcal{L}_2$.

5.5 $K \triangleright K$

Let us consider the l-product $K \triangleright K$. The modal logic K is determined by the class of all frames. In this respect, the l-product $\mathcal{F} = (W, S_1, S_2)$ of a frame $\mathcal{F}_1 = (W_1, R_1)$ and a frame $\mathcal{F}_2 = (W_2, R_2)$ satisfies the following first-order sentences:

- $\forall u \forall v (\exists w (u \ S_1 \ w \wedge w \ S_2 \ v) \to u \ S_2 \ v)$,
- $\forall u \forall v (\exists w (w \ S_1 \ u \wedge w \ S_2 \ v) \to u \ S_2 \ v)$,
- $\forall u \forall v (\exists w (u \ S_2 \ w \wedge w \ S_1 \ v) \to u \ S_2 \ v)$.

Nevertheless, there exists countable rooted frames $\mathcal{F} = (W, S_1, S_2)$ satisfying the above first-order sentences and such that for all frames $\mathcal{F}_1 = (W_1, R_1)$, $\mathcal{F}_2 = (W_2, R_2)$, $\mathcal{F}$ is not a bounded morphic image of $\mathcal{F}_1 \triangleright \mathcal{F}_2$. Take the case of the frame $\mathcal{F} = (W, S_1, S_2)$ defined in figure 6.

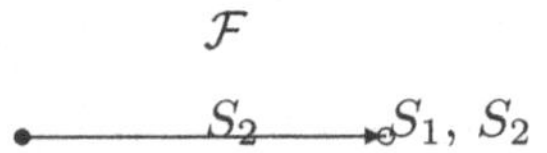

$$\mathcal{F}$$

$$\bullet \!\!\!\!\!\!\!\!\!\!\!\xrightarrow{\qquad S_2 \qquad} \!\!\!\bullet S_1, S_2$$

Fig. 6.

We demonstrate that for all frames $\mathcal{F}_1 = (W_1, R_1)$, $\mathcal{F}_2 = (W_2, R_2)$, $\mathcal{F}$ is not a bounded morphic image of $\mathcal{F}_1 \triangleright \mathcal{F}_2$. Assume there exists frames $\mathcal{F}_1 = (W_1, R_1)$, $\mathcal{F}_2 = (W_2, R_2)$ such that $\mathcal{F}$ is a bounded morphic image of $\mathcal{F}_1 \triangleright \mathcal{F}_2$. Since, $\mathcal{F}_1 \triangleright \mathcal{F}_2 \models \Box_1 \bot \to \Box_2 \bot \vee \Diamond_2 \Box_1 \bot$ and $\mathcal{F} \not\models \Box_1 \bot \to \Box_2 \bot \vee \Diamond_2 \Box_1 \bot$, then by the lemma of bounded morphism, $\mathcal{F}$ is not a bounded morphic image of $\mathcal{F}_1 \triangleright \mathcal{F}_2$: a contradiction. Hence, for all frames $\mathcal{F}_1 = (W_1, R_1)$, $\mathcal{F}_2 = (W_2, R_2)$, $\mathcal{F}$ is not a bounded morphic image of $\mathcal{F}_1 \triangleright \mathcal{F}_2$. The truth of the matter is that

Proposition 30. *Let $\mathcal{F}_1$ and $\mathcal{F}_2$ be frames. Let m be a non-negative integer, $\alpha_1, \ldots, \alpha_m \in \{1, 2\}$, n be a non-negative integer, $\beta_1, \ldots, \beta_n \in \{1, 2\}$ and ϕ be a variable-free formula in the language $\mathcal{L}_1$. $\mathcal{F}_1 \triangleright \mathcal{F}_2 \models \Diamond_{\alpha_1} \ldots \Diamond_{\alpha_m} \phi \to \Box_{\beta_1} \ldots \Box_{\beta_n} (\Box_2 \bot \vee \Diamond_2 \phi)$.*

We do not know whether $K \triangleright K$ is finitely axiomatizable. Nevertheless,

Proposition 31. *$K \triangleright K$ is a conservative extension of K in the language $\mathcal{L}_2$.*

6   Axiomatization/Completeness

Let $\mathcal{L}_1 = (BV, \{1\})$ and $\mathcal{L}_2 = (BV, \{2\})$. Taking into account what we have observed in the previous section, the most obvious properties that hold in the l-product $\mathcal{F}_1 \triangleright \mathcal{F}_2 = (W_1 \times W_2, S_1, S_2)$ of a frame $\mathcal{F}_1 = (W_1, R_1)$ and a frame $\mathcal{F}_2 = (W_2, R_2)$ can be described by the following first-order sentences:

- $\forall u \forall v (\exists w (u \, S_1 \, w \wedge w \, S_2 \, v) \to u \, S_2 \, v)$,
- $\forall u \forall v (\exists w (w \, S_1 \, u \wedge w \, S_2 \, v) \to u \, S_2 \, v)$,
- $\forall u \forall v (\exists w (u \, S_2 \, w \wedge w \, S_1 \, v) \to u \, S_2 \, v)$.

By the completeness theorem of Sahlqvist, they can also be described by the following modal formulas:

- $\Box_2 p \to \Box_1 \Box_2 p$,
- $\Diamond_2 p \to \Box_1 \Diamond_2 p$,
- $\Box_2 p \to \Box_2 \Box_1 p$.

Frames of the form (W, S_1, S_2) will be called standard iff they satisfy the above first-order sentences. It is worth noting at this point the following: there exists standard frames that are not bounded morphic images of l-products of any frames. See section 5.5 for an example of such a standard frame. Let L_1 and L_2 be two Kripke complete modal logics formulated in languages $\mathcal{L}_1$ and $\mathcal{L}_2$. We define the l-union of L_1 and L_2 as the modal logic

$$L_1 \sqcup L_2 = (L_1 \otimes L_2) \oplus \{\Box_2 p \to \Box_1 \Box_2 p, \Diamond_2 p \to \Box_1 \Diamond_2 p, \Box_2 p \to \Box_2 \Box_1 p\}$$

in the language $\mathcal{L}_1 \otimes \mathcal{L}_2$, that is to say: $L_1 \sqcup L_2$ is the least modal logic for $(BV, \{1, 2\})$ containing L_1, L_2, $\Box_2 p \to \Box_1 \Box_2 p$, $\Diamond_2 p \to \Box_1 \Diamond_2 p$ and $\Box_2 p \to \Box_2 \Box_1 p$. Modal logics L_1 and L_2 for which $L_1 \triangleright L_2 = L_1 \sqcup L_2$ will be called l-product-matching. According to what we have observed in section 5, it follows that

- $S5$ and $S5$ are l-product-matching,
- $S4.3$ and $S4.3$ are l-product-matching,
- T and T are l-product-matching,
- $DAlt$ and $DAlt$ are not l-product-matching,
- K and K are not l-product-matching.

For all $i \in \{1, 2\}$, we shall say that a formula ϕ of $\mathcal{L}_i$ is a Horn formula iff there exists a positive formula $\varphi_\phi(u, v, \boldsymbol{w})$ in the first-order language with equality based on the binary predicate R_i such that for all frames $\mathcal{F}_i = (W_i, R_i)$, $\mathcal{F}_i \models \phi$ iff $\mathcal{F}_i \models \forall u \forall v (\exists \boldsymbol{w} \varphi_\phi(u, v, \boldsymbol{w}) \rightarrow R_i(u, v))$. A modal logic L for $\mathcal{L}_i$ is said to be Horn axiomatizable iff there exists a subset L_{vff} of the set of variable-free formulas of $\mathcal{L}_i$ and there exists a subset L_{hf} of the set of Horn formulas of $\mathcal{L}_i$ such that L is the least modal logic for $\mathcal{L}_i$ containing L_{vff} and L_{hf}. We show first that

Proposition 32. *Let L_1 and L_2 be two consistent Kripke complete modal logics formulated in languages $\mathcal{L}_1$ and $\mathcal{L}_2$ such that $\square_1 p \rightarrow p \in L_1$, $\square_2 p \rightarrow p \in L_2$ and L_1 and L_2 are Horn axiomatizable. L_1 and L_2 are l-product-matching.*

Obviously, for all $i \in \{1, 2\}$, for all consistent Kripke complete modal logics L_i formulated in language $\mathcal{L}_i$ such that L_i is in $\{S5, S4, B, T\}$, $\square_i p \rightarrow p \in L_i$ and L_i is Horn axiomatizable. Hence, by applying proposition 32, we obtain the following result as a corollary:

> for all consistent Kripke complete modal logics L_1 and L_2 formulated in languages $\mathcal{L}_1$ and $\mathcal{L}_2$ such that L_1 and L_2 are in $\{S5, S4, B, T\}$, L_1 and L_2 are l-product-matching.

We shall say that the consistent Kripke complete modal logics L_1 and L_2 formulated in languages $\mathcal{L}_1$ and $\mathcal{L}_2$ are compatible iff $\mathcal{F}_1 \rhd \mathcal{F}_2 \models L_2$ for each frame $\mathcal{F}_1 = (W_1, R_1)$ such that $\mathcal{F}_1 \models L_1$, for each frame $\mathcal{F}_2 = (W_2, R_2)$ such that $\mathcal{F}_2 \models L_2$. Now, we show that

Proposition 33. *Let L_1 and L_2 be two consistent Kripke complete modal logics formulated in languages $\mathcal{L}_1$ and $\mathcal{L}_2$ such that L_1 is canonical, $S5 \subseteq L_2 \subseteq Triv$ and L_1 and L_2 are compatible. L_1 and L_2 are l-product-matching.*

In actual fact, for all consistent Kripke complete modal logics L_1 and L_2 formulated in languages $\mathcal{L}_1$ and $\mathcal{L}_2$ such that L_1 is canonical and $S5 \subseteq L_2 \subseteq Triv$, L_1 and L_2 are compatible iff $S5 = L_2$. Hence, referring to proposition 33, we obtain the following result as a corollary:

> for all consistent Kripke complete modal logics L_1 and L_2 formulated in languages $\mathcal{L}_1$ and $\mathcal{L}_2$ such that L_1 is canonical and $S5 = L_2$, L_1 and L_2 are l-product-matching.

For all $i \in \{1, 2\}$, a canonical formula ϕ of $\mathcal{L}_i$ is said to be nice iff there exists a sentence φ_ϕ in the first-order language without equality based on the binary predicate R_i such that for all frames $\mathcal{F}_i = (W_i, R_i)$, $\mathcal{F}_i \models \phi$ iff $\mathcal{F}_i \models \varphi_\phi$. A modal logic L_i for $\mathcal{L}_i$ is said to be nice iff there exists a subset L_{nf} of the set of nice formulas of $\mathcal{L}_i$ such that L_i is the least modal logic for $\mathcal{L}_i$ containing L_{nf}. We show finally that

Proposition 34. *Let L_1 and L_2 be two consistent Kripke complete modal logics formulated in languages $\mathcal{L}_1$ and $\mathcal{L}_2$ such that $S5 = L_1$ and L_2 is nice. L_1 and L_2 are l-product-matching.*

Obviously, for all consistent Kripke complete modal logics L_2 formulated in language $\mathcal{L}_2$ such that L_2 is in $\{S5, KB4, S4, B, K4, KB, T, K\}$, L_2 is nice. Hence, by applying proposition 34, we obtain the following result as a corollary:

for all consistent Kripke complete modal logics L_1 and L_2 formulated in languages $\mathcal{L}_1$ and $\mathcal{L}_2$ such that $S5 = L_1$ and L_2 is in $\{S5, KB4, S4, B, K4, KB, T, K\}$, L_1 and L_2 are l-product-matching.

7 Open Problems

The formation of fusion has nice features, seeing that, for instance, the Kripke completeness of modal logics L_1 and L_2 and the decidability of modal logics L_1 and L_2 are transferred to their fusion $L_1 \otimes L_2$. See [10,18] for a detailed study of fusions of modal logics. There are many open questions about the formation of l-unions. For instance, it is not known whether the Kripke completeness of modal logics L_1 and L_2 or the decidability of modal logics L_1 and L_2 are transferred to their l-union $L_1 \sqcup L_2$.

The axiomatization/completeness issue of l-products remains far from being solved. For example, although it is easy to completely axiomatize the self-l-product of a non-self-l-product-matching logic like $DAlt$, it seems difficult to completely axiomatize the self-l-product of a non-self-l-product-matching logic like K. A related question is whether the set $\{(\phi_1, \phi_2): \phi_1$ is a Sahlqvist formula in the language $\mathcal{L}_1$ and ϕ_2 is a Sahlqvist formula in the language $\mathcal{L}_2$ such that $K \oplus \{\phi_1\}$ and $K \oplus \{\phi_2\}$ are l-product-matching$\}$ is decidable.

As for the decidability/complexity issue of l-products, much remains to be done. For instance, although we know from proposition 29 and the $PSPACE$ lower bound of D, see [13] for details, that the NP upper bound of $DAlt$ is not inherited by its self l-product, we do not know whether the $PSPACE$ upper bound of K is inherited by its self l-product. In other respects, the question whether the lower bound of Kripke complete modal logics L_1 and L_2 is transferred to their l-product $L_1 \rhd L_2$ remains open.

Within the context of time representation and temporal reasoning, in a language based on $\square_1$ and $\square_2$, there is the question of the modal logic characterized by the l-product of two given temporal orderings. We have been able to demonstrate in [3] that the modal logics characterized by the l-products of two given temporal orderings among $(\mathbb{R}, \leq)$, $(\mathbb{Q}, \leq)$ and $(\mathbb{Z}, \leq)$ are nothing but the modal logic $S4.3 \rhd S4.3$. As for the modal logics characterized by the l-products of two given temporal orderings among $(\mathbb{R}, <)$, $(\mathbb{Q}, <)$ and $(\mathbb{Z}, <)$, nothing is known.

Acknowledgements

We make a point of thanking the colleagues of the *Institut de recherche en informatique de Toulouse* who, by the discussions we had with them, contributed to the development of the work we present today. In particular, we want to thank Yannick Chevalier, Andreas Herzig, Philippe Palanque and François Schwarzentruber for their helpful comments and their useful suggestions.

References

1. Balbiani, P.: Time representation and temporal reasoning from the perspective of non-standard analysis. In: Brewka, G., Lang, J. (eds.) Eleventh International Conference on Principles of Knowledge Representation and Reasoning. Association for the Advancement of Artificial Intelligence, pp. 695–704 (2008)
2. Balbiani, P.: Axiomatization and completeness of lexicographic products of modal logics (long version). Research Report IRIT/RR–2009-20–FR+ of the Institut de recherche en informatique de Toulouse (2009)
3. Balbiani, P.: Lexicographic products of modal logics with linear frames (to appear)
4. Blackburn, P., de Rijke, M., Venema, Y.: Modal Logic. Cambridge University Press, Cambridge (2001)
5. Van Ditmarsch, H., van der Hoek, W., Kooi, B.: Dynamic Epistemic Logic. Springer, Heidelberg (2007)
6. Euzenat, J., Montanari, A.: Time granularity. In: Fisher, M., Gabbay, D., Vila, L. (eds.) Handbook of Temporal Reasoning in Artificial Intelligence, pp. 59–118. Elsevier B.V., Amsterdam (2005)
7. Fagin, R., Halpern, J., Moses, Y., Vardi, M.: Reasoning About Knowledge. MIT Press, Cambridge (1995)
8. Fine, K.: The logics containing $S4.3$. Zeitschrift für mathematische Logik und Grundlagen der Mathematik 17, 371–376 (1971)
9. Gabbay, D., Kurucz, A., Wolter, F., Zakharyaschev, M.: Many-Dimensional Modal Logics: Theory and Applications. Elsevier B.V., Amsterdam (2003)
10. Gabbay, D., Shehtman, V.: Products of modal logics, part 1. Logic Journal of the IGPL 6, 73–146 (1998)
11. Hemaspaandra, E.: The price of universality. Notre Dame Journal of Formal Logic 37, 174–203 (1996)
12. Kurucz, A.: Combining modal logics. In: Blackburn, P., van Benthem, J., Wolter, F. (eds.) Handbook of Modal Logic, pp. 869–924. Elsevier B.V., Amsterdam (2007)
13. Ladner, R.: The computational complexity of provability in systems of modal propositional logic. SIAM Journal on Computing 6, 467–480 (1977)
14. Nagle, M.: The decidability of normal $K5$ logics. Journal of Symbolic Logic 46, 319–328 (1981)
15. Nagle, M., Thomason, S.: The extensions of the modal logic $K5$. Journal of Symbolic Logic 50, 102–109 (1985)
16. Oztürk, M., Tsoukiàs, A., Vincke, P.: Preference modelling. In: Figueira, J., Greco, S., Ehrgott, M. (eds.) Multiple Criteria Decision Analysis, pp. 27–71. Springer, Heidelberg (2005)
17. Palanque, P., Paternò, F. (eds.): Formal Methods in Human-Computer Interaction. Springer, Heidelberg (1998)
18. Wolter, F.: Fusions of modal logics revisited. In: Kracht, M., de Rijke, M., Wansing, H., Zakharyaschev, M. (eds.) Advances in Modal Logic, pp. 361–379. CSLI Publications, Stanford (1998)

Automating Theories in Intuitionistic Logic

Guillaume Burel

Nancy-Université & LORIA[*]
guillaume.burel@ens-lyon.org
http://www.loria.fr/~burel/

Abstract. Deduction modulo consists in applying the inference rules of a deductive system modulo a rewrite system over terms and formulæ. This is equivalent to proving within a so-called compatible theory. Conversely, given a first-order theory, one may want to internalize it into a rewrite system that can be used in deduction modulo, in order to get an analytic deductive system for that theory. In a recent paper, we have shown how this can be done in classical logic. In intuitionistic logic, however, we show here not only that this may be impossible, but also that the set of theories that can be transformed into a rewrite system with an analytic sequent calculus modulo is not co-recursively enumerable. We nonetheless propose a procedure to transform a large class of theories into compatible rewrite systems. We then extend this class by working in conservative extensions, in particular using Skolemization.

1 Introduction

Mathematical propositions are seldom proved in pure first-order logic, but more often within a particular theory, e.g. arithmetic or Euclidean geometry. In general, this is performed using an axiomatization of these theories, but this has drawbacks. First, this is rather inefficient from an automated-proof-search point of view, in particular when computations are involved. To be convinced of this, one may try to prove a simple result such as "2+2=4" in Peano's arithmetic. Second, some interesting properties of deductive systems may be lost when proving using axioms. In particular, in a constructive setting, the disjunction property, that says that from a proof of $P \vee Q$ one can find a proof of P or a proof of Q, and the witness property, that says that from a proof of $\exists x.\ P(x)$ one can find a witness term t and a proof of $P(t)$, no longer hold when using axioms.

Dowek, Hardin and Kirchner [12] proposed an alternative way of proving within a theory: in deduction modulo, the inference rules used to prove a formula are applied modulo a rewrite system. This system can rewrite terms, but also atomic formulæ to formulæ. For instance, given the (propositional) rule $x \times y = 0 \rightarrow x = 0 \vee y = 0$, we can build the following proof of $\forall x.\ x \times x = 0 \Rightarrow x = 0$ in the sequent calculus modulo:

---

[*] UMR 7503 CNRS–INPL–INRIA–Nancy2–UHP.

S. Ghilardi and R. Sebastiani (Eds.): FroCoS 2009, LNAI 5749, pp. 181–197, 2009.
© Springer-Verlag Berlin Heidelberg 2009

$$\text{Ax.} \cfrac{\cfrac{\text{Ax.} \cfrac{}{x = 0 \vdash x = 0}}{x \times x = 0 \vdash x = 0} \qquad \text{Ax.} \cfrac{}{x = 0 \vdash x = 0} \quad x \times x = 0 \longrightarrow x = 0 \vee x = 0}{\cfrac{\vdash x \times x = 0 \Rightarrow x = 0}{\vdash \forall x.\ x \times x = 0 \Rightarrow x = 0}} \vdash\forall$$

We can see that proving in the sequent calculus modulo this rule is equivalent to proving in the theory $\forall x\ y.\ x \times y = 0 \Leftrightarrow x = 0 \vee y = 0$. Propositions 1.6 and 1.8 of [12] tell us that given a rewrite system, it is always possible to find a theory such that proving modulo the rewrite system is equivalent to proving in the theory. Presentations of that theory are then called compatible with the rewrite system.

We are interested here in the converse problem: given a theory, how is it possible to internalize it into a rewrite system usable in deduction modulo? In which case, we will also say that the rewrite system is compatible with the theory. Proof search methods based on deduction modulo, e.g. ENAR [12] and TaMed [5] can then be used to find proofs in those theories. These methods are complete only if the sequent calculus modulo the compatible rewrite system admits cut. Indeed, it may not be the case in deduction modulo, as shown by the consistent example $A \to A \Rightarrow B$: B possesses the following proof

$$\text{Cut} \cfrac{\cfrac{\text{Ax.} \cfrac{}{A \Rightarrow B \vdash B, A}}{A \vdash B} \Rightarrow\vdash \ * \quad \text{Ax.} \cfrac{}{B \vdash B} \ *}{\vdash B} \qquad \cfrac{\cfrac{A \vdash B}{\vdash B, A} \vdash\Rightarrow}{} \ *$$

where the inference rules applied modulo $A \to A \Rightarrow B$ are marked by $*$. But B cannot be proved without cut. We therefore want to find compatible rewrite systems ensuring the cut admissibility. This was for instance successfully done by hand for arithmetic [14] and Zermelo's set theory [13]. However, to be sure that the deductive system modulo admits cuts, some tricks are used that seems difficult to automate. This paper studies the automation of the transformation of the presentation of an intuitionistic first-order theory into a rewrite system that is applied modulo.

In a submitted paper [8], we proposed a complete solution in the case of classical logic: First, we have shown how to transform any presentation of a theory into a compatible rewrite system; Then, we have defined a completion procedure that transforms the resulting rewrite system to ensure that the sequent calculus modulo the final rewrite system admits cut. In intuitionistic logic, however, there are theories that cannot be transformed into a compatible rewrite system, as we will soon show, and we cannot separate the production of the rewrite system and its completion that ensures the cut admissibility.

To better explain how we will proceed in the intuitionistic case, let us recall how theories can be internalized in classical logic. The main technical complication arises because in deduction modulo, left hand sides of proposition rewrite rules must be atomic formulæ. To transform an axiom into such a rule, the idea is therefore to apply the inference rules of a sequent calculus to decompose the axiom and pick out one of its atomic subformula. To remain in the same theory, the inference rules that we are using must preserve the provability. Therefore, we are only allowed to apply invertible rules —recall that an inference rule is called invertible if whenever its conclusion is derivable, its premises also are. Fortunately, there exists sequent calculi for classical logic where all inference rules are invertible, e.g. the system G4 of Kleene [20], so that the transformation is always possible in classical logic. For instance, the theory presented by $\forall x.\ \exists y.\ A(x, y)$ is decomposed into the sequent $\vdash A(x, y), \exists y.\ A(x, y)$ which is in turn oriented into the rewrite rule $A(x, y) \rightarrow A(x, y) \vee \neg \exists y.\ A(x, y)$. The transformation of sequents into rewrite rules relies on classical tautologies, so that in intuitionistic logic, we cannot hope to obtain such a result. Indeed, if you consider the theory presented by the simple axiom $A \vee B$ with A and B some distinct atomic formulæ, you can prove neither A nor B. However, were it possible to find a rewrite system for that theory such that the sequent calculus modulo this system admits cuts, this deductive system would have the disjunction property (see Proposition 3). As by compatibility $A \vee B$ could be proven, either A or B should be provable, hence the contradiction. Note that in classical logic, the axiom $A \vee B$ would produce the rule $A \rightarrow A \vee \neg B$, but it is not intuitionistically equivalent to $A \vee B$. We would like to be able to characterize the presentations that have a compatible rewrite system such that the sequent calculus modulo this system admits cuts, but we prove that the set of such presentations is not co-recursively enumerable, that is, cannot be decided. Nevertheless, we propose a procedure that transforms a large class of theories into compatible rewrite systems. This procedure is a nontrivial generalization of the procedure for classical logic, because we have to mix the transformation into rewrite rules and the completion that ensures the cut admissibility, and because we must develop new techniques to avoid being stuck with examples such as $A \vee (B \Rightarrow A)$.

The same kind of counterexample as $A \vee B$ can be obtained from a theory presented by an axiom of the form $\exists x.\ A(x)$, using the witness property. In that case however, it is possible to use Skolemization to work in a conservative extension of the theory that has a compatible rewrite system such that the sequent calculus modulo this rewrite system admits cuts. As Skolemization does not always lead to a conservative extension in intuitionistic logic, this means that this will not always be possible. In this paper, we investigate in which cases it is possible to transform the presentation of a theory into a compatible rewrite system, possibly using conservative extensions of the theory.

In the following section we recall some sequent calculi for intuitionistic logic maximizing the number of invertible rules, and we introduce deduction modulo. In Section 3 we prove that the set of presentations that have a compatible rewrite system such that the sequent calculus modulo this system admits cut is not co-recursively enumerable. Section 4 presents a procedure that tries to transform a presentation into a compatible rewrite system. Then in Section 5, we extend the domain where this procedure succeeds by considering infinite presentations, equality and Skolemization. Finally, Section 6 provides an example application extracted from the Intuitionistic Logic Theorem Proving library [25].

2   Preliminaries

2.1   Sequent Calculi for Intuitionistic Logic

We use standard definitions for terms, predicates, propositions (with connectors $\bot, \top, \Rightarrow, \wedge, \vee$ and quantifiers $\forall, \exists$), substitutions, term rewrite rules and term rewriting, as can be found in [1,15]. The set of terms built from a signature Σ and a set of variables V is denoted by $\mathcal{T}(\Sigma, V)$, the replacement of a variable x by a term t in a proposition P by $\{t/x\}P$, the application of a substitution σ in a proposition P by σP, the free variables occurring in P by $FV(P)$. $\neg P$ is a shorthand for $P \Rightarrow \bot$, and when $\Gamma = P_1, \ldots, P_n$, then $\bigwedge \Gamma$, $\bigvee \Gamma$ and $\neg \Gamma$ are notations for $P_1 \wedge \cdots \wedge P_n$, $P_1 \vee \cdots \vee P_n$ and $\neg P_1, \ldots, \neg P_n$. $P \Leftrightarrow Q$ denotes $(P \Rightarrow Q) \wedge (Q \Rightarrow P)$.

The reader is referred to [15] for an introduction to sequent calculi. A sequent is a pair (Γ, Δ) of multisets of formulæ, denoted by $\Gamma \vdash \Delta$. A logical rule of a sequent calculus decomposes a formula, which is called *principal*, appearing in a sequent, into its direct subformulæ, which are called the *side formulæ*. For instance, in

$$\Rightarrow\vdash \frac{\Gamma \vdash X, \Delta \qquad \Gamma, Y \vdash \Delta}{\Gamma, X \Rightarrow Y \vdash \Delta}$$

$X \Rightarrow Y$ is the principal formula, X and Y are the side formulæ, and the other formulæ, those appearing in Γ and Δ, are called the *extra formulæ*. An inference rule $\dfrac{H_1 \quad \cdots \quad H_n}{C}$ is said *invertible* if whenever C can be proved, then so can all H_i for $1 \le i \le n$. A logical rule r permutes over a logical rule r' if whenever there is a proof ending with

$$r \frac{H_1 \quad \cdots \quad H_n}{r' \frac{C \qquad\qquad I_1 \ \cdots \ I_m}{D}}$$

where the principal formula of r is not a side formula of r', it is possible to build a proof with r below r'. If an inference rule permutes with all the other rules, it can be proved that it is invertible. A double horizontal line indicates several application of an inference rule. We will also consider *derivations*, that is, partial proofs where leafs are not all closed by Ax. The sequents appearing in the open leafs of a derivation are called its *premises*.

The usual sequent calculus for intuitionistic logic, LJ, was introduced by Gentzen [16]. It consists in allowing at most one formula to the right of the sequents of the sequent calculus for classical logic LK. However, this has drawbacks, because many rules cannot be permuted contrarily to classical logic, so that almost all rules are not invertible. Therefore, it has been proposed to keep multiple conclusions in the sequents, but to restrict only the rules where it is needed, i.e. for the right rules for $\Rightarrow$ and $\forall$. The resulting system is called L'J [22], LB [27] or LJm [24], with little differences between versions. We represent the system LB in Fig. 1, as it appears in [27]. It is shown [27] that the only cases of

Identity rules

$$\text{Ax.} \frac{}{\Gamma, X \vdash X, \Delta} \qquad\qquad \text{Cut} \frac{\Gamma, X \vdash \Delta \qquad \Gamma \vdash X, \Delta}{\Gamma \vdash \Delta}$$

Structural rules

$$\vdots\vdash \frac{\Gamma, X, X \vdash \Delta}{\Gamma, X \vdash \Delta} \qquad\qquad \vdash\vdots \frac{\Gamma \vdash X, X, \Delta}{\Gamma \vdash X, \Delta}$$

$$\cdot\vdash \frac{\Gamma \vdash \Delta}{\Gamma, X \vdash \Delta} \qquad\qquad \vdash\cdot \frac{\Gamma \vdash \Delta}{\Gamma \vdash X, \Delta}$$

Logical rules

$$\Rightarrow\vdash \frac{\Gamma \vdash X, \Delta \qquad \Gamma, Y \vdash \Delta}{\Gamma, X \Rightarrow Y \vdash \Delta} \qquad\qquad \vdash\Rightarrow \frac{\Gamma, X \vdash Y}{\Gamma \vdash X \Rightarrow Y}$$

$$\wedge\vdash \frac{\Gamma, X, Y \vdash \Delta}{\Gamma, X \wedge Y \vdash \Delta} \qquad\qquad \vdash\wedge \frac{\Gamma \vdash X, \Delta \qquad \Gamma \vdash Y, \Delta}{\Gamma \vdash X \wedge Y, \Delta}$$

$$\vee\vdash \frac{\Gamma, X \vdash \Delta \qquad \Gamma, Y \vdash \Delta}{\Gamma, X \vee Y \vdash \Delta} \qquad\qquad \vdash\vee_1 \frac{\Gamma \vdash X, Y, \Delta}{\Gamma \vdash X \vee Y, \Delta}$$

$$\forall\vdash \frac{\Gamma, X(t) \vdash \Delta}{\Gamma, \forall x, X(x) \vdash \Delta} \qquad\qquad \vdash\forall \frac{\Gamma \vdash X(y)}{\Gamma \vdash \forall x, X(x)} \; \begin{array}{l} y \text{ not free in} \\ \Gamma, X(x), \Delta \end{array}$$

$$\exists\vdash \frac{\Gamma, X(y) \vdash \Delta}{\Gamma, \exists x, X(x) \vdash \Delta} \; \begin{array}{l} y \text{ not free in} \\ \Gamma, X(x), \Delta \end{array} \qquad\qquad \vdash\exists \frac{\Gamma \vdash X(t), \Delta}{\Gamma \vdash \exists x, X(x), \Delta}$$

$$\perp\vdash \frac{}{\perp \vdash C} \qquad\qquad \vdash\top \frac{}{\vdash \top}$$

Fig. 1. Inference rules of LB [27]

$$\Rightarrow\vdash \frac{\Gamma, X \Rightarrow Y \vdash X, \Delta \qquad \Gamma, Y \vdash \Delta}{\Gamma, X \Rightarrow Y \vdash \Delta} \qquad\qquad \vdash\Rightarrow \frac{\Gamma, X \vdash Y}{\Gamma \vdash X \Rightarrow Y, \Delta}$$

$$\forall\vdash \frac{\Gamma, X(t), \forall x, X(x) \vdash \Delta}{\Gamma, \forall x, X(x) \vdash \Delta} \qquad\qquad \vdash\forall \frac{\Gamma \vdash X(y)}{\Gamma \vdash \forall x, X(x), \Delta} \; \begin{array}{l} y \text{ not free in} \\ \Gamma, X(x), \Delta \end{array}$$

$$\exists\vdash \frac{\Gamma, X(y) \vdash \Delta}{\Gamma, \exists x, X(x) \vdash \Delta} \; \begin{array}{l} y \text{ not free in} \\ \Gamma, X(x), \Delta \end{array} \qquad\qquad \vdash\exists \frac{\Gamma \vdash X(t), \exists x, X(x), \Delta}{\Gamma \vdash \exists x, X(x), \Delta}$$

$$\perp\vdash \frac{}{\Gamma, \perp \vdash \Delta} \qquad\qquad \vdash\perp \frac{\Gamma \vdash \Delta}{\Gamma \vdash \perp, \Delta}$$

$$\top\vdash \frac{\Gamma \vdash \Delta}{\Gamma, \top \vdash \Delta} \qquad\qquad \vdash\top \frac{}{\Gamma \vdash \top, \Delta}$$

Fig. 2. Logical rules of LBi

rules that do not permute are $\forall \vdash$ over $\vdash \forall$; $\forall \vdash$ and $\vdash \exists$ over $\exists \vdash$; and $\Rightarrow \vdash$ over $\vdash \Rightarrow$ and $\vdash \forall$. This means that the only logical rules that are not invertible are $\forall \vdash$, $\vdash \exists$ and $\Rightarrow \vdash$.

To make these rules invertible, one solution is to apply a contraction ($\because \vdash$ or $\vdash \because$) to the active formula just before applying the logical rule. This is what is done in classical logic to obtain the system G4 [20] from LK. It can be shown [24] that for $\Rightarrow \vdash$ it is only necessary to apply a contraction in the left premise. We also want to get rid of the weakening rules ($. \vdash$ and $\vdash .$), that are of course non invertible. To do so, we have to allow extra formulæ in $\perp \vdash$ and $\vdash \top$, to add a left rule for $\top$ and a right rule for $\perp$, and to allow weakening below an application of $\vdash \Rightarrow$ and $\vdash \forall$ and into premises of derivations. In so doing, it can be proved that all structural rules are admissible (see the full version of this paper [7]). The system that we use here will be called LBi ("i" standing for invertible and not intuitionistic). Its logical rules are presented in Fig. 2, except the rules for $\wedge$ and $\vee$ that are the same than in LB. Note that LBi has *no* structural rules. However, LBi is equivalent to LB (see the proof in the full version of this paper [7]).

Proposition 1. *All inference rules of LBi but $\vdash \Rightarrow$ and $\vdash \forall$ are invertible. Nonetheless, when there is no extra formula on the right hand side of their conclusion, $\vdash \Rightarrow$ and $\vdash \forall$ are also invertible.*

2.2 Deduction Modulo

An introduction on term rewriting can be found in [1]. We consider two kinds of rules: the usual term rewrite rules, and proposition rewrite rules defined below. An atomic formula $A(s_1, \ldots, s_i, \ldots, s_n)$ can be rewritten to the atomic formula $A(s_1, \ldots, t_i, \ldots, s_n)$ by a term rewrite rule $l \rightarrow r$ if s_i can be rewritten to t_i by $l \rightarrow r$. This rewrite relation is extended to non-atomic formulæ by congruence.

A *proposition rewrite rule* is the pair of an atomic proposition A and a proposition P, such that all free variables of P appear in A. It is denoted $A \rightarrow P$. A *proposition rewrite system* is a set of proposition rewrite rules. A formula P can be rewritten to a formula Q by the rule $A \rightarrow O$ at the position p with substitution σ if the subterm of P at position p equals σA and Q is P where its subterm at position p is replaced by σO.

In the following, a *rewrite system* $\mathcal{R}$ will be the disjoint union of a term rewrite system and a proposition rewrite system. $P \xrightarrow[\mathcal{R}]{} Q$ denotes the fact that P can be rewritten to Q by some term or proposition rewrite rule in $\mathcal{R}$, and $\xrightarrow[\mathcal{R}]{*}$ (resp. $\xleftrightarrow[\mathcal{R}]{*}$) denotes the reflexive and transitive (resp. reflexive, symmetric and transitive) closure of $\xrightarrow[\mathcal{R}]{}$.

As said above, deduction modulo consists in applying the inference rules of a deductive system modulo a rewrite system. For instance, in LBi modulo $\mathcal{R}$, the left rule for $\Rightarrow$ becomes

$$\Rightarrow \vdash \frac{\Gamma, Z \vdash X, \Delta \qquad \Gamma, Y \vdash \Delta}{\Gamma, Z \vdash \Delta} \; Z \xleftrightarrow[\mathcal{R}]{*} X \Rightarrow Y$$

Proving modulo a rewrite system $\mathcal{R}$ is equivalent to proving inside some theory whose presentations are called compatible with $\mathcal{R}$:

Definition 2. *A presentation is a set of formulæ with no free variables. The theory presented by a presentation Γ is the set of formulæ P such that $\Gamma' \vdash P$ can be proved in the sequent calculus for some finite subset Γ' of Γ.*

Given a rewrite system $\mathcal{R}$, its associated theory is the set of formulæ P such that $\vdash P$ can be proved in the sequent calculus modulo $\mathcal{R}$.

A presentation and a rewrite system $\mathcal{R}$ are said to be compatible *if they are associated with the same theory.*

Note that these definitions depend on the considered logic (e.g. classical or intuitionistic). Propositions 1.6 and 1.8 of [12] prove that a rewrite system always has a compatible presentation. This shows that the theory associated with a rewrite system is a theory in the standard meaning, that is, a deductively closed set of formulæ.

Some automated theorem-proving procedures have been designed based on deduction modulo, e.g. ENAR [12], generalizing resolution, as well as Tamed [5], a tableau method. These methods are complete only if the sequent calculus modulo admits cut. In fact, as proved by Hermant [18], the proofs found by these methods are exactly the cut-free proofs of the asymmetric sequent calculus modulo [10], a variant of the sequent calculus modulo where rewriting can only be applied from bottom to top in the proofs. For instance the left rule for $\Rightarrow$ becomes

$$\Rightarrow\vdash \frac{\Gamma, X \Rightarrow Y \vdash X, \Delta \qquad \Gamma, Y \vdash \Delta}{\Gamma, Z \vdash \Delta} \; Z \xrightarrow[\mathcal{R}]{*} X \Rightarrow Y$$

It can also be useful to distinguish which rules can be applied to the left and to the right of a sequent, or more precisely at positive and negative position in a sequent. Recall that a position in a formula is positive (resp. negative) if it is in the left subformula of an even (resp. odd) number of $\Rightarrow$. Suppose that the rewrite rules are associated with polarities. We denote by $A \to^+ P$ the rewrite rule $A \to P$ associated with a positive polarity, and dually for $-$. A proposition P can be positively rewritten to Q in $\mathcal{R}$ $\left(P \xrightarrow[\mathcal{R} \, +]{} Q \right)$ if P can be rewritten to Q by a positive rule at a positive position or by a negative rule at a negative position. A proposition P can be negatively rewritten to Q in $\mathcal{R}$ $\left(P \xrightarrow[\mathcal{R} \, -]{} Q \right)$ if P can be rewritten to Q by a negative rule at a positive position or by a positive rule at a negative position. In the polarized sequent calculus modulo [9], formulæ in the left (resp. right) of a sequent can only be negatively (resp. positively) rewritten, so that the Ax. rule, for instance, becomes

$$\mathsf{Ax.} \; \frac{}{\Gamma, X \vdash Y, \Delta} \; X \xrightarrow[\mathcal{R} \, -]{} \xleftarrow[\mathcal{R} \, +]{} Y$$

In [8] we proved that for classical logic, the polarized sequent calculus is equivalent to the asymmetric sequent calculus, also w.r.t. the cut admissibility. This also holds for LBi (see the full version of this paper [7]). The latter is equivalent to the original version of the sequent calculus modulo, but if we are also concerned with cut admissibility, they are equivalent if and only if the rewrite system is confluent. Given a sequent $\Gamma \vdash \Delta$, we denote by $\Gamma \vdash_{\mathcal{R}}^{S} \Delta$ the fact that for finite subsets Γ' and Δ' of Γ and Δ, the sequent $\Gamma' \vdash \Delta'$ can be derived from premises in the set of sequents S, in the polarized LBi modulo $\mathcal{R}$. If S and $\mathcal{R}$ are empty, we write $\Gamma \vdash \Delta$, which therefore means that there is a proof of $\Gamma' \vdash \Delta'$ in LBi without modulo.

A (polarized) rewrite system $\mathcal{R}$ is called *analytic* if the polarized sequent calculus modulo $\mathcal{R}$ admits cut, that is, if $\Gamma \vdash_{\mathcal{R}} \Delta$ then $\Gamma \vdash \Delta$ can be proved in the polarized LBi modulo $\mathcal{R}$ without Cut. In other words, adding Cut does not increase the set of theorems.

Proposition 3 (Disjunction and witness property). *Consider an analytic rewrite system* $\mathcal{R}$.

– *If* $\vdash_{\mathcal{R}} P \vee Q$ *then either* $\vdash_{\mathcal{R}} P$ *or* $\vdash_{\mathcal{R}} Q$.
– *If* $\vdash_{\mathcal{R}} \exists x. P$ *then for some* $t \in T(\Sigma, V)$, *we have* $\vdash_{\mathcal{R}} \{t/x\}P$.

Proof. If $\vdash_{\mathcal{R}} P \vee Q$, because $\mathcal{R}$ is analytic there is a cut-free proof of $\vdash P \vee Q$ in the polarized LBi modulo $\mathcal{R}$, and therefore also in the polarized LJ modulo $\mathcal{R}$ (see
the full version of this paper [7]). As the left hand side of proposition rewrite rules are atomic formulæ, if $P \vee Q \xrightarrow[\mathcal{R}\ +]{*} O$ then the connector at the root of O has to be $\vee$, so that the only rule that can be applied is $\vdash\vee$, hence the conclusion. The proof of the witness property is similar.   □

3   Undecidability of the Automation

As we saw in the introduction, the theory $A \vee B$ with A and B atomic cannot be transformed into an analytic compatible rewrite system. Therefore, we may want to characterize the theories that have an analytic compatible rewrite system, and to find an algorithm to build such rewrite systems. We prove in this section that it cannot be done through a decidable characterization, because the set of such theories is no co-recursively enumerable. In other words, if we have a procedure that transforms a presentation into an analytic compatible rewrite system, it would either be incomplete, that is, the procedure would not answer for some theories that do have an analytic compatible rewrite system, or it would not always terminate.

Theorem 4. *The set of presentations that can be transformed into an analytic compatible rewrite system is not co-recursively enumerable.*

Proof. Recall that the set of valid formulæ in classical first-order logic is not co-recursively enumerable. Using the double-negation translation, neither is the set of valid formulæ in intuitionistic first-order logic. We prove that a formula P

is intuitionistically valid iff the presentation $\{(A \Rightarrow P) \vee A\}$ can be transformed into an analytic compatible rewrite system.

Let P be a formula and A an atomic formula not appearing in P. We do not have $(A \Rightarrow P) \vee A \vdash A$: it does not hold in classical logic, so neither does it hold in intuitionistic logic.

Suppose that P is intuitionistically valid. Then so is $(A \Rightarrow P) \vee A$. Consequently, the theory presented by $(A \Rightarrow P) \vee A$ is the theory presented by an empty set of axioms. Consider the empty rewrite system. It is therefore compatible with $(A \Rightarrow P) \vee A$, and the sequent calculus modulo the empty rewrite system admits cuts. Thus, the theory presented by $(A \Rightarrow P) \vee A$ has an analytic compatible rewrite system.

Conversely, suppose that the theory presented by $(A \Rightarrow P) \vee A$ has an analytic compatible rewrite system $\mathcal{R}$. By compatibility, $\vdash_{\mathcal{R}} (A \Rightarrow P) \vee A$. By Proposition 3, either $\vdash_{\mathcal{R}} A \Rightarrow P$ or $\vdash_{\mathcal{R}} A$. In the latter case, that would mean by compatibility that $(A \Rightarrow P) \vee A \vdash A$, but this does not hold as mentioned above. Hence $\vdash_{\mathcal{R}} A \Rightarrow P$ and by compatibility $(A \Rightarrow P) \vee A \vdash A \Rightarrow P$. Because $\vee_\vdash$ is invertible, $A \vdash A \Rightarrow P$. Because $\vdash_\Rightarrow$ is invertible when there is only one formula on the right hand side, $A \vdash P$. Because A is atomic and does not appear in P, it cannot be used in this proof, so that $\vdash P$. By soundness of LBi, P is valid.

We therefore reduced the problem of deciding validity in intuitionistic first-order logic to the problem of deciding whether a theory has an analytic compatible rewrite system. The set of theories having one is therefore not co-recursively enumerable.   □

4   A Procedure to Produce Compatible Rewrite Systems

In this section, we try to find a way to transform the presentation of a theory into a compatible rewrite system, whishing this rewrite system to be analytic. Because of Theorem 4, it is not possible to find a terminating algorithm producing such a rewrite system in all cases where it is possible to find one. The procedure that we propose does not contradict this because it may not terminate. However, we try to avoid cases where it would unnecessarily fail.

To ease the description, we present the procedure by a set of transition rules as is traditional for completion procedures, e.g. in [3]. The procedure is therefore non-deterministic and may not terminate, in particular when the theory does not have a compatible rewrite system. Transition rules, which are given below in Procedure 1, transform a set of sequents S and a set of polarized rewrite rules $\mathcal{R}$. Given a presentation Θ, the input to the procedure is $\{\vdash P : P \in \Theta\}$ for the set of sequents, and the empty rewrite system. Let us describe the transition rules. **Orient+** and **Orient−** transform a sequent containing an atomic formula into rewrite rules. These are the base cases. Note that in **Orient+** the right hand side only contains one formula. Sequents with several formulæ on the right and no atomic formula on the left are therefore the potential failure cases. To obtain sequents in which there are atomic formulæ, one may apply the inference rules

Procedure 1. Transition rules to compute a compatible rewrite system

Orient+	$S \cup \{\Gamma \vdash A\}, \mathcal{R} \rightsquigarrow S, \mathcal{R} \cup \{A \rightarrow^+ \exists x_1, \ldots, x_n. \bigwedge \Gamma\}$
	if A atomic and $\{x_1, \ldots, x_n\} = FV(\Gamma) \setminus FV(A)$
Orient−	$S \cup \{\Gamma, A \vdash \Delta\}, \mathcal{R} \rightsquigarrow S, \mathcal{R} \cup \{A \rightarrow^- \forall x_1, \ldots, x_n. \bigwedge \Gamma \Rightarrow \bigvee \Delta\}$
	if A atomic and $\{x_1, \ldots, x_n\} = FV(\Gamma, \Delta) \setminus FV(A)$
Decompose	$S \cup \{\Gamma \vdash \Delta\}, \mathcal{R} \rightsquigarrow S \cup \bigcup_{1 \leq i \leq n} \{\Gamma_i \vdash \Delta_i\}, \mathcal{R}$

$$\text{if } r \frac{\Gamma_1 \vdash \Delta_1 \quad \cdots \quad \Gamma_n \vdash \Delta_n}{\Gamma \vdash \Delta} \text{ is invertible}$$

Discard	$S \cup \{\Gamma \vdash P, \Delta\}, \mathcal{R} \rightsquigarrow S \cup \{\Gamma \vdash \Delta\}, \mathcal{R}$	if $\Gamma, P \vdash^S_{\mathcal{R}} \Delta$
Delete	$S \cup \{\Gamma \vdash \Delta\}, \mathcal{R} \rightsquigarrow S, \mathcal{R}$	if $\Gamma \vdash^S_{\mathcal{R}} \Delta$ without Cut
Deduce	$S, \mathcal{R} \rightsquigarrow S \cup \{\Gamma \vdash \Delta\}, \mathcal{R}$	if $\Gamma \vdash \Delta \in CP(\mathcal{R})$

of LBi. This is what **Decompose** does, with the proviso that the inference rules are invertible to remain in the same theory. Contrary to classical logic, there remains sequents that cannot be transformed into rewrite rules even though there exists a compatible rewrite system. **Discard** and **Delete** permit to deal with these sequents. **Delete** is not really necessary, but it permits to eliminate redundancies in the construction of the rewrite system. In particular, it gets rid of tautologies such as those used in the proof of Theorem 4. The rewrite systems produced by all these rules may nevertheless not admit cuts, as shown by the example $A \Leftrightarrow A \Rightarrow B$ which can lead to the rewrite rules $A \rightarrow^+ A \Rightarrow B$ and $A \rightarrow^- A \Rightarrow B$ (see the introduction). **Deduce** completes the theory to recover the cut admissibility. The set $CP(\mathcal{R})$ is the set of conclusions of critical proofs

of $\mathcal{R}$. A critical proof of $\mathcal{R}$ is a proof of the form $\text{Cut} \dfrac{\overset{\pi}{\Gamma, P \vdash \Delta} \quad \overset{\pi'}{\Gamma \vdash Q, \Delta}}{\Gamma \vdash \Delta}$

where

- P, Q is a critical pair of $\mathcal{R}$, i.e. there exists A atomic such that $P \underset{\mathcal{R}}{\longleftarrow} A \underset{\mathcal{R}}{\longrightarrow} Q$;
- π and π' are cut-free;
- P (resp. Q) is the principal formula of the last inference rule of π (resp. π');
- all formulæ in Γ, Δ are principal in one of the inference rules of π or π';
- there is no cut-free proof of $\Gamma \vdash \Delta$ modulo $\mathcal{R}$.

Example 5. Given the axiom $A \vee (B \Rightarrow A)$, we apply **Decompose** to get $\vdash A, B \Rightarrow A$. Because $A \vdash B \Rightarrow A$, we can apply **Discard** to change $\vdash A, B \Rightarrow A$ into $\vdash B \Rightarrow A$. We apply **Decompose** to get $B \vdash A$. We have the choice between **Orient+** and **Orient−** to get either the rewrite rule $B \rightarrow^- A$ or the rule $A \rightarrow^+ B$, both of them which are analytical rewrite systems compatible with $A \vee (B \Rightarrow A)$.

Example 6. Consider the axioms $A \Rightarrow B \Rightarrow \bot$ and $(A \Rightarrow B \Rightarrow \bot) \Rightarrow A$. If we apply **Decompose** and **Orient−** on the former, we obtain the rule 1: $A \rightarrow^- B \Rightarrow \bot$. On the latter, we can apply **Decompose** and **Orient+** to get the rule 2: $A \xrightarrow{+} A \Rightarrow B \Rightarrow \perp$. There is a critical proof with the two rules we have obtained (numbers indicate which rewrite rules are used modulo):

$$\text{Cut} \dfrac{\Rightarrow \vdash \dfrac{\text{Ax.} \dfrac{}{B \Rightarrow \perp, B \vdash B} \quad \perp \vdash \dfrac{}{\perp, B \vdash}}{B \Rightarrow \perp, B \vdash}}{B \vdash} \qquad \vdash \Rightarrow \dfrac{\text{Ax.} \dfrac{}{B, A \vdash B \Rightarrow \perp} \; 1}{B \vdash A \Rightarrow B \Rightarrow \perp} \; 1,2$$

Using **Deduce**, we therefore add $B \vdash$ to S. It can be oriented into 3: $B \xrightarrow{-} \perp$. The resulting rewrite system, consisting of the rules 1 to 3, is compatible with the input axioms and is analytical.

We first prove that the procedure produces compatible rewrite systems:

Proposition 7. *If* $S, \mathcal{R} \rightsquigarrow S', \mathcal{R}'$ *then for all sequents* $\Gamma \vdash \Delta$, *we have* $\Gamma \vdash^S_{\mathcal{R}} \Delta$ *iff* $\Gamma \vdash^{S'}_{\mathcal{R}'} \Delta$.
 Moreover, if the derivation of $\Gamma \vdash^S_{\mathcal{R}} \Delta$ *is* Cut*-free, so is the derivation of* $\Gamma \vdash^{S'}_{\mathcal{R}'} \Delta$.

Proof. We prove it by cases on the transition rules. For **Orient+**, for the "only if" direction, it is enough to show that $\Gamma \vdash A$ can be proved without Cut in $A \rightarrow^+ \exists x_1, \ldots, x_n. \bigwedge \Gamma$, which is easy. For the "if" direction, we proceed by induction on the lexicographic order of the number of rewrite steps using the rule $A \rightarrow^+ \exists x_1, \ldots, x_n. \bigwedge \Gamma$ and the structure of the proof. Except for Cut, the application of an inference rule in LBi modulo $\mathcal{R}$ can be decomposed into an application of r without modulo followed by an explicit conversion rule (two for Ax.) of the form

$$\uparrow^* \vdash \dfrac{\Gamma, Q \vdash \Delta}{\Gamma, P \vdash \Delta} \; P \xrightarrow{*}_{\mathcal{R}-} Q \qquad \text{or} \qquad \vdash \uparrow^* \dfrac{\Gamma \vdash Q, \Delta}{\Gamma \vdash P, \Delta} \; P \xrightarrow{*}_{\mathcal{R}+} Q \quad .$$

For Cut, we need two explicit conversions above the application of Cut without modulo. Consider the last application of an inference rule in a derivation of $\Gamma' \vdash \Delta'$ modulo $\mathcal{R} \cup \{A \rightarrow^+ \exists x_1, \ldots, x_n. \bigwedge \Gamma\}$, and decompose it as shown above. If the explicit conversion step does not use $A \rightarrow^+ \exists x_1, \ldots, x_n. \bigwedge \Gamma$, then we proceed by structural induction on the proof. Otherwise, suppose that $\Gamma' = P, \Sigma$ where P is negatively rewritten by $A \rightarrow^+ \exists x_1, \ldots, x_n. \bigwedge \Gamma$ into Q. By the induction hypothesis, we obtain a derivation of $Q, \Sigma \vdash \Delta$ in $\mathcal{R}$. From $\Gamma \vdash A$ we can derive $\exists x_1, \ldots, x_n. \bigwedge \Gamma \vdash A$, and by induction on the rewrite position, we know how to build a derivation of $P \vdash Q$. Using a Cut, we therefore have a derivation of $P, \Sigma \vdash \Delta$, as expected. The case where the rewriting occurs in Δ is dual.

The case of **Orient−** is dual.

For **Decompose**, this results from the fact that r is supposed invertible.

For **Discard**, for the "only if" part is obtained by weakening. For the "if" direction, we replace the premise $\Gamma \vdash \Delta$ by a Cut between the premise $\Gamma \vdash P, \Delta$ and the derivation of $\Gamma, P \vdash^S_{\mathcal{R}} \Delta$.

For **Delete**, for the "if" part is trivial. For the "only if" direction, replace the premises $\Gamma \vdash \Delta$ by the cut-free derivation $\Gamma \vdash^S_{\mathcal{R}} \Delta$.

For **Deduce**, the "only if" part is trivial. For the "if" direction, because $\Gamma \vdash \Delta \in CP(\mathcal{R})$, it is the conclusion of a proof modulo $\mathcal{R}$. We can therefore replace the premises $\Gamma \vdash \Delta$ by this proof.

Remark that for the "only if" direction, we never added Cuts. □

Corollary 8. *Given a presentation Θ, if $\{\vdash P : P \in \Theta\}, \emptyset \rightsquigarrow^* \emptyset, \mathcal{R}$, then Θ and $\mathcal{R}$ are compatible.*

Proof. A proof $\Theta \vdash Q$ can be seen as a derivation $\vdash^{\{\vdash P : P \in \Theta\}} Q$ by replacing $\text{Ax.} \dfrac{}{\Theta \vdash P}$ where $P \in \Theta$ by the premise $\vdash P$. □

As usual in completion procedures, we need a fairness condition to ensure that all critical proofs are dealt with. This condition is the following: at any moment, if $\Gamma \vdash \Delta \in CP(\mathcal{R}) \setminus S$ then **Deduce** will eventually add $\Gamma \vdash \Delta$ in the set of sequents.

Proposition 9. *Under this fairness condition, if the procedure terminates and produces $\emptyset, \mathcal{R}$, then $\mathcal{R}$ is analytic.*

Proof. Suppose that $\mathcal{R}$ is not analytic. There exists a sequent that can be proved with Cut but not without. Consider proofs as trees of couple of inference rules and principal formula, and define the recursive path ordering defined by the following precedence: $(\text{Cut}, P) > (\text{Ax.}, Q) > (r, R)$ for all inference rules r different from Cut and Ax., and all formulæ P, Q, R; and $(\text{Cut}, P) > (\text{Cut}, Q)$ and $(\text{Ax.}, P) > (\text{Ax.}, Q)$ if Q is a subformula of P. As the precedence is well-founded, so is this ordering. By induction on this ordering, and following the cut-elimination procedure as

described in [17], we can find a proof of the form $\text{Cut} \dfrac{\overset{\pi}{\Gamma, P \vdash \Delta} \quad \overset{\pi'}{\Gamma \vdash Q, \Delta}}{\Gamma \vdash \Delta}$

where

- P, Q is a critical pair of $\mathcal{R}$, i.e. there exists A atomic such that $P \underset{\mathcal{R}}{\longleftarrow} A \underset{\mathcal{R}}{\longrightarrow} Q$;
- π and π' are cut-free;
- P (resp. Q) is the principal formula of the last inference rule of π (resp. π');
- there is no cut-free proof of $\Gamma \vdash \Delta$ modulo $\mathcal{R}$.

In this proof, we can prune all formulæ that are not principal in one of the inference rules of π or π', and we therefore obtain a critical proof. By the fairness assumption, the sequent $\Gamma \vdash \Delta$ has been added to S during the procedure. By Proposition 7, the Cut-free derivation $\Gamma \vdash \Delta$ using the premise $\Gamma \vdash \Delta$ has been transformed by the procedure into a Cut-free derivation using premises in $\emptyset$ and rewrite rules in $\mathcal{R}$. We therefore have a Cut-free *proof* of $\Gamma \vdash \Delta$ modulo $\mathcal{R}$, hence the contradiction. □

Note that Procedure 1 is not computable, in the sense that **Discard**, **Delete** and **Deduce** use oracles that are not recursive. Indeed, the sets $\vdash^S_{\mathcal{R}}$ and $CP(\mathcal{R})$ are not co-recursively enumerable in general. Nonetheless, we believe that it is not possible to do better, because we conjecture the set described in Theorem 4 to be Σ^0_3-complete in the arithmetical hierarchy (see [4, Chapter C.1] for an introduction on the arithmetical hierarchy), that is, it is not even recursively enumerable. Once this conjecture has been proved, we could try to prove that our procedure with oracles is complete, that is, for all presentations that can be transformed into an analytic rewrite system, the procedure terminates without failure. Of course, in the case where the procedure fails, we can keep the remaining sequents in S and use them either as premises, or, if we only want to work with proofs and not derivations, we can transform these sequents $\Gamma \vdash \Delta$ into axioms $\forall x_1, \ldots, x_n. \bigwedge \Gamma \Rightarrow \bigvee \Delta$ with $\{x_1, \ldots, x_n\} = FV(\Gamma, \Delta)$.

5   Extensions

In this section, we present some extensions to the procedure presented in the previous section. For lack of space, we only briefly discuss them.

Axiom Schemata. Theories are often presented not only by axioms but also by axiom schemata. An axiom schema is a formula in which proposition variables can appear. The instance of an axiom schema are the formulæ where these proposition variables are substituted by formulæ. For instance, the induction principle in Peano's arithmetic $\forall x. (X(0) \wedge \forall y. X(y) \Rightarrow X(s(y))) \Rightarrow X(x)$ is an axiom schema with the proposition variable $X(x)$. An instance of this axiom schema is $\forall x. (0 + 0 = 0 \wedge \forall y. y + 0 = y \Rightarrow s(y) + 0 = s(y)) \Rightarrow x + 0 = x$ where $X(x)$ being substituted by $x + 0 = x$.

Axiom schemata can be seen as the infinite set of their instances, so that our procedure works on such presentations. However, in that case, $\mathcal{R}$ may be infinite. The rewrite relation would therefore not be implementable as it is. If the theory is presented by a finite set of axiom schemata, we can use the work of Kirchner [19] who shows how to get a finitely presented conservative extension of the theory. We can then apply Procedure 1 to this finite presentation and obtain a finite rewrite system if it terminates.

Equalities. First-order theories often use equality, for instance in Peano's arithmetic we have the axiom $\forall x. 0 + x = x$. Such axioms are better represented by term rewrite rules instead of proposition rewrite rules. In this example, $0 + x \rightarrow x$ is better than $0 + x = x \rightarrow \top$. Therefore, given a presentation, before applying our procedure, a better approach is to take away the equational logic subset of the presentation (axioms of the form $\forall x_1, \ldots, x_n. s = t$) and to apply standard tools to it, for instance Knuth-Bendix completion [21], to obtain a compatible confluent term rewrite system for that subset. Then, we apply Procedure 1 to the remaining axioms.

Skolemization. The theory presented by $\exists x. A(x)$ has no analytic compatible rewrite system, because it does not have the witness property. However, for some new constant c not appearing in the original signature, $A(c)$ is a presentation of a conservative extension of this theory that does have an analytic compatible rewrite system, e.g. $A(c) \rightarrow^+ \top$. Nevertheless, contrary to classical logic, Skolemization does not always lead to a conservative extension in intuitionistic logic. Mints [23] characterizes the presentations that can be correctly Skolemized. One improvement is therefore to apply Skolemization on those cases before applying Procedure 1. Nevertheless, even doing so, we will not be able to handle presentations such as $\neg\neg\exists x.\ A(x)$.

Baaz and Iemhoff [2] propose a generalization of Skolemization which works every time. To sum up the idea, formulæ are translated into their semantic in a Kripke structure. As the semantic of a Kripke model is defined in classical logic, the translated formulæ can be Skolemized. For our purpose, we do not even need to Skolemize these formulæ. Instead, we can apply the completion procedure for classical logic described in [8] to the translated presentation. Indeed, Baaz and Iemhoff proved that a formula is valid in intuitionistic logic iff its translation is valid in classical logic [2, Lemma 11]. However, we think that this is probably highly inefficient, in particular because of the transitivity of the accessibility relation in Kripke structures.

6   Example of Application

We can apply Procedure 1 to one of the axiom sets proposed in the Intuitionistic Logic Theorem Proving library [25], for instance the presentation of constructive geometry derived from [26] (files `GEJxxx+1.ax`). We obtain an analytic compatible rewrite system including among others the three following rules:

$$x \neq_p y \to^- \neg x \notin ln(x,y) \qquad\qquad \text{(GEJ002+1.ax, a1)}$$

$$x \neq_p y \to^- \neg y \notin ln(x,y) \qquad\qquad \text{(GEJ002+1.ax, a2)}$$

$$x \neq_p y \to^- \forall u\ v.\ u \neq_l v \Rightarrow (x \notin u \vee x \notin v \vee y \notin u \vee y \notin v) \quad \text{(GEJ003+1.ax, a1)}$$

The theorem proposed in the problem `GEJ001+1.p` therefore has the following proof in which Γ stands for $x \neq_p y, \neg x \notin z, \neg y \notin z, z \neq_l ln(x,y)$ and the inference rules that are applied modulo are marked by *:

$$
\begin{array}{c}
\cfrac{
  \cfrac{
    \text{Ax.}\ \cfrac{z \neq_l ln(x,y) \vdash z \neq_l ln(x,y)}{}\ \Rightarrow\vdash
    \quad
    \cfrac{
      \cfrac{\text{Ax.}\ \cfrac{x \notin z \vdash x \notin z}{x \notin z, \neg x \notin z \vdash}\ \neg\vdash \quad \cdots \quad \text{Ax.}\ \cfrac{y \notin ln(x,y) \vdash y \notin ln(x,y)}{x \neq_p y, y \notin ln(x,y) \vdash}\ \neg\vdash}{x \notin z \vee x \notin ln(x,y) \vee y \notin z \vee y \notin ln(x,y), \Gamma \vdash}\ \vee\vdash
    }{}
  }{
    \cfrac{z \neq_l ln(x,y) \Rightarrow (x \notin z \vee x \notin ln(x,y) \vee y \notin z \vee y \notin ln(x,y)), \Gamma \vdash}{
      \cfrac{\Gamma \vdash}{
        \cfrac{x \neq_p y, \neg x \notin z, \neg y \notin z \vdash \neg z \neq_l ln(x,y)}{
          \cfrac{x \neq_p y \wedge \neg x \notin z \wedge \neg y \notin z \vdash \neg z \neq_l ln(x,y)}{
            \cfrac{\vdash (x \neq_p y \wedge \neg x \notin z \wedge \neg y \notin z) \Rightarrow \neg z \neq_l ln(x,y)}{\vdash \forall x\ y\ z.\ (x \neq_p y \wedge \neg x \notin z \wedge \neg y \notin z) \Rightarrow \neg z \neq_l ln(x,y)}\ \vdash\forall
          }\ \vdash\Rightarrow
        }\ \wedge\vdash
      }\ \vdash\Rightarrow
    }\ \forall\vdash
  }\ \ast
}{}
\end{array}
$$

7   Conclusion

We have proposed a method to find automated theorem proving procedures adapted to proof search in a particular intuitionistic theory. The idea is to transform a presentation of the theory into a rewrite system, and to combine the inference rules of a sequent calculus with rewriting. We first proved that it is not decidable to transform the presentation of a theory into a rewrite system with an analytic sequent calculus modulo. We nonetheless proposed a (possibly non-terminating) procedure to do so, covering a large class of presentations. We then extended the domain of applicability of this procedure by working in conservative extensions of the theories we want to automate, to get finite presentations, to better handle equality and to partially authorize Skolemization. This work opens new challenges that we are now considering.

First, we would like to know the precise hardness in the arithmetical hierarchy of the transformation of a presentation into a compatible analytic rewrite system, and to prove that Procedure 1 is complete, or to find a complete procedure, in order to be able to transform all presentations that can be. Besides, the procedure only guarantees the Cut admissibility, and not the strong normalization. It would be interesting to refine the procedure to also have it, for instance because strong normalization helps at conceiving proof checkers. Note that if we are only interested in automated proof search, the normalization is less crucial, because the admissibility of cuts suffices to ensure the completeness of the proof-search procedures. Also, remark that the rewrite system produced by Procedure 1 may be not confluent. The original version of the sequent calculus modulo may therefore not be equivalent to the polarized version. Nonetheless, this is not problematic because we are mainly interested in the automated proving procedures based on deduction modulo, which are equivalent to the cut-free portion of the polarized version. Another interesting point is the combination of theories. Given two theories whose presentations have been transformed into analytic compatible rewrite systems, in which cases would the union of the rewrite system still be analytic? Investigating this question implies the study of modularity in deduction modulo.

We also need to implement Procedure 1. To control its non-termination, we can resort to iterative deepening, that is, incrementally limiting the number of times that $\Rightarrow\vdash$, $\forall\vdash$ and $\vdash\exists$ can be applied. We should link this implementation with a theorem prover based on deduction modulo that will serve as an oracle to compute $\vdash^S_{\mathcal{R}}$ and $CP(\mathcal{R})$.

Finally, we have researched how theories can be presented in deduction modulo. We could also examine how deductive systems can be encoded in it, in order to use deduction modulo as a logical framework. It was already proven that deduction modulo can encode HOL [11] and every functional pure type system [6]. An interesting issue is to automate how to find out such encodings.

Acknowledgments. This work was partly supported by the Inria ARC Corias. The author wishes to thank C. Kirchner for his support and helpful discussions about this topic, and M. Boespflug for his useful comments.

References

1. Baader, F., Nipkow, T.: Term Rewriting and all That. Cambridge University Press, Cambridge (1998)
2. Baaz, M., Iemhoff, R.: On Skolemization in constructive theories. The Journal of Symbolic Logic 73, 969–998 (2008)

3. Bachmair, L., Dershowitz, N.: Completion for rewriting modulo a congruence. In: Lescanne, P. (ed.) RTA 1987. LNCS, vol. 256, pp. 192–203. Springer, Heidelberg (1987)
4. Barwise, J. (ed.): Handbook of Mathematical Logic, 4th edn. Elsevier Science Publishers B. V., North-Holland (1985)
5. Bonichon, R., Hermant, O.: On constructive cut admissibility in deduction modulo. In: Altenkirch, T., McBride, C. (eds.) TYPES 2006. LNCS, vol. 4502, pp. 33–47. Springer, Heidelberg (2007)
6. Burel, G.: A first-order representation of pure type systems using superdeduction. In: Pfenning, F. (ed.) LICS, pp. 253–263. IEEE Computer Society, Los Alamitos (2008)
7. Burel, G.: Automating theories in intuitionistic logic (2009), http://hal.inria.fr/inria-00395934/
8. Burel, G., Kirchner, C.: Regaining cut admissibility in deduction modulo using abstract completion (2008) (submitted)
9. Dowek, G.: What is a theory? In: Alt, H., Ferreira, A. (eds.) STACS 2002. LNCS, vol. 2285, pp. 50–64. Springer, Heidelberg (2002)
10. Dowek, G.: Confluence as a cut elimination property. In: Nieuwenhuis, R. (ed.) RTA 2003. LNCS, vol. 2706, pp. 2–13. Springer, Heidelberg (2003)
11. Dowek, G., Hardin, T., Kirchner, C.: HOL-$\lambda\sigma$ an intentional first-order expression of higher-order logic. Mathematical Structures in Computer Science 11, 1–25 (2001)
12. Dowek, G., Hardin, T., Kirchner, C.: Theorem proving modulo. Journal of Automated Reasoning 31, 33–72 (2003)
13. Dowek, G., Miquel, A.: Cut elimination for Zermelo's set theory. Available on authors' web page (2006)
14. Dowek, G., Werner, B.: Arithmetic as a theory modulo. In: Giesl, J. (ed.) RTA 2005. LNCS, vol. 3467, pp. 423–437. Springer, Heidelberg (2005)
15. Gallier, J.H.: Logic for Computer Science: Foundations of Automatic Theorem Proving. Computer Science and Technology Series, vol. 5. Harper & Row, New York (1986), http://www.cis.upenn.edu/~jean/gbooks/logic.html, Revised On-Line Version (2003)
16. Gentzen, G.: Untersuchungen über das logische Schliessen. Mathematische Zeitschrift 39, 176–210, 405–431 (1934)
17. Girard, J.Y., Lafont, Y., Taylor, P.: Proofs and Types. Cambridge Tracts in Theoretical Computer Science, vol. 7. Cambridge University Press, Cambridge (1989)
18. Hermant, O.: Semantic cut elimination in the intuitionistic sequent calculus. In: Urzyczyn, P. (ed.) TLCA 2005. LNCS, vol. 3461, pp. 221–233. Springer, Heidelberg (2005)
19. Kirchner, F.: A finite first-order theory of classes. In: Altenkirch, T., McBride, C. (eds.) TYPES 2006. LNCS, vol. 4502, pp. 188–202. Springer, Heidelberg (2007)
20. Kleene, S.C.: Mathematical Logic. John Wiley, New York (1967)
21. Knuth, D.E., Bendix, P.B.: Simple word problems in universal algebras. In: Leech, J. (ed.) Computational Problems in Abstract Algebra, pp. 263–297. Pergamon Press, Oxford (1970)
22. Maehara, S.: Eine Darstellung der intuitionistischen Logik in der klassischen. Nagoya Mathematical Journal 7, 45–64 (1954)
23. Mints, G.: The Skolem method in intuitionistic calculi. Proc. Steklov Inst. Math. 121, 73–109 (1974)

24. Mints, G.: A Short Introduction to Intuitionistic Logic. The University series in mathematics. Kluwer Academic Publishers, Dordrecht (2000)
25. Raths, T., Otten, J., Kreitz, C.: The ILTP problem library for intuitionistic logic, release v1.1. Journal of Automated Reasoning 38, 261–271 (2007), http://www.iltp.de/
26. von Plato, J.: The axioms of constructive geometry. Annals of Pure and Applied Logic 76, 169–200 (1995)
27. Waaler, A., Wallen, L.: Tableaux for Intuitionistic Logics. In: Handbook of Tableau Methods. Kluwer Academic Publishers, Boston (1999)

Taming the Complexity of Temporal Epistemic Reasoning

Clare Dixon, Michael Fisher, and Boris Konev

Department of Computer Science, University of Liverpool, Liverpool, U.K.
{CLDixon,MFisher,Konev}@liverpool.ac.uk

Abstract. Temporal logic of knowledge is a combination of temporal and epistemic logic that has been shown to be very useful in areas such as distributed systems, security, and multi-agent systems. However, the complexity of the logic can be prohibitive. We here develop a refined version of such a logic and associated tableau procedure with improved complexity but where important classes of specification can still be described. This new logic represents a combination of an "exactly one" temporal logic with an S5 multi-modal logic again restricted to the "exactly one" form.

1 Introduction

While temporal logic has been shown to be very useful, particularly in the areas of formal specification and verification [16,14], there are two problems with its use:

1. *there are cases where* full *temporal logic is* too *expressive*
   — in particular, if we wish to describe the temporal properties of a restricted number of components, only one of which can occur at any moment in time, then the full temporal language forces us to describe the behaviour of all these components and their interactions explicitly;
2. *many applications require the extension of temporal logic with different modalities*
   — in particular, extensions with various modal logics (such as those describing knowledge or belief) are *very* useful.

Taking (2) first, there has been considerable work on defining, mechanising and applying combined temporal and modal logics.

A very popular modal approach is to use a logic of *knowledge*, i.e. an *epistemic* logic (typically S5 modal logic), in order to represent the knowledge that any player/agent/process has [7]. Involving multiple players/agents/processes leads us to *multi-dimensional* logics of knowledge [9] where multiple agents each have an associated notion of knowledge. We can then reason not only about the agent's knowledge of the situation, but also about the agent's knowledge of other agents, the agent's knowledge of other agents' situation, the agent's knowledge of other agents' knowledge about the situation, and so on.

This naturally leads on to *temporal logic of knowledge* [7], which is the combination of propositional discrete, linear temporal logic (LTL) with (S5) modal

S. Ghilardi and R. Sebastiani (Eds.): FroCoS 2009, LNAI 5749, pp. 198–213, 2009.

logic, which has been shown to be very useful in areas such as distributed systems [11,8], security [4], and multi-agent systems [20,17]. However, the complexity of such a combined logic is quite high, in particular even with a simple combination such as the fusion of LTL and multi-modal S5 the complexity of satisfiability is PSPACE [7].

In the meantime we have been working on (1). In [6], it was shown that, simply by incorporating *"exactly one" constraints* into a propositional temporal logic, much better computational complexity could be achieved. Essentially sets of propositions were allowed as part of the input (termed *"exactly one"* or *"constrained"* sets) where exactly one proposition from each set must hold at every moment in time. Normal unconstrained propositions were also allowed. Not only did this allow the concise specification of examples such as the representation of automata, basic planning problems, and agent negotiation protocols, but also greatly reduced the complexity of the associated decision procedure [5,6]. Essentially, this is because (as the name suggests) *exactly* one element of each "exactly one" set must be satisfied at every temporal state. This allowed polynomial complexity concerning the constrained sets within the decision procedure.

In this paper we will now make the obvious connection between (1) and (2) above. Specifically, we here:

- define an "exactly-one" temporal logic of knowledge;
- define a complete tableau system for this new logic;
- explore the computational complexity of the tableau system; and
- explore potential applications of the approach.

Thus, the paper builds on our previous work on "exactly one" temporal logics [6] and tableaux for temporal logics of knowledge [26], but provides a new logic, new tableau system, and significant complexity improvements with potential applications. The tableau algorithm replaces traditional alpha and beta rules with a DPLL-like construction [2] which ensures the exactly one sets hold. The complexity results show how careful organisation of the problem can, in many cases, greatly reduce exponential bounds.

The paper is organised as follows. In Section 2 we introduce XL5, a constrained temporal logic of knowledge. The complexity of satisfiability for this logic is considered in Section 3. In Section 4 we present a tableau algorithm for XL5 and prove its completeness and refined complexity. In Sections 5 and Section 6, we demonstrate the tableau algorithm in practice and identify areas where we believe XL5 may be useful. Finally, in Section 7, we provide concluding remarks and discuss related and future work.

2   A Constrained Temporal Logic of Knowledge

The logic we consider is called "XL5", and its syntax and semantics are essentially that of a propositional temporal logic of knowledge [7], which is in turn a *fusion* of propositional (linear, discrete) temporal logic [10] and an S5 modal logic of knowledge [12]. The models of such a logic are essentially a set of *timelines*, isomorphic to the Natural Numbers, at which modal relations (of the S5 variety) can link to points (a state occurring at a particular time in a timeline) in other timelines.

The main novelty in XL5 is that formulae of $XL5(\mathcal{P}^1, \mathcal{P}^2, \ldots)$ are constructed under the restrictions that *exactly* one proposition from every set $\mathcal{P}^i$ is true in every state. Note that propositions may appear in more than one set $\mathcal{P}^i$, i.e. $\mathcal{P}^i \cap \mathcal{P}^j$ may be non-empty for $i \neq j$. Furthermore, we assume that there exists a set of propositions, $\mathcal{A}$, in addition to those defined by the parameters $\mathcal{P}^i$, where for all i, $\mathcal{A} \cap \mathcal{P}^i = \emptyset$, and that these propositions are unconstrained as normal. Thus, XL5() is essentially a standard propositional, linear temporal logic of knowledge, while $XL5(\mathcal{P}, \mathcal{Q}, \mathcal{R})$ is a temporal logic of knowledge containing at *least* the propositions $\mathcal{P} \cup \mathcal{Q} \cup \mathcal{R}$, where $\mathcal{P} = \{p_1, p_2, \ldots, p_l\}$, $\mathcal{Q} = \{q_1, q_2, \ldots, q_m\}$, and $\mathcal{R} = \{r_1, r_2, \ldots, r_n\}$ and any state in a $XL5(\mathcal{P}, \mathcal{Q}, \mathcal{R})$ model must satisfy exactly one of $p_1, p_2, \ldots, p_l$; exactly one of $q_1, q_2, \ldots, q_m$; and exactly one of $r_1, r_2, \ldots, r_n$.

2.1 Syntax

The alphabet of $XL5(\mathcal{P}^1, \mathcal{P}^2, \ldots, \mathcal{P}^m)$ contains the following symbols:

1. the "exactly one" sets $\mathcal{P}^i = \{p_1^i, p_2^i, \ldots\}$ of atomic propositions and a set of unconstrained propositions $\mathcal{A}$ such that $\mathcal{P}^1 \cup \mathcal{P}^2 \cup \ldots \cup \mathcal{P}^m \cup \mathcal{A} = \text{PROP}$;
2. basic classical connectives, $\wedge$, $\vee$, $\Rightarrow$, $\neg$, F and T;
3. a set $\mathsf{Ag} = \{1, \ldots, n\}$ of agents;
4. the unary modal connectives K_i, where $i \in \mathsf{Ag}$; and
5. the temporal connectives, $\bigcirc$ (next), $\square$ (always), $\Diamond$ (sometime), and $\mathcal{U}$ (until).

2.2 Semantics

The semantics of XL5 is based upon *timelines* which are themselves composed of *points*. These are defined as follows. A *timeline*, l, is an infinitely long, linear, discrete sequence of states, indexed by the Natural Numbers. We assume that $\mathcal{TL}$ is the set of all timelines. A *point*, p, is a pair $p = (l, u)$, where $l \in \mathcal{TL}$ is a timeline and $u \in \mathbb{N}$ is a temporal index into l.

Any point (l, u) will uniquely identify a state $l(u)$. Let the set of all points be *Points*. We then let an agent's knowledge accessibility relation R_i hold over *Points*, i.e., $R_i \subseteq Points \times Points$, for all $i \in Ag$. This captures the idea of an agent being uncertain both about which timeline it is in, and how far along that timeline it is. A *valuation* for XL5 is a function that takes a point and a proposition, and says whether that proposition is true (T) or false (F) at that point.

We can now define model structures for XL5. A *model structure*, M, for XL5 is a structure $M = \langle TL, R_1, \ldots, R_n, \pi \rangle$, where:

- $TL \subseteq \mathcal{TL}$ is a set of timelines;
- R_i, for all $i \in Ag$, is an agent accessibility relation over *Points*, i.e., $R_i \subseteq Points \times Points$ such that R_i is an equivalence relation; and
- $\pi : Points \times \text{PROP} \to \{T, F\}$ is a valuation which satisfies the "exactly one" sets, i.e. makes exactly one element of each set $\mathcal{P}^i$ true.

$$\langle M, (l, u)\rangle \models T$$

$\langle M, (l, u)\rangle \models p$	iff	$\pi((l, u), p) = T$ (where $p \in \text{PROP}$)
$\langle M, (l, u)\rangle \models \neg\varphi$	iff	$\langle M, (l, u)\rangle \not\models \varphi$
$\langle M, (l, u)\rangle \models \varphi \vee \psi$	iff	$\langle M, (l, u)\rangle \models \varphi$ or $\langle M, (l, u)\rangle \models \psi$
$\langle M, (l, u)\rangle \models K_i\varphi$	iff	$\forall l' \in TL, \forall v \in \mathbb{N}$, if $((l, u), (l', v)) \in R_i$ then $\langle M, (l', v)\rangle \models \varphi$
$\langle M, (l, u)\rangle \models \bigcirc\varphi$	iff	$\langle M, (l, u+1)\rangle \models \varphi$
$\langle M, (l, u)\rangle \models \varphi \mathcal{U} \psi$	iff	$\exists v \in \mathbb{N}$ such that $(v \geq u)$ and $\langle M, (l, v)\rangle \models \psi$, and $\forall w \in \mathbb{N}$, if $(u \leq w < v)$ then $\langle M, (l, w)\rangle \models \varphi$

Fig. 1. Semantics of XL5

As usual, we define the semantics of the language via the satisfaction relation '$\models$'. For XL5, this relation holds between pairs of the form $\langle M, (l, u)\rangle$ (where M is a model structure and $(l, u) \in Points$), and XL5 formulae. The rules defining the satisfaction relation for selected operators (others can be defined from these) are given in Fig. 1. Other Boolean and temporal operators can be obtained with the usual equivalences. For the operators '$\Diamond$' and '$\Box$' these are $\Diamond\psi \equiv T \mathcal{U} \psi$ and $\Box\psi \equiv \neg\Diamond\neg\psi$.

We assume that for each $(l, u) \in Points$ the valuation π satisfies the "exactly one" sets, i.e. makes exactly one element of each set $\mathcal{P}^i$ true. Notice that the logical symbols of XL5 do not allow us to express such global requirements (eg everywhere exactly one of p, q, and r hold), and to represent such constraints *within* the logic, the set of logical operators would have to be extended with universal modalities. In other words, global restrictions on models give more expressivity to the logic.

A formula φ is *satisfied* in a model M if there exist a timeline l such that $\langle M, (l, 0)\rangle \models \varphi$. A formula is satisfiable if there exists a model in which it is satisfied. A formula is valid if its negation is unsatisfiable.

3   Complexity of XL5

When it comes to the complexity of reasoning, if only the length of a given formula is taken into account, XL5 does not have any advantages over an unrestricted fusion of $S5_n$ and LTL.

Theorem 1. *The satisfiability problem for XL5($\mathcal{P}$), even if all variables belong to the single constrained set $\mathcal{P}$, is PSPACE-complete.*

Proof. The PSPACE upper bound can be obtained from the complexity of temporal epistemic logic [7]. To prove the lower bound, we reduce the PSPACE-complete satisfiability of multi-modal $S5_n$ to satisfiability of XL5. Let φ be a multi-modal $S5_n$-formula constructed over $\{p_0, \ldots, p_m\}$. Consider a XL5($\{s, p_0', \ldots, p_m'\}$)-formula φ' obtained from φ by replacing every occurrence of a proposition p_i with $\Diamond p_i'$ for all p_i, $0 \leq i \leq m$, where s and $p_0', \ldots, p_m'$ are new propositions, which do not occur to φ. Notice that the size of φ' is linear in the size of φ. We show that φ is satisfiable if, and only if, φ' is satisfiable.

Clearly, if φ' is satisfiable then φ is satisfiable. Suppose now that φ has a model. Since φ does not contain temporal operators, its model $M = \langle TL, R_1, \ldots, R_n, \pi \rangle$ is such that, for any j, we have $((l_1, u_1), (l_2, u_2)) \in R_j$ implies $u_1 = u_2 = 0$. A model for φ' is $M' = \langle TL, R_1, \ldots, R_n, \pi' \rangle$, where $\pi'((l, u), p_i') = T$ if, and only if, $u = i$ and $\pi((l, 0), p_i) = T$; and $\pi'((l, u), s) = T$ if, and only if, $u > n$ or $\pi((l, 0), p_u) = F$ (that is, we set in M' the i-th proposition p_i' true in the i-th moment of time whenever in M the proposition p_i is true in the beginning of time; if p_i' is set to be false in M' in the i-th moment of time, s is true in the same moment). Clearly, M' satisfies the exactly one restriction $\{s, p_0, \ldots, p_m\}$ and $\langle M, (l, 0) \rangle \models p_i$ if, and only if, $\langle M', (l, 0) \rangle \models \Diamond p_i'$. Thus, $M' \models \varphi'$.   □

Theorem 2. *The satisfiability problem for two fragments of XL5($\mathcal{P}$)*

- *all variables belong to the single constrained set $\mathcal{P}$, there is one agent and temporal operators are not used; and*
- *all variables belong to the single constrained set $\mathcal{P}$ and modal operators are not used*

is NP-hard.

Proof. To prove the lower NP bound for the class of single-agent formulae without temporal operators, we reduce the Boolean satisfiability problem to satisfiability of XL5 formulae. Let φ be a Boolean formula over variables $p_1, \ldots, p_n$. Let $\psi = s \wedge \varphi'$, where s is a new proposition and φ' is obtained from φ by replacing every occurrence of a proposition p_i with the expression $K \neg p_i'$, where p_i' is a new proposition not used in φ, and let $\mathcal{X} = \{s, p_1', \ldots, p_n'\}$ be the 'exactly one' constraint.

Suppose that an assignment $\mathcal{I}$ satisfies φ. We show how to construct a model $\mathcal{M} = \langle TL, R, \pi \rangle$. The set of timelines $TL = \{l_0, l_1, \ldots, l_n\}$ (recall that n is the number of variables in φ), the relation R is the full relation of the set of points, and the valuation π is defined as follows

- for all $u \in \mathbb{N}$, $\pi((l_0, u), s) = T$ and for all $i, 1 \leq i \leq n$, $\pi((l_0, u), p_i') = F$.
- for every $i, 1 \leq i \leq n$ and every $u \in \mathbb{N}$ we have
  - $\pi((l_i, u), p_j') = F$ for all $j \neq i$
  - $\pi((l_i, u), p_i') = T$ if, and only if, $\mathcal{I}(p_i) = F$
  - $\pi((l_i, u), s) = T$ if, and only if, $\mathcal{I}(p_i) = T$.

Notice that $\langle \mathcal{M}, (l_0, 0) \rangle \models K \neg p_i'$ if, and only if, $\mathcal{I}(p_i) = T$. Since φ' is obtained from φ by renaming every occurrence of x_i with $K \neg x_i'$ we have $\langle \mathcal{M}, (l_0, 0) \rangle \models \psi$.

The NP lower bound for the subclass of XL5 formulae, in which modal operators are not used, can be obtained from the PSPACE lower bound above by considering propositional formulae instead of $S5_n$ formulae.   □

Theorem 3 later demonstrates, however, that XL5 reasoning is tractable if the number of occurrences of temporal and modal operators is bounded.

4 Tableau for XL5

Consider an XL5 formula φ that is to be shown to be satisfiable. The tableau algorithm constructs sets of *extended assignments* of propositions and modal subformulae i.e. a mapping to true or false, that satisfy both the "exactly one" sets and φ. However, rather than using the standard alpha and beta rules (see for example the modal tableau in [12,26]) these are constructed using a DPLL-based expansion [2]. Next the algorithm attempts to satisfy modal formulae, of the form $\neg K_i \psi$, and temporal formulae, of the form $\bigcirc \psi$ and $\psi_1 \mathcal{U} \psi_2$ (or their negations), made true in such an extended assignment by constructing R_i and "next time" successors which are themselves extended assignments which must satisfy particular subformulae (and the exactly one sets). We begin with some definitions.

Definition 1. *If φ is an XL5 formula, then $sub(\varphi)$ is the set of all subformulae of φ:*

$$sub(\varphi) = \begin{cases} \{\varphi\} & \text{if } \varphi \in \text{PROP } or \ \varphi = T \ or \ \varphi = F \\ \{\neg\psi\} \cup sub(\psi) & \text{if } \varphi = \neg\psi \\ \{\psi * \chi\} \cup sub(\psi) \cup sub(\chi) & \text{if } \varphi = \psi * \chi \text{ where } * \text{ is } \vee, \wedge \text{ or } \Rightarrow \\ \{K_i\psi\} \cup sub(\psi) & \text{if } \varphi = K_i\psi \\ \{\bigcirc\psi\} \cup sub(\psi) & \text{if } \varphi = \bigcirc\psi \\ \{\psi_1 \mathcal{U} \psi_2\} \cup sub(\psi_1) \cup sub(\psi_2) & \text{if } \varphi = \psi_1 \mathcal{U} \psi_2 \end{cases}$$

A formula $\psi \in sub(\varphi)$ is a modal subformula *of φ if, and only if, ψ is of the form $K_i\psi'$ for some ψ'. A formula $\psi \in sub(\varphi)$ is a* temporal subformula *of φ if, and only if, ψ is of the form $\bigcirc\psi'$ or $\psi_1' \mathcal{U} \psi_2'$ for some ψ', ψ_1', ψ_2'.*

Definition 2. *Let φ be an XL5 formula, $\text{PROP}(\varphi)$ be the set of all propositions occurring in φ, $\text{MOD}(\varphi)$ be the set of all modal subformulae of φ, and $\text{TEMP}(\varphi)$ be the set of all temporal subformulae of φ. We assume, without loss of generality, that $\mathcal{P}^i \subseteq \text{PROP}(\varphi)$ for $i : 1 \leq i \leq n$. An* extended assignment ν *for φ is a mapping from $\Sigma(\varphi) = \text{PROP}(\varphi) \cup \text{MOD}(\varphi) \cup \text{TEMP}(\varphi)$ to $\{T, F\}$.*

Every extended assignment ν can be represented by a set of formulae

$$\Delta_\nu = \bigcup_{\substack{\psi \in \Sigma(\varphi) \\ \nu(\psi) = T}} \{\psi\} \ \cup \ \bigcup_{\substack{\psi \in \Sigma(\varphi) \\ \nu(\psi) = F}} \{\neg\psi\}$$

Let ψ be a XL5 formula such that $\text{PROP}(\psi) \subseteq \text{PROP}(\varphi)$, $\text{MOD}(\psi) \subseteq \text{MOD}(\varphi)$ and $\text{TEMP}(\psi) \subseteq \text{TEMP}(\varphi)$. An extended assignment ν *for φ is* compatible *with ψ if, and only if, the following conditions hold.*

- *For every set $\mathcal{P}^i$, there exists exactly one proposition $p \in \mathcal{P}^i$ such that $\nu(p) = T$ (and so $\nu(q) = F$ for all $q \in \mathcal{P}^i, q \neq p$).*
- *The result of replacing every occurrence of a proposition $p \in \text{PROP}(\psi)$ in ψ with $\nu(p)$, every occurrence of a modal subformula $\psi' \in \text{MOD}(\psi)$, such that ψ' is not in the scope of another modal or temporal operator in ψ, with $\nu(\psi')$, and every occurrence of a temporal subformula $\chi \in \text{TEMP}(\psi)$, such that χ is not in the scope of another modal or temporal operator in ψ, with $\nu(\chi)$, evaluates to T.*
- *If $\nu(K_j\chi) = T$, for some modal subformula $K_j\chi$ of ψ, then ν is compatible with χ.*
- *If $\nu(\chi_1 \mathcal{U} \chi_2) = T$, for some temporal subformula $\chi_1 \mathcal{U} \chi_2$ of ψ, then ν is compatible with χ_1 or χ_2.*
- *If $\nu(\chi_1 \mathcal{U} \chi_2) = F$, for some temporal subformula $\chi_1 \mathcal{U} \chi_2$ of ψ, then ν is compatible with $\neg\chi_2$.*

We denote by $\mathcal{N}(\varphi)$ the set of all extended assignments of φ.

Example 1. Within XL5($\{p, q\}$), let $\varphi = \neg K_1(p \wedge \bigcirc K_2 \neg p)$. Suppose ψ is φ itself. Consider the extended assignment ν_1 represented by the set $\Delta_{\nu_1} = \{p, \neg q, \neg K_1(p \wedge K_2 \neg p), \bigcirc K_2 \neg p, K_2 \neg p\}$. Then the first two conditions of compatibility with ψ hold true. Notice, however, that ν_1 is not compatible with ψ since $\nu_1(K_2 \neg p) = T$ but $\neg p$ evaluates to F under ν_1. The extended assignment ν_2 represented by the set $\Delta_{\nu_2} = \{p, \neg q, \neg K_1(p \wedge K_2 \neg p), \bigcirc K_2 \neg p, \neg K_2 \neg p\}$ is compatible with ψ.

Lemma 1. *Let φ be an XL5 formula and ψ be its subformula. Then the set of all extended assignments for φ compatible with ψ can be computed in $O\left(|\mathcal{P}^1| \times \ldots \times |\mathcal{P}^n| \times 2^{|\mathcal{A}|} \times 2^k \times 2^t\right)$ time, where $|\mathcal{P}^i|$ is the size of the set $\mathcal{P}^i$ of constrained propositions, $|\mathcal{A}|$ is the size of the set $\mathcal{A}$ of non-constrained propositions, k is the number of modal operators in φ, and t is the number of temporal operators in φ.*

Proof. The set of all extended assignments compatible with ψ can be constructed by the DPLL algorithm, where we first split on elements of $\mathcal{P}^i$ (that requires $O(|\mathcal{P}^1| \times \ldots \times |\mathcal{P}^n|)$ time) and then on elements of $\mathcal{A}$, $\text{MOD}(\varphi)$, and $\text{TEMP}(\varphi)$. $\square$

Note 1. The complexity of TLX (linear time logic parametrised by exactly one sets) given in [6] is polynomial in the size of the number of constrained propositions (that is, propositions belonging to an exactly one set) and does not depend on the number of temporal operators occurring to the formula. This is because [6] only considers formulae in a normal form where temporal operators only occur in the form $\square(\varphi_1 \Rightarrow \bigcirc\varphi_2)$, and $\square\diamondsuit\varphi_2$, where φ_1 is a conjunction of literals and φ_2 is a disjunction of literals. Reduction to the normal form introduces unconstrained propositions, therefore, the complexity result for XL5 is not worse than for TLX. Notice further that in many practical applications (for example, when modelling transition systems), parts of the formula are in the normal form and no reduction is necessary. Thus, in practice, the bound in Lemma 1 may not be reached. Indeed, if x and y belong to the same exactly one set, $\bigcirc x$ and $\bigcirc y$ are also mutually exclusive.

The tableau algorithm constructs a *structure* $H = (S, \eta, R_1, \ldots, R_n, L)$, where:

- S is a set of states;
- $\eta \subseteq S \times S$ is a binary *next-time* relation on S;
- $R_i \subseteq S \times S$ represents an accessibility relation over S for agent $i \in Ag$;
- $L : S \to \mathcal{N}(\varphi)$ labels each state with an extended assignment for φ.

We try to construct a structure from which a model may be extracted, and then delete states in this structure that are labelled with formulae such as $\neg K_i p$, $p \,\mathcal{U}\, q$, which are not satisfied in the structure. Expansion uses the formulae in the labels of each state to build R_i successors and η successors.

Given the XL5 formula φ to be shown unsatisfiable, we now perform the following tableau construction steps.

1. *Initialisation.*
   First, set
   $$S = \eta = R_1 = \cdots = R_n = L = \emptyset.$$

   Construct $\mathcal{F}$, the set of all extended assignments for φ compatible with φ. For each $\nu_i \in \mathcal{F}$ create a new state s_i and let $L(s_i) = \nu_i$ and $S = S \cup \{s_i\}$.

2. *Creating R_i successors.* For any state s labelled by an extended assignment ν, i.e. $L(s) = \nu$ for each formula of the form $\neg K_i \psi \in \Delta_{L(s)}$ create a formula

   $$\psi' = \neg\psi \wedge \bigwedge_{K_i\chi \in \Delta_{L(s)}} \chi \wedge \bigwedge_{K_i\chi \in \Delta_{L(s)}} K_i\chi \wedge \bigwedge_{\neg K_i\chi \in \Delta_{L(s)}} \neg K_i\chi$$

   For each ψ' above construct $\mathcal{F}$, the set of all extended assignments for φ compatible with ψ' and for each member $\nu \in \mathcal{F}$ if there exists a state $s'' \in S$ such that $\nu = L(s'')$ then add (s, s'') to R_i, otherwise add a new state s' to S, labelled by $L(s') = \nu$, and add (s, s') to R_i.

3. *Creating η successors.* Let ν be an extended assignment for φ. Then $next(\nu)$ is the smallest subset of Δ_ν such that whenever:-

   - $\bigcirc\chi \in \Delta_\nu$ then $\chi \in next(\nu)$;
   - $\neg\bigcirc\chi \in \Delta_\nu$ then $\neg\chi \in next(\nu)$;
   - $\chi_1 \,\mathcal{U}\, \chi_2 \in \Delta_\nu$ but ν is not compatible with χ_2, then $\chi_1 \,\mathcal{U}\, \chi_2 \in next(\nu)$; and
   - $\neg(\chi_1 \,\mathcal{U}\, \chi_2) \in \Delta_\nu$ but ν is not compatible with $\neg\chi_1$, then $\neg(\chi_1 \,\mathcal{U}\, \chi_2) \in next(\nu)$.

   For any state s labelled by an extended assignment ν, i.e. $L(s) = \nu$ create the set of formulae $\Delta = next(L(s))$. Let ψ' be the conjunction of formulae in Δ. For the formula ψ' above construct $\mathcal{F}$, the set of all extended assignments for φ compatible with ψ' and for each member $\nu \in \mathcal{F}$ if there exists a state $s'' \in S$ such that $\nu = L(s'')$ then add (s, s'') to η, otherwise add a new state s' to S, labelled by $L(s') = \nu$, and add (s, s') to η.

4. *Contraction.*
   Continue deleting any state s where
   - there exists a formula $\psi \in \Delta_{L(s)}$ such that ψ is of the form $\neg K_i \chi$ and there is no state $s' \in S$ such that $(s, s') \in R_i$ and $L(s')$ is compatible with $\neg \chi$,
   - $next(\nu)$ is not empty but there is no $s' \in S$ such that $(s, s') \in \eta$, or
   - there exists a formula $\psi \in \Delta_{L(s)}$ such that ψ is of the form $\chi_1 \, \mathcal{U} \, \chi_2$ and $\nexists s' \in S$ such that $(s, s') \in \eta^*$ and $L(s')$ is compatible with χ_2, where η^* is the transitive reflexive closure of η.
   until no further deletions are possible.

If φ is a formula then we say the tableau algorithm is *successful* if, and only if, the structure returned contains a state s such that φ is compatible with $L(s)$. We claim that a formula φ is XL5 satisfiable if, and only if, the tableau algorithm performed on φ is successful.

Theorem 3. *Let $\mathcal{P}^1, \ldots, \mathcal{P}^n$ be sets of constrained propositions, and φ be an $XL5(\mathcal{P}^1, \ldots, \mathcal{P}^n)$ formula such that $\bigcup_{i=1}^{n} \mathcal{P}^i \subseteq \mathrm{PROP}(\varphi)$. Then*

- *φ is satisfiable if, and only if, the tableau algorithm applied to φ returns a structure $(S, \eta, R_1, \ldots, R_n, L)$ in which there exists a state $s \in S$ such that φ is compatible with $L(s)$.*
- *The tableau algorithm runs in time polynomial in $\big((k + t) \times |\mathcal{P}^1| \times \ldots \times |\mathcal{P}^n| \times 2^{|\mathcal{A}| + k + t}\big)$, where $|\mathcal{P}^i|$ is the size of the set $\mathcal{P}^i$ of constrained propositions, $|\mathcal{A}|$ is the size of the set $\mathcal{A}$ of non-constrained propositions, k is the number of modal operators in φ, and t is the number of temporal operators in φ.*

Proof. The correctness and completeness of the tableau algorithm can be proved by adapting the correctness and completeness proof given in [26]. The main difference between the two algorithms is that the algorithm in [26] applies propositional tableau expansion rules to formulae and the one given above uses DPLL-based expansion.

For the second part of the theorem, notice that the number of nodes in any structure does not exceed $\big(|\mathcal{P}^1| \times \ldots \times |\mathcal{P}^n| \times 2^{|\mathcal{A}| + k + t}\big)$. When creating R_i successors, we consider at most k formulae of the form $\neg K_i \psi \in \Delta_\nu$, and, by Lemma 1, the set of all extended assignments for φ compatible with ψ' can be computed in $O\big(|\mathcal{P}^1| \times \ldots \times |\mathcal{P}^n| \times 2^{|\mathcal{A}| + k + t}\big)$ time. Similarly, when creating η successors, we consider at most t formulae in $next(\nu)$. Building the structure and applying the contraction rule can be implemented in time polynomial in the structure size. $\square$

5   Example

We now consider a longer example. We base this[1] on the simple card-playing scenario from [22].

---

[1] A version of this example was presented as part of *"WiebeFest 2009 — A Celebration of Prof. Wiebe van der Hoek's 50th Birthday"*; hence the principle agent is called 'Wiebe'!

Here, an agent (called Wiebe) can hold one of three cards. Each of these cards is in a different suit: *hearts*, *spades*, or *clubs*. The cards are dealt so that Wiebe holds one, one is on the table, and the final one is in a holder (*aka* deck). Following [22] we use simple propositions to represent the position of the cards. So, if $spades_w$ is true, then Wiebe holds a spade, if $clubs_t$ is true, then the clubs card is on the table, if $hearts_h$ is true, then the hearts card is in the holder, etc. Similarly, $K_w spades_w$ means that Wiebe *knows* he holds a spade. And so on.

Now, if we were to specify this scenario in a standard temporal logic of knowledge, we would be forced to specify much background information. For example:

- Wiebe's card is spades or hearts or clubs: $(spades_w \vee clubs_w \vee hearts_w)$
- but Wiebe cannot hold both spades and clubs, both spades and hearts, or both clubs and spades:

$$\neg(spades_w \wedge clubs_w) \wedge \neg(spades_w \wedge hearts_w) \wedge \neg(clubs_w \wedge hearts_w)$$

- And Wiebe knows both of the above, e.g.: $K_w(spades_w \vee clubs_w \vee hearts_w)$
- Similarly for the *holder* and the *table*.
- The spades card must be either held by Wiebe or be in the holder or be on the table: $(spades_w \vee spades_h \vee spades_t)$
- but cannot be in more than one place:

$$\neg(spades_w \wedge spades_h) \wedge \neg(spades_w \wedge spades_t) \wedge \neg(spades_h \wedge spades_t)$$

- And again Wiebe knows the above, e.g.: $K_w(spades_w \vee spades_h \vee spades_t)$
- Similarly for both the *hearts* and *clubs* cards.
- All the above statements hold globally.

However, we can model this scenario with six "exactly one" sets within XL5($\mathcal{P}^1$, $\mathcal{P}^2$, $\mathcal{P}^3$, $\mathcal{P}^4$, $\mathcal{P}^5$, $\mathcal{P}^6$) where

- $\mathcal{P}^1 = \{spades_w, clubs_w, hearts_w\}$ — Wiebe has exactly one card.
- $\mathcal{P}^2 = \{spades_h, clubs_h, hearts_h\}$ — exactly one card is in the holder.
- $\mathcal{P}^3 = \{spades_t, clubs_t, hearts_t\}$ — exactly one card is on the table.
- $\mathcal{P}^4 = \{spades_w, spades_h, spades_t\}$ — the spades card is in exactly one place.
- $\mathcal{P}^5 = \{clubs_w, clubs_h, clubs_t\}$ — the clubs card is in exactly one place.
- $\mathcal{P}^6 = \{hearts_w, hearts_h, hearts_t\}$ — the hearts card is in exactly one place.

Thus, all the formulae at the beginning of this section are unnecessary.

Now let us try to establish something using the tableau construction. Given the basic scenario, we add some temporal evolution. Specifically, we add the fact that Wiebe comes to know more about the scenario as time passes. Thus, we add:

- originally Wiebe has been dealt the clubs card (but has not looked at the card so doesn't know this yet), so $clubs_w$;
- at the next step Wiebe looks at his card so he knows that he has the *clubs* card, so $\bigcirc K_w clubs_w$.

So, one statement we may try to establish from this is that given the above, sometime Wiebe knows that either the hearts card or the spades card is in the holder.

$$(clubs_w \wedge \bigcirc K_w \, clubs_w) \Rightarrow \Diamond K_w(hearts_h \vee spades_h).$$

We replace $\Diamond K_w(hearts_h \vee spades_h)$ by $T \mathcal{U} K_w(hearts_h \vee spades_h)$ and negate the above, giving

$$\varphi = \neg((clubs_w \wedge \bigcirc K_w \, clubs_w) \Rightarrow T \mathcal{U} K_w(hearts_h \vee spades_h))$$

and begin constructing the tableau for φ.

First we construct the set of extended assignments for φ compatible with φ. To save space we assume that any propositions not mentioned are false. Let

$$\mathcal{I}_0 = \{clubs_w, \bigcirc K_w \, clubs_w, \neg(T \mathcal{U} K_w(hearts_h \vee spades_h)), \neg K_w(hearts_h \vee spades_h)\}.$$

Notice that any extended assignment that does not contain $\mathcal{I}_0$ is not compatible with φ.

$$\Delta_{L(s_0)} = \mathcal{I}_0 \cup \{K_w \, clubs_w, hearts_h, spades_t\}$$
$$\Delta_{L(s_1)} = \mathcal{I}_0 \cup \{K_w \, clubs_w, hearts_t, spades_h\}$$
$$\Delta_{L(s_2)} = \mathcal{I}_0 \cup \{\neg K_w \, clubs_w, hearts_h, spades_t\}$$
$$\Delta_{L(s_3)} = \mathcal{I}_0 \cup \{\neg K_w \, clubs_w, hearts_t, spades_h\}$$

Next we create R_w successors. For s_0 and s_1 let

$$\psi' = K_w \, clubs_w \wedge \neg K_w(hearts_h \vee spades_h) \wedge clubs_w \wedge \neg(hearts_h \vee spades_h).$$

There are no extended assignments of φ which are compatible with ψ' (essentially $\neg(hearts_h \vee spades_h)$ and $\mathcal{P}^2$ forces $clubs_h$ to hold which contradicts with $clubs_w$ and $\mathcal{P}^5$). Hence during the deletion phase s_0 and s_1 will be deleted as there are no R_w successors of s_0 and s_1 compatible with $\neg(hearts_h \vee spades_h)$. We can, however, construct a number of R_w successors for s_2 and s_3. When we attempt to construct η successors for s_2 and s_3 for $i = 2, 3$ we obtain

$$next(L(s_i)) = \{K_w \, clubs_w, \neg(T \mathcal{U} K_w(hearts_h \vee spades_h))\}$$

and

$$\psi'' = K_w \, clubs_w \wedge \neg(T \mathcal{U} K_w(hearts_h \vee spades_h))\}.$$

Let

$$\mathcal{I}_1 = \{\neg \bigcirc K_w \, clubs_w, \neg(T \mathcal{U} K_w(hearts_h \vee spades_h))\}.$$

We construct the extended assignments for φ which are compatible with ψ'' obtaining $L(s_0)$, $L(s_1)$ and

$$\Delta_{L(s_4)} = \mathcal{I}_1 \cup \{K_w \, clubs_w, \neg(K_w(hearts_h \vee spades_h)), clubs_w, hearts_h, spades_t\}$$
$$\Delta_{L(s_5)} = \mathcal{I}_1 \cup \{K_w \, clubs_w, \neg(K_w(hearts_h \vee spades_h)), clubs_w, hearts_t, spades_h\}$$

We add $(s_j, s_0), (s_j, s_1), (s_j, s_4), (s_j, s_5)$ to η for $j = 2, 3$.

If we try to construct R_w successors of s_4 and s_5 we construct ψ' as previously and obtain no extended assignments of φ that satisfy ψ' from the reasons given before. Hence during deletions s_4 and s_5 will be deleted as they have no state s such that $(s_4, s) \in R_w$ or $(s_5, s) \in R_w$ such that $L(s)$ is compatible with $\neg(hearts_h \vee spades_h)$. Hence as s_0 and s_1 have already been deleted for similar reasons then s_2 and s_3 have no η successors and so are deleted. As there is no remaining state compatible with φ the tableau is unsuccessful and so φ is unsatisfiable and $(clubs \wedge \bigcirc K_w clubs_w) \Rightarrow \Diamond K_w(hearts_h \vee spades_h)$ is valid.

6   Potential Application Areas

Temporal logics of knowledge are important in both mainstream Computer Science and AI. Thus, with a variety of such logics with lower complexity, we can potentially target a number of areas.

6.1   Distributed Systems

Temporal logics of knowledge are typically used for the specification and verification of distributed systems and are also used in *knowledge-based protocols* [7]. Here, the idea is that when designing a distributed system, one often makes use of statements such as "if process a_1 knows that process a_2 has received message m_1, then a_1 should *eventually* send message m_2". Temporal logics of knowledge are used to formalise this kind of reasoning; knowledge is given a precise interpretation, in terms of the states of a process.

Thus, the "exactly one" variant can come into its own when we have epistemic or temporal states that are constrained in this way. Most obviously, if a process can be in only one particular mode (e.g. *running, suspended,* or *stopped*) then a logic describing this process can utilise the "exactly one" set {*running, suspended, stopped*}. Crucially, the process *knows* that its mode must be one of these, and every other process also knows this. For example, a process a in reasoning about its knowledge might construct formulae such as the following (about process b) $K_a K_b(running_a \vee suspended_a \vee stopped_a)$ and so on. Formulae such as these are implicit within the XL5 parametrised by appropriate "exactly one" sets.

6.2   Learning and Knowledge Evolution

As we saw in Section 5, temporal formulae can easily be used to describe how an agent's knowledge changes, for example due to learning, observation or announcements by other agents. Thus, many of the examples given in [23] in terms of *dynamic epistemic logic* [22] can be described in a more concise and efficient manner. We note that many of the examples given in [22] have quite low numbers of modal/dynamic operators and so we might expect a reasonable complexity within our logic. Similarly, the representation of the game Cluedo provided in [3] is concerned with how players' knowledge evolves over time and contains "exactly one" sets relating to the representation of the cards of each player and of the murderer.

6.3 Security

Not only do we gain similar advantages as in the area of distributed systems described above, but can also utilise the "exactly one" sets (and knowledge about them) to simplify security descriptions given in temporal logics of knowledge [4]. For example, reasoning about the fact that a message was sent by exactly one of "*expected_sender*", "*intruder*", or "*error_process*" can be simplified.

6.4 Robotics

Robot swarms are collections of, often simple, robots usually with some task to perform. Although the algorithm controlling each robot is fairly simple it is often challenging to prove desirable properties of the swarm, for example that the group of robots does stay in a connected group and some robot doesn't go off on its own and get lost, or that the task is completed successfully etc.

In [24] a swarm algorithm is specified using temporal logic. Underlying this algorithm we can see a number of "exactly one" sets relating to the robot direction (North, South, East, West); the location of the robot; and related to the robot's internal state. In [15] a swarm of foraging robots is defined. Underlying this description is a transition system that describes the different states a robot can pass through whilst foraging for food, for example leaving the nest, random walk, scanning for food, returning home, depositing food, resting etc. It is clear that, for each robot each of these will form an "exactly one" set. Knowledge may be used here to model the robot's awareness of nearby robots etc. Thus a logic such as XL5 may well help specify and prove properties of more complex robot swarms.

6.5 Planning and Knowledge Representation

The planning problem is given a set of initial conditions, a set of actions and a goal to find a suitable sequence of actions that can take us from the initial conditions to the goal. The planning problem can be represented as a temporal logic satisfiability problem, see for example [1]. Initial conditions can be represented as formulae holding in the initial state, actions can be modelled by making a next step and recording that the action that has been taken, goals can be represented using eventualities ($\Diamond$-formulae) and invariants can be modelled using the $\Box$ operator. Given a representation of the initial conditions and consequences of actions in temporal logic ($SPEC$) and the representation of the goal in temporal logic ($GOAL$) if we can show that $SPEC \Rightarrow GOAL$ is satisfiable in a model then the model can be inspected to see what sequence of actions was used to reach the goal producing the required plan.

"Exactly one" sets seem to occur often in this domain, for example recording that exactly one action may occur at any moment. Further in the domains of interest, for example blocksworld, transportation and scheduling, exactly one sets also occur widely (for example that the location of transportation vehicles may be at one place at any moment, etc).

7 Concluding Remarks

We have taken recent ideas relating to temporal logics which allow the input of sets of proposition where exactly one from each set must hold and have adapted them to the framework of multi-modal temporal logics of knowledge. We have motivated the need for such constraints by considering a number of application areas. We have provided a tableau based algorithm to prove XL5 formulae which replaces the usual alpha and beta rules with a DPLL-based expansion and analysed its complexity. This shows that the tableau is useful when applied to problems with a large number of constrained propositions and a comparatively low number of unconstrained propositions, modal and temporal operators in the formula to be proved.

7.1 Related and Further Work

This paper defines a logic combining linear-time temporal logic and epistemic modal logic but allowing a number of constrained sets as input. In [21] the authors try and specify implicit facts and knowledge for (non-temporal) games of the form given in Section 5 for the modal logic $S5_n$. This is given in terms of a minimal (in some sense) set of formulae that are satisfied in every world for any model for the problem. However that work focuses on the specification of these facts and knowledge rather than looking at the complexity and decision procedure for a logic with constraints as input.

Here we define a tableau for a temporal logic of knowledge allowing the input of constraints. Tableau for modal logics have been given in [12] for example and tableau for propositional linear-time temporal logics have been given in [25,19,13]. The tableau we present here uses a DPLL-like construction to construct tableau states rather than the usual alpha and beta rules. The construction of modal and temporal successors follows what is usually done for modal and temporal tableau.

The authors of this paper have considered decision procedures for propositional linear-time temporal logics allowing the input of constrained sets in [5,6]. Both assume the temporal formulae are in a normal form with clauses relating to the initial moment, conditions on the next moment given the current state, and eventualities. This is different than the approach here where, as usual, the tableau algorithm can be applied to any XL5 formula and does not require translation into normal form. In [5] a tableau-like structure (known as an Incremental Behaviour Graph) is constructed and allows more expressive constraints than we do here (eg exactly n from a set holding or less than n from a set holding). The paper [6] defines a resolution calculus. We note that with constrained logics just involving temporal logic we can express the constraints within the logic itself using the □-operator. However for XL5 we cannot express the constraints without adding a universal modality to the syntax, so we extend the expressivity of the logic.

Regarding further work, primarily we are interested in implementing the tableau system and applying the logical framework to applications outlined in

Section 6. In addition, we would explore different combinations of logics. For example, tableau-based methods have been used for the Belief, Desire, Intention (BDI) logics of Rao and Georgeff in [18]. Whilst here we have considered propositional-linear time temporal logics combined with the modal logic of knowledge it would be fairly easy to amend this to combine with belief logics (KD45) or the logics KD for desire or intention.

Acknowledgements

The work of Fisher was partially supported by EPSRC grant EP/F033567 ("Verifying Interoperability Requirements in Pervasive Systems") and the work of Dixon was partially supported by EPSRC grant EP/D060451 ("Practical Reasoning Approaches for Web Ontologies and Multi-Agent Systems").

References

1. Cerrito, S., Mayer, M.C.: Using linear temporal logic to model and solve planning problems. In: Giunchiglia, F. (ed.) AIMSA 1998. LNCS (LNAI), vol. 1480, pp. 141–152. Springer, Heidelberg (1998)
2. Davis, M., Logemann, G., Loveland, D.: A Machine Program for Theorem-Proving. Commun. ACM 5(7), 394–397 (1962)
3. Dixon, C.: Using Temporal Logics of Knowledge for Specification and Verification– a Case Study. Journal of Applied Logic 4(1), 50–78 (2006)
4. Dixon, C., Fernández Gago, M.C., Fisher, M., van der Hoek, W.: Temporal Logics of Knowledge and their Applications in Security. Electronic Notes in Theoretical Computer Science, vol. 186, pp. 27–42 (2007)
5. Dixon, C., Fisher, M., Konev, B.: Temporal Logic with Capacity Constraints. In: Konev, B., Wolter, F. (eds.) FroCos 2007. LNCS (LNAI), vol. 4720, pp. 163–177. Springer, Heidelberg (2007)
6. Dixon, C., Fisher, M., Konev, B.: Tractable Temporal Reasoning. In: Proc. Int. Joint Conference on Artificial Intelligence (IJCAI), AAAI Press, Menlo Park (2007)
7. Fagin, R., Halpern, J., Moses, Y., Vardi, M.: Reasoning About Knowledge. MIT Press, Cambridge (1995)
8. Fagin, R., Halpern, J.Y., Vardi, M.Y.: What Can Machines Know? On the Properties of Knowledge in Distributed Systems. Journal of the ACM 39, 328–376 (1996)
9. Gabbay, D., Kurucz, A., Wolter, F., Zakharyaschev, M.: Many-Dimensional Modal Logics: Theory and Applications. Studies in Logic and the Foundations of Mathematics, vol. 148. Elsevier Science, Amsterdam (2003)
10. Gabbay, D., Pnueli, A., Shelah, S., Stavi, J.: The Temporal Analysis of Fairness. In: Proc. Seventh ACM Symposium on the Principles of Programming Languages (POPL), January 1980, pp. 163–173 (1980)
11. Halpern, J.Y., Moses, Y.: Knowledge and Common Knowledge in a Distributed Environment. J. ACM 37(3), 549–587 (1990)
12. Halpern, J.Y., Moses, Y.: A Guide to Completeness and Complexity for Modal Logics of Knowledge and Belief. Artificial Intelligence 54, 319–379 (1992)
13. Janssen, G.: Logics for Digital Circuit Verification: Theory, Algorithms, and Applications. PhD thesis, Eindhoven University of Technology, Eindhoven, The Netherlands (1999)

14. Lamport, L.: Specifying Systems: The TLA+ Language and Tools for Hardware and Software Engineers. Addison Wesley Professional, Reading (2003)
15. Liu, W., Winfield, A., Sa, J., Chen, J., Dou, L.: Strategies for energy optimisation in a swarm of foraging robots. In: Şahin, E., Spears, W.M., Winfield, A.F.T. (eds.) SAB 2006 Ws 2007. LNCS, vol. 4433, pp. 14–26. Springer, Heidelberg (2007)
16. Manna, Z., Pnueli, A.: The Temporal Logic of Reactive and Concurrent Systems: Specification. Springer, New York (1992)
17. Moore, R.C.: Logic and Representation. Lecture Notes. Center for the Study of Language and Information, CSLI (1994)
18. Rao, A.S., Georgeff, M.: BDI Agents: from theory to practice. In: Proc. First Int. Conference on Multi-Agent Systems (ICMAS), San Francisco, USA, pp. 312–319 (1995)
19. Schwendimann, S.: Aspects of Computational Logic. PhD thesis, University of Bern, Switzerland (1998)
20. van der Hoek, W.: Systems for Knowledge and Beliefs. Journal of Logic and Computation 3(2), 173–195 (1993)
21. van Ditmarsch, H., van der Hoek, W., Kooi, B.: Descriptions of game states. In: Games, Logic, and Constructive Sets. CSLI Lecture Notes, vol. 161, pp. 43–58. CSLI Publications, Stanford (2003)
22. van Ditmarsch, H., van der Hoek, W., Kooi, B.: Playing Cards with Hintikka — An Introduction to Dynamic Epistemic Logic. Australasian Journal of Logic 3, 108–134 (2005)
23. van Ditmarsch, H., van der Hoek, W., Kooi, B.: Dynamic Epistemic Logic. Synthese Library Series, vol. 337. Springer, Heidelberg (2007)
24. Winfield, A., Sa, J., Fernández-Gago, M.-C., Dixon, C., Fisher, M.: On Formal Specification of Emergent Behaviours in Swarm Robotic Systems. Int. Journal of Advanced Robotic Systems 2(4), 363–370 (2005)
25. Wolper, P.: The Tableau Method for Temporal Logic: An Overview. Logique et Analyse, 110–111, 119–136 (June-September 1985)
26. Wooldridge, M., Dixon, C., Fisher, M.: A Tableau-Based Proof Method for Temporal Logics of Knowledge and Belief. Journal of Applied Non-Classical Logics 8(3), 225–258 (1998)

Putting ABox Updates into Action

Conrad Drescher, Hongkai Liu, Franz Baader, Steffen Guhlemann,
Uwe Petersohn, Peter Steinke, and Michael Thielscher

Department of Computer Science,
Dresden University of Technology
Nöthnitzer Str. 46, 01187 Dresden, Germany

Abstract. When trying to apply recently developed approaches for updating Description Logic ABoxes in the context of an action programming language, one encounters two problems. First, updates generate
so-called *Boolean* ABoxes, which cannot be handled by traditional Description Logic reasoners. Second, iterated update operations result in
very large Boolean ABoxes, which, however, contain a huge amount of
redundant information. In this paper, we address both issues from a
practical point of view.

1 Introduction

Agent programming languages such as Golog [1] and Flux [2] employ actions
whose effects are defined in a logic-based calculus to describe and implement
the behaviour of intelligent agents. In the so-called progression approach, the
agent starts with a (possibly incomplete) description of the initial state of the
world. When an action is performed, it updates this description to take into
account the effects of this action. Reasoning about the description of the current
state of the world is then, for example, used in the control structures of the
agent program to decide which action to apply. The calculi underlying Golog
and Flux (situation calculus and fluent calculus, respectively) employ full first-
order predicate logic, which makes the computation of exact updates as well as
the use of decision procedures for reasoning about descriptions of the state of the
world impossible. To overcome this problem, recent papers [3,4] have proposed to
employ a decidable Description Logic (DL) [5] in place of full first-order predicate
logic. In particular, states of the world are then described using a DL ABox. In
[4], a method for updating DL ABoxes has been developed, and in [6] it was
shown that this notion of an update conforms with the semantics employed by
Golog and Flux.

In practice, however, there are two obstacles towards employing the update
approach from [4] in the context of agent programs. First, using the update
procedures in the form described in [4] quickly leads to unmanageably large
ABoxes. However, there is quite some room for optimizations since the updated
ABoxes contain a lot of redundant information. The second problem is that
the updated ABoxes are so-called Boolean ABoxes, which cannot be directly
handled by traditional DL reasoners. The main contributions of this paper are,

S. Ghilardi and R. Sebastiani (Eds.): FroCoS 2009, LNAI 5749, pp. 214–229, 2009.

on the one hand, that we propose and evaluate different optimization approaches for computing more concise updated ABoxes. On the other hand, we compare different approaches for reasoning with Boolean ABoxes, among them one based on the DPLL(T) approach.

The rest of this paper is organized as follows. In Section 2, we recall the basic notions for DLs and ABox updates. In Sections 3 we present optimizations that enable the construction of more concise updated ABoxes, and in Section 4 we discuss reasoning with Boolean ABoxes. In Section 5, the approaches introduced in the previous two sections are empirically evaluated. This paper is also available as a longer technical report [7].

2   Preliminaries

In DLs, knowledge is represented with the help of concepts (unary predicates) and roles (binary predicates). Complex concepts and roles are inductively defined starting with a set N_C of *concept names*, a set N_R of *role names*, and a set N_I of *individual names*. The expressiveness of a DL is determined by the set of available *constructors* to build *concepts* and *roles*. The concept and role constructors of the DLs $\mathcal{ALCO}^@$ and $\mathcal{ALCO}^+$ that form the base of our work on ABox update are shown in Table 1, where C, D are concepts, q, r are roles, and a, b are individual names. The DL that allows only for negation, conjunction, disjunction, and universal and existential restrictions is called $\mathcal{ALC}$. By adding nominals $\mathcal{O}$, we obtain $\mathcal{ALCO}$, which is extended to $\mathcal{ALCO}^@$ by the @-constructor from hybrid logic [8], and to $\mathcal{ALCO}^+$ by the Boolean constructors on roles and the nominal role [4]. We will use $\top$ ($\bot$) to denote arbitrary tautological (unsatisfiable) concepts and roles. By $\mathsf{sub}(\phi)$ we denote the set of all subconcepts and subroles of a concept or role ϕ, respectively.

Table 1. Syntax and semantics of $\mathcal{ALCO}^@$ and $\mathcal{ALCO}^+$

Name	Syntax	Semantics
negation	$\neg C$	$\Delta^\mathcal{I} \setminus C^\mathcal{I}$
conjunction	$C \sqcap D$	$C^\mathcal{I} \cap D^\mathcal{I}$
disjunction	$C \sqcup D$	$C^\mathcal{I} \cup D^\mathcal{I}$
universal restriction	$\forall r.C$	$\{x \mid \forall y.((x,y) \in r^\mathcal{I} \rightarrow y \in C^\mathcal{I})\}$
existential restriction	$\exists r.C$	$\{x \mid \exists y.((x,y) \in r^\mathcal{I} \wedge y \in C^\mathcal{I})\}$
nominal	$\{a\}$	$\{a^\mathcal{I}\}$
@ constructor	$@_a C$	$\Delta^\mathcal{I}$ if $a^\mathcal{I} \in C^\mathcal{I}$, and $\emptyset$ otherwise
role negation	$\neg r$	$(\Delta^\mathcal{I} \times \Delta^\mathcal{I}) \setminus r^\mathcal{I}$
role conjunction	$q \sqcap r$	$q^\mathcal{I} \cap r^\mathcal{I}$
role disjunction	$q \sqcup r$	$q^\mathcal{I} \cup r^\mathcal{I}$
nominal role	$\{(a,b)\}$	$\{(a^\mathcal{I}, b^\mathcal{I})\}$

The semantics of concepts and roles is given via *interpretations* $\mathcal{I} = (\Delta^{\mathcal{I}}, \cdot^{\mathcal{I}})$. The *domain* $\Delta^{\mathcal{I}}$ is a non-empty set and the *interpretation function* $\cdot^{\mathcal{I}}$ maps each concept name $A \in N_C$ to a subset $A^{\mathcal{I}}$ of $\Delta^{\mathcal{I}}$, each role name $r \in N_R$ to a binary relation $r^{\mathcal{I}}$ on $\Delta^{\mathcal{I}}$, and each individual name $a \in N_I$ to an individual $a^{\mathcal{I}} \in \Delta^{\mathcal{I}}$. The interpretation function $\cdot^{\mathcal{I}}$ is inductively extended to complex concepts and roles as shown in Table 1.

An *ABox assertion* is of the form $C(a)$, $r(a, b)$, or $\neg r(a, b)$ with r a role, C a concept and a, b individual names. A *classical ABox*, or an *ABox* for short, is a finite conjunction of ABox assertions. A *Boolean ABox* is a Boolean combination of ABox assertions. For convenience we will also sometimes represent classical and Boolean ABoxes as finite sets of assertions by breaking the toplevel conjunctions. An interpretation $\mathcal{I}$ is a *model* of an assertion $C(a)$ if $a^{\mathcal{I}} \in C^{\mathcal{I}}$. $\mathcal{I}$ is a model of an assertion $r(a, b)$ (resp. $\neg r(a, b)$) if $(a^{\mathcal{I}}, b^{\mathcal{I}}) \in r^{\mathcal{I}}$ (resp. $(a^{\mathcal{I}}, b^{\mathcal{I}}) \notin r^{\mathcal{I}}$). A model of a (Boolean) ABox is defined in the obvious way. We use $M(\mathcal{A})$ to denote the set of models of a Boolean ABox $\mathcal{A}$. A (Boolean) ABox $\mathcal{A}$ is *consistent* if $M(\mathcal{A}) \neq \emptyset$. Two (Boolean) ABoxes $\mathcal{A}$ and $\mathcal{A}'$ are *equivalent*, denoted by $\mathcal{A} \equiv \mathcal{A}'$, if $M(\mathcal{A}) = M(\mathcal{A}')$. An assertion α is *entailed* by a Boolean ABox $\mathcal{A}$, written as $\mathcal{A} \models \alpha$, if $M(\mathcal{A}) \subseteq M(\{\alpha\})$. Classical $\mathcal{ALCO}^{@}$-ABoxes can equivalently be compiled to Boolean $\mathcal{ALCO}$-ABoxes (and vice versa) — the translation in the first direction is exponential, in the other direction it is linear [4]. *Consistency checking* and *entailment* for classical ABoxes are standard inference problems and supported by all DL reasoners[1], while, to the best of our knowledge, no state of the art reasoner directly supports these inferences for Boolean ABoxes. Reasoning in $\mathcal{ALCO}^+$ is NExpTime complete [9]; for $\mathcal{ALCO}^{@}$ it is PSpace complete [10].

ABox Update. An ABox can be used to represent knowledge about the state of some world. An *update* contains information on changes that have taken place in that world.

Definition 1 (Update). *An* update $\mathcal{U} = \{\delta(\bar{t})\}$ *contains a single literal, i.e.* $\delta(\bar{t})$ *is of the form* $A(a)$, $\neg A(a)$, $r(a, b)$, *or* $\neg r(a, b)$ *with A a concept name, r a role name, and a, b individual names.*[2]

Intuitively, an update literal $\delta(\bar{t})$ says that this literal holds after the change of the world state. The formal semantics of updates given in [4] defines, for every interpretation $\mathcal{I}$, a successor interpretation $\mathcal{I}^{\mathcal{U}}$ obtained by changing this model according to the update. Given an ABox $\mathcal{A}$, all its models are considered to be possible current states of the world. The goals is then to find an updated ABox $\mathcal{A} * \mathcal{U}$ that has exactly the successor of the models of $\mathcal{A}$ as its models, i.e., $\mathcal{A} * \mathcal{U}$ must be such that $M(\mathcal{A} * \mathcal{U}) = \{\mathcal{I}^{\mathcal{U}} \mid \mathcal{I} \in M(\mathcal{A})\}$. In general, such an updated ABox need not exists.

---

[1] A list of DL reasoners is available at
http://www.cs.man.ac.uk/~sattler/reasoners.html

[2] In [4], an update is defined as a consistent set of literals, not as a single literal. Updating an ABox $\mathcal{A}$ with a set of literals can in our setting be achieved by iteratively updating $\mathcal{A}$ with the individual literals.

$$(\exists r.C)^{\mathcal{U}} = (\bigsqcap_{a \in \mathrm{Obj}(\mathcal{U})} \neg\{a\} \sqcap \exists r.C^{\mathcal{U}}) \sqcup \exists r.(\bigsqcap_{a \in \mathrm{Obj}(\mathcal{U})} \neg\{a\} \sqcap C^{\mathcal{U}})$$

$$\sqcup \bigsqcup_{a,b \in \mathrm{Obj}(\mathcal{U}),\, r(a,b) \notin \mathcal{U}} (\{a\} \sqcap \exists r.(\{b\} \sqcap C^{\mathcal{U}})) \sqcup \bigsqcup_{\neg r(a,b) \in \mathcal{U}} (\{a\} \sqcap @_b C^{\mathcal{U}})$$

$$(\forall r.C)^{\mathcal{U}} = (\bigsqcup_{a \in \mathrm{Obj}(\mathcal{U})} \{a\} \sqcup \forall r.C^{\mathcal{U}}) \sqcap \forall r.(\bigsqcup_{a \in \mathrm{Obj}(\mathcal{U})} \{a\} \sqcup C^{\mathcal{U}})$$

$$\sqcap \bigsqcap_{a,b \in \mathrm{Obj}(\mathcal{U}),\, r(a,b) \notin \mathcal{U}} (\neg\{a\} \sqcup \forall r.(\neg\{b\} \sqcup C^{\mathcal{U}})) \sqcap \bigsqcap_{\neg r(a,b) \in \mathcal{U}} (\neg\{a\} \sqcup @_b C^{\mathcal{U}})$$

Fig. 1. Constructing $C^{\mathcal{U}}$ for $\mathcal{ALCO}^{@}$

The minimal DLs that contain both the basic DL $\mathcal{ALC}$ and are closed under ABox updates are $\mathcal{ALCO}^{@}$ and Boolean $\mathcal{ALCO}$. For $\mathcal{ALCO}^{@}$, updated ABoxes are exponential in the size of the original ABox and the update. The DL $\mathcal{ALCO}^{+}$ admits updated ABoxes that are exponential in the size of the update, but polynomial in the size of the original ABox. This is the reason why, in this work, we focus on $\mathcal{ALCO}^{+}$ and $\mathcal{ALCO}^{@}$. The following two propositions, which are simplified and streamlined versions of the ones given in [4], tell us how updated ABoxes can be computed for these two DLs:

Proposition 1 (Updated ABox for $\mathcal{ALCO}^{+}$). *Let $\alpha^{\mathcal{U}}$ be the concept (role) obtained by replacing every occurrence of*

- *A by $A \sqcap \neg\{a\}$ if $\mathcal{U} = \{A(a)\}$; and by $A \sqcup \{a\}$ if $\mathcal{U} = \{\neg A(a)\}$;*
- *r by $r \sqcap \neg\{(a,b)\}$ if $\mathcal{U} = \{r(a,b)\}$; and by $r \sqcup \{(a,b)\}$ if $\mathcal{U} = \{r(a,b)\}$.*

Let the ABox $\mathcal{A}'$ be defined as

$$\mathcal{A}' = \bigwedge(\mathcal{A} \cup \mathcal{U}) \vee \bigwedge(\mathcal{A}^{\mathcal{U}} \cup \mathcal{U}), \tag{1}$$

where the ABox $\mathcal{A}^{\mathcal{U}}$ is defined as $\mathcal{A}^{\mathcal{U}} = \{\alpha^{\mathcal{U}}(\bar{t}) \mid \alpha(\bar{t}) \in \mathcal{A}\}$. Then $\mathcal{A} * \mathcal{U} \equiv \mathcal{A}'$.

Intuitively, there is one disjunct $(\mathcal{A} \cup \mathcal{U})$ for the case that the update already held before the update, and one disjunct $(\mathcal{A}^{\mathcal{U}} \cup \mathcal{U})$ for the case that its negation did.

The DL $\mathcal{ALCO}^{@}$ lacks role operators, and, hence, the construction of the updated quantifier concepts is complicated — it is depicted in Figure 1. Here $\mathrm{Obj}(\mathcal{U})$ denotes all the individuals that occur in the update $\mathcal{U}$. For concept names the construction is as in $\mathcal{ALCO}^{+}$.

Proposition 2 (Updated ABox for $\mathcal{ALCO}^{@}$). *For $\mathcal{ALCO}^{@}$ the ABox $\mathcal{A}^{\mathcal{U}}$ is defined as*

$$\mathcal{A}^{\mathcal{U}} = \{C^{\mathcal{U}}(a) \mid C(a) \in \mathcal{A}\} \cup \{r(a,b) \mid r(a,b) \in \mathcal{A} \wedge \neg r(a,b) \notin \mathcal{U}\} \cup$$
$$\{\neg r(a,b) \mid \neg r(a,b) \in \mathcal{A} \wedge r(a,b) \notin \mathcal{U}\}.$$

Let $\mathcal{A}'$ be as defined in (1). Then $\mathcal{A} * \mathcal{U} \equiv \mathcal{A}'$.

In the following, we want to illustrate the usefulness of ABox updates by a simple example. In this example, it is convenient to use also a TBox. TBoxes are a very useful feature of DLs that allow us to introduce abbreviations for complex concepts. A TBox $\mathcal{T}$ is a finite set of concept definitions of the form $A \equiv C$, where A is a concept name (called a defined concept) and C is a complex concept. This TBox is acyclic if it does not contains multiple or cyclic definitions. Acyclic TBoxes introduce abbreviations for complex concepts, but these abbreviations can be expanded out [5]. This makes it possible to work with ABox updates also in the presence of acyclic TBoxes as long as defined concept names do not occur in the update. This restriction avoids semantic problems [3] such as the ramification problem.

Example 1 (Medical Record – Acetylsalicylic Acid). The following concept definitions could be part of a bigger medical ontology for pain treatment. It states under what conditions a treatment with acetylsalicylic acid (ASA) is indicated for a patient, in terms of both anamnesis and diagnosis results, under the additional safety condition that there must not be a contraindication for "similar" patients:[3]

ASA-indicated $\equiv$ ASA-tolerant $\sqcap$ ASA-Diagnosis $\sqcap$
                          $\forall$similar_patient.ASA-tolerant
ASA-tolerant $\equiv$ ¬Pregnant $\sqcap$ ¬Atopic $\sqcap$ ¬Infant $\sqcap$ ¬Child
ASA-Diagnosis $\equiv$ (Migraine $\sqcup$ Tension_Headache $\sqcup$ Cluster_Headache $\sqcup$
                          Drug-induced_Headache $\sqcup$ Impingement_Syndrome $\sqcup$

                          $\vdots$

                          HIV_Peripheral_Neuropathy) $\sqcap$
                          ¬Bleeding_Diathesis $\sqcap$ ¬Heart_Disease $\sqcap$
                          ¬Renal_Disease $\sqcap$ ¬Peptic_Ulcer
Migraine $\equiv \ldots$

Assume that the ABox describing the medical record of the patient Mary, who has come to the hospital because she suffers from migraine, includes the ABox assertions in the first line below. In addition, assume that this ABox contains the information that the patient Jane is similar to Mary:

ASA-Diagnosis $\sqcap$ ASA-tolerant(Mary), $\forall$similar_patient.ASA-tolerant(Mary),
        similar_patient(Mary, Jane), similar_patient(Jane, Mary).

The DL reasoner can infer from this information that Mary belongs to the concept ASA-indicated, and that Jane belongs to the concept ASA-tolerant. But assume that, at her next visits, Mary tells the doctor that she is now pregnant. If her medical record is *updated* with {Pregnant(Mary)}, then we can conclude that an ASA treatment is no longer possible for Mary since the updated ABox implies ¬ASA-indicated(Mary). However, it also implies ¬ASA-indicated(Jane) since there is now a patient similar to Jane (i.e., Mary) that is not ASA tolerant. To avoid this (obviously unintended) consequence, we must additionally update the ABox with ¬similar_patient(Mary, Jane) and ¬similar_patient(Jane, Mary) (unless we have learnt that Jane is now also pregnant).

---

[3] We assume here that the (reflexive and symmetric) similarity relation between patients is computed by some separate, non-DL mechanism [11].

3   Optimizations for ABox Updates

It turns out that a naive implementation of the update algorithms based on Proposition 1 or 2 is not practical. Even for very simple update problems — where simple means e.g. small initial ABoxes containing only literals — after only a few updates we obtain ABoxes so huge and redundant that the reasoners cannot handle them anymore. In this section we propose a range of techniques for obtaining less redundant updated ABoxes.

In particular we are looking for ABoxes that are smaller than, but equivalent to, the updated ABoxes. In principle this could be done by enumerating ever bigger ABoxes, and checking for equivalence to the updated ABox. This is not likely to be practical, though. Instead we focus on logical transformations for obtaining smaller updated ABoxes. Since these transformations can be computationally expensive themselves, we also identify fragments of the transformations that we expect to be relatively cheap. The proposed techniques are each motivated by avoidable redundancy that we observed in practical examples. We present the various techniques for obtaining smaller updated ABoxes individually; they can be combined in a modular fashion.

Updating Boolean ABoxes. Updating an ABox according to Proposition 1 or 2 results in a Boolean ABox. In [4] this updated ABox is transformed to a non-Boolean ABox using the @-constructor, before it is updated again. The following observation shows that Boolean ABoxes can directly be updated again by updating the individual assertions, avoiding the transformation.

Observation 1 (Distributivity of Update). *Update distributes over the connectives conjunction and disjunction in Boolean ABoxes; i.e.*

$$(\mathcal{A}_1 \boxtimes \mathcal{A}_2) * \mathcal{U} \equiv (\mathcal{A}_1 * \mathcal{U}) \boxtimes (\mathcal{A}_2 * \mathcal{U}),$$

where $\boxtimes$ denotes either $\wedge$ or $\vee$ (negation can be pushed inside the assertions).

By updating a Boolean ABox directly we also obtain a slightly more compact representation than the original one — the update $\mathcal{U}$ is no longer contained in two disjuncts:

Observation 2 (Updating Boolean ABoxes). *For a Boolean ABox $\mathcal{A}$ (we assume negation has been pushed inside the assertions), let the updated ABox $\mathcal{A}'$ be defined as*

$$\mathcal{A}' = (\mathcal{A} \circledast \mathcal{U}) \wedge \bigwedge \mathcal{U}.$$

Here $\mathcal{A} \circledast \mathcal{U}$ is defined recursively as

$$
\begin{aligned}
\alpha \circledast \mathcal{U} &= \alpha \vee \alpha^{\mathcal{U}} \\
(\alpha \boxtimes \mathcal{B}) \circledast \mathcal{U} &= (\alpha \circledast \mathcal{U}) \boxtimes (\mathcal{B} \circledast \mathcal{U})
\end{aligned}
$$

where $\boxtimes$ denotes $\wedge$ or $\vee$, α is an assertion, and $\{\alpha\}^{\mathcal{D}}$ is defined as in Proposition 1 (or 2) for $\mathcal{ALCO}^+$ (or for $\mathcal{ALCO}^{@}$, respectively). Then $\mathcal{A} * \mathcal{U} \equiv \mathcal{A}'$.

Determinate Updates. Looking at the construction of updated ABoxes, we see that from an ABox $\mathcal{A}$ by an update we get a disjunction $\mathcal{A} \vee \mathcal{A}^{\mathcal{U}}$. This causes a rapid growth of the updated ABox. If, however, either the update or its negation is entailed by the ABox $\mathcal{A}$, then one of the disjuncts is inconsistent and can be removed:

Observation 3 (Determinate Updates). *For Boolean ABox $\mathcal{A}$, update $\mathcal{U} = \{\delta\}$, and updated ABox $\mathcal{A}'$ we have that $\mathcal{A}' \equiv \mathcal{A}$ if $\mathcal{A} \models \delta$; and $\mathcal{A}' \equiv \mathcal{U} \cup \mathcal{A}^{\mathcal{U}}$ if $\mathcal{A} \models \neg\delta$.[4] Otherwise, if neither $\mathcal{A} \models \delta$ nor $\mathcal{A} \models \neg\delta$, both $\mathcal{A}^{\emptyset}$ and $\mathcal{A}^{\mathcal{U}}$ are consistent with $\mathcal{U}$.*

Detecting this type of situation requires up to two reasoning steps: $\mathcal{A} \models \delta$ and $\mathcal{A} \models \neg\delta$, resulting in a tradeoff between time and space efficiency.

Exploiting the Unique Name Assumption. The common unique name assumption (UNA) means that no two individual names may denote the same object. The constructions from Proposition 1 and 2 do not take the UNA into account; but we can construct simpler updated ABoxes by keeping track of the individuals $\bar{s}$ and $\bar{t}$ that an assertion $\gamma(\bar{s})$ refers to when updating it with $\delta(\bar{t})$:

Example 2 (Exploiting UNA). If we update the ABox $\mathcal{A} = \{A(i)\}$ with $\mathcal{U} = \{\neg A(j)\}$, we can easily obtain $A(i)$, instead of $A \sqcup \{j\}(i)$ using the standard construction. But next consider the ABox $\mathcal{A} = \{\forall r.(\{j\} \sqcap A)(i)\}$, updated by $\mathcal{U} = \{A(k)\}$. As part of the update construction we obtain $\forall r.(\{j\} \sqcap (A \sqcap \neg\{k\}))(i)$ which can be simplified using UNA to $\forall r.(\{j\} \sqcap A)(i)$. Our implemented method for exploiting UNA cannot detect this latter case.

This UNA-based construction is not costly at all. It cannot identify all cases where the UNA admits a more concise updated ABox, though.

Omitting Subsuming Disjuncts and Entailed Assertions. Intuitively, in a disjunction we can omit the "stronger" of two disjuncts: Let the disjunction $(\mathcal{A} \vee \mathcal{A}^{\mathcal{U}})$ be part of an updated ABox. If $\mathcal{A} \models \mathcal{A}^{\mathcal{U}}$ (or $\mathcal{A}^{\mathcal{U}} \models \mathcal{A}$) then $(\mathcal{A} \vee \mathcal{A}^{\mathcal{U}}) \equiv \mathcal{A}^{\mathcal{U}}$ (or $(\mathcal{A} \vee \mathcal{A}^{\mathcal{U}}) \equiv \mathcal{A}$). Detecting subsuming disjuncts in general requires reasoning. But by a simple, syntactic check we can detect beforehand some cases where one of the disjuncts $\mathcal{A}^{\mathcal{U}}$ and $\mathcal{A}$ will subsume the other. Then the computation of subsuming disjuncts can be avoided. We say that an occurrence of a concept or role name δ in an assertion is *positive*, if it is in the scope of an even number of negation signs, and *negative* otherwise; δ *occurs only positively (negatively)* in an assertion if every occurrence of δ is positive (negative).

Observation 4 (Detecting Subsuming Disjuncts). *If for an ABox $\mathcal{A}$, updated with update $\mathcal{U} = \{(\neg)\delta(\bar{t})\}$, we have that:*

(1) if the update is positive (i.e. $\delta(\bar{t})$) then
- *if δ occurs only positively in $\mathcal{A}$ then $\mathcal{A}^{\mathcal{U}} \models \mathcal{A}$; and*
- *if δ occurs only negatively in $\mathcal{A}$ then $\mathcal{A} \models \mathcal{A}^{\mathcal{U}}$.*

---

[4] The latter of these two observations is from [4].

(2) if the update is negative (i.e. $\neg\delta(\bar{t})$) then
  - *if δ occurs only positively in $\mathcal{A}$ then $\mathcal{A} \models \mathcal{A}^{\mathcal{U}}$; and*
  - *if δ occurs only negatively in $\mathcal{A}$ then $\mathcal{A}^{\mathcal{U}} \models \mathcal{A}$.*

Conversely, we can also avoid updating entailed assertions: Let $\mathcal{A}$ be an ABox and $\mathcal{U}$ an update. If $\mathcal{U} \models \alpha$ or $\mathcal{A} \setminus \{\alpha\} \models \alpha$ for some assertion $\alpha \in \mathcal{A}$, then $\mathcal{A} * \mathcal{U} \equiv (\mathcal{A} \setminus \{\alpha\}) * \mathcal{U}$. Removing all entailed assertions might be too expensive in practice; one might try doing this periodically.

Propositional ABoxes. Sometimes we do not need the full power of DL reasoning, but propositional reasoning is enough: We call a Boolean ABox *propositional* if it does not contain quantifiers. For propositional ABoxes we could in principle use progression algorithms for propositional logic [12] and efficient SAT-technology, since an updated propositional ABox is propositional, too.

Independent Assertions. Next we address the question under which conditions an assertion in an ABox is not affected by an update. We say that assertion α in an ABox $\mathcal{A}$ is independent from update $\mathcal{U} = \{\delta\}$ iff $\mathcal{A} * \mathcal{U} \equiv \alpha \wedge (\mathcal{B} * \mathcal{U})$ where $\mathcal{B} = \mathcal{A} \setminus \{\alpha\}$. The more independent assertions we can identify, the more compact our ABox representation becomes.

Detecting this in all cases requires reasoning steps and thus is costly. It is easy, though, to syntactically detect some of the independent assertions:

Observation 5 (Independent Assertion). *For an ABox $\mathcal{A}$ in negation normal form and update $\mathcal{U} = \{(\neg)\delta(\bar{t}_1)\}$, the assertion $\alpha(\bar{t}_2) \in \mathcal{A}$ is independent if $\delta \notin$ sub(α). It is also independent if $\mathcal{A} \models \bar{t}_1 \neq \bar{t}_2$, δ occurs in α only outside the scope of a quantifier, and for all subconcepts $@_i C$ of α the assertion $C(i)$ is independent of $\mathcal{U}$.*

4 Reasoning with Boolean ABoxes

As we have seen in the previous sections, updated ABoxes are Boolean $\mathcal{ALCO}^{@}$- or $\mathcal{ALCO}^{+}$-ABoxes, so that an intelligent agent built on top of ABox update needs Boolean ABox reasoning. Reasoning with $\mathcal{ALC}$-LTL formulas [13] requires Boolean ABox reasoning, too. However, Boolean ABox reasoning is not directly supported by DL reasoners. In this section, we present four different reasoning methods that can handle Boolean ABoxes:

  - one where a DL reasoner operates on single disjuncts of an ABox in DNF;
  - one which uses Otter, a first-order theorem prover;
  - one which uses a consistency preserving reduction from a Boolean ABox to a non-Boolean ABox; and
  - one which is based on propositional satisfiability testing modulo theories — the DPLL(T) approach.

Replacing every assertion in a Boolean ABox $\mathcal{A}$ with a propositional letter results in a propositional formula $F_{\mathcal{A}}$. The ABox $\mathcal{A}$ is a *Boolean ABox in CNF (resp. DNF)* if $F_{\mathcal{A}}$ is in CNF (resp. DNF). The first approach works on Boolean ABoxes in DNF while the other approaches are based on CNF.

We do not use the equivalence-preserving, exponential transformation from [4] for compiling the @ constructor away. Instead we simulate the @-operator by a universal role [14]; this consistency-preserving transformation is linear.

We use Pellet as a DL reasoner because it supports nominals, query-answering and pinpointing [15].

The DNF Approach. A Boolean ABox in DNF is consistent iff it contains a consistent disjunct. We can employ a DL reasoner to decide the consistency of each disjunct. We refer to this approach as Pellet-DNF. A drawback of this approach is that we will see that the less redundant updated ABoxes are in CNF, and thus require a costly translation to DNF (using de Morgan's laws).

The Theorem Prover Approach. The DL $\mathcal{ALCO}^+$ admits smaller updated ABoxes than $\mathcal{ALCO}^@$ [4]; however, its role operators are not supported by current mature DL reasoners. By translating $\mathcal{ALCO}^+$ to first order logic [16] we can use theorem provers that can cope with Boolean role constructors. We chose to use Otter [17] because it supports query-answering via answer literals [18]; this is useful e.g. for parametric actions, which are to be instantiated to concrete actions. After a few experiments we chose to configure Otter to use hyperresolution combined with Knuth-Bendix-rewriting, plus the set-of-support strategy.

The Reduction Approach. We can linearly compile Boolean $\mathcal{ALCO}^@$-ABoxes to classical $\mathcal{ALCO}^@$-ABoxes [4]. Then, simulating the @-operator by a universal role, we can directly use a standard DL reasoner; this approach is henceforth called Pellet-UR.

The DPLL(T) Approach. Most modern SAT-solvers [19,20] are variants of the Davis-Putnam-Logemann-Loveland (DPLL) procedure [21,22]. Such a SAT-solver exhaustively applies transition rules[5] to generate and extend a partial interpretation and thus decides satisfiability of a propositional formula in CNF. One of the strengths of the DPLL procedures is that they can efficiently prune the search space by building and learning backjump clauses [24].

The DPLL(T) approach combines a DPLL procedure with a theory solver that can handle conjunctions of literals in the theory to solve the satisfiability problem modulo theories (SMT) [23]. In DPLL(T) a DPLL procedure works on the propositional formula obtained by replacing the theory atoms with propositional letters. Whenever the DPLL procedure extends the current partial interpretation by a new element the theory solver is invoked to check consistency of the conjunction of the theory atoms corresponding to the partial, propositional interpretation. If the theory solver reports an inconsistency, the DPLL procedure will backjump and thus the search space is pruned.

The consistency problem of Boolean ABoxes can be viewed as an instance of SMT where ABox assertions are the theory atoms and a DL reasoner serves as theory solver.

---

[5] See [23] for the details.

The non-standard DL inference of pinpointing [25,26] is highly relevant to this approach. Explaining why an ABox is inconsistent is an instance of the pinpointing problem, where an explanation is a minimal sub-conjunction of the input ABox, containing only those assertions that are responsible for the inconsistency. Based on these explanations in the DPLL(T) approach we can build better backjump clauses [23].

We implemented an algorithm based on the DPLL(T) approach with the strategy of MINISAT [19]. Pellet was chosen as the theory solver because it supports pinpointing. Henceforth we call this approach Pellet-DPLL.

Propositional Reasoning. For the case where we can identify propositional ABoxes we have developed and implemented a simple, specialized method. Reasoning there is reduced to efficient list operations. This reasoner is used to supplement the other reasoning approaches (if possible).

5   Experimental Results

In this section, we evaluate the efficiency of the different update and reasoning mechanisms. The relevant measures are the time needed for computing the updated ABox together with its size, and the efficiency of reasoning with it.

An update algorithm based on Proposition 1 or 2 generates Boolean ABoxes in DNF, while an algorithm based on Proposition 2 outputs ABoxes in CNF. Of course, every Boolean ABox can equivalently be represented in CNF or in DNF; however, this transformation (using De Morgan's laws) is rather expensive. The performance of reasoning with updated ABoxes strongly depends on the choice of underlying representation. We use several types of testing data:

- we use a set of randomly generated Boolean ABoxes in CNF;
- we use a set of random ABoxes, Updates, and Queries; and
- we use the Wumpus world [27].

We distinguish two main types of update algorithms that we implemented:

- In one we compute updated ABoxes in DNF; we call this the DNF approach.
- Or we compute updated ABoxes in CNF; we call this the CNF approach.

Both approaches are further parametrized by using different reasoners, and a different combination of optimization techniques. We have implemented the different ABox update algorithms in ECLiPSe-Prolog.

The reasoning methods have already been described in Section 4. We call a reasoning method *hybrid* if it resorts to our propositional reasoner whenever possible; for example, we then speak of hybrid Pellet-UR.

5.1   Representation: DNF or CNF?

We have used both the Wumpus world and the random update examples to compare DNF and CNF based update algorithms (with and without optimizations). CNF representation consistently proved to be superior: The DNF approach quickly drowns in redundant information. This is because to compute an updated ABox in DNF is to include both the update and all the non-affected information in both disjuncts. Detecting subsuming disjuncts and determinate updates alleviates this problem, but does not eliminate it. By avoiding this redundancy we immediately obtain an updated ABox in CNF. On DNF-based updated ABoxes Pellet-DNF performs best — the other methods suffer from the expensive conversion to CNF. In the following we only consider the CNF-based representation of updated ABoxes.

5.2 Consistency Checking for Boolean ABoxes in CNF

We implemented a random generator of Boolean $\mathcal{ALC}$-ABoxes, which randomly generates a propositional formula in CNF and then assigns a randomly generated assertion to each propositional letter. Several parameters are used to control the shape of the generated Boolean ABoxes (the numbers in parentheses indicate the upper bound on the parameters we used): the number n_1 of literals in a clause (53), the number n_2 of propositional letters (36), the number n_3 of clauses (83), the number d of nested roles in a concept assertion (23), the number ncs of the constructors in a concept assertion (106), the numbers nc, nr, and ni of concept names, role names, and individual names in an assertion (12 each), and the probability pr of generating a role assertion (0.2).

In Figure 2, we plot the runtimes of Pellet-DPLL and Pellet-UR on these testing data against the number of symbols in the Boolean ABox. The points plotted as + indicate the runtime of Pellet-DPLL while those plotted as × indicate the runtime of Pellet-UR. We depict the performance on consistent and inconsistent Boolean ABoxes separately — the testing data contained more consistent than inconsistent Boolean ABoxes.

We can see that the runtime of Pellet-UR linearly increases with the size of the input (the bar from the lower left to the upper right corner). On inconsistent ABoxes Pellet-DPLL also exhibits a linear increase in runtime, while on consistent ABoxes the runtime is less predictable. Pellet-DPLL performs better on all of the inconsistent Boolean ABoxes. On most of the consistent ABoxes, the Pellet-UR approach does better. This is due to the fact that in Pellet-DPLL

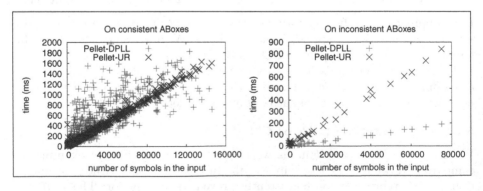

Fig. 2. Experimental Results for Pellet-DPLL and Pellet-UR

the frequent invocations of the theory solver Pellet are more likely to pay off if inconsistency of the current, partial model can be detected often: We then can build a back-jump clause that helps to prune the search space. The runtimes of Pellet-UR are about the same on both consistent and inconsistent input data.

For Otter the conversion from ABoxes in CNF to full first order CNF proved to be a big obstacle, as did the conversion to DNF for Pellet-DNF.

5.3   Random Updates

We have extensively experimented with a set of randomly generated ABoxes and updates. Initial ABoxes were between two and thirty assertions in size.We were mostly interested in runtime and space consumption for iterated updates. We could make a number of interesting observations:

- The cheap UNA-based concept update construction always paid.
- The reasoning needed to identify determinate updates pays in the long run.
- Syntactically detecting subsuming disjuncts worked, too. Doing so using a reasoner proved to be too expensive.
- Identifying all entailed assertions to shrink the ABoxes proved to be too expensive, too.
- Resorting to our dedicated propositional reasoner whenever possible resulted in significantly better performance.
- We can keep updated ABoxes much smaller at a low cost by syntactically identifying independent assertions.

Updating an ABox according to [4] is a purely syntactic procedure. But if we iteratively update ABoxes, then in the long run we get both a lower space and time consumption by calling a reasoner to identify determinate updates. Using our propositional reasoner whenever possible for this resulted in better performance. If identifying determinate updates required DL reasoning then Pellet-UR performed slightly better than Pellet-DPLL. This is due to the fact that less updates were determinate than not, and thus inconsistency was not detected often. On a subset of the random examples where there were more determinate updates Pellet-DPLL performed better than Pellet-UR. The runtimes for Otter widely varied: converting CNF-ABoxes to full first order CNF proved the bottleneck. Pellet-DNF was not competitive because of the expensive conversion to DNF.

We could also identify characteristics of initial ABoxes that allow to predict performance: If the initial ABox does not contain nested quantifiers then performance is acceptable; e.g. we can iteratively apply 300 singleton updates to a fifteen assertion ABox in 90 seconds, without a significant increase in size. If the initial ABox contains nested quantifiers space consumption quickly grows out of bounds. This is because we then cannot cheaply identify independent assertions and use the UNA-based concept update construction. For nested quantifiers using $\mathcal{ALCO}^+$ instead of $\mathcal{ALCO}^@$ helps to reduce space consumption; but this still does not result in satisfactory overall performance.

5.4   The Wumpus World

The Wumpus World [27] is a well-known challenge problem in the reasoning about action community. It consists of a grid-like world: cells may contain pits, one cell contains gold, and one the fearsome Wumpus. The agent dies if she enters a cell containing a pit or the Wumpus. But she carries one arrow so that she can shoot the Wumpus from an adjacent cell. If the agent is next to a cell containing a pit (Wumpus), she can detect that one of the surrounding cells contains a pit (the Wumpus), but doesn't know which one. She knows the contents of the already visited cells. Getting the gold without getting killed is the agent's goal.

At each step, the agent performs sensing to learn whether one of the adjacent cells contains a pit or the Wumpus. Since the sensing results are disjunctive, we cannot treat them via ABox updates. But the properties sensed are static (i.e., cannot change once we know them): We can simply adjoin the sensing results to the ABox serving as the agent's current world model. The effects of the agent's (non-sensing) actions (like moving to another cell) are modelled as ABox update.

The Wumpus World can be modelled in different ways. In the simplest model, the initial ABox contains the connections between the cells, the agent's location, and the facts that the agent carries an arrow, and that the Wumpus is alive (Model PL1). For this, Boolean combinations of concept/role literals are enough. In Model PL2, we include the fact that the Wumpus is at exactly one location by enumerating all possible cases in a big disjunction. We turn PL1 into a DL problem by including the information $\exists at.\top(wumpus)$ (Model DL1). Model DL2 is obtained from PL2 by adding this same assertion, which here is redundant. Table 2 shows the runtimes, where n/a stands for unavailable expressivity and * for non-termination in 15 minutes. For the propositional models we also used the action programming language Flux [2].

Pellet-DNF, and to a lesser extent also Otter, again had difficulties with the necessary input conversion. Pellet-UR proved to be the best DL reasoner in this setting. This is due to the fact that this domain requires query-answering: The agent e.g. needs to know for which values of x and y we have that at(agent, x) $\wedge$ connected(x, y). Pellet-DPLL is the only reasoner that lacks direct support for query-answering. Thus, for query $C(x)$, we check for every individual name $i \in \mathsf{N_I}$ whether $C(i)$ holds — this results in bad performance for Pellet-DPLL.

The propositional reasoner performs quite well on the propositional models. Including more information wrt. the Wumpus' location results in worse performance. We used Model DL2 to see if it pays to identify all entailed assertions: after omitting the entailed $\exists at.\top(wumpus)$ the model is propositional again.

Table 2. Runtimes for the Wumpus World

Model	Prop	hybrid Otter	hybrid Pellet-UR	Flux
8x8 PL1	0.26 s	0.26 s	0.26 s	14.9 s
8x8 PL2	16.9 s	16.9 s	16.9 s	n/a
4x4 DL1	n/a	36.4 s	5.5 s	n/a
4x4 DL2	n/a	*	23.93 s	n/a

In practice this proved too costly. The other observations from Section 5.3 also hold in this domain. Removing assertions entailed by the update sometimes did help, though: Once the Wumpus is found, the assertion $\exists$at.$\top$(wumpus) is entailed by the respective update and we can then resort to efficient propositional reasoning.

6   Summary and Future Work

In this work, we have investigated implementation techniques for ABox update, and for reasoning with (updated) Boolean ABoxes. We have introduced and evaluated several optimizations of the ABox update algorithms in [4]. The lessons learnt were: Using CNF-representation of updated ABoxes is strongly recommended. The (incomplete) syntactic techniques for exploiting the unique name assumption, and detecting subsuming disjuncts and independent assertions have also resulted in an improved performance. The benefit of identifying determinate updates made up for the associated reasoning costs. Other techniques requiring DL reasoning in general proved to be too expensive; but removing some entailed assertions helped in the Wumpus world.

Regarding the investigated reasoning methods for Boolean ABoxes, we have come to the following conclusions. Pellet-DNF is the best reasoner for Boolean ABoxes in DNF. For consistency checking of ABoxes in CNF, Pellet-DPLL and Pellet-UR worked best. Pellet-DPLL did better for detecting an actual inconsistency, while it performed worse than Pellet-UR on most of the consistent Boolean ABoxes. On the randomly generated update examples, Pellet-UR also performed slightly better than Pellet-DPLL because inconsistency was not detected often. On a subset where the updates were mostly determinate, Pellet-DPLL outperformed Pellet-UR. If query-answering is among the reasoning tasks, then Pellet-UR is to be preferred over Pellet-DPLL because of Pellet's direct support for this inference.

It would be interesting to develop heuristics for finding suitable individual names as well as other optimizations for query-answering in the DPLL(T) approach. The performance of the DPLL(T) approach also depends on the performance of the SAT solver and the pinpointing service. Thus Pellet-DPLL can benefit from more efficient implementation of these tasks as well.

The tests on the Wumpus world confirmed that resorting to our dedicated propositional reasoner whenever possible is useful. In the Wumpus world, removing entailed assertions helped a lot. In contrast, for the randomly generated update examples, finding entailed assertions did not pay off.

Using Otter as a theorem prover might be considered somewhat unfair (to the theorem proving approach), since it is no longer actively maintained and optimized. The conversion to full first order CNF proved to be the biggest obstacle for Otter. We chose to use Otter because it supports query-answering, which is not supported by most current provers [28], but vital in some domains. If this is to change,[6] we can try to resort to state-of-the art theorem provers for reasoning

---

[6] cf. www.cs.miami.edu/~tptp/TPTP/Proposals/AnswerExtraction.html

in $\mathcal{ALCO}^+$. This may allow us to really exploit the fact that $\mathcal{ALCO}^+$ admits smaller updated ABoxes than $\mathcal{ALCO}^@$. Alternatively, one could also try to use a more dedicated reasoning system for $\mathcal{ALCO}^+$ [29].

Acknowledgments. Many thanks to Albert Oliveras for his help regarding the construction of a backjump clause in the DPLL(T) approach.

References

1. Levesque, H., Reiter, R., Lespérance, Y., Lin, F., Scherl, R.: GOLOG: A logic programming language for dynamic domains. Journal of Logic Programming (1997)
2. Thielscher, M.: FLUX: A Logic Programming Method for Reasoning Agents. Theory and Practice of Logic Programming (2005)
3. Baader, F., Lutz, C., Milicic, M., Sattler, U., Wolter, F.: Integrating Description Logics and Action Formalisms: First Results. In: Proceedings of the Twentieth National Conference on Artificial Intelligence (AAAI 2005). AAAI Press, Menlo Park (2005)
4. Liu, H., Lutz, C., Milicic, M., Wolter, F.: Updating Description Logic ABoxes. In: Proceedings of the Tenth International Conference on Principles of Knowledge Representation and Reasoning (KR 2006). AAAI Press, Menlo Park (2006)
5. Baader, F., Calvanese, D., Mcguinness, D.L., Nardi, D., Patel-Schneider, P.F. (eds.): The Description Logic Handbook: Theory, Implementation, and Applications. Cambridge University Press, Cambridge (2003)
6. Drescher, C., Thielscher, M.: Integrating Action Calculi and Description Logics. In: Hertzberg, J., Beetz, M., Englert, R. (eds.) KI 2007. LNCS (LNAI), vol. 4667, pp. 68–83. Springer, Heidelberg (2007)
7. Drescher, C., Liu, H., et al.: Putting abox updates into action. LTCS-Report 09-01, Dresden University of Technology, Germany (2009), http://lat.inf.tu-dresden.de/research/reports.html
8. Areces, C., de Rijke, M.: From Description Logics to Hybrid Logics, and Back. In: Advances in Modal Logic (2001)
9. Tobies, S.: Complexity Results and Practical Algorithms for Logics in Knowledge Representation. PhD thesis, RWTH-Aachen, Germany (2001)
10. Areces, C., Blackburn, P., Marx, M.: A road-map on complexity for hybrid logics. In: Flum, J., Rodríguez-Artalejo, M. (eds.) CSL 1999. LNCS, vol. 1683, pp. 307–321. Springer, Heidelberg (1999)
11. Zezula, P., Batko, M., Dohnal, V., Amato, G.: Similarity Search: The Metric Space Approach. Springer, Heidelberg (2006)
12. Amir, E., Russell, S.J.: Logical Filtering. In: IJCAI 2003, Proceedings of the Eighteenth International Joint Conference on Artificial Intelligence. Morgan Kaufmann, San Francisco (2003)
13. Baader, F., Ghilardi, S., Lutz, C.: LTL over Description Logic Axioms. In: Proceedings of the 11th International Conference on Principles of Knowledge Representation and Reasoning, KR 2008 (2008)
14. Bong, Y.: Description Logic ABox Updates Revisited. Master thesis, TU Dresden, Germany (2007)
15. Sirin, E., Parsia, B., Grau, B.C., Kalyanpur, A., Katz, Y.: Pellet: A practical OWL-DL reasoner. Journal of Web Semantics (2007)

16. Borgida, A.: On the Relative Expressiveness of Description Logics and Predicate Logics. Artificial Intelligence (1996)
17. McCune, W.: OTTER 3.3 Manual. Computing Research Repository (2003)
18. Green, C.: Theorem Proving by Resolution as a Basis for Question-answering Systems. Machine Intelligence (1969)
19. Een, N., Sörensson, N.: An Extensible SAT-solver. In: Giunchiglia, E., Tacchella, A. (eds.) SAT 2003. LNCS, vol. 2919, pp. 502–518. Springer, Heidelberg (2004)
20. de Moura, L., Bjørner, N.: Z3: An efficient SMT Solver. In: Ramakrishnan, C.R., Rehof, J. (eds.) TACAS 2008. LNCS, vol. 4963, pp. 337–340. Springer, Heidelberg (2008)
21. Davis, M., Putnam, H.: A Computing Procedure for Quantification Theory. Journal of the ACM (1960)
22. Davis, M., Logemann, G., Loveland, D.: A Machine Program for Theorem-proving. Communications of the ACM (1962)
23. Nieuwenhuis, R., Oliveras, A., Rodríguez-Carbonell, E., Rubio, A.: Challenges in Satisfiability Modulo Theories. In: Baader, F. (ed.) RTA 2007. LNCS, vol. 4533, pp. 2–18. Springer, Heidelberg (2007)
24. Zhang, L., Madigan, C.F., Moskewicz, M.H., Malik, S.: Efficient Conflict Driven Learning in a Boolean Satisfiability Solver. In: International Conference on Computer-Aided Design, ICCAD 2001 (2001)
25. Schlobach, S.: Non-Standard Reasoning Services for the Debugging of Description Logic Terminologies. In: Proceedings of the Eighteenth International Joint Conference on Artificial Intelligence (IJCAI 2003). Morgan Kaufmann, San Francisco (2003)
26. Baader, F., Peñaloza, R.: Automata-Based Axiom Pinpointing. In: Armando, A., Baumgartner, P., Dowek, G. (eds.) IJCAR 2008. LNCS (LNAI), vol. 5195, pp. 226–241. Springer, Heidelberg (2008)
27. Russell, S.J., Norvig, P.: Artificial Intelligence: A Modern Approach. Prentice Hall, Englewood Cliffs (2003)
28. Waldinger, R.J.: Whatever happened to deductive question answering? In: Dershowitz, N., Voronkov, A. (eds.) LPAR 2007. LNCS (LNAI), vol. 4790, pp. 15–16. Springer, Heidelberg (2007)
29. Schmidt, R.A., Tishkovsky, D.: Using tableau to decide expressive description logics with role negation. In: Aberer, K., Choi, K.-S., Noy, N., Allemang, D., Lee, K.-I., Nixon, L.J.B., Golbeck, J., Mika, P., Maynard, D., Mizoguchi, R., Schreiber, G., Cudré-Mauroux, P. (eds.) ASWC 2007 and ISWC 2007. LNCS, vol. 4825, pp. 438–451. Springer, Heidelberg (2007)

A Declarative Agent Programming Language Based on Action Theories

Conrad Drescher, Stephan Schiffel, and Michael Thielscher

Department of Computer Science
Dresden University of Technology
{conrad.drescher,stephan.schiffel,mit}@inf.tu-dresden.de

Abstract. We discuss a new concept of agent programs that combines logic programming with reasoning about actions. These *agent logic programs* are characterized by a clear separation between the specification of the agent's strategic behavior and the underlying theory about the agent's actions and their effects. This makes it a generic, declarative agent programming language, which can be combined with an action representation formalism of one's choice. We present a declarative semantics for agent logic programs along with (two versions of) a sound and complete operational semantics, which combines the standard inference mechanisms for (constraint) logic programs with reasoning about actions.

1 Introduction

Action theories, like the classical Situation Calculus [1], provide the foundations for the design of artificial, intelligent agents capable of reasoning about their own actions. Research in this area has led to mature action theories, including the modern Situation Calculus [2] or the Event Calculus [3], which allow to endow agents with knowledge of complex dynamic environments. Despite the existence of elaborate action theories today, surprisingly few attempts have been made to integrate these into actual programming languages for intelligent agents. Existing agent programming languages such as [4,5,6] use nothing but a very basic concept of reasoning about actions, where the belief base of an agent is updated in a STRIPS-like [7] fashion upon executing an action. Moreover, the agent programmer always has to provide this belief update as part of the behavioral strategy, rather than having the agent use a separate, behavior-independent action theory to reason about its actions and their effects.

Two exceptions to this notable gap between practical agent programming languages on the one hand and elaborate action theories on the other hand, are GOLOG [2] and FLUX [8], which have been built on top of two action theories, namely, the Situation Calculus and the Fluent Calculus. Both languages are procedural in nature: the semantics of FLUX is defined on the basis of Prolog computation trees, while GOLOG (= Algol in Logic) combines standard elements from imperative programming with reasoning about actions. Especially for Artificial Intelligence applications, however, declarative programming languages have

S. Ghilardi and R. Sebastiani (Eds.): FroCoS 2009, LNAI 5749, pp. 230–245, 2009.
© Springer-Verlag Berlin Heidelberg 2009

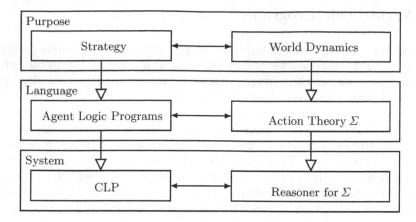

Fig. 1. Strategic Behavior in Dynamic Worlds with Agent Logic Programs

proved a useful alternative to the procedural programming paradigm (see, e.g., [9]). An open research issue, therefore, is the development of a declarative agent programming language based on action theories.

In this paper, we investigate *agent logic programs*, which are obtained by combining the logic programming paradigm with action theories. These programs are characterized by a clear separation between the specification of the agent's strategic behavior (given as a logic program) and the underlying theory about the agent's actions and their effects (see Figure 1). This makes it a fully generic agent programming language, which can be combined with a variety of action formalisms, including the Situation-, Event-, and Fluent Calculus. Specifically,

- we give a generic, declarative semantics for agent logic programs;
- we provide a sound operational semantics which combines the standard inference mechanisms for logic programs with reasoning about actions; and
- we provide completeness results for the operational semantics by investigating increasingly expressive classes of agent logic programs and by incorporating concepts derived from constraint logic programming.

Agent programs can be used in two distinct ways: If executed online they directly control the behavior of an intelligent agent. By executing them offline the agent can infer plans that achieve strategic goals. We will see that agent logic programs go beyond established agent programming languages by being capable of inferring conditional plans for open-world planning problems.

The rest of this paper is organized as follows. In the next section, we give the basic formal definitions of an agent logic program and illustrate these by means of an example that will be used throughout the paper. We then show how the usual declarative reading of a logic program can be combined with an action theory to provide a declarative semantics for agent logic programs. Thereafter we present two operational semantics and prove their soundness and completeness. In the ensuing section we discuss the use of agent logic programs for planning. We conclude with a brief discussion of the results and future work.

2   Agent Logic Programs

The purpose of agent logic programs is to provide high-level control programs for agents using a combination of declarative programming with reasoning about actions. The syntax of these programs shall be kept very simple: standard (definite) logic programs are augmented with just two special predicates, one — written $do(\alpha)$ — to denote the execution of an action by the agent, and one — written $?(\varphi)$ — to verify properties against (the agent's model of) the state of its environment. This model, and how it is affected by actions, is defined in a separate action theory. This allows for a clear separation between the agent's strategic behavior (given by the agent logic program itself) and the underlying theory about the agent's actions and their effects. Prior to giving the formal definition, let us illustrate the idea by an example agent logic program.

Example 1.   Consider an agent whose task is to find gold in a maze. For the sake of simplicity, the states of the environment shall be described by a single *fluent* (i.e., state property): $At(u, x)$ to denote that $u \in \{Agent, Gold\}$ is at location x. The agent can perform the action $Go(y)$ of going to location y, which is possible if y is adjacent to, and accessible from, the current location of the agent. The fluent and action are used as basic elements in the following agent logic program. It describes a simple search strategy based on two parameters: a given list of locations (choice points) that the agent may visit, and an ordered collection of backtracking points.[1]

```
explore(Choicepoints,Backtrack) :-          % finished, if
    ?(at(agent,X)), ?(at(gold,X)).          % gold is found

explore(Choicepoints,Backtrack) :-
    ?(at(agent,X)),
    select(Y,Choicepoints,NewChoicepoints), % choose available direction
    do(go(Y)),                              % go in this direction
    explore(NewChoicepoints,[X|Backtrack]). % store it for backtracking

explore(Choicepoints,[X|Backtrack]) :-      % go back one step
    do(go(X)),
    explore(Choicepoints,Backtrack).

select(X,[X|Xs],Xs).
select(X,[Y|Xs],[Y|Ys]) :- select(X,Xs,Ys).
```

Suppose we are given a list of choice points C, then the query :- explore(C,[]) lets the agent systematically search for gold from its current location: the first clause describes the base case where the agent is successful; the second clause lets the agent select a new location from the list of choice points and go to this location (the declarative semantics and proof theory for $do(\alpha)$ will require that

---

[1] Below, we follow the Prolog convention according to which variables are indicated by a leading uppercase letter.

the action is possible at the time of execution); and the third clause sends the agent back using the latest backtracking point.

The example illustrates two distinct features of agent logic programs. First, an agent strategy is defined by a logic program that may use arbitrary function and predicate symbols in addition to the signature of the underlying action theory. Second, and in contrast to usual BDI-style programming languages like, e.g. AgentSpeak [6], the update of the agent's belief according to the effects of its actions is not part of the strategy. The formal definition of agent logic programs is as follows.

Definition 1. Consider an action theory signature Σ, including the pre-defined sorts ACTION and FLUENT, and a logic program signature Π.

- *Terms* are from $\Sigma \cup \Pi$.
- If p is an n-ary relation symbol from Π and $t_1, ..., t_n$ are terms, then $p(t_1, ..., t_n)$ is a *program atom*.
- $do(\alpha)$ is a *program atom* if α is an ACTION term in Σ.
- $?(\varphi)$ is a *program atom* if φ is a *state property* in Σ, that is, a formula (represented as a term) based on the FLUENTs in Σ.
- Clauses, programs, and queries are then defined as usual for definite logic programs, with the restriction that the two special atoms cannot occur in the head of a clause.   ∎

It is easy to verify that our example program complies with this definition given the aforementioned action theory signature and the usual list notation.

3   Semantics: Program + Action Theory

The semantics of an agent logic program is given in two steps. First, the program needs to be "temporalized," by making explicit the state change that is implicit in the use of the two special predicates, $do(\alpha)$ and $?(\varphi)$. Second, the resulting program is combined with an action theory as the basis for evaluating these two special predicates. The overall declarative semantics is the classical logical semantics of the expanded program together with the action theory.

Time is incorporated into a program through macro-expansion: two arguments of sort TIME[2] are added to every regular program atom $p(\bar{x})$, and then $p(\bar{x}, s_1, s_2)$ is understood as restricting the truth of the atom to the temporal interval between (and including) s_1 and s_2. The two special atoms receive special treatment: atom $?(\varphi)$ is re-written to $Holds(\varphi, s)$, with the intended meaning that φ is true at s; and $do(\alpha)$ is mapped onto $Poss(\alpha, s_1, s_2)$, meaning that action α can be executed at s_1 and that its execution ends in s_2. The formal definition is as follows.

---

[2] Which specific concept of time is being used depends on how the sort TIME is defined in the underlying action theory, which may be branching (as, e.g., in the Situation Calculus) or linear (as, e.g., in the Event Calculus).

Definition 2. For a clause $H \text{:-} B_1, \ldots, B_n$ $(n \geq 0)$, let $s_1, \ldots, s_{n+1}$ be variables of sort TIME.

- For $i = 1, \ldots, n$, if B_i is of the form
  - $p(t_1, \ldots, t_m)$, expand to $P(t_1, \ldots, t_m, s_i, s_{i+1})$.
  - $do(\alpha)$, expand to $Poss(\alpha, s_i, s_{i+1})$.
  - $?(\varphi)$, expand to $Holds(\varphi, s_i)$ and let $s_{i+1} = s_i$.[3]
- The head atom $H = p(t_1, \ldots, t_m)$ is expanded to $P(t_1, \ldots, t_m, s_1, s_{n+1})$.
- The resulting clauses are understood as universally quantified implications.

Queries are expanded exactly like clause bodies, except that

- a special constant S_0 — denoting the earliest time-point in the underlying action theory — takes the place of s_1;
- the resulting conjunction is existentially quantified. ■

Example 1 (continued). The example program of the preceding section is understood as the following axioms:

$$(\forall) Explore(c, b, s, s) \subset Holds(At(Agent, x), s) \land Holds(At(Gold, x), s)$$
$$(\forall) Explore(c, b, s_1, s_4) \subset Holds(At(Agent, x), s_1) \land Select(y, c, c', s_1, s_2) \land$$
$$Poss(Go(y), s_2, s_3) \land Explore(c', [x|b], s_3, s_4)$$
$$(\forall) Explore(c, [x|b], s_1, s_3) \subset Poss(Go(x), s_1, s_2) \land Explore(c, b, s_2, s_3)$$
$$(\forall) Select(x, [x|x'], x', s, s) \subset true$$
$$(\forall) Select(x, [y|x'], [y|y'], s_1, s_2) \subset Select(x, x', y', s_1, s_2)$$

The resulting theory constitutes a purely logical axiomatization of the agent's strategy, which provides the basis for logical entailment. For instance, macro-expanding the query :- explore(C,[]) from the above example results in the temporalized formula $(\exists s) Explore(C, [], S_0, s)$. If this formula follows from the axioms above, then that means that the strategy can be successfully executed, starting at S_0, for the given list of choice points C. Whether this is actually the case of course depends on the additional action theory that is needed to evaluate the special atoms *Holds* and *Poss* in a macro-expanded program. ■

Macro-expansion provides the first part of the declarative semantics of an agent logic program; the second part is given by an action theory in form of a logical axiomatization of actions and their effects. The overall declarative semantics of agent logic programs is given by the axiomatization consisting of the action theory and the expanded program.

In principle, agent logic programs can be combined with any action formalism that features the predicates $Poss(a, s_1, s_2)$ and $Holds(\phi, s)$. However, in the formal definitions we make some assumptions that existing action formalisms either already satisfy or can be made to satisfy: We stipulate that action theories are based on many-sorted first order logic with equality and the four sorts TIME,

---

[3] Setting $s_{i+1} = s_i$ is a convenient way of saying that the expansion of $?(\varphi)$ "consumes" only one TIME variable, in which case less than $n + 1$ different variables for a clause with n body atoms are needed.

FLUENT, OBJECT, and ACTION.[4] Fluents are reified, and the standard predicates $Holds(f, s)$ and $Poss(a, s_1, s_2)$ are included. For actions, objects, and fluents unique name axioms have to be included. We abstract from a particular time structure: an axiomatization of the natural or the positive real numbers (providing the linear time structure of e.g. the Event Calculus), or of situations (the branching time structure of Situation and Fluent Calculus) can be included.

Definition 3. [Action Theory Formula Types] We stipulate that the following formula types are used by action theories:

- State formulas express what is true at particular times: A *state formula* $\Phi[\bar{s}]$ *in* $\bar{s}$ is a first-order formula with free variables $\bar{s}$ where
  - for each occurrence of $Holds(f, s)$ we have $s \in \bar{s}$;
  - predicate *Poss* does not occur.
- A *state property* ϕ is an expression built from the standard logical connectives and terms $F(\bar{x})$ of sort FLUENT. With a slight abuse of notation, by $Holds(\phi, s)$ we denote the state formula obtained from state property ϕ by replacing every occurrence of a fluent f by $Holds(f, s)$.[5] State properties are used by agent logic programs in ?(Phi) atoms.
- An *action precondition axiom* is of the form $(\forall)Poss(A(\bar{x}), s_1, s_2) \equiv \pi_A[s_1]$, where $\pi_A[s_1]$ is a state formula in s_1 with free variables among $s_1, s_2, \bar{x}$.
- *Effect axioms* have to be of the form $Poss(A(\bar{x}), s_1, s_2) \supset \phi[\bar{x}, s_1, s_2]$. This assumption is implicit in the macro-expansion of do(A) to $Poss(a, s_1, s_2)$.

For illustration, the following is a background axiomatization for our example scenario. Essentially it is a basic Fluent Calculus theory in the sense of [10], with a simple syntactic modification to meet the requirements just given.

Example 1   (continued)
- Initial state axiom

$$Holds(At(Agent, 1), S_0) \wedge Holds(At(Gold, 4), S_0)$$

- Precondition axiom

$$Poss(Go(y), s_1, s_2) \equiv (\exists x)(Holds(At(Agent, x), s_1) \wedge (y = x + 1 \vee y = x - 1))$$
$$\wedge s_2 = Do(Go(y), s_1)$$

- Effect axiom

$$Poss(Go(y), s_1, s_2) \supset$$
$$(\exists x)(Holds(At(Agent, x), s_1) \wedge$$
$$[(\forall f)Holds(f, s_2) \equiv (Holds(f, s_1) \vee f = At(Agent, y)) \wedge f \neq At(Agent, x)]).$$

---

[4] By convention variable symbols s, f, x, and a are used for terms of sort TIME, FLUENT, OBJECT, and ACTION, respectively.

[5] In an expanded program Π we always treat $Holds(\phi, s)$ as atomic.

Given this (admittedly very simple, for the sake of illustration) specification of the background action theory, the axiomatization of the agent's strategy from above entails, for example, $(\exists s)\, Explore([2, 3, 4, 5], [\,], S_0, s)$, because the background theory allows to conclude that

$$Holds(At(Agent, 4), S) \wedge Holds(At(Gold, 4), S),$$

where S denotes the situation term $Do(Go(4), Do(Go(3), Do(Go(2), S_0)))$. It follows that $Explore([5], [3, 2, 1], S, S)$ according to the first clause of our example ALP. Consider, now, the situation $S' = Do(Go(3), Do(Go(2), S_0))$, then action theory and strategy together imply

$$Holds(At(Agent, 3), S') \wedge Select(4, [4, 5], [5], S', S') \wedge Poss(Go(4), S', S)$$

By using this in turn, along with $Explore([5], [3, 2, 1], S, S)$ from above, we obtain $Explore([4, 5], [2, 1], S', S)$, according to the second program clause. Continuing this line of reasoning, it can be shown that

$$Explore([3, 4, 5], [1], Do(Go(2), S_0), S)$$
$$\text{and hence, } Explore([2, 3, 4, 5], [\,], S_0, S)$$

This proves the claim that $(\exists s)\, Explore([2, 3, 4, 5], [\,], S_0, s)$. On the other hand e.g. the query $(\exists s)\, Explore([2, 4], [\,], S_0, s)$ is *not* entailed under the given background theory: Without location 3 among the choice points, the strategy does not allow the agent to reach the only location that is known to house gold. ∎

The example illustrates how an agent logic program is interpreted logically by first adding an explicit notion of time and then combining the result with a suitable action theory. As indicated above, most action formalisms can be used directly or can be extended to serve as a background theory. Languages like the Planning Language PDDL [11] or the Game Description Language GDL [12] require the addition of a time structure before they can be employed.

4   Generic Proof Calculus

In this section, we provide an operational counterpart to the declarative semantics given in the preceding section, beginning with the simple integration of reasoning about actions with standard SLD-resolution.

4.1   Elementary Case: LP($\mathcal{D}$)

The basic proof calculus for agent logic programs is obtained as an adaptation of SLD-resolution: for action domain $\mathcal{D}$, expanded agent logic program Π and query $(\exists)\Gamma$, we prove that $\mathcal{D} \cup \Pi \models (\exists)\Gamma$ by proving unsatisfiability of $\mathcal{D} \cup \Pi \cup \{(\forall)\neg\Gamma\}$. As a fully generic proof calculus, for the two special atoms in queries and clause bodies the inference steps $\mathcal{D} \models Holds(\varphi, s)$ and $\mathcal{D} \models Poss(\alpha, s_1, s_2)$ are treated as atomic, which allows to integrate any reasoner for $\mathcal{D}$.

Definition 4. The proof calculus is given by two inference rules on *states*, which are of the form $\langle \neg\Gamma, \theta \rangle$:

- *Normal Goals* (with G_i different from *Holds* and *Poss*):

$$\frac{\langle (\neg G_1 \vee \ldots \vee \neg G_{i-1} \vee \neg G_i \vee \neg G_{i+1} \vee \ldots \vee \neg G_n), \; \theta_1 \rangle}{\langle (\neg G_1 \vee \ldots \vee \neg G_{i-1} \vee \bigvee_{j=1..m} \neg B_j \vee \neg G_{i+1} \vee \ldots \vee \neg G_n)\theta_2, \; \theta_1\theta_2 \rangle}$$

where $H \subset B_1 \wedge \ldots \wedge B_m$ is a fresh variant of a clause in Π such that G_i and H unify with most general unifier θ_2.

- *Special Goals* ($G_i = Holds(\varphi, s)$ or $Poss(\alpha, s_1, s_2)$):

$$\frac{\langle (\neg G_1 \vee \ldots \vee \neg G_{i-1} \vee \neg G_i \vee \neg G_{i+1} \vee \ldots \vee \neg G_n), \; \theta_1 \rangle}{\langle (\neg G_1 \vee \neg G_{i-1} \vee \neg G_{i+1} \vee \neg G_n)\theta_2, \; \theta_1\theta_2 \rangle}$$

such that $\mathcal{D} \vDash (\forall)G_i\theta_2$ with substitution θ_2 on the variables in G_i. ∎

For illustration, the reader may verify that the agent logic program in Example 1, together with the background theory given in the preceding section, admits a derivation starting from $\langle \neg Explore([2, 3, 4, 5], [], S_0, s), \varepsilon \rangle$ and ending with $\langle \Box, \theta \rangle$ [6] such that the replacement $s/Do(Go(4), Do(Go(3), Do(Go(2), S_0)))$ is part of the resulting substitution θ.

Under the assumption that the underlying reasoning about actions is sound, soundness of the basic proof calculus follows easily from the corresponding result in standard logic programming (see, e.g., [9]).

Proposition 1 (Soundness). *Let Π be an expanded agent logic program, $\mathcal{D}$ a background domain axiomatization, and $(\exists)\Gamma$ an expanded query. If there exists a derivation starting from $\langle (\forall)\neg\Gamma, \varepsilon \rangle$ and ending in $\langle \Box, \theta \rangle$, then $\Pi \cup \mathcal{D} \vDash (\forall)\Gamma\theta$.*

While being sound, the use of standard SLD-resolution in combination with reasoning about actions is incomplete in general. This can be illustrated with a simple example, which highlights the influence of the background action theory on the existence of computed answers to queries for an agent logic program.

Example 2. Suppose we are given the following disjunctive knowledge of the initial state:

$$Holds(At(Gold, 4), S_0) \vee Holds(At(Gold, 5), S_0) \tag{1}$$

Consider the query `:- ?(at(gold,X))`, corresponding to the question whether $(\exists x) Holds(At(Gold, x), S_0)$ is entailed. This is obviously the case given (1), but there is no *answer substitution* θ such that $Holds(At(Gold, x), S_0)\theta$ is implied. The same phenomenon can be observed in the presence of state knowledge that is merely "de dicto," as in $(\exists y) Holds(At(Gold, y), S_0)$ in place of (1).

In case of classical logic programming, the computational completeness of SLD-resolution hinges on the fact that whenever a program Π entails $(\exists)Q$ then there also exists a substitution θ such that $\Pi \vDash (\forall)Q\theta$. For this reason, we introduce the following restricted class of background action theories.

---

[6] The symbols $\Box$ and ε stand for the empty query and the empty substitution.

Definition 5. An action domain axiomatization $\mathcal{D}$ is *query-complete* if and only if $\mathcal{D} \models (\exists)Q$ implies that there exists a substitution θ such that $\mathcal{D} \models (\forall)Q\theta$, for any Q of the form $Holds(\varphi, s)$ or $Poss(\alpha, s_1, s_2)$.

Under the assumption that the underlying reasoning about actions is complete *and* that the background action theory is query-complete, the basic proof calculus for agent logic programs can be shown to be complete.

Definition 6. A *computation rule* is a function selecting an atom from a non-empty negated query to continue the derivation with.

Proposition 2 (Completeness). *Let Π be an expanded agent logic program, $\mathcal{D}$ a background domain axiomatization, and $(\exists)\Gamma$ an expanded query. If $\Pi \cup \mathcal{D} \models (\forall)\Gamma\theta_1$ for some θ_1, then there exists a successful derivation via any computation rule starting with $\langle \neg(\exists)\Gamma, \varepsilon \rangle$ and ending in $\langle \Box, \theta_2 \rangle$. Furthermore, there is a substitution θ_3 such that $\Gamma\theta_1 = \Gamma\theta_2\theta_3$.*

Proof. The claim can be proved by a straightforward adaptation of Stärk's proof of the completeness of plain SLD-resolution [13]: his concept of an implication tree is extended by allowing instances of the two special atoms, *Holds* and *Poss*, to occur as leaves just in case they are entailed by the background theory. The base case in the completeness proofs then follows for these two atoms from the assumption of a query-complete theory.

It is worth pointing out that the restriction to query-completeness is not the same as the following, more common notion: A first-order theory is called *complete* iff for every sentence ϕ either ϕ or $\neg\phi$ is in the theory. Referring to Example 2, say, if the initial state axiom does not contain any information at all concerning the location of gold, then this theory *is* query-complete (while it is not complete in the above sense). Thus the completeness of the basic proof calculus does extend to action domains with incomplete information.

On the other hand, query-complete action domains cannot express disjunctive or mere existential information. Because this is exactly one of the strong-points of general action calculi, we next present a proof theory for agent logic programs that is suitable for the general case.

4.2   General Case: CLP($\mathcal{D}$)

We address the problem of incompleteness of the basic proof calculus by moving to the richer framework of constraint logic programming [14]. Denoted by CLP(X), constraint logic programming constitutes a family of languages where, in addition to the syntax of standard logic programs, special *constraints* are used and evaluated against the background constraint theory X. We instantiate this general framework to CLP($\mathcal{D}$)—constraint logic programming over action domains $\mathcal{D}$—where the two special atoms of agent logic programs, $Poss(\alpha, s_1, s_2)$ and $Holds(\varphi, s)$, are taken as constraints.

As illustrated by Example 2, it is the lack of a most general answer substitution that causes the incompleteness of the basic proof calculus in case of domains that are not query-complete. This motivates the use of the following, more expressive notion of answer substitutions (see, e.g., [15]).

Definition 7. A *disjunctive substitution* is a set $\Theta = \{\theta_1, \ldots, \theta_n\}$ of substitutions. The *application* of a disjunctive substitution Θ to a clause c results in the disjunction $\bigvee_{i=1,\ldots,n} c\theta_i$. The *composition* $\Theta_1\Theta_2$ of two disjunctive substitutions is defined as $\{\theta_i\theta_j \mid \theta_i \in \Theta_1 \text{ and } \theta_j \in \Theta_2\}$. A substitution $\Theta_1 = \{\theta_1, \ldots, \theta_k\}$ is *more general* than a substitution $\Theta_2 = \{\theta_{k+1}, \ldots, \theta_l\}$ if for every $\theta_i \in \Theta_1$ there exist $\theta_j \in \Theta_2$ and θ such that $\theta_i\theta = \theta_j$.

Every disjunctive substitution Θ determines a formula in disjunctive normal form consisting of equality atoms. With a little abuse of notation we will denote this formula by Θ, too; e.g. we treat $\Theta = \{\{x/3\}, \{x/4\}\}$ and $x = 3 \vee x = 4$ interchangeably. These equational formulas, together with *Holds* and *Poss* atoms, constitute the elements of the *constraint store*, which replaces the simple substitutions in the derivation states used in $\mathrm{LP}(\mathcal{D})$.

In $\mathrm{CLP}(\mathsf{X})$, the derivation rule that handles constraint atoms G is based on the logical equivalence $G \wedge \mathcal{S} \equiv \mathcal{S}'$, where $\mathcal{S}$ and $\mathcal{S}'$ denote the constraint store prior to and after the rule application, respectively. In our setting $\mathrm{CLP}(\mathcal{D})$, where G is either *Holds* or *Poss*, the resulting constraint store $\mathcal{S}'$ is obtained based on the following equivalences:

- if there is a substitution Θ such that $\mathcal{D} \vDash (\forall) \bigvee_{\theta \in \Theta} G\theta$ then we can exploit that
$$\mathcal{D} \vDash (G \wedge \mathcal{S}) \equiv ((G \wedge \Theta) \wedge \mathcal{S}); \text{ and} \tag{2}$$

- if $\mathcal{D}$ does not entail that the constraint is unsatisfiable (i.e. $\mathcal{D} \nvDash \neg\mathcal{S} \wedge G$) we can use the following trivial equivalence
$$\mathcal{D} \vDash G \wedge \mathcal{S} \equiv G \wedge \mathcal{S}. \tag{3}$$

Prior to defining the CLP-based proof calculus for agent logic programs, let us discuss how disjunctive substitutions are applied. Most $\mathrm{CLP}(\mathsf{X})$-languages come with an additional *Solve* transition, which maps derivation states into simpler, equivalent ones. A typical example is the application of substitutions, which, for instance, allows to transform the state $\langle \neg P(x), x = 1 \rangle$ into the simpler $\langle \neg P(1), \textit{true} \rangle$.

The application of a disjunctive substitution $\Theta = \{\theta_1, \ldots, \theta_k\}$ is a bit more involved: In the definition of our $\mathrm{CLP}(\mathcal{D})$ calculus, if we have obtained a disjunctive substitution $\Theta = \{\theta_1, \ldots, \theta_n\}$ for special atom G, we employ reasoning by cases: we split the current substate of the derivation into a disjunction of substates, one for each θ_i. We extend the substates by an additional argument $\mathcal{C}$ (the case store), for recording the case $G \wedge \theta_i$. In a substate $< \text{Negative Clause}, \mathcal{S}, \mathcal{C} >$ special atoms are evaluated against the action theory augmented by the respective case — $\mathcal{D} \cup \{\mathcal{C}\}$. It is crucial to observe that the disjunction of the action theories $\mathcal{D}_i$ augmented by the respective cases $\mathcal{C}_i$ is equivalent to the original $\mathcal{D}$.

A *derivation state* in $\mathrm{CLP}(\mathcal{D})$ is a disjunction, denoted by $\dot\vee$, of sub-states $\langle \neg G_1 \vee \ldots \vee \neg G_n, \mathcal{S}, \mathcal{C} \rangle$. The derivation rules of the proof calculus are depicted

Substitution Rule:

$$\frac{< (\neg G_1 \vee \ldots \vee \neg G_{j-1} \vee \neg G_j \vee \neg G_{j+1} \vee \ldots \vee \neg G_n), \mathcal{S}, \mathcal{C} >}{< \dot{\bigvee}_i < (\neg G_1 \vee \ldots \vee \neg G_{j-1} \vee \neg G_{j+1} \vee \ldots \vee \neg G_n), \mathcal{S} \wedge G_j \wedge \theta_i, \mathcal{C} \wedge G_j \wedge \theta_i >}$$

where $\mathcal{D} \cup \{\mathcal{C}\} \models (\forall) \bigvee_{\theta_i \in \Theta} G_j \theta_i$ with most general disjunctive substitution Θ

Constraint Rule:

$$\frac{< (\neg G_1 \vee \ldots \vee \neg G_{j-1} \vee \neg G_j \vee \neg G_{j+1} \vee \ldots \vee \neg G_n), \mathcal{S}, \mathcal{C} >}{< (\neg G_1 \vee \ldots \vee \neg G_{j-1} \vee \neg G_{j+1} \vee \ldots \vee \neg G_n), \mathcal{S} \wedge G_j, \mathcal{C} >}$$

if $\mathcal{D} \cup \{\mathcal{C}\} \not\models \neg(\exists) \mathcal{S} \wedge G_j$.

Fig. 2. Inference rules for $\mathrm{CLP}(\mathcal{D})$ (the given rules operate on single sub-states)

in Figure 2. Due to lack of space, we omit the straightforward rule for regular program atoms. A *derivation* of a query Γ starts with $\langle \neg\Gamma, true, true \rangle$ and, if successful, ends in a state $\langle \Box, \mathcal{S}_1, \mathcal{C}_1 \rangle \dot{\vee} \ldots \dot{\vee} \langle \Box, \mathcal{S}_m, \mathcal{C}_m \rangle$, ($m \geq 1$). The formula $\mathcal{S}_1 \vee \ldots \vee \mathcal{S}_m$ is the *computed answer*. A *failed* derivation ends with a sub-state to which none of the rules can be applied.

Example 2 (continued). Recall that this action domain contains the initial state axiom $Holds(At(Gold, 4), S_0) \vee Holds(At(Gold, 5), S_0)$. Further, consider the simple program clause

$$\text{p(Y) :- ?(at(gold,Y)).} \tag{4}$$

along with the query :- ?(at(gold,X)), p(X). Obviously there exists x such that $Holds(At(Gold, x), S_0)$ and $P(x, S_0, S_0)$. This is a successful derivation:[7]

$$\langle \neg Holds(At(Gold, x), S_0) \vee \neg P(x, S_0, s), true \rangle$$

$$\mapsto$$

$$\langle \neg P(4, S_0, s), Holds(At(Gold, x), S_0) \wedge x = 4 \rangle$$
$$\dot{\vee} \langle \neg P(5, S_0, s), Holds(At(Gold, x), S_0) \wedge x = 5 \rangle$$

$$\mapsto$$

$$\langle \neg Holds(At(Gold, 4), S_0), Holds(At(Gold, 4), S_0) \wedge \theta_1 \rangle$$
$$\dot{\vee} \langle \neg Holds(At(Gold, 5), S_0), Holds(At(Gold, 5), S_0) \wedge \theta_2 \rangle$$

$$\mapsto$$

$$\langle \Box, Holds(At(Gold, 4), S_0) \wedge \theta_1 \rangle$$
$$\dot{\vee} \langle \Box, Holds(At(Gold, 5), S_0) \wedge \theta_2 \rangle$$

where θ_1 is $x = 4 \wedge s = S_0$, and θ_2 is $x = 5 \wedge s = S_0$. This example illustrates the necessity of reasoning by cases: in both sub-states, the last step would not be possible without adding the case store to the domain axioms prior to verifying the respective *Holds* instance. ∎

---

[7] We only show one of the constraint and case store (always identical in this example).

Piggybacking on the general proofs for $CLP(X)$, and based on the equivalences in (2) and (3), the $CLP(\mathcal{D})$ approach is sound and complete in the following sense, provided that the underlying reasoning about actions is sound and complete. In the following, let Π be an expanded agent logic program, $\mathcal{D}$ a background domain axiomatization, and Γ an expanded query.

Theorem 1 (Soundness of $CLP(\mathcal{D})$). *If Γ has a successful derivation with computed answer $\bigvee_{i=1..k} S_i$, then $\Pi \cup \mathcal{D} \models (\forall) \bigvee_{i=1..k} S_i \supset \Gamma$.*

Theorem 2 (Completeness of $CLP(\mathcal{D})$). *If $\Pi \cup \mathcal{D} \models (\forall)S \supset \Gamma$ and S is satisfiable wrt. $\mathcal{D}$, then there are successful derivations for Γ with computed answers $S_1, \ldots, S_n$ such that $\mathcal{D} \models (\forall)(S \supset (S_1 \vee \ldots \vee S_n))$.*

5   Planning with ALPs

Agent logic programs can be used to solve two complementary tasks: They can be used to control an intelligent agent online; or the agent may use them to infer a plan that helps it achieve its goals. For online agent control it is a sound strategy to non-deterministically pick one path in the proof tree of agent logic programs, restricted to non-disjunctive substitutions. Essentially, this is the same as what is being done in GOLOG and FLUX. In this section we consider how agent logic programs can be utilized by agents for offline deliberation on planning problems.

5.1   Inferring Plans

It is surprisingly easy to formulate a generic agent logic program for arbitrary planning problems:

Example 3. [Generic ALP for Planning] The following is the generic ALP for planning problems, where `Phi` shall denote the respective goal description:

```
plan :- ?(Phi).
plan :- do(A), plan.
```

Put in words, we execute arbitrary actions until the goal ϕ is reached.

The soundness and completeness results from the previous section assure us that the query `?-plan.` can be proved if and only if it is entailed by this ALP together with the action theory. Somewhat surprisingly, there remains the question on how the inferred plan — if it exists — can be communicated to the programmer. The usual notion of a computed answer in logic programming does not provide any information concerning the plan inferred by deriving this query. In situation-based action theories $\mathcal{D}$ we could simply print out the final situations. If the natural or the real numbers serve as time structures this does not work, though.

For solving planning problems the sequence of the evaluated $Poss(a, s_1, s_2)$ atoms provides the programmer with the desired information (or, in the case of disjunctive plans, the corresponding tree does). The construction of such a planning tree is easily included into our proof calculi: In the case of $CLP(\mathcal{D})$ the constraint stores already contain this information, and in the case of query complete domains the calculus is easily extended to construct this sequence.

5.2 Planning Completeness

The soundness and completeness results from the previous section assure us that a query can be proved if and only if it is entailed by the ALP together with the action theory. In this section we consider the following question: Assume that the action theory entails that some goal is achievable. Does the ALP from example 3 allow to infer a plan achieving this goal? It turns out that, unfortunately, in general the query ?-plan. need not have a successful derivation, even if the action theory entails that the goal is achievable, i.e. $\mathcal{D} \models (\exists s) Holds(\phi, s)$. We next identify a number of natural conditions on action theories that will preclude this kind of situation.

Definition 8. [Properties of Action Theories] An action theory with precondition axioms $\mathcal{D}_{Poss}$ and time structure axiomatization $\mathcal{D}_{Time}$ is

- *progressing* if $\mathcal{D}_{Poss} \cup \mathcal{D}_{Time} \models Poss(a, s_1, s_2) \supset s_1 < s_2$.
- *sequential* if it is progressing and no two actions overlap; that is

$$\mathcal{D}_{Poss} \cup \mathcal{D}_{Time} \models Poss(a, s_1, s_2) \wedge Poss(a', s_1', s_2') \supset$$
$$(s_2 < s_2' \supset s_2 \leq s_1') \wedge (s_2 = s_2' \supset a = a' \wedge s_1 = s_1').$$

- *temporally determined* if all precondition axioms are of the form

$$Poss(A(\bar{x}), s_1, s_2) \equiv \pi_A[s_1] \wedge \bigvee_i \varphi_i, \tag{5}$$

where $\pi_A[s_1]$ does not mention s_2, and each φ_i is an equality atom equating the time variable s_2 to a function with arguments among s_1 and $\bar{x}$.
- *anytime* if it is sequential and action applicability is not tied to a specific time-point; that is $\mathcal{D}_{Poss} \cup \mathcal{D}_{Time}$ entail

$$(\forall)(\exists s_2)(Poss(a, s_1, s_2) \wedge [Holds(f, s_1) \equiv Holds(f, s_1')]) \supset (\exists s_2') Poss(a, s_1', s_2').$$

Let us illustrate the last two of these notions by the following example:

Example 4. [Properties of Action Theories] A precondition axiom is not temporally determined if it is e.g. of the form $(\forall) Poss(A, s_1, s_2) \equiv s_2 > s_1$. Next, consider the precondition axioms $Poss(A, s_1, s_2) \equiv s_1 = 0 \wedge s_2 = 1$ and $Poss(B, s_1, s_2) \equiv s_1 = 2 \wedge s_2 = 3$, violating the conditions for a anytime action theories. The query ?- do(a), do(b) is macro-expanded to $(\exists) Poss(A, 0, s_1') \wedge Poss(B, s_1', s_2')$, which does not follow under the given precondition axioms.

Define an action theory to be admissible if it satisfies all of the above properties. Now, if an admissible action theory entails that there exists a time where a goal holds, by an agent logic program a plan achieving that goal can be inferred:

Theorem 3 (Planning Completeness of ALPs). *Let $\mathcal{D}$ be an admissible action theory. Further, let Π be the generic planning ALP from example 3, and let the query Γ be ?- plan.. Assume that $\mathcal{D} \models (\exists s) \mathrm{Holds}(\phi, s)$ for planning* goal ϕ, and $\Pi \cup \mathcal{D} \vDash (\forall)\mathcal{S} \supset \Gamma$ and $\mathcal{S}$ is satisfiable wrt. $\mathcal{D}$. We then know that there exist successful derivations of the query $Plan(S_0, s)$ in $CLP(\mathcal{D})$ with computed answers $\mathcal{S}_1, \ldots, \mathcal{S}_n$ such that $\mathcal{D} \vDash (\forall)(\mathcal{S} \supset (\mathcal{S}_1 \vee \ldots \vee \mathcal{S}_n))$. The plans computed by these derivations can be combined into a plan achieving the goal ϕ. Note that this plan can be disjunctive, and conditional on the constraint store. For $LP(\mathcal{D})$ and query-complete action theories $\mathcal{D}$ a similar result holds.

Admissible action theories are not overly restrictive: while some of the expressivity of the Event Calculus and concurrent planning languages like full PDDL is lost, most standard agent and planning languages, as well as all of the basic Fluent and Situation Calculus are preserved.[8]

The correspondence between goal achievability and the existence of disjunctive plans is a well-known property of the Situation Calculus [16,17]. Interestingly, GOLOG, which is based on Situation Calculus action theories, cannot be used to infer disjunctive plans. Agent logic programs, on the other hand, instantiated with any admissible action theory can handle this task.

Example 5. [Disjunctive Plan] Consider a further simplified version of the action theory from example 1, where the agent can move instantaneously to any location: The precondition of moving is axiomatized as

$$Poss(Go(y), s, t) \equiv (\exists x)(Holds(At(Agent, x), s) \wedge t = Do(Go(y), s),$$

and the effect axiom is as before. Let the initial state be given by

$$Holds(At(Agent, 1), S_0) \wedge (Holds(At(Gold, 4), S_0) \vee Holds(At(Gold, 5), S_0)).$$

On top of this action theory, consider the following agent logic program:

```
goToGold :- ?(at(gold,X)), do(go(X)).
```

It is not hard to see that there exists a successful derivation of the query ?-goToGold., from which the plan $Poss(Go(4), S_0) \vee Poss(Go(5), S_0)$ can be extracted, informing us that the agent should go to either location 4 or 5 to achieve its goal.

6 Conclusion

We have developed a declarative programming paradigm which can be used to specify agent strategies on top of underlying background action theories. A declarative semantics in pure classical logic has been given and complemented with a sound and complete operational semantics for two different settings: one, where we admit only query-complete background theories and which, as a consequence, harmonizes with basic logic programming; and one that is fully general, appealing to constraint logic programming. Agent logic programs are generic

---

[8] Discussing in detail which (parts of) existing action formalisms are admissible is beyond the scope of this paper.

in that they can be used in combination with different (sufficiently expressive) action calculi. This paves the way for implementations of agent logic programs which combine SLD-resolution (or CLP-implementation techniques) with existing reasoners for actions. Specifically, we are currently developing an implementation of agent logic programs on the basis of recent results on how to build a decidable action calculus on top of Description Logics[18,19,20].

It is worth pointing out that the declarative semantics we have used in this paper is not the only meaningful interpretation of an agent logic program. In fact, macro-expansion via Definition 2 implicitly requires an agent to execute actions in a strictly sequential order. For future work, we intend to investigate alternative interpretations, which support overlapping actions and temporal gaps between two actions. This will allow us to broaden the class of action theories on which agent logic programs are planning complete.

With regard to related work, GOLOG [2] and FLUX [8] are two major exponents of agent programming languages based on general action calculi. In contrast to agent logic programs, GOLOG is a procedural language, whose elements derive from the classical programming language Algol. GOLOG has been implemented in Prolog on the basis of a Situation Calculus-style axiomatization of its programming elements. We believe that this can form the basis of a generic agent logic program for GOLOG, which would then provide a nice reconciliation of the procedural and the declarative programming paradigms. FLUX programs, on the other hand, are full Prolog programs together with a sound implementation of a fragment of the Fluent Calculus. As a consequence, they only admit an operational semantics based on the notion of Prolog computation trees [8]. However, FLUX restricted to pure definite logic programs is an example of a sound implementation of a fragment of agent logic programs.

A prominent feature of agent logic programs that is absent from existing agent programming languages are the disjunctive substitutions in $CLP(\mathcal{D})$, which can be viewed as conditional plans. Agent logic programs also stand apart by their clear separation between world dynamics and employed strategy.

References

1. McCarthy, J., Hayes, P.: Some philosophical problems from the standpoint of artificial intelligence. Machine Intelligence 4, 463–502 (1969)
2. Reiter, R.: Knowledge in Action. MIT Press, Cambridge (2001)
3. Mueller, E.: Commonsense Reasoning. Morgan Kaufmann, San Francisco (2006)
4. Dastani, M., de Boer, F., Dignum, F., Meyer, J.J.: Programming agent deliberation: An approach illustrated using the 3APL language. In: Proceedings of the International Conference on Autonomous Agents and Multiagent Systems (AAMAS), pp. 97–104 (2003)
5. Morley, D., Meyers, K.: The SPARK agent framework. In: Proceedings of the International Conference on Autonomous Agents and Multiagent Systems (AAMAS), pp. 714–721 (2004)
6. Bordini, R., Hübner, J., Wooldridge, M.: Programming Multi-Agent Systems in AgentSpeak using Jason. Wiley, Chichester (2007)

7. Fikes, R.E., Nilsson, N.J.: STRIPS: A new approach to the application of theorem proving to problem solving. Artificial Intelligence 2, 189–208 (1971)
8. Thielscher, M.: FLUX: A logic programming method for reasoning agents. Theory and Practice of Logic Programming 5, 533–565 (2005)
9. Lloyd, J.: Foundations of Logic Programming. Springer, Heidelberg (1987)
10. Thielscher, M.: Reasoning Robots: The Art and Science of Programming Robotic Agents. Applied Logic Series, vol. 33. Kluwer, Dordrecht (2005)
11. McDermott, D.: The 1998 AI planning systems competition. AI Magazine 21, 35–55 (2000)
12. Genesereth, M., Love, N., Pell, B.: General game playing: Overview of the AAAI competition. AI Magazine 26, 62–72 (2005)
13. Stärk, R.: A direct proof for the completeness of SLD-resolution. In: Third Workshop on Computer Science Logic (1990)
14. Jaffar, J., Lassez, J.L.: Constraint logic programming. In: Proceedings of the 14th ACM Principles of Programming Languages Conference, Munich (1987)
15. Green, C.: Theorem proving by resolution as a basis for question-answering systems. Machine Intelligence 4, 183–205 (1969)
16. Reiter, R.: The frame problem in the situation calculus: A simple solution (sometimes) and a completeness result for goal regression. In: Lifschitz, V. (ed.) Artificial Intelligence and Mathematical Theory of Computation, pp. 359–380. Academic Press, London (1991)
17. Savelli, F.: Existential assertions and quantum levels on the tree of the situation calculus. Artificial Intelligence 170, 643–652 (2006)
18. Liu, H., Lutz, C., Milicic, M., Wolter, F.: Updating description logic ABoxes. In: Proceedings of the Tenth International Conference on Principles of Knowledge Representation and Reasoning (KR 2006), Lake District of the UK (2006)
19. Baader, F., Lutz, C., Milicic, M., Sattler, U., Wolter, F.: Integrating description logics and action formalisms: First results. In: Proceedings of the AAAI National Conference on Artificial Intelligence, Pittsburgh, pp. 572–577 (2005)
20. Drescher, C., Liu, H., Baader, F., Guhlemann, S., Petersohn, U., Steinke, P., Thielscher, M.: Putting abox updates into action. In: Ghilardi, S., Sebastiani, R. (eds.) FroCoS 2009. LNCS (LNAI), vol. 5749, pp. 214–229. Springer, Heidelberg (2009)

Termination Modulo Combinations of Equational Theories

Francisco Durán[1], Salvador Lucas[2], and José Meseguer[3]

[1] LCC, Universidad de Málaga, Spain
[2] DSIC, Universidad Politécnica de Valencia, Spain
[3] CS Dept. University of Illinois at Urbana-Champaign, IL, USA

Abstract. Rewriting with rules R modulo axioms E is a widely used technique in both rule-based programming languages and in automated deduction. Termination methods for rewriting systems modulo specific axioms E (e.g., associativity-commutativity) are known. However, much less seems to be known about termination methods that can be modular in the set E of axioms. In fact, current termination tools and proof methods cannot be applied to commonly occurring combinations of axioms that fall outside their scope. This work proposes a modular termination proof method based on semantics- and termination-preserving transformations that can reduce the proof of termination of rules R modulo E to an equivalent proof of termination of the transformed rules modulo a typically much simpler set B of axioms. Our method is based on the notion of variants of a term recently proposed by Comon and Delaune. We illustrate its practical usefulness by considering the very common case in which E is an arbitrary combination of associativity, commutativity, left- and right-identity axioms for various function symbols.

1 Introduction

Many declarative languages and formal reasoning systems support rewriting modulo combinations of equational theories, where different function symbols may satisfy different axioms. Although well-known modularity results exist for matching and unification modulo combinations of equational theories, e.g. [1,23,27], the modularity aspects of termination modulo combinations of such theories do not seem to have been systematically studied. Indeed, at present there is a practical impossibility of proving many rewrite systems terminating, because current tools do not support termination proofs modulo combinations of many frequently used theories. Many of the current difficulties can be illustrated by means of the following TRS, which we use as a running example.

Example 1. Consider the (order-sorted) TRS specified in Maude with self-explanatory syntax in Figure 1. It has four sorts: Bool, Nat, List, and Set, with Nat included in both List and Set as a subsort. That is, a natural number n is simultaneously regarded as a list of length 1 and as a singleton set. The terms of each sort are, respectively, Booleans, natural numbers (in Peano notation), lists of natural numbers, and finite sets of natural numbers. The rewrite

S. Ghilardi and R. Sebastiani (Eds.): FroCoS 2009, LNAI 5749, pp. 246–262, 2009.

```
fmod LIST&SET is
  sorts Bool Nat List Set .
  subsorts Nat < List Set .
  ops true false : -> Bool .
  ops _and_ _or_ : Bool Bool -> Bool [assoc comm] .
  op 0 : -> Nat .
  op s_ : Nat -> Nat .
  op _;_ : List List -> List [assoc] .
  op null : -> Set .
  op __ : Set Set -> Set [assoc comm id: null] .
  op _in_ : Nat Set -> Bool .
  op _==_ : List List -> Bool [comm] .
  op list2set : List -> Set .
  var  B : Bool .            vars N M : Nat .
  vars L L' : List .         var  S : Set .
  eq N N = N .
  eq true and B = B .        eq false and B = false .
  eq true or B = true .      eq false or B = B .
  eq 0 == s N = false .      eq s N == s M = N == M .
  eq N ; L == M = false .    eq N ; L == M ; L' = (N == M) and L == L' .
  eq L == L = true .
  eq list2set(N) = N .       eq list2set(N ; L) = N list2set(L) .
  eq N in null = false .     eq N in M S = (N == M) or N in S .
endfm
```

Fig. 1. Example in Maude syntax

rules in this module then define various functions such as _and_ and _or_, a function list2set associating to each list its corresponding set, the set membership predicate _in_, and an equality predicate _==_ on lists. Furthermore, the idempotency of set union is specified by the first equation. All these equations rewrite terms *modulo* the equational axioms declared in the module. Specifically, _and_ and _or_ have been declared associative and commutative with the assoc and comm keywords, the list concatenation operator _;_ has been declared associative using the assoc keyword; the set union operator __ has been declared associative, commutative and with null as its identity using the assoc, comm, and id: keywords; and the _==_ equality predicate has been declared commutative using the comm keyword. The succinctness of this specification is precisely due to the power of rewriting modulo axioms, which typically uses considerably fewer rules that standard rewriting.

As we shall see, this module is terminating. However, at present we are not aware of any termination tools that could handle termination proofs modulo the combinations of axioms used: in the best cases associative-commutative symbols are supported, but even the set union operator __ is outside the scope of such tools because of the identity axiom for null, which is explicitly exploited in some of the module's rewrite rules such as the second rule for _in_. The difficulty is not just a pragmatic one of current tools not supporting some known methods.

Unfortunately, *it applies also to termination methods themselves.* For example, perhaps the most general termination modulo proof method known, namely, the Giesl-Kapur dependency pairs modulo E method [13] assumes that E has *non-collapse* equational axioms (thus excluding the identity axiom for $\_\_$) and a *finitary* E-unification algorithm (which also excludes the associativity axiom for the list concatenation operator $\_ ; \_$).

The main contribution of this paper is a new technique that greatly increases the capacity of proving termination of term rewriting systems modulo axioms. This is accomplished by *decomposing* the set of axioms E that we are rewriting modulo into smaller theories, and using such *modular decompositions* to ultimately reduce termination proofs to proofs for specifications that can be handled by existing termination tools and methods. A first key idea is to *decompose* the equational axioms E as a union $\Delta \cup B$, where Δ is a set of rewrite rules that are convergent and (strongly) coherent modulo the axioms B. We then automatically transform our original TRS (Σ, E, R), whose rules R are applied modulo E, into a *semantically equivalent* TRS (for both termination and confluence purposes) $(\Sigma, B, \widehat{R} \cup \Delta)$, whose rules $\widehat{R} \cup \Delta$ are now applied modulo the potentially much simpler set of equational axioms B.

The second key idea is to generate the transformed rules $\widehat{R}$ by computing the Δ, B-*variants* of the left-hand sides l for the rules $l \rightarrow r$ in R. The notion of variant has been proposed by Comon and Delaune [5] and has been further developed in [9,10]. Intuitively, given a term t, a Δ, B-variant of t is a Δ, B-canonical form u of an instance of t by some substitution θ; more precisely, it is a pair (u, θ). Some variants are more general than others, so that variants form a preorder in an appropriate generalization order. The key requirement for the theory transformation $(\Sigma, E, R) \mapsto (\Sigma, B, \widehat{R} \cup \Delta)$ to be effectively usable is that each term l for $l \rightarrow r$ in R has a *finite set* of most general Δ, B-variants. Although the sufficient condition that $\Delta \cup B$ has the *finite variant property* [5] can be checked under some assumptions using the method in [9], we show in this paper that the finiteness of variants can be either ensured, or often achieved in practice, for quite general cases where the axioms B may not have a finitary unification algorithm (for example the case of associativity), and/or the finite variant property may fail for $\Delta \cup B$.

One important feature of our method is its high degree of *modularity*, which we could describe as being both *vertical* and *horizontal.* Vertically, we can go on and apply a similar variant-based decomposition to our transformed theory $(\Sigma, B, \widehat{R} \cup \Delta)$ by further decomposing B as, say, $\Lambda \cup D$, with the rules Λ convergent and (strongly) coherent modulo D. That is, *the transformation using variants can be repeated several times* to yield increasingly simpler sets of axioms: from E to B, to D, and so on. Horizontally, we may decompose a given $E = \biguplus E_i$ into a *disjoint union* of theories E_i.

To illustrate the power and usefulness of our modular transformation methods for proving termination modulo axioms, we study in detail the very common case when $E = \biguplus E_i$ is a modular combination of theories where $E_i \subseteq \{A_i, C_i, LU_i, RU_i\}$ is *any* subset of associativity (A), commutativity (C), left-identity (LU), and right-identity (RU) axioms for a symbol f_i. We show successive termination-equivalent transformations where first LU and RU axioms are removed, then A-only axioms can sometimes be removed, and, finally, C (but not AC) axioms are also removed. In the end, therefore, we can often obtain semantically equivalent theories whose termination proofs can be handled by existing termination methods and tools. We illustrate all these transformations using our running LIST&SET example. Throughout, we treat the case of *order-sorted* term rewriting systems for two reasons. First, it is *more general* than unsorted and many-sorted rewriting, which are contained as special cases. Second, as explained in § 4.1, order-sortedness can greatly facilitate the elimination of associative-only axioms.

The paper is organized as follows. § 2 contains preliminaries on term rewriting, rewriting modulo axioms, and variants. § 3 introduces our variant-based theory transformation. § 4 illustrates the use of such a transformation to rewriting modulo combinations of associativity, commutativity, and left and right identities. § 5 comments on the current tool support, and § 6 covers related work and conclusions. All proofs of technical results can be found in [7].

2   Preliminaries

2.1   Order-Sorted Term Rewriting

We summarize here material from [15,19] on order-sorted algebra and order-sorted rewriting. We start with a partially ordered set $(S, \leq)$ of *sorts*, where $s \leq s'$ is interpreted as *subsort inclusion*. The *connected components* of $(S, \leq)$ are the equivalence classes $[s]$ corresponding to the least equivalence relation $\equiv_\leq$ containing $\leq$. When a connected component $[s]$ has a top element, we will also denote by $[s]$ the top element of the connected component $[s]$. An order-sorted signature $(\Sigma, S, \leq)$ consists of a poset of sorts $(S, \leq)$ and a $S^* \times S$-indexed family of sets $\Sigma = \{\Sigma_{w,s}\}_{(w,s) \in S^* \times S}$, which are sets of *function symbols* with given string of argument sorts and result sort. If $f \in \Sigma_{s_1 \ldots s_n, s}$, then we display the function symbol f as $f : s_1 \ldots s_n \longrightarrow s$. This is called a *rank* declaration for symbol f. Some of these symbols f can be *subsort-overloaded*, i.e., they can have several rank declarations related in the $\leq$ ordering [15].

Given an S-sorted set $\mathcal{X} = \{\mathcal{X}_s \mid s \in S\}$ of *disjoint* sets of variables, the set $\mathcal{T}(\Sigma, \mathcal{X})_s$ of terms of sort s is the least set such that $\mathcal{X}_s \subseteq \mathcal{T}(\Sigma, \mathcal{X})_s$; if $s' \leq s$, then $\mathcal{T}(\Sigma, \mathcal{X})_{s'} \subseteq \mathcal{T}(\Sigma, \mathcal{X})_s$; and if $f : s_1 \ldots s_n \longrightarrow s$ is a rank declaration for symbol f and $t_i \in \mathcal{T}(\Sigma, \mathcal{X})_{s_i}$ for $1 \leq i \leq n$, then $f(t_1, \ldots, t_n) \in \mathcal{T}(\Sigma, \mathcal{X})_s$. The set $\mathcal{T}(\Sigma, \mathcal{X})$ of order-sorted terms is $\mathcal{T}(\Sigma, \mathcal{X}) = \cup_{s \in S} \mathcal{T}(\Sigma, \mathcal{X})_s$. An element of any set $\mathcal{T}(\Sigma, \mathcal{X})_s$ is called a *well-formed* term. A simple syntactic condition on $(\Sigma, S, \leq)$ called *prokregularity* [15] ensures that each well-formed term t has always a *least-sort* possible among all sorts in S, which is denoted $ls(t)$. Terms are viewed as labelled trees in the usual way. Positions $p, q, \ldots$ are represented by chains of positive natural numbers used to address subterm positions of t. The set of positions of a term t is denoted $\mathcal{P}os(t)$. Positions of non-variable symbols in t are denoted as $\mathcal{P}os_\Sigma(t)$, and $\mathcal{P}os_\mathcal{X}(t)$ are the positions of variables.

The subterm at position p of t is denoted as $t|_p$ and $t[u]_p$ is the term t with the subterm at position p replaced by u. We write $t \unrhd u$, read u *is a subterm of* t, if $u = t|_p$ for some $p \in \mathcal{P}os(t)$ and $t \rhd u$ if $t \unrhd u$ and $t \neq u$.

An order-sorted substitution σ is an S-sorted mapping $\sigma = \{\sigma : \mathcal{X}_s \to \mathcal{T}(\Sigma, \mathcal{X})_s\}_{s \in S}$ from variables to terms. The application of an OS-substitution σ to t (denoted $t\sigma$) consists of simultaneously replacing the variables occurring in t by corresponding terms according to the mapping σ. A *specialization* ν is an OS-substitution that maps a variable x of sort s to a variable x' of sort $s' \leq s$. We denote $\mathcal{D}om(\sigma)$ and $\mathcal{R}ng(\sigma)$ the domain and range of a substitution σ.

An (order-sorted) rewrite rule is an ordered pair (l, r), written $l \to r$, with $l, r \in \mathcal{T}(\Sigma, \mathcal{X})$, $l \notin \mathcal{X}$, $\mathcal{V}ar(r) \subseteq \mathcal{V}ar(l)$ (and $ls(l) \equiv_{\leq} ls(r)$ for order-sorted rules). If for all specializations ν, $ls(\nu(l)) \geq ls(\nu(r))$, then we say that the OS-rule $l \to r$ is *sort-decreasing*. An OS-TRS is a pair $\mathcal{R} = (\Sigma, R)$ where R is a set of OS-rules. We say that $\mathcal{R}$ is sort-decreasing if all rules in R are so. A term $t \in \mathcal{T}(\Sigma, \mathcal{X})$ rewrites to u (at position $p \in \mathcal{P}os(t)$ and using the rule $l \to r$), written $t \xrightarrow{p}_{l \to r} s$ (or just $t \to_{\mathcal{R}} s$ or even $t \to s$ if no confusion arises), if $t|_p = \sigma(l)$ and $s = t[\sigma(r)]_p$, for some OS-substitution σ; if $\mathcal{R}$ is *not* sort-decreasing, we also require that $t[\sigma(r)]_p$ is a well-formed term.

2.2   Rewriting Modulo Axioms

A *rewrite theory* is a triple $\mathcal{R} = (\Sigma, E, R)$ with Σ a preregular order-sorted signature such that each connected component has a top sort, E a set of Σ-equations, and R a set of Σ-rules. We furthermore assume throughout that each equation $u = v$ in E is *regular* (i.e., $\mathcal{V}ar(u) = \mathcal{V}ar(v)$), and *linear* (neither u nor v have repeated variables). Furthermore, the variables $\{x_1, \ldots, x_n\} = \mathcal{V}ar(u) = \mathcal{V}ar(v)$ have *top sorts* $[s_1], \ldots, [s_n]$.

Given a rewrite theory $\mathcal{R}$ as above, $t \to_{R/E} t'$ iff there exist u, v such that $t =_E u$ and $u \to_R v$ and $v =_E t'$. In general, of course, given terms t and t' with sorts in the same connected component, the problem of whether $t \to_{R/E} t'$ holds is undecidable. For this reason, a much simpler relation $\to_{R,E}$ is defined, which becomes decidable if an E-matching algorithm exists. For any terms u, v with sorts in the same connected component, the relation $u \to_{R,E} v$ holds if there is a position p in u, a rule $l \to r$ in R, and a substitution σ such that $u|_p =_E l\sigma$ and $v = u[r\sigma]_p$ (see [26]).

Of course, $\to_{R,E} \subseteq \to_{R/E}$. The important question is the *completeness* question: can any $\to_{R/E}$-step be simulated by a $\to_{R,E}$-step? We say that $\mathcal{R}$ satisfies the *E-completeness* property if for any u, v with sorts in the same connected component we have:

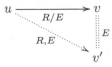

where here and in what follows dotted lines indicate existential quantification.

It is easy to check that E-completeness is equivalent to the following (strong) E-coherence[1] (or just *coherence* when E is understood) property:

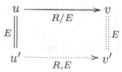

If a theory $\mathcal{R}$ is not coherent, we can try to make it so by completing the set of rules R to a set of rules $\widetilde{R}$ by a Knuth-Bendix-like completion procedure that computes critical pairs between equations in E and rules in R (see, e.g., [17,29] for the *strong* coherence completion that we use here, and [13] for the equivalent notion of extension completion). As we will further discuss in § 4, for theories E that are combinations of A, C, LU, and RU axioms, the coherence completion procedure always terminates and has a very simple description.

We say that $\mathcal{R} = (\Sigma, E, R)$ is E-*confluent*, resp. E-*terminating*, if the relation $\to_{R/E}$ is confluent, resp. terminating. If $\mathcal{R}$ is E-coherent, then E-confluence is equivalent to asserting that, for any $t \to^*_{R,E} u$, $t \to^*_{R,E} v$, we have:

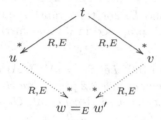

and E-termination is equivalent to the termination of the $\to_{R,E}$ relation.

The fact that we are performing *order-sorted* rewriting makes one more requirement necessary. When E-matching a subterm $t|_p$ against a rule's left-hand side to obtain a matching substitution σ, we need to check that σ is well-sorted, that is, that if a variable x has sort s, then the term $x\sigma$ has also sort s. This may however fail to be the case even though there is a term $w \in [x\sigma]_E$ which does have sort s, where $[t]_E$ denotes the E-equivalence class of term t. We call an order-sorted signature E-*preregular* if the set of sorts $\{s \in S \mid \exists w' \in [w]_E \text{ s.t. } w' \in \mathcal{T}(\Sigma, \mathcal{X})_s\}$ has a least upper bound, denoted $ls[w]_E$ which can be effectively computed.[2] Then we can check the well-sortedness of the substitution σ not based on $x\sigma$ above, but, implicitly, on all the terms in $[w]_E$.

---

[1] Note that the assumption of E being regular and linear is essential for one $\to_{R/E}$-step to exactly correspond to one $\to_{R,E}$-step. For this reason, some authors (e.g., [17,29]) call conditions as the one above *strong coherence*, and consider also weaker notions of coherence.

[2] The Maude system automatically checks the E-preregularity of a signature Σ for E any combination of A, C, LU, and RU axioms (see [4, Chapter 22.2.5]).

Yet another property required for the good behavior of confluent and terminating rewrite theories modulo E is their being *E-sort-decreasing*. This means that $\mathcal{R}$ is E-preregular, and for each rewrite rule $l \to r$, and for each specialization substitution ν we have $ls[r\nu]_E \leq ls[l\nu]_E$.

3   A Variant-Based Theory Transformation

Consider a rewrite theory $\mathcal{E} = (\Sigma, B, \Delta)$ satisfying the conditions in § 2.2, and such that $\mathcal{E}$ is B-confluent, B-terminating, B-preregular, B-sort-decreasing, and B-coherent. Then, we can view $\mathcal{E}$ as an order-sorted equational theory $(\Sigma, \widetilde{\Delta} \cup B)$, where $\widetilde{\Delta} = \{l = r \mid l \to r \in \Delta\}$ and we can use the B-confluence, B-termination, B-preregularity, and B-sort-decreasingness of $\mathcal{E}$ to make the $\widetilde{\Delta} \cup B$-equality relation decidable by $\to_{\Delta,B}$-rewriting. The first key idea in the present work is to greatly simplify the problem of proving termination for a rewrite theory $\mathcal{R} = (\Sigma, E, R)$ by decomposing E into a union $E = \widetilde{\Delta} \cup B$ such that the axioms B are simpler and the rewrite theory $\mathcal{E}_E = (\Sigma, B, \Delta)$ is B-confluent, B-terminating, B-preregular, B-sort-decreasing, and B-coherent.

The second key idea is to then transform $\mathcal{R} = (\Sigma, E, R)$ into a semantically equivalent rewrite theory $\widehat{\mathcal{R}} = (\Sigma, B, \widehat{R} \cup \Delta)$ so that $\mathcal{R}$ terminates modulo E iff $\widehat{\mathcal{R}} \cup \Delta$ terminates modulo B. For this transformation $\mathcal{R} \mapsto \widehat{\mathcal{R}}$, Comon and Delaune's notion of *variant*, proposed in [5] and further developed in [9,10], is very useful.

Definition 1. (Variant [5,9,10]). *Let $\mathcal{E}_E = (\Sigma, B, \Delta)$ be an order-sorted rewrite theory satisfying the requirement in § 2.2 plus being B-confluent, B-terminating, B-preregular, B-sort-decreasing, and B-coherent. Given any Σ-term t, a Δ, B-variant of t is a pair of the form $(t\theta\downarrow_{\Delta,B}, \theta)$ where $t\theta\downarrow_{\Delta,B}$ (abbreviated to $t\theta\downarrow$ in what follows) denotes a canonical form for t, i.e., a term w such that $t \to^*_{\Delta,B} w$ and w cannot be further rewritten with $\to_{\Delta,B}$. By confluence, this makes $t\theta\downarrow$ unique up to equality modulo B.* $\square$

Definition 2. (Most General Variants [5,9,10]). *We denote by $[\![t]\!]^*_{\Delta,B}$ the set of Δ, B-variants of t. This set is ordered by a preorder relation of generalization, $(u, \theta) \sqsubseteq_{\Delta,B} (v, \sigma)$, meaning that (v, σ) is a more general variant than (u, θ), that holds iff there is a substitution ρ such that $u =_B v\rho$, and $\theta\downarrow =_B \sigma\rho$ (that is, for each variable $x \in \mathcal{D}om(\theta)$ we have $x\theta\downarrow =_B x\sigma\rho$). In this preordered set we denote by $[\![t]\!]_{\Delta,B}$ a subset of $[\![t]\!]^*_{\Delta,B}$ such that for any $(u, \theta) \in [\![t]\!]^*_{\Delta,B}$ there exists $(v, \sigma) \in [\![t]\!]_{\Delta,B}$ such that $(u, \theta) \sqsubseteq_{\Delta,B} (v, \sigma)$, and if $(v, \sigma) \in [\![t]\!]_{\Delta,B}$ there is no $(v', \sigma') \neq (v, \sigma) \in [\![t]\!]^*_{\Delta,B}$ such that $(v, \sigma) \sqsubseteq_{\Delta,B} (v', \sigma')$. That is, $[\![t]\!]_{\Delta,B}$ is a choice of a complete set of maximal elements in the preordered set $([\![t]\!]^*_{\Delta,B}, \sqsubseteq_{\Delta,B})$. We say that $\mathcal{E}_E$ has the finite variant property if for any Σ-term t we can find a finite complete set of most general variants $[\![t]\!]_{\Delta,B}$.* $\square$

As already mentioned, we transform $\mathcal{R}$ into $\widehat{\mathcal{R}} = (\Sigma, B, \Delta \cup \widehat{R})$, where the rules $\widehat{R}$ will be appropriate Δ, B-variants of the rules R, and show that $\mathcal{R}$ and $\widehat{\mathcal{R}}$ are *semantically equivalent* rewrite theories, for deduction, confluence, and termination purposes. The transformation can be defined in general. Furthermore, if B has a finitary unification algorithm it can be implementd by *variant-narrowing* [11], which when $\mathcal{E}_E$ has the finite variant property makes $\widehat{R}$ *finite* if R is finite.

Definition 3 ($\mathcal{R} \mapsto \widehat{\mathcal{R}}$ transformation). *Let $\mathcal{R} = (\Sigma, E, R)$ be an order-sorted rewrite theory where E satisfies the requirements in § 2.2, Σ is E-preregular, R is E-coherent, and such that E can be decomposed as a B-confluent, B-terminating, B-preregular, B-sort-decreasing and B-coherent rewrite theory $\mathcal{E}_E = (\Sigma, B, \Delta)$. We then define the Δ, B-variant of $\mathcal{R}$, denoted $\widehat{\mathcal{R}} = (\Sigma, B, \Delta \cup \widehat{R})$, where $\widehat{R}$ is obtained from R as the B-coherence completion of the set of rules $\{\hat{l} \to r\alpha \mid l \to r \in R,$ and $(\hat{l}, \alpha) \in [\![l]\!]_{\Delta,B}\}$.*

Essentially, $\mathcal{R}$ and $\widehat{\mathcal{R}}$ have the same deductive power. The only difference is that $\widehat{\mathcal{R}}$ accomplishes the same deductions as $\mathcal{R}$ (up to E-equality) by simpler means: modulo B instead of modulo E.

Theorem 1 (Semantic equivalence). *Let $\mathcal{R}$ be as in Definition 3. Then:*

1. *For any two terms such that $t_0 =_E t'_0$ and any rewrite sequence*

$$t_0 \to_{R,E} t_1 \to_{R,E} t_2 \cdots t_{n-1} \to_{R,E} t_n$$

with $n \geq 0$ there is a corresponding sequence

$$t'_0 \to^!_{\Delta,B} t'_0{\downarrow} \to_{\widehat{R},B} t'_1 \to^!_{\Delta,B} t'_1{\downarrow} \to_{\widehat{R},B} t'_2 \cdots t'_{n-1}{\downarrow} \to_{\widehat{R},B} t'_n \to^!_{\Delta,B} t'_n{\downarrow}$$

with $t_i =_E t'_i$, $0 \leq i \leq n$.

2. *Conversely, for any $t'_0 =_E t_0$ and for any sequence*

$$t'_0 \to^*_{\Delta,B} t''_0 \to_{\widehat{R},B} t'_1 \to^*_{\Delta,B} t''_1 \to_{\widehat{R},B} t'_2 \cdots t'_{n-1} \to^*_{\Delta,B} t''_{n-1} \to_{\widehat{R},B} t'_n \to^*_{\Delta,B} t''_n$$

with $n \geq 0$ there is a sequence

$$t_0 \to_{R,E} t_1 \to_{R,E} t_2 \cdots t_{n-1} \to_{R,E} t_n$$

with $t_i =_E t'_i$, $1 \leq i \leq n$.

Corollary 1. *Let $\mathcal{R} = (\Sigma, E, R)$ be a TRS as in Definition 3. Then:*

1. *$\mathcal{R}$ is E-terminating iff $\widehat{\mathcal{R}}$ is B-terminating.*
2. *$\mathcal{R}$ is E-confluent iff $\widehat{\mathcal{R}}$ is B-confluent.*

4   Application to Rewriting Modulo Combinations of *A*, *C*, *LU*, and *RU* Theories

Let $\mathcal{R} = (\Sigma, E, R)$ be a rewrite theory such that E satisfies the conditions in § 2.2, Σ is E-preregular, R is E-coherent, and such that E has the modular decomposition $E = \bigcup_{f:[s_1]\cdots[s_n]\to[s]\in\Sigma} E_f$, where if $n \neq 2$, then $E_f = \emptyset$, and if $n = 2$, then $E_f \subseteq \{A_f, C_f, LU_f, RU_f\}$, where:

- A_f is the axiom $f(f(x,y),z) = f(x,f(y,z))$,
- C_f is the axiom $f(x,y) = f(y,x)$,
- LU_f is the axiom $f(e,x) = x$, for e a given ground term[3] of sort $[s_1]$, and
- RU_f is the axiom $f(x,e') = x$, for e' a given ground term of sort $[s_2]$,

and where the variables x, y, z are all of the appropriate top sorts. Note that A_f is only possible when $[s_1] = [s_2] = [s]$. Instead, we can have C_f with $[s] \neq [s_1], [s_2]$, but whenever C_f holds we assume that $[s_1] = [s_2]$. Also, if LU_f holds, then $[s_2] = [s]$; and if RU_f holds, then $[s_1] = [s]$. If $LU_f, RU_f \in E_f$, then $[s_1] = [s_2] = [s]$, and $e = e'$. Note that if $LU_f, C_f \in E_f$ (resp. $RU_f, C_f \in E_f$), then $E_f \vdash RU_f$ (resp. $E_f \vdash LU_f$), and $[s_1] = [s_2] = [s]$. We write:

$$ALU_f = \{A_f, LU_f\} \quad ARU_f = \{A_f, RU_f\} \qquad AU_f = \{A_f, LU_f, RU_f\}$$
$$AC_f = \{A_f, C_f\} \quad ACU_f = \{A_f, C_f, LU_f, RU_f\} \quad CU_f = \{C_f, LU_f, RU_f\}$$

of course, we may have $E_f = \emptyset$ for any given $f : [s_1] \cdots [s_n] \to [s]$, or even $E = \emptyset$.

We are interested in greatly simplifying proofs of termination for the $\to_{R,E}$ relation as proofs of termination for the $\to_{\widehat{R}\cup\widetilde{U},B}$ relation, where we obtain the following modular decomposition of E as the rewrite theory $\mathcal{E} = (\Sigma, B, \widetilde{U})$, with:

$$B = \bigcup_{f:[s_1]\cdots[s_n]\to[s]\in\Sigma} B_f \quad B_f = E_f \cap \{A_f, C_f\}$$
$$U = \bigcup_{f:[s_1]\cdots[s_n]\to[s]\in\Sigma} U_f \quad U_f = E_f \cap \{LU_f, RU_f\}$$

with LU_f and RU_f understood as rewrite rules $f(e,x) \to x$, and $f(x,e) \to x$, and where $\widetilde{U}$ is the B-coherence completion of U, which has the following modular description as a union $\widetilde{U} = \bigcup_{f:[s_1]\cdots[s_n]\to[s]\in\Sigma} \widetilde{U}_f$. If $A_f \notin B_f$, or $A_f, C_f \in B_f$, then $\widetilde{U}_f = U_f$. Otherwise, if $A_f \in B_f$, but $C_f \notin B_f$, then, if $LU_f \in U_f$, then we add the rule $f(x, f(e,y)) \to f(x,y)$ and if $RU_f \in U_f$, then we add the rule $f(f(x,e'),y) \to f(x,y)$.

By well-known results about A-coherence (see, e.g., [26]), this makes the rules $\widetilde{U}$ B-coherent, and of course we have $\to_{U,B}\subseteq\to_{\widetilde{U},B}\subseteq\to_{U/B}$. An important result about the rewrite theory $\mathcal{E} = (\Sigma, B, \widetilde{U})$ is the following.

Proposition 1. *Assuming that the rewrite theory $\mathcal{E} = (\Sigma, B, \widetilde{U})$ is B-sort decreasing and the signature Σ is B-preregular, then the rules $\widetilde{U}$ are B-terminating and B-confluent.*

Let $\mathcal{R} = (\Sigma, E, R)$ be a rewrite theory satisfying the conditions in this section, so that $E = \bigcup_f E_f$, and $E_f \subseteq \{A_f, C_f, LU_f, RU_f\}$, and such that the decomposition $\mathcal{E} = (\Sigma, B, \widetilde{U})$ is B-preregular and B-sort decreasing. Then, as $\widetilde{U}$ is B-coherent and by Proposition 1, $\mathcal{R}$ satisfies the requirements in Definition 3,

---

[3] We do not require e and e' to be *constants*. For example, we may allow the term $s\ 0$ to be the identity element for multiplication of natural numbers. However, we will assume and require that the top function symbol of e, resp. e', as left, resp. right, identity of f is *different* from f itself.

and by Theorem 1 we can transform $\mathcal{R}$ into the semantically equivalent rewrite theory $\widehat{\mathcal{R}} = (\widehat{\Sigma}, B, \widetilde{U} \cup \widehat{R})$, so that $\mathcal{R}$ is terminating modulo E iff $\widehat{\mathcal{R}}$ is terminating modulo B. The only question remaining is whether $\mathcal{E} = (\Sigma, B, \widetilde{U})$ has the finite variant property, so that we can obtain an explicit finitary description of $\widehat{\mathcal{R}}$ when R is finite.

Theorem 2. *If* $\mathcal{E} = (\Sigma, B, \widetilde{U})$ *has a finite set of sorts, is B-preregular and B-sort decreasing, then $\mathcal{E}$ has the finite variant property.*

Example 2. Let us apply our transformation to our running example to remove the identity element of the __ operator from the equational part of the specification. The variants of the rules can still be computed thanks to Theorem 2. Specifically, we get a variant for one of the equations defining _in_. The application of our transformation therefore removes the id: null annotation, and, with X a new variable of kind [List,Set],[4] adds the following two rules:

```
eq null X = X .                    eq N in M = (N == M) or N in null .
```

4.1   Eliminating the *A* But Not *AC* Axioms

Although certain termination methods can be used to prove termination of rewriting modulo associativity, we are not aware of termination tools that allow direct input of a general TRS with some symbols declared as associative but not associative-commutative. It is therefore of practical interest to study theory transformations that yield a semantically equivalent theory (also for termination purposes) where if $B_f = \{A_f\}$, then A_f is removed and turned into a rule. That is, given axioms B, where for each f we have $B_f \subseteq \{A_f, C_f\}$, we now define a rewrite theory (Σ, B°, A), where for each $f \in \mathcal{F}$ we have $B_f^\circ = B_f$ if $B_f \neq \{A_f\}$, and $B_f^\circ = \emptyset$ if $B_f = \{A_f\}$, and where A consists of rules of either the form

$$f(f(x, y), z) \rightarrow f(x, f(y, z)) \tag{1}$$

or the form

$$f(x, f(y, z)) \rightarrow f(f(x, y), z) \tag{2}$$

for each $f \in \Sigma$ such that $B_f = \{A_f\}$. That is, for any such f we *choose* a rule associating f to the right or to the left (but only *one* of these two possibilities).

Proposition 2. *The theory* (Σ, B°, A) *is confluent and terminating modulo B°.*

Therefore, assuming that (Σ, B°, A) is B°-sort-decreasing and B°-preregular, the obvious idea is to apply again the transformation $\mathcal{R} \mapsto \widehat{\mathcal{R}}$, but now with $E = B$, $B = B^\circ$, and $\Delta = A$ to obtain from a theory $\mathcal{R} = (\Sigma, B, R)$ a semantically

---

[4] Maude automatically adds top sorts, called *kinds*, and implicitly lifts all operators to their top sorts. Although they can be denoted in different forms, Maude prints kinds using a comma-separated list of the *maximal elements* of the connected component.

equivalent $\mathcal{R}_A = (\Sigma, B^\circ, R_A \cup A)$, where the rules R_A are the A, B°-*variants* of the rules $\mathcal{R}$. Indeed, this is perfectly correct, and all the good properties of Theorem 1 and its corollaries apply. There is, however, a remaining problem, namely, that in general R_A may be *infinite*, even when R is not. This is obviously the case because the theory (Σ, B°, A) does *not* have the finite variant property. Indeed, if (Σ, B°, A) were to have the finite variant property, we would obtain a *finitary* A-unification algorithm by variant narrowing (see [11]), which is well-known to be impossible.

What can we do? The key observation is that the fact that a theory lacks the finite variant property does *not* imply that any term lacks a finite complete set of most general variants. For practical purposes, it may very well be the case that the terms we care about *do* have a finite complete set of variants. For the variants involved in $\mathcal{R}_A$ this may often happen for two good reasons:

1. the terms appearing on left-hand sides often describe recursive function definitions, in which the patterns (or subpatterns) involving associative-only symbols are very simple, and are in A, B°-normal form, and
2. an order-sorted type structure makes many potential unifiers impossible.

Observations (1)-(2) apply very nicely to our running example, where we do not just have $\mathcal{R}_A$ finite, but we actually have the set identity $R = R_A$. To illustrate why this is the case, let us consider the rules for the `list2set` and `_==_` functions. We obtain the variants of a term by *variant narrowing*, which is a special narrowing strategy [11]. But the only left-hand sides that could potentially be narrowed with the rule (X ; Y) ; Z = X ; (Y ; Z) are the left-hand sides of the rules

```
eq list2set(N ; L) = N list2set(L) .
eq N ; L == M = false .
eq N ; L == M ; L' = (N == M) and L == L' .
```

However, no such narrowing steps are possible, since the terms N ; L and (X ; Y) ; Z have *no* order-sorted unifiers (likewise for M ; L').

Therefore, a useful semi-algorithm to attempt the $\mathcal{R} \mapsto \mathcal{R}_A$ transformation can proceed as follows:

1. Group all the rules according to a partition $R = R_1 \uplus \cdots \uplus R_k$ where for each R_i the function symbols f with $B_f = \{A_f\}$ appearing in the left-hand sides of rules in R_i are, say, $\{f_i^1, \ldots, f_i^{n_i}\}$.
2. For each rule $l \to r$ in R_i, try to compute a complete, finite set of variants for l with **all** possible orientations of the associativity rules for the function symbols $\{f_i^1, \ldots, f_i^{n_i}\}$. This should be done with a *timeout*. That is, either the variant narrowing algorithm terminates before the timeout, or we abandon that choice of orientation for the associativity rule.
3. If for each R_i an orientation A_i of the associativity rules succeeds in generating a finite set of variants $R_{i,A}$ for the rules R_i, then define $R_A = \bigcup_i R_{i,A_i}$, $A = \bigcup_i A_i$, and $\mathcal{R}_A = (\widehat{\Sigma}, B^\circ, R_A \cup A)$

Example 3. Since for our running example we have $R_A = R$, we obtain the transformed module by removing the *assoc* attribute from _;_, and by adding the following associativity rule, given new variables X, Y, and Z of kind [List,Set].

```
eq (X ; Y) ; Z = X ; (Y ; Z) .
```

4.2 Eliminating the C But Not AC Cases

We are not aware of termination tools supporting proofs of termination for symbols f such that $B_f = \{C_f\}$. Instead, the case $B_f = \{A_f, C_f\}$ is well-supported by termination proof methods and tools. It may therefore be desirable to develop an additional theory transformation $\mathcal{R} = (\Sigma, B, R) \mapsto \mathcal{R}_C = (\Sigma_C, B_C, R_C)$ where $B = \bigcup_f B_f$, with $B_f \subseteq \{A_f, C_f\}$, and where $B_C = \bigcup_f B_{C_f}$, where if $B_f = \{A_f, C_f\}$, then $B_{C_f} = B_f$, and otherwise $B_{C_f} = \emptyset$. We define this transformation for $\mathcal{R} = (\Sigma, B, R)$ an order-sorted theory where the rules R are B-coherent and such that all the variables in their left-hand sides are C-linear (i.e., they do not have any C-nonlinear variables).

Definition 4. *Given a rewrite rule $l \rightarrow r$ in R, where we of course assume $Var(r) \subseteq Var(l)$, we call a variable $x \in Var(l)$ of sort s C-nonlinear if (1) it is nonlinear in l, and (2) there exists a Σ-term t with $ls[t]_B \leq s$ with a position p such that $t|_p = f(u,v)$, with $B_f = \{C_f\}$. It is easy to determine whether a variable x is C-nonlinear by a simple fixpoint computation.*

Our transformation considers an OS rewrite theory[5] $\mathcal{R} = (\Sigma, B, R)$ where Σ is B-preregular and the rules R are B-coherent, with $B = \bigcup_f B_f$ such that $B_f \subseteq \{A_f, C_f\}$, and such that all the variables in their left-hand sides are C-linear. The transformation $\mathcal{R} \mapsto \mathcal{R}_C$ is defined with $\mathcal{R}_C = (\Sigma, B_C, R_C)$, where:

1. For each $f \in \Sigma$, if $B_f \neq \{C_f\}$, then $B_{C_f} = B_f$, and if $B_f = \{C_f\}$, then $B_{C_f} = \emptyset$, that is, we remove the commutativity axiom from all commutative but not associative operators. We also require that Σ_C is B_C-*preregular*[6].
2. $\mathcal{R}_C$ contains the rules $\widetilde{l'} \rightarrow r$ for each $\widetilde{l'} \in [l']_{\widehat{C}}$ where $\widehat{C} = \bigcup_f \widehat{C}_f$, and $\widehat{C}_f = \{C_f\}$ if $B_f = \{C_f\}$, and $\widehat{C}_f = \emptyset$ otherwise. Note that the equivalence class $[l']_{\widehat{C}}$ is *finite*, and consists of permuting all the subterms of l' of the form $f(u,v)$ with $B_f = \{C_f\}$ in all possible ways.

The main result about this transformation is:

Theorem 3. *For $\mathcal{R} = (\Sigma, B, R)$ satisfying the requirements in the above transformation $\mathcal{R} \mapsto \mathcal{R}_C$, the following properties hold:*

1. *For each $t_0 =_B t'_0$ and each rewrite sequence*

$$t_0 \rightarrow_{R,B} t_1 \cdots t_{n-1} \rightarrow_{R,B} t_n$$

---

[5] Satisfying the extra B_C-preregularity requirement in (1) below.
[6] B_C-*preregularity* can be easily checked, for example by Maude [4].

there is a rewrite sequence

$$t'_0 \rightarrow_{R_C, B_C} t'_1 \cdots t'_{n-1} \rightarrow_{R_C, B_C} t'_n$$

with $t_i =_B t'_i$, $1 \le i \le n$.

2. *Conversely, for each* $t_0 =_B t'_0$ *and each rewrite sequence*

$$t'_0 \rightarrow_{R_C, B_C} t'_1 \cdots t'_{n-1} \rightarrow_{R_C, B_C} t'_n$$

there is a rewrite sequence

$$t_0 \rightarrow_{R, B} t_1 \cdots t_{n-1} \rightarrow_{R, B} t_n$$

with $t_i =_B t'_i$, $1 \le i \le n$.

3. $\mathcal{R}$ *is terminating modulo* B *iff* $\mathcal{R}_C$ *is terminating modulo* B_C.

Example 4. Since none of the equations in the specification in Example 3 is C-nonlinear, the application of the transformation to remove the commutativity attributes to our running example is reduced to the addition of equations resulting from permuting all those subterms with a commutative-only operator at their top. The equations to be added are therefore the following:

```
eq s N == 0 = false .              eq M == N ; L = false .
```

5   Tool Support

All the transformations presented in this paper (with a check for a sufficient condition instead of the full transformation for the A-only case) are currently part of an alpha version of Full Maude, where several commands are available so that the different transformations and checks can be executed. The different versions of the running example have been obtained with these commands, and then MTT has been used to obtain a version of the specification in TPDB notation, which was used to prove its AC-termination using AProVE [14]. Specifically, the specification proved was the one obtained using the C;Uk;B transformation in MTT (see [8] for details on this transformation). Notice that sort information is key to prove the termination of the resulting specification.

6   Related Work and Conclusions

This work is related to a wide body of work on termination methods for term rewriting systems modulo axioms. We cannot survey all such methods here: just for AC termination alone there is a substantial body of termination orderings and methods. However, we can mention sample references such as [18,3,28,12,22,25,13]. The paper closest in spirit to ours is probably the one by Giesl and Kapur [13], in that it also aims at developing proof methods modulo some generic class E of equational axioms. They point out that the notion of coherence in [17] (what we call *weak coherence*) does not give an equivalence between the termination of $\rightarrow_{R/E}$ and that of $\rightarrow_{R,E}$. They then propose a completion-like method to generate the set of "E-extensions" of a set of rules R and show that the termination of $\rightarrow_{R/E}$ is equivalent to that of $\rightarrow_{Ext(R),E}$. The exact relation of their extension construction to our work is as follows. Our notion of (**strong**) coherence is equivalent to the condition in their Lemma 10 (which is just our notion of E-completeness), so that their $Ext(R)$ completion is in fact a very useful algorithm for **strong coherence completion**. Therefore for us, as for them with a different formulation, when R is (strongly) E-coherent, $\rightarrow_{R/E}$ terminates iff $\rightarrow_{R,E}$ terminates. Their E-dependency pairs proof method is nicely complementary to ours. As they indicate, their method cannot handle collapse equations and assumes a finitary E-unification algorithm, so that, for example, identity axioms and associativity-only axioms are outside the scope of their method. What is nice is that our method can transform a TRS modulo axioms E that contain collapse equations and may not have a finitary unification algorithm into an equivalent TRS modulo axioms B to which their B-dependency pairs method can be applied. In fact, this is exactly how our running example is proved.

Our work bears also some relationship to modularity methods for termination of TRSs. A very good survey of the literature on such methods up to 2002 can be found in [24]. They are very much orthogonal to ours. They consider the problem of when two TRSs, $\mathcal{R}_1$ and $\mathcal{R}_2$, both terminating, are such that $\mathcal{R}_1 \cup \mathcal{R}_2$ is also terminating. Most of the literature seems to focus on the free case, that is: if $(\Sigma, \emptyset, R)$ and $(\Sigma', \emptyset, R')$ are terminating, when is $(\Sigma \cup \Sigma', \emptyset, R \cup R')$ terminating? However, this can be generalized to terminating rewrite theories (Σ, E, R) and (Σ', E', R'), asking whether $(\Sigma \cup \Sigma', E \cup E', R \cup R')$ is terminating, which would require considering a combination of axioms $E \cup E'$, perhaps using our methods, plus methods in the style of those surveyed in [24] but generalized to the modulo case to deal with the termination of $\rightarrow_{R \cup R'/E \cup E'}$.

There is also a rich body of related work on rewriting modulo E and coherence issues, including the just-discussed [13]. Early papers include those by Huet [16], and particularly by Peterson and Stickel [26], who first studied the coherence of rewriting modulo A and AC axioms. Their ideas were later extended to general sets E of axioms in, e.g., [17,2]. Perhaps the two papers closest in spirit to ours are those by Marché [21] and Viry [29], since in both of them the idea of decomposing a set of axioms E as a union $\Delta \cup B$ with Δ convergent and coherent modulo B is used. In particular, [29] developed in detail the treatment of strong coherence (what we just call E-coherence in this paper) and gave a completion-like procedure to try to make a set of rules (strongly) coherent. The main differences with [21] and [29] are that termination issues were not systematically studied, and the fact that both papers relied on general "critical pair" methods for coherence completion whose termination is hard to characterize. In this regard, our work presents a new viewpoint and a simpler way of achieving strong coherence by introducing what we might call a "variant-based strong coherence completion method," whose termination properties can be studied using the recently introduced variant-based methods and results [5,9,10].

In conclusion, we have presented a new variant-based method to prove termination modulo combinations of sets of equational axioms. Our method is modular both vertically, in the sense that it can be applied repeatedly to reduce such termination proofs modulo increasingly simpler sets of axioms which in the end can be handled by existing termination methods and tools, and horizontally, since it can naturally handle unions of different sets of axioms for different function symbols. We have illustrated its usefulness in the very common case where the axioms E are an arbitrary combination of associativity, commutativity, left- and right-identity axioms for various function symbols, but of course our method is fully general and applies to other axioms E, provided they are regular and linear. Note that it follows from Corollary 1 that the transformation $\mathcal{R} \mapsto \widehat{\mathcal{R}}$ *can also be used for proofs of confluence* modulo E. For example, computation of critical pairs can now be carried out modulo a much simpler theory B for which a finitary unification algorithm may exist.

Much work remains ahead both in terms of generalizations and in tool support. We are currently working on an extension of these methods to the case of conditional rewrite theories. It would also be very useful to explore how the requirements on E can be relaxed to handle even more general sets of axioms. The generalization of modular termination methods for unions of term rewriting sytems modulo the unions of their corresponding axioms sketched above is yet another promising research direction in which two orthogonal types of modularity could be synergistically combined. Regarding tool support for the method we have presented, our current experimental prototype should be extended and integrated within the MTT tool [6]. In this way, our termination technique modulo combinations of axioms will become applicable to an even wider range of rewrite theories, that can be transformed into order-sorted ones by non-termination-preserving transformations [8,20].

Acknowledgements. F. Durán and S. Lucas were partially supported by Spanish MEC grants TIN 2008-03107 and TIN 2007-68093-C02, respectively. J. Meseguer was partially supported by NSF grants CNS 07-16638 and CNS 08-31064.

References

1. Baader, F., Schulz, K.U.: Unification Theory. In: Automated Deduction. Applied Logic Series, vol. I, 8, pp. 225–263. Kluwer, Dordrecht (1998)
2. Bachmair, L., Dershowitz, N.: Completion for rewriting modulo a congruence. Theor. Comput. Sci. 67(2,3), 173–201 (1989)
3. Cherifa, A.B., Lescanne, P.: Termination of rewriting systems by polynomial interpretations and its implementation. Sci. Comput. Program. 9(2), 137–159 (1987)
4. Clavel, M., Durán, F., Eker, S., Lincoln, P., Martí-Oliet, N., Meseguer, J., Talcott, C.: All About Maude - A High-Performance Logical Framework. LNCS, vol. 4350. Springer, Heidelberg (2007)

5. Comon, H., Delaune, S.: The Finite Variant Property: How to Get Rid of Some Algebraic Properties. In: Giesl, J. (ed.) RTA 2005. LNCS, vol. 3467, pp. 294–307. Springer, Heidelberg (2005)
6. Durán, F., Lucas, S., Meseguer, J.: MTT: The Maude Termination Tool (System Description). In: Armando, A., Baumgartner, P., Dowek, G. (eds.) IJCAR 2008. LNCS (LNAI), vol. 5195, pp. 313–319. Springer, Heidelberg (2008)
7. Durán, F., Lucas, S., Meseguer, J.: Termination Modulo Combinations of Equational Theories (Long Version). University of Illinois Tech. Rep. (June 2009), http://hdl.handle.net/2142/12311
8. Durán, F., Lucas, S., Meseguer, J., Marché, C., Urbain, X.: Proving operational termination of membership equational programs. Higher-Order and Symbolic Computation 21(1-2), 59–88 (2008)
9. Escobar, S., Meseguer, J., Sasse, R.: Effectively Checking the Finite Variant Property. In: Voronkov, A. (ed.) RTA 2008. LNCS, vol. 5117, pp. 79–93. Springer, Heidelberg (2008)
10. Escobar, S., Meseguer, J., Sasse, R.: Variant Narrowing and Equational Unification. In: Proc. of WRLA 2008. ENTCS (2008) (to appear, 2009)
11. Escobar, S., Meseguer, J., Sasse, R.: Variant Narrowing and Extreme Termination. University of Illinois Tech. Rep. UIUCDCS-R-2009-3049 (March 2009)
12. Ferreira, M.C.F.: Dummy elimination in equational rewriting. In: Ganzinger, H. (ed.) RTA 1996. LNCS, vol. 1103. Springer, Heidelberg (1996)
13. Giesl, J., Kapur, D.: Dependency Pairs for Equational Rewriting. In: Middeldorp, A. (ed.) RTA 2001. LNCS, vol. 2051, pp. 93–108. Springer, Heidelberg (2001)
14. Giesl, J., Schneider-Kamp, P., Thiemann, R.: APROVE 1.2: Automatic Termination Proofs in the Dependency Pair Framework. In: Furbach, U., Shankar, N. (eds.) IJCAR 2006. LNCS (LNAI), vol. 4130, pp. 281–286. Springer, Heidelberg (2006)
15. Goguen, J., Meseguer, J.: Order-sorted algebra I: Equational deduction for multiple inheritance, overloading, exceptions and partial operations. Theor. Comput. Sci. 105, 217–273 (1992)
16. Huet, G.: Confluent reductions: Abstract properties and applications to term rewriting systems. Journal of the ACM 27, 797–821 (1980)
17. Jouannaud, J.-P., Kirchner, H.: Completion of a Set of Rules Modulo a Set of Equations. SIAM Journal of Computing 15(4), 1155–1194 (1986)
18. Jouannaud, J.-P., Marché, C.: Termination and completion modulo associativity, commutativity and identity. Theor. Comput. Sci. 104(1), 29–51 (1992)
19. Kirchner, C., Kirchner, H., Meseguer, J.: Operational Semantics of OBJ3. In: Lepistö, T., Salomaa, A. (eds.) ICALP 1988. LNCS, vol. 317, pp. 287–301. Springer, Heidelberg (1988)
20. Lucas, S., Meseguer, J.: Operational Termination of Membership Equational Programs: the Order-Sorted Way. In: Proc. of WRLA 2008. ENTCS (2008) (to appear, 2009)
21. Marché, C.: Normalised rewriting and normalised completion. In: Proc. LICS 1994, pp. 394–403. IEEE, Los Alamitos (1994)
22. Marché, C., Urbain, X.: Termination of associative-commutative rewriting by dependency pairs. In: Nipkow, T. (ed.) RTA 1998, vol. 1379, pp. 241–255. Springer, Heidelberg (1998)
23. Nipkow, T.: Combining Matching Algorithms: The Regular Case. Journal of Symbolic Computation 12, 633–653 (1991)

24. Ohlebusch, E.: Advanced Topics in Term Rewriting. Springer, Heidelberg (2002)
25. Ohsaki, H., Middeldorp, A., Giesl, J.: Equational termination by semantic labelling. In: Clote, P.G., Schwichtenberg, H. (eds.) CSL 2000. LNCS, vol. 1862, pp. 457–471. Springer, Heidelberg (2000)
26. Peterson, G.E., Stickel, M.E.: Complete Sets of Reductions for Some Equational Theories. Journal of the ACM 28(2), 233–264 (1981)
27. Ringeissen, C.: Combination of matching algorithms. In: Enjalbert, P., Mayr, E.W., Wagner, K.W. (eds.) STACS 1994. LNCS, vol. 775, pp. 187–198. Springer, Heidelberg (1994)
28. Rubio, A., Nieuwenhuis, R.: A total AC-compatible ordering based on RPO. Theor. Comput. Sci. 142(2), 209–227 (1995)
29. Viry, P.: Equational rules for rewriting logic. Theor. Comp. Sci. 285, 487–517 (2002)

Combinations of Theories for Decidable Fragments of First-Order Logic*

Pascal Fontaine

Université de Nancy, Loria
Nancy, France
Pascal.Fontaine@loria.fr

Abstract. The design of decision procedures for first-order theories and their combinations has been a very active research subject for thirty years; it has gained practical importance through the development of SMT (satisfiability modulo theories) solvers. Most results concentrate on combining decision procedures for data structures such as theories for arrays, bitvectors, fragments of arithmetic, and uninterpreted functions. In particular, the well-known Nelson-Oppen scheme for the combination of decision procedures requires the signatures to be disjoint and each theory to be stably infinite; every satisfiable set of literals in a stably infinite theory has an infinite model.

In this paper we consider some of the best-known decidable fragments of first-order logic with equality, including the Löwenheim class (monadic FOL with equality, but without functions), Bernays-Schönfinkel-Ramsey theories (finite sets of formulas of the form $\exists^*\forall^*\varphi$, where φ is a function-free and quantifier-free FOL formula), and the two-variable fragment of FOL. In general, these are not stably infinite, and the Nelson-Oppen scheme cannot be used to integrate them into SMT solvers. Noticing some elementary results about the cardinalities of the models of these theories, we show that they can nevertheless be combined with almost any other decidable theory.

1 Introduction

Among automated deduction techniques for the verification of computer systems, SMT solvers (Satisfiability Modulo Theories) are nowadays attracting a lot of interest. These solvers are built on top of SAT solvers for propositional logic and include decision procedures for different first-order theories, thus providing more expressive input languages. Usually, SMT solvers implement a combination of a fixed number of theories such as linear arithmetic, uninterpreted symbols, list operators, bit vectors, etc., based on the classical Nelson-Oppen framework [16,21] for combining decidable theories. This framework covers combinations of disjoint theories provided they are stably infinite: if a set of quantifier-free formulas has a model with respect to a theory, it should also have an infinite model. For instance, a combination of decision procedures for integer linear arithmetic

---

* This work is partly supported by the ANR project DECERT.

and for the empty theory (equality and uninterpreted symbols) can detect the unsatisfiability of the formula

$$x \leq y \wedge y \leq x + f(x) \wedge P(h(x) - h(y)) \wedge \neg P(0) \wedge f(x) = 0.$$

The Bernays-Schönfinkel-Ramsey (BSR) class [4,17] is certainly the most well-known decidable class of first-order theories. A BSR theory is a finite set (conjunction) of formulas of the form $\exists^* \forall^* \varphi$, where the first-order formula φ is function-free and quantifier-free. Many verification problems generate formulas in this class (see for instance [11]). The CASC competition [20] for first-order theorem provers has a dedicated division (EPR, Effectively Propositional) for this class. BSR theories are in general not stably infinite. As a trivial example, consider the BSR theory $\forall x \forall y . x = y$ that only accepts models with singleton domains. The Nelson-Oppen framework does not apply to combinations including BSR theories.

A Löwenheim theory with equality is a finite set of closed formulas in a language containing only unary predicates, and no function except constants. This class is also known as first-order relational monadic logic, and it is decidable. The theory $\forall x \forall y . x = y$ also belongs to the Löwenheim class, and hence the Nelson-Oppen framework does not apply to this class.

The last decidable class we study in this paper is the class of finitely axiomatized first-order theories built in a language with equality, only two variables, and no functions (except constants). Again $\forall x \forall y . x = y$ belongs to this class, and the Nelson-Oppen framework is not appropriate.

The objective of the present paper is to lay the ground for incorporating theories from these three well-known classes into SMT solvers.

We are not aware of previous combination results about the full Löwenheim class with equality or the full two-variable fragment with equality. However, it has already been observed [23] that, thanks to its finite model property, a BSR theory can be combined with a theory $\mathcal{T}$ provided the following conditions hold:

- if a set of ground literals L is $\mathcal{T}$-satisfiable, then the minimal cardinality of $\mathcal{T}$-models for L can be computed;
- $\mathcal{T}$ only has finite models.

The second requirement is quite strong. In particular, it is not satisfied by combinations including decidable fragments of arithmetic, which admit only infinite models. For example, the combination scheme of [23] cannot be used to decide the satisfiability of the set of literals such as

$$\{a > 0, a < 2, a + b = 2, b > 0, A(f(a)), \neg C(f(b))\}$$

(where $a, b, f(a), f(b)$ are integers and $+, <, >, 0, 2$ have their usual meaning over integers) with respect to the BSR theory

$$\mathcal{T} = \{\forall x \, [(A(x) \vee B(x)) \equiv (C(x) \vee D(x))]\}.$$

The classical Nelson-Oppen combination scheme and that of [23] introduce rather strong requirements on the theories in the combination, and these requirements ensure that component theories agree on model cardinalities. For instance, the stably infinite requirement ensures that both theories will agree on the cardinality $\aleph_0$ for their models. But essentially, the combination process is a matter of matching the interpretation of shared symbols (by exchanging disjunction of equalities), and cardinalities of the models of the theories [12,23,9].

We observe in this paper that it is possible to compute all the cardinalities of models admitted by a theory in the BSR, Löwenheim, or two-variable classes with equality. The set of cardinalities accepted by such theories even has a very particular structure. In section 3 we characterize this structure, and show that any decidable theory that verifies this property can be combined with a decidable theory $\mathcal{T}$ provided $\mathcal{T}$ fulfils very liberal constraints. These constraints are trivially met in most practical cases.

For convenience, the results in this paper are presented in an *unsorted* framework, although most SMT-solvers work in a many-sorted logic framework (see for instance [8]). Our results could be transferred to a many-sorted framework, at the expense of heavier notations.

The remainder of this paper is structured as follows: Section 2 introduces basic concepts and notations. Section 3 presents the general scheme for combining (not necessarily stably infinite) theories, and introduces the required notions for the new combination results with the considered first-order decidable classes. Sections 4, 5 and 6 respectively present essential cardinality results about the Löwenheim, BSR, and two-variables classes. We do not claim that the results in those three sections are original. Some of them can be found in classical Model Theory books [5,6,7]. But some of them are less known. This paper thus presents them together, and relates them to the combination scheme. Section 7 presents a simple example, and Section 8 concludes the paper.

2   Notations

A first-order language is a tuple $\mathcal{L} = \langle \mathcal{V}, \mathcal{F}, \mathcal{P} \rangle$ such that $\mathcal{V}$ is an enumerable set of variables, $\mathcal{F}$ and $\mathcal{P}$ are sets of function and predicate symbols. Every function and predicate symbol is assigned an arity. Nullary predicates are propositions, and nullary functions are constants. Terms and formulas over the language $\mathcal{L}$ are defined in the usual way. A ground term is a term without variables. An atomic formula is either $t = t'$ where t and t' are terms, or a predicate symbol applied to the right number of terms. Formulas are built from atomic formulas, Boolean connectives ($\neg$, $\wedge$, $\vee$, $\Rightarrow$, $\equiv$), and quantifiers ($\forall$, $\exists$). A formula with no free variables is closed. A theory is a set of closed formulas. Two theories are disjoint if no predicate symbol in $\mathcal{P}$ or function symbol in $\mathcal{F}$ appears in both theories. A finite theory or a finitely axiomatized theory is a finite set of formulas.

An interpretation $\mathcal{I}$ for a first-order language provides a domain D, a total function $\mathcal{I}[f] : D^r \to D$ of appropriate arity for every function symbol f, a predicate $\mathcal{I}[p] : D^r \to \{\top, \bot\}$ of appropriate arity for every predicate symbol p, and an element $\mathcal{I}[x] \in D$ for every variable x. By extension, an interpretation defines a value in D for every term, and a truth value for every formula. The notation $\mathcal{I}_{x_1/d_1,\ldots,x_n/d_n}$ stands for the interpretation that agrees with $\mathcal{I}$, except that it associates the elements d_i to the variables x_i.

A model of a formula (or a theory) is an interpretation in which the formula (resp., every formula in the theory) evaluates to true. A formula or theory is satisfiable if it has a model, and it is unsatisfiable otherwise. A formula G is $\mathcal{T}$-satisfiable if it is satisfiable in the theory $\mathcal{T}$, that is, if $\mathcal{T} \cup \{G\}$ is satisfiable. A $\mathcal{T}$-model of G is a model of $\mathcal{T} \cup \{G\}$. A formula G is $\mathcal{T}$-unsatisfiable if it has no $\mathcal{T}$-models.

The cardinality of an interpretation is the cardinality of its domain. The restriction of a predicate p on domain D to domain $D' \subseteq D$ is the predicate p' with domain D' such that p and p' have the same truth value for all arguments in D'.

A formula is universal if it is of the form $\forall x_1 \ldots \forall x_n.\varphi$ where φ is quantifier-free. A Skolem formula is a formula where all universal quantifiers appear with a positive polarity, and all existential quantifiers appear with a negative polarity. It is always possible to transform a given formula into an equisatisfiable Skolem formula, using Skolemization. We refer to [2] for Skolemization.

3   Combination of Theories

Assume we want to study the satisfiability of the set of literals

$$L = \{a \le b, b \le a + f(a), P(h(a) - h(b)), \neg P(0), f(a) = 0\}$$

in the combination of the integer linear arithmetic theory $\mathcal{T}_1$ and the empty theory (i.e. the theory of uninterpreted symbols) $\mathcal{T}_2$. First, a *separation* is built by introducing fresh uninterpreted constants[1], to produce the equisatisfiable problem

$$L_1 = \{a \le b,\, b \le a + v_1,\, v_1 = 0,\, v_2 = v_3 - v_4,\, v_5 = 0\}$$
$$L_2 = \{P(v_2),\, \neg P(v_5),\, v_1 = f(a),\, v_3 = h(a),\, v_4 = h(b)\}.$$

The set L_1 only contains arithmetic symbols and uninterpreted constants. The symbols in L_2 are all uninterpreted. The only shared symbols are the uninterpreted constants in the set $S = \{a, b, v_1, v_2, v_3, v_4, v_5\}$. Notice that although L is unsatisfiable in $\mathcal{T}_1 \cup \mathcal{T}_2$, L_1 is $\mathcal{T}_1$-satisfiable, and L_2 is $\mathcal{T}_2$-satisfiable; it is not sufficient for the decision procedures for $\mathcal{T}_1$ and $\mathcal{T}_2$ to only examine the satisfiability of their part of the separation. Indeed, the decision procedures also have to "agree on the common part". This can be captured using the notion of arrangement:

Definition 1. *An arrangement $\mathcal{A}$ for a set of constant symbols S is a maximal satisfiable set of equalities and inequalities $a = b$ or $a \ne b$, with $a, b \in S$.*

The following theorem (other formulations can be found in [22,23,12]) then states the completeness of the combination of decision procedures:

---

[1] Traditionally combination schemes use variables for this role. Since variables will be used in quantifiers in the following sections, for consistency and clarity we will rather use uninterpreted constants here.

Theorem 1. *Assume T_1 and T_2 are theories over the disjoint languages $\mathcal{L}_1$ and $\mathcal{L}_2$, and L_i ($i = 1, 2$) is a set of literals in $\mathcal{L}_i$ augmented by a finite set of fresh constant symbols S. Then $L_1 \cup L_2$ is $T_1 \cup T_2$-satisfiable if and only if there exist an arrangement $\mathcal{A}$ of S, a cardinality k, and a T_i-model $\mathcal{M}_i$ of $\mathcal{A} \cup L_i$ with cardinality k for $i = 1, 2$.*

Proof. Assume $\mathcal{I}$ is an interpretation on domain D for a language $\mathcal{L}$, and $\mathcal{L}'$ is a sub-language of $\mathcal{L}$, i.e. the set of variable, function, and predicate symbols in $\mathcal{L}'$ are subsets of their counterpart in $\mathcal{L}$. We say that the interpretation $\mathcal{I}'$ on domain D for language $\mathcal{L}'$ is the restriction of $\mathcal{I}$ if $\mathcal{I}'$ and $\mathcal{I}$ give the same interpretation for the symbols in $\mathcal{L}'$.

The condition is necessary. Assume $\mathcal{M}$ is a $T_1 \cup T_2$-model for $L_1 \cup L_2$. $\mathcal{M}$ perfectly defines an arrangement $\mathcal{A}$ of S: indeed $a = b \in \mathcal{A}$ with $a, b \in S$ iff $a = b$ is true according to $\mathcal{M}$. The restriction of $\mathcal{M}$ to $\mathcal{L}_i$ augmented with the constant symbols S is a T_i-model for $\mathcal{A} \cup L_i$, $i = 1, 2$.

The condition is sufficient. Assume that $\mathcal{A}$ is an arrangement for S, $\mathcal{M}_1$ on domain D_1 is a T_1-model for $\mathcal{A} \cup L_1$, $\mathcal{M}_2$ on domain D_2 is a T_2-model for $\mathcal{A} \cup L_2$, and $|D_1| = |D_2|$. Since both $\mathcal{M}_1$ and $\mathcal{M}_2$ are models of $\mathcal{A}$, there exist two interpretations $\mathcal{M}_1'$ and $\mathcal{M}_2'$ on the same domain that are respectively isomorphic to $\mathcal{M}_1$ and $\mathcal{M}_2$ and such that $\mathcal{M}_1'[a] = \mathcal{M}_2'[a]$ for every $a \in S$. It is then possible to build an interpretation $\mathcal{M}$ such that its restriction to the language $\mathcal{L}_i$ augmented with S is $\mathcal{M}_i'$, $i = 1, 2$. $\mathcal{M}$ is a $T_1 \cup T_2$-model of $L_1 \cup L_2$. □

Checking the existence of a model is the task of the decision procedures for the decidable theories in the combination. The previous theorem however also imposes a restriction on cardinalities: the two decision procedures should exhibit a model with the same cardinality. A theory T is said to be stably infinite when every T-satisfiable set of literals has a model with cardinality $\aleph_0$. Combining only stably infinite theories is a radical solution to the cardinality requirement in the previous theorem; k can always be $\aleph_0$. Since the empty theory and the theory of integer linear arithmetic are both stably infinite, the set of literals L in our example is $T_1 \cup T_2$-satisfiable if and only if there exists an arrangement $\mathcal{A}$ of the seven variables in S such that $\mathcal{A} \cup L_i$ is T_i-satisfiable for $i = 1$ and $i = 2$. No such arrangements exist, and indeed, L is $T_1 \cup T_2$-unsatisfiable.

The first-order decidable classes considered in this paper contain theories that are not stably infinite. For instance the formula $\forall x\, (x = a \lor x = b)$ belongs to the BSR, Löwenheim and two variable classes, and it only accepts models with at most two elements. A combination scheme to handle such theories requires to carefully examine cardinalities. The notion of spectrum is helpful for this task:

Definition 2. *The spectrum of a theory T is the set of cardinalities k such that T is satisfiable in a model of cardinality k.*[2]

Using this definition and Theorem 1, a combination scheme for disjoint theories (not necessarily stably infinite) can thus be easily expressed:

---

[2] The spectrum of a theory is usually defined as the set of the *finite* cardinalities of its models. We here slightly extend the definition for convenience.

Corollary 1. *Given two theories T_1 and T_2 over the disjoint languages $\mathcal{L}_1$ and $\mathcal{L}_2$, the $T_1 \cup T_2$-satisfiability problem for sets of literals (written in the union of the languages $\mathcal{L}_1$ and $\mathcal{L}_2$) is decidable if, for any sets of literals L_1 and L_2 (respectively written in the languages $\mathcal{L}_1$ and $\mathcal{L}_2$ augmented with a finite set of fresh uninterpreted constants) it is possible to compute if the intersection of the spectrums for $T_1 \cup L_1$ and for $T_2 \cup L_2$ is non-empty.*

In the case of stably infinite decidable theories, it is guaranteed that, if $T_1 \cup L_1$ and $T_2 \cup L_2$ are satisfiable, both spectrums contain cardinality $\aleph_0$, and so their intersection is trivially non-empty.

To characterize the spectrum of the decidable classes considered in this paper, we introduce the following property:

Definition 3. *A theory T is gentle if, for every set L of literals in the language of T (augmented by a finite number of fresh constants), the spectrum of $T \cup L$ can be computed and is either*

- *a finite set of finite cardinalities*
- *the union of a finite set of finite cardinalities and all the (finite and infinite) cardinalities greater than a computable finite cardinality; it is thus co-finite.*

A gentle theory is decidable. In the following sections, we show that the BSR theories, the Löwenheim theories, and finite theories with only two variables are gentle. The empty theory, as a special case of a BSR theory, is gentle. Shiny theories in general (see [23]) are gentle. We also have the following result:

Theorem 2. *The union of disjoint gentle theories is a gentle theory.*

Proof. The case for the union of any number of disjoint gentle theories can be proved by induction, and using the case for two gentle theories.

The intersection of two spectrums of gentle theories is also either a finite set of finite cardinalities, or the union of a finite set of finite cardinalities and all the (finite and infinite) cardinalities greater than a (computable) finite cardinality. The case for two gentle theories is thus a direct consequence of Theorem 1. □

We point out that a theory T taking part in a combination of theories has some interesting property about its spectrum. Since the T-satisfiability problem for sets of literals (written in the language of the theory plus fresh constants) is decidable, it is also possible to assess for any set of literals L if $T \cup L$ has a model of cardinality greater than a given number k. Indeed it suffices to introduce k new constants $a_1, \ldots, a_k$ and check the satisfiability of $T \cup L \cup \{a_i \neq a_j \mid i \neq j, \; i, j = 1, \ldots, k\}$. Also notice that it is always possible to decide if a finite first-order theory admits a model of a given finite cardinality. Indeed there are only a finite number of interpretations for a finite language, and it takes a finite time to check if a given finite interpretation is a model of the finite theory.

Some widely used theories are not gentle, but in practical cases they can be combined with gentle theories:

Theorem 3. *Given a gentle theory T and another disjoint theory T', the $T \cup T'$-satisfiability problem for sets of literals written in the union of their language is decidable if one of the following cases holds:*

- T' *is gentle;*
- T' *is a decidable finitely axiomatixed first-order theory;*
- T' *is a decidable theory that only admits a fixed finite (possibly empty) known set of finite cardinalities for its models, and possibly infinite models.*

Proof. Assume $L \cup L'$ is the separation to check for $T \cup T'$-satisfiability. If an arrangement $\mathcal{A}$ is such that $\mathcal{A} \cup L$ is T-satisfiable, and $\mathcal{A} \cup L'$ is T'-satisfiable, then it is possible to compute the spectrum S of $T \cup \mathcal{A} \cup L$. Either S is a finite set of finite cardinalities, or it is a union of a finite set of finite cardinalities and the set of all cardinalities greater than a number k.

If T' is also gentle, it is possible to compute the spectrum of $T' \cup \mathcal{A} \cup L'$, and the intersection of the two spectrums can easily be computed.

If T' is a decidable finite first-order theory, it is possible to check if $T' \cup \mathcal{A} \cup L'$ admits a cardinality in the finite part of S, and, if S is infinite, it is possible to check if $T' \cup \mathcal{A} \cup L'$ admits a cardinality greater than k.

If T' is a decidable theory that only admits a fixed finite known set of cardinalities for its models, it suffices to check if one of these cardinalities is in the spectrum S. The considered theories are first-order, and the Löwenheim-Skolem theorem states that, if a theory has an infinite model, it has models for every infinite cardinality. Infinite cardinalities can thus be understood as one cardinality. □

For instance, the real or integer linear arithmetic theories (or combinations involving real or integer linear arithmetic) fall into the last case, and the usual theories for arrays fall into the second one.

4   The Löwenheim Class with Equality

A Löwenheim theory is a finite set of closed formulas in a language containing only unary predicates, and no functions except constants. This class is also known as first-order relational monadic logic. Usually one distinguishes the Löwenheim class with and without equality. The Löwenheim class has the finite model property (and is thus decidable) even with equality. Full monadic logic *without equality*, i.e. the class of finite theories over a language containing symbols (predicates and functions) of arity at most 1, also has the finite model property. Considering monadic logic with equality, the class of finite theories over a language containing only unary predicates and just two unary functions is already undecidable. With only one unary function however the class remains decidable, but does not have the finite model property anymore. Since the spectrum for this last class is significantly more complicated [14] than for the Löwenheim class we will here only concentrate on the Löwenheim class with equality (only classes with equality are relevant in our context). More can be found about monadic first-order logic in [5,6]. In particular, the following Theorem can be found in [6]:

Theorem 4. *Assume T is a Löwenheim theory with equality with n distinct unary predicates. Let q be the number of constants plus the maximum number of nested quantifiers in T. If T has a model of some cardinality $\geq q\,2^n$, then T has models of every cardinality $> q\,2^n$.*

Proof. For simplicity, assume T is constant-free and is a single formula. Because T is finite, it is always possible to get back to such a case by taking the conjunction of all formulas in T, and then quantify existentially over all constants in the formula.

Let $p_1, \ldots, p_n$ be the unary predicates used in T. Given an interpretation $\mathcal{I}$ on domain D for T, every element $d \in D$ has a color $c(d) = c_1 \ldots c_n \in \{\top, \bot\}^n$ where $c_i = \mathcal{I}[p_i](d)$. We denote by $D_c \subseteq D$ the set of elements with color c.

Two interpretations $\mathcal{I}$ (on domain D) and $\mathcal{I}'$ (on domain D') for a formula ψ are *similar* if

– either $D_c = D'_c$ or $|D_c \cap D'_c| \geq q$ for every color $c \in \{\top, \bot\}^n$;
– $D_c \cap D'_{c'} = \emptyset$ for any two distinct colors $c, c' \in \{\top, \bot\}^n$;
– $\mathcal{I}[x] = \mathcal{I}'[x]$ for every variable free in ψ.

We first prove that, given a formula ψ, two similar interpretations for ψ give the same truth value to ψ and to every sub-formula of ψ.

This is proved by induction on the structure of the (sub-)formula ψ. It is obvious if ψ is atomic, since similar interpretations assign the same value to variables, and since ψ is variable-free. If ψ is $\neg\varphi_1$, $\varphi_1 \vee \varphi_2$, $\varphi_1 \wedge \varphi_2$ or $\varphi_1 \Rightarrow \varphi_2$, the result holds if it also holds for φ_1 and φ_2.

Assume $\mathcal{I}$ makes true the formula $\psi = \exists x \, \varphi(x)$. Then there exists some $d \in D$ such that $\mathcal{I}_{x/d}$ is a model of $\varphi(x)$. If $d \in D'$, then $\mathcal{I}'_{x/d}$ is similar to $\mathcal{I}_{x/d}$ and, by the induction hypothesis, it is a model of $\varphi(x)$; $\mathcal{I}'$ is thus a model of ψ. If $d \notin D'$, it means that $D_{c(d)} \cap D'_{c(d)} \geq q$. Furthermore, since the whole formula contains at most q nested quantifiers, $\varphi(x)$ contains at most $q - 1$ free variables. Let $x_1, \ldots, x_m$ be those variables. There exists some $d' \in D_{c(d)} \cap D'_{c(d)}$ such that $d' \neq \mathcal{I}[x_i]$ for every $i \in \{1, \ldots, m\}$. By structural induction, it is easy to show that $\mathcal{I}_{x/d}$ and $\mathcal{I}_{x/d'}$ give the same truth value to $\varphi(x)$. Furthermore $\mathcal{I}_{x/d'}$ and $\mathcal{I}'_{x/d'}$ are similar. $\mathcal{I}'$ is thus a model of ψ. To summarize, if $\mathcal{I}$ is a model of ψ, $\mathcal{I}'$ is also a model of ψ. By symmetry, if $\mathcal{I}'$ is a model of ψ, $\mathcal{I}$ is also a model of ψ. Thus, if $\psi = \exists x \, \varphi(x)$, the results hold if it also holds for $\varphi(x)$. The proof for formulas of the form $\forall x \, \varphi(x)$ is dual.

If $\mathcal{M}$ on domain D is a model for T with cardinality $\geq q \, 2^n$, then there exists a color c such that $|D_c| \geq q$. For any cardinality $k \geq q \, 2^n$ one can build a model $\mathcal{M}'$ of cardinality k for T, similar to $\mathcal{M}$. $\qquad\square$

Corollary 2. *The Löwenheim class has the finite model property.*

Proof. Assume T is a Löwenheim theory, with n distinct unary predicates. Let q be the maximum number of nested quantifiers in T. Let $\mathcal{I}$ be a model of T. According to Theorem 4, if $\mathcal{I}$ has an infinite cardinality ($\geq q \, 2^n$), T also has a finite model (e.g. of cardinality $q \, 2^n$). $\qquad\square$

Corollary 3. *The satisfiability problem for the Löwenheim class is decidable.*

Proof. It is well-known that any class of finite first-order theories that has the finite model property is also decidable. The decidability of the Löwenheim class can also be easily proved directly. Assume T is a Löwenheim theory, with n distinct unary predicates. Let q be the maximum number of nested quantifiers in T. There exist only a finite number of interpretations of a finite theory for a given cardinality. It is thus decidable to check if T has a model of cardinality $q\,2^n$. If such a model exists T is satisfiable. If no such models exist, Theorem 4 states that T has no models of cardinality $\geq q\,2^n$. It remains to decide if T has a model of cardinality $< q\,2^n$, i.e. it remains to examine a finite number of interpretations.   □

Corollary 4. *The spectrum of a Löwenheim theory can be computed and expressed either as a finite set of naturals, or as the union of a finite set of naturals with the set of all the (finite or infinite) cardinalities greater than a natural. The Löwenheim theories are gentle.*

5   The Bernays-Schönfinkel-Ramsey Class

A Bernays-Schönfinkel-Ramsey theory (BSR) is a finite set of formulas of the form $\exists^*\forall^*\varphi$, where φ is a first-order formula which is function-free (but constants are allowed) and quantifier-free. Bernays and Schönfinkel first proved the decidability of this class without equality; Ramsey later proved that it remains decidable with equality. The results about the spectrum of BSR theories are less known, but were also originally found by Ramsey.

For simplicity, we will assume that existential quantifiers are Skolemized. In the following, a BSR theory is thus a finite closed set of universal function-free first-order formulas.

Theorem 5. *Let T be a BSR theory, and let k_c be the number of constants in T, or $k_c = 1$ if T is constant-free. If T has a model with cardinality $k \geq k_c$, then T has a model for every cardinality i, with $k \geq i \geq k_c$.*

Proof. Given a model $\mathcal{M}$ for a BSR theory T with domain D, then any interpretation $\mathcal{M}'$ such that

- the domain of $\mathcal{M}'$ is a non-empty set $D' \subseteq D$ such that $\mathcal{M}'[a] = \mathcal{M}[a] \in D'$ for every constant a in T, and
- for every predicate p, $\mathcal{M}'[p]$ is the restriction of $\mathcal{M}[p]$ to the domain D'

is also a model of T. Intuitively, this states that the elements in the domain that are not assigned to ground terms (i.e. the constants) can be eliminated in a model of a BSR theory. Since $\mathcal{M}$ is a model of T, for each closed formula $\forall x_1 \ldots x_n.\varphi$ in T (where φ is function-free and quantifier-free), and for all $d_1, \ldots, d_n \in D' \subseteq D$, $\mathcal{M}_{x_1/d_1,\ldots,x_n/d_n}$ is a model of φ. This also means that, for all $d_1, \ldots, d_n \in D'$, $\mathcal{M}'_{x_1/d_1,\ldots,x_n/d_n}$ is a model of φ, and finally that $\mathcal{M}'$ is a model of $\forall x_1 \ldots x_n.\varphi$.   □

Theorem 6. *There exists a computable function f such that, for any BSR theory T, if T has a model of some cardinality $\geq f(T)$, then it has a model for every cardinality $\geq f(T)$.*

Proof. The proof is quite long and requires a non trivial theorem on hypergraph coloring. A partial proof can be found in [6], and a full self-contained proof can be found in the full version of the paper [10].   □

The proofs of the following corollaries are similar to the corresponding proofs for the Löwenheim class.

Corollary 5. *The BSR class has the finite model property.*

Corollary 6. *The satisfiability problem for the BSR class is decidable.*

Corollary 7. *The spectrum of a BSR theory can be computed and expressed either as a finite set of naturals, or as the union of a finite set of naturals with the set of all the (finite or infinite) cardinalities greater than a natural. BSR theories are gentle.*

6   First-Order Logic with Two Variables

Following [7], we will denote by FO^2 the class of finite theories built over a language with only two variables, and no functions (except constants). The satisfiability problem for FO^2 is known to be decidable with and without equality (see for instance [5,7,13]). Again, we will only concentrate here on the language with equality. This class has the finite model property, and also has very nice properties concerning the cardinalities of its models.

The Scott class is a subset of FO^2: it is the class of finite theories over a language with only two variables, and no functions (except constants) such that every formula in the theory is of the form $\forall x \forall y \, \varphi(x, y)$ or $\forall x \exists y \, \varphi(x, y)$ where $\varphi(x, y)$ is quantifier-free. The satisfiability problem for FO^2 (with equality) is traditionally translated into the satisfiability problem for the Scott class, using the following theorem (see [5,7] for equivalent theorems):

Theorem 7. *There exists an algorithm that, for each finite theory T of FO^2, constructs a theory T' in the Scott class such that T has a model of a given cardinality if and only if T' has a model of the same cardinality. The size of T' is linear with respect to the size of T.*

Proof. First notice that formula $\forall x \, (R(x) \equiv Qy \, \varphi(x,y))$ where Q is either $\exists$ or $\forall$ can be rewritten as a set of formulas in the required form:

- $\forall x \, (R(x) \equiv \forall y \, \varphi(x,y)) \longleftrightarrow \forall x \forall y \, (R(x) \Rightarrow \varphi(x,y)) \wedge \forall x \exists y \, (\varphi(x,y) \Rightarrow R(x))$
- $\forall x \, (R(x) \equiv \exists y \, \varphi(x,y)) \longleftrightarrow \forall x \exists y \, (R(x) \Rightarrow \varphi(x,y)) \wedge \forall x \forall y \, (\varphi(x,y) \Rightarrow R(x))$

The theory T can thus be rewritten into a suitable theory T' by iteratively applying the following step until no more formulas of unsuitable form exist in the theory:

- select a formula ψ in the theory that does not have the required form;
- choose a sub-formula of form $Qy \, \varphi(x,y)$ of ψ where Q is $\exists$ or $\forall$ and $\varphi(x,y)$ is quantifier-free;
- take a new unary predicate R not used in the theory;

- define the formula ψ' as ψ where $Qy\,\varphi(x,y)$ has been substituted by $R(x)$;
- remove ψ from the theory, and add ψ', and the formulas in the required form for $\forall x\,(R(x) \equiv Qy\,\varphi(x,y))$. □

The following theorem is left as an exercice in [7]. For completeness we here give the full proof.

Theorem 8. *There exists a computable function f such that, for any Scott theory $\mathcal{T}$, if $\mathcal{T}$ has a model of some cardinality $\geq f(\mathcal{T})$, then $\mathcal{T}$ has models for every cardinality $\geq f(\mathcal{T})$.*

Proof. We first assume that every formula ψ_i in $\mathcal{T}$ ($i = 1, \ldots, m$) of the form $\forall x \exists y\,\varphi(x,y)$ is such that every model of $\varphi(x,y)$ is a model of $x \neq y$. This assumption is acceptable if $f(\mathcal{T}) \geq 2$ for all Scott theories $\mathcal{T}$ since for all models with at least two elements $\forall x \exists y\,\varphi(x,y)$ is equivalent to $\forall x \exists y\,.\,x \neq y \wedge (\varphi(x,y) \vee \varphi(x,x))$.

For the rest of the proof, we assume that the Scott theory $\mathcal{T}$ has a model $\mathcal{M}$ on domain D. We define the sets $A = \{\mathcal{M}[a] : a$ is a constant in $\mathcal{T}\}$ and $B = D \setminus A$. We establish that if B is larger than a computable cardinality $\geq f(\mathcal{T})$, one can build a model for every cardinality $\geq f(\mathcal{T})$.

Given a first-order language $\mathcal{L}$, a k-table[3] $T[x_1, \ldots, x_k]$ over the variables $x_1, \ldots, x_k$ is a maximal satisfiable set of atomic formulas and negation of atomic formulas using only variables $x_1, \ldots, x_k$. Given an interpretation $\mathcal{I}$ on domain D and k elements $d_1, \ldots, d_k$ of D, the k-table of $d_1, \ldots, d_k$ (denoted $T_{\mathcal{I}}[d_1, \ldots, d_k]$) is the unique k-table $T[x_1, \ldots, x_k]$ such that the interpretation $\mathcal{I}_{x_1/d_1, \ldots, x_k/d_k}$ is a model of $T[x_1, \ldots, x_k]$. Notice that there are only a finite number of k-tables, for a finite language with no functions except constants. In particular if A is the set of constants, a 1-table is determined by at most $b = \sum_p (|A| + 1)^{\mathrm{arity}(p)}$ Boolean values, where the sum ranges over all predicates in the language. Indeed, given a predicate p of arity r, there are at most $(|A| + 1)^r$ terms that can be built with p and $A \cup \{x\}$. Thus the number of different 1-tables is bounded by $C = 2^b$.

For every formula $\psi_i = \forall x \exists y\,\varphi_i(x,y)$ in $\mathcal{T}$ ($i = 1, \ldots, m$), there exists a total function g_i on domain D ranging on D such that $\mathcal{M}[\varphi_i](d, g_i(d))$ is true for every $d \in D$. The set K (commonly referred as the set of kings) is defined as the union of A and of the possibly empty set of all elements of $d \in D$ such that the 1-table of d is unique, i.e. $T_{\mathcal{M}}[d'] \neq T_{\mathcal{M}}[d]$ for every $d' \in D$ such that $d' \neq d$. The set C (commonly referred as the court) is the possibly empty set $C = K \cup \{g_i(d) \mid d \in K, i = 1, \ldots, m\}$. The set S is defined as $T_{\mathcal{M}}[D] \setminus T_{\mathcal{M}}[C]$ where $T_{\mathcal{M}}[D]$ is the set of all 1-tables of elements in D (and similarly for $T_{\mathcal{M}}[C]$). We choose a function h on domain S that ranges on D such that $T_{\mathcal{M}}[h(t)] = t$.

The set D' is defined as $C \cup (S \times \{1, \ldots, m\} \times \{0, 1, 2\})$. A model $\mathcal{M}'$ on D' for $\mathcal{T}$ is defined such that:

- $T_{\mathcal{M}'}[d_1, \ldots, d_k] = T_{\mathcal{M}}[d_1, \ldots, d_k]$ for $d_1, \ldots d_k \in C$, $k \in \mathbb{N}$;
- $T_{\mathcal{M}'}[(t, i, j)]$ is t, for every $(t, i, j) \in D' \setminus C$;
- if $g_i(h(t)) \in K$ then $T_{\mathcal{M}'}[(t, i, j), g_i(h(t))] = T_{\mathcal{M}}[h(t), g_i(h(t))]$;

---

[3] We here adopt the notation of [5]. The same notion is also called (atomic) k-type, for instance in [13].

- if $g_i(h(t)) \notin K$ then $T_{\mathcal{M}'}[(t,i,j),(T_{\mathcal{M}}(g_i(h(t))),i,(j+1) \mod 3)]$ is equal to $T_{\mathcal{M}}[h(t),g_i(h(t))]$
- if not yet defined $T_{\mathcal{M}'}[d'_1,d'_2]$ is $T_{\mathcal{M}}[d_1,d_2]$, where d_i is chosen such that $T_{\mathcal{M}}[d_i] = T_{\mathcal{M}'}[d'_i]$ $(i=1,2)$.

The undefined interpretations are not relevant for interpreting the theory and can be arbitrarily defined. The previous assignments are non-conflicting, i.e. 2-tables are never defined twice inconsistently.

Assume $\forall x \forall y \, \varphi(x,y)$ belongs to $\mathcal{T}$. Then $\mathcal{M}'_{x/d'_1,y/d'_2}\varphi(x,y) = \top$ since there exists d_1 and d_2 such that $T_{\mathcal{M}}[d_1,d_2] = T_{\mathcal{M}'}[d'_1,d'_2]$. It remains to prove that $\mathcal{M}'$ is a model of every formula $\forall x \exists y \, \varphi_i(x,y)$ in $\mathcal{T}$, or equivalently, that for every $d \in D'$, $\mathcal{M}'_{x/d}$ is a model of $\exists y \, \varphi_i(x,y)$:

- if $d \in K$, $g_i(d) \in C \subseteq D'$, and $\mathcal{M}'_{x/d,y/g_i(d)}$ is a model of $\varphi_i(x,y)$;
- if $d \in C \setminus K$, if $g_i(d) \in C$ then $\mathcal{M}'_{x/d,y/g_i(d)}$ is a model of $\varphi_i(x,y)$;
- if $d \in C \setminus K$, if $g_i(d) \notin C$ then $T_{\mathcal{M}'}[d,(T_{\mathcal{M}}(g_i(d)),i,0)] = T_{\mathcal{M}}[d,g_i(d)]$, and thus $\mathcal{M}'_{x/d,y/(T_{\mathcal{M}}(g_i(d)),i,0)}$ is a model of $\varphi_i(x,y)$;
- if $d = (t,i,j) \in D' \setminus C$, if $g_i(h(t)) \in K$ then $T_{\mathcal{M}'}[(t,i,j),g_i(h(t))] = T_{\mathcal{M}}[h(t),g_i(h(t))]$, and thus $\mathcal{M}'_{x/d,y/g_i(h(t))}$ is a model of $\varphi_i(x,y)$;
- if $d = (t,i,j) \in D' \setminus C$, if $g_i(h(t)) \notin K$ then $T_{\mathcal{M}'}[(t,i,j),(T_{\mathcal{M}}(g_i(h(t))),i,(j+1) \mod 3)] = T_{\mathcal{M}}[h(t),g_i(h(t)]$, and thus $\mathcal{M}'_{x/d,y/(T_{\mathcal{M}}(g_i(h(t))),i,(j+1) \mod 3)}$ is a model of $\varphi_i(x,y)$.

Finally notice that $D \setminus K$ is necessarily non-empty if $|D| \geq 2^b + 1 + |A|$. In the process of building $\mathcal{M}'$, any element $(t,i,0)$ may be duplicated, thus creating models of arbitrary size $\geq 3m\, 2^b + (m+1)|A|$ where m is the number of formulas of the form $\forall x \exists y \, \varphi(x,y)$ in $\mathcal{T}$.   □

Corollary 8. *There exists a computable function f such that, for any finite theory $\mathcal{T}$ of FO^2, if $\mathcal{T}$ has a model of some cardinality $\geq f(\mathcal{T})$, then $\mathcal{T}$ has models for every cardinality $\geq f(\mathcal{T})$.*

Corollary 9. *The class of finite theories of FO^2 has the finite model property.*

Corollary 10. *The satisfiability problem for finite theories of FO^2 is decidable.*

Corollary 11. *The spectrum of a finite theory of FO^2 can be computed and expressed as a finite set of naturals, or as the union of a finite set of naturals with the set of all the (finite or infinite) cardinalities greater than a natural. The finite theories of FO^2 are gentle.*

7   An Example

Assume that one wants to study the satisfiability of the simple example given in the introduction:

$$\{a > 0, a < 2, a + b = 2, b > 0, A(f(a)), \neg C(f(b))\}$$

in the combination of the theories

$$T_1 = \forall x \left[(A(x) \lor B(x)) \equiv (C(x) \lor D(x)) \right]$$

and T_2, where T_2 is itself the combination of the theory of uninterpreted functions and linear arithmetic over the integers. The theory T_2 is decidable, and a decision procedure can be built using the standard Nelson-Oppen scheme since both components are stably infinite. The domain of the models of T_2 is always the set of integers, thus all models have cardinality $\aleph_0$. The theory T_1 belongs to the BSR, Löwenheim, and two-variables classes and is thus gentle.[4] The third case of Theorem 3 is fulfilled. First, a separation is built, to produce the equisatisfiable problem $L_1 \cup L_2$ with

$$L_1 = \{A(t), \neg C(u)\}$$
$$L_2 = \{a > 0, a < 2, a + b = 2, b > 0, t = f(a), u = f(b)\}.$$

The set $L_1 \cup L_2$ is $T_1 \cup T_2$-satisfiable if and only if there exists a T_1-model $\mathcal{M}_1$ for L_1 and a T_2-model $\mathcal{M}_2$ for L_2, such that $\mathcal{M}_1$ and $\mathcal{M}_2$ agree on which shared constant symbols (i.e. t and u) are equal, and agree on cardinalities (Theorem 1). The first requirement is fulfilled by checking every arrangement of the variables (here: $t = u$ or $t \neq u$): $\{t \neq u\} \cup L_2$ is T_2-unsatisfiable, but $\{t = u\} \cup L_1$ and $\{t = u\} \cup L_2$ are both satisfiable in their respective theory. It remains to check if it is possible for both models to agree on cardinalities. The theory of integer linear arithmetic only accepts models of cardinality $\aleph_0$, therefore $L_1 \cup L_2$ is $T_1 \cup T_2$-satisfiable if and only if $T_1 \cup \{t = u\} \cup L_1$ has a model of cardinality $\aleph_0$.

The theory $T_1 \cup \{t = u\} \cup L_1$ uses only one quantified variable, four predicate symbols (A, B, C, D), and two constants (t, u). Using for instance the fact that this theory is a Löwenheim theory, one can use Theorem 4 to check if it has an infinite model. The theory contains two constants, at most one "nested" quantifier, and four unary predicates. If there is a model with cardinality 3×2^4, then there is an infinite model. It can easily be showed that $T_1 \cup \{t = u\} \cup L_1$ indeed accepts such a model with cardinality 48. Similar bounds exist for BSR and two-variable theories, but unfortunately they are also large compared to the size of this toy example.

There exists another criteria to check if a BSR theory has an infinite model. Indeed, a BSR theory with n variables has an infinite model if and only if it has a n-repetitive model (see the full version of the paper [10]). Checking if $T_1 \cup \{t = u\} \cup L_1$ has a 1-repetitive model simply amounts to check if $T_1 \cup \{t = u\} \cup L_1 \cup \{v \neq t, v \neq u\}$ is satisfiable.

As a final remark, notice that the example used in this section encodes the set of formulas

$$\{a > 0, a < 2, a + b = 2, b > 0, f(a) \in A, f(b) \notin C, A \cup B = C \cup D\}$$

in a language that combines integer linear arithmetic, uninterpreted function symbols, and elementary set-theoretic operations. One motivation for the work reported in this paper is indeed to augment the languages accepted by SMT

---

[4] T_1 is also stably infinite, but we ignore this fact to illustrate the generic approach.

solvers with certain operators on sets or relations, which can conveniently be represented by BSR theories over their characteristic predicates.

8   Conclusion

In this paper we observed that one can express completely the spectrum, i.e. the set of the cardinalities of the models, for Löwenheim theories, BSR theories, and finite theories in the two-variables fragment. We characterise those theories as *gentle*. Gentle theories can be combined with almost any decidable theory, including gentle theories, integer or real linear arithmetic, finite first-order theories, and some combinations of these.

It remains to develop algorithmic techniques to make this combination work in practice. The results presented here are prohibitively expensive, the finite cardinalities that guarantee the existence of an infinite model grow very rapidly with the size of the theories. In that sense, the combination scheme presented in this paper is really at the frontiers of combining decision procedures. It is certainly not practical to first extract all cardinalities of the gentle theories in the combination, just like, in the Nelson-Oppen combination scheme, it is not practical to check every arrangement one by one. Rather than guessing arrangements, SMT solvers use, among other techniques, equality propagation. Equality propagation can thus be seen as the negotiation of an arrangement. A practical way to agree on cardinality could also rely on negotiation. This negotiation would often be trivial, for instance if one theory puts very strong constraints on cardinalities, or if most theories are on the contrary very permissive. Another approach to handle the same classes of theories can be found in [24]: it consists in reducing each part of the separation to a formula in a common decidable language including Presbruger arithmetics; this approach has the drawback of being much more complex, but as a counterpart the language handled is in some aspects much more expressive.

Usually, SMT solvers implement a combination of a fixed set of theories, which are known *a priori*, and are also known to have the right properties according to cardinalities (typically, being stably infinite). Here, we show that every theory in the major well-known first-order decidable classes can be integrated in a combination. Since it can be shown that assertions over sets or relations and elementary set-theoretic operations like ∪, ∩, etc. just introduce one more BSR theory in the combination, the problem remains decidable even if this theory is not fixed a priori. We mainly target formal methods based on set theory such as B [1] and TLA$^+$ [15]. We believe that the results in this paper can help automating the proof of some parts of the verification conditions, which often mix arithmetic symbols, uninterpreted functions, and elementary set theory. Verification conditions generated within those formal methods are usually small and should be most of the time within reach of a decision procedure, even if it is inefficient.

An interesting direction for further research is to investigate how to use the techniques embedded in state-of-the-art first order provers (for instance [3,18,19]) to efficiently handle the first-order theories within a combination of decision procedures.

Acknowledgments. We are grateful to Yves Guiraud, Yuri Gurevich, Stephan Merz, Silvio Ranise, Christophe Ringeissen, Michaël Rusinowitch, and Duc-Khanh Tran for helpful remarks and interesting discussions. We also thank the anonymous reviewers for their comments.

References

1. Abrial, J.-R.: The B-Book: Assigning Programs to Meanings. Cambridge University Press, Cambridge (1996)
2. Baaz, M., Egly, U., Leitsch, A.: Normal form transformations. In: Robinson, J.A., Voronkov, A. (eds.) Handbook of Automated Reasoning, ch. 5, vol. I, pp. 273–333. Elsevier Science B.V, Amsterdam (2001)
3. Baumgartner, P., Fuchs, A., Tinelli, C.: Implementing the Model Evolution Calculus. In: Schulz, S., Sutcliffe, G., Tammet, T. (eds.) Special Issue of the International Journal of Artificial Intelligence Tools (IJAIT). International Journal of Artificial Intelligence Tools, vol. 15 (2005)
4. Bernays, P., Schönfinkel, M.: Zum Entscheidungsproblem der mathematischen Logik. Math. Annalen 99, 342–372 (1928)
5. Börger, E., Grädel, E., Gurevich, Y.: The Classical Decision Problem. Perspectives in Mathematical Logic. Springer, Berlin (1997)
6. Dreben, B., Goldfarb, W.D.: The Decision Problem: Solvable Classes of Quantificational Formulas. Addison-Wesley, Reading (1979)
7. Ebbinghaus, H.-D., Flum, J.: Finite Model Theory. Perspectives in Mathematical Logic. Springer, Berlin (1995)
8. Enderton, H.B.: A Mathematical Introduction to Logic, Orlando, Florida. Academic Press Inc., London (1972)
9. Fontaine, P.: Combinations of theories and the Bernays-Schönfinkel-Ramsey class. In: Beckert, B. (ed.) 4th International Verification Workshop - VERIFY 2007, Bremen (15/07/07-16/07/07) (July 2007)
10. Fontaine, P.: Combinations of theories for decidable fragments of first-order logic (2009), http://www.loria.fr/~fontaine/Fontaine12b.pdf
11. Fontaine, P., Gribomont, E.P.: Decidability of invariant validation for parameterized systems. In: Garavel, H., Hatcliff, J. (eds.) TACAS 2003. LNCS, vol. 2619, pp. 97–112. Springer, Heidelberg (2003)
12. Fontaine, P., Gribomont, E.P.: Combining non-stably infinite, non-first order theories. In: Ahrendt, W., Baumgartner, P., de Nivelle, H., Ranise, S., Tinelli, C. (eds.) Selected Papers from the Workshops on Disproving and the Second International Workshop on Pragmatics of Decision Procedures (PDPAR 2004), July 2005. Electronic Notes in Theoretical Computer Science, vol. 125, pp. 37–51 (2005)
13. Grädel, E., Kolaitis, P.G., Vardi, M.Y.: On the decision problem for two-variable first-order logic. The Bulletin of Symbolic Logic 3(1), 53–69 (1997)
14. Gurevich, Y., Shelah, S.: Spectra of monadic second-order formulas with one unary function. In: LICS 2003: Proceedings of the 18th Annual IEEE Symposium on Logic in Computer Science, pp. 291–300. IEEE Computer Society, Washington (2003)
15. Lamport, L.: Specifying Systems. Addison-Wesley, Boston (2002)
16. Nelson, G., Oppen, D.C.: Simplifications by cooperating decision procedures. ACM Transactions on Programming Languages and Systems 1(2), 245–257 (1979)
17. Ramsey, F.P.: On a Problem of Formal Logic. Proceedings of the London Mathematical Society 30, 264–286 (1930)

18. Riazanov, A., Voronkov, A.: The design and implementation of Vampire. AI Communications 15(2), 91–110 (2002)
19. Schulz, S.: System Abstract: E 0.61. In: Goré, R.P., Leitsch, A., Nipkow, T. (eds.) IJCAR 2001. LNCS (LNAI), vol. 2083, pp. 370–375. Springer, Heidelberg (2001)
20. Sutcliffe, G., Suttner, C.: The State of CASC. AI Communications 19(1), 35–48 (2006)
21. Tinelli, C., Harandi, M.T.: A new correctness proof of the Nelson–Oppen combination procedure. In: Baader, F., Schulz, K.U. (eds.) Frontiers of Combining Systems (FroCoS), Applied Logic, pp. 103–120. Kluwer Academic Publishers, Dordrecht (1996)
22. Tinelli, C., Ringeissen, C.: Unions of non-disjoint theories and combinations of satisfiability procedures. Theoretical Computer Science 290(1), 291–353 (2003)
23. Tinelli, C., Zarba, C.G.: Combining non-stably infinite theories. Journal of Automated Reasoning 34(3), 209–238 (2005)
24. Wies, T., Piskac, R., Kuncak, V.: Combining theories with shared set operations. In: Ghilardi, S., Sebastiani, R. (eds.) FroCoS 2009. LNCS (LNAI), vol. 5749, pp. 366–382. Springer, Heidelberg (2009)

Products of Modal Logics with Diagonal Constant Lacking the Finite Model Property

Agi Kurucz

Department of Computer Science
King's College London
agi.kurucz@kcl.ac.uk

Abstract. Two-dimensional products of modal logics having at least one 'non-transitive' component, such as $\mathbf{K} \times \mathbf{K}$, $\mathbf{K} \times \mathbf{K4}$, and $\mathbf{K} \times \mathbf{S5}$, are often known to be decidable and have the finite model property. Here we show that by adding the diagonal constant to the language this might change: one can have formulas that are only satisfiable in infinite 'abstract' models for these logics.

1 Introduction

The formation of Cartesian products of various structures (vector and topological spaces, algebras, etc.) is a standard mathematical way of modelling the multi-dimensional character of our world. In modal logic, products of Kripke frames are natural constructions allowing us to reflect interactions between modal operators representing time, space, knowledge, actions, etc. The product construction as a combination method on modal logics has been used in applications in computer science and artificial intelligence (see [2,10] and references therein) ever since its introduction in the 1970s [15,16].

If the component frames are unimodal, then the modal language speaking about product frames has two interacting box operators (and the corresponding diamonds), one coming from each component. Product logics are Kripke complete logics in this language, determined by classes of product frames. In general they can also have other, non-product, frames. So one can consider two different kinds of the *finite model property* (fmp): one w.r.t. arbitrary ('abstract' or 'non-standard') frames, and a stronger one, w.r.t. product frames only. As the fmp can be an important tool in establishing decidability of a modal logic, it has been extensively studied in connection with product logics as well. In particular, if one of the component logics is either $\mathbf{K}$ or $\mathbf{S5}$, then many product logics are known to be decidable and have the fmp [3,2,17]. Product logics like $\mathbf{K} \times \mathbf{K}$, $\mathbf{K} \times \mathbf{S5}$ and $\mathbf{S5} \times \mathbf{S5}$ even have the fmp w.r.t. product frames [4,2,13]. On the other hand, when both component logics have transitive frames only, such as $\mathbf{K4}$, $\mathbf{S4}$, $\mathbf{GL}$, then product logics are usually undecidable and lack the 'abstract' fmp [5,6,14].

Here we take the first steps in investigating the expressive power of extensions of decidable product logics with 'dimension-connecting' connectives. Perhaps

S. Ghilardi and R. Sebastiani (Eds.): FroCoS 2009, LNAI 5749, pp. 279–286, 2009.

the simplest and most natural operation of this sort is the *diagonal constant* δ. The main reason for introducing such a constant has been to give a 'modal treatment' of equality of classical first-order logic. Modal algebras for the product logic **S5** × **S5** extended with diagonal constant are called *representable cylindric algebras of dimension 2* and have been extensively studied in the algebraic logic literature [8]. '**S5** × **S5** plus δ' is known to be decidable and has the finite model property, even w.r.t. product frames [13]. Adding the diagonal constant does not even change the NEXPTIME-completeness of the **S5** × **S5**-satisfiability problem [7,12]. Here we show that, rather surprisingly, products of other decidable modal logics may behave differently (see Theorem 3 below). Though, say, **K** × **S5** also has a NEXPTIME-complete satisfiability problem and has the fmp w.r.t. product frames [3,12,2], by adding the diagonal constant to the language one can find some formula such that *any* frame for **K** × **S5** satisfying it must be infinite.

As concerns our formulas and the technique used in the proofs below, we would like to emphasise that—unlike [14,5,6,2]—in general here we are *neither* dealing with transitive frames, *nor* having some kind of universal modality in the language. So the fact that infinity can be forced by a formula is quite unusual. We hope that the formulas below will either help in encoding some undecidable problem and showing that decidable product logics like **K** × **K**, **K** × **S5** and **K** × **K4** become undecidable if we add the diagonal constant, or give some hints on how their infinite models can be represented by some finite means, say, using mosaics or loop-controlled tableaux, in order to prove decidability.

2   Products and δ-Products

We assume as known the fundamental notions of modal logic (such as uni- and multimodal Kripke frames and models, satisfiability and validity of formulas, generated subframes, etc.) and their basic properties, and use a standard notation.

Let us begin with introducing the product construction and its extension with a diagonal element. Given unimodal Kripke frames $\mathfrak{F}_0 = (W_0, R_0)$ and $\mathfrak{F}_1 = (W_1, R_1)$, their *product* is the bimodal frame

$$\mathfrak{F}_0 \times \mathfrak{F}_1 = (W_0 \times W_1, R_h, R_v),$$

where $W_0 \times W_1$ is the Cartesian product of sets W_0 and W_1 and the binary relations R_h and R_v are defined by taking, for all $u, u' \in W_0$, $v, v' \in W_1$,

$$(u, v)R_h(u', v') \quad \text{iff} \quad uR_0u' \text{ and } v = v',$$
$$(u, v)R_v(u', v') \quad \text{iff} \quad vR_1v' \text{ and } u = u'.$$

The δ-*product* of $\mathfrak{F}_0$ and $\mathfrak{F}_1$ is the 3-modal frame

$$\mathfrak{F}_0 \times^\delta \mathfrak{F}_1 = (W_0 \times W_1, R_h, R_v, D),$$

where $(W_0 \times W_1, R_h, R_v) = \mathfrak{F}_0 \times \mathfrak{F}_1$ and

$$D = \{(u, u) : u \in W_0 \cap W_1\}.$$

The respective modal languages speaking about product and δ-product frames are defined as follows.

$$\mathcal{L}_2: \qquad \psi = p \mid \top \mid \bot \mid \neg\psi \mid \psi_1 \wedge \psi_2 \mid \Diamond_0\psi \mid \Box_0\psi \mid \Diamond_1\psi \mid \Box_1\psi$$

$$\mathcal{L}_2^\delta: \qquad \psi = p \mid \top \mid \bot \mid \neg\psi \mid \psi_1 \wedge \psi_2 \mid \Diamond_0\psi \mid \Box_0\psi \mid \Diamond_1\psi \mid \Box_1\psi \mid \delta$$

For $i = 0, 1$, let L_i be a Kripke complete unimodal logic in the language using the modal operators $\Diamond_i$ and $\Box_i$. The product and δ-product of L_0 and L_1 are defined, respectively, as

$$L_0 \times L_1 = \{\psi \in \mathcal{L}_2 : \psi \text{ is valid in } \mathfrak{F}_0 \times \mathfrak{F}_1, \ \mathfrak{F}_i \text{ is a frame for } L_i, \ i = 0, 1\}$$

$$L_0 \times^\delta L_1 = \{\psi \in \mathcal{L}_2^\delta : \psi \text{ is valid in } \mathfrak{F}_0 \times^\delta \mathfrak{F}_1, \ \mathfrak{F}_i \text{ is a frame for } L_i, \ i = 0, 1\}.$$

The following proposition shows that we can define δ-products differently, in a way that might look more natural to some:

Proposition 1. *For all Kripke complete logics L_0 and L_1,*

$$L_0 \times^\delta L_1 = \{\psi \in \mathcal{L}_2^\delta : \psi \text{ is valid in } \mathfrak{F}_0 \times^\delta \mathfrak{F}_1, \ \mathfrak{F}_i \text{ is a frame for } L_i,$$

$$i = 0, 1, \ \mathfrak{F}_0 \text{ and } \mathfrak{F}_1 \text{ have the same set of worlds}\}.$$

Proof. One inclusion is obvious. For the other, suppose $\psi \notin L_0 \times^\delta L_1$, that is, $\mathfrak{F}_0 \times^\delta \mathfrak{F}_1 \not\models \psi$, where $\mathfrak{F}_i = (W_i, R_i)$ is a frame for L_i, $i = 0, 1$. We define frames $\mathfrak{G}_0$ and $\mathfrak{G}_1$ such that:

1. $\mathfrak{G}_i$ is a frame for L_i, for $i = 0, 1$.
2. $\mathfrak{G}_0$ and $\mathfrak{G}_1$ have the same set of worlds, $W_0 \cup W_1$.
3. $\mathfrak{F}_0 \times^\delta \mathfrak{F}_1$ is a generated subframe of $\mathfrak{G}_0 \times^\delta \mathfrak{G}_1$.

To this end, for $i = 0, 1$, let $\mathfrak{H}_i$ be either the one-element irreflexive or the one-element reflexive frame, depending on which of these two is a frame for L_i. (As a Kripke complete logic is always consistent, by Makinson's theorem [11] at least one of them would do for sure.) Now, for $\{i, j\} = \{0, 1\}$, let $\mathfrak{G}_i$ be the disjoint union of $\mathfrak{F}_i$ and $(W_j - (W_0 \cap W_1))$-many copies of $\mathfrak{H}_i$.

The proof of the following statement is straightforward from the definitions:

Proposition 2. *$L_0 \times^\delta L_1$ is a conservative extension of $L_0 \times L_1$.*

At first sight, the diagonal constant can only be meaningfully used in applications where the domains of the two component frames consist of objects of similar kinds, or at least overlap. However, as modal languages cannot distinguish between isomorphic frames, in fact *any* subset $D \subseteq W_0 \times W_1$ can be considered as an interpretation of the diagonal constant, once it has the following properties:

$$\forall x \in W_0, \forall y, y' \in W_1 \ ((x, y), (x, y') \in D \implies y = y'),$$

$$\forall x, x' \in W_0, \forall y \in W_1 \ ((x, y), (x', y) \in D \implies x = x').$$

So, say, when a product frame represents the movement of some objects in time, then the diagonal constant can be used for collecting a set of special time-stamped objects, provided no special object is chosen twice and at every moment of time at most one special object is chosen.

3 Main Results

Although δ-product logics are determined by classes of δ-product frames, of course there are other, non-δ-product, frames for them. As usual, a multimodal logic L (in particular, a δ-product logic $L_0 \times^\delta L_1$) is said to have the (*abstract*) *finite model property* (*fmp*, for short) if, for every formula φ in the language of L, if $\varphi \notin L$ then there is a finite frame $\mathfrak{F}$ for L such that $\mathfrak{F} \not\models \varphi$. (By a standard argument, this means that $\mathfrak{M} \not\models \varphi$ for some *finite model* $\mathfrak{M}$ for L; see, e.g., [1].) Below we show that many δ-product logics (with $\mathbf{K} \times^\delta \mathbf{K}$, $\mathbf{K} \times^\delta \mathbf{K4}$ and $\mathbf{K} \times^\delta \mathbf{S5}$ among them) lack the fmp.

Let φ_∞ be the conjunction of the following three (variable-free) $\mathcal{L}_2^\delta$-formulas:

$$\Diamond_1 \Diamond_0 (\delta \wedge \Box_0 \bot) \tag{1}$$

$$\Box_1 \Diamond_0 (\neg \delta \wedge \Diamond_0 \top \wedge \Box_0 \delta) \tag{2}$$

$$\Box_0 \Diamond_1 \delta \tag{3}$$

First we show that *any* frame for δ-product logics satisfying φ_∞ should be *infinite*. To this end, we have a closer look at arbitrary (not necessarily δ-product) frames for δ-product logics. It is straightforward to see that δ-product frames always have the following first-order properties:

$$\forall xyz \left(xR_v y \wedge yR_h z \rightarrow \exists u \, (xR_h u \wedge uR_v z) \right)$$

$$\forall xyz \left(xR_h y \wedge yR_v z \rightarrow \exists u \, (xR_v u \wedge uR_h z) \right)$$

$$\forall xyz \left(xR_v y \wedge xR_h z \rightarrow \exists u \, (yR_h u \wedge zR_v u) \right)$$

$$\forall xyzu \left(xR_h y \wedge xR_h z \wedge zR_h u \wedge D(y) \wedge D(u) \rightarrow y = u \right)$$

These properties are modally definable by the respective $\mathcal{L}_2^\delta$-formulas:

(lcom) $\Diamond_1 \Diamond_0 p \rightarrow \Diamond_0 \Diamond_1 p$

(rcom) $\Diamond_0 \Diamond_1 p \rightarrow \Diamond_1 \Diamond_0 p$

(chr) $\Diamond_0 \Box_1 p \rightarrow \Box_1 \Diamond_0 p$

(diag) $\Diamond_0 (\delta \wedge p) \rightarrow \Box_0 \Box_0 (\delta \rightarrow p)$

Theorem 1. *Let* $\mathfrak{F} = (W, R_0, R_1, \Delta)$ *be any frame validating* (lcom), (rcom), (chr) *and* (diag). *If* φ_∞ *is satisfied in* $\mathfrak{F}$, *then* $\mathfrak{F}$ *should be infinite.*

Proof. Let $\mathfrak{F} = (W, R_0, R_1, \Delta)$ be as required and suppose that φ_∞ is satisfied at point r of a model $\mathfrak{M}$ based on $\mathfrak{F}$. We define inductively four infinite sequences

$$x_0, x_1, x_2, \ldots, \quad y_0, y_1, y_2, \ldots, \quad u_0, u_1, u_2, \ldots \quad \text{and} \quad v_0, v_1, v_2, \ldots$$

of points from W such that, for every $i < \omega$,

(gen1) $(\mathfrak{M}, x_i) \models \delta$,

(gen2) $(\mathfrak{M}, y_i) \models \neg \delta \wedge \Diamond_0 \top \wedge \Box_0 \delta$

(gen3) $rR_1 u_i$, $u_i R_0 x_i$, $u_i R_0 y_i$, and $y_i R_0 x_i$

(gen4)   if $i > 0$ then $rR_0 v_i$, $v_i R_1 x_i$ and $v_i R_1 y_{i-1}$,

see Fig. 1. (We do not claim at this point that, say, all the x_i are distinct.)

To begin with, by (1), there are u_0, x_0 such that $rR_1u_0R_0x_0$ and

$$(\mathfrak{M}, x_0) \models \delta \wedge \Box_0 \bot. \tag{4}$$

By (2), there is y_0 such that $u_0R_0y_0$ and $(\mathfrak{M}, y_0) \models \neg\delta \wedge \Diamond_0\top \wedge \Box_0\delta$. By (diag), we have that $y_0R_0x_0$, and so **(gen1)**–**(gen3)** hold for $i = 0$.

Now suppose that, for some $n < \omega$, x_i and y_i with **(gen1)**–**(gen4)** have already been defined for all $i \leq n$. By **(gen3)** for $i = n$ and by (lcom), there is v_{n+1} such that $rR_0v_{n+1}R_1y_n$. So by (3), there is x_{n+1} such that $(\mathfrak{M}, x_{n+1}) \models \delta$ and $v_{n+1}R_1x_{n+1}$. Now by (rcom), there is u_{n+1} such that $rR_1u_{n+1}R_0x_{n+1}$. So, by (2), there is y_{n+1} such that $u_{n+1}R_0y_{n+1}$ and $(\mathfrak{M}, y_{n+1}) \models \neg\delta \wedge \Diamond_0\top \wedge \Box_0\delta$, and so by (diag) $y_{n+1}R_0x_{n+1}$, as required (see Fig. 1).

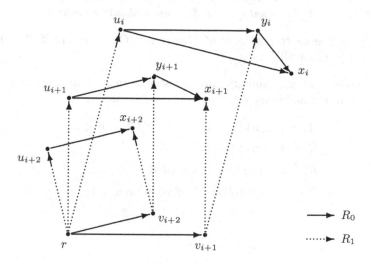

Fig. 1. Generating the points x_i, y_i, u_i and v_i

Now we will prove that in fact all the x_n are different. We claim that, for all $n < \omega$,

$$(\mathfrak{M}, x_n) \models \Diamond_0^n\top \wedge \Box_0^{n+1}\bot \quad \text{and} \quad (\mathfrak{M}, y_n) \models \Diamond_0^{n+1}\top \wedge \Box_0^{n+2}\bot \tag{5}$$

(here $\Diamond_0^0\top = \top$, $\Diamond_0^{n+1}\top = \Diamond_0\Diamond_0^n\top$, $\Box_0^0\bot = \bot$ and $\Box_0^{n+1}\bot = \Box_0\Box_0^n\bot$). In order to prove this claim, first observe that, by **(gen1)**–**(gen3)** and (diag), we have

$$\forall z\, (y_iR_0z \rightarrow z = x_i), \tag{6}$$

for all $i < \omega$. Now we prove (5) by induction on n. For $n = 0$: Obviously, we have $(\mathfrak{M}, x_0) \models \top$, and $(\mathfrak{M}, x_0) \models \Box_0\bot$ by (4). $(\mathfrak{M}, y_0) \models \Diamond_0\top$ by **(gen2)**, and $(\mathfrak{M}, y_0) \models \Box_0^2\bot$ by (6) and $(\mathfrak{M}, x_0) \models \Box_0\bot$.

Now suppose that (5) holds for n. As $(\mathfrak{M}, y_n) \models \Diamond_0^{n+1}\top$, by (lcom), (chr) and **(gen4)** we have $(\mathfrak{M}, x_{n+1}) \models \Diamond_0^{n+1}\top$. Therefore, we obtain $(\mathfrak{M}, y_{n+1}) \models \Diamond_0^{n+2}\top$ by **(gen3)**. As $(\mathfrak{M}, y_n) \models \Box_0^{n+2}\bot$, we have $(\mathfrak{M}, x_{n+1}) \models \Box_0^{n+2}\bot$ by (lcom), (chr) and **(gen4)**. Therefore, by (6), we have $(\mathfrak{M}, y_{n+1}) \models \Box_0^{n+3}\bot$, as required.

Next, we consider a variant of φ_∞ that is satisfiable in δ-product frames with a reflexive second component. (The idea is a version of the 'chessboard-trick' of [6].) We introduce a fresh propositional variable v, and define φ_∞^r as the conjunction of the following $\mathcal{L}_2^\delta$-formulas:

$$\Box_1(\Diamond_0 v \to v)$$
$$\Diamond_1\big(v \wedge \Diamond_0(\delta \wedge \Box_0\bot)\big)$$
$$\Box_1\big(v \to \Diamond_0(\neg\delta \wedge \Diamond_0\top \wedge \Box_0\delta)\big)$$
$$\Box_0\Diamond_1(v \wedge \delta)$$

Theorem 2. *Let* $\mathfrak{F} = (W, R_0, R_1, \Delta)$ *be any frame validating* (lcom), (rcom), (chr) *and* (diag). *If* φ_∞^r *is satisfied in* $\mathfrak{F}$, *then* $\mathfrak{F}$ *should be infinite.*

Proof. It is analogous to the proof of Theorem 1. Observe that if $(\mathfrak{M}, r) \models \varphi_\infty^r$ then $(\mathfrak{M}, u_i) \models v$, for all $i < \omega$.

Next, we show that φ_∞ and φ_∞^r are satisfiable in certain infinite δ-product frames. Indeed, define binary relations on $\omega + 1$ by taking

$$R_0 = \{(\omega, n) : n < \omega\} \cup \{(n + 1, n) : n < \omega\},$$
$$R_1 = \{(\omega, n) : n < \omega\},$$
$$R_1^{refl} = \text{reflexive closure of } R_1,$$
$$R_1^{univ} = \text{the universal relation on } \omega + 1,$$

and let

$$\mathfrak{H}_0 = (\omega + 1, R_0),$$
$$\mathfrak{H}_1 = (\omega + 1, R_1),$$
$$\mathfrak{H}_1^{refl} = (\omega + 1, R_1^{refl}),$$
$$\mathfrak{H}_1^{univ} = (\omega + 1, R_1^{univ}).$$

Theorem 3. *Let* L_0 *be any Kripke complete unimodal logic such that* $\mathfrak{H}_0$ *is a frame for* L_0 *(such as, e.g.,* **K***) and let* L_1 *be any Kripke complete unimodal logic such that either* $\mathfrak{H}_1$ *or* $\mathfrak{H}_1^{refl}$ *or* $\mathfrak{H}_1^{univ}$ *is a frame for* L_1 *(such as, e.g.,* **K, K4, GL, T, S4, Grz, B, S5***). Then* $L_0 \times^\delta L_1$ *does not have the 'abstract' finite model property.*

Proof. It is straightforward to see that φ_∞ is satisfiable at the root (ω, ω) of $\mathfrak{H}_0 \times^\delta \mathfrak{H}_1$. As concerns the other cases, take the following model $\mathfrak{M}$, either over $\mathfrak{H}_0 \times^\delta \mathfrak{H}_1^{refl}$ or $\mathfrak{H}_0 \times^\delta \mathfrak{H}_1^{univ}$:

$$\mathfrak{M}(v) = \{(n, m) : n \leq \omega, \, m < \omega\}.$$

Then, in both cases, $\big(\mathfrak{M}, (\omega, \omega)\big) \models \varphi_\infty^r$.

Now the theorem follows from Theorems 1 and 2.

4   Discussion

1. Let us emphasise that some results in Theorem 3 are rather surprising, as the corresponding (diagonal-free) products do have the fmp. It is shown in [3,17] (using filtration) that if L_0 is either **K** or **S5**, and L_1 is axiomatisable by formulas having Horn first-order correspondents (such as e.g., **K**, **K4**, **T**, **S4**, **B**, **S5**), then $L_0 \times L_1$ has the fmp. Moreover, **K** $\times$ **K** and **K** $\times$ **S5** even have the fmp w.r.t. product frames [4,2].

2. Let us next summarise what is known about the fmp of δ-products that are out of the scope of Theorem 3. If *both* components L_0 and L_1 are logics having only transitive frames of arbitrary depth and width (such as, e.g., **K4**, **GL**, **S4**, **Grz**), then it is shown in [5,6] that already $L_0 \times L_1$ lacks the fmp. So by Prop. 2, $L_0 \times^\delta L_1$ does not have the fmp either. It is not clear, however, whether the 'chessboard-trick' of [6] can be used to extend the proofs of our Theorems 1–3 to cover δ-products with a reflexive (but not necessarily transitive) first component, like e.g. **T** $\times^\delta$**T**.

3. Though representable diagonal-free cylindric algebras of dimension 2 are the modal algebras of **S5** $\times$ **S5**, two-dimensional *representable cylindric algebras* are not exactly the modal algebras of **S5** $\times^\delta$**S5**, but those of

$$\textbf{S5} \times^{\delta'} \textbf{S5} = \{\psi \in \mathcal{L}_2^\delta : \psi \text{ is valid in } (W, W \times W) \times^\delta (W, W \times W),$$

$$W \text{ is a non-empty set}\}.$$

(That is, unlike in Prop. 1, only δ-product frames of *rooted* **S5**-frames sharing a common set of worlds are considered in this definition.) It is straightforward to see that **S5**$\times^\delta$**S5** $\subseteq$ **S5**$\times^{\delta'}$**S5** and that this inclusion is proper: for instance, $\diamond_0\delta$ belongs to **S5**$\times^{\delta'}$**S5** but not to **S5**$\times^\delta$**S5**. The propositional modal logic **S5** $\times^{\delta'}$ **S5** is also connected to two-variable first-order logic with equality, so there are several known proofs showing that **S5** $\times^{\delta'}$ **S5** is decidable and has the fmp, even w.r.t. 'δ-squares' of universal frames [13,7]. Perhaps the same is true for **S5** $\times^\delta$**S5**.

4. As concerns the decision problem for δ-product logics other than **S5** $\times^{\delta'}$ **S5**, not much is known. It is straightforward to extend the proof given in [3] for product logics to δ-products, and show that $L_0 \times^\delta L_1$ is recursively enumerable whenever the class of all frames for each of L_0 and L_1 is recursively first-order definable. However, even having the fmp would not necessarily help in solving the decision problems. It is shown in [9] that, for many component logics L_0 and L_1 (with **K**, **T**, **K4**, **S4** among them), $L_0 \times^\delta L_1$ is not only not finitely axiomatisable, but it cannot be axiomatised by any set of $\mathcal{L}_2^\delta$-formulas containing finitely many propositional variables. It is not known, however, whether there is some other way of deciding if a finite frame is a frame for such a δ-product logic.

Acknowledgement. Thanks are due to Stanislav Kikot for the problem and interesting discussions.

References

1. Chagrov, A., Zakharyaschev, M.: Modal Logic. Oxford Logic Guides, vol. 35. Clarendon Press, Oxford (1997)
2. Gabbay, D., Kurucz, A., Wolter, F., Zakharyaschev, M.: Many-Dimensional Modal Logics: Theory and Applications. Studies in Logic and the Foundations of Mathematics, vol. 148. Elsevier, Amsterdam (2003)
3. Gabbay, D., Shehtman, V.: Products of modal logics. Part I. Journal of the IGPL 6, 73–146 (1998)
4. Gabbay, D., Shehtman, V.: Products of modal logics. Part II. Journal of the IGPL 2, 165–210 (2000)
5. Gabelaia, D., Kurucz, A., Zakharyaschev, M.: Products of transitive modal logics without the (abstract) finite model property. In: Schmidt, R., Pratt-Hartmann, I., Reynolds, M., Wansing, H. (eds.) Proceedings of AiML 2004, Manchester, U.K (September 2004)
6. Gabelaia, D., Kurucz, A., Wolter, F., Zakharyaschev, M.: Products of 'transitive' modal logics. Journal of Symbolic Logic 70, 993–1021 (2005)
7. Grädel, E., Kolaitis, P., Vardi, M.: On the decision problem for two-variable first order logic. Bulletin of Symbolic Logic 3, 53–69 (1997)
8. Henkin, L., Monk, D., Tarski, A.: Cylindric Algebras, Part II. Studies in Logic and the Foundations of Mathematics, vol. 115. North-Holland, Amsterdam (1985)
9. Kikot, S.: On axiomatising products of Kripke frames with diagonal constant. Manuscript (submitted 2008) (in Russian)
10. Kurucz, A.: Combining modal logics. In: Blackburn, P., van Benthem, J., Wolter, F. (eds.) Handbook of Modal Logic. Studies in Logic and Practical Reasoning, vol. 3, pp. 869–924. Elsevier, Amsterdam (2007)
11. Makinson, D.: Some embedding theorems for modal logic. Notre Dame Journal of Formal Logic 12, 252–254 (1971)
12. Marx, M.: Complexity of products of modal logics. Journal of Logic and Computation 9, 197–214 (1999)
13. Mortimer, M.: On languages with two variables. Zeitschrift für Mathematische Logik und Grundlagen der Mathematik 21, 135–140 (1975)
14. Reynolds, M., Zakharyaschev, M.: On the products of linear modal logics. Journal of Logic and Computation 11, 909–931 (2001)
15. Segerberg, K.: Two-dimensional modal logic. Journal of Philosophical Logic 2, 77–96 (1973)
16. Shehtman, V.: Two-dimensional modal logics. Mathematical Notices of the USSR Academy of Sciences 23, 417–424 (1978) (Translated from Russian)
17. Shehtman, V.: Filtration via bisimulation. In: Schmidt, R., Pratt-Hartmann, I., Reynolds, M., Wansing, H. (eds.) Advances in Modal Logic, vol. 5, pp. 289–308. King's College Publications (2005)

Improving Coq Propositional Reasoning Using a Lazy CNF Conversion Scheme

Stéphane Lescuyer[1,2] and Sylvain Conchon[1,2]

[1] INRIA Saclay-Île de France, ProVal, Orsay F-91893
[2] LRI, Université Paris-Sud, CNRS, Orsay F-91405

Abstract. In an attempt to improve automation capabilities in the Coq proof assistant, we develop a tactic for the propositional fragment based on the DPLL procedure. Although formulas naturally arising in interactive proofs do not require a state-of-the-art SAT solver, the conversion to clausal form required by DPLL strongly damages the performance of the procedure. In this paper, we present a reflexive DPLL algorithm formalized in Coq which outperforms the existing tactics. It is tightly coupled with a lazy CNF conversion scheme which, unlike Tseitin-style approaches, does not disrupt the procedure. This conversion relies on a lazy mechanism which requires slight adaptations of the original DPLL. As far as we know, this is the first formal proof of this mechanism and its Coq implementation raises interesting challenges.

1   Introduction

Interactive provers like the Coq Proof Assistant [8] offer a rich and expressive language that allows one to formalize complex objects and mathematical properties. Unfortunately, using such provers can be really laborious since users are often required to delve into vast amounts of proof details that would just be ignored in a pencil-and-paper proof. Specific decision procedures have been implemented in Coq in an attempt to improve its automation capabilities and assist users in their task. For instance, tactics like omega, tauto and congruence respectively address linear arithmetic, propositional logic and congruence closure, but they still lack co-operation with each other.

Our long-term goal is to design a tactic integrating techniques from the Satisfiability Modulo Theories (SMT) community in Coq in order to automatize the combination of different decision procedures. This would be a drastic improvement over the current situation where combination has to be manually driven by the user. As a first step in that direction, we design a tactic based on a SAT solver, the procedure at the heart of most SMT solvers. This procedure can be used to decide the validity of propositional formulas in Conjunctive Normal Form (CNF). In order for our tactic to be able to deal with the full propositional fragment of Coq's logic and be useful in practice, we must perform a conversion into CNF before applying the procedure. This conversion step can be critical for the efficiency of the whole system since it can transform a rather easy problem into one that is much too hard for our decision procedure. A possible solution

S. Ghilardi and R. Sebastiani (Eds.): FroCoS 2009, LNAI 5749, pp. 287–303, 2009.

is to rely on a lazy conversion mechanism such as Simplify's [15]. Because this mechanism must be tightly coupled to the decision procedure, this rules out the use of an external tool and leads us to an approach of proof by reflection.

In this paper, we present a reflexive tactic for deciding validity in the propositional fragment of Coq's logic. We show how to adapt a fully certified standard DPLL procedure in order to take a lazy conversion scheme into account. In Sect. 2, we start by some preliminary considerations about reflection and CNF conversion techniques. We describe our abstraction of the lazy CNF conversion method in Sect. 3 as well as the necessary modifications to the DPLL procedure. Section 4 then presents how the lazy CNF conversion can be efficiently implemented in Coq. Finally, we compare our tactic with other methods in Sect. 5 and argue about its advantages and how they could be useful in other settings.

The whole Coq development is browsable online at `http://www.lri.fr/~lescuyer/unsat`. In the electronic version of this paper, statements and objects that have been formalized are marked with ✓, which are hyperlinks to the corresponding documented code.

2   Motivations

2.1   Integrating Decision Procedures in Proof Assistants

Interactive provers in general ensure their correctness by following the so-called LCF-style approach: every proof must be checked by a small, trusted part of the system. Thus, a complex decision procedure for an interactive prover shall not only decide if a formula is provable or not, but it must also generate an actual proof object, which can be checked by the prover's kernel. There have been several different approaches to the problem of integrating decision procedures in interactive provers.

A first possible approach is to use an external state-of-the-art decision procedure. This requires the external tool to be able to return *proof traces* of its proof search. Work must then be done in the interactive prover in order to reconstruct a suitable proof object from the output of the external tool. For instance, Weber and Amjad [28] have successfully integrated two leading SAT solvers, zChaff [23] and MiniSat [18], with Higher Order Logic theorem provers. Integrations of resolution-based provers have also been realized in Coq [1,2] and Isabelle [22]. This approach's main advantage is the ability to use a very efficient external tool.

Another approach is to implement one's own decision procedure in the sources of the interactive prover. It is actually the one being used for most of Coq's automation tactics, including `tauto` by Muñoz [16], `omega` [26] by Crégut and `congruence` by Corbineau [9]. This approach is not as optimized as a mature external tool, but can be specifically designed for the prover in order to have a more efficient proof construction.

The last approach is the so-called *proof by reflection* [3] and is summarized in Fig. 1. It consists in implementing the decision procedure directly as a function in the prover's logic, along with its correctness properties. If a formula Φ can

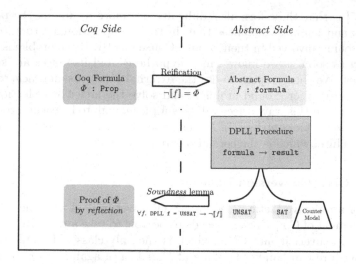

Fig. 1. An overview of our reflexive tactic

be *reified* into an abstract representation f, proving Φ amounts to applying the soundness theorem and executing the procedure on f. For instance, the tactics `ring` [20] and `field` [14], which respectively solve expressions on ring and field structures, are built along this reflection mechanism. The main advantage of the reflexive approach is the size of the generated proof term, which only consists in one application of the correctness property. The trade-off is that typechecking the proof term includes executing the decision procedure, therefore reflection can be used favourably in cases where the proof traces would not be comparatively simpler than the proof search itself.

2.2 A Mixed Approach Based on Reflection

Although traces-based approaches allow the use of state-of-the-art decision procedures, they raise a couple of practical issues nonetheless. The main difficulty consists in finding the adequate level of detail to describe the reasoning steps performed by the decision procedure. Fine-grained traces make for an easier proof reconstruction but require a substantial amount of work in the decision procedure, including justifying steps that are often implicit in an efficient implementation. On the other hand, coarse-grained traces make proof reconstruction much harder since all implicit steps must be implemented in the proof assistant, for instance using reflection. Looking for an intermediate approach, Corbineau and Contejean [6] and Contejean *et al.* [7] proposed integrations mixing traces and reflection.

Our project of integrating an SMT solver in Coq follows this mixed approach, giving a more prominent role to reflection. Indeed, we are especially interested in proving proof obligations from program verification, similar to AUFLIA and AUFLIRA divisions of the SMT competition. Our experience with our own prover

Alt-Ergo [5] is that these formulas' difficulty lies more in finding the pertinent hypotheses and lemmas' instances than in their propositional structure or the theory reasoning involved in their proofs. Consequently, these problems become rather easy as soon as we know which hypotheses and instances are sufficient for the proof. We thus propose to use the external prover as an oracle to reduce a formula to an easier ground problem, and solve the latter by reflection in the proof assistant. In this way, traces will be simple enough to be easily provided by any SMT solver. Our contribution in this paper is a reflexive, carefully designed, DPLL procedure, which is the core of our reflexive solver.

2.3   The CNF Conversion Issue

In order for a reflexive tactic based on a SAT solver to deal with the full propositional fragment of Coq's logic, it needs to be able to take any arbitrary formula in input and convert it into CNF, which is the only class of formulas that the DPLL procedure can handle. Looking at Fig. 1 once again, there are two possibilities as to where this CNF conversion can occur : on the Coq side or on the abstract side, *i.e.* before or after the formula is reified into an abstract Coq object. When conversion is performed on the Coq side✓, every manipulation of the formula is actually a logical rewriting step and ends up in the proof term. Moreover, it is very slow in practice because the matching mechanism used to rewrite the formula is not very efficient. Altogether, this CNF conversion can yield really big proof terms on average-sized formulas and it even ends up taking much longer than the proof search itself — we experimented it in earlier versions of our system [21]. Performing the CNF conversion on the abstract side, however, can be summarized in the following way:

- we implement a function `conversion : formula → formula` that transforms an abstract formula as wanted✓ ;
- we show that for all formula `F`, `conversion F` is in CNF✓ and is equivalent✓ (or at least equisatisfiable) to `F` itself.

This method ensures that the CNF conversion takes constant size in the final proof term, and can be performed efficiently since it is executed by Coq's virtual machine.

Once we decide to implement the CNF conversion as a function on abstract formulas, there are different well-known techniques that can be considered and that we implemented.

1. The first possibility is to do a naive, traditional, CNF conversion✓ that uses de Morgan laws in order to push negations through the formula to the atoms' level, and distributes disjunctions over conjunctions until the formula is in CNF. For instance, this method would transform the formula $A \lor (B \land C)$ in $(A \lor B) \land (A \lor C)$. It is well-known that the resulting formula can be exponentially bigger than the original.

2. Another technique✓ that avoids the exponential blow-up of the naive conversion is to use Tseitin's conversion [27]. It adds intermediate variables for

subformulas and *definitional clauses* for these variables such that the size of the resulting CNF formula is linear in the size of the input. On the $A \lor (B \land C)$ formula above, this method returns $(A \lor X) \land (\bar{X} \lor B) \land (\bar{X} \lor C) \land (X \lor \bar{B} \lor \bar{C})$ where X is a new variable.

3. A refinement of the previous technique✓ is to first convert the formula to negation normal form and use Plaisted and Greenbaum's CNF conversion [25] to add half as many definitional clauses for the Tseitin variables. In the above example, the resulting formula is $(A \lor X) \land (\bar{X} \lor B) \land (\bar{X} \lor C)$.

The Need for Another CNF Conversion. The CNF conversion techniques that we have considered so far remain unsatisfactory. The first one can cause an exponential increase in the size of the formula, and the other two add many new variables and clauses to the problem. All of them also fail to preserve the high-level logical structure of the input formula, in the sense that they make the problem more difficult than it was before. There has been lots of work on more advanced CNF conversion techniques but their implementation in Coq raises some issues. For instance, Plaisted and Greenbaum's method was originally intended to preserve the structure of formulas, but in order to do so requires that equal subformulas be shared. Other optimization techniques [24,12] are based on renaming parts of the subformula to increase the potential sharing. However, it is hard to implement such methods efficiently as a Coq function, ie. in a pure applicative setting with structural recursion. Even proving the standard Tseitin conversion proved to be more challenging than one would normally expect.

For the same reason, it is undeniable that a reflexive Coq decision procedure cannot reach the same level of sheer performance and tuning than state-of-the-art tools, which means that we cannot afford a CNF conversion that adds too many variables, disrupts the structure of the formula, in a word that makes a given problem look harder than it actually is. Results presented in Sect. 5 show that this concern is justified. Constraints due to CNF conversion also arise in Isabelle where formulas sent to the Metis prover are limited to 64 clauses. In the description of their Simplify theorem prover [15], Nelson *et al.* describe a lazy CNF conversion method they designed so as to prevent the performance loss due to Tseitin-style CNF conversion. Their experience was that "introducing lazy CNF into Simplify avoided such a host of performance problems that [..] it converted a prover that didn't work in one that did." In the remaining sections of this paper, we describe how we formalized and integrated this lazy CNF conversion mechanism in our DPLL procedure.

3   A DPLL Procedure with Lazy CNF Conversion

In this section, we formally describe how a DPLL procedure can be adapted to deal with literals that represent arbitrary formulas. We start by recalling a formalization of the basic DPLL procedure.

$$\text{UNIT } \frac{\Gamma, l \vdash \Delta}{\Gamma \vdash \Delta, l} \qquad \text{RED } \frac{\Gamma, l \vdash \Delta, C}{\Gamma, l \vdash \Delta, \bar{l} \vee C} \qquad \text{ELIM } \frac{\Gamma, l \vdash \Delta}{\Gamma, l \vdash \Delta, l \vee C}$$

$$\text{CONFLICT } \frac{}{\Gamma \vdash \Delta, \emptyset} \qquad \text{SPLIT } \frac{\Gamma, l \vdash \Delta \quad \Gamma, \bar{l} \vdash \Delta}{\Gamma \vdash \Delta}$$

Fig. 2. The standard DPLL procedure

3.1   Basic Modular DPLL

The DPLL procedure [11,10], named after its inventors Davis, Putnam, Logemann and Loveland, is one of the oldest decision procedures for the problem of checking the satisfiability of a propositional formula. DPLL deals with CNF formulas, ie. conjunctions of disjunctions of literals. A formula in CNF can thus be written $\bigwedge_{i=1}^{n}(l_{i,1} \vee \cdots \vee l_{i,k_i})$ where each $l_{i,j}$ is a propositional variable or its negation.

We give a formalization of this basic DPLL procedure as a set of five inference rules, presented in Fig. 2. The current state of the algorithm is represented as a sequent $\Gamma \vdash \Delta$ where Γ is the set of literals that are assumed to be true, and Δ is the current formula, seen as a set of clauses, i.e. a set of sets of literals. We use the comma to denote conjunction, $\vee$ for disjunction and $\bar{l}$ for the negation of literal l. The CONFLICT rule corresponds to the case where a clause has been reduced to the empty clause: this rule terminates a branch of the proof search and forces the algorithm to backtrack in order to find another valuation. UNIT implements *unit propagation*: if a clause is reduced to the literal l, this literal can be added to the context before proof search goes on. ELIM and RED each perform one kind of boolean constraint propagation by simplifying the current set of clauses. The last rule is the rule that actually performs the branching, and thus the "proof search". SPLIT picks any literal l and adds it to the context Γ. If no instantiation is found on this side (i.e. all the branches end with CONFLICT), then $\bar{l}$ is supposed true instead and the right branch is explored. If there exists a derivation for a CNF formula F starting with an empty context $\emptyset \vdash F$, this means that the whole tree has been explored and that the formula F is unsatisfiable.

In Coq, we can implement this formalization in a modular way using the module system [4]. The DPLL procedure can be implemented as a functor parameterized by a module for literals. Such a module for literals contains a type equipped with a negation function, comparisons, and various properties:

Module Type LITERAL.
   Parameter t : Set.
   Parameter mk_not : $t \to t$.
   Axiom mk_not_invol : $\forall l$, mk_not (mk_not l) = l.

   ...
   (* Equality, comparisons, ... *)
   Parameter eq : $t \to t \to$ Prop.
   Parameter lt : $t \to t \to$ Prop.

   ...
End LITERAL.

For more details about a Coq formalization of the basic DPLL procedure, the reader can refer to our previous work [21]. We will now proceed to extend this signature of literals and introduce our abstraction of the lazy CNF conversion.

3.2   Expandable Literals

In a Tseitin-style CNF conversion, new literals are added that represent subformulas of the original formula. To denote this fact, clauses must be added to the problem that link the new literals to the corresponding subformulas. The idea behind lazy CNF conversion is that new literals should not merely *represent* subformulas, but they should *be* the subformulas themselves. This way, there would be no need for additional definitional clauses. Detlefs et al. [15] present things a bit differently, using a separate set of *definitions* for new variables (which they call *proxies*), and make sure the definitions of a given proxy variable are only added to the current context when this variable is assigned a boolean value by the procedure. Our abstraction will require less changes to the DPLL procedure.

In order for literals to be able to stand for arbitrary complex subformulas, we extend the signature of literals given in Sect. 3.1 in the following way√ :

```
Module Type LITERAL.
   Parameter t : Set.
   Parameter expand : t → list (list t).
   (* Negation, Equality... as before *)
   ...
End LITERAL.
```

In other words, literals always come with negation, comparison, and various properties, but they have an additional *expansion* function, named **expand**, which takes a literal and returns a list of lists of literals, in other words a CNF of literals. For a genuine literal which just stands for itself, this list is simply the empty list []. For another literal that stands for a formula F, ie. a proxy F, this function allows one to unfold this literal and reveal the underlying structure of F. This underlying structure must be expressed as a conjunction (list) of disjunctions (lists) of literals, but since these literals can stand for subformulas of F themselves, this CNF does not have to be the full conjunctive normal form of F: it can undress the logical structure of F one layer at a time, using literals to represent the direct subformulas of F. This means that the CNF conversion of formula F can be performed step after step, in a *call-by-need* fashion. In [15], the **expand** function would be a look-up in the set of proxy definitions.

As an example, let us consider the formula $A \lor (B \land C)$ once again. A proxy literal for this formula could expand to its full CNF, namely the list of lists $[[A; C]; [B; C]]$. But more interestingly, it may also reveal only one layer at a time and expand to the simpler list $[[A; X]]$, where X itself expands to $[[B]; [C]]$. Note that this variable X is not a new variable in the sense of Tseitin conversion, it is just a way to denote the *unique* literal that expands to $[[B]; [C]]$, and which therefore stands for the formula $B \land C$. This unicity will be the key to

$$\text{UNIT } \frac{\Gamma, l \vdash \Delta, \text{expand}(l)}{\Gamma \vdash \Delta, l} \qquad \text{RED } \frac{\Gamma, l \vdash \Delta, C}{\Gamma, l \vdash \Delta, \bar{l} \vee C} \qquad \text{ELIM } \frac{\Gamma, l \vdash \Delta}{\Gamma, l \vdash \Delta, l \vee C}$$

$$\text{CONFLICT } \frac{}{\Gamma \vdash \Delta, \emptyset} \qquad \text{SPLIT } \frac{\Gamma, l \vdash \Delta, \text{expand}(l) \quad \Gamma, \bar{l} \vdash \Delta, \text{expand}(\bar{l})}{\Gamma \vdash \Delta}$$

Fig. 3. The DPLL procedure adapted to expandable literals

the structural sharing provided by this method. In Sect. 4, we will describe how these expandable literals can be implemented in such a way that common operations are efficient, but for now let us see how the DPLL procedure should be adapted.

3.3 Adaptation of the DPLL Procedure

In order to use expandable literals in the DPLL procedure, we have to adapt the rules presented in Sect. 3.1. Let us consider a proxy literal f for a formula F. If this proxy is assigned a true value at some point during the proof search, this means that the formula F is assumed to be true. Therefore, something should be added to the current problem that reflects this fact in order to preserve the semantic soundness of the procedure. To this end, we use the expand function on f in order to unveil the structure of F, and add the resulting list of clauses $\text{expand}(f)$ to the current problem.

The revised version of our inference rules system is given in Fig. 3. The only modifications between this system and the one presented in Fig. 2 concern rules which change the current assignment Γ : UNIT and SPLIT. When a literal l is assumed in the current context, it is expanded and the resulting clauses are added to the current problem Δ. Intuitively, if l is a proxy for F, $\text{expand}(l)$ can be seen as "consequences" of F and must be added in order to reflect the fact that F shall now be satisfied. Now, given an arbitrary formula F, instead of explicitly converting it into a CNF Δ_F and searching a derivation for $\emptyset \vdash \Delta_F$, it is enough to build a proxy literal l_F for F and attempt to find a derivation for $\emptyset \vdash l_F$ instead. This allows us to use a DPLL decision procedure with the lazy conversion mechanism. Note that correctness does not require proxy literals to be added to the current assignment Γ; however, doing so has a dramatic effect on formulas that can benefit from sharing, e.g. $l \wedge \neg l$, where l stands for a big formula F. Such formulas are not as anecdotal as they seem, and we discuss this further in Sect. 5.2.

We have implemented this system✓ in Coq as a functor parameterized by a module for literals and have proved its soundness✓ and completeness✓. We have also implemented a correct and complete proof-search function✓ that tries to build a derivation for a given formula, returns Unsat if it succeeds and a counter-model satisfying the formula otherwise.

4   Implementing Lazy Literals in Coq

In this section, we show how to design a suitable literal module on which we can instantiate the procedure we described in Sect. 3.3.

4.1   Raw Expandable Literals✓

Expandable literals are either standard propositional atoms, or proxies for a more complex formula. Because a proxy shall be uniquely determined by its expansion (in other words, proxies that expand to the same formula stand for the same formula, and therefore should be equal), we choose to directly represent proxies as their expansion. This leads us to the following definition✓ as a Coq inductive type:

```
Inductive t : Type :=
| Proxy (pos neg : list (list t))
| L (idx : index) (b : bool)
| LT | LF.
```

Standard literals are represented by the L constructor which takes a propositional variable idx and its sign b as argument. The last two constructors LT and LF are just the true and false literals; they are handled specially for practical reasons and we will mostly ignore them in the following. More interestingly, the Proxy constructor expects two arguments: the first one represents the formula that the proxy literal stands for, while the other one corresponds to the expansion of its negation. We proceed this way in order to be able to compute the negation of a literal in constant time, whether it is a proxy or not. Thus, the second parameter of Proxy should just be seen as a memoization of the negation function. As a matter of fact, we can easily define✓ the negation function:

```
Definition mk_not (l : t) : t :=
  match l with
  | Proxy pos neg ⇒ Proxy neg pos
  | L idx b ⇒ L idx b̄
  | LT ⇒ LF | LF ⇒ LT
  end.
```

Negating a standard literal is just changing its sign, while negating a proxy amounts to swapping its arguments. This memoization of the negation of a proxy literal is really critical for the efficiency of the method because literals are negated many times over the course of the DPLL procedure. In Sect. 4.3, we show how these proxies are created in linear time.

The implementation of the expansion function✓ is straightforward and requires no further comment:

```
Definition expand (l : t) : list (list t) :=
  match l with
  | Proxy pos _ ⇒ pos
  | L _ _ | LT | LF ⇒ []
  end.
```

We are left with implementing the comparison functions✓ on these literals. For instance, the equality test goes like this:

```
Fixpoint eq_dec (x y : t) : bool :=
  match x, y with
  | LT, LT | LF, LF ⇒ true
  | L idx b, L idx' b' ⇒ index_eq idx idx' && beq b b'
  | Proxy xpos _, Proxy ypos _ ⇒ ll_eq_dec eq_dec xpos ypos
  | _, _ ⇒ false
  end.
```

In this definition index_eq and beq respectively test equality for indices and booleans, while ll_eq_dec recursively applies this equality test point-wise to lists of lists of literals. The part that is worth noticing is that we only compare proxies' first component and we skip the negated part. This of course ensures that the comparison of proxies is linear in the size of the formula they stand for; had we compared the second component as well, it would have been exponential in practice. The issue with such optimizations is that we have to convince Coq that they make sense, and the next section is devoted to that point.

4.2   Adding Invariants to Raw Literals✓

When implementing expandable literals in the previous section, we made a strong implicit assumption about a proxy Proxy pos neg, namely that neg was indeed containing the "negation" of pos. We need to give a formal meaning to this sentence and to ensure this invariant is verified by all literals. It is not only needed for semantical proofs about literals and the DPLL procedure, but for the correctness of the simplest operations on literals, starting with comparisons. Indeed, considering the equality function eq_dec presented above, it is basically useless unless we can prove the two following properties:

Property eq_dec_true : ∀(x y : t), eq_dec x y = true → x = y.
Property eq_dec_false : ∀(x y : t), eq_dec x y = false → x ≠ y.

Proving the first property for standard literals is straightforward, but as far as proxies are concerned, the fact that the equality test returns true only tells us that the first component of the proxies are equal: there is no guarantee whatsoever on the second component. Therefore, this property is not provable as is and we need to add some relation between the two components of a proxy. This relation also ought to be symmetric since the mk_not function swaps the first and second component, and should of course preserve the invariant as well.

We are going to link the two components of a proxy literal by ensuring that each one is the image of the other by an adequate function $\mathcal{N}$. Intuitively, this function $\mathcal{N}$ must negate a conjunction of disjunction of literals and return another conjunction of disjunction of literals ; it can be recursively defined in the following way

$$\mathcal{N}((\bigvee_{i=1}^{n} x_i) \wedge C) = \bigwedge_{i=1}^{n} \bigwedge_{D \in \mathcal{N}(C)} (\bar{x}_i \vee D)$$

where the x_i are literals and C is a CNF formula. Once this function is implemented✓, we can define an inductive predicate that specifies *well-formed* literals:✓

```
Inductive wf_lit : t → Prop :=
| wf_lit_lit : ∀idx b, wf_lit (L idx b)
| wf_lit_true : wf_lit LT
| wf_lit_false : wf_lit LF
| wf_lit_proxy : ∀pos neg, N pos = neg → N neg = pos →
    (∀ t, l ∈ pos → t ∈ l → wf_lit t) →
    (∀ t, l ∈ neg → t ∈ l → wf_lit t) → wf_lit (Proxy pos neg).
```

The first three constructors express that the true and false literals, as well as all atomic literals, are well-formed. The last one brings up requirements on proxy literals : not only should the two components be each other's image by N [1], but all literals appearing in these expansions should recursively be well-formed. In particular, if two proxies are well-formed, their second components are equal if and only if their first components are equal, which means that we can establish the needed properties about the comparison function.

Packing everything together. In Coq, one can use *dependent types* in order to define a type of objects that meet certain specifications. We use this feature in our Coq development in order to define a module of well-formed literals✓. In this module, the type of literals is the dependent type of raw literals packed with a proof that they are well-formed:✓

Definition t : **Type** := {l | wf_lit l}.

We then have to redefine the required operations on literals. In most cases, it is just a matter of "lifting" to well-formed literals the definition we made for raw literals by showing that the operation preserves well-formedness. For instance, the negation function is (re)defined this way:✓

Property wf_mk_not : ∀l, wf_lit l → wf_lit (mk_not l).
Proof. ..... **Qed.**
Definition mk_not (l:t):t := exist (mk_not $\pi_1(l)$) (wf_mk_not $\pi_1(l)$ $\pi_2(l)$).

where π_1 and π_2 respectively access to the raw literal and its well-formedness proof in a well-formed literal. We have presented a simplified version here and the real development contains more invariants that are required throughout various proofs about literals and their operations. Altogether, we obtain a module with the signature of literals as expected by the DPLL procedure, and where every operation is totally certified.

4.3   Converting Formulas to Lazy Literals✓

Once we have a module implementing lazy literals as described above, we are left with the task of constructing such literals out of an input formula.

First, note that we should not build arbitrary literals but only literals that are well-formed. Therefore we have to make sure that the proxies we build respect the invariants that we introduced in the last section. Assume we want to build a

---

[1] This constraints the form of possible proxies since N is not involutive in general.

Proxy	*pos*	*neg*
$X \equiv P$	$\{P\}$	$\{\bar{P}\}$
$X \equiv F \vee G$	$\{F \vee G\}$	$\{\bar{F}\}\{\bar{G}\}$
$X \equiv F \wedge G$	$\{F\}\{G\}$	$\{\bar{F} \vee \bar{G}\}$
$X \equiv (F \rightarrow G)$	$\{\bar{F} \vee G\}$	$\{F\}\{\bar{G}\}$
$X \equiv (F_1 \vee F_2 \vee \ldots \vee F_n)$	$\{F_1 \vee F_2 \vee \ldots \vee F_n\}$	$\{\bar{F}_1\}\{\bar{F}_2\}\ldots\{\bar{F}_n\}$
$X \equiv (F_1 \wedge F_2 \wedge \ldots \wedge F_n)$	$\{F_1\}\{F_2\}\ldots\{F_n\}$	$\{\bar{F}_1 \vee \bar{F}_2 \vee \ldots \vee \bar{F}_n\}$

Fig. 4. Proxy construction for each logical connective

proxy for a formula $F = F_1 \vee F_2$ and we know how to build proxies l_1 and l_2 for the formulas F_1 and F_2. A suitable proxy for F is the one that expands positively to the list $[[l_1; l_2]]$, and to the list $[[\bar{l}_1]; [\bar{l}_2]]$ negatively. We can check that these two lists are indeed each other's image by $\mathcal{N}$. In practice, we define a function✓ constructing such a proxy and we prove that its result a well-formed:✓

> **Definition** `mk_or_aux` f g := `Proxy` [[f;g]] [[`mk_not` f];[`mk_not` g]].
> **Property** `wf_mk_or` : $\forall (l \ l' : t)$, `wf_lit` (`mk_or_aux` l l').
> **Proof.** ..... **Qed.**
> **Definition** `mk_or` f g : t := `exist` (`mk_or_aux` f g) (`wf_mk_or` f g).

The last command uses `mk_or_aux` and `wf_mk_or` to define a function that creates a well-formed proxy literal for the disjunction of two well-formed literals. We create such smart constructors for each logical connective : the table in Fig. 4 sums up how proxies are constructed for the usual logical connectives. Creating a proxy for an arbitrary formula is then only a matter of recursively applying these smart constructors by following the structure of the formula. We have implemented✓ such a function named `mk_form` and proved✓ that for every formula F, `mk_form` F $\leftrightarrow$ F. This theorem is very important since it is the first step that must be done when applying the tactic : it allows us to replace the current formula by a proxy✓ before calling the DPLL procedure. Note that the converted formula is *equivalent* to the original because no new variables have been added, whereas with Tseitin-like methods, the converted formula is only *equisatisfiable*.

Constructing proxies for N-ary operators. Figure 4 also contains proxy definitions for n-ary versions of the $\wedge$ and $\vee$ operators. We have implemented an alternative version✓ of the `mk_form` function above which tries to add as few levels of proxies as possible. When constructing a proxy for a disjunction (resp. conjunction), it tries to regroup all the disjunctive (resp. conjunctive) top-level structure in one single proxy. In this setting, equivalences are interpreted either as conjunctions or as disjunctions[2] in order to minimize the number of proxies.

---

[2] The equivalence $F \leftrightarrow G$ is logically equivalent to the conjunction $(F \rightarrow G) \wedge (G \rightarrow F)$ and the disjunction $(F \wedge G) \vee (\bar{F} \wedge \bar{G})$.

5 Results and Discussion

5.1 Benchmarks

The whole Coq development is available at http://www.lri.fr/~lescuyer/ unsat/unsat.tgz and can be compiled with Coq v8.2. It represents about 10000 lines of proofs and definitions and provides two different proof search strategies and all six variants of CNF conversion✓ that were discussed in this paper. No result has been admitted and no axioms have been assumed, therefore proofs made with our tactics are closed under context.[3] Because our development is highly modular, the procedure can be instantiated to decide boolean formulas as well as propositional formulas.

	tauto	CNF_C	CNF_A	Tseitin	Tseitin2	Lazy	LazyN
hole3	–	0.72	0.06	0.24	0.21	0.06	**0.05**
hole4	–	3.1	0.23	3.5	6.8	0.32	**0.21**
hole5	–	10	2.7	80	–	1.9	**1.8**
deb5	83	–	0.04	0.15	0.10	0.09	**0.03**
deb10	–	–	0.10	0.68	0.43	0.66	**0.09**
deb20	–	–	**0.35**	4.5	2.5	7.5	**0.35**
equiv2	0.03	–	0.06	1.5	1.0	**0.02**	**0.02**
equiv5	61	–	–	–	–	0.44	**0.42**
franzen10	0.25	16	0.05	0.05	0.03	**0.02**	**0.02**
franzen50	–	–	0.40	1.4	0.80	**0.34**	0.35
schwicht20	0.48	–	0.12	0.43	0.23	**0.10**	**0.10**
schwicht50	8.8	–	0.60	4.3	2.2	**0.57**	0.7
partage	–	–	–	13	19	**0.04**	0.06
partage2	–	–	–	–	–	0.12	**0.11**

Fig. 5. Comparison of different tactics and CNF conversion methods. Timings are given in seconds and – denote time-outs (>120s).

We benchmarked our tactic and the different CNF conversion methods on valid and unsatisfiable formulas✓ described by Dyckhoff [17] ; for instance *holen* stands for the pigeon-hole formula with n holes. We used two extra special formulas in order to test sharing of subformulas : *partage* is the formula *hole3* $\wedge$ $\neg hole3$, while *partage2* is *deb3* where atoms have been replaced by pigeon-hole formulas with varying sizes. Results are summarized in Fig. 5, where CNF_C and CNF_A are naive translations respectively on the Coq side and on the abstract side, Tseitin and Tseitin2 are the two variants of Tseitin conversion described in Sect. 2.3, and LazyN is our lazy conversion with proxies for n-ary operators. These results show that our tactic outperforms tauto in every single case (see discussion below for differences between our tactic and tauto), solving in less

---

[3] We discuss the possible use of the excluded-middle in Sect. 5.2. In any case, users can use the new Print Asssumptions command in order to check if their proofs depend on any axioms or not.

than a second goals that were beyond reach with the existing tactic. About the different CNF conversions, it turns out that the Tseitin conversion is almost always worse than the naive CNF conversion because of the extra clauses and variables. The lazy tactics always perform at least as well as CNF_A and in many cases they perform much better, especially when some sharing is required.

5.2 Discussion and Limitations

Comparison with tauto/intuition. In Coq, the tactic tauto is actually a customized version of the tactic intuition. intuition relies on an intuitionistic decision procedure and, when it can't solve a goal completely, is able to take advantage of the search-tree built by the decision procedure in order to simplify the current goal in a set of (simpler) subgoals ; tauto simply calls intuition and fails if any subgoals are generated. Unlike intuition, our tactic is unable to return a simplified goal when it cannot solve it completely, and in that sense it can be considered as less powerful. However, intuition's performance often becomes an issue in practice[4], therefore we are convinced that the two tactics can prove really complementary in practice, with intuition being used as a simplifier and our tactic as a solver.

Classical reasoning in an intuitionistic setting. The DPLL procedure is used to decide classical propositional logic whereas Coq's logic is intuitionistic. In our development, we took great care in not using the excluded-middle for our proofs so that Coq users who do not want to assume the excluded-middle in their development can still use our tactic. The reason we were able to do so lies in the observation that the formula $\forall A. \neg\neg (A \vee \neg A)$ is intuitionnistically provable: when the current goal is False, this lemma can be applied to add an arbitrary number of ground instances of the excluded-middle to the context. In other words, if a ground formula Φ is a classical tautology, $\neg\neg\Phi$ is an intuitionistic tautology[5]. Noticing that $\neg\neg\neg\Phi$ implies $\neg\Phi$ in intuitionistic logic, this means that if $\neg\Phi$ is classically valid, it is also a tautology in intuitionistic logic. Because the DPLL procedure proceeds by refuting the context Φ, ie. proving $\neg\Phi$, we can use it in intuitionsitic reasoning even if it relies on classical reasoning.

In practice, the use of classical reasoning in our development is mainly for the correctness of the SPLIT rule and of the different CNF conversion rules (*e.g.* $F \rightarrow G \equiv \bar{F} \vee G$). This led us to proving many intermediate results and lemmas in double-negation style because they were depending on some classical reasoning steps, but the nice consequence is that our tactic produces intuitionistic refutation proofs and thus can really replace tauto when the context becomes inconsistent. Users of classical reasoning can use our tactic for classical validity by simply refuting the negation of the current goal.

---

[4] As Coq users, we often let tauto run for 10 seconds to make sure that a goal is provable, but if tauto didn't succeed immediately, we then proceed to manually prove it or simplify it in easier subgoals.

[5] This is not true for first-order formulas, because the formula $\neg\neg(\forall A.A \vee \neg A)$, where the quantification lies below the double negation, is not intuitionnistically provable.

Impact of sharing. The results presented above show that the number of proxies has less effect on the performance than the sharing they provide. Depending on the formula, it may not be the best idea to minimize the number of proxies as LazyN does, because this minimizes the number of subformulas that are shared. Once again, we can use our modular development to provide these different alternatives as options to the user. We wrote in Sect. 3.3 that adding proxies to the current assignment made it possible to reduce a whole subformula of a the problem in one single step, and this is why sharing is beneficial. We gave the obvious, rather crafted, example of $l \wedge \bar{l}$ where l is a big formula, but there is a less obvious and much more frequent situation where it happens. Formalizations often involve predicate definitions $p(x_1, \ldots, x_n) = \Phi(x_1, \ldots, x_n)$ where Φ can be a big formula, p is then used as a shortcut for Φ throughout the proofs. Now, when calling a DPLL procedure, one has to decide whether occurrences of p should be considered as atoms or should be unfolded to Φ. There is no perfect strategy, since proofs sometimes depend on p being unfolded and sometimes do not, but always unfolding p in the latter case leads to performance losses. Proxies make the DPLL procedure completely oblivious to such intermediate definitions, and this is a great asset when dealing with proof obligations from program verification.

5.3   Application to Other Systems

The advantages of the CNF conversion that we have implemented go beyond the scope of our tactic. It generally allows subformulas to be structurally shared which can give a big performance boost to the procedure. Moreover, in standard programming languages, proxies can be compared in constant time by using *hash-consing* [19], which removes the main cost of using lazy literals.

Lazy literals also provide a solution to a problem that is specific to SMT solvers : definitional clauses due to Tseitin-style variables appearing in contexts where they are not relevant can not only cause the DPLL procedure to perform many useless splits, but they also add ground terms that can be used to generate instances of lemmas. De Moura and Bjorner report on this issue in [13], where they use a notion of *relevancy* in order to only consider definitional clauses at the right time. Lazy CNF conversion is a solution to this issue, and it is the method we currently use in our own prover Alt-Ergo [5].

Finally, one may wonder whether this method can be adapted to state-of-the-art decision procedures, including common optimizations like backjumping and conflict clause learning. Adapting such procedures can be done in the same way that we adapted the basic DPLL and is really straightforward ; an interesting question though is the potential impact that lazy CNF conversion could have on the dependency analysis behind these optimizations. We have not yet thoroughly studied this question but our experience with Alt-Ergo suggests that lazy CNF conversion remains a very good asset even with a more optimized DPLL.

6   Conclusion

We have presented a new Coq tactic for solving propositional formulas which outperforms the existing `tauto`. It is based on a reflexive DPLL procedure that we have entirely formalized in the Coq proof assistant. We have used a lazy conversion scheme in order to bring arbitary formulas into clausal form without deteriorating the performance of the procedure. The results are very encouraging and we are planning on extending this tactic with decision procedures for specific theories in the same spirit as SMT solvers.

References

1. Bezem, M., Hendriks, D., de Nivelle, H.: Automated proof construction in type theory using resolution. JAR 29(3), 253–275 (2002)
2. Bonichon, R., Delahaye, D., Doligez, D.: Zenon: An extensible automated theorem prover producing checkable proofs. In: Dershowitz, N., Voronkov, A. (eds.) LPAR 2007. LNCS, vol. 4790, pp. 151–165. Springer, Heidelberg (2007)
3. Boutin, S.: Using reflection to build efficient and certified decision procedures. In: Abadi, M., Ito, T. (eds.) TACS 1997. LNCS, vol. 1281, pp. 515–529. Springer, Heidelberg (1997)
4. Chrząszcz, J.: Implementation of modules in the Coq system. In: Basin, D., Wolff, B. (eds.) TPHOLs 2003. LNCS, vol. 2758, pp. 270–286. Springer, Heidelberg (2003)
5. Conchon, S., Contejean, E.: The Alt-Ergo Prover, http://alt-ergo.lri.fr/
6. Contejean, E., Corbineau, P.: Reflecting Proofs in First-Order Logic with Equality. In: Nieuwenhuis, R. (ed.) CADE 2005. LNCS (LNAI), vol. 3632, pp. 7–22. Springer, Heidelberg (2005)
7. Contejean, E., Courtieu, P., Forest, J., Pons, O., Urbain, X.: Certification of automated termination proofs. In: Konev, B., Wolter, F. (eds.) FroCos 2007. LNCS (LNAI), vol. 4720, pp. 148–162. Springer, Heidelberg (2007)
8. The Coq Proof Assistant, http://coq.inria.fr/
9. Corbineau, P.: Deciding equality in the constructor theory. In: Altenkirch, T., McBride, C. (eds.) TYPES 2006. LNCS, vol. 4502, pp. 78–92. Springer, Heidelberg (2007)
10. Davis, M., Logemann, G., Loveland, D.: A machine program for theorem-proving. Communication of the ACM 5(7), 394–397 (1962)
11. Davis, M., Putnam, H.: A computing procedure for quantification theory. J. ACM 7(3), 201–215 (1960)
12. de la Tour, T.B.: Minimizing the number of clauses by renaming. In: Stickel, M.E. (ed.) CADE-10 1990. LNCS (LNAI), vol. 449, pp. 558–572. Springer, Heidelberg (1990)
13. de Moura, L.M., Bjørner, N.: Efficient E-matching for SMT solvers. In: Pfenning, F. (ed.) CADE 2007. LNCS, vol. 4603, pp. 183–198. Springer, Heidelberg (2007)
14. Delahaye, D., Mayero, M.: Field: une procédure de décision pour les nombres réels en Coq. In: JFLA, Pontarlier (France), INRIA, Janvier (2001)
15. Detlefs, D., Nelson, G., Saxe, J.B.: Simplify: a theorem prover for program checking. J. ACM 52(3), 365–473 (2005)
16. Dyckhoff, R.: Contraction-free sequent calculi for intuitionistic logic. J. Symb. Log. 57(3), 795–807 (1992)
17. Dyckhoff, R.: Some benchmark formulae for intuitionistic propositional logic (1997)
18. Eén, N., Sörensson, N.: An extensible sat-solver. In: Giunchiglia, E., Tacchella, A. (eds.) SAT 2003. LNCS, vol. 2919, pp. 502–518. Springer, Heidelberg (2004)
19. Filliâtre, J.-C., Conchon, S.: Type-safe modular hash-consing. In: Kennedy, A., Pottier, F. (eds.) ML, pp. 12–19. ACM, New York (2006)

20. Grégoire, B., Mahboubi, A.: Proving equalities in a commutative ring done right in Coq. In: Hurd, J., Melham, T. (eds.) TPHOLs 2005. LNCS, vol. 3603, pp. 98–113. Springer, Heidelberg (2005)
21. Lescuyer, S., Conchon, S.: A Reflexive Formalization of a SAT Solver in Coq. In: TPHOLS 2008 Emerging Trends (2008)
22. Meng, J., Quigley, C., Paulson, L.C.: Automation for interactive proof: first prototype. Inf. Comput. 204(10), 1575–1596 (2006)
23. Moskewicz, M.W., Madigan, C.F., Zhao, Y., Zhang, L., Malik, S.: Chaff: engineering an efficient sat solver. In: DAC 2001, pp. 530–535. ACM Press, New York (2001)
24. Nonnengart, A., Rock, G., Weidenbach, C.: On generating small clause normal forms. In: Kirchner, C., Kirchner, H. (eds.) CADE 1998. LNCS, vol. 1421, pp. 397–411. Springer, Heidelberg (1998)
25. Plaisted, D.A., Greenbaum, S.: A structure-preserving clause form translation. J. Symb. Comput. 2(3), 293–304 (1986)
26. Pugh, W.: The omega test: a fast and practical integer programming algorithm for dependence analysis. Communications of the ACM 8, 4–13 (1992)
27. Tseitin, G.S.: On the complexity of derivations in the propositional calculus, Part II. Studies in Mathematics and Mathematical Logic, pp. 115–125 (1968)
28. Weber, T., Amjad, H.: Efficiently Checking Propositional Refutations in HOL Theorem Provers. Journal of Applied Logic 7, 26–40 (2009)

Combining Instance Generation and Resolution

Christopher Lynch and Ralph Eric McGregor

Clarkson University
www.clarkson.edu/projects/carl

Abstract. We present a new inference system for first-order logic, SIG-Res, which couples together SInst-Gen and ordered resolution into a single inference system. Given a set F of first order clauses we create two sets, P and R, each a subset of F. Under SIG-Res, P is saturated by SInst-Gen and resolution is applied to pairs of clauses in $P \cup R$ where at least one of the clauses is in R. We discuss the motivation for this inference system and prove its completeness. We also discuss our implementation called Spectrum and give some initial results.

1 Introduction

The most efficient propositional logic SAT solvers are those based on the DPLL procedure [5, 4]. Given the incredible efficiency of these solvers, a great deal of research has centered around ways to utilize the efficiency of SAT solvers for first-order logic theorem proving. Toward this pursuit, some have lifted the DPLL procedure to first-order logic in the form of the model evolution calculus [3]. Others have used SAT solvers as auxiliary tools to determine the satisfiability of certain fragments (or all) of first-order logic via propositional encodings [11,22,7]. A third use of SAT solvers in first-order logic theorem proving has been in saturation-based instance generation methods which repeatedly call upon a SAT solver to find so-called *conflicts* between clauses and use instance generation inferences to resolve these conflicts. Notable in this last line of research are the works by Jeroslow [12, 13] who developed the saturation-based instance generation method called *Partial Instantiation* (PI), Hooker (et.al) who developed the first complete PI method for the full first-order logic called *Primal PI* [10] and Ganzinger and Korovin who among many other contributions formalized and proved the completeness of the instance generation inference rule, Inst-Gen, and the extention SInst-Gen (Inst-Gen with semantic selection and hyper inferences) in [9]. The efficiency of saturation-based instance generation methods is demonstrated by Korovin's implementation called IProver [15, 24].

Another well known line of research in first-order logic theorem proving began with Robinson's landmark paper [20] which describes his resolution principle and unification. Since then, many refinements have been made, e.g. ordered resolution and semantic resolution [18, 16, 1]. Recent implementations of resolution have been shown to be the top performer in the CASC competition [24].

A key benefit of resolution is the ability to restrict the search space with the use of *ordered* resolution. Here, resolution inferences are only necessary on

S. Ghilardi and R. Sebastiani (Eds.): FroCoS 2009, LNAI 5749, pp. 304–318, 2009.

maximal literals. Selection rules can also be applied which also restrict the search space. Ordered resolution can be efficient in practice, because it tends to produce literals in the conclusion of an inference that are smaller than in the premises. This is not always the case however, because the most general unifier may prevent that, but it often happens in practice. For the simplest example, consider a set of clauses consisting of one non-ground clause $C = \neg P(x) \vee P(f(x))$ and any number of ground clauses. Any inference among two ground clauses will produce another ground clause which does not introduce any new literals. Any inference between a ground clause and C will produce a new ground clause where an occurrence of the symbol f has disappeared. This will clearly halt. However, if this set of clauses is fed to an instantiation-based prover, it may run forever, depending on the model created by the SAT solver. In our experiments, this does run forever in practice.

Although resolution methods appear to be more efficient in practice, there are some classes of problems that are suited better for instantiation-based methods. Instantiation-based methods work especially well on problems that are close to propositional problems, because then the key technique is the DPLL procedure in the SAT solver. There is even a class of first-order logic problems, problems which contain no function symbols, called Effectively Propositional (EPR) for which instantiation-based methods form a decision procedure, whereas resolution methods may run forever.

Here we show that we can combine both instance generation and resolution into a single inference system while retaining completeness with the aim of getting the best of both methods. The inference system SIG-Res, given in this paper, combines semantic selection instance generation (SInst-Gen) with ordered resolution. Each clause in the given set of clauses is determined, by some heuristic, to be an instantiation clause and placed in the set P or a resolution clause and placed in the set R or placed in both P and R. Clauses from P are given to a SAT solver and inferences among them are treated as in SInst-Gen, while any inference which involves a clause in R is a resolution inference.

Our combination of instance generation and resolution differs from the method used in the instantiation-based theorem prover IProver which uses resolution inferences to simplify clauses, i.e. if a conclusion of a resolution inference strictly subsumes one if its premise then the conclusion is added to the set of clauses sent to the SAT solver and the subsumed premise is removed. Our inference system also allows for the use of resolution for the simplification of the clauses in P, but differs from IProver in that it restricts certain clauses, the clauses in R, from any instance generation inference.

Our idea is similar to the idea of Satisfiability Modulo Theories (SMT), where clauses in P represent data, and the clauses in R represent a theory. This is similar to the SMELS inference system [17] and the DPLL($\Gamma + T$) inference system [19]. The difference between those inference systems and ours is that in those inference systems, P must only contain ground clauses, and the theory is all the nonground clauses, whereas in our case we allow nonground clauses in P.

In the pages that follow, we prove the completeness of our inference system, discuss our implementation, called Spectrum, and we present our initial implementation results.

2   Preliminaries

We begin by defining the terminology used in this paper as is in [9,1]. The setting we are considering is classical first order logic. Variables and constant symbols are *terms* and if f is any n-ary function symbol and $t_1, \ldots, t_n$ are terms then $f(t_1, \ldots, t_n)$ is a term. If P is a predicate symbol and $t_1, \ldots, t_n$ are terms then $P(t_1, \ldots, t_n)$ is an *atom*. Formulas are constructed using the logical connectives $\neg$ (negation), $\vee$ (disjunction), $\wedge$ (conjunction) under the standard rules of formula construction. A *literal* is either an atom (positive literal) or the negation of an atom (negative literal). If A is an atom we say that A and $\neg A$ are *complements* and we denote the complement of a literal L by $\overline{L}$. A *clause* is a disjunction of literals, however we often view a clause as a multiset of literals. A *ground clause* is a clause that contains no variables. We consider a formula to be a conjunction of clauses in conjunctive normal form and often view a formula as a set of clauses. We denote by $\varnothing$ the empty set and denote the empty clause by $\square$.

An ordering $<$ on terms is any strict partial ordering that is well-founded, stable under substitution and total on ground terms. We extend $<$ to atoms in such a way so that for any atom A we have $A < \neg A$. The ordering $<$ is extended to clauses by considering a clause as a multiset of literals. Given a clause C, a literal $L \in C$ is *maximal* in C if there is no $K \in C$ such that $K > L$. We define a mapping, max from clauses to multisets of literals such that $\max(C) = \{L | L \text{ is maximal in } C\}$.

A *substitution* is a mapping from variables to terms, almost everywhere the identity. We denote an application of a substitution σ to a clause C as $C\sigma$. A clause C *subsumes* another clause D if there exists a substitution σ such that $C\sigma \subseteq D$. A *unifier* of two literals L and K is a substitution σ such that $L\sigma = K\sigma$. If such a unifier exists, we say that L and K are *unifiable*. A *most general unifier* of L and K, denoted $\mathrm{mgu}(L, K)$, is a unifier, σ, of L and K such that for every unifier, τ, of L and K, there exists some substitution ρ such that $\tau = \sigma\rho$ over the variables of L and K. A *renaming* is an injective substitution that maps variables to variables and we say that two literals are *variants* if there exists a renaming which unifies them.

A substitution that maps at least one variable of an expression E to a nonvariable term is called a *proper instantiator* of E. We say that a clause C is a (proper) *instance* of clause C' if there exists some (proper instantiator) substitution σ such that $C = C'\sigma$. For a set of clauses S, we denote the set of all ground instances of the clauses in S as $Gr(S)$.

$\perp$ is used to denote a distinguished constant and the substitution which maps all variables to $\perp$. If L is a literal then $L\perp$ denotes the ground literal obtained by applying the $\perp$-substitution to L and if P is a set of clauses then $P\perp$ denotes the set of ground clauses obtained by applying the $\perp$-substitution to the clauses in P.

A *Herbrand interpretation*, I, is a consistent set of ground literals. We say that a ground literal is *undefined* in I if neither it nor its complement is in I. If a ground literal L is in I then we say that L is *true* in I and $\overline{L}$ is *false* in I. I is a *total interpretation* if no ground literal is undefined in I. A ground clause C is true in a partial interpretation I if there exists some literal L in C that is true in I, and we say that C is satisfied by I.

A *closure* is denoted by the pair $C' \cdot \sigma$, where C' is a clause and σ is a substitution. Suppose $C = C' \cdot \sigma$ is a closure. As an abuse of notation we may also refer to C as the instance of C' under the substitution σ, that is $C'\sigma$. We say that C is a *ground closure* if $C'\sigma$ is ground. If S is a set of clauses and $C' \in S$ we say that $C'\sigma$ is an *instance of* S. A *closure ordering* is any well founded and total (modulo renaming) ordering on closures.

3   Instance Generation and Resolution

The main idea behind all saturation-based instance generation methods is to augment a set of clauses with sufficiently many proper instances so that the satisfiability of the set can be determined by a SAT solver. Additional instances are generated using some form of the Inst-Gen [9] inference rule. An instance generation with semantic selection inference system (SInst-Gen) (See Figure 1) uses a selection function and the notion of *conflicts* to determine exactly which clauses are to be used as premises in the instance generation inferences.

Let P be a set of first order clauses and view $P\perp$ as a set of propositional clauses. Under this setting, if $P\perp$ is unsatisfiable, then P is unsatisfiable and our work is done. Otherwise a model for $P\perp$ is denoted as $I_\perp$ and we define a selection function, $\text{sel}(C, I_\perp)$, which maps each clause $C \in P$ to a singleton set $\{L\}$ such that $L \in C$ and $L\perp$ is true in $I_\perp$.

We say, given a model $I_\perp$, that two clauses $\Gamma \vee L$ and $\Delta \vee \overline{K}$ *conflict* if

(i) $L \in sel(\Gamma \vee L, I_\perp)$ and $\overline{K} \in \text{sel}(\Delta \vee \overline{K}, I_\perp)$
(ii) L and K are unifiable

Instance generation with semantic selection methods saturate a set of clauses P by repeatedly calling apon a SAT solver to obtain a model for $P\perp$ and resolving all conflicts with SInst-Gen inferences[1]. If $P\perp$ is ever found unsatisfiable, P is unsatisfiable. If, on the other hand, $P\perp$ is satisfiable and no conflicts exist then P is satisfiable. SInst-Gen is refutationally complete [9] but may not halt.

The ordered resolution and factoring inference rules are well known in the literature. For completeness they are given in Figure 2. The strength of ordered resolution is in its ability to reduce the search space by requiring only inferences between clauses which conflict where max is the selection function.

The satisfiablity of a set R is determined by applying resolution and factoring inferences rules to the clauses in R in a fair manner until either the empty clause ($\square$) is resolved, in which case R is unsatisfiable, or the set is saturated and $\square \notin R$,

---

[1] Instance generation with selection functions mapping to singleton sets and resolving conflicts based on these selected literals is precisely the Primal Pl method in [10].

SInst-Gen

$$\frac{\Gamma \vee L \qquad \Delta \vee \overline{K}}{(\Gamma \vee L)\tau \qquad (\Delta \vee \overline{K})\tau}$$

where (i) $L \in sel(\Gamma \vee L, I_\perp)$ and $\overline{K} \in sel(\Delta \vee \overline{K}, I_\perp)$
(ii) $\tau = \mathrm{mgu}(L, \overline{K})$

Fig. 1. SInst-Gen Inference Rule

in which case R is satisfiable. As is the case with SInst-Gen, ordered resolution with factoring is refutationally complete, but for some satisfiable problems may not halt.

Ordered Resolution

$$\frac{\Gamma \vee L \qquad \Delta \vee \overline{K}}{(\Gamma \vee \Delta)\tau}$$

where (i) $L \in \max(\Gamma \vee L)$ and $\overline{K} \in \max(\Delta \vee \overline{K})$
(ii) $\tau = \mathrm{mgu}(L, K)$

Factoring

$$\frac{\Gamma \vee L \vee K}{(\Gamma \vee L)\tau}$$

where $\tau = \mathrm{mgu}(L, K)$

Fig. 2. Ordered Resolution and Factoring Inference Rules

4   SIG-Res

The inferences in SIG-Res are variations of SInst-Gen, ordered resolution and factoring (see Figure 3). SIG-Res is an inference system that requires two sets of clauses. Given a set of clauses, S, which we wish to prove satisfiable or unsatisfiable, we create two sets of clauses, $P \subseteq S$ and $R \subseteq S$, not necessarily disjoint, such that $P \cup R = S$. Given some clause $C \in S$, C is designated as either a clause in P, a clause in R, or both, according to any distribution heuristic of our choosing, so long as $P \cup R = S$.

The distribution heuristic is a key mechanism in this inference system as it determines which inferences are applied to the clauses. Under SIG-Res, a distribution heuristic can, at one end of the spectrum, insert all the clauses of S in P, leaving R empty, which would make the system essentially a instance generation inference system. On the other end of the spectrum, the distribution heuristic can distribute all the clauses to R, leaving P empty, making the system a resolution system. This flexibility allows any number of heuristics to be used and heuristics to be tailored to specific classes of problems. An open question is which heuristics perform best and for which classes of problems. In Section 6 we describe one general heuristic, GSM, which we have incorporated into our implementation.

The selection function, $\text{sel}(C, I_\perp)$, where $C \in P \cup R$ and $I_\perp$ is a model for $P\perp$, is defined as follows. For clarity, we note that $\text{sel}(C, I_\perp)$ returns a singleton set if $C \in P$ and a non-empty set if $C \in R$.

$$\text{sel}(C, I_\perp) = \begin{cases} \{L\} \text{ for some } L \in C \text{ such that } L\perp \in I_\perp & \text{if } C \in P \\ \max(C) & \text{if } C \in R \end{cases}$$

We will have the usual redundancy notions for saturation inference systems. We can define deletion rules to say that a clause can be deleted if it is implied by zero or more smaller clauses. For example, tautologies can be deleted. The clause ordering, as we will define it in the next section, will restrict what subsumptions can be done. In particular, if a clause C is in R, we say that C is subsumed by a clause D if there exists a substitution σ such that $D\sigma$ is a subset of C. If C is a clause in P, we say that C is subsumed by D if there exists a substitution σ such that $D\sigma$ is a proper subset of C.

We will define saturation in the next section, to take into account the model $I_\perp$. Saturation of S under SIG-Res is achieved by ensuring that all possible inferences are made (fairness). One way to ensure fairness, as is done in the Primal Partial Instantiation method, is to increment a counter and only allow inferences with premises having depth less than or equal to the counter. An alternative method is to perform all possible inferences with the exception that we restrict conclusions generated during each iteration from being considered as premises until the next iteration. We have implmented IG-Res in a theorem prover called Spectrum. Our implementation uses the latter method and follows Algorithm 1.

5 Completeness

Let S be a set of clauses. We begin by defining an ordering $\prec$ on the closures in S. Given an ordering on terms, $<$, we denote by $\prec_C$ any closure ordering with the following properties: for any closures $C \cdot \sigma$ and $D \cdot \tau$, $C \cdot \sigma \prec_C D \cdot \tau$ if

> i. $C\sigma < D\tau$ or
> ii. $C\sigma = D\tau$ and $C = D\rho$ where ρ is a proper instantiator of D

We denote by $\prec_S$ any (subsumption) closure ordering with the following property: for any closures $C \cdot \sigma$ and $D \cdot \tau$, $C \cdot \sigma \prec_S D \cdot \tau$ if

> i. $C\sigma < D\tau$ or
> ii. $C\sigma = D\tau$ and $C\rho = D$ where ρ is a proper instantiator of C

Given a set of clauses $S = P \cup R$ and orderings $\prec_C$ and $\prec_S$ we define the ordering $\prec$ on the closures of S as follows. For all closures C and D of S, $C \prec D$ iff

SInst-Gen

$$\frac{\Gamma \vee L \qquad \Delta \vee \overline{K}}{(\Gamma \vee L)\tau \qquad (\Delta \vee \overline{K})\tau}$$

where (i) $\Gamma \vee L \in P$ and $\Delta \vee \overline{K} \in P$
   (ii) $L \in \text{sel}(\Gamma \vee L, I_\perp)$ and $\overline{K} \in \text{sel}(\Delta \vee \overline{K}, I_\perp)$
   (iii) $\tau = \text{mgu}(L, K)$
   (iv) $(\Gamma \vee L)\tau \in P$ and $(\Delta \vee \overline{K})\tau \in P$

Ordered Resolution

$$\frac{\Gamma \vee L \qquad \Delta \vee \overline{K}}{(\Gamma \vee \Delta)\tau}$$

where (i) $\Gamma \vee L \in R$ or $\Delta \vee \overline{K} \in R$
   (ii) $L \in \text{sel}(\Gamma \vee L, I_\perp)$ and $\overline{K} \in \text{sel}(\Delta \vee \overline{K}, I_\perp)$
   (iii) $\tau = \text{mgu}(L, K)$
   (iv) $(\Gamma \vee \Delta)\tau \in P$ if $\Gamma \vee L \notin R$ or $\Delta \vee \overline{K} \notin R$

Factoring

$$\frac{\Gamma \vee L \vee K}{(\Gamma \vee L)\tau}$$

where (i) $\tau = \text{mgu}(L, K)$
   (ii) $(\Gamma \vee L)\tau \in P$ if $\Gamma \vee L \vee K \notin R$

Fig. 3. SIG-Res Inference Rules

 i. C and D are closures of P and $C \prec_C D$ or
 ii. C and D are closures of R and $C \prec_S D$ or
 iii. C is a closure of P and D is a closure of R

$C \cdot \sigma$ is a *minimal closure* in S if C is a closure in S and C is the minimal representation of $C'\sigma$ in S under $\prec$.

A ground clause C is *redundant* in S if there are clauses $C_1, \cdots, C_n$ in set $Gr(S)$ such that $C_i \prec C$ holds for all i, $1 \leq i \leq n$ and $C_1, \cdots, C_n \vDash C$. A clause C is redundant in S if all of the ground instances of C are redundant in $Gr(S)$. A *derivation* of an inference system is a sequence $(S_0, I_0, \text{sel}_0), \cdots, (S_i, I_i, \text{sel}_i), \cdots$, where each S_i is a multiset of clauses divided into sets P_i and R_i, I_i is a model of $P_i \perp$, sel_i is a selection function based on the model I_i, and S_{i+1} results from applying an inference rule or deletion rule on S_i. The sequence has as its limit the set of *persistent clauses* $S_\infty = \bigcup_{i \geq 0} \bigcap_{j \geq i} S_j$. By definition of redundancy, if a clause is redundant in some S_i it is redundant in S_∞.

We define a *persistent model* I_∞ in the following way. Let $A_1, A_2, \cdots$ be an enumeration of all the atoms. Let D_0 be the derivation sequence. For each i, let D_i be the subsequence of D_{i-1} such that (i) if A is true in an infinite number of I_j then D_i is the subsequence of D_{i-1} that only contains tuples (S_j, I_j, sel_j) where

I_j makes A true, else (ii) if A is not true in an infinite number of S_j then D_i is the subsequence of D_{i-1} that only contains tuples (S_j, I_j, sel_j) where I_j makes A false. If $D_\infty = (S_0, I_0, \text{sel}_0), \cdots, (S_i, I_i, \text{sel}_i), \cdots$, then we define $I_\infty = \bigcup_{j \geq 0} I_j$.

S_∞ is called *saturated* if the conclusion of every inference of $(S_\infty, I_\infty, \text{sel}_\infty)$ is in S_∞ or is redundant in S_∞. A derivation is *fair* if no inference is ignored forever, i.e. the conclusion of every inference among persistent clauses is persistent or redundant in S_∞. A fair derivation produces a saturated set.

Now we define the construction of a candidate model for the ground instances of S. Given a clause ordering $\prec$ on the closures of a set of clauses, $S = P \cup R$, for every ground closure, C, of S, we define ϵ_C as a set of zero or more literals in C. We say that C is *productive* if $\epsilon_C \neq \varnothing$, otherwise we say that C is not productive.

Let D be a ground closure in S. We define $I_D = \bigcup_{C \prec D} \epsilon_C$ where C is a ground closure of S and define $I^D = I_D \cup \epsilon_D$. It follows that if $C \prec D$ then $I_C \subseteq I_D$. We define $I_S = \bigcup_C \epsilon_C$ where C is a ground closure in S.

Suppose that $P\bot$ is satisfied by the model $I_\bot$ and let $\prec$ be a closure ordering on the closures of S. We construct a candidate model for the ground instances of S as follows. For all ground closures $C = C' \cdot \sigma$ we define $\epsilon_C = \{L\sigma\}$ if

   i. $C'\sigma$ is not true in I_C and
   ii. $L\sigma$ is undefined in I_C and
   iii. $(C' \in P$ and $L\bot \in I_\bot)$ or $(C' \in R$ and $\max(C'\sigma) = \{L\sigma\})$

Otherwise $\epsilon_C = \varnothing$.

Theorem 1. *Let $S = P \cup R$ be a multiset of clauses saturated under SIG-Res. If $P\bot$ is satisfied by $I_\bot$ then the set of ground instances of P is satisfiable in the candidate model I_S.*

Proof. Let $S = P \cup R$ be a multiset of clauses saturated under SIG-Res and suppose $P\bot$ is satisfied by $I_\bot$. By the completeness of SInst-Gen [9], I_P is a model of the ground instances of P. As $I_P \subseteq I_S$ and I_S is consistent, it follows that the set of ground instances of P is satisfiable in the candidate model I_S.

Theorem 2. *Let $S = P \cup R$ be a multiset of clauses saturated under SIG-Res. S is satisfiable if $P\bot$ is satisfied by $I_\bot$ and S does not contain the empty clause.*

Proof. Let $S = P \cup R$ be a multiset of clauses saturated by SIG-Res. Suppose $P\bot$ is satisfied by $I\bot$ and S does not contain the empty clause. We claim that I_S is a model of all ground instances of S.

Suppose on the contrary that I_S is not a model for the set of ground instances of S. Let $C = C' \cdot \sigma$ be the minimal ground closure of S that is false or undefined in I_S.

As $P\bot$ is satisfied by $I_\bot$, it follows that the set of ground instances of P is satisfiable in the candidate model I_S. Therefore it must be the case that $C' \in R$.

Let $L\sigma \in \max(C)$. Now, suppose $L\sigma$ is undefined in I_S. Then as $C'\sigma$ is not true in I_S, C is productive, a contradiction. Hence, $L\sigma$ is false in I_S. If $L\sigma$ is a duplicate in $C'\sigma$ then let B' be the conclusion resulting from the factoring of C'. Then $B'\sigma$ is smaller than $C'\sigma$, thus contradicting the minimality of $C'\sigma$.

Therefore, let us assume that $L\sigma$ is not a duplicate and let $C' = C'' \vee L$ for some C''.

As C is not productive and $L\sigma$ is false in I_S there exists some productive minimal ground closure $D = D' \cdot \sigma$ [2] such that $D \prec C$ and $\epsilon_D = \{\overline{L\sigma}\}$. Therefore $D' = D'' \vee K$ where $K\sigma = \overline{L\sigma}$ and $.D''\sigma$ is not true in I^D.

Let $B' = (D'' \vee C'')\tau$ where $\tau = \mathrm{mgu}(\overline{K}, L)$ be the conclusion of the resolution inference with premises $D' = D'' \vee K$ and $C' = C'' \vee L$ and let B be the minimal representative of $B'\sigma$. Therefore B is a ground instance of B'.

Now $D' \in P$ or $D' \in R$ so we proceed by cases.

Case 1: Suppose that $D' \in P$. Since S is saturated by SInst-Gen and $C' \in R$, then the conclusion of the resolution inference between D' and C', i.e. B', is in P or is redundant.

If B' is in P then $B'\sigma$ is satisfied in I_S. If B' is redundant then there exists $B_1, B_2, ..., B_n \in P$ such that $B_1, B_2, \cdots, B_n \models B'$ and for all i, $1 \leq i \leq n$, B_i is smaller than B'. Since for all i, $1 \leq i \leq n$, $B_i\sigma$ is satisfied in I_S then $B'\sigma$ is satisfied in I_S.

Since $B'\sigma = (D'' \vee C'')\sigma$ is true in I_S and $C''\sigma$ is not true in I_S then $D''\sigma$ must be satisfied in I_S. Now as $D''\sigma$ is not true in I^D, then it follows that $D \prec B$. Therefore $(D'' \vee K)\sigma$ is smaller than $(D'' \vee C'')\sigma$. Hence $K\sigma = \overline{L\sigma}$ is smaller than $C''\sigma$, which is a contradiction as $L\sigma \in \max(C)$.

Case 2: Suppose now that $D' \in R$. Since $\epsilon_D = \{K\sigma\}$, $K\sigma \in \max(D)$. Therefore $D''\sigma$ is smaller than $K\sigma$. Hence B' is strictly smaller than C. And as $D''\sigma$ is not true in I_S and $C''\sigma$ is not true in I_S we have $B'\sigma$ is not true in I_S. If B' is in S, this contradicts the minimality of C.

If B' is redundant in S then there exists clauses $B_1, B_2, \cdots, B_n \in S$ each smaller than B' such that $B_1, B_2, \cdots, B_n \models B'$. It follows that there exists some $0 \leq i \leq n$ such that $B_i\sigma$ is false in I_S, hence a contradiction. $\qquad\square$

Since SIG-Res is refutationally complete and the inferences are sound, it should be clear that it is only necessary that *at some point in time* we insert the conclusions of SIG-Res inferences into the appropriate set as defined by the inference rules. Prior to that time, without affecting completeness, we can insert conclusions from inferences into P or R with disregard to the algorithm if by doing so we can find a solution quicker.

6   Spectrum

We have implemented SIG-Res in a theorem prover for first order logic called Spectrum. The name comes from the fact that given a set of clauses, our choices to construct the sets P and R are among a spectrum.

Spectrum is written in C++, has a built-in parser for CNF problems in the TPTP format [25] and outputs results in accordance to the SZS ontology [23]. It takes as arguments a filename and mode and outputs satisfiable or unsatisfiable. The modes determine how the clauses will be distributed to the sets P and R.

---

[2] As clauses are standardized apart we use a single substitution σ.

There are a number of distribution modes which Spectrum can be run in. When running Spectrum with the -p flag, Spectrum places all clauses in P, hence makes Spectrum run essentially as an instantiation-based theorem prover. The flag -r makes Spectrum run essentially as a resolution theorem prover by placing all the clauses in R. Running spectrum without a mode flag runs our default heuristic we call Ground-Single Max (GSM).

It is well known that in general, SAT solvers are more efficient in solving ground instances than resolution. Our GSM heuristic takes advantage of this by placing all ground clauses in P. GSM also places all clauses with more than one maximal literal in P. GSM places all other clauses in R.

When the program begins, the program distributes the clauses to the two sets P and R in accordance with the distribution mode and if a clause is inserted in R, its maximal literals are identified. After distributing the clauses, Spectrum follows Algorithm 1.

As we begin the instance generation phase on the set P, Yices [8] is used to check the satisfiability of the ground instances of $P\perp$. If Yices reports the problem as inconsistent, Spectrum reports unsatisfiable and halts. However, if Yices reports the problem is consistent (satisfiable) we retrieve a model from Yices and select for each clause the first literal in the clause whose propositional abstraction is true in the model. These are the selected literals that we use for determining if conflicts exist. If a conflict exists we instantiate the new clauses and check to see if the new clauses already exist in P. If not, we add them to P. To ensure that we do not run the instance generation phase forever we do not allow conclusions to SInst-Gen inferences to be premises until after the next call to the SAT solver.

Following the instance generation phase, we check for resolution inferences. We first resolve all unchecked pairs of clauses where both clauses are in R, and then for the unchecked pairs where one clause is in P and the other is in R. To ensure fairness, we exclude from being premises SInst-Gen conclusions that were added during the previous instantiation phase and conclusions from resolution and factoring inferences that are added in the current iteration. If an inference is made, we check to see if it is the empty clause. If so, Spectrum reports unsatisfiable and halts. Otherwise, if one of the premises is in P we perform the simple redundancy check as stated above and when appropriate add the conclusion to P. If, on the other hand, both premises are in R we check for factors. If a factor is slated for R we determine if it already exists in R and if it is forwardly-subsumed by some clause in R. If it is slated for P we only check to see if it already exists in P.

If no new clause is added during an iteration, Spectrum reports Satisfiable and halts, otherwise it repeats the process.

7   Experimental Results and Example

We have tested Spectrum on 450 unsatisfiable problems rated *easy* in the TPTP library. These problems, in general, are not challenging for *state of the art*

Algorithm 1. Spectrum(P,R)

---

while true do
  $N_P := \varnothing$
  $N_R := \varnothing$

  Run SAT on $P\perp$
  if $P\perp$ is unsatisfiable **then**
    return UNSATISFIABLE
  for all $C_1, C_2 \in P$ **do**
    if conflict$(C_1, C_2) = true$ **then**
      $N_P := N_P \cup (\text{SInst-Gen}(C_1, C_2) \setminus P)$

  for all $C_1 \in P, C_2 \in R$ **do**
    $D := \text{Resolution}(C_1, C_2)$
    if $\square \in D$ **then**
      return UNSATISFIABLE
    else if $D \neq \varnothing$ **then**
      $N_P := N_P \cup (D \setminus P)$

  for all $C_1, C_2 \in R$ **do**
    $D := \text{Resolution}(C_1, C_2)$
    if $\square \in D$ **then**
      return UNSATISFIABLE
    else if $D \neq \varnothing$ **then**
      for all $C \in D$ **do**
        $F := \text{Factor}(C)$
        for all $B \in F$ **do**
          $T := \text{distribute}(B)$
          $N_T := N_T \cup (\{B\} \setminus T)$

  if $N_P = \varnothing$ and $N_R = \varnothing$ **then**
    return SATISFIABLE
  else
    Set $P = P \cup N_P$
    Set $R = R \cup N_R$

---

threorem provers, but allow us to compare the different modes of our implementation and give us simple proofs to analyze. Of the 450 problems we tested, Spectrum run in GSM mode for 300 seconds solved 192 problems[3]. Of these 192 problems when given the same time limit, 18 could not be solved by Spectrum run in -p mode where the problem is solved using only instance generation or in -r mode where only resolution inferences are allowed. Interestingly, 16 of these are in the LCL class of problems, the class of Propositional Logic Calculi. Many of these problems contain the axioms of propositional logic which have clauses that are similar to the transitivity property. These can produce a large number

---

[3] These results reflect that our implementation is not yet competitive and lacks some key processes such as robust redundancy deletion.

of clauses under resolution. These clauses, when run under our heuristic, are put in P to avoid this condition. Also present are clauses which we call *growing clauses* because their tendency to produce larger and larger clauses. These growing clauses, e.g. $\neg P(x) \vee P(f(x))$, contain pairs of complementary literals where each argument in the first is a subterm of the second and there exists at least one argument that is a proper subterm. Growing clauses, under our heuristic, since they have only a single maximal literal, are put in R which avoids this problem.

One problem in the TPTP library that illustrates another benefit of SIG-Res with the GSM heuristic is problem GRP006-1. Spectrum using our heuristic solved this problem in less than 1 second, but did not find a solution using instantiation or resolution alone. The initial distribution of clauses and an SIG-Res proof are given in Figure 4. As can be seen, by placing the clauses with more than one maximal literal, specifically clauses *3* and *4*, in P we avoid many resolution inferences that are not necessary for the proof. We also avoid generating many SInst-Gen inferences by placing clause 4 in P and clause 6 in R.

Before determining the problem unsatisfiable, Spectrum makes 3 passes through the while loop generating 32 clauses. During the initial iteration, no conflicts are found and resolution and factoring inferences produce a total of 9 new clauses. During the second iteration, 2 conflicts produce 2 new clauses

Clauses in P

1. $\neg E(inv(a))$
2. $E(a)$
3. $\neg P(x,y,z) \vee \neg P(y,w,v) \vee \neg P(x,v,t) \vee P(z,w,t)$
4. $\neg P(x,y,z) \vee \neg P(y,w,v) \vee \neg P(z,w,t) \vee P(x,v,t)$

Clauses in R

5. $\neg E(x) \vee \neg E(y) \vee \neg P(x,inv(y),z) \vee E(z)$
6. $P(inv(x),x,id)$
7. $P(x,inv(x),id)$
8. $P(x,id,x)$
9. $P(id,x,x)$

$$\textbf{Res(5,7)} \quad \frac{\neg E(x) \vee \neg E(y) \vee \neg P(x,inv(y),z) \vee E(z) \qquad P(x,inv(x),id)}{10.\ \neg E(x) \vee \neg E(x) \vee E(id)}$$

$$\textbf{Factor(10)} \quad \frac{\neg E(x) \vee \neg E(x) \vee E(id)}{11.\ \neg E(x) \vee E(id)}$$

$$\textbf{Res(5,9)} \quad \frac{\neg E(x) \vee \neg E(y) \vee \neg P(x,inv(y),z) \vee E(z) \qquad P(id,x,x)}{12.\ \neg E(id) \vee \neg E(x) \vee E(inv(x))}$$

$$\textbf{SInst-Gen(2,11)} \quad \frac{E(a) \qquad \neg E(x) \vee E(id)}{13.\ \neg E(a) \vee E(id)}$$

$$\textbf{Res(1,12)} \quad \frac{\neg E(inv(a)) \qquad \neg E(id) \vee \neg E(x) \vee E(inv(x))}{14.\ \neg E(id) \vee \neg E(a)}$$

Fig. 4. Proof of GRP006-1

and resolution and factoring produce 21 new clauses. During the third iteration, Yices returns back unsatisfiable as clause 2, 13 and 14 are inconsistent. This example shows that the clauses in a problem may have different properties and that by controlling the types of inferences that are applied to the clauses we may eliminates unnecessary inferences and may produce a solution sooner than if using resolution or instantiation inferences alone.

8   Conclusion

In this paper, we have developed an inference system which combines instance generation and resolution. We have proved its completeness and provide some preliminary experimental results from our implementation. The key feature of our inference system is that clauses are partitioned into two sets: P and R. SInst-Gen inferences are performed between members of P, while resolution is performed between clauses when one is from R.

It is important to provide a good heuristic to decide which clauses should be in P and which ones should be in R. Ground clauses ought to be in P, because the SAT solver processes ground clauses most efficiently. Our heuristic puts clauses with more than one maximal literal into P, because ordered resolution generally does not handle these clauses well. For example, ordered resolution with the Transitivity Axiom does not halt. In our heuristic, we put clauses with a single maximal literal into R, because ordered resolution with those literals will generally reduce the size of the other premise.

Our implementation is rudimentary and does not contain all the useful features of state of the art theorem provers but is still useful for comparison purposes. There are several examples from LCL, and also the GRP problem we illustrate, where our heuristic performs better than solely using instance generation or resolution. The GRP problem is an example that contains clauses that can cause infinite growth, so it is not good for instance generation. While at the same time, it contains clauses similar to Transitivity where ordered resolution is explosive. We believe these examples show the use of our technique and the potential for further research into this area.

9   Future Work

We are continuing our experiments to determine which distribution heuristics perform best on general sets of problems and for certain classes of problems. We are also continuing the development of Spectrum. As a rudimentary theorem prover, there is room for improving Spectrum's performance by incorporating more sophisticated data structures, heuristics and techniques that are in the literature, e.g. implementing a more sophisticated method for choosing selected literals for clauses in P, restricting SInst-Gen inference using *dismatching constraints*, using more efficient factoring and redundancy elimination techniques, etc.

The Completeness Proof for SIG-Res relies on ordered resolution. It may be interesting to determine if the completeness proof for SIG-Res can be extended to ordered resolution with selection and if so, how it affects the implementation's performance.

We are also interested in investigating if the partitioning idea can be extended to equalities. Specifically, given a problem, we are interested in developing a method which uses a SMT solver to solve the ground equalities and Rewriting techniques to solve the non-ground equalities.

Another area that might be worthy of investigating is determining for which classes of problems is SIG-Res a decision procedure and for those classes, what is the complexity?

References

1. Bachmair, L., Ganzinger, H.: Resolution Theorem Proving. In: Robinson, J.A., Voronkovs, A. (eds.) Handbook of Automated Reasoning, ch. 2, vol. 1, pp. 19–99. Elsevier and MIT Press (2001)
2. Baumgartner, P.: Logical Engineering With Instance-Based Methods. In: Pfennings, F. (ed.) CAV 2007. LNCS, vol. 4590, pp. 298–302. Springer, Heidelberg (2007)
3. Baumgartner, P., Tinelli, C.: The Model Evolution Calculus as a First-Order DPLL Method. Artificial Intelligence 172, 591–632 (2008)
4. Davis, M., Logemann, G., Loveland, D.: A Machine Program for Theorem Proving. Communications of the ACM 5(7), 394–397 (1962)
5. Davis, M., Putnam, H.: A Computing Procedure for Quantification Theory. Journal of the ACM 7(3), 201–215 (1960)
6. de Moura, L., Bjørner, N.S.: Z3: An Efficient SMT Solver. In: Ramakrishnan, C.R., Rehof, J. (eds.) TACAS 2008. LNCS, vol. 4963, pp. 337–340. Springer, Heidelberg (2008)
7. Deshane, T., Hu, W., Jablonski, P., Lin, H., Lynch, C., McGregor, R.E.: Encoding First Order Proofs in SAT. In: Pfenning, F. (ed.) CADE 2007. LNCS, vol. 4603, pp. 476–491. Springer, Heidelberg (2007)
8. B. Dutertre, L. de Moura. The Yices SMT Solver, http://yices.csl.sri.com/tool-paper.pdf
9. Ganzinger, H., Korovin, K.: New Directions in Instantiation-Based Theorem Proving. In: Proc. 18th IEEE Symposium on Logic in Computer Science (LICS 2003), pp. 55–64. IEEE Computer Society Press, Los Alamitos (2003)
10. Hooker, J.N., Rago, G., Chandru, V., Shrivastava, A.: Partial Instantiation Methods for Inference in First Order Logic. Journal of Automated Reasoning 28(4), 371–396 (2002)
11. Jackson, D.: Automating First-Order Relational Logic. ACM SIGSOFT Software Engineering Notes 25(6), 130–139 (2000)
12. Jeroslow, R.G.: Computation-Oriented Reductions of Predicate to Propositional Logic. In: Decision Support Systems, vol. 4, pp. 183–197. Elsevier Science, Amsterdam (1988)
13. Jeroslow, R.G.: Logic-Based Decision Support: Mixed Integer Model Formulation. In: Annals of Discrete Mathematics, vol. 40. North-Holland, Amsterdam (1989)
14. Korovin, K.: An Invitation to Instantiation-Based Reasoning: From Theory to Practice. Volume in Memoriam of Harald Ganzinger. LNCS (to appear)

15. Korovin, K.: System Description: iProver - An Instantiation-Based Theorem Prover for First-Order Logic. In: Armando, A., Baumgartner, P., Dowek, G. (eds.) IJCAR 2008. LNCS (LNAI), vol. 5195, pp. 292–298. Springer, Heidelberg (2008)
16. Leitsch, A.: The Resolution Calculus. Springer, Heidelberg (1997)
17. Lynch, C., Tran, D.: SMELS: Satisfiability Modulo Equality with Lazy Superposition. In: Cha, S(S.), Choi, J.-Y., Kim, M., Lee, I., Viswanathan, M. (eds.) ATVA 2008. LNCS, vol. 5311, pp. 186–200. Springer, Heidelberg (2008)
18. Loveland, D.W.: Automated Theorem Proving: a Logical Basis. Fundamental Studies in Computer Science. Elsevier/North-Holland (1978)
19. Paola Bonacina, M., Lynch, C., de Moura, L.: On Deciding Satisfiability by DPLL(Gamma+T) and Unsound Theorem Proving. In: Schmidt, R.A. (ed.) CADE 2009. LNCS (LNAI), vol. 5663, pp. 35–50. Springer, Heidelberg (2009)
20. Robinson, J.A.: A Machine-Oriented Logic Based on the Resolution Principle. J. Association for Computing Machinery 12, 23–41 (1965)
21. Slagle, J.R.: Automatic Theorem Proving with Renamable and Semantic Resolution. Journal of the ACM 14(4), 687–697 (1967)
22. Strichman, O., Seshia, S.A., Bryant, R.E.: Deciding Separation Formulas With SAT. In: Brinksma, E., Larsen, K.G. (eds.) CAV 2002. LNCS, vol. 2404, pp. 113–124. Springer, Heidelberg (2002)
23. Sutcliffe, G.: The SZS Ontology, http://www.cs.miami.edu/~tptp
24. Sutcliffe, G.: The CADE-21 Automated Theorem Proving System Competition. AI Communications 21(1), 71–82
25. Sutcliffe, G., Suttner, C.B.: The TPTP Problem Library: CNF Release v1.2.1. Journal of Automated Reasoning 21(2), 177–203 (1998)

Data Structures with Arithmetic Constraints: A Non-disjoint Combination*

Enrica Nicolini, Christophe Ringeissen, and Michaël Rusinowitch

LORIA & INRIA Nancy Grand Est, France
FirstName.LastName@loria.fr

Abstract. We apply an extension of the Nelson-Oppen combination method to develop a decision procedure for the non-disjoint union of theories modeling data structures with a counting operator and fragments of arithmetic. We present some data structures and some fragments of arithmetic for which the combination method is complete and effective. To achieve effectiveness, the combination method relies on particular procedures to compute sets that are representative of all the consequences over the shared theory. We show how to compute these sets by using a superposition calculus for the theories of the considered data structures and various solving and reduction techniques for the fragments of arithmetic we are interested in, including Gauss elimination, Fourier-Motzkin elimination and Groebner bases computation.

1 Introduction

Many verification problems can be reduced to checking the satisfiability of formulae modulo a combination of theories including arithmetic operators, the theory of equality, and sophisticated data structures such as lists, arrays, trees, etc. Even uninterpreted function symbols (in other words, the theory of equality) can be used as a possible abstraction to store elements. The classical Nelson-Oppen combination method [13] allows us to combine this very basic data structure with fragments of arithmetic, and the arithmetic with uninterpreted function symbols represents a popular case study due to its practical interest for verification. But the Nelson-Oppen method can be used also to combine the arithmetic with more sophisticated data structures, as shown for lists and arrays in [13]. More recently, the development of combination methods and decision procedures has received a lot of interest for its application to solvers for the problem of Satisfiability Modulo Theories (SMT). To improve the applicability of SMT solvers, it is important to develop general uniform methods to combine and to build decision procedures. Hence, equational theorem proving has been successfully applied to build decision procedures for various data structures including lists and arrays [2,1,3,12,5]. More precisely, a superposition calculus [18] based on rewriting techniques can be used for this purpose. Then, the Nelson-Oppen method can be applied to combine the theory of a data structure with a theory

---

* This work is partly funded by the ANR project "DeCert".

S. Ghilardi and R. Sebastiani (Eds.): FroCoS 2009, LNAI 5749, pp. 319–334, 2009.

of arithmetic [9]. However, the genuine Nelson-Oppen has a severe limitation since it applies only to signature-disjoint theories.

Recently, a non-disjoint extension of the Nelson-Oppen framework has been designed in [7,8,14]. In this paper, we show how to use this non-disjoint combination method to build a decision procedure for the union of (1) a theory modeling a data structure with a successor function to express some counting capabilities, and (2) the linear or non-linear arithmetic over the rationals augmented by the successor function. Both theories share the successor function s and have a common subtheory, called the theory of Increment, axiomatizing the acyclicity and the injectivity of s. This paper is the continuation of a previous work, where we studied the combination of superposition-based decision procedures for the union of two data structures sharing the theory of Integer Offsets [17]. Unfortunately, it was not possible in [17] to integrate standard procedures for reasoning about arithmetic. Here, we focus on the union of theories modeling data structures and fragments of arithmetic sharing the theory of Increment. This union allows us to handle more expressive arithmetic constraints and to obtain a combined decision procedure in which the procedures for the individual theories can be constructed by using an appropriate superposition calculus for data structures but also by classical solving techniques for reasoning about arithmetic (Gauss/Fourier-Motzkin elimination, Groebner bases computation). Our aim is to consider arithmetic constraints over non-necessarily positive numbers, and so the theory of Integer Offsets is not the right axiomatization. Formally, the theory of Increment is the theory of Integer Offsets minus the axiom $\forall x \; 0 \neq s(x)$, that is true in $\mathbb{N}$ but not in $\mathbb{Z}$ nor in $\mathbb{Q}$. In this paper, we adapt to the theory of Increment the superposition calculus developed for the Integer Offsets in [17]. For the theories we are interested in, we check that all the assumptions for applying the non-disjoint combination method are satisfied. To be effective, the combination method relies on procedures able to compute the logical consequences over the shared signature that are exchanged in the main loop of the method. A major contribution of this paper is to build these procedures by using classical solving techniques for arithmetic constraints.

The paper is organized as follows. Section 2 introduces the basic definitions and notations. In Section 3, we present several data structures for which a superposition calculus modulo the theory of Increment can be turned into a decision procedure. In Sections 4 and 5, we present two fragments of arithmetic and the related decision procedures. Section 6 shows how to instantiate the non-disjoint combination method for our need, when the theory of Increment is used as the shared theory. This combination method makes use of procedures for computing all the shared logical consequences to be exchanged. We explain how to compute the required consequences by using the proposed superposition calculus. For the two considered fragments of arithmetic, we show how to compute the needed consequences by using respectively Gauss/Fourier-Motzkin elimination and Groebner bases computation. Eventually, in Section 7, we conclude with some final remarks. Omitted proofs can be found in [16].

2   Preliminaries

We consider a many-sorted language. A *signature* Σ is a set of sorts, functions and predicate symbols (each endowed with the corresponding arity and sort). We assume that, for each sort s, the equality "$=_s$" is a logical constant that does not occur in Σ and that is always interpreted as the identity relation over (the interpretation of) s; moreover, as a notational convention, we will often omit the subscript and the symbol $\bowtie$ will denote either $=$ or $\neq$. The signature obtained from Σ by adding a set $\underline{a}$ of new constants (i.e., 0-ary function symbols, each of them again equipped with its sort) is denoted by $\Sigma^{\underline{a}}$ and named a *simple expansion* of Σ. Σ-*atoms*, Σ-*literals*, Σ-*clauses*, and Σ-*formulae* are defined in the usual way. A set of Σ-literals is called a Σ-*constraint*. Terms, literals, clauses and formulae are called *ground* whenever no variable appears in them; *sentences* are formulae in which free variables do not occur. Given a function symbol f, a f-rooted term is a term whose top-symbol is f.

From the semantic side, we have the standard notion of a Σ-*structure* $\mathcal{M}$: it consists of non-empty pairwise disjoint domains M_s for every sort s and a sort- and arity-matching interpretation $\mathcal{I}$ of the function and predicate symbols from Σ. The truth of a Σ-formula in $\mathcal{M}$ is defined in any of the standard ways. If $\Sigma_0 \subseteq \Sigma$ is a subsignature of Σ and if $\mathcal{M}$ is a Σ-structure, the Σ_0-*reduct* of $\mathcal{M}$ is the Σ_0-structure $\mathcal{M}_{|\Sigma_0}$ obtained from $\mathcal{M}$ by forgetting the interpretation of the symbols from $\Sigma \setminus \Sigma_0$.

A collection of Σ-sentences is a Σ-theory, and a Σ-theory T admits *quantifier elimination* iff for every formula $\varphi(\underline{x})$ there is a quantifier-free formula (over the same free variables $\underline{x}$) $\varphi'(\underline{x})$ such that $T \models \varphi(\underline{x}) \leftrightarrow \varphi'(\underline{x})$. A Σ-theory T is *convex* if for any set of Σ-literals and any Σ-atoms $\alpha_1, \ldots, \alpha_n$, we have that $T \models \Gamma \rightarrow (\alpha_1 \vee \cdots \vee \alpha_n)$ implies $T \models \Gamma \rightarrow \alpha_i$ for some i. In the following, all considered theories are convex.

In this paper, we are concerned with the *(constraint) satisfiability problem* for a theory T, also called the T-satisfiability problem, which is the problem of deciding whether a Σ-constraint is satisfiable in a model of T (and, if so, we say that the constraint is T-satisfiable). Notice that a constraint may contain variables: since these variables may be equivalently replaced by free constants, we can reformulate the constraint satisfiability problem as the problem of deciding whether a finite conjunction of ground literals in a simply expanded signature $\Sigma^{\underline{a}}$ is true in a $\Sigma^{\underline{a}}$-structure whose Σ-reduct is a model of T. Given an idempotent substitution $\sigma = \{x_i \mapsto t_i\}_{i \in I}$, $\widehat{\sigma}$ denotes the constraint $\bigwedge_{i \in I} x_i = t_i$. Note that this constraint in *solved form* is satisfiable in any model. The special symbol $\perp$ denotes a literal which is unsatisfiable in any model.

3   Theories

All the examples of data structures we are interested in involve also a successor function (denoted by s) that satisfies the axioms formalizing the properties of injectivity and acyclicity.

Theory of Increment.

$\boxed{T_S}$ denotes the theory of Increment defining the behaviour of the successor function s and the constant 0. T_S has the mono-sorted signature $\Sigma_S := \{0 : \text{NUM}, \text{s} : \text{NUM} \rightarrow \text{NUM}\}$, and it is axiomatized as follows:

$$\forall x, y \quad \text{s}(x) = \text{s}(y) \rightarrow x = y$$
$$\forall x \quad x \neq \text{s}^n(x) \quad \text{for all } n \text{ in } \mathbb{N}^+$$

We consider below some theories T corresponding to standard data structures and we focus on the constraint satisfiability problem for $T \cup T_S$.

Lists.

$\boxed{T_{LS}}$ is a theory of lists endowed with length. The many-sorted signature of T_{LS} is Σ_S plus the set of function symbols $\{\text{nil} : \text{LISTS}, \text{car} : \text{LISTS} \rightarrow \text{ELEM}, \text{cdr} : \text{LISTS} \rightarrow \text{LISTS}, \text{cons} : \text{ELEM} \times \text{LISTS} \rightarrow \text{LISTS}, \ell : \text{LISTS} \rightarrow \text{NUM}\}$ and the predicate symbol atom : LISTS. The axioms[1] of T_{LS} are:

$$\text{car}(\text{cons}(x, y)) = x \qquad\qquad \neg\text{atom}(x) \rightarrow \text{cons}(\text{car}(x), \text{cdr}(x)) = x$$
$$\text{cdr}(\text{cons}(x, y)) = y \qquad\qquad \neg\text{atom}(\text{cons}(x, y))$$
$$\ell(\text{nil}) = 0 \qquad\qquad\qquad\quad \text{atom}(\text{nil})$$
$$\ell(\text{cons}(x, y)) = \text{s}(\ell(y))$$

The theory T'_{LS} corresponds to a slight variant of T_{LS} where the sort ELEM coincides with the sort NUM. It is important to notice that, by applying some standard reasoning (see, e.g., [17]), we can substitute T_{LS} (resp. T'_{LS}) with its subset of purely equational axioms, say T_{ELS} (resp. T'_{ELS}), and enrich the set of ground literals G we want to test for satisfiability modulo T_{LS} (resp. T'_{LS}), to a set of literals H in such a way that $T_{LS} \cup G$ is equisatisfiable to $T_{ELS} \cup H$ (resp. $T'_{LS} \cup G$ is equisatisfiable to $T'_{ELS} \cup H$). In this way we can still consider T_{LS} and T'_{LS} as *equational* theories.

Records.

$\boxed{T_{RS}}$ denotes a theory of records with increment defined as follows. We consider records in which all the attribute identifiers are associated to the sort NUM or to sorts ELEM_i, and suppose we want to be able to increment by a unity every value of sort NUM stored into the record. To formalize this situation, the signature of T_{RS} is Σ_S plus the function symbols defined as follows. Let $Id = \{id_1, id_2, \ldots, id_n\}$ be a set of attribute identifiers id_i associated to NUM or ELEM_i. Let NI be the set of elements $i \in \{1, \ldots, n\}$ such that id_i is associated to NUM, and let $\overline{NI}$ be $\{1, \ldots, n\} \backslash NI$. Let us name REC the sort of records; for every attribute identifier $id_1, id_2, \ldots, id_n$ we have a couple of functions $\text{rselect}_i : \text{REC} \rightarrow \text{NUM}$ and $\text{rstore}_i : \text{REC} \times \text{NUM} \rightarrow \text{REC}$ for $i \in NI$; $\text{rselect}_i : \text{REC} \rightarrow \text{ELEM}_i$ and $\text{rstore}_i : \text{REC} \times \text{ELEM}_i \rightarrow \text{REC}$ for $i \in \overline{NI}$. Moreover, there is also an increment function incr : $\text{REC} \rightarrow \text{REC}$ that increments the elements of sort NUM. The axioms of T_{RS} are:

---

[1] All the axioms should be considered as universally quantified.

for every i, j such that $1 \leq i, j \leq n$, $i \neq j$

$$\mathsf{rselect}_i(\mathsf{rstore}_i(x, y)) = y$$
$$\mathsf{rselect}_j(\mathsf{rstore}_i(x, y)) = \mathsf{rselect}_j(x)$$
$$\wedge_{i=1}^{n}(\mathsf{rselect}_i(x) = \mathsf{rselect}_j(y)) \to x = y \qquad \text{(extensionality)}$$

for any $i \in NI$, $\mathsf{rselect}_i(\mathsf{incr}(x)) = \mathsf{s}(\mathsf{rselect}_i(x))$ and for any $i \in \overline{NI}$, $\mathsf{rselect}_i(\mathsf{incr}(x)) = \mathsf{rselect}_i(x)$.

The theory T'_{RS} denotes the particular case where all elements of records are of sort NUM, i.e. $\overline{NI} = \emptyset$. Moreover, following the same argument used in [1], it is possible to check the satisfiability forgetting the extensionality axioms, thus again the theory of records can be still considered as an *equational* one.

Trees.

$\boxed{T_{BS}}$ corresponds to a theory of binary trees endowed with size functions. The many-sorted signature of T_{BS} is Σ_S plus the set of function symbols $\{\mathsf{bin} :$ ELEM $\times$ TREES $\times$ TREES $\to$ TREES, null : TREES, size_L : TREES $\to$ NUM, size_R : TREES $\to$ NUM$\}$. The axioms of T_{BS} are:

$$\mathsf{size}_L(\mathsf{null}) = 0 \qquad\qquad\qquad \mathsf{size}_R(\mathsf{null}) = 0$$
$$\mathsf{size}_L(\mathsf{bin}(e, t_1, t_2)) = \mathsf{s}(\mathsf{size}_L(t_1)) \qquad \mathsf{size}_R(\mathsf{bin}(e, t_1, t_2)) = \mathsf{s}(\mathsf{size}_R(t_2))$$

The function size_L (resp. size_R) computes the length of the left (resp. right) branch of the input binary tree.

The theory T'_{BS} denotes the particular case where ELEM and NUM coincide.

3.1 Decision Procedure Using a Superposition Calculus

Consider the theory of Increment T_S defined in Section 3. We want to develop a calculus able to take into account the axioms of T_S in a framework based on superposition. To this aim, we adapt the calculus presented in [17]. Let us consider a presentation of the superposition calculus specialized for reasoning over sets of literals, whose rules are described in Figures 1 and 2, augmented with the three more rules over ground terms presented in Figure 3.

We call the so introduced calculus $\mathcal{SP}_S$ and, from now on, we assume that the ordering we consider when performing any application of $\mathcal{SP}_S$ is T_S-*good*.

Definition 1. *We say that an ordering $\succ$ over terms on a signature containing Σ_S is T_S-good whenever it satisfies the following requirements:*

(i) $\succ$ is a simplification ordering that is total on ground terms;
(ii) whenever two terms t_1 and t_2 are not s-rooted it happens that $\mathsf{s}^{n_1}(t_1) \succ \mathsf{s}^{n_2}(t_2)$ iff either $t_1 \succ t_2$ or ($t_1 \equiv t_2$ and n_1 is bigger than n_2).

It is easy to build a T_S-*good* ordering: for example, it is enough to consider a lexicographic path ordering (LPO) with a precedence $>$ over the symbols in the signature such that $f > \mathsf{s}$ for all the symbols f in the signature different from s.

$$\text{Superposition} \quad \frac{l[u'] = r \quad u = t}{(l[t] = r)\sigma} \quad (i),(ii)$$

$$\text{Paramodulation} \quad \frac{l[u'] \neq r \quad u = t}{(l[t] \neq r)\sigma} \quad (i),(ii)$$

$$\text{Reflection} \quad \frac{u' \neq u}{\bot}$$

where σ is the most general unifier of u and u', u' is not a variable in *Superposition* and *Paramodulation*, and the following hold: *(i)* $u\sigma \not\preceq t\sigma$, *(ii)* $l[u']\sigma \not\preceq r\sigma$.

Fig. 1. Expansion Inference Rules

$$\text{Subsumption} \quad \frac{S \cup \{L, L'\}}{S \cup \{L\}} \quad \text{if } L\vartheta \equiv L' \text{ for some substitution } \vartheta$$

$$\text{Simplification} \quad \frac{S \cup \{L[l'], l = r\}}{S \cup \{L[r\vartheta], l = r\}} \quad \begin{array}{l} \text{if } l' \equiv l\vartheta, \, r\vartheta \prec l\vartheta, \text{ and} \\ (l\vartheta = r\vartheta) \prec L[l\vartheta] \end{array}$$

$$\text{Deletion} \quad \frac{S \cup \{t = t\}}{S}$$

where L and L' are literals and S is a set of literals.

Fig. 2. Contraction Inference Rules

$$\text{R1} \quad \frac{S \cup \{\mathsf{s}(u) = \mathsf{s}(v)\}}{S \cup \{u = v\}} \quad \text{if } u \text{ and } v \text{ are ground terms}$$

$$\text{R2} \quad \frac{S \cup \{\mathsf{s}(u) = t, \mathsf{s}(v) = t\}}{S \cup \{\mathsf{s}(v) = t, u = v\}} \quad \begin{array}{l} \text{if } u, v \text{ and } t \text{ are ground terms and} \\ \mathsf{s}(u) \succ t, \quad \mathsf{s}(v) \succ t \text{ and } u \succ v \end{array}$$

$$\text{C1} \quad \frac{S \cup \{\mathsf{s}^n(t) = t\}}{S \cup \{\mathsf{s}^n(t) = t\} \cup \{\bot\}} \quad \text{if } t \text{ is a ground term and } n \in \mathbb{N}^+$$

where S is a set of literals.

Fig. 3. Ground reduction Inference Rules

Theorem 1. *Let T be a Σ-theory presented as a finite set of unit clauses such that $\Sigma \supseteq \Sigma_S$, and assume there is an ordering over terms that is T_S-good. $\mathcal{SP}_S$ induces a decision procedure for the constraint satisfiability problem w.r.t. $T \cup T_S$ if, for any set G of ground literals:*

- *the saturation of $Ax(T) \cup G$ w.r.t. $\mathcal{SP}_S$ is finite,*
- *the saturation of $Ax(T) \cup G$ w.r.t. $\mathcal{SP}_S$ does not contain non-ground equations whose maximal term is s-rooted, or equations whose maximal term is a variable of sort* NUM.

Corollary 1. *For any theory $T \in \{T_{LS}, T'_{LS}, T_{RS}, T'_{RS}, T_{BS}, T'_{BS}\}$, $\mathcal{SP}_S$ induces a decision procedure for the constraint satisfiability problem w.r.t. $T \cup T_S$.*

4   Theory of Linear Rational Arithmetic

A very natural extension of the theory of Increment is the linear arithmetic over the rationals. In more detail, let us fix the signature over the sort NUM $\Sigma_{\mathbb{Q}} :=$ $\{0, 1, +, -, \{f_q\}_{q \in \mathbb{Q}}, \mathsf{s}, <\}$, where $0, 1$ are constants, $-$, f_q, s are unary function symbols, $+$ is a binary one and $<$ is a binary predicate symbol. Let $T_{\mathbb{Q}}$ be the set of all the $\Sigma_{\mathbb{Q}}$-sentences that are true in $\mathbb{Q}$ considered as an ordered $\mathbb{Q}$-vector space, under the obvious convention that $0, 1, -, +, <$ are interpreted in their intended meaning, s is the function that to each rational q associates the rational $q + 1$, and the f_q's represent the external product of the $\mathbb{Q}$-vector spaces.

We can observe that in all the models of $T_{\mathbb{Q}}$ the function for the successor function symbol s has an explicit definition using only the symbol 1 and $+$, since $T_{\mathbb{Q}} \models \forall x, y \ (y = \mathsf{s}(x) \leftrightarrow y = x + 1)$. This observation can be useful in order to rewrite all the formulae over $\Sigma_{\mathbb{Q}}$ discarding the symbol s.

4.1   Decision Procedure

To build a $T_{\mathbb{Q}}$-satisfiability procedure, a possible solution is to transform equalities and disequalities into inequalities and then to apply the Fourier-Motzkin elimination procedure for checking the satisfiability of the resulting set inequalities. But for efficiency reasons, it is more convenient to keep the initial form of literals. Moreover, we are interested in a decision procedure enhanced with the capability of computing some particular entailed equalities. To this aim, we use the notions of solver and canonizer introduced by Shostak [19]. A solver (*solve*) for $T_{\mathbb{Q}}$ computes a solved form (an idempotent substitution) of a set of equalities given by the Gauss elimination procedure, and a canonizer (*canon*) for $T_{\mathbb{Q}}$ is the classical normalization of arithmetic expressions (assuming an ordering over free constants). Any set of literals denoted by Γ is partitioned into a set of equalities $\Gamma^=$, a set of disequalities $\Gamma^{\neq}$ and a set of inequalities $\Gamma^{\leq}$. Since $T_{\mathbb{Q}}$ is convex, it is possible to take into account disequalities in an easy way. To handle inequalities, we use Fourier-Motzkin elimination to derive (1) unsatisfiable inequalities $q \leq 0$ where q is a strictly positive rational and (2) implicit equalities.

Equalities and Disequalities. The convexity of $T_{\mathbb{Q}}$ justifies the following lemma.

Lemma 1. *Let $\Gamma^=$ be a $T_{\mathbb{Q}}$-satisfiable set of equalities, and let $\Gamma^{\neq}$ be a set of disequalities. $\Gamma^= \wedge \Gamma^{\neq}$ is $T_{\mathbb{Q}}$-unsatisfiable iff there is some $s \neq t \in \Gamma^{\neq}$ such that $canon(s\gamma) = canon(t\gamma)$, where $\gamma = solve(\Gamma^=)$.*

Inequalities. It is well-known that Fourier-Motzkin elimination provides a $T_{\mathbb{Q}}$-satisfiability procedure for inequalities. Moreover, it can be slightly adapted to derive "implicit" equalities. Given a set of inequalities $\Gamma^{\leq}$, an inequality $s \leq t$ in $\Gamma^{\leq}$ is an *implicit equality* if $T_{\mathbb{Q}} \models \Gamma^{\leq} \rightarrow s = t$. These implicit equalities can be derived by Fourier-Motzkin elimination and are propagated to the Gauss elimination procedure. The use of Fourier-Motzkin is justified by results expressed in [10,11] for the case of the reals. These results hold also when the rationals are considered:

- An inequality in $\Gamma^{\leq}$ is an implicit equality iff it appears in a derivation computed by Fourier-Motzkin leading to the inequality $0 \leq 0$.
- If an equality is entailed by $\Gamma^{\leq}$, then it is entailed by the implicit equalities of $\Gamma^{\leq}$.

A $T_{\mathbb{Q}}$-satisfiability procedure can be obtained by using an architecture with the following components:

GE (Gauss). The solver is applied to compute a solved form for the set of equalities. Solved variables are substituted in disequalities and inequalities.

DH (Disequalities Handler). The canonizer is used to check whether a disequality $s \neq t$ is canonized into a trivially unsatisfiable disequality $u \neq u$.

FME (Fourier-Motzkin). Provided that Gauss does not apply, Fourier-Motzkin is used to derived unsatisfiable (ground) inequalities or implicit equalities. Fourier-Motzkin eliminates successively the variables occurring in the inequalities. Eventually, if it derives an inequality $q \leq 0$ such that q is a strictly positive rational, then the unsatisfiability is reported. If it derives an inequality $0 \leq 0$, then the implicit equalities used in the derivation of $0 \leq 0$ are sent to **GE**.

This procedure is terminating because neither **GE** nor **FME** introduces new variables and **GE** strictly decreases the number of unsolved variables. By analysing more precisely this procedure, one can remark that it is sufficient to apply **FME** only once. When we assume that **GE** (resp. **FME**) is applied on the whole set of equalities (resp. inequalities), sending to **GE** the implicit equalities found by **FME** does not help to find further implicit equalities by applying **FME** again, but it computes a solved form used to check the satisfiability of disequalities.

It is easy to show the correctness and completeness of this procedure. Indeed, if $false$ is derived then the input is unsatisfiable (since all inferences are obviously correct). Otherwise, it produces eventually a conjunction of the form $\widehat{\sigma} \wedge \Phi^{\neq} \wedge \Phi^{\leq}$ such that (1) $\widehat{\sigma}$ is a solved form such that every variable in the domain of the substitution σ occurs only once in $\widehat{\sigma} \wedge \Phi^{\neq} \wedge \Phi^{\leq}$, (2) $\Phi^{\neq}$ is a set of disequalities such that for any $s \neq t \in \Phi^{\neq}$, $canon(s) \neq canon(t)$, and (3) $\Phi^{\leq}$ is a $T_{\mathbb{Q}}$-satisfiable set of inequalities containing no implicit equalities. Thanks to (3), $\Phi^{\neq} \wedge \Phi^{\leq}$ is $T_{\mathbb{Q}}$-satisfiable too, and then by (1), we can conclude that $\widehat{\sigma} \wedge \Phi^{\neq} \wedge \Phi^{\leq}$ is $T_{\mathbb{Q}}$-satisfiable.

5   Theory of $\mathbb{Q}$-Algebras

We can consider now another extension of the theory of Increment, namely we can see T_S as subtheory of the theory of (non-degenerate) $\mathbb{Q}$-algebras. More in detail, we fix as a signature $\Sigma_{\mathbb{Q}\text{-}alg}$ the set consisting of the constants $0, 1$, the two binary function symbols $+, \times$, the unary function symbols $-$ and the $\mathbb{Q}$-indexed family of unary function symbols f_q. As a notational convention, of course we use the infix notation for $+$ and write qv, v_1v_2 for $f_q(v)$, $\times(v_1, v_2)$, respectively. The theory of $\mathbb{Q}$-algebras, denoted by $T_{\mathbb{Q}\text{-}alg}$, is described using the axioms of abelian groups for $+$ (stating the associativity, the commutativity of $+$, the existence of the inverse $-v$ for each v and the fact that 0 is the unity of $+$), the axioms of abelian monoids for $\times$ (asserting the associativity and the commutativity of $\times$, and that 1 is the unity of $\times$), the fact that 0 is different from 1 and the other six axioms relating the behaviour of $+$ and $\times$

for every q, q_1 and q_2 in $\mathbb{Q}$

$$\forall x, y, z \ (x + y)z = xz + yz \tag{1}$$
$$\forall x, y \ q(x + y) = qx + qy \tag{2}$$
$$\forall x \ (q_1 \oplus q_2)x = q_1 x + q_2 x \tag{3}$$
$$\forall x \ (q_1 \cdot q_2)x = q_1(q_2 x) \tag{4}$$
$$\forall x \ 1_{\mathbb{Q}} x = x \tag{5}$$
$$\forall x, y \ q(xy) = x(qy) \tag{6}$$

where $\oplus$ and $\cdot$ are respectively the sum and multiplication operation in $\mathbb{Q}$, and $1_{\mathbb{Q}}$ is the multiplicative unit of $\mathbb{Q}$.

Again, the symbol s admits in $T_{\mathbb{Q}\text{-}alg}$ the explicit definition as in the previous example: we have $T_{\mathbb{Q}\text{-}alg} \models \forall x, y \ (y = \mathsf{s}(x) \leftrightarrow y = x + 1)$. Injectivity of s is guaranteed by the group structure (i.e., it holds $T_{\mathbb{Q}\text{-}alg} \models \forall x, y \ (x + 1 = y + 1 \leftrightarrow x = y)$), and the acyclicity of s is guaranteed by the fact that $1 \neq 0$ and by the axiom (4).

5.1   Decision Procedure

Given a set $\underline{a}$ of n fresh constants, the ground atoms over $\Sigma_{\mathbb{Q}\text{-}alg}^{\underline{a}}$ are polynomials in at most n indeterminates whose normalized representation is of the kind $p(\underline{a}) = 0$. Given the convexity of $T_{\mathbb{Q}\text{-}alg}$, The constraint satisfiability problem in $T_{\mathbb{Q}\text{-}alg}$ is just the problem of deciding whether an equation $p(\underline{a}) = 0$ is a logical consequence of a finite number of equations $\{p_1(\underline{a}) = 0, \ldots, p_m(\underline{a}) = 0\}$. Since the polynomial ring $\mathbb{Q}[a_1, \ldots, a_n]$ is the free $\mathbb{Q}$-algebra over n generators, this problem is equivalent to the membership of the polynomial p to the ideal $\langle p_1, \ldots, p_m \rangle$ generated by the polynomials $p_1, \ldots, p_m$. The Buchberger algorithm solves the problem by computing the Groebner basis associated to the ideal $\langle p_1, \ldots, p_m \rangle$ [4].

6   Non-disjoint Combination of Theories

It would be interesting for us to take into account constraints that involve symbols used to describe the data structures and symbols for the arithmetic. Usually, these constraints are handled relying on a framework that allows to combine the already available decision procedures for the theories of the data structures and the arithmetic, provided that the theories are formalized on signatures that share only the equality predicate symbol.

In the examples we have considered in Section 3, if we imagine to deal with constraints involving also arithmetical symbols, the requirement for the signatures to be disjoint cannot be satisfied, since every theory in the above examples presents some axioms involving the successor function symbol s. Note that, even if for the arithmetic the symbol s may not be used, in order to have a meaningful answer for the satisfiability of constraints, it is necessary to recall the axiom that links s and $+$, i.e. the axioms that defines s by the formula $\forall x, y\, (y = \mathsf{s}(x) \leftrightarrow y = x + 1)$.

At this point, we have at our disposal satisfiability procedures for $T_{\mathbb{Q}}$, $T_{\mathbb{Q}\text{-}alg}$ and for the theories of some data structures. Since all these theories share the theory T_S over the signature $\Sigma_S = \{0, \mathsf{s}\}$, we look if the general framework for the combination of non-disjoint theories developed in [8] could be applied. This framework extends the well-known Nelson-Oppen methodology, and can guarantee, under the conditions described in the following, the transfer of the decidability of the satisfiability problem.

Theorem 2. *[8] Consider two theories T_1, T_2 in signatures Σ_1, Σ_2 and suppose that:*

1. *both T_1, T_2 have decidable constraint satisfiability problem;*
2. *there is some theory T_0 in the signature $\Sigma_1 \cap \Sigma_2$ such that:*
   - *T_0 is universal;*
   - *T_1, T_2 are both T_0-compatible;*
   - *T_0 is Noetherian;*
   - *T_1, T_2 are both effectively Noetherian extensions of T_0.*

Then the $(\Sigma_1 \cup \Sigma_2)$-theory $T_1 \cup T_2$ also has decidable constraint satisfiability problem.

We will not enter into the detail of the conditions required by the theorem; we will simply specialize them when the theory of Increment T_S plays the role of the shared theory between a theory modeling a data structure as in Section 3 and the arithmetic over the rationals (in both the cases $T_{\mathbb{Q}}$ and $T_{\mathbb{Q}\text{-}alg}$).

T_S is a universal theory; moreover, if we add to T_S the axiom $\forall x \exists y\; x = \mathsf{s}(y)$, we obtain a theory $T_S^\star$ that admits quantifier elimination (it is easy, e.g., to adapt the procedure in [6]) and such that every constraint that is satisfiable in a model of T_S is satisfiable also in a model of $T_S^\star$. To justify the last claim, it is sufficient to observe that each model of T_S can be extended to a model of $T_S^\star$ simply by adding recursively to each element a "predecessor". Now, for any theory $T \supseteq T_S$ over a signature $\Sigma \supseteq \Sigma_S$ the T_S-compatibility requirement simply reduces to the following definition.

Definition 2 (T_S-compatibility). *Let T be a theory in the signature $\Sigma \supseteq \Sigma_S$. We say that T is T_S-compatible iff $T_S \subseteq T$ and every Σ-constraint which is satisfiable in a model of T is satisfiable also in a model of $T_S^\star \cup T$.*

In our case, Definition 2 requires that the satisfiability problem has the same answer in the models of T and in the models of $T \cup \{\forall x \exists y\; x = \mathsf{s}(y)\}$.

It is immediate now to verify that $T_{\mathbb{Q}}$ is a T_S-compatible theory, since all the models of $T_{\mathbb{Q}}$ are already models of T_S^*: indeed, for each element r in a model of $T_{\mathbb{Q}}$, the (unique) element t such that r is equal to the (interpretation of the) successor of t is simply (the interpretation of) $r - 1$. The same kind of argument can be applied also to show the T_S-compatibility of $T_{\mathbb{Q}\text{-}alg}$, since, in each model of $T_{\mathbb{Q}\text{-}alg}$, for each element t the (unique) element v such that t is equal to the (interpretation of the) successor of v is again (the interpretation of) $t - 1$. As far as the other theories presented in Section 3 for the lists, the records and the trees are concerned, it is easy to see that the T_S-compatibility requirement holds again, because the eventual adjunction of predecessors to the elements in the sort NUM does not affect the satisfiability of constraints; more details can be found in [17].

Let us analyze the third requirement of Theorem 2. Roughly speaking, the property of being Noetherian for T_S means that, fixed a finite number of fresh constants, there exists only a finite number of Σ_S-atoms over those constants that are not redundant when reasoning modulo T_S.

Definition 3 (Noetherian Theory). *T_S is Noetherian if and only if for every finite set of free constants $\underline{a}$, every infinite ascending chain $\Theta_1 \subseteq \Theta_2 \subseteq \cdots \subseteq \Theta_n \subseteq \cdots$ of sets of ground $\Sigma_S^{\underline{a}}$-atoms is eventually constant modulo T_S, i.e. there is an n such that $T_S \cup \Theta_n \models \alpha$, for every natural number m and atom $\alpha \in \Theta_m$.*

Since it is possible to prove (see, e.g. [20]) that all the theories whose signature contains only constants and one unary function symbol are Noetherian, it follows that the theory of Increment T_S enjoys this property.

Exactly as it happens for the original Nelson-Oppen procedure, the result of Theorem 2 strongly relies on the capability of deducing logical consequences over the shared signature. To this aim, let us consider a convex theory $T \supseteq T_S$ with signatures $\Sigma \supseteq \Sigma_S$, and suppose we want to discover, given an arbitrary set of ground literals Γ over Σ, a "complete set" of logical positive consequences of Γ over Σ_S, formalized by the notion of T_S-*basis*.

Definition 4 (T_S-basis). *Given a convex Σ-theory $T \supseteq T_S$ and a finite set Γ of ground literals (built out of symbols from Σ and possibly further free constants) and a finite set of free constants $\underline{a}$, a T_S-basis modulo T for Γ w.r.t. $\underline{a}$ is a set Δ of ground $\Sigma_S^{\underline{a}}$-atoms such that*

(i) $T \cup \Gamma \models \alpha$, for all $\alpha \in \Delta$ and
(ii) if $T \cup \Gamma \models \alpha$ then $T_S \cup \Delta \models \alpha$, for every ground $\Sigma_S^{\underline{a}}$-atom α.

The Noetherianity of T_S guarantees that, for every set of Σ-literals Γ and for every set $\underline{a}$ of constants, a finite T_S-basis Δ for Γ w.r.t. $\underline{a}$ always exists. Note that if Γ is T-unsatisfiable then w.l.o.g. $\Delta = \{\bot\}$. Unfortunately, a basis does not need to be computable; this motivates the following definition corresponding to the last hypothesis of Theorem 2.

Definition 5. *A convex theory T is an* effectively Noetherian extension *of T_S if and only if T_S is Noetherian and a T_S-basis modulo T is computable for every set of literals and every finite set $\underline{a}$ of free constants.*

Now we are ready to give a more detailed picture of the procedure that is the core of Theorem 2, and that extends the Nelson-Oppen combination method to theories over non disjoint signatures. In the algorithm below, Γ_i denotes a set of ground literals built out of symbols of Σ_i (for $i = 1, 2$), a set of shared free constants $\underline{a}$ and possibly further free constants.

Algorithm 1. Extending Nelson-Oppen

---

1. If $T_S\text{-basis}_{T_i}(\Gamma_i) = \Delta_i$ and $\bot \notin \Delta_i$ for each $i \in \{1, 2\}$, then
    1.1. For each $D \in \Delta_i$ such that $T_j \cup \Gamma_j \not\models D$, $(i \neq j)$, add D to Γ_j
    1.2. If Γ_1 or Γ_2 has been changed in **1.1**, then rerun **1**.
  Else **return** *"unsatisfiable"*
2. Return *"satisfiable"*.

The requirement of being effectively Noetherian extension of T_S for $T_{\mathbb{Q}}$, $T_{\mathbb{Q}\text{-}alg}$ and the theories of the data structures in Section 3 is the last condition that remains to be guaranteed. In the following we show how the decision procedures that we have already presented can be used to this aim.

6.1   Computing T_S-Bases for Data Structures

In this section we show that the superposition calculus $\mathcal{SP}_S$ allows us to build T_S-bases modulo theories that are axiomatized by unit clauses.

Assume that $G(\underline{a}, \underline{b})$ is a set of ground literals over an expansion of Σ with the finite sets of fresh constants $\underline{a}, \underline{b}$. The theory $T \cup T_S$ is convex because it is a Horn theory. At this point, Proposition 1 shows how $\mathcal{SP}_S$ can be used in order to derive T_S-bases.

Proposition 1. *Let S_ω be a finite saturation of $T \cup G(\underline{a}, \underline{b})$ w.r.t $\mathcal{SP}_S$ using a T_S-good ordering over the terms in the signature $\Sigma \cup \{\underline{a}, \underline{b}\}$ such that (i) every term over the subsignature $\Sigma_S^{\underline{a}}$ is smaller than any term that contains a symbol in $(\Sigma \setminus \Sigma_S) \cup \{\underline{b}\}$, (ii) not containing $\bot$, and such that (iii) s-rooted terms can be maximal just in ground equations in S_ω and (iv) variables of sort NUM are never the maximal term in the equations. The set $\Delta(\underline{a})$ of all the ground equations over $\Sigma_S^{\underline{a}}$ in S_ω is a T_S-basis for T.*

Corollary 2. *$\mathcal{SP}_S$ is able to compute T_S-bases for the theories $T \cup T_S$, where T varies in $\{T_{LS}, T'_{LS}, T_{RS}, T'_{RS}, T_{BS}, T'_{BS}\}$ as presented in Section 3.*

6.2   Computing T_S-Bases for Fragments of Arithmetic

In this section we will show how to derive T_S-bases when we consider the theory $T_{\mathbb{Q}}$ and the theory $T_{\mathbb{Q}\text{-}alg}$. First of all, we recall that both $T_{\mathbb{Q}}$ and $T_{\mathbb{Q}\text{-}alg}$ are convex theories and we will see that, in both cases, given a set of atoms, the respective decision procedures are able to derive a "representative set" of the linear equalities, i.e. equalities in the shape $q_1 x_1 + \cdots + q_n x_n = 0$, $q_i \in \mathbb{Q}$, that are implied.

Our aim is, at that point, to describe a procedure that, given a generic constraint over $\Sigma_{\mathbb{Q}}$ (resp. $\Sigma_{\mathbb{Q}\text{-}alg}$), say Γ, is able to derive a set of ground atoms over an expansion $\Sigma_S^{\underline{a}}$, say Δ, such that $T_{\mathbb{Q}} \cup \Gamma \models \Delta$ (resp. $T_{\mathbb{Q}\text{-}alg} \cup \Gamma \models \Delta$), and such that, for every $\Sigma_S^{\underline{a}}$-atom e it holds that $T_{\mathbb{Q}} \cup \Gamma \models e$ iff $T_S \cup \Delta \models e$ (resp. $T_{\mathbb{Q}\text{-}alg} \cup \Gamma \models e$ iff $T_S \cup \Delta \models e$).

We start by recalling that all the literals in Γ that are not atoms, i.e. that are the negation of some atoms, are irrelevant in order to compute the set Δ.

Lemma 2. *Let T be a convex theory, let P be a set of atoms, let N be a set of negative literals, i.e. a set consisting only of negations of atoms, and let α be an atom. If $P \wedge N$ is T-satisfiable, it holds $T \models (P \wedge N) \rightarrow \alpha$ iff $T \models P \rightarrow \alpha$.*

Let us now introduce $T_{\mathbb{Q}}^=$, the theory of the (non-degenerate) $\mathbb{Q}$-vector spaces. This theory is a subtheory of both $T_{\mathbb{Q}}$ and $T_{\mathbb{Q}\text{-}alg}$, it is built on the signature $\Sigma_{\mathbb{Q}^=} := \{0, 1, +, -, \{f_q\}_{q \in \mathbb{Q}}, \mathsf{s}\}$, and it is ruled by the axioms of abelian groups over $+$, the requirement that $1 \neq 0$ and the axioms (3) – (6) in Section 5. Again, we require the relationship $\forall x, y \ (y = \mathsf{s}(x) \leftrightarrow y = x + 1)$ to hold in all the structures that are models of $T_{\mathbb{Q}}^=$.

Lemma 3. *Let $\underline{a}$, $\underline{b}$ be two sets of free constants such that $\underline{a} \subseteq \underline{b}$. Given a $T_{\mathbb{Q}}^=$-satisfiable set of linear equalities P over the signature $\Sigma_{\mathbb{Q}^=}^{\underline{b}}$, it is possible to derive a T_S-basis modulo $T_{\mathbb{Q}}^=$ for P w.r.t. $\underline{a}$.*

Proof. Any $\Sigma_S^{\underline{a}}$-equation is of the form $\mathsf{s}^{n_1}(a_1) = \mathsf{s}^{n_2}(a_2)$ for some n_1, n_2 in $\mathbb{N}$ and for some a_1, a_2 in $\underline{a} \cup \{0\}$. Due to the injectivity axiom for the s function symbol, any equation can be equivalently rewritten in the form $a_1 = \mathsf{s}^{n_2 - n_1}(a_2)$ whenever $n_2 \geq n_1$, or in the form $\mathsf{s}^{n_1 - n_2}(a_1) = a_2$ whenever $n_1 \geq n_2$. Thus, for any couple of constants a_1, a_2 in $\underline{a}$, it is sufficient to detect if $T_{\mathbb{Q}}^= \cup P \models a_1 = a_2 + n$ for some $n \in \mathbb{N}$, or if $T_{\mathbb{Q}}^= \cup P \models a_2 = a_1 + n$ (for some $n \in \mathbb{N}$, again). While running the Gauss elimination procedure on P and computing $\sigma = solve(P)$, we obtain:

$$T_{\mathbb{Q}}^= \cup P \models a_1 = a_2 + n \text{ iff } canon(a_1\sigma - a_2\sigma) = n$$

Let Δ be the set of $\Sigma_S^{\underline{a}}$-equations obtained by collecting all the equations of the form $a_1 = \mathsf{s}^n(a_2)$ for which $canon(a_1\sigma - a_2\sigma) = n$. The properties (i) and (ii) of Definition 4 for T_S-bases are straightforward.

Example 1. Consider $P = \{a_1 - 1 = a_3 + 1, 2b_2 + a_3 = b_2 + 2b_1 + b_2, a_2 - 1 = 2a_3 - 2b_1\}$. A solved form for P is given by $\sigma = \{a_1 \mapsto 2b_1 + 2, a_2 \mapsto 2b_1 + 1, a_3 \mapsto 2b_1\}$. By using the method given in the proof of Lemma 3, we can derive that $a_1 = \mathsf{s}^2(a_3), a_2 = \mathsf{s}(a_3)$ and these equalities define a T_S-basis modulo $T_{\mathbb{Q}}^=$ for P w.r.t. $\{a_1, a_2, a_3\}$.

The $T_{\mathbb{Q}}$ Case. While running over a constraint Γ the procedure presented in Section 4.1, we have already pointed out that, if Γ is satisfiable, the procedure halts returning a conjunction of the form $\hat{\sigma} \wedge \Phi^{\neq} \wedge \Phi^{\leq}$, where $\hat{\sigma}$ is a set of linear equalities that, thanks to the results in [10,11] and Lemma 2, satisfies the following two properties:

1. $T_{\mathbb{Q}} \cup \Gamma \models \widehat{\sigma}$;
2. if e is a linear equality such that $T_{\mathbb{Q}} \cup \Gamma \models e$, then $T_{\overline{Q}}^{\overline{=}} \cup \widehat{\sigma} \models e$.

The $T_{\mathbb{Q}\text{-}alg}$ Case. In Section 5.1, we have recalled that the satisfiability problem modulo $T_{\mathbb{Q}\text{-}alg}$ can be solved by running the Buchberger algorithm for computing the Groebner basis associated to a set Γ of polynomials. Actually, the Groebner basis computation can be considered as a way to obtain a confluent and terminating rewriting system for deciding the universal fragment of the theory of $\mathbb{Q}$-algebras. In [14], it is shown how a little tuning on the ordering of the rules in the term rewriting system is able to produce in the final Groebner basis associated to Γ a set, say P, of linear polynomials such that:

1. $T_{\mathbb{Q}\text{-}alg} \cup \Gamma \models P$;
2. if e is a linear polynomial such that $T_{\mathbb{Q}\text{-}alg} \cup \Gamma \models e$, then $T_{\overline{Q}}^{\overline{=}} \cup P \models e$.

Proposition 2. *Let $\underline{a}, \underline{b}$ be two sets of free constants such that $\underline{a} \subseteq \underline{b}$. Given a constraint Γ over the signature $\Sigma_{\mathbb{Q}}^{\underline{b}}$ (resp. $\Sigma_{\mathbb{Q}\text{-}alg}^{\underline{b}}$, $(\Sigma_{\mathbb{Q}} \cup \Sigma_{\mathbb{Q}\text{-}alg})^{\underline{b}}$), it is possible to compute a T_S-basis modulo $T_{\mathbb{Q}}$ (resp. $T_{\mathbb{Q}\text{-}alg}$, $T_{\mathbb{Q}} \cup T_{\mathbb{Q}\text{-}alg}$) for Γ w.r.t. $\underline{a}$.*

Proof.

$\boxed{T_{\mathbb{Q}}}$ Let us run the decision procedure for testing the satisfiability of Γ w.r.t. $T_{\mathbb{Q}}$. If it reports unsatisfiability, then the T_S-basis is simply $\{\bot\}$. Otherwise collect all the equalities (say $\widehat{\sigma}$) as described in Section 4.1, and apply on $\widehat{\sigma}$ the procedure described in Lemma 3. Thanks to the properties 1. and 2. recalled in the paragraph above about the $T_{\mathbb{Q}}$ case, the set Δ is a T_S-basis. Indeed, since $T_{\mathbb{Q}} \cup \Gamma \models \widehat{\sigma}$ and $T_{\overline{Q}}^{\overline{=}} \cup \widehat{\sigma} \models \Delta$, it follows (i) $T_{\mathbb{Q}} \cup \Gamma \models \Delta$ (recall that $T_{\overline{Q}}^{\overline{=}} \subset T_{\mathbb{Q}}$); moreover it holds the following chain of implications: for any e s.t. $T_{\mathbb{Q}} \cup \Gamma \models e$, then the set of equalities $\widehat{\sigma}$ derived using Fourier-Motzkin and Gauss elimination procedures is such that $T_{\overline{Q}}^{\overline{=}} \cup \widehat{\sigma} \models e$, and thus, by Lemma 3, also (ii) $T_S \cup \Delta \models e$.

$\boxed{T_{\mathbb{Q}\text{-}alg}}$ The case to compute a T_S-basis for Γ is analogous, taking into account the fact that the set P of representative linear polynomials is given by running the Buchberger algorithm as described in [14], and again the properties 1. and 2. in the paragraph above about the $T_{\mathbb{Q}\text{-}alg}$ case.

$\boxed{T_{\mathbb{Q}} \cup T_{\mathbb{Q}\text{-}alg}}$ The proofs of Lemma 3 and the two cases above make clear that, once we are able to guarantee the derivation of a set of linear equalities P that satisfy the properties of the kind 1. and 2., we are also able to compute T_S-bases. Since it is possible to isolate such a set w.r.t. $T_{\mathbb{Q}}$ and $T_{\mathbb{Q}\text{-}alg}$, it is possible to apply Theorem 1.3.12 in [20] to derive, given a set of literals Γ over $(\Sigma_{\mathbb{Q}} \cup \Sigma_{\mathbb{Q}\text{-}alg})^{\underline{b}}$, a set P' of linear equalities such that, again,

1. $T_{\mathbb{Q}} \cup T_{\mathbb{Q}\text{-}alg} \cup \Gamma \models P'$;
2. if e is a linear equality such that $T_{\mathbb{Q}} \cup T_{\mathbb{Q}\text{-}alg} \cup \Gamma \models e$, then $T_{\overline{Q}}^{\overline{=}} \cup P' \models e$.

At this point, it is immediate to apply again Lemma 3 to compute a T_S-basis modulo $T_{\mathbb{Q}} \cup T_{\mathbb{Q}\text{-}alg}$.

6.3   Applying the Combination Method

At the beginning of Section 6, we have pointed out that the theory of Increment T_S is Noetherian and that it can be "enlarged" to T_S^*, which admits quantifier elimination and behaves the same w.r.t. the satisfiability of constraints; moreover we have also shown that $T_{\mathbb{Q}}, T_{\mathbb{Q}\text{-}alg}$ and all the theories for the data structures we have introduced in Section 3 are T_S-compatible. Since the T_S-compatibility is a modular property (cf. Proposition 4.4 in [7]), also $T_{\mathbb{Q}} \cup T_{\mathbb{Q}\text{-}alg}{}^2$ is T_S-compatible. Moreover, in Section 6.1 we have shown how to compute T_S-bases modulo the theories for the considered data structures, and in Section 6.2 we have shown how to compute T_S-bases modulo the three fragments of arithmetic we are taking into account. Hence, all the hypotheses of Theorem 2 are satisfied.

Theorem 3. *Let DST be the set of theories* $\{T_{LS}, T'_{LS}, T_{RS}, T'_{RS}, T_{BS}, T'_{BS}\}$ *defined in Section 3. For any Σ_1-theory $T_1 \in DST$ and any Σ_2-theory $T_2 \in \{T_{\mathbb{Q}}, T_{\mathbb{Q}\text{-}alg}, T_{\mathbb{Q}} \cup T_{\mathbb{Q}\text{-}alg}\} \cup DST$ such that $\Sigma_1 \cap \Sigma_2 = \Sigma_S$, $T_1 \cup T_S \cup T_2$ has a decidable constraint satisfiability problem.*

7   Conclusion

We have presented a way to instantiate the non-disjoint extension of the Nelson-Oppen method in order to combine various theories corresponding to data structures with some fragments of arithmetic. Our approach allows us to consider arbitrary arithmetic constraints even if the shared signature is restricted to the successor function. We have focused on fragments over the rationals, but the same results hold in the case we replace the rationals with the reals. On the other hand, the fragments over the integers are more problematic, since first of all the convexity is lost, and secondly it is not so clear how to extract from the existing decision procedures the sets that are representative of the logical consequences involving only the successor function symbol. This is a problem left for future work.

Another interesting issue is to study how to handle more complex connecting axioms between the data structure and the arithmetic, and to try to enlarge the shared signature. In [17], the shared theory is a more precise approximation of the theory of integers, but on the other hand there is no integration of standard techniques for reasoning about arithmetic. In [15], we show how to combine data structures sharing the theory of abelian groups. In a similar way to what is investigated here, it would be interesting to study the combination of a data structure with some fragments of arithmetic when the shared theory is the one of abelian groups.

References

1. Armando, A., Bonacina, M.-P., Ranise, S., Schulz, S.: New results on rewrite-based satisfiability procedures. ACM Trans. on Computational Logic 10(1) (2009)
2. Armando, A., Ranise, S., Rusinowitch, M.: A rewriting approach to satisfiability procedures. Information and Computation 183(2), 140–164 (2003)

---

^{2} The satisfiability problem w.r.t. $T_{\mathbb{Q}} \cup T_{\mathbb{Q}\text{-}alg}$ can be decided through an appropriate application of Theorem 2: for the details we refer to [14].

3. Bonacina, M.P., Echenim, M.: On variable-inactivity and polynomial T-satisfiability procedures. Journal of Logic and Computation 18(1), 77–96 (2008)
4. Buchberger, B.: A theoretical basis for the reduction of polynomials to canonical forms. ACM SIGSAM Bull. 10(3), 19–29 (1976)
5. de Moura, L.M., Bjørner, N.: Engineering DPLL(T) + Saturation. In: Armando, A., Baumgartner, P., Dowek, G. (eds.) IJCAR 2008. LNCS, vol. 5195, pp. 475–490. Springer, Heidelberg (2008)
6. Enderton, H.B.: A Mathematical Introduction to Logic. Academic Press, New York-London (1972)
7. Ghilardi, S.: Model theoretic methods in combined constraint satisfiability. Journal of Automated Reasoning 33(3-4), 221–249 (2004)
8. Ghilardi, S., Nicolini, E., Zucchelli, D.: A comprehensive combination framework. ACM Transactions on Computational Logic 9(2), 1–54 (2008)
9. Kirchner, H., Ranise, S., Ringeissen, C., Tran, D.-K.: On superposition-based satisfiability procedures and their combination. In: Van Hung, D., Wirsing, M. (eds.) ICTAC 2005. LNCS, vol. 3722, pp. 594–608. Springer, Heidelberg (2005)
10. Lassez, J.-L., Maher, M.J.: On Fourier's algorithm for linear arithmetic constraints. Journal of Automated Reasoning 9(3), 373–379 (1992)
11. Lassez, J.-L., McAloon, K.: A canonical form for generalized linear constraints. Journal of Symbolic Computation 13(1), 1–24 (1992)
12. Lynch, C., Tran, D.-K.: Automatic decidability and combinability revisited. In: Pfenning, F. (ed.) CADE 2007. LNCS, vol. 4603, pp. 328–344. Springer, Heidelberg (2007)
13. Nelson, G., Oppen, D.C.: Simplification by cooperating decision procedures. ACM Transaction on Programming Languages and Systems 1(2), 245–257 (1979)
14. Nicolini, E.: Combined decision procedures for constraint satisfiability. PhD thesis. Università degli Studi di Milano (2007)
15. Nicolini, E., Ringeissen, C., Rusinowitch, M.: Combinable extensions of abelian groups. In: Schmidt, R.A. (ed.) CADE 2009. LNCS (LNAI), vol. 5663, pp. 51–66. Springer, Heidelberg (2009)
16. Nicolini, E., Ringeissen, C., Rusinowitch, M.: Data structures with arithmetic constraints: a non-disjoint combination. Report, INRIA, RR-6963 (2009)
17. Nicolini, E., Ringeissen, C., Rusinowitch, M.: Satisfiability procedures for combination of theories sharing integer offsets. In: Kowalewski, S., Philippou, A. (eds.) TACAS 2009. LNCS, vol. 5505, pp. 428–442. Springer, Heidelberg (2009)
18. Nieuwenhuis, R., Rubio, A.: Paramodulation-based theorem proving. In: Robinson, A., Voronkov, A. (eds.) Handbook of Automated Reasoning, ch. 7, vol. I, pp. 371–443. Elsevier Science, Amsterdam (2001)
19. Shostak, R.E.: Deciding combinations of theories. J. of the ACM 31, 1–12 (1984)
20. Zucchelli, D.: Combination methods for software verification. PhD thesis, Università degli Studi di Milano and Université Henri Poincaré - Nancy 1 (2008)

Efficient Combination of Decision Procedures for MUS Computation

Cédric Piette[1], Youssef Hamadi[2], and Lakhdar Saïs[1]

[1] Université Lille-Nord de France, Artois
CRIL-CNRS UMR 8188
F-62307 Lens Cedex, France
{piette,sais}@cril.fr
[2] Microsoft Research
7 J J Thomson Avenue
Cambridge, United Kingdom
youssefh@microsoft.com

Abstract. In recent years, the problem of extracting a MUS (Minimal Unsatisfiable Subformula) from an unsatisfiable CNF has received much attention. Indeed, when a Boolean formula is proved unsatisfiable, it does not necessarily mean that all its clauses take part to the inconsistency; a small subset of them can be conflicting and make the whole set without any solution. Localizing a MUS can thus be extremely valuable, since it enables to circumscribe a minimal set of constraints that represents a cause for the infeasibility of the CNF. In this paper, we introduce a novel, original framework for computing a MUS. Whereas most of the existing approaches are based on complete algorithms, we propose an approach that makes use of both local and complete searches. Our combination is empirically evaluated against the current best techniques on a large set of benchmarks.

1 Introduction

The concept of Minimally Unsatisfiable Subformula (MUS for short) proves more and more valuable in many applications of SAT, such as bounded model checking (see e.g. [1,2]) or knowledge-base validation. Indeed, when a Boolean formula is proved unsatisfiable, it does not necessarily mean that all its clauses take part to the inconsistency; a small subset of them can be conflicting and make the whole set without any solution. Localizing a MUS can thus be extremely valuable, since it enables to circumscribe a minimal set of constraints that represents a cause for the infeasibility of a CNF formula. For instance, in [3], an abstraction-based approach for deciding the satisfiability of finite-precision bit-vector is presented. Roughly, this method consists in generating an under-approximation such that if this latter one is satisfiable, so is the original problem. In the opposite case, an approximation of MUS (also called core) of this CNF formula is computed for generating an over-approximation whose unsatisfiability proves that the original problem has no solution. Experimental results clearly show that this way is more efficient than running a complete DPLL-like procedure on the whole original formula.

S. Ghilardi and R. Sebastiani (Eds.): FroCoS 2009, LNAI 5749, pp. 335–349, 2009.
© Springer-Verlag Berlin Heidelberg 2009

SAT solving has made a wonderful progress in the recent years, and some problems considered out-of-reach a decade ago can now be solved in a few seconds. A natural consequence of those algorithmic improvements is the modeling of larger problems whose reasons for unsatisfiability can be very difficult to catch. One way to explain inconsistency is to extract a Minimally Unsatisfiable Subformula, which represents an irreducible (w.r.t. the involved clauses) cause of the unsatisfiability. With the recent increase in formulae sizes, the problem of extracting one or several MUS has received much attention these last years. However, the current approaches which are based on complete search algorithms (DPLLs) often deliver an unsatisfiable subformula, which is not guaranteed to be minimal. Among these techniques, let us mention AMUSE [4] which consists in marking clauses during the exploration of a DPLL-related search tree. Another technique called zCore [5], the core extractor related to the well-known solver zChaff, is able to localize an unsatisfiable subformula by analyzing the resolution graph of a complete search procedure. Indeed, the source clauses from which is derived the empty one by the resolution process, simulated by modern solvers, forms a non-minimal core of the CNF formula.

More recently, a new technique called AOMUS [6] has also been introduced. It makes an original use of local search and relies on a so-called critical clause concept, to progressively focus on the difficult parts of a problem. This allows AOMUS to compute the upper-approximation of a MUS. Finally, an approach based on a serie of redundancy checks is presented in [7]. Let us also note that the problem of finding a Minimal Unsatisfiable Core (MUC) in the CSP framework is also the subject of many publications [8,9].

Although these approaches are based on different algorithmic principles, they are *destructive* by nature, in the sense that they consider the whole formula to *remove* parts which have been shown useless in a particular proof of unsatisfiability. In this paper, we are concerned with a new *constructive* framework. Indeed, this approach starts without any clause and builds a core by adding some particular clauses regularly, until an unsatisfiable set of clauses (which represents an approximated MUS) has been obtained. This framework makes an incomplete search – in charge of delivering sets of models – and an exhaustive technique act together. This can be opposed to destructive approaches which often imply the ability to prove a CNF unsat before starting a core extraction process. For applications like MaxSat solving through detection of cores [10], this could be an issue, though. Our constructive method does not suffer from this drawback, as it only requires to check the unsatisfiability of the discovered core instead of repetitively proving the whole CNF and some of its suformulae inconsistent.

To reduce the number of calls to a complete DPLL solver, our combination exploits the power of stochastic local search (SLS) for both finding models (proving the consistency of the current subformula) and for selecting the set of relevant clauses that might be added to the current subformula. A call to a complete solver is only done when the SLS method is not able to prove the consistency of the formula.

The paper is organized as follows. After some preliminary definitions and notations about SAT and MUS, we describe in section 3 the constructive framework. In section 4, an implementation of the framework is presented and experimented in section 5. Finally, we conclude by providing some interesting future lines of research.

2   Technical Background

Let L be the propositional language of formulas defined in the usual inductive way from a set P of propositional symbols (represented using plain letters like a, b, c, etc.), the Boolean constants $\top$ and $\bot$, and the standard connectives $\neg$, $\wedge$, $\vee$, $\Rightarrow$ and $\Leftrightarrow$. A SAT instance is a propositional formula in conjunctive normal form (CNF for short), i.e. a conjunction of clauses, where a clause is a disjunction of literals, a literal being a possibly negated propositional variable.

An interpretation is a function that assigns values from $\{true, false\}$ to every Boolean variable. An interpretation is called *model* w.r.t. a particular CNF if it satisfies this formula, namely if this interpretation makes it *true*. SAT is the well-known NP-complete problem that consists in deciding whether a propositional CNF is satisfiable or not, i.e. whether the formula admits at least one model. In this paper, CNF formulae are represented using a set (interpreted as a conjunction) of clauses, where a clause is a set (interpreted as a disjunction) of literals.

When a CNF is satisfiable, most of the current approaches are able to provide a model, which is a certificate of its satisfiability. By opposite, in case of inconsistency, these approaches only ensure that no satisfying interpretation exists. However, this is not very informing. The user might prefer to localize, if there exists, a small part of the CNF which triggers the inconsistency of the whole problem. In this respect, the concept of MUS (Minimally Unsatisfiable Subformula) is extremely valuable.

Definition 1. *Let Σ be a CNF formula. Γ is a MUS (Minimally Unsatisfiable Subformula) of Σ iff:*

1. *$\Gamma \subseteq \Sigma$;*
2. *Γ is unsatisfiable;*
3. *for each $\Gamma' \subset \Gamma$, Γ' is satisfiable.*

Extracting of MUS from an unsatisfiable CNF is a highly complex problem. For instance, checking if a CNF is a MUS is DP-complete [11] (where DP is the class composed of the union of a language in NP and another one in CoNP), while checking whether a set of clauses belongs to at least one MUS of an unsatisfiable CNF is Σ_2^p-hard [12].

Despite these not encouraging complexity results, many approaches for extracting a *core* (i.e. an approximated MUS) have already been proposed. In the next section, we propose a new constructive framework to extract cores from unsatisfiable formulae.

3   A Constructive Framework

3.1   Presentation

Most of the current approaches are destructive, in the sense that they consider the whole formula to progressively reduce it toward a core. In order to present the ideas of this new framework in comparison to the destructive one, we introduce here some notations that will be used in the remaining of this paper. First of all, let us denote Σ the CNF from which a MUS (or an approximation) is to be extracted. We also denote Γ another set of clauses which will contain the computed core. This set contains at any step of the procedure a subset of original formula Σ. Generally, the algorithms for computing a MUS are based on the iteration of the same function. So, let f be a function that takes Σ and Γ as input to produce a subformula Γ_N.

With destructive methods, Γ is initially set to Σ. In addition, f is a function that takes Σ and Γ as input to produce a subformula Γ_N of Γ, the most often by analyzing a proof of unsatisfiability. The resulting CNF Γ_N is then a subset of Γ. This new CNF is then used as Γ with respect to f, to obtain a potentially even smaller CNF. This iteration is performed until the delivered formula is Γ itself, namely until a fix point is reached.

For the constructive method, we propose to start the computation considering Γ as the empty set, and to progressively add clauses from Σ in Γ. So, a core is *built* thanks to f which returns a superset Γ_N of Γ which contains new clauses from $\Sigma \backslash \Gamma$. This operation is repeated until Γ becomes unsatisfiable and represents a core for Σ. The following table summarizes the main differences between those general frameworks.

	Constructive	Destructive
Initial Γ	$\emptyset$	Σ
$f(\Sigma,\Gamma){=}\Gamma_N$	$\Gamma \subseteq \Gamma_N$ and $\Gamma_N \subseteq \Sigma$	$\Gamma_N \subseteq \Gamma$
Stopping Condition	Γ is UNSAT	$f(\Sigma,\Gamma){=}\Gamma$

Actually, constructive procedures have already been studied for the problem of minimizing an unsatisfiable system toward a minimal one, in order to extract an exact cause of its infeasibility. For example, this approach is known for a long time in the mathematical programming [13] and CSP [14] communities. However, it is not used in practice any more, because of its complexity in the worst case. Indeed, by considering the number of calls to a complete procedure and denoting n the number of constraints of the CNF, and c_n the number of constraints of the biggest MUS (in number of constraints), the constructive approach exhibits a worst case complexity in $\mathcal{O}(n \times c_n)$, whereas the worst case complexities of destructive and dichotomic approaches are only $\mathcal{O}(n)$ and $\mathcal{O}(log(n) \times c_n)$ [8], respectively.

Fortunately, this is only true for systematic complete procedures that aim at returning a minimal set of clauses; in this paper, we focus on approaches that aim at approximating a MUS (delivering an upper set of clauses). Consequently, they do not suffer from this bad complexity result. In the next section, we discuss about particular clauses that can be safely added to Γ without discarding any MUS of the formula.

3.2   The Role of Necessary Clauses

In a recent study which aims at categorizing the clauses of a formula w.r.t. their role in its unsatisfiability [15], different classes of clauses have been established. Roughly, a clause is called *necessary* if it belongs to all MUS of a formula. Clearly, those clauses participate to any proof of inconsistency, and removing any one of them makes the CNF recover satisfiability. A clause is *potentially necessary* if it is not a necessary clause but the removal of some particular clause(s) can make it necessary. Those clauses appear in at least one MUS of the formula. Finally, a clause which is neither necessary nor potentially necessary is *never necessary* and does not belong to any MUS. They can be used in a proof of unsatisfiability, but all of them can be removed from the CNF keeping it unsatisfiable.

Necessary clauses are computationally hard to be extracted: indeed, for an unsatisfiable CNF Σ and a clause $c \in \Sigma$, if $\Sigma \backslash \{c\}$ is satisfiable, then c is necessary with respect to Σ. A linear number of calls of a complete algorithm is thus needed to exhaustively extract all necessary clauses of a given CNF. Fortunately, an inexpensive technique [6] can find them in an incomplete way. During the exploration of a local search for the satisfiability of Σ, if all its clauses are satisfied except one, the falsified clause is clearly necessary and is marked as *protected*. As necessary clauses represent global minima for the objective function of the local search, this notion proves really efficient for most of benchmarks, in an empirical point of view. Actually, most of the necessary clauses can be computed through the protected clause concept on many instances, but the approach cannot ensure they have all been delivered.

Nevertheless, an unsatisfiable CNF can exhibit no necessary clause. Indeed, containing two independent causes of unsatisfiability, namely two MUS with an empty intersection, is a sufficient condition for not exhibiting such clauses. However, most of realistic CNF which are expected to be satisfiable are not of this form. As said previously, a necessary clause of a formula belongs to any of its MUS and can therefore be safely added to Γ, in our constructive framework.

The main difference between destructive procedures is the strategy used to select the subset of clauses of Γ (represented previously by the function f). With respect to a constructive policy, a lot of possible techniques can also be imagined for augmenting Γ. However, when f only considers particular clauses to be added, interesting properties can be established. The interest of such particular functions are described in the next section.

3.3   The Non-redundancy Property

Our technique is based on the following proposition, which is a straight consequence of the definition of MUS itself:

Proposition 1. *Let Σ be a CNF formula, and ω an interpretation of Σ. $\forall M \in \Sigma$ s.t. M is a MUS, $\exists c \in M$ s.t. $\omega \nvDash c$.*

Clearly enough, as a MUS is an irreducible unsatisfiable set of clauses, any interpretation of a formula falsifies at least one clause from each of its MUSes. Accordingly, when considering a large number of interpretations, the most often falsified clauses are heuristically a good approximation of clauses belonging to MUSes. The highest score clauses are then added to the growing core. Thus, we associate a score (initialized to 0) to each clause, and while a large number of interpretations are considered, the score of each falsified clause is increased by 1.

A lot of different constructive algorithms can be created, choosing various strategies to enumerate interpretations. Those ones can be randomly generated, but it appears reasonable to attempt to reduce the number of clauses falsified by the explored interpretations. Indeed, some falsified clauses may not appear in any MUS and are just "noise" for the heuristic. Attempting to reduce the number of falsified clauses limits this phenomenon. Hence, meta-heuristics designed for optimisation problems (simulated annealing, genetic algorithms, etc.) can be used in this context.

Moreover, if the scoring function only considers falsified clauses of Σ with respect to models of Γ, then the following proposition ensures that no clause redundant with Γ can be added to this set of clauses. Those redundant clauses are clearly superfluous when considering the growing core.

Proposition 2. *Let us consider the CNF formulae Σ, Γ and the function f_{S_ω} defined previously in the constructive context. f_{S_ω} depends on a set of explored interpretations S_ω. The following proposition holds:*

if $f_{S_\omega}(\Sigma, \Gamma) \subseteq \Gamma \cup \{c \in \Sigma \backslash \Gamma \mid \exists \omega \in S_\omega$ s.t. $\omega \vDash \Gamma$ and $\omega \nvDash c\}$
then $\nexists c \in (f(\Sigma, \Gamma) \backslash \Gamma)$ such that $\Gamma \vDash c$.

Thus, within this condition, it is not possible for our constructive policy to add to the built core, the clauses which are redundant with Γ, namely clauses which "cover" the same part of the search space. This feature is obviously not shared by destructive methods. However, if f enables to add several clauses at the same time, a subset of them can clearly be redundant with another one in conjunction of Γ. Nevertheless, this is only possible for clauses added at the same time. The number of added clauses after each iteration can be tuned through the definition of f itself. If it is small, a bigger number of iterations would be necessary to construct a core, but this one would exhibit a good quality. In the opposite, with a big number of clauses added, only a few iterations are sufficient to obtain a core, but it will probably not be fine-grained. This property makes the constructive approaches very flexible, since it provides a parameter that represents a trade off between the quality of the obtained core and the time spent for its computation. Destructive approaches cannot propose to the user such a parameter. Let us illustrate the non-redundancy property through an example.

Example 1. Let Σ be a CNF formula made of 13 clauses, involving 4 variables such that:

$$\Sigma = \begin{cases} c_1 & : & (\neg a \lor c \lor d) & c_2 & : & (a \lor b \lor c) \\ c_3 & : & (\neg a \lor \neg b \lor c) & c_4 & : & (c \lor \neg d) \\ c_5 & : & (\neg a \lor \neg c \lor d) & c_6 & : & (\neg b \lor d) \\ c_7 & : & (a \lor \neg c \lor d) & c_8 & : & (a \lor \neg b \lor \neg c) \\ c_9 & : & (b \lor \neg c) & c_{10} & : & (\neg b \lor \neg c \lor \neg d) \\ c_{11} & : & (a \lor \neg c \lor \neg d) & c_{12} & : & (a \lor c \lor d) \\ c_{13} & : & (\neg a \lor b \lor \neg d) \end{cases}$$

The search space induced by those 4 variables is represented through a Karnaugh map in Figure 1a, together with each clause of Σ falsified by the different possible interpretations. Let us note that Σ is clearly unsatisfiable, since every interpretation is falsified by at least one clause of the CNF. As an example, $\omega_1 = \{\neg a, b, c, d\}$ falsifies the clauses c_8 and c_{10}.

Let us note that some interpretations are only falsified by a unique clause. For instance, $\omega_2 = \{\neg a, b, \neg c, d\}$ is only violated by c_4. Accordingly, this clause is necessary [15], since without it, ω_2 would become a model of Σ. c_4 thus participates to all sources of inconsistency of Σ and belongs to all its MUS. Σ exhibits two other necessary clauses, which are c_1 and c_9. Indeed, we can observe in Figure 1a that there exists at least one interpretation which is only "covered" (i.e. falsified) by one of these clauses.

Assume that those necessary clauses are first computed, as presented previously. Γ is then set to $\Gamma = \{c_1, c_4, c_9\}$. Consequently, only the models of this latter CNF are now considered for selecting the other clauses of Σ. The set of models of $\Gamma = \{c_1, c_4, c_9\}$ is represented in Figure 1b using white cells, the interpretations that falsify this CNF being in gray. For instance, the clauses c_3 and c_{13} cannot be added to Γ any more, since they are falsified iff at least one necessary clause is also falsified. Hence, they do not belongs to any MUS of Σ. With destructive methods, proofs of inconsistency can use these clauses which can then be present in the delivered core.

Thus, if f only considers the falsified clauses of Σ with respect to models of Γ, then c_{12} would be candidate to the built core and in this case would also prevent c_2 and c_6 from being added in the future, since these latter clauses cannot be falsified w.r.t. a model of $\Gamma \cup \{c_{12}\}$.

However, if f enables to add simultaneously several clauses, c_2 and c_{12} could be both added to Γ, whereas c_2 is a logical consequence of $\Gamma \cup \{c_{12}\}$ (c_2 covers an underset of interpretations covered by $\Gamma \cup \{c_{12}\}$ in Figure 1a).

Moreover, the traditional approaches aiming at extracting a MUS, or an approximation, from an unsatisfiable CNF delivers an arbitrary one, based on the refutation proof obtained. However, a propositional formula can contain several MUS (actually an exponential number of MUS in the worst case), and the user might prefer to extract a core that contains specific information, or clauses. Such a computation can be very useful: as an example, in FPGA routing task, in order to check if a particular part of the circuit is involved in the inroutability of the layout. Classical approaches cannot perform such a computation, and the only way to do this until now was to use a complete procedure, namely an approach that computes the exhaustive set of MUS, like [16] does, for instance.

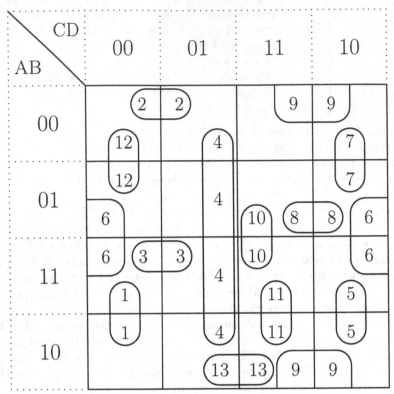

(a) Karnaugh map of Example 1

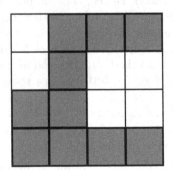

(b) Models of the CNF composed of necessary clauses of Σ

Fig. 1. Graphical representation of example 1

The constructive policy which respects the non-redundancy property offers such a choice to the user by guiding a search toward a specific core. To this purpose, instead of starting the computation with the empty formula, it suffices to begin with the chosen clauses. Let us denote Δ the set of clauses selected by the user to build a core. As shown previously, some clauses can be redundant w.r.t. the rest of the formula, and the constructive approach ensures that none of them can be added by the algorithm. Hence, by setting the first set of clauses to Δ, no other constraint redundant with it can be considered by the procedure. The following example shows the interest and the limitation of this kind of approach.

Example 2. Let us consider the CNF presented in the Example 1. Assume the user wants to compute a core involving the set of clauses $\{c_1, c_3, c_8, c_{12}\}$.

First, c_1 is a necessary clause, and thus belongs to all MUS/cores of Σ anyway. On the opposite, c_3 is a *never necessary* clause (w.r.t. the terminology of [15]) and does not belongs to any MUS. Consequently, the user's choice implies a non-optimal construction of core. c_8 and c_{12} are *potentially necessary* clauses, and belong to at least one MUS of the CNF. By adding those clauses before the first iteration, assuming that the 3 necessary clauses are first detected, Γ contains the clauses $\{c_1, c_3, c_4, c_8, c_9, c_{12}\}$. Using this "partial core", the only clauses that can be falsified with respect to these models are c_5, c_6, c_{10} and c_{11}, and some of them will then be added to Γ to construct a core. If c_5 and c_{11} are selected, the resulting core can only be minimized by removing c_3 and all the clauses chosen by the user (except this last one) do participate to the computed MUS. Unfortunately, the potential choice of c_6 and c_{10} to start the core construction would make c_8 redundant, and not belong to all its MUS.

This example shows the constructive approach's flexibility. It enables the end-user to guide the computation toward a specific core, and might be driven by the user's expertise on the problem. Clearly, the proposed process is not limited to the initial core, and different user-interactions during the construction of the core can be imagined. However, this is done without ensuring that the chosen clauses will actually be a part of all MUS of this core. We believe that this incomplete computation is a good tradeoff in front of the very high complexity of such a problem. Indeed, assuming $P \neq NP$, we cannot expect the development of an efficient complete procedure, since checking whether a formula belongs to the set of MUS of an unsatisfiable SAT instance is in Σ_2^p (a consequence of theorem 8.2 of [12]). In the next section, we present a first implementation of this constructive approach which uses local search for adding new clauses to Γ.

4   A First Implementation: constructMUS

In this section, we present a particular implementation of the constructive framework that respects the non-redundancy property. The function f is based on local search for choosing clauses to be added. Initially, this stochastic technique is used for extracting protected clauses, and initialize Γ [6].

We then perform multiple runs of a local search on Γ and consider the discovered models. We then consider the falsified clauses of Σ and increment a related score, initially set to 0 for each clause. As at least one clause of each set that could complement Γ to form a MUS is falsified, it suffices to consider the clauses that have obtained the highest score and add them to the approximation of the

---

Algorithm 1. `construct_MUS`

Input: an unsatisfiable CNF: Σ
Output: a core of Σ: Γ

1 **begin**
2      $call\_DPLL \leftarrow false$;
3      $\Gamma \leftarrow \emptyset$;
4      $\Gamma \leftarrow$ search_protected_clauses() ;
5      $\Sigma \leftarrow \Sigma \backslash \Gamma$;
6   **while** *true* **do**
7   **if** *call_DPLL* **then**
8   **if** $DPLL(\Gamma) = UNSAT$ **then**
9   **return** Γ ;
10   **else**
11                  $seed \leftarrow$ found_model ;
12                  $call\_DPLL \leftarrow false$;
13   **else**
14              $seed \leftarrow$ random_interpretation() ;
15          $S_\omega \leftarrow$ LS_finds_models(Γ,*seed*) ;
16   **if** $S_\omega = \emptyset$ **then**
17              $call\_DPLL \leftarrow true$;
18   **else**
19              $\Phi \leftarrow$ select_most_falsified_clauses(Σ, S_ω, p) ;
20              $\Gamma \leftarrow \Gamma \cup \Phi$;
21              $\Sigma \leftarrow \Sigma \backslash \Phi$;
22 **end**

MUS. Accordingly, at the end of the incomplete procedure, Γ is augmented with these "high-score clauses" and these operations are repeated, searching models to the new set of clauses.

This process is iterated until no model can be found to the growing formula Γ. However, due to the incomplete nature of the local search, this computed set of clauses is not guaranteed to be unsatisfiable, even if in practice this case occurs quite often. To ensure the completeness of this algorithm, when the local search fails to find a model of Γ, we run a DPLL complete method on this formula. If Γ is proved unsatisfiable, then Γ is returned as the computed MUS approximation. Otherwise, a model ω which represents a certificate of the satisfiability of Γ, is discovered by the complete approach; in this case, the model is used by the local search as its first explored interpretation, ensuring at least one model will be discovered. Moreover, as local search has not found a model previously, this means that this part of the search space has probably not been explored by the incomplete method. Forcing the model as the seed enables to diversify the search, and to find other "close" models.

With these features, the proposed constructive algorithm is sound for the problem of extracting an unsatisfiable subformula from any CNF. This approach is synthesized in the Algorithm 1. As explained previously, the considered "core" Γ is initially set of the empty formula, and only clauses found necessary (in a very cheap way) through the protected clause concept (line 4) are added. A flag $call\_DPLL$ is set initially to $false$, which implies the computation of a sample of models of Γ by a local search call (line 14). The p most falsified clauses of the remaining part of the formula are added to Γ (lines 18-19). Let us note that this parameter plays a role in the quality of the core and in the runtime of the procedure, since it provides the number of added clauses at each iteration. These operations are iterated until no model can be found by LS to Γ.

If no model is found by LS, then the flag $call\_DPLL$ is set to $true$ (line 16) and a complete approach is run on Γ (line 8). If Γ is unsatisfiable, it is returned as the computed core; in the opposite case, a model is found by the procedure and is used as a "seed" in the next call of the local search (line 11). In the next section, this first implementation of the constructive framework is empirically evaluated.

5   Experiments

In order to assess the ability of the proposed constructive framework to efficiently extract cores, we have implemented the ideas described in the previous sections, and compared them to three state-of-the-art approaches on various instances from SATLIB and the SAT competitions. As a case study, we have used the RSAPS [17] local search. For the complete approach, Minisat [18] has been chosen, since it is recognized by the community as one of the best complete solver. Based on empirical tuning, the parameter p of constructMUS procedure has been set to $(1 + \#cla_\Sigma \times 3\%)$ and the flips limit devoted to the local search runs at each iteration of the algorithm has been set to $((1 + \#cla_\Gamma) \times 100)$, where $\#cla_\Sigma$ is the number of clauses of Σ not added to Γ, and $\#cla_\Gamma$ the number of clauses of the current sub-formula Γ.

We compare constructMUS to 3 state-of-the-art approaches: zCore [5], AMUSE [4] and AOMUS [6]. The Table 1 reports these experiments. For each result, the size (in terms of number of clauses) of the delivered approximation of MUS is reported together with the time needed for the computation. Moreover, for those two values, the best obtained one is given in bold. All experiments have been conducted on Pentium IV, 3 Ghz with 1 GB of memory, and for each tested benchmark, a 10,000 seconds timeout has been respected.

First of all, only AMUSE cannot succeed to precisely localize in a few seconds the single MUS of the {23,42}.shuffled benchmarks, which come from bounded model checking. These ones actually encode formal verification of the open-source Sun PicoJava II microprocessor, and as emphasized in [19], the discovered MUS enables to identify the relevant components of the system for the checked property. We also have performed some experimental tests on various benchmarks from the graph coloring problem ({3,4}col-*). On those CNFs, the finding of a core enables to localize a sub-graph that cannot be colored with the given number of colors, and make the whole problem infeasible. The constructive approach appears to be the best when we consider the size of the returned

Table 1. Experimental evaluation of a constructive implementation

Instances			zCore		constructMUS		AMUSE		AOMUS	
Name	#var	#cla	#cla	time	#cla	time	#cla	time	#cla	time
23.shuffled	198	474	**221**	0.05	**221**	4.83	230	**0.04**	**221**	2.05
42.shuffled	378	904	**421**	0.08	**421**	5.00	434	0.09	**421**	3.80
3col20_5_5	40	176	46	**0.04**	**42**	19.6	60	0.06	46	13.8
3col20_5_6	40	176	43	0.07	**40**	18.3	46	**0.06**	66	7.15
3col20_5_7	40	176	**40**	0.05	**40**	18.5	60	0.06	**40**	9.39
3col20_5_8	40	176	52	**0.05**	**40**	18.6	46	0.06	55	8.96
4col100_9_5	200	1806	*time out*		**1462**	335	1566	**56.4**	1512	1550
4col100_9_6	200	1806	1458	7030	**1451**	351	1505	**79.9**	1506	5222
4col100_9_7	200	1806	1596	3165	**1461**	352	1472	**38.7**	*time out*	
4col100_9_8	200	1806	1618	6694	**1455**	356	1510	**71.5**	1502	2638
4col100_9_9	200	1806	1556	5202	**1458**	377	1527	**45.1**	1484	2973
5cnf...30f4	30	419	316	0.65	**237**	127	369	**0.13**	340	26.7
5cnf...40f1	40	608	601	0.86	**397**	189	593	**0.34**	418	39.5
am_4_4	433	1458	929	6.3	944	25.6	**902**	**3.95**	929	29.2
am_5_5	1076	3677	**2046**	7614	2244	**62.5**	**2046**	765	2140	76.4
ca008	130	370	276	0.17	**255**	4.83	283	**0.08**	**255**	1.93
ca016	272	780	584	0.72	**559**	8.73	646	**0.30**	**559**	5.33
ca032	558	1606	**1176**	**2.66**	1230	14.4	1316	3.46	1281	52.9
ca064	1132	3264	**2421**	**4.29**	2793	20.2	2687	22.9	2613	141
ezfact16_1	193	1113	**41**	0.19	169	20.4	100	**0.10**	**41**	383
ezfact16_2	193	1113	**47**	**0.07**	169	20.8	55	0.09	**41**	382
gt-012	144	1398	1356	7.4	**1124**	171	1219	**1.40**	1205	162
gt-014	196	2289	2113	53.4	1940	301	**1713**	**5.27**	1989	581
hanoi4u	1312	16856	*time out*		7605	**300**	6434	9670	*time out*	
homer06	180	830	**415**	14.2	461	50.2	**415**	38.1	**415**	**9.66**
homer07	198	1012	506	19.2	531	62.3	506	38.6	**415**	**13.9**
homer08	216	1212	606	39.5	650	79.0	506	54.4	**415**	**20.3**
hwb-n20-01	134	630	**624**	1248	**624**	93.6	627	**58.8**	**624**	351
hwb-n20-02	134	630	625	1270	**624**	142	628	**50.6**	625	508
hwb-n20-03	134	630	626	272	**622**	**58.6**	626	180	625	191
linvrinv2	24	61	51	**0.05**	**50**	6.03	51	**0.05**	53	0.10
linvrinv3	90	262	250	0.15	**239**	16.9	253	**0.09**	244	0.30
linvrinv4	224	689	689	16.4	**653**	42.3	689	**4.46**	657	14.2
mm-2x2-5-5-s.1	324	2064	**1290**	136	1857	152	1791	**40.4**	2064	259

sub-formula. In addition, this result is obtained in a reasonable time, even if generally AMUSE provides a rougher core in a shorter time. As an example, for 4col100_9_8, constructMUS extracts a 1455-clause core in less than 6 minutes whereas zCore only localizes a core made of 1618 clauses in about one hour and a half. AMUSE and AOMUS provide sets of 1510 and 1502 clauses in 1 and 23 minutes, respectively. Let us note that on this family of benchmarks, our constructive method is systematically more accurate than the destructive ones.

More generally, our results show that this first implementation of the algorithm constructMUS delivers very satisfying results on various CNF, compared to state-of-the-art approaches (see e.g. hwb-*, gt-*). However, AOMUS appears to be a very good approach for some industrial problems (homer), while DPLL-based procedures are more adapted on various families, such that the am_*_* one. Consulting the presented results, the developed approach is validated, but let us note that the four tested methods deliver orthogonal results with respect to the considered CNF. Each one of them appears the best appropriate technique for some families of benchmarks, but no one clearly outperforms the others. Obviously, the fact that the result is here multi-criterion (size of the approximation and run time) is not helpful for the comparison.

In [20], it is suggested to use the notion of *velocity*, which is defined as the ratio between the size of the delivered core and the time needed for the computation. This element enables to know how many clauses are "eliminated" per second, then to know the *best* approach. However, this choice is not completely satisfying. Indeed, let us assume that a CNF formula exhibits 2 MUS that contain a different number of clauses. Is a method which extracts exactly the bigger MUS less efficient that another one which delivers roughly the smaller one (and then, a smaller set of clauses) ?

Deciding the best approach is still intrinsically a problem, that appears to be difficult to deal with objectively without considering any particular application domain. Nevertheless, the behaviour of our implementation appears to be very satisfying for various benchmarks, in comparison to the "best" current approaches. This added to its flexibility (parameter to control the precision, possibility to start with a guess) makes it very interesting as a new general framework for MUS extraction.

6   Conclusion

In this paper, an original framework called *constructive* has been presented for the problem of computing an approximated MUS, or *core*. The presented technique is based on a combination of a local search procedure and an exhaustive DPLL-like algorithm. It exhibits interesting features. For instance, it does not need to be able to solve the whole CNF for extracting a core; moreover, the procedure gives rooms to user's expertise and allows him to guide the search toward a specific core. This is not possible with classical approaches that always compute arbitrary cores. Preliminary experiments show that in many cases, an instance of this framework proves competitive, and can outperform previous approaches. Particularly, our implementation delivers very satisfying results in terms of the size of core.

This first implementation opens many interesting perspectives. The concept of a critical clause, presented in [6], has been proved useful for another local-search-based extractor. This concept cannot be used as such, due to the nature of the approach, but a possible adaptation could improve the accuracy of the delivered core. Other hybridizations of this constructive framework, based for instance on a genetic algorithm for providing sets of models, are also planned as further works. Finally, a combination of a constructive and a destructive approaches could also be explored to combine the best of both worlds.

References

1. McMillan, K.L., Amla, N.: Automatic abstraction without counterexamples. In: Garavel, H., Hatcliff, J. (eds.) TACAS 2003. LNCS, vol. 2619, pp. 2–17. Springer, Heidelberg (2003)
2. Gupta, A., Ganai, M., Yang, Z., Ashar, P.: Iterative abstraction using SAT-based BMC with proof analysis. In: Proceedings of the IEEE/ACM international conference on Computer-aided design (ICCAD 2003), Washington, DC, USA, pp. 416–423 (2003)
3. Bryant, R.E., Kroening, D., Ouaknine, J., Seshia, S.A., Strichman, O., Brady, B.: Deciding bit-vector arithmetic with abstraction. In: Grumberg, O., Huth, M. (eds.) TACAS 2007. LNCS, vol. 4424, pp. 358–372. Springer, Heidelberg (2007)
4. Oh, Y., Mneimneh, M.N., Andraus, Z.S., Sakallah, K.A., Markov, I.L.: AMUSE: a minimally-unsatisfiable subformula extractor. In: DAC 2004: Proceedings of the 41st annual conference on Design automation, pp. 518–523. ACM Press, New York (2004)
5. Zhang, L., Malik, S.: Extracting small unsatisfiable cores from unsatisfiable boolean formula. In: Sixth international conference on theory and applications of satisfiability testing (SAT 2003), Portofino, Italy (2003)
6. Gregoire, E., Mazure, B., Piette, C.: Extracting MUSes. In: Proceedings of the 17th European Conference on Artificial Intelligence (ECAI 2006), Trento (Italy), pp. 387–391 (2006)
7. van Maaren, H., Wieringa, S.: Finding guaranteed MUSes fast. In: Kleine Büning, H., Zhao, X. (eds.) SAT 2008. LNCS, vol. 4996, pp. 291–304. Springer, Heidelberg (2008)
8. Hemery, F., Lecoutre, C., Saïs, L., Boussemart, F.: Extracting MUCs from constraint networks. In: Proceedings of the 17th European Conference on Artificial Intelligence (ECAI 2006), Trento (Italy), pp. 113–117 (2006)
9. Junker, U.: QuickXplain: Preferred explanations and relaxations for over-constrained problems. In: Proceedings of the 19th National Conference on Artificial Intelligence (AAAI 2004), pp. 167–172 (2004)
10. Marques-Silva, J., Planes, J.: Algorithms for maximum satisfiability using unsatisfiable cores. In: Design, Automation and Test in Europe (DATE 2008), pp. 408–413 (2008)
11. Papadimitriou, C.H.: Computational Complexity. Addison-Wesley, New York (1994)
12. Eiter, T., Gottlob, G.: On the complexity of propositional knowledge base revision, updates and counterfactual. Artificial Intelligence 57, 227–270 (1992)
13. Chinneck, J.W.: Feasibility and viability. In: Advances in Sensitivity Analysis and Parametric Programming. International Series in Operations Research and Management Science, vol. 6, Kluwer Academic Publishers, Dordrecht (1997)
14. de Siqueira, J.L., Puget, J.F.: Explanation-based generalisation of failures. In: Proceedings of the 8th European Conference on Artificial Intelligence, pp. 339–344 (1988)
15. Kullmann, O., Lynce, I., Marques Silva, J.P.: Categorisation of clauses in conjunctive normal forms: Minimally unsatisfiable sub-clause-sets and the lean kernel. In: Biere, A., Gomes, C.P. (eds.) SAT 2006. LNCS, vol. 4121, pp. 22–35. Springer, Heidelberg (2006)

16. Gregoire, E., Mazure, B., Piette, C.: Boosting a complete technique to find mss and mus thanks to a local search oracle. In: Proceedings of the 20th International Joint Conference on Artificial Intelligence (IJCAI 2007), Hyderabad (India), January 2007, vol. 2, pp. 2300–2305 (2007)
17. Hutter, F., Tompkins, D.A.D., Hoos, H.H.: Scaling and probabilistic smoothing: Efficient dynamic local search for SAT. In: Van Hentenryck, P. (ed.) CP 2002. LNCS, vol. 2470, pp. 233–248. Springer, Heidelberg (2002)
18. Eén, N., Sorensson, N.: Minisat home page,
    http://www.cs.chalmers.se/cs/research/formalmethods/minisat
19. McMillan, K.L.: Applications of Craig interpolants in model checking. In: Halbwachs, N., Zuck, L.D. (eds.) TACAS 2005. LNCS, vol. 3440, pp. 1–12. Springer, Heidelberg (2005)
20. Gershman, R., Koifman, M., Strichman, O.: Deriving small unsatisfiable cores with dominators. In: Proceedings of Computer-Aided Verification, Seattle (USA), pp. 109–122 (2006)

Learning to Integrate Deduction and Search in Reasoning about Quantified Boolean Formulas

Luca Pulina and Armando Tacchella*

DIST, Università di Genova, Viale Causa, 13 – 16145 Genova, Italy
Luca.Pulina@unige.it, Armando.Tacchella@unige.it

Abstract. In this paper we study the problem of integrating deduction and search with the aid of machine learning techniques to yield practically efficient decision procedures for quantified Boolean formulas (QBFs). We show that effective on-line policies can be learned from the observed performances of deduction and search on representative sets of formulas. Such policies can be leveraged to switch between deduction and search during the solving process. We provide empirical evidence that learned policies perform better than either deduction and search, even when the latter are combined using hand-made policies based on previous works. The fact that even with a proof-of-concept implementation, our approach is competitive with sophisticated state-of-the-art QBF solvers shows the potential of machine learning techniques in the integration of different reasoning methods.

1 Introduction

Quantified Boolean formulas (QBFs) are known to yield compact encodings of many automated reasoning problems, including formal property verification of circuits (see, e.g., [1]), symbolic planning (see, e.g. [2]) and reasoning about knowledge (see, e.g., [3]). Because of this property, reasoning about QBFs attracted a lot of interest in recent years, leading to the development of decision procedures based on various methods, including search (see, e.g., [4]), skolemization [5], resolution [6,7], as well as multi-engine [8] and multi-heuristics [9] solvers. However, in spite of such a considerable effort, the current implementations of QBF reasoners still cannot handle many instances of practical interest. This is witnessed, e.g., by the results of the 2008 QBF solver competition (QBFE-VAL'08) where even the most sophisticated solvers failed to decide encodings obtained from real-world applications [10].

In this paper we study the problem of building decision procedures for QBFs by integrating deduction and search with the aid of Machine Learning techniques. In particular, we consider on-line switching between deduction – in the form of variable elimination by means of Q-resolution [11] – and search – with backjumping as in [12], where selection policies are learned from observed performances of

---

* We wish to thank the Italian Ministry of University and Research for its financial support, and the anonymous reviewers for helpful suggestions on how to improve the paper.

the two different reasoning methods on representative sets of formulas. We show that learned policies can leverage a small set of informative features which can be efficiently computed, and we empirically demonstrate that such features are relevant in order to synthesize effective policies. While in principle a large set of features coming from diverse representations of the input formula could be used (see, e.g., [8]), it is known, see, e.g., [13], that variable elimination on plain Boolean formulas may require computational resources that are exponential in the treewidth.[1] This connection has been studied also for quantified formulas in [15,16,17] where extensions of treewidth are shown to be related to the efficiency of reasoning about quantified Boolean constraints, of which QBFs are a subclass. In theory, treewidth could be informative enough for our purposes, but, in practice, since computing treewidth is an NP-complete problem and QBFs of some interest for applications may have thousands of variables, even approximations of treewidth can be too expensive to compute on-the-fly [18]. We overcome this problem by considering alternative parameters that are both computable without a prohibitive overhead, and informative as much as treewidth in many situations. Concerning policy synthesis, we accomplish this by analyzing the performances of two inductive models: a symbolic one, i.e., decision trees [19], and a functional one, i.e., Support Vector Machines (SVMs) [20]. We consider these two methods because they are both fairly robust, efficient, and are not subject to stringent hypothesis on the training data. They are also "orthogonal", since the algorithms they use are based on radically different approaches to the dataset.

To test our approach, we implemented it in QuReS (**Qu**antified **R**esolution and **S**earch solver), a proof-of-concept tool consisting of about 2K lines of C++ code. We have experimented with QuReS on the QBFEVAL'08 dataset [10], which is comprised of more than three thousands QBF encodings in various application domains – the largest publicly available collection of QBFs to date. Here, we show that exploiting learned policies to dynamically integrate deduction and search enables QuReS to solve QBFs which, all other things being equal, cannot be solved by the deductive and search components of QuReS alone. In this, QuReS outranks both the experimental control, i.e., policies based on random switching between resolution and search, and the hand-coded heuristic proposed in [13]. Moreover, QuReS is competitive with respect to current QBF solvers, as it would have ranked third best among QBFEVAL'08 competitors if considering the number of problems solved within a given amount of resources.

Approaches similar to ours have been proposed for plain Boolean satisfiability in [13], and for non-quantified constraint satisfaction in [21], but in these cases the policies were hand-coded instead of automatically synthesized. On the other hand, Machine Learning techniques have been used in [8] to combine different QBF engines and in [9] to combine different heuristics, but in these cases the polices were synthesized to select the best solver for a given instance, or the best heuristic to search in a given subproblem, respectively. This is thus the first time that an approach integrating deduction and search with the aid of

---

[1] Induced width, as defined in [13], is shown to be equivalent to treewidth in [14].

Machine Learning techniques to synthesize on-line switching policies is designed, implemented and empirically tested for QBFs.

The paper is structured as follows. In Section 2 we lay down the foundations of our work considering relevant definitions and known results. In Section 3 we define the basic QURES algorithms, including search, resolution and their combination, while in Section 4 we present the methodology implemented in QURES devoted to compute on-line policies to discriminate between deduction and search and their usage during the solving process. In Section 5 we describe our experiments and we conclude in Section 6 summarizing our current results and future research directions.

2   Groundwork

A *variable* is an element of a set P of propositional letters and a *literal* is a variable or the negation thereof. We denote with $|l|$ the variable occurring in the literal l, and with $\bar{l}$ the *complement* of l, i.e., $\neg l$ if l is a variable and $|l|$ otherwise. A *clause* C is an n-ary $(n \geq 0)$ disjunction of literals such that, for any two distinct disjuncts l, l' of C, it is not the case that $|l| = |l'|$. A *propositional formula* is a k-ary $(k \geq 0)$ conjunction of clauses. A *quantified Boolean formula* is an expression of the form $Q_1 z_1 \ldots Q_n z_n \Phi$ where, for each $1 \leq i \leq n$, z_i is a variable, Q_i is either an existential quantifier $Q_i = \exists$ or a universal one $Q_i = \forall$, and Φ is a propositional formula in the variables $Z = \{z_1, \ldots, z_n\}$. The expression $Q_1 z_1 \ldots Q_n z_n$ is the *prefix* and Φ is the *matrix*. A literal l is *existential* if $|l| = z_i$ for some $1 \leq i \leq n$ and $\exists z_i$ belongs to the prefix, and it is *universal* otherwise. A prefix $p = Q_1 z_1 \ldots Q_n z_n$ can be viewed as the concatenation of h *quantifier blocks*, i.e., $p = Q_1 Z_1 \ldots Q_h Z_h$, where the sets Z_i with $1 \leq i \leq h$ are a partition of Z, and consecutive blocks have different quantifiers. To each variable z we can associate a *level* $lvl(z)$ which is the index of the corresponding block, i.e., $lvl(z) = i$ for all the variables $z \in Z_i$. We also say that variable z *comes after* a variable z' in p if $lvl(z) \geq lvl(z')$.

The semantics of a QBF φ can be defined recursively as follows. A QBF clause is *contradictory* exactly when it does not contain existential literals. If φ contains a contradictory clause then φ is false. If φ has no conjuncts then φ is true. If $\varphi = Qz\psi$ is a QBF and l is a literal, we define φ_l as the QBF obtained from ψ by removing all the conjuncts in which l occurs and removing $\bar{l}$ from the others. Then we have two cases. If φ is $\exists z\psi$, then φ is true exactly when φ_z or $\varphi_{\neg z}$ are true. If φ is $\forall z\psi$, then φ is true exactly when φ_z and $\varphi_{\neg z}$ are true. The QBF decision problem (QSAT) can be stated as the problem of deciding whether a given QBF is true or false.

Given a QBF φ on the set of variables $Z = \{z_1, \ldots, z_n\}$, its *Gaifman graph* has a vertex set equal to Z with an edge (z, z') for every pair of different elements $z, z' \in Z$ that occur together in some clause of φ. A *scheme* for a QBF φ having prefix p is a supergraph (Z, E) of the Gaifman graph of φ along with an ordering $z'_1, \ldots, z'_n$ of the elements of Z such that (i) the ordering $z'_1, \ldots, z'_n$ preserves the order of p, i.e., if $i < j$ then z'_j comes after z'_i in p, and (ii) for any z'_k, its lower numbered neighbors form a clique, that is, for all k, if $i < k$, $j < k$, $(z'_i, z'_k) \in E$

and $(z'_j, z'_k) \in E$, then $(z'_i, z'_j) \in E$. The *width* $w_p(\varphi)$ of a scheme is the maximum, over all vertices z_k, of the size of the set $\{i : i < k, (z_i, z_k) \in E\}$, i.e., the set containing all lower numbered neighbors of z_k. The *treewidth* $tw_p(\varphi)$ of a QBF φ is the minimum width over all schemes for φ.

Clause resolution [11] for a QBF φ is an operation whereby given two clauses $Q \vee x$ and $R \vee \neg x$ of φ, the clause $\min(Q \vee R)$ can be derived, where (i) Q and R are disjunctions of literals, (ii) x is an existential variable, (iii) Q and R do not share any literal l such that l occurs in Q and $\bar{l}$ occurs in R, and (iv) $\min(C)$ is obtained from C by removing the universal literals coming after all the existential literals in C. *Variable elimination* is a control strategy for resolution defined as follows. Given a QBF φ on the set of variables $Z = \{z_1, \ldots, z_n\}$, we consider a scheme for φ and the associated *elimination ordering* $Z' = \{z'_1, \ldots, z'_n\}$. Starting from $z = z'_n$ and scanning the elimination ordering in reverse, we *eliminate* the variables as follows. If z is existential, and assuming that φ contains $k > 0$ clauses in the form $Q \vee z$ and $h > 0$ clauses in the form $R \vee \neg z$, then we add at most $k \cdot h$ clauses to φ obtained by performing all the resolutions on z, and eliminating all clauses in which z occurs. In the case where either $k = 0$ or $h = 0$, no operation is performed. If z is universal, we simply skip to the next variable. If all the variables in φ can be eliminated without generating a contradictory clause, then φ is true, else it is false.

Backtracking search [22] for a QBF φ is a depth-first exploration of an *AND-OR tree* defined as follows. Initially, the current QBF is φ. If the current QBF is of the form $\exists x \psi$ then we create an *OR-node*, whose children are obtained by checking recursively whether φ_x is true or $\varphi_{\neg x}$ is true. If the current QBF is of the form $\forall y \psi$ then we create an *AND-node*, whose children are obtained by checking recursively whether both φ_y and $\varphi_{\neg y}$ are true. We call φ_l a *branch* (also, an *assignment*), and since we explore the tree in a depth-first fashion, a node wherein only the first branch was taken is said to be *open*, and *closed* otherwise. The leaves are of two kinds: If the current QBF contains a contradictory clause we have a *conflict*, while if the current QBF contains no conjuncts we have a *solution*. Backtracking from a conflict amounts to reaching back to the deepest open OR-node: if there is no such node, then φ is false; backtracking from a solution amounts to reaching back to the deepest open AND-node: if there is no such node, then φ is true.

Unit propagation [22] is an optimization that can be added on top of basic variable elimination and search. A clause C is *unit* in a QBF φ exactly when (i) C contains only one existential literal l (*unit literal*) and, (ii) all the universal literals in C have a level greater than $lvl(l)$ in the prefix of φ. If φ contains a unit literal l, then φ is true if and only if φ_l is true. Unit propagation is the process whereby we keep assigning unit literals until no more such literals can be found.

Backjumping is an optimization that can be added on top of search. According to [4] the computation performed by a QBF search algorithm corresponds to a particular kind of deductive proof, i.e., a tree wherein clause resolution and *term resolution* alternate, where a *term* is a conjunction of literals, and term resolution is the "symmetric" operation of clause resolution – see [4] for details. The clause/term tree resolution proof corresponding to search for a QBF φ can be reconstructed as follows. In case of a conflict, there must be two clauses, say $Q \lor x$ and $R \lor \neg x$ such that all the literals in Q and R have been deleted by previous assignments. We can always resolve such clauses to obtain the *working reason* $\min(Q \lor R)$ – where $Q \lor x$ and $R \lor \neg x$ are the *initial* working reasons. The other clauses can be derived from the working reason when backtracking over any existential literal l such that $|l|$ occurs in the working reason. There are three cases: (i) If l is a unit literal, then there is a clause C where l occurs – the *reason* of assigning l – and we obtain a new working reason by resolving the current one with C; (ii) If l is an open branch, then proof reconstruction stops, because we must branch on $\bar{l}$, and the reason of this assignment is the current working reason; (iii) If l is a closed branch, then its reason was computed before, and it can be treated as in (1). In case of a solution, the initial working reason is a term which is the conjunction of (a subset of) all the literals assigned from the root of the search tree, down to the current leaf, i.e., a Boolean implicant of the matrix of φ. The other terms can be derived when backtracking over any universal literal l such that l is in the working reason, considering cases (ii) and (iii) above, and using term instead of clause resolution.[2] Given the above, it is easy to see that closing branches over existential (resp. universal) literals that do not appear in the current working reason is useless, i.e., they are not responsible for the current conflict (resp. solution). Backjumping can thus be described as the process whereby useless branches are skipped while backtracking.

3   A Framework to Integrate Resolution and Search

In Figure 1 we present QuRES basic routines in pseudo-code format. All the routines take as by-reference parameters the data structure φ which encodes the input QBF, and a stack Γ which keeps track of the steps performed. We consider the following primitives for φ:

- DOASSIGN(φ, l) implements φ_l as in Section 2, where clauses and literals are disabled rather than deleted.
- DOELIMINATE(φ, v) implements variable elimination as in Section 2, with the addition that clauses subsumed by some clause already in φ are not added – a process named *forward subsumption* in [6]; as in the case of DOASSIGN, the eliminated variables and the clauses where they occur are disabled.
- FINDUNIT(φ), returns a pair $\langle l, r \rangle$ if l is a unit literal in φ and r is a unit clause in which l occurs, or a pair $\langle \text{NIL}, \text{NIL} \rangle$ if no such literal exists in φ.
- CHOOSELIT(φ, Γ) returns a literal l subject to the constraint that all the remaining variables of φ which do not appear in Γ come after $|l|$.
- CHOOSEVAR(φ, Γ) returns a variable v subject to the constraint that v comes after all the remaining variables of φ which do not appear in Γ.

---

[2] Case (1) will not apply unless terms are learned, and thus unit propagation may involve universal variables as well – see [4] for the technical details.

```
SEARCH(φ, Γ)                          PROPAGATE(φ, Γ)
   l ← CHOOSELIT(φ, Γ)                   ⟨l, r⟩ ← FINDUNIT(φ)
   push(Γ, ⟨l, LS, NIL⟩)                 while l ≠ NIL do
   DOASSIGN(φ, l)                           push(Γ, ⟨l, FL, r⟩)
                                            DOASSIGN(φ, l)
ELIMINATE(φ, Γ)                             ⟨l, r⟩ ← FINDUNIT(φ)
   v ← CHOOSEVAR(φ, Γ)
   push(Γ, ⟨v, VE, NIL⟩)              BACKJUMP(φ, Γ, q)
   DOELIMINATE(φ, v)                     wr ← INITREASON(φ, Γ, q)
                                         while Γ ≠ EMPTY do
                                            ⟨l, m, r⟩ ← top(Γ)
BACKTRACK(φ, Γ, q)                          if m = VE then
   while Γ ≠ EMPTY do                          UNDOELIMINATE(φ, l)
      ⟨l, m, _ ⟩ ← top(Γ)                   else
      if m = VE then                          UNDOASSIGN(φ, l)
         UNDOELIMINATE(φ, l)               pop(Γ)
      else                                 if ISBOUND(q, l, φ) then
         UNDOASSIGN(φ, l)                     if OCCURS(|l|, wr) then
      pop(Γ)                                     if m = LS then
      if ISBOUND(q, l, φ) then                      push(Γ, ⟨l̄, FL, wr⟩)
         if m = LS then                             DOASSIGN(φ, l̄)
            push(Γ, ⟨l̄, FL, NIL⟩)                   return FALSE
            DOASSIGN(φ, l̄)                 else if m = FL then
            return FALSE                      UPDATEREASON(wr, r)
   return TRUE                           return TRUE
```

Fig. 1. Pseudo-code of QuReS basic routines

Because updates in DOASSIGN and DOELIMINATE are not destructive, we can further assume that their effects can be reversed by "undo" functions, i.e., UNDOASSIGN and UNDOELIMINATE.

The routines SEARCH and ELIMINATE (Figure 1, top-left) perform one step of search and variable elimination, respectively. SEARCH (resp. ELIMINATE), asks CHOOSELIT (resp. CHOOSEVAR) for a literal l (resp. a variable v) and then it (i) pushes l (resp. v) onto the stack and (ii) it updates φ. In both cases step (i) amounts to push a triple $\langle u, m, r \rangle$ in Γ where r is always NIL, u is the literal being assigned or the variable being eliminated, and m is the *mode* of the assignment, where LS ("L"eft "S"plit) indicates an open branch in the search tree, and VE ("V"ariable "E"limination) indicates the corresponding resolution step. The task of PROPAGATE (Figure 1, top-right) is to perform unit propagation in φ. For each unit literal l, PROPAGATE pushes a record $\langle l, \text{FL}, r \rangle$ in Γ, where l and r are the results of FINDUNIT, and the mode is always FL ("F"orced "L"iteral). BACKTRACK (Figure 1 bottom-left) and BACKJUMP (Figure 1, bottom-right) are alternative backtracking procedures to be invoked at the leaves of the search tree with an additional parameter q, where $q = \exists$ if the current leaf is a conflict, and $q = \forall$ otherwise. BACKTRACK goes back in the stack Γ, popping records for search (LS) or deduction steps (VE, FL), and undoing the corresponding effects on φ. Notice that, if BACKTRACK is a component of a plain search solver, then VE-type records will not show up in Γ. BACKTRACK stops when an open branch (LS) corresponding to a literal l bound by the quantifier q is found (ISBOUND(q, l, φ)=TRUE). In this case, BACKTRACK closes the branch by assigning $\bar{l}$ with mode FL and returning FALSE to indicate that search should not stop. On the other hand, if all the records are popped from Γ without finding an open branch

QuReS(φ, Γ)
   stop $\leftarrow$ FALSE
   while $\neg stop$ **do**
     PROPAGATE(φ, Γ)
     if ISTRUE(φ) **then**
       result $\leftarrow$ TRUE
       stop $\leftarrow$ BACKJUMP(φ, Γ, $\forall$)
     else if ISFALSE(φ) **then**
       result $\leftarrow$ FALSE
       stop $\leftarrow$ BACKJUMP(φ, Γ, $\exists$)
     else
       if PREFERSEARCH(φ) **then** SEARCH(φ, Γ)
       else ELIMINATE(φ, Γ)
   return *result*

Fig. 2. Pseudo-code of QuReS

then search is over and BACKTRACK returns TRUE. BACKJUMP implements back-jumping as in Section 2 on top of the following primitives:

- INITREASON(φ, Γ, q) initializes the working reason wr. If $q = \exists$, then we have two cases: (*i*) If **top**(Γ) is a FL-type record, then wr is any clause in φ which is contradictory because all of its existential literals have been disabled. (*ii*) If **top**(Γ) is a VE-type record, this means that a contradictory clause C has been derived when eliminating a variable, and thus wr is C. If $q = \forall$, then wr is a term obtained considering a subset of the literals in Γ such that the number of universal literals in the term is minimized – VE-type records are disregarded in this process.
- UPDATEREASON(wr, r) updates wr by resolving it with r, i.e., the reason of the assignment which is being undone.

When BACKJUMP is invoked in lieu of BACKTRACK, it first initializes the working reason, and then it pops records from Γ until either the stack is empty, or some open branch is found – the return values in these cases are the same as BACK-TRACK. BACKJUMP stops at open branches (LS) only if they correspond to some literal l which is bound by the quantifier q and such that $|l|$ occurs in the current working reason wr (OCCURS($|l|$, wr)=TRUE). Also, when popping records $\langle l, \text{FL}, r \rangle$ such that l occurs in the working reason, the procedure UPDATEREASON is invoked to update the current working reason wr. As described in Section 2, all the literals bound by q that are not in the current working reason are irrelevant to the current conflict/solution and are simply popped from Γ without further ado.

On top of the basic algorithms of Figure 1, we define the main algorithm of QuReS[3] shown in Figure 2, where we consider some additional primitives on φ: ISTRUE(φ) returns TRUE exactly when all clauses in φ have been disabled; ISFALSE(φ) returns TRUE exactly when there is at least one contradictory

---

[3] QuReS can be downloaded from http://www.mind-lab.it/projects

clause in φ; finally, PREFERSEARCH(φ) implements the policy to switch between search and variable elimination. In the following, we consider also two "stripped-down" versions of QuReS, namely QuReS-BJ, and QuReS-VE: QuReS-BJ is obtained by replacing the call to PREFERSEARCH with TRUE and it implements a pure search-based solver with backjumping, whereas QuReS-VE is obtained by replacing the call to PREFERSEARCH with FALSE and it implements a pure variable-elimination based solver.

4   Learning to Integrate Resolution and Search

We now consider the implementation of PREFERSEARCH in more detail. Computing an effective policy to switch between search and variable elimination is a key point for the efficiency of QuReS. Here we approach the problem by synthesizing policies with the aid of Machine Learning techniques, with the ultimate goal of obtaining an automatic implementation of PREFERSEARCH that can outperform hand-coded ones. In order to do that, there are three main design issues to address:

1. Choosing the set of QBFs on which the analysis will be based.
2. Choosing informative parameters on which PREFERSEARCH is based, i.e., a set of features which characterizes the input QBF, yet it can be computed without a prohibitive overhead.
3. Choosing the inductive model to synthesize PREFERSEARCH

Concerning the first design issue, our analysis is based on the formulas of the QBFEVAL'08 dataset, which is comprised of 3326 formulas divided into 17 suites and 71 families (suites may be comprised of more than one family). All the formulas considered are QBF encodings of some automated reasoning task [10]. In order to identify a core subset of formulas whereon our investigation is to be focused, we run QuReS-BJ and QuReS-VE on the whole QBFEVAL'08 dataset[4] granting 600s of CPU time and 3GB of memory to both solvers. Overall, QuReS-BJ is able to solve 614 formulas, while QuReS-VE solves 528 of them. Noticeably, there are 272 formulas solved by QuReS-BJ only, and 186 formulas solved by QuReS-VE only, i.e., there is a pool of 458 formulas such that either search is effective and variable elimination is totally ineffective, or the contrary is true. We believe that the dataset obtained considering all the formulas in this pool — that we call QBFEVAL'08-unique — provides an excellent starting point for our analysis, because it contains exactly those cases in which variable elimination alone is most effective and those where search alone is most effective.

As for our second design issue, we wish to compute features that discriminate between variable elimination and search. In the following, we denote with $\varphi_1, \varphi_2, \ldots$ the sequence of subproblems generated by QuReS when solving the

---

[4] All the experimental results that we present are obtained on a family of identical Linux workstations comprised of 10 Intel Core 2 Duo 2.13 GHz PCs with 4GB of RAM.

input formula $\varphi = \varphi_0$. In Section 1 we have mentioned that the treewidth $tw_p(\psi)$ where $\psi \in \{\varphi_0, \varphi_1, \varphi_2, \ldots\}$ is a candidate feature, but it is also prohibitively expensive to compute in most cases.[5] Therefore, we require alternative measures which can be computed efficiently and which are able to provide us with treewidth-like information in our cases of interest. Analyzing the behaviour of QuReS-ve and QuReS-bj on the QBFEVAL'08-unique dataset, we noticed that the following three measures seem to meet our requirements. If x is any variable that qualifies for elimination, n_x (resp. $n_{\neg x}$) is the number of clauses where x (resp. $\neg x$) occurs, and l_x (resp. $l_{\neg x}$) is the sum of the literals in each clause where x (resp. $\neg x$) occurs, then we consider:

- the number of occurrences of x, denoted as $occs(x)$ and computed as $occs(x)$ $= n_x + n_{\neg x}$;
- the diversity [13] of x, denoted as $div(x)$ and computed as $div(x) = n_x \cdot n_{\neg x}$; and
- the companion literals of x, denoted as $lits(x)$ and computed as $lits(x) = l_x \cdot l_{\neg x}$.

In Figure 3 we present the result of an experiment aimed to confirm the relevance of the features above when it comes to discriminate between QuReS-ve and QuReS-bj on the QBFEVAL'08-unique dataset. In the experiment, we run QuReS-ve on all the formulas of the dataset, and we collected $occs(x)$, $div(x)$ and $lits(x)$ for each variable x eliminated by QuReS-ve. Then, we consider the distributions of such values distinguishing between formulas solved by QuReS-bj and those solved by QuReS-ve. In Figure 3 we visualize the distributions of the three features using boxplots, one for each combination of solver and feature. Looking at the leftmost plot in the figure, we can see that the median value related to $occs$ for QuReS-bj (141.5) is two orders of magnitude higher than the same value for QuReS-ve (7). Considering now the results related to div (center), we find a very similar picture: the median value for QuReS-ve is 5, and the one of QuReS-bj is 488. The motivation behind this result is clear: the efficiency of eliminating a variable x is very sensitive to the size of $n_x \cdot n_{\neg x}$ because this is an (over)estimate of the number of clauses that will be added by Q-resolution on x. Similar results and conclusions hold also for the distribution of $lits$ in Figure 3 (right): here the median value of the distribution for QuReS-bj is 65274, while the one for QuReS-ve is 784. From this experiment, we can conclude that $occs$, div and $lits$ meet the requirement of being easy to compute, yet discriminative enough for our purposes, and they are thus candidate inputs for PREFERSEARCH.

The last design issue concerns the inductive models to use in PREFERSEARCH. An inductive model is comprised of a *classifier*, i.e., a function that maps an unlabeled formula – described by some combination of $occs$, div and $lits$ values – to a label – whether search is preferred or not, and an *inducer*, i.e., an algorithm that

---

[5] Deciding if treewidth is bounded by a constant can be done in asymptotic linear time [23], but an actual implementation of such algorithm would be too slow to be of practical use.

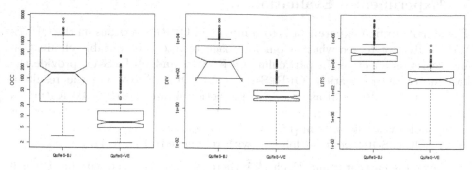

Fig. 3. Distributions of the features *occs* (left), *div* (center), and *lits* (right), considering formulas in the QBFEVAL'08-unique dataset solved by QURES-BJ (distribution on the left of each plot) and QURES-VE (distribution of the right of each plot). For each distribution, we show a box-and-whiskers diagram representing the median (bold line), the first and third quartile (bottom and top edges of the box), the minimum and maximum (whiskers at the top and the bottom) of a distribution. Values laying farther away than the median ±1.5 times the interquartile range are considered outliers and shown as dots on the plot. In case outliers are detected, the whiskers extend up to the median +1.5 (resp. −1.5) times the interquartile range, while the maximum (resp. minimum) value becomes the highest (resp. lowest) outlier. An approximated 95% confidence interval for the difference in the two medians is represented by the notches cut in the boxes: if the notches of two plots do not overlap, this is strong evidence that the two medians differ. The y-axes of each plot is in logarithmic scale.

builds the classifier. While there is an overwhelming number of inductive models in the literature (see, e.g., [24]), we can somewhat limit the choice considering that QURES has to deal with numerical features. Moreover, we would like to avoid formulating specific hypothesis of normality or (in)dependence among the features. Considering all the above, we choose to experiment with two inductive models in QURES, namely:

Decision trees. (QURES-C4.5) A classifier arranged in a tree structure, wherein each inner node contains a test on some attributes, and each leaf node contains a label; we use C4.5 [19] to induce decision trees.

Support vector machines. (QURES-SVM) Support Vector Machines performs classification by constructing an N-dimensional hyperplane that optimally separates the data into two categories in a high-dimensional projection of the input space [20].

The above methods are fairly robust, efficient, and are not subject to stringent hypothesis on the training data. They are also "orthogonal", since the algorithms they use are based on radically different approaches to the dataset. The implementation of QURES-C4.5 is based on the WEKA library [24], while QURES-SVM is built on top of the LIBSVM library [25].

5   Experimental Evaluation

The aim of our first experiment is to compare all QURES versions on the QBFE-VAL'08 dataset to see whether our approach to integrate variable elimination and search is effective. In particular, QURES-BJ and QURES-VE provide the baseline of the evaluation, QURES-C4.5 and QURES-SVM are the result of learning PREFERSEARCH as described in Section 4, and QURES-HM features a hand-coded implementation of PREFERSEARCH similar to the one proposed for plain Boolean satisfiability in [13], and for non-quantified constraint satisfaction in [21]. QURES-HM works as follows (with reference to Figure 1):

1. Given the current φ and Γ, check if there is any existential variable x which respects CHOOSEVAR's constraints. If it exists, compute the degree of x in the Gaifman graph of φ and check if it is less than a given bound k.
2. If condition (1) is met for some x, then check if the diversity of x is less than a predefined threshold d.

If both conditions above are met for some x, then PREFERSEARCH returns FALSE, and CHOOSEVAR is instructed to return x. If either condition is not met, then PREFERSEARCH returns TRUE. We mention that this criteria is also the same used by our incomplete QBF solver QUBIS [18] to check whether a given variable qualifies for elimination. Finally, we also consider QURES-RND, a version of QURES which is meant to provide experimental control: given a variable that respects CHOOSEVAR's constraints, the implementation of PREFERSEARCH in QURES-RND decides, uniformly at random with equal probability, whether to return TRUE or FALSE. The purpose of QURES-RND is to make sure that the performances of the learned versions of PREFERSEARCH are not the mere effect of chance. In the following, we say that solver A *dominates* solver B whenever the set of problems solved by A is a superset of the problems solved by B; we say that two solvers are *incomparable* when neither one dominates the other.

In Table 1 we report the results of the above experiment on the QBFEVAL'08 dataset excluding formulas used to train the inductive models, while in Table 2 we report the results considering the whole QBFEVAL'08 dataset.

A quick glance at Table 2 reveals that solvers featuring integration of variable elimination and search are *always* superior to the baseline versions. In more detail, QURES-VE can deal with 16% of the dataset, and QURES-BJ tops at 18%. Only 342 problems (10% of the dataset) are solved by both QURES-BJ and QURES-VE, which are incomparable. As for the other versions, we see that all of them are more efficient than the baseline versions: QURES-RND can solve 20% of the dataset[6], QURES-HM[7] tops at 27%, while QURES-SVM and QURES-C4.5 can solve 38% and 39% of the dataset, respectively. In particular, QURES-C4.5 and QURES-SVM, turn out to be the most efficient among QURES versions. Moreover, the total number of problems solved by QURES-SVM and QURES-C4.5 is more than the set of problems solved by at least one of QURES-BJ and

---

[6] QURES-RND performances are obtained by running the solver several times and considering the median value.

[7] We run QURES-HM with $k = 20$ and $div = 2000$.

Table 1. Results of QuReS versions on the QBFEVAL'08 dataset excluding the formulas contained in QBFEVAL'08-unique. The table reports the number of problems solved ("#") and the cumulative CPU seconds ("Time") when considering overall results ("Solved"), as well as "True" and "False" formulas separately.

Solver	Solved		True		False	
	#	Time	#	Time	#	Time
QuReS-c4.5	994	34110	453	22722	541	11388
QuReS-svm	975	42343	438	25859	537	16484
QuReS-hm	615	44756	258	26323	357	18433
QuReS-rnd	374	8622	149	4166	225	4456
QuReS-ve	342	8016	128	2398	214	5618
QuReS-bj	342	10566	128	4682	214	5884

QuReS-ve (800). This means that there are 449 (resp. 482) problems which cannot be solved by either QuReS-ve or QuReS-bj, and which can be solved by QuReS-svm (resp. QuReS-c4.5). Considering QuReS-hm, we report that it is also able to outperform the best combination between QuReS-bj and QuReS-ve, but the total number of problems solved is about 30% less than QuReS-c4.5 and QuReS-svm. The result of QuReS-rnd confirms that learned policies owe their performances to the fact that the inducer built a classifier encoding a sensible model of the formula. That this can be done, is also confirmed by the fact that both QuReS-c4.5 and QuReS-svm feature relatively similar performances. Another key aspect is that resolution and search alternate quite heavily inside both QuReS-c4.5 and QuReS-svm, so that it would be difficult to replicate their results with a hand-made policy, unless it was using, e.g., the very same rules synthesized by QuReS-c4.5. This fact is confirmed by the analysis of the distributions of variable elimination and search steps, and how these two steps alternate. If we consider, e.g., QuReS-c4.5, we report that the number of variable elimination steps ranges from 0 to 1.32×10^7, while the number of search steps ranges from 0 to 8.88×10^6, with a median value of 4974 and 108, respectively. Considering the number of times in which QuReS-c4.5 switches between variable elimination and search, the values range from 0 to 6.63×10^5, with a median value of 100. Moreover, if we restrict our attention to the formulas which can be solved by either QuReS-bj or QuReS-ve, we see that the proportion of variable elimination vs. search steps varies depending on whether the formula is best solved by search or variable elimination alone.

One last set of considerations about Table 2 regards dominance relationships. In particular, QuReS-c4.5 is incomparable with both QuReS-bj and QuReS-ve. In particular, there are 71 problems solved by QuReS-bj that QuReS-c4.5 cannot solve, whereof 57 are from the family blackbox-01X-QBF. These instances are characterized by the largest number of quantifier blocks among formulas in the dataset, and search is already quite efficient on them. QuReS-ve can solve 84 formulas in which QuReS-c4.5 fails, of which 70 are from the suite Pan. Looking at the results of recent QBFEVAL events, we can see that solvers performing variable elimination are always more efficient on these formulas. QuReS-c4.5

Table 2. Results of QuReS versions on the whole QBFEVAL'08 dataset. The structure of the table is the same of Table 1.

Solver	Solved		True		False	
	#	Time	#	Time	#	Time
QuReS-c4.5	1282	53812	569	27547	713	26265
QuReS-svm	1249	68423	548	30592	702	37831
QuReS-hm	883	64062	382	32989	501	31073
QuReS-rnd	670	24640	260	8428	410	16212
QuReS-bj	614	31543	208	13099	406	18444
QuReS-ve	528	12834	228	6384	300	6450

Table 3. QuReS-c4.5 vs. state-of-the-art QBF solvers on the whole QBFEVAL'08 dataset. The structure of the table is the same of tables 1 and 2.

Solver	Solved		True		False	
	#	Time	#	Time	#	Time
AQME	2434	43987	977	19747	1457	24240
QuBE6.1	2144	32414	828	18248	1316	14166
sKizzo	1887	40864	631	17550	1256	23314
QuReS-c4.5	1282	53812	569	27547	713	26265
QuBE3.0	1077	16700	406	6536	671	10164
NENOFEX	985	22360	459	13853	526	8507
QUANTOR	972	15718	485	10418	487	5300
sSolve	965	23059	450	9866	515	13193
yQuaffle	948	16708	389	9058	559	7650
2clsQ	780	21287	391	13234	389	8053
QMRes	704	13576	360	7722	344	5853

is also incomparable with QuReS-hm because there are 78 problems that the latter cannot solve, whereof 27 are from the family `terminator` and 39 are from the suite `Pan`. Finally, we report that QuReS-c4.5 dominates QuReS-rnd. Also QuReS-svm is incomparable with both QuReS-bj and QuReS-ve; in this case, there are 80 problems solved by QuReS-bj that QuReS-c4.5 cannot solve, whereof 59 are from the family `blackbox-01X-QBF`, and 92 formulas solved by QuReS-ve, whereof 76 are again from the suite `Pan`. As for QuReS-c4.5, QuReS-svm does not dominate QuReS-hm because QuReS-svm cannot solve 91 problems, whereof the greater parts are from the family `tipfixpoint` (15), `terminator` (28) and from the suite `Pan` (47). Finally, we report that QuReS-svm dominates QuReS-rnd. As last consideration, QuReS-c4.5 does not dominate QuReS-svm because of two formulas only.

We conclude this section with Table 3, wherein we compare QuReS-c4.5 with other state-of-the-art QBF solvers. We have considered all the competitors of QBFEVAL'08 [10], namely AQME, QuBE6.1, NENOFEX, QUANTOR, and sSolve. To them, we have added the solvers sKizzo [5] which is representative of skolemization-based approaches, QuBE3.0 [4] which is the same as

QuBE6.1 but without preprocessing, yQUAFFLE [26] and 2CLSQ [27] which are also search-based solvers, and QMRES [7] which features symbolic variable elimination. Although QuRES-c4.5 is just a proof-of-concept solver, Table 3 reveals that it would have ranked third best considering only the participants to QBFE-VAL'08, and it ranks as fourth best in Table 3. Moreover, there are 22 instances that can be solved only by QuRES-c4.5. If we consider that AQME is a multi-engine solver combining the ability of several engines (including QuBE6.1 and sKizzo), and that both QuBE6.1 and sKizzo are fairly sophisticated pieces of software, we can conclude that QuRES-c4.5 performances are very satisfactory. From an implementation point of view, QuRES is somewhat limited by its unsophisticated data structures and, in particular, by the forward subsumption algorithm. On one hand, disabling forward subsumption, even in its present form, decreases by 15% the number of problems solved by QuRES. On the other hand, forward subsumption accounts for 8% of the total time spent by QuRES on the formulas that it can solve, but for 20% of the total time on the formulas that it cannot solve. Indeed, increasing the time limit to 1200 seconds allows QuRES to solve about 10% additional problems, indicating that the efficiency of basic operations such as forward subsumption is currently a limiting factor for QuRES. These limitations beg the question of whether QuRES – featuring a "white-box" approach to integration – has any chance of being more effective than AQME – featuring a "black-box" approach . Indeed, while AQME can leverage state-of-the-art implementations and QuRES does not, at least in its present form, AQME will always be limited by the performances collectively expressed by current QBF solvers. On the other hand, even with a proof-of-concept implementations, QuRES is able to solve problems that are not within the reach of its basic engines QuRES-BJ and QuRES-VE. If we were to adopt a "black-box" integration schema in QuRES, we would not have managed to solve the additional 482 problems that separate the ideal combination of QuRES-BJ and QuRES-VE from QuRES-c4.5. In this sense, investigation of white-box integration seems to be more promising towards the solution of challenging encodings.

6   Conclusions and Future Work

Summing up, the combination of search and resolution featured by QuRES seems to offer a gateway to effective reasoning in QBFs. The two key results of our work are (i) showing that automatically synthesized policies to integrate search and resolution can outperform both baseline solvers and hand-made policies, and (ii) showing that QuRES is competitive with other state-of-the-art solvers. We believe that these results can be improved by pursuing an efficient implementation of QuRES. The fact that QuRES, however unsophisticated, is able to solve 22 problems that cannot be solved by other state-of-the-art QBF solvers is promising in this sense. Other improvements would be leveraging different structural features and approximations thereof, and/or integrating on-line self-adaptive techniques to synthesize PREFERSEARCH policies.

References

1. Mneimneh, M., Sakallah, K.: Computing Vertex Eccentricity in Exponentially Large Graphs: QBF Formulation and Solution. In: Giunchiglia, E., Tacchella, A. (eds.) SAT 2003. LNCS, vol. 2919, pp. 411–425. Springer, Heidelberg (2004)
2. Ansotegui, C., Gomes, C.P., Selman, B.: Achille's heel of QBF. In: Proc. of AAAI, pp. 275–281 (2005)
3. Egly, U., Eiter, T., Tompits, H., Woltran, S.: Solving Advanced Reasoning Tasks Using Quantified Boolean Formulas. In: Seventeenth National Conference on Artificial Intelligence (AAAI 2000), pp. 417–422. MIT Press, Cambridge (2000)
4. Giunchiglia, E., Narizzano, M., Tacchella, A.: Clause-Term Resolution and Learning in Quantified Boolean Logic Satisfiability. Artificial Intelligence Research 26, 371–416 (2006), http://www.jair.org/vol/vol26.html
5. Benedetti, M.: sKizzo: a Suite to Evaluate and Certify QBFs. In: Nieuwenhuis, R. (ed.) CADE 2005. LNCS (LNAI), vol. 3632, pp. 369–376. Springer, Heidelberg (2005)
6. Biere, A.: Resolve and Expand. In: Hoos, H.H., Mitchell, D.G. (eds.) SAT 2004. LNCS, vol. 3542, pp. 59–70. Springer, Heidelberg (2005)
7. Pan, G., Vardi, M.Y.: Symbolic Decision Procedures for QBF. In: Wallace, M. (ed.) CP 2004. LNCS, vol. 3258, pp. 453–467. Springer, Heidelberg (2004)
8. Pulina, L., Tacchella, A.: A self-adaptive multi-engine solver for quantified Boolean formulas. Constraints 14(1), 80–116 (2009)
9. Samulowitz, H., Memisevic, R.: Learning to Solve QBF. In: Proc. of 22nd Conference on Artificial Intelligence (AAAI 2007), pp. 255–260 (2007)
10. Peschiera, C., Pulina, L., Tacchella, A.: 6th QBF solvers evaluation (2008), http://www.qbfeval.org/2008
11. Kleine-Büning, H., Karpinski, M., Flögel, A.: Resolution for Quantified Boolean Formulas. Information and Computation 117(1), 12–18 (1995)
12. Giunchiglia, E., Narizzano, M., Tacchella, A.: Backjumping for Quantified Boolean Logic Satisfiability. In: Seventeenth International Joint Conference on Artificial Intelligence (IJCAI 2001). Morgan Kaufmann, San Francisco (2001)
13. Rish, I., Dechter, R.: Resolution versus search: Two strategies for sat. Journal of Automated Reasoning 24(1/2), 225–275 (2000)
14. Gottlob, G., Leone, N., Scarcello, F.: A comparison of structural CSP decomposition methods. Artificial Intelligence 124, 243–282 (2000)
15. Chen, H., Dalmau, V.: From Pebble Games to Tractability: An Ambidextrous Consistency Algorithm for Quantified Constraint Satisfaction. In: Ong, L. (ed.) CSL 2005. LNCS, vol. 3634, pp. 232–247. Springer, Heidelberg (2005)
16. Gottlob, G., Greco, G., Scarcello, F.: The Complexity of Quantified Constraint Satisfaction Problems under Structural Restrictions. In: IJCAI 2005, Proceedings of the Nineteenth International Joint Conference on Artificial Intelligence, pp. 150–155. Professional Book Center (2005)
17. Pan, G., Vardi, M.Y.: Fixed-Parameter Hierarchies inside PSPACE. In: 21th IEEE Symposium on Logic in Computer Science (LICS 2006), pp. 27–36. IEEE Computer Society, Los Alamitos (2006)
18. Pulina, L., Tacchella, A.: Treewidth: A useful marker of empirical hardness in quantified boolean logic encodings. In: Cervesato, I., Veith, H., Voronkov, A. (eds.) LPAR 2008. LNCS (LNAI), vol. 5330, pp. 528–542. Springer, Heidelberg (2008)
19. Quinlan, J.R.: C4.5: Programs for Machine Learning. Morgan Kaufmann Publishers, San Francisco (1993)

20. Vapnik, V.: The nature of statistical learning. Springer, New York (1995)
21. Larrosa, J., Dechter, R.: Boosting Search with Variable Elimination in Constraint Optimization and Constraint Satisfaction Problems. Constraints 8(3), 303–326 (2003)
22. Cadoli, M., Giovanardi, A., Schaerf, M.: An algorithm to evaluate quantified boolean formulae. In: Proc. of AAAI (1998)
23. Bodlaender, H.L.: A linear time algorithm for finding tree-decompositions of small treewidth. In: 25th Annual ACM Symposium on Theory of Computing, pp. 226–234 (1993)
24. Witten, I.H., Frank, E.: Data Mining, 2nd edn. Morgan Kaufmann, San Francisco (2005)
25. Chang, C.-C., Lin, C.-J.: LIBSVM – A Library for Support Vector Machines (2005), http://www.csie.ntu.edu.tw/~cjlin/libsvm/
26. Yu, Y., Malik, S.: Verifying the Correctness of Quantified Boolean Formula(QBF) Solvers: Theory and Practice. In: ASP-DAC (2005)
27. Samulowitz, H., Bacchus, F.: Binary Clause Reasoning in QBF. In: Biere, A., Gomes, C.P. (eds.) SAT 2006. LNCS, vol. 4121, pp. 353–367. Springer, Heidelberg (2006)

Combining Theories with Shared Set Operations

Thomas Wies, Ruzica Piskac, and Viktor Kuncak

EPFL School of Computer and Communication Sciences, Switzerland

Abstract. Motivated by applications in software verification, we explore automated reasoning about the non-disjoint combination of theories of infinitely many finite structures, where the theories share set variables and set operations. We prove a combination theorem and apply it to show the decidability of the satisfiability problem for a class of formulas obtained by applying propositional connectives to formulas belonging to: 1) Boolean Algebra with Presburger Arithmetic (with quantifiers over sets and integers), 2) weak monadic second-order logic over trees (with monadic second-order quantifiers), 3) two-variable logic with counting quantifiers (ranging over elements), 4) the Bernays-Schönfinkel-Ramsey class of first-order logic with equality (with $\exists^*\forall^*$ quantifier prefix), and 5) the quantifier-free logic of multisets with cardinality constraints.

1 Introduction

Constraint solvers based on satisfiability modulo theories (SMT) [4, 8, 13] are a key enabling technique in software and hardware verification systems[2, 3]. The range of problems amenable to such approaches depends on the expressive power of the logics supported by the SMT solvers. Current SMT solvers implement the combination of quantifier-free stably infinite theories with disjoint signatures, in essence following the approach pioneered by Nelson and Oppen [24]. Such solvers serve as decision procedures for quantifier-free formulas, typically containing uninterpreted function symbols, linear arithmetic, and bit vectors. The limited expressiveness of SMT prover logics translates into a limited class of properties that automated verification tools can handle.

To support a broader set of applications, this paper considers decision procedures for the combination of *possibly quantified* formulas in *non-disjoint* theories. The idea of combining rich theories within an expressive language has been explored in interactive provers [5, 7, 23, 25]. Such integration efforts are very useful, but do not result in complete decision procedures for the combined logics. The study of completeness for non-disjoint combination is relatively recent [32] and provides foundations for the general problem. Under certain conditions, such as local finiteness, decidability results have been obtained even for non-disjoint theories [14]. Our paper considers a case of combination of non-disjoint theories sharing operations on *sets of uninterpreted elements*, a case that was not considered before. The theories that we consider have the property that the tuples of cardinalities of Venn regions over shared set variables in the models of a formula are a semilinear set (i.e., expressible in Presburger arithmetic).

S. Ghilardi and R. Sebastiani (Eds.): FroCoS 2009, LNAI 5749, pp. 366–382, 2009.

Reasoning about combinations of decidable logics. The idea of deciding a combination of logics is to check the satisfiability of a conjunction of formulas $A \wedge B$ by using one decision procedure, D_A, for A, and another decision procedure, D_B, for B. To obtain a complete decision procedure, D_A and D_B must communicate to ensure that a model found by D_A and a model found by D_B can be merged into a model for $A \wedge B$.

Reduction-based decision procedure. We follow a reduction approach to decision procedures. The first decision procedure, D_A, computes a *projection*, S_A, of A onto *shared* set variables, which are free in both A and B. This projection is semantically equivalent to existentially quantifying over predicates and variables that are free in A but not in B; it is the strongest consequence of A expressible only using the shared set variables. D_B similarly computes the projection S_B of B. This reduces the satisfiability of $A \wedge B$ to satisfiability of the formula $S_A \wedge S_B$, which contains only set variables.

A logic for shared constraints on sets. A key parameter of our combination approach is the logic of sets used to express the projections S_A and S_B. A suitable logic depends on the logics of formulas A and B. We consider as the logics for A, B several expressive logics we consider useful based on our experience with the Jahob verification system [34, 36]. Remarkably, the smallest logic needed to express the projection formulas in these logics has the expressive power of Boolean Algebra with Presburger Arithmetic (BAPA), described in [21] and in Fig. 3. We show that the decision procedures for these four logics can be naturally extended to a reduction to BAPA that captures precisely the constraints on set variables. The existence of these reductions, along with quantifier elimination [20] and NP membership of the quantifier-free fragment [21], make BAPA an appealing reduction target for expressive logics.

Contribution summary. We present a technique for showing decidability of theories that share sets of elements. Furthermore, we show that the logics

1. Boolean Algebra with Presburger Arithmetic [9, 20, 21],
2. weak monadic second-order logic of two successors WS2S [31],
3. two-variable logic with counting C^2 [29],
4. Bernays-Schönfinkel-Ramsey class [30], and
5. quantifier-free multisets with cardinality constraints [27, 28]

all meet the conditions of our combination technique. Consequently, we obtain the decidability of quantifier-free combination of formulas in these logics.[1]

2   Example: Proving a Verification Condition

Our example shows a verification condition formula generated when verifying an unbounded linked data structure. The formula belongs to our new decidable class obtained by combining several decidable logics.

---

[1] Further details are provided in [35].

tree [left , right] $\wedge$ left p = null $\wedge$ p $\in$ nodes $\wedge$
nodes={x. (root,x) $\in$ {(x,y). left x = y| right x = y}^*} $\wedge$
content={x. $\exists$ n. n $\neq$ null $\wedge$ n $\in$ nodes $\wedge$ data n = x} $\wedge$
e $\notin$ content $\wedge$ nodes $\subseteq$ alloc $\wedge$
tmp $\notin$ alloc $\wedge$ left tmp = null $\wedge$ right tmp = null $\wedge$
data tmp = null $\wedge$ ($\forall$ y. data y $\neq$ tmp) $\wedge$
nodes1={x. (root,x) $\in$ {(x,y). (left (p:=tmp)) x = y) | right x = y} $\wedge$
content1={x. $\exists$ n. n $\neq$ null $\wedge$ n $\in$ nodes1 $\wedge$ (data(tmp:=e)) n = x} $\rightarrow$
         card content1 = card content + 1

Fig. 1. Verification condition

SHARED SETS: nodes, nodes1, content, content1, {e}, {tmp}

WS2S FRAGMENT: tree[left,right] $\wedge$ left p = null $\wedge$ p $\in$ nodes $\wedge$ left tmp = null $\wedge$
   right tmp = null $\wedge$ nodes={x. (root,x) $\in$ {(x,y). left x = y| right x = y}^*} $\wedge$
   nodes1={x. (root,x) $\in$ {(x,y). (left (p:=tmp)) x = y) | right x = y}
CONSEQUENCE: nodes1=nodes $\cup$ {tmp}

C2 FRAGMENT: data tmp = null $\wedge$ ($\forall$ y. data y $\neq$ tmp) $\wedge$ tmp $\notin$ alloc $\wedge$
   nodes $\subseteq$ alloc $\wedge$ content={x. $\exists$ n. n $\neq$ null $\wedge$ n $\in$ nodes $\wedge$ data n = x} $\wedge$
   content1={x. $\exists$ n. n $\neq$ null $\wedge$ n $\in$ nodes1 $\wedge$ (data(tmp:=e)) n = x}
CONSEQUENCE: nodes1 $\neq$ nodes $\cup$ {tmp} $\vee$ content1 = content $\cup$ {e}

BAPA FRAGMENT: e $\notin$ content $\wedge$ card content1 $\neq$ card content + 1
CONSEQUENCE: e $\notin$ content $\wedge$ card content1 $\neq$ card content + 1

Fig. 2. Negation of Fig. 1, and consequences on shared sets

Decidability of the verification condition. Fig. 1 shows the verification condition formula for a method (`insertAt`) that inserts a node into a linked list. The validity of this formula implies that invoking a method in a state satisfying the precondition results in a state that satisfies the postcondition of `insertAt`. The formula contains the transitive closure operator, quantifiers, set comprehensions, and the cardinality operator. Nevertheless, there is a (syntactically defined) decidable class of formulas that contains the verification condition in Fig. 1. This decidable class is a set-sharing combination of three decidable logics, and can be decided using the method we present in this paper.

To understand the method for proving the formula in Fig. 1, consider the problem of showing the unsatisfiability of the negation of the formula. Fig. 2 shows the conjuncts of the negation, grouped according to three decidable logics to which the conjuncts belong: 1) weak monadic second-order logic of two successors (WS2S) 2) two-variable logic with counting C^2 3) Boolean Algebra with Presburger Arithmetic (BAPA). For the formula in each of the fragments, Fig. 2 also shows a consequence formula that contains only shared sets and statements about their cardinalities. (We represent elements as singleton sets, so we admit formulas sharing elements as well.)

A decision procedure. Note that the conjunction of the consequences of three formula fragments is an unsatisfiable formula. This shows that the original verification condition is valid. In general, our decidability result shows that the decision procedures of logics such as WS2S and C^2 can be naturally extended to compute strongest consequences of formulas involving given shared sets. These consequences are all expressed in BAPA, which is decidable. In summary, the following is a decision procedure for satisfiability of combined formulas: 1) split the formula into fragments (belonging to WS2S, C^2, or BAPA); 2) for each fragment compute its strongest BAPA consequence; 3) check the satisfiability of the conjunction of consequences.

3 Syntax and Semantics of Formulas

Higer-order logic. We present our problem in a fragment of classical higher-order logic [1, Chapter 5] with a particular set of types, which we call sorts. We assume that formulas are well-formed according to sorts of variables and logical symbols. Each variable and each logical symbol have an associated sort. The primitive sorts we consider are 1) bool, interpreted as the two-element set $\{\mathsf{true}, \mathsf{false}\}$ of booleans; 2) int, interpreted as the set of integers $\mathbb{Z}$; and 3) obj, interpreted as a non-empty set of elements. The only sort constructors is the binary function space constructor '$\rightarrow$'. We represent a function mapping elements of sorts $s_1, \ldots, s_n$ into an element of sort s_0 as a term of sort $s_1 \times \ldots \times s_n \rightarrow s_0$ where $s_1 \times s_2 \times \ldots \times s_n \rightarrow s_0$ is a shorthand for $s_1 \rightarrow (s_2 \rightarrow \ldots (s_n \rightarrow s_0))$. When $s_1, \ldots, s_n$ are all the same sort s, we abbreviate $s_1 \times \ldots \times s_n \rightarrow s_0$ as $s^n \rightarrow s_0$. We represent a relation between elements of sorts $s_1, \ldots, s_n$ as a function $s_1 \times \ldots \times s_n \rightarrow \mathsf{bool}$. We use set as an abbreviation for the sort $\mathsf{obj} \rightarrow \mathsf{bool}$. We call variables of sort set *set variables*. The equality symbol applies only to terms of the same sort. We assume to have a distinct equality symbol for each sort of interest, but we use the same notation to denote all of them. Propositional operations connect terms of sort bool. We write $\forall x{:}s.F$ to denote a universally quantified formula where the quantified variable has sort s (analogously for $\exists x{:}s.F$ and $\exists x{:}s^K.F$ for counting quantifiers of Section 5.2). We denote by $\mathsf{FV}(F)$ the set of all free variables that occur free in F. We write $\mathsf{FV}_s(F)$ for the free variables of sort s. Note that the variables can be higher-order (we will see, however, that the shared variables are of sort set). A *theory* is simply a set of formulas, possibly with free variables.

Structures. A structure α specifies a finite set, which is also the meaning of obj, and we denote it $\alpha(\mathsf{obj})$.[2] When α is understood we use $[\![X]\!]$ to denote $\alpha(X)$, where X denotes a sort, a term, a formula, or a set of formulas. If S is a set of formulas then $\alpha(S) = \mathsf{true}$ means $\alpha(F) = \mathsf{true}$ for each $F \in X$. In every structure we let $[\![\mathsf{bool}]\!] = \{\mathsf{false}, \mathsf{true}\}$. Instead of $\alpha(F) = \mathsf{true}$ we often write simply $\alpha(F)$. We interpret terms of the sort $s_1 \times \ldots \times s_n \rightarrow s_0$ as total functions $[\![s_1]\!] \times \ldots [\![s_n]\!] \rightarrow [\![s_0]\!]$. For a set A, we identify a function $f : A \rightarrow \{\mathsf{false}, \mathsf{true}\}$

---

[2] We focus on the case of finite $\alpha(\mathsf{obj})$ primarily for simplicity; we believe the extension to the case where domains are either finite or countable is possible and can be done using results from [20, Section 8.1], [29, Section 5], [31].

with the subset $\{x \in A \mid f(x) = \text{true}\}$. We thus interpret variables of the sort $\text{obj}^n \to \text{bool}$ as subsets of $[\![\text{obj}]\!]^n$. If s is a sort then $\alpha(s)$ depends only on $\alpha(\text{obj})$ and we denote it also by $[\![s]\!]$. We interpret propositional operations $\wedge, \vee, \neg$ as usual in classical logic. A quantified variable of sort s ranges over all elements of $[\![s]\!]$. (Thus, as in standard model of HOL [1, Section 54], quantification over variables of sort $s_1 \to s_2$ is quantification over all total functions $[\![s_1]\!] \to [\![s_2]\!]$.)

3.1 Boolean Algebra with Presburger Arithmetic

It will be convenient to enrich the language of our formulas with operations on integers, sets, and cardinality operations. These operations could be given by a theory or defined in HOL, but we choose to simply treat them as built-in logical symbols, whose meaning must be respected by all structures α we consider. Fig. 3 shows the syntax of Boolean Algebra with Presburger Arithmetic (BAPA) [9, 20]. The sorts of symbols appearing in BAPA formulas are as expected, e.g., $\subseteq : \text{set}^2 \to \text{bool}$, $< : \text{int}^2 \to \text{bool}$, $\text{dvd}_K : \text{int} \to \text{bool}$ for each integer constant K, singleton : obj $\to$ set (with singleton(x) denoted as $\{x\}$), and complement : set $\to$ set (with complement(A) denoted by A^c).

$$F ::= A \mid F_1 \wedge F_2 \mid F_1 \vee F_2 \mid \neg F \mid \forall x{:}s.F \mid \exists x{:}s.F$$
$$s ::= \text{int} \mid \text{obj} \mid \text{set}$$
$$A ::= B_1 = B_2 \mid B_1 \subseteq B_2 \mid T_1 = T_2 \mid T_1 < T_2 \mid K \,\text{dvd}\, T$$
$$B ::= x \mid \emptyset \mid \text{Univ} \mid \{x\} \mid B_1 \cup B_2 \mid B_1 \cap B_2 \mid B^c$$
$$T ::= x \mid K \mid \text{CardUniv} \mid T_1 + T_2 \mid K \cdot T \mid \text{card}(B)$$
$$K ::= \ldots -2 \mid -1 \mid 0 \mid 1 \mid 2 \ldots$$

Fig. 3. Boolean Algebra with Presburger Arithmetic (BAPA)

We sketch the meaning of the less common among the symbols in Fig. 3. Univ denotes the universal set, that is, $[\![\text{Univ}]\!] = [\![\text{obj}]\!]$. card$(A)$ denotes the cardinality of the set A. CardUniv is interpreted as card(Univ). The formula $K \,\text{dvd}\, t$ denotes that the integer constant K divides the integer t. We note that the condition $x \in A$ can be written in this language as $\{x\} \subseteq A$. Note that BAPA properly extends the first-order theory of Boolean Algebras over finite structures, which in turn subsumes the first-order logic with unary predicates and no function symbols, because e.g. $\exists x{:}\text{obj}.F(x)$ can be written as $\exists X{:}\text{set}.\,\text{card}(X){=}1 \wedge F'(X)$ where in F' e.g. $P(x)$ is replaced by $X \subseteq P$.

BAPA-definable relations between sets. A *semilinear set* is a finite union of *linear sets*. A linear set is a set of the form $\{a + k_1 b_1 + \ldots + k_n b_n \mid k_1, \ldots, k_n \in \{0, 1, 2 \ldots\}\}$ where $a, b_1, \ldots, b_n \in \mathbb{Z}^M$ (a is a *base* and b_i are *step* vectors). We represent a linear set by its generating vectors $a, b_1, \ldots, b_n$, and a semilinear set by the finite set of representations of its linear sets. It was shown in [15] that a set of integer vectors $S \subseteq \mathbb{Z}^M$ is a solution set of a Presburger arithmetic formula P i.e. $S = \{(v_1, \ldots, v_n).P\}$ iff S is a semilinear set. We then have the following characterization of relationships between sets expressible in BAPA, which follows from [20].

Lemma 1 (BAPA-expressible   means   Venn-cardinality-semilinear). *Given a finite set U and a relation $\rho \subseteq (2^U)^p$ the following are equivalent:*

1. *there exists a BAPA formula F whose free variables are $A_1, \ldots, A_p$, and have the sort* set*, such that $\rho = \{(s_1, \ldots, s_p) \mid \{A_1 \mapsto s_1, \ldots, A_p \mapsto s_p\}(F)\}$;*
2. *the following subset of $\mathbb{Z}^M$ for $M = 2^p$ is semilinear:*
   $$\{(|s_1^c \cap s_2^c \cap \ldots \cap s_p^c|, |s_1 \cap s_2^c \cap \ldots \cap s_p^c|, \ldots, |s_1 \cap s_2 \cap \ldots \cap s_p|) \mid (s_1, \ldots, s_p) \in \rho\}.$$

Structures of interest in this paper.   In the rest of this paper we consider structures that interpret the BAPA symbols as defined above. Because the meaning of BAPA-specific symbols is fixed, a structure α that interprets a set of formulas is determined by a finite set $\alpha(\mathsf{obj})$ as well as the values $\alpha(x)$ for each variable x free in the set of formulas. Let $\{\mathsf{obj} \mapsto u, x_1 \mapsto v_1, \ldots, x_n \mapsto v_n\}$ denote the structure α with domain u that interprets each variable x_i as v_i.

4   Combination by Reduction to BAPA

The Satisfiability Problem.   We are interested in an algorithm to determine whether there exists a structure $\alpha \in \mathcal{M}$ in which the following formula is true

$$B(F_1, \ldots, F_n) \tag{1}$$

where

1. $F_1, \ldots, F_n$ are formulas with $\mathsf{FV}(F_i) \subseteq \{A_1, \ldots, A_p, x_1, \ldots, x_q\}$.
2. $V_S = \{A_1, \ldots, A_p\}$ are variables of sort set, whereas $x_1, \ldots, x_q$ are the remaining variables.[3]
3. Each formula F_i belongs to a given class of formulas, $\mathcal{F}_i$. For each $\mathcal{F}_i$ we assume that there is a corresponding theory $T_i \subseteq \mathcal{F}_i$.
4. $B(F_1, \ldots, F_n)$ denotes a formula built from $F_1, \ldots, F_n$ using the propositional operations $\wedge, \vee$.[4]
5. As the set of structures $\mathcal{M}$ we consider all structures α of interest (with finite $[\![\mathsf{obj}]\!]$, interpreting BAPA symbols in the standard way) for which $\alpha(\cup_{i=1}^n T_i)$.
6. (Set Sharing Condition) If $i \neq j$, then $\mathsf{FV}(\{F_i\} \cup T_i) \cap \mathsf{FV}(\{F_j\} \cup T_j) \subseteq V_S$.

Note that, as a special case, if we embed a class of first-order formulas into our framework, we obtain a framework that supports sharing unary predicates, but not e.g. binary predicates.

Combination Theorem.   The formula B in (1) is satisfiable iff one of the disjuncts in its disjunctive normal form is satisfiable. Consider a disjunct $F_1 \wedge$

---

[3] For notational simplicity we do not consider variables of sort obj because they can be represented as singleton sets, of sort set.

[4] The absence of negation is usually not a loss of generality because most $\mathcal{F}_i$ are closed under negation so B is the negation-normal form of a quantifier-free combination.

$\dots \wedge F_m$ for $m \leq n$. By definition of the satisfiability problem (1), $F_1 \wedge \dots \wedge F_m$ is satisfiable iff there exists a structure α such that for each $1 \leq i \leq m$, for each $G \in \{F_i\} \cup T_i$, we have $\alpha(G) = \text{true}$. Let each variable x_i have some sort s_i (such as $\text{obj}^2 \rightarrow \text{bool}$). Then the satisfiability of $F_1 \wedge \dots \wedge F_m$ is equivalent to the following condition:

$$\exists \text{ finite set } u. \ \exists a_1, \dots, a_p \subseteq u. \ \exists v_1 \in [\![s_1]\!]^u. \dots \ \exists v_q \in [\![s_q]\!]^u. \ \bigwedge_{i=1}^{m} \{\text{obj} \rightarrow u, A_1 \mapsto a_1, \dots, A_p \mapsto a_p, x_1 \mapsto v_1, \dots, x_q \mapsto v_q\}(\{F_i\} \cup T_i) \qquad (2)$$

By the set sharing condition, each of the variables $x_1, \dots, x_q$ appears only in one conjunct and can be moved inwards from the top level to this conjunct. Using x_{ij} to denote the j-th variable in the i-th conjunct we obtain the condition

$$\exists \text{ finite set } u. \ \exists a_1, \dots, a_p \subseteq u. \ \bigwedge_{i=1}^{m} C_i(u, a_1, \dots, a_p) \qquad (3)$$

where $C_i(u, a_1, \dots, a_p)$ is

$$\exists v_{i1}. \dots \exists v_{iw_i}. \ \{\text{obj} \rightarrow u, A_1 \mapsto a_1, \dots, A_p \mapsto a_p, x_{i1} \mapsto v_{i1}, \dots, x_{iw_i} \mapsto v_{iw_i}\}(\{F_i\} \cup T_i)$$

The idea of our combination method is to simplify each condition $C_i(u, a_1, \dots, a_p)$ into the truth value of a BAPA formula. If this is possible, we say that there exists a BAPA reduction.

Definition 2 (BAPA Reduction). *If $\mathcal{F}_i$ is a set of formulas and $T_i \subseteq \mathcal{F}_i$ a theory, we call a function $\rho : \mathcal{F}_i \rightarrow \mathcal{F}_{\text{BAPA}}$ a BAPA reduction for $(\mathcal{F}_i, T_i)$ iff for every formula $F_i \in \mathcal{F}_i$ and for all finite u and $a_1, \dots, a_p \subseteq u$, the condition*

$$\exists v_{i1} \dots \exists v_{iw_i}. \ \{\text{obj} \rightarrow u, A_1 \mapsto a_1, \dots, A_p \mapsto a_p, x_{i1} \mapsto v_{i1}, \dots, x_{iw_i} \mapsto v_{iw_i}\}(\{F_i\} \cup T_i)$$

is equivalent to the condition $\{\text{obj} \rightarrow u, A_1 \mapsto a_1, \dots, A_p \mapsto a_p\}(\rho(F_i))$.

A computable BAPA reduction is a BAPA reduction which is computable as a function on formula syntax trees.

Theorem 3. *Suppose that for every $1 \leq i \leq n$ for $(\mathcal{F}_i, T_i)$ there exists a computable BAPA reduction ρ_i. Then the problem (1) in Section 4 is decidable.*

Specifically, to check satisfiability of $B(F_1, \dots, F_n)$, compute $B(\rho_1(F_1), \dots, \rho_n(F_n))$ and then check its satisfiability using a BAPA decision procedure [20, 21].

5   BAPA Reductions

5.1   Monadic Second-Order Logic of Finite Trees

Figure 4 shows the syntax of (our presentation of) monadic second-order logic of finite trees (FT), a variant of weak monadic second-order logic of two successors

$$F ::= P \mid F_1 \wedge F_2 \mid F_1 \vee F_2 \mid \neg F \mid \forall x{:}s.F \mid \exists x{:}s.F$$
$$s ::= \mathsf{obj} \mid \mathsf{set}$$
$$P ::= B_1 = B_2 \mid B_1 \subseteq B_2 \mid r(x, y)$$
$$r ::= \mathsf{succ}_L \mid \mathsf{succ}_R$$
$$B ::= x \mid \epsilon \mid \emptyset \mid \mathsf{Univ} \mid \{x\} \mid B_1 \cup B_2 \mid B_1 \cap B_2 \mid B^c$$

Fig. 4. Monadic Second-Order Logic of Finite Trees (FT)

(WS2S) [18, 31]. The following are the sorts of variables specific to FT formulas: $\mathsf{succ}_L, \mathsf{succ}_R : \mathsf{obj}^2 \to \mathsf{bool}$.

We interpret the sort obj over finite, prefix-closed sets of binary strings. More precisely, we use $\{1, 2\}$ as the binary alphabet, and we let $[\![\mathsf{obj}]\!] \subset \{1, 2\}^*$ such that

$$\forall w \in \{1, 2\}^*. \ (w1 \in [\![\mathsf{obj}]\!] \vee w2 \in [\![\mathsf{obj}]\!]) \to w \in [\![\mathsf{obj}]\!]$$

In each model, $[\![\mathsf{set}]\!]$ is the set of all subsets of $[\![\mathsf{obj}]\!]$. We let $[\![\epsilon]\!]$ be the empty string which we also denote by ϵ. We define

$$[\![\mathsf{succ}_L]\!] = \{(w, w1) \mid w1 \in [\![\mathsf{obj}]\!]\} \quad \text{and} \quad [\![\mathsf{succ}_R]\!] = \{(w, w2) \mid w2 \in [\![\mathsf{obj}]\!]\}$$

The remaining constants and operations on sets are interpreted as in BAPA.

Let $\mathcal{F}_{\mathsf{FT}}$ be the set of all formulas in Figure 4. Let $\mathcal{M}_{\mathsf{FT}}$ be the set of all (finite) structures described above. We define $\mathcal{T}_{\mathsf{FT}}$ as the set of all formulas $F \in \mathcal{F}_{\mathsf{FT}}$ such that F is true in all structures from $\mathcal{M}_{\mathsf{FT}}$.

Note that any FT formula $F(x)$ with a free variable x of sort obj can be transformed into the equisatisfiable formula $\exists x : \mathsf{obj}.y = \{x\} \wedge F(x)$ where y is a fresh variable of sort set. For conciseness of presentation, in the rest of this section we only consider FT formulas F with $\mathsf{FV}_{\mathsf{obj}}(F) = \emptyset$.

Finite tree automata. In the following, we recall the connection between FT formulas and finite tree automata. Let Σ be a finite ranked alphabet. We call symbols of rank 0 constant symbols and a symbol of rank $k > 0$ a k-ary function symbol. We denote by $\mathsf{Terms}(\Sigma)$ the set of all terms over Σ. We associate a position $p \in \{1, \ldots, r_{\max}\}^*$ with each subterm in a term t where $r_{\max}$ is the maximal rank of all symbols in Σ. We denote by $t[p]$ the topmost symbol of the subterm at position p. For instance, consider the term $t = f(g(a, b, c), a)$ then we have $t[\epsilon] = f$ and $t[13] = c$.

A finite (deterministic bottom-up) tree automaton A for alphabet Σ is a tuple (Q, Q_f, ι) where Q is a finite set of states, $Q_f \subseteq Q$ is a set of final states, and ι is a function that associates with each constant symbol $c \in \Sigma$ a state $\iota(c) \in Q$ and with each k-ary function symbol $f \in \Sigma$ a function $\iota(f) : Q^k \to Q$. We homomorphically extend ι from symbols in Σ to Σ-terms. We say that A accepts a term $t \in \mathsf{Terms}(\Sigma)$ if $\iota(t) \in Q_f$. The language $\mathcal{L}(A)$ accepted by A is the set of all Σ-terms accepted by A.

Let F be an FT formula and let $\mathsf{SV}(F)$ be the set $\mathsf{SV}(F) = \mathsf{FV}(F) \cup \{\mathsf{Univ}\}$. We denote by Σ_F the alphabet consisting of the constant symbol $\bot$ and all binary function symbols f_ν where ν is a function $\nu : \mathsf{SV}(F) \to \{0, 1\}$. We inductively associate a Σ_F-term $t_{\alpha, w}$ with every structure $\alpha \in \mathcal{M}_{\mathsf{FT}}$ and string $w \in \{1, 2\}^*$ as follows:

$$t_{\alpha, w} = \begin{cases} f_{\nu_{\alpha, w}}(t_{\alpha, w1}, t_{\alpha, w2}) & \text{if } w \in \alpha(\mathsf{obj}) \\ \bot & \text{otherwise} \end{cases}$$

such that for all $x \in \mathsf{SV}(F)$, $\nu_{\alpha, w}(x) = 1$ iff $w \in \alpha(x)$. The language $\mathcal{L}(F) \subseteq \mathsf{Terms}(\Sigma_F)$ of F is then defined by $\mathcal{L}(F) = \{ t_{\alpha, \epsilon} \mid \alpha \in \mathcal{M}_{\mathsf{FT}} \wedge \alpha(F) \}$.

Parikh image. We recall Parikh's commutative image [26]. The Parikh image for an alphabet Σ is the function $\mathsf{Parikh} : \Sigma^* \to \Sigma \to \mathbb{N}$ such that for any word $w \in \Sigma^*$ and symbol $\sigma \in \Sigma$, $\mathsf{Parikh}(w)(\sigma)$ is the number of occurrences of σ in w. The Parikh image is extended pointwise from words to sets of words: $\mathsf{Parikh}(W) = \{ \mathsf{Parikh}(w) \mid w \in W \}$. In the following, we implicitly identify $\mathsf{Parikh}(W)$ with the set of integer vectors $\{ (\chi(\sigma_1), \ldots, \chi(\sigma_n)) \mid \chi \in \mathsf{Parikh}(W) \}$ where we assume some fixed order on the symbols $\sigma_1, \ldots, \sigma_n$ in Σ.

We generalize the Parikh image from words to terms as expected: the Parikh image for a ranked alphabet Σ is the function $\mathsf{Parikh} : \mathsf{Terms}(\Sigma) \to \Sigma \to \mathbb{N}$ such that for all $t \in \mathsf{Terms}(\Sigma)$ and $\sigma \in \Sigma$, $\mathsf{Parikh}(t)(\sigma)$ is the number of positions p in t such that $t[p] = \sigma$. Again we extend this function pointwise from terms to sets of terms.

BAPA Reduction. In the following, we prove the existence of a computable BAPA reduction for the theory of monadic second-order logic of finite trees.

Let F be an FT formula and let Σ_F^2 be the set of all binary function symbols in Σ_F, i.e., $\Sigma_F^2 \stackrel{\text{def}}{=} \Sigma_F \setminus \{\bot\}$. We associate with each $\sigma_\nu \in \Sigma_F^2$ the *Venn region* $\mathsf{vr}(\sigma_\nu)$, which is given by a set-algebraic expression over $\mathsf{SV}(F)$: let $\mathsf{SV}(F) = \{x_1, \ldots, x_n\}$ then

$$\mathsf{vr}(\sigma_\nu) \stackrel{\text{def}}{=} x_1^{\nu(x_1)} \cap \cdots \cap x_n^{\nu(x_n)} .$$

Hereby x_i^0 denotes x_i^c and x_i^1 denotes x_i. Let $\alpha \in \mathcal{M}_{\mathsf{FT}}$ be a model of F. Then the term $t_{\alpha, \epsilon}$ encodes for each $w \in \alpha(\mathsf{obj})$ the Venn region to which w belongs in α, namely $\mathsf{vr}(t_{\alpha, \epsilon}[w])$. Thus, the Parikh image $\mathsf{Parikh}(t_{\alpha, \epsilon})$ encodes the cardinality of each Venn region over $\mathsf{SV}(F)$ in α.

Lemma 4. *Let F be an FT formula then*

$$\mathsf{Parikh}(\mathcal{L}(F))|_{\Sigma_F^2} = \{ \{ \sigma \mapsto |\alpha(\mathsf{vr}(\sigma))| \mid \sigma \in \Sigma_F^2 \} \mid \alpha \in \mathcal{M}_{\mathsf{FT}} \wedge \alpha(F) \} .$$

Following [31, Theorem 17] we can construct a finite tree automaton A_F over Σ_F such that $\mathcal{L}(F) = \mathcal{L}(A_F)$. From [26, Theorem 2] follows that $\mathsf{Parikh}(\mathcal{L}(F))$ is a semilinear set whose finite representation in terms of base and step vectors is effectively computable from A_F. From this finite representation we can construct a Presburger arithmetic formula ϕ_F over free integer variables $\{ x_\sigma \mid \sigma \in \Sigma_F \}$ whose set of solutions is the Parikh image of $\mathcal{L}(F)$, i.e.

$$\mathsf{Parikh}(\mathcal{L}(F)) = \{ \{ \sigma \mapsto k_\sigma \mid \sigma \in \Sigma_F \} \mid \{ x_\sigma \mapsto k_\sigma \mid \sigma \in \Sigma \}(\phi_F) \} \quad (4)$$

Using the above construction of the Presburger arithmetic formula ϕ_F for a given FT formula F, we define the function $\rho_{FT} : \mathcal{F}_{FT} \rightarrow \mathcal{F}_{BAPA}$ as follows:

$$\rho_{FT}(F) \stackrel{\text{def}}{=} \exists \boldsymbol{x}_\sigma . \phi_F \wedge \bigwedge_{\sigma \in \Sigma_F^2} \mathsf{card}(\mathsf{vr}(\sigma)) = x_\sigma$$

where $\boldsymbol{x}_\sigma$ are the free integer variables of ϕ_F.

Theorem 5. *The function ρ_{FT} is a BAPA reduction for $(\mathcal{F}_{FT}, \mathcal{T}_{FT})$.*

5.2   Two-Variable Logic with Counting

Figure 5 shows the syntax of (our presentation of) two-variable logic with counting (denoted C^2) [29]. As usual in C^2, we require that every sub-formula of a formula has at most two free variables. In the atomic formula $r(x_1, x_2)$, variables x_1, x_2 are of sort obj and r is a relation variable of sort $\mathsf{obj}^2 \rightarrow \mathsf{bool}$. The formula $\{x\} \subseteq A$ replaces $A(x)$ in predicate-logic notation, and has the expected meaning, with the variable x is of sort obj and A of sort set. The interpretation of the counting quantifier $\exists^K x{:}\mathsf{obj}.F$ for a positive constant K is that there exist at least K distinct elements x for which the formula F holds.

$$F ::= P \mid F_1 \wedge F_2 \mid F_1 \vee F_2 \mid \neg F \mid \exists^K x{:}\mathsf{obj}.F$$
$$P ::= x_1 = x_2 \mid \{x\} \subseteq A \mid r(x_1, x_2)$$

Fig. 5. Two-Variable Logic with Counting (C^2)

Let $\mathcal{F}_{C2}$ be the set of all formulas in Figure 5. Let $\mathcal{M}_{C2}$ be the set of structures that interpret formulas in $\mathcal{F}_{C2}$. We define $\mathcal{T}_{C2}$ as the set of all formulas $F \in \mathcal{F}_{C2}$ such that F is true in all structures from $\mathcal{M}_{C2}$. Modulo our minor variation in syntax and terminology (using relation and set variables instead of predicate symbols), $\mathcal{T}_{C2}$ corresponds to the standard set of valid C^2 formulas over finite structures.

BAPA Reduction. We next build on the results in [29] to define a BAPA reduction for C^2. We fix set variables $A_1, \ldots, A_p$ and relation variables $r_1, \ldots, r_q$. Throughout this section, let $\Sigma_A = \{A_1, \ldots, A_p\}$, $\Sigma_R = \{r_1, \ldots, r_q\}$, and $\Sigma_0 = \Sigma_A \cup \Sigma_R$. We call $\Sigma_A, \Sigma_R, \Sigma_0$ signatures because they correspond to the notion of signature in the traditional first-order logic formulation of C^2.

Model theoretic types. Define the model-theoretic notion of n-type π_Σ $(x_1, \ldots, x_n)$ in the signature Σ as the maximal consistent set of non-equality literals in Σ whose obj-sort variables are included in $\{x_1, \ldots, x_n\}$. Given a structure α such that $\alpha(x_1), \ldots, \alpha(x_n)$ are all distinct, α *induces* an n-type We also define the set of n-tuples for which a type π holds in a structure α:

$$S^\alpha(\pi(x_1, \ldots, x_n)) = \{(e_1, \ldots, e_n) \in \alpha(\mathsf{obj})^n \mid \alpha(x_1 := e_1, \ldots, x_n := e_n)(\pi)\}$$

If $\Sigma \subseteq \Sigma'$ and π' is an n-type in signature Σ', by $\pi'|_\Sigma$ we denote the subset of π containing precisely those literals from π whose sets and relations belong to Σ. The family of sets $\{S^\alpha(\pi') \mid \pi'|_\Sigma = \pi\}$ is a partition of $S^\alpha(\pi')$. We will be particularly interested in 1-types. We identify a 1-type $\pi(x)$ in the signature Σ_A with the corresponding Venn region

$$\bigcap\{A_i \mid (\{x\} \subseteq A_i) \in \pi(x)\} \cap \bigcap\{A_i^c \mid (\neg(\{x\} \subseteq A_i)) \in \pi(x)\}.$$

If $\pi_1, \ldots, \pi_m$ is the sequence of all 1-types in the signature Σ and α is a structure, let $I^\alpha(\Sigma) = (|S^\alpha(\pi_1)|, \ldots, |S^\alpha(\pi_m)|)$. If $\mathcal{M}$ is a set of structures let $I^{\mathcal{M}}(\Sigma) = \{I^\alpha(\Sigma) \mid \alpha \in \mathcal{M}\}$.

Observation 6. *If π is a 1-type in Σ and π' a 1-type in Σ' for $\Sigma \subseteq \Sigma'$, then*

$$|I^\alpha(\pi)| = \sum_{\pi'|_\Sigma = \pi} |I^\alpha(\pi')|$$

Making structures differentiated, chromatic, sparse preserves 1-types.
Let ϕ be a C^2 formula with signature Σ_0 of relation symbols. By Scott normal form transformation [29, Lemma 1] it is possible to introduce fresh set variables and compute another C^2 formula ϕ^* in an extended signature $\Sigma^* \supseteq \Sigma_0$, and compute a constant C_ϕ such that, for all sets u with $|u| \geq C_\phi$: 1) if α_0 is a Σ_0 interpretation with domain u such that $\alpha_0(\phi)$, then there exists its Σ^* extension $\alpha^* \supseteq \alpha_0$ such that $\alpha^*(\phi^*)$, and 2) if α^* is a Σ^* interpretation with domain u such that $\alpha^*(\phi^*)$, then for its restriction $\alpha_0 = \alpha^*|_\Sigma$ we have $\alpha_0(\phi)$. By introducing further fresh set- and relation- symbols, [29, lemmas 2 and 3] shows that we can extend the signature from Σ^* to Σ such that each model α^* in Σ^* extends to a model α in Σ, where α satisfies some further conditions of interest: α is *chromatic* and *differentiated*. [29, Lemma 10] then shows that it is possible to transform a model of a formula into a so-called X-*sparse* model for an appropriately computed integer constant X. What is important for us is the following.

Observation 7. *The transformations that start from α_0 with $\alpha_0(\phi)$, and that produce a chromatic, differentiated, X-sparse structure α with $\alpha(\phi)$, have the property that, for structures of size C_ϕ or more,*

1. *the domain remains the same: $\alpha_0(\mathsf{obj}) = \alpha(\mathsf{obj})$,*
2. *the induced 1-types in the signature Σ_0 remain the same: for each 1-type π in signature Σ_0, $S^{\alpha_0}(\pi) = S^\alpha(\pi)$.*

Star types. [29, Definition 9] introduces a star-type (π, v) (denoted by letter σ) as a description of a local neighborhood of a domain element, containing its induced 1-type π as well as an integer vector $v \subseteq \mathbb{Z}^N$ that counts 2-types in which the element participates, where N is a function of the signature Σ. A star type thus gives a more precise description of the properties of a domain element than a 1-type. Without repeating the definition of star type [29, Definition 9], we note that we can similarly define the set $S^\alpha((\pi, v))$ of elements that realize a given star type $(\pi, \boldsymbol{v})$. Moreover, for a given 1-type π, the family of the non-empty among the sets $S^\alpha((\pi, \boldsymbol{v}))$ partitions the set $S^\alpha(\pi)$.

Frames. The notion of Y-*bounded chromatic frame* [29, Definition 11] can be thought of as a representation of a disjunct in a normal form for the formula ϕ^*. It summarizes the properties of elements in the structure and specifies (among others), the list of possible star types $\sigma_1, \ldots, \sigma_N$ whose integer vectors $\boldsymbol{v}$ are bounded by Y. For a given ϕ^*, it is possible to effectively compute the set of C_ϕ-bounded frames $\mathcal{F}$ such that $\mathcal{F} \models \phi^*$ holds. The '$\models$' in $\mathcal{F} \models \phi^*$ is a certain syntactic relation defined in [29, Definition 13].

For each frame $\mathcal{F}$ with star-types $\sigma_1, \ldots, \sigma_N$, [29, Definition 14] introduces an effectively computable Presburger arithmetic formula $P_\mathcal{F}$ with N free variables. We write $P_\mathcal{F}(w_1, \ldots, w_N)$ if $P_\mathcal{F}$ is true when these variables take the values $w_1, \ldots, w_N$. The following statement is similar to the main [29, Theorem 1], and can be directly recovered from its proof and the proofs of the underlying [29, lemmas 12,13,14].

Theorem 8. *Given a formula ϕ^*, and the corresponding integer constant C_ϕ, there exists a computable constant X such that if $N \leq X$, if $\sigma_1, \ldots, \sigma_N$ is a sequence of star types in Σ whose integer vectors are bounded by C_ϕ, and $w_1, \ldots, w_N$ are integers, then the following are equivalent:*

1. *There exists a chromatic differentiated structure α such that $\alpha(\phi^*)$, $w_i = |S^\alpha(\sigma_i)|$ for $1 \leq i \leq N$, and $\alpha(\mathsf{obj}) = \bigcup_{i=1}^N S^\alpha(\sigma_i)$.*
2. *There exists a chromatic frame $\mathcal{F}$ with star types $\sigma_1, \ldots, \sigma_N$, such that $\mathcal{F} \models \phi^*$ and $P_\mathcal{F}(w_1, \ldots, w_N)$.*

We are now ready to describe our BAPA reduction. Fix $V_1, \ldots, V_M$ to be the list of all 1-types in signature Σ_A; let $s_1, \ldots, s_M$ be variables corresponding to their counts. By the transformation of models into chromatic, differentiated, X-sparse ones, the observations 7, 6, and Theorem 8, we obtain

Corollary 9. *If $\mathcal{M} = \{\alpha \mid \alpha(\phi^*)\}$, then there is a computable constant X such that $I^\mathcal{M}(\Sigma_A) = \{(s_1, \ldots, s_M) \mid F_{\phi^*}(s_1, \ldots, s_M)\}$ where $F_{\phi^*}(s_1, \ldots, s_M)$ is the following Presburger arithmetic formula*

$$\bigvee_{N, \sigma_1, \ldots, \sigma_N, \mathcal{F}} \exists w_1, \ldots, w_N. \; P_\mathcal{F}(w_1, \ldots, w_N) \wedge \bigwedge_{j=1}^M s_j = \sum \{w_i \mid V_j = (\pi_i|_{\Sigma_A})\}$$

where N ranges over $\{0, 1, \ldots, X\}$, $\sigma_1, \ldots, \sigma_N$ range over sequences of C_ϕ-bounded star types, and where $\mathcal{F}$ ranges over the C_ϕ-bounded frames with star types $\sigma_1, \ldots, \sigma_N$ such that $\mathcal{F} \models \phi^*$.

By adjusting for the small structures to take into account Scott normal form transformation, we further obtain

Corollary 10. *If* $\mathcal{M} = \{\alpha \mid \alpha(\phi)\}$, *then* $I^{\mathcal{M}}(\Sigma_A) = \{(s_1, \ldots, s_M) \mid G_\phi(s_1, \ldots, s_M)\}$ *where* $G_\phi(s_1, \ldots, s_M)$ *is the Presburger arithmetic formula*

$$\sum_{i=1}^{M} s_i \geq C_\phi \wedge F_{\phi^*}(s_1, \ldots, s_M) \quad \bigvee$$

$$\bigvee \{\bigwedge_{i=1}^{M} s_i = d_i \mid \exists \alpha. \; |\alpha(\mathsf{obj})| < C_\phi \; \wedge (d_1, \ldots, d_M) \in I^\alpha(\Sigma_A)\}$$

Theorem 11. *The following is a BAPA reduction for* C^2 *over finite models to variables* Σ_A: *given a two-variable logic formula* ϕ, *compute the BAPA formula* $\exists s_1, \ldots, s_M. \; G_\phi(s_1, \ldots, s_M) \; \wedge \bigwedge_{i=1}^{M} \mathsf{card}(V_i) = s_i$.

5.3   Bernays-Schönfinkel-Ramsey Fragment of First-Order Logic

Figure 6 shows the syntax of (our presentation of) the Bernays-Schönfinkel-Ramsey fragment of first-order logic with equality [6], often called effectively propositional logic (EPR). The interpretation of atomic formulas is analogous as for C^2 in previous section. Quantification is restricted to variables of sort obj and must obey the usual restriction of $\exists^*\forall^*$-prenex form that characterizes the Bernays-Schönfinkel-Ramsey class.

$$F ::= \exists z_1:\mathsf{obj}. \ldots \exists z_n:\mathsf{obj}. \; \forall y_1:\mathsf{obj}. \ldots \forall y_m:\mathsf{obj}. \; B$$
$$B ::= P \mid B_1 \wedge B_2 \mid B_1 \vee B_2 \mid \neg B$$
$$P ::= x_1 = x_2 \mid \{x\} \subseteq A \mid r(x_1, \ldots, x_k)$$

Fig. 6. Bernays-Schönfinkel-Ramsey Fragment of First-Order Logic

BAPA Reduction. Our BAPA reduction for the Bernays-Schönfinkel-Ramsey fragment (EPR) is in fact a reduction from EPR formulas to *unary* EPR formulas, in which all free variables have the sort set. To convert a unary EPR formula into BAPA, treat first-order variables as singleton sets and apply quantifier elimination for BAPA [20].

Theorem 12 (BAPA Reduction for EPR). *Let* ϕ *be a quantifier-free formula whose free variables are: 1)* $A_1, \ldots, A_p$, *of sort* set, *2)* $r_1, \ldots, r_q$, *each* r_i *of sorts* $\mathsf{obj}^{K(i)} \to \mathsf{bool}$ *for some* $K(i) \geq 2$, *3)* $z_1, \ldots, z_n, y_1, \ldots, y_m$, *of sort* obj. *Then*

$$\exists r_1, \ldots r_q. \; \exists z_1, \ldots, z_n. \; \forall y_1, \ldots, y_m. \; \phi$$

is equivalent to an effectively computable BAPA formula.

The proof of Theorem 12 builds on and generalizes, for finite models, the results on the spectra of EPR formulas [10, 11, 30]. We here provide some intuition. The key insight [30] is that, when a domain of a model of an EPR formula has sufficiently many elements, then the model contains an induced submodel S of m nodes such that for every $0 \leq k < m$ elements $e_1, \ldots, e_k$ outside S the m-type induced by $e_1, \ldots, e_k$ and any $m - k$ elements in S is the same. Then an element of S can be replicated to create a model with more elements, without changing the set of all m-types in the model and thus without changing the truth value of the formula. Moreover, every sufficiently large model of the EPR formula that has a submodel S with more than m such symmetric elements can be shrunk to a model by whose expansion it can be generated. This allows us to enumerate a finite (even if very large) number of characteristic models whose expansion generates all models. The expansion of a characteristic model increases by one the number of elements of some existing 1-type, so the cardinalities of Venn regions of models are a semilinear set whose base vectors are given by characteristic models and whose step vectors are given by the 1-types being replicated.

5.4   Quantifier-Free Mutlisets with Cardinality Constraints

The satisfiability of the quantifier-free fragment of multisets with cardinality operators is decidable [27]. There is, in fact, also a BAPA reduction from a quantifier-free multiset formula over multiset and set variables to a BAPA formula ranging only over the set variables. Multiset formula are built from multiset variables, multiset operations, and cardinality constraints on multisets. Multiset variables have sort $\mathsf{obj} \to \mathsf{int}$ and are interpreted as functions from $[\![\mathsf{obj}]\!]$ to the nonnegative integers (for details see [35]).

Let F be a multiset constraint containing sets $A_1, \ldots, A_p$ and multisets $M_1, \ldots, M_q$. To obtain a BAPA reduction, we apply the decision procedure in [27] to the formula $F \wedge \bigwedge_{i=1}^{w} \mathsf{card}(V_i){=}k_i$ with fresh integer variables $k_1, \ldots, k_w$, where $V_1, \ldots, V_w$ are the Venn regions over sets $A_1, \ldots, A_p$. The result is a Presburger arithmetic formula P with $\{k_1, \ldots, k_w\} \subseteq \mathsf{FV}(P)$. If $x_1, \ldots, x_n$ are the variables in P other than $k_1, \ldots, k_w$, the result of the BAPA reduction is then the formula

$$P_F \stackrel{\mathrm{def}}{=} \exists k_1. \ldots . \exists k_w. \; (\bigwedge_{i=1}^{w} \mathsf{card}(V_i){=}k_i) \wedge (\exists x_1{:}\mathsf{int}. \ldots . \exists x_n{:}\mathsf{int.} \; P)$$

Theorem 13. *The function mapping a multiset formula F to the BAPA formula P_F is a BAPA reduction for the theory of multisets with cardinalities.*

6   Further Related Work

There are combination results for the disjoint combinations of non-stably infinite theories [10, 11, 19, 33]. These results are based on the observation that such combinations are possible whenever one can decide for each component theory whether a model of a specific cardinality exists. Our combination result takes into account not only the cardinality of the models, i.e. the interpretation of the universal set, but cardinalities of Venn regions over the interpretations of arbitrary shared set variables. It is a natural generalization of the disjoint case restricted to theories that share the theory of finite sets, thus, leading to a non-disjoint combination of non-stably infinite theories.

Ghilardi [14] proposes a model-theoretic condition for decidability of the non-disjoint combination of theories based on quantifier elimination and local finiteness of the shared theory. Note that BAPA is not locally finite and that, in general, we need the full expressive power of BAPA to compute the projections on the shared set variables. For instance, consider the C^2 formula

$$(\forall x. \exists^{=1} y.r(x,y)) \wedge (\forall x. \exists^{=1} y.r(y,x)) \wedge (\forall y.\ y \in B \leftrightarrow (\exists x.x \in A \wedge r(x,y)))$$

where r is a binary relation variable establishing the bijection between A and B. This constraint expresses $|A| = |B|$ without imposing any additional constraint on A and B. Similar examples can be given for weak monadic second-order logic of finite trees.

The reduction approach to combination of decision procedures has previously been applied in the simpler scenario of reduction to propositional logic [22]. Like propositional logic, quantifier-Free BAPA is NP-complete, so it presents an appealing alternative for combination of theories that share sets.

Gabbay and Ohlbach [12] present a procedure, called SCAN, for second-order quantifier elimination. However, [12] gives no characterization of when SCAN terminates. We were therefore unable to use SCAN to derive any BAPA reductions.

The general combination of weak monadic second-order logics with linear cardinality constraints has been proven undecidable by Klaedtke and Rueß[16, 17]. They introduce the notion of Parikh automata to identify decidable fragments of this logic which inspired our BAPA reduction of MSOL of finite trees. Our combined logic is incomparable to the decidable fragments identified by Klaedtke and Rueß because it supports non-tree structures as well. However, by applying projection to C^2 and the Bernays-Schönfinkel-Ramsey class, we can combine our logic with [16, 17], obtaining an even more expressive decidable logic.

7   Conclusion

We have presented a combination result for logics that share operations on sets. This result yields an expressive decidable logic that is useful for software verification. We therefore believe that we made an important step in increasing the class of properties that are amenable to automated verification.

References

1. Andrews, P.B.: An Introduction to Mathematical Logic and Type Theory: To Truth Through Proof, 2nd edn. Springer (Kluwer), Heidelberg (2002)
2. Ball, T., Podelski, A., Rajamani, S.K.: Relative completeness of abstraction refinement for software model checking. In: Katoen, J.-P., Stevens, P. (eds.) TACAS 2002. LNCS, vol. 2280, p. 158. Springer, Heidelberg (2002)
3. Barnett, M., DeLine, R., Fähndrich, M., Leino, K.R.M., Schulte, W.: Verification of object-oriented programs with invariants. Journal of Object Technology 3(6), 27–56 (2004)

4. Barrett, C., Tinelli, C.: CVC3. In: Damm, W., Hermanns, H. (eds.) CAV 2007. LNCS, vol. 4590, pp. 298–302. Springer, Heidelberg (2007)
5. Basin, D., Friedrich, S.: Combining WS1S and HOL. In: FroCoS (1998)
6. Börger, E., Grädel, E., Gurevich, Y.: The Classical Decision Problem. Springer, Heidelberg (1997)
7. Boyer, R.S., Moore, J.S.: Integrating decision procedures into heuristic theorem provers: A case study of linear arithmetic. In: Machine Intelligence, vol. 11. Oxford University Press, Oxford (1988)
8. de Moura, L., Bjørner, N.: Z3: An efficient SMT solver. In: Ramakrishnan, C.R., Rehof, J. (eds.) TACAS 2008. LNCS, vol. 4963, pp. 337–340. Springer, Heidelberg (2008)
9. Feferman, S., Vaught, R.L.: The first order properties of products of algebraic systems. Fundamenta Mathematicae 47, 57–103 (1959)
10. Fontaine, P.: Combinations of theories and the bernays-schönfinkel-ramsey class. In: VERIFY (2007)
11. Fontaine, P.: Combinations of theories for decidable fragments of first-order logic. In: Ghilardi, S., Sebastiani, R. (eds.) FroCoS 2009. LNCS (LNAI), vol. 5749, pp. 263–278. Springer, Heidelberg (2009)
12. Gabbay, D.M., Ohlbach, H.J.: Quantifier elimination in second-order predicate logic. In: Nebel, B., Rich, C., Swartout, W. (eds.) Principles of Knowledge Representation and Reasoning. Morgan-Kaufmann, San Francisco (1992)
13. Ge, Y., Barrett, C., Tinelli, C.: Solving quantified verification conditions using satisfiability modulo theories. In: Pfenning, F. (ed.) CADE 2007. LNCS (LNAI), vol. 4603, pp. 167–182. Springer, Heidelberg (2007)
14. Ghilardi, S.: Model theoretic methods in combined constraint satisfiability. Journal of Automated Reasoning 33(3-4), 221–249 (2005)
15. Ginsburg, S., Spanier, E.: Semigroups, Pressburger formulas and languages. Pacific Journal of Mathematics 16(2), 285–296 (1966)
16. Klaedtke, F., Rueß, H.: Parikh automata and monadic second-order logics with linear cardinality constraints. Technical Report 177, Institute of Computer Science at Freiburg University (2002)
17. Klaedtke, F., Rueß, H.: Monadic second-order logics with cardinalities. In: Baeten, J.C.M., Lenstra, J.K., Parrow, J., Woeginger, G.J. (eds.) ICALP 2003. LNCS, vol. 2719. Springer, Heidelberg (2003)
18. Klarlund, N., Møller, A.: MONA Version 1.4 User Manual. BRICS Notes Series NS-01-1, Department of Computer Science. University of Aarhus (January 2001)
19. Krstic, S., Goel, A., Grundy, J., Tinelli, C.: Combined satisfiability modulo parametric theories. In: Grumberg, O., Huth, M. (eds.) TACAS 2007. LNCS, vol. 4424, pp. 602–617. Springer, Heidelberg (2007)
20. Kuncak, V., Nguyen, H.H., Rinard, M.: Deciding Boolean Algebra with Presburger Arithmetic. J. of Automated Reasoning (2006)
21. Kuncak, V., Rinard, M.: Towards efficient satisfiability checking for Boolean Algebra with Presburger Arithmetic. In: Pfenning, F. (ed.) CADE 2007. LNCS (LNAI), vol. 4603, pp. 215–230. Springer, Heidelberg (2007)
22. Lahiri, S.K., Seshia, S.A.: The UCLID decision procedure. In: Alur, R., Peled, D.A. (eds.) CAV 2004. LNCS, vol. 3114, pp. 475–478. Springer, Heidelberg (2004)
23. McLaughlin, S., Barrett, C., Ge, Y.: Cooperating theorem provers: A case study combining HOL-Light and CVC Lite. In: PDPAR. ENTCS, vol. 144(2) (2006)
24. Nelson, G., Oppen, D.C.: Simplification by cooperating decision procedures. ACM TOPLAS 1(2), 245–257 (1979)

25. Owre, S., Rushby, J.M., Shankar, N.: PVS: A prototype verification system. In: Kapur, D. (ed.) 11th CADE, June 1992. LNCS (LNAI), vol. 607, pp. 748–752 (1992)
26. Parikh, R.J.: On context-free languages. J. ACM 13(4), 570–581 (1966)
27. Piskac, R., Kuncak, V.: Decision procedures for multisets with cardinality constraints. In: Logozzo, F., Peled, D.A., Zuck, L.D. (eds.) VMCAI 2008. LNCS, vol. 4905, pp. 218–232. Springer, Heidelberg (2008)
28. Piskac, R., Kuncak, V.: Linear arithmetic with stars. In: Gupta, A., Malik, S. (eds.) CAV 2008. LNCS, vol. 5123, pp. 268–280. Springer, Heidelberg (2008)
29. Pratt-Hartmann, I.: Complexity of the two-variable fragment with counting quantifiers. Journal of Logic, Language and Information 14(3), 369–395 (2005)
30. Ramsey, F.P.: On a problem of formal logic. Proc. London Math. Soc. s2-30, 264–286 (1930), doi:10.1112/plms/s2-30.1.264
31. Thatcher, J.W., Wright, J.B.: Generalized finite automata theory with an application to a decision problem of second-order logic. Mathematical Systems Theory 2(1), 57–81 (1968)
32. Tinelli, C., Ringeissen, C.: Unions of non-disjoint theories and combinations of satisfiability procedures. Th. Comp. Sc. 290(1), 291–353 (2003)
33. Tinelli, C., Zarba, C.: Combining nonstably infinite theories. Journal of Automated Reasoning 34(3) (2005)
34. Wies, T.: Symbolic Shape Analysis. PhD thesis. University of Freiburg (2009)
35. Wies, T., Piskac, R., Kuncak, V.: On Combining Theories with Shared Set Operations. Technical Report LARA-REPORT-2009-002, EPFL (May 2009)
36. Zee, K., Kuncak, V., Rinard, M.: Full functional verification of linked data structures. In: ACM Conf. Programming Language Design and Implementation, PLDI (2008)

Author Index